T0364929

Vauxhall/Opel Meriva
Owners Workshop Manual

John S. Mead

(4893 - 416)

Models covered

Meriva 'A' MPV
Petrol: 1.4 litre (1364cc), 1.6 litre (1598cc) non-turbo & 1.8 litre (1796cc)
Turbo-Diesel: 1.3 litre (1248cc) & 1.7 litre (1686cc)

Does NOT cover 1.6 litre turbo VXR models
Does NOT cover new Meriva 'B' range introduced June 2010

© Haynes Publishing 2011

ABCDE
FGHIJ
KLM

A book in the **Haynes Owners Workshop Manual Series**

ISBN **978 0 85733 980 5**

British Library Cataloguing in Publication Data
A catalogue record for this book is available from the British Library.

Printed in Malaysia

Haynes Publishing
Sparkford, Yeovil, Somerset BA22 7JJ, England

Haynes North America, Inc
859 Lawrence Drive, Newbury Park, California 91320, USA

*Printed using NORBRITE BOOK 48.8gsm (CODE: 40N6533) from NORPAC; procurement system certified under Sustainable Forestry Initiative
standard. Paper produced is certified to the SFI Certified Fiber Sourcing Standard (CERT - 0094271)*

Contents

Contents

The Vauxhall/Opel Meriva was introduced in the UK in early 2003. The Meriva is available with only one body style, that of a 5-door mini multi-purpose vehicle (MPV), and with 1.4, 1.6 and 1.8 litre petrol engines, and 1.3 and 1.7 litre diesel engines. All engines are of the four-cylinder double overhead camshaft (DOHC) configuration, in-line type, with the exception of one of the 1.6 litre petrol engines which is a single overhead camshaft (SOHC) unit. The engines all have fuel injection and are fitted with a range of emission control systems.

The manual gearbox is of the five-speed all synchromesh type, with an 'Easytronic' manual/automatic transmission optionally available on 1.6 and 1.8 litre petrol engine models.

All models have front-wheel-drive with fully-independent front suspension, and semi-independent rear suspension with a torsion beam and trailing arms.

A wide range of standard and optional equipment is available within the Meriva range to suit most tastes, including electric power steering, air conditioning, remote central locking, electric windows, electric sunroof, anti-lock braking system, electronic alarm system and supplemental restraint systems.

For the home mechanic, the Meriva is a relatively straightforward vehicle to maintain, and most of the items requiring frequent attention are easily accessible.

Your Vauxhall/Opel Meriva manual

The aim of this manual is to help you get the best value from your vehicle. It can do so in several ways. It can help you decide what work must be done (even should you choose to get it done by a garage), provide information on routine maintenance and servicing, and give a logical course of action and diagnosis when random faults occur. However, it is hoped that you will use the manual by tackling the work yourself. On simpler jobs, it may even be quicker than booking the car into a garage and going there twice, to leave and collect it. Perhaps most important, a lot of money can be saved by avoiding the costs a garage must charge to cover its labour and overheads.

The manual has drawings and descriptions to show the function of the various components, so that their layout can be understood. Then the tasks are described and photographed in a clear step-by-step sequence.

References to the 'left' or 'right' are in the sense of a person in the driver's seat, facing forward.

Project vehicles

The main vehicle used in the preparation of this manual, and which appears in many of the photographic sequences, was a Vauxhall/Opel Meriva with a 1.6 litre DOHC petrol engine. Additional work was carried out on a variety of petrol and diesel engine models.

Acknowledgements

Certain illustrations are the copyright of Vauxhall Motors Limited, and are used with their permission. Thanks are also due to Draper Tools Limited, who provided some of the workshop tools, and to all those people at Sparkford who helped in the production of this manual.

We take great pride in the accuracy of information given in this manual, but vehicle manufacturers make alterations and design changes during the production run of a particular vehicle of which they do not inform us. No liability can be accepted by the authors or publishers for loss, damage or injury caused by any errors in, or omissions from, the information given.

Working on your car can be dangerous. This page shows just some of the potential risks and hazards, with the aim of creating a safety-conscious attitude.

General hazards

Scalding

• Don't remove the radiator or expansion tank cap while the engine is hot.
• Engine oil, transmission fluid or power steering fluid may also be dangerously hot if the engine has recently been running.

Burning

• Beware of burns from the exhaust system and from any part of the engine. Brake discs and drums can also be extremely hot immediately after use.

Crushing

• When working under or near a raised vehicle, always supplement the jack with axle stands, or use drive-on ramps. *Never venture under a car which is only supported by a jack*.

• Take care if loosening or tightening high-torque nuts when the vehicle is on stands. Initial loosening and final tightening should be done with the wheels on the ground.

Fire

• Fuel is highly flammable; fuel vapour is explosive.
• Don't let fuel spill onto a hot engine.
• Do not smoke or allow naked lights (including pilot lights) anywhere near a vehicle being worked on. Also beware of creating sparks (electrically or by use of tools).
• Fuel vapour is heavier than air, so don't work on the fuel system with the vehicle over an inspection pit.
• Another cause of fire is an electrical overload or short-circuit. Take care when repairing or modifying the vehicle wiring.
• Keep a fire extinguisher handy, of a type suitable for use on fuel and electrical fires.

Electric shock

• Ignition HT and Xenon headlight voltages can be dangerous, especially to people with heart problems or a pacemaker. Don't work on or near these systems with the engine running or the ignition switched on.

• Mains voltage is also dangerous. Make sure that any mains-operated equipment is correctly earthed. Mains power points should be protected by a residual current device (RCD) circuit breaker.

Fume or gas intoxication

• Exhaust fumes are poisonous; they can contain carbon monoxide, which is rapidly fatal if inhaled. Never run the engine in a confined space such as a garage with the doors shut.
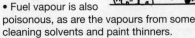
• Fuel vapour is also poisonous, as are the vapours from some cleaning solvents and paint thinners.

Poisonous or irritant substances

• Avoid skin contact with battery acid and with any fuel, fluid or lubricant, especially antifreeze, brake hydraulic fluid and Diesel fuel. Don't syphon them by mouth. If such a substance is swallowed or gets into the eyes, seek medical advice.
• Prolonged contact with used engine oil can cause skin cancer. Wear gloves or use a barrier cream if necessary. Change out of oil-soaked clothes and do not keep oily rags in your pocket.
• Air conditioning refrigerant forms a poisonous gas if exposed to a naked flame (including a cigarette). It can also cause skin burns on contact.

Asbestos

• Asbestos dust can cause cancer if inhaled or swallowed. Asbestos may be found in gaskets and in brake and clutch linings. When dealing with such components it is safest to assume that they contain asbestos.

Special hazards

Hydrofluoric acid

• This extremely corrosive acid is formed when certain types of synthetic rubber, found in some O-rings, oil seals, fuel hoses etc, are exposed to temperatures above 4000C. The rubber changes into a charred or sticky substance containing the acid. *Once formed, the acid remains dangerous for years. If it gets onto the skin, it may be necessary to amputate the limb concerned*.
• When dealing with a vehicle which has suffered a fire, or with components salvaged from such a vehicle, wear protective gloves and discard them after use.

The battery

• Batteries contain sulphuric acid, which attacks clothing, eyes and skin. Take care when topping-up or carrying the battery.
• The hydrogen gas given off by the battery is highly explosive. Never cause a spark or allow a naked light nearby. Be careful when connecting and disconnecting battery chargers or jump leads.

Air bags

• Air bags can cause injury if they go off accidentally. Take care when removing the steering wheel and trim panels. Special storage instructions may apply.

Diesel injection equipment

• Diesel injection pumps supply fuel at very high pressure. Take care when working on the fuel injectors and fuel pipes.

 Warning: Never expose the hands, face or any other part of the body to injector spray; the fuel can penetrate the skin with potentially fatal results.

Remember...

DO

• Do use eye protection when using power tools, and when working under the vehicle.
• Do wear gloves or use barrier cream to protect your hands when necessary.
• Do get someone to check periodically that all is well when working alone on the vehicle.
• Do keep loose clothing and long hair well out of the way of moving mechanical parts.
• Do remove rings, wristwatch etc, before working on the vehicle – especially the electrical system.
• Do ensure that any lifting or jacking equipment has a safe working load rating adequate for the job.

DON'T

• Don't attempt to lift a heavy component which may be beyond your capability – get assistance.
• Don't rush to finish a job, or take unverified short cuts.
• Don't use ill-fitting tools which may slip and cause injury.
• Don't leave tools or parts lying around where someone can trip over them. Mop up oil and fuel spills at once.
• Don't allow children or pets to play in or near a vehicle being worked on.

The following pages are intended to help in dealing with common roadside emergencies and breakdowns. You will find more detailed fault finding information at the back of the manual, and repair information in the main chapters.

If your car won't start and the starter motor doesn't turn

☐ Open the bonnet and make sure that the battery terminals are clean and tight.

☐ Switch on the headlights and try to start the engine. If the headlights go very dim when you're trying to start, the battery is probably flat. Get out of trouble by jump starting (see next page) using a friend's car.

If your car won't start even though the starter motor turns as normal

☐ Is there fuel in the tank?

☐ Is there moisture on electrical components under the bonnet? Switch off the ignition, then wipe off any obvious dampness with a dry cloth. Spray a water-repellent aerosol product (WD-40 or equivalent) on ignition and fuel system electrical connectors like those shown in the photos.

1 On petrol engines, check that the wiring to the ignition module is connected firmly.

2 Check that the airflow meter or air temperature sensor wiring is connected securely.

3 Check the security and condition of the battery connections.

Check that electrical connections are secure (with the ignition switched off) and spray with water dispersant if you suspect a problem due to damp.

4 Check all multiplugs and wiring connectors for security.

5 Check that all fuses are still in good condition and none have blown.

Jump starting

When jump-starting a car using a booster battery, observe the following precautions:

✔ Before connecting the booster battery, make sure that the ignition is switched off.

Caution: Remove the key in case the central locking engages when the jump leads are connected

✔ Ensure that all electrical equipment (lights, heater, wipers, etc) is switched off.

✔ Take note of any special precautions printed on the battery case.

✔ Make sure that the booster battery is the same voltage as the discharged one in the vehicle.

✔ If the battery is being jump-started from the battery in another vehicle, the two vehicles MUST NOT TOUCH each other.

✔ Make sure that the transmission is in neutral (or PARK, in the case of automatic transmission).

 HAYNES HiNT *Jump starting will get you out of trouble, but you must correct whatever made the battery go flat in the first place. There are three possibilities:*

1 *The battery has been drained by repeated attempts to start, or by leaving the lights on.*

2 *The charging system is not working properly (alternator drivebelt slack or broken, alternator wiring fault or alternator itself faulty).*

3 *The battery itself is at fault (electrolyte low, or battery worn out).*

1 Connect one end of the red jump lead to the positive (+) terminal of the flat battery

2 Connect the other end of the red lead to the positive (+) terminal of the booster battery.

3 Connect one end of the black jump lead to the negative (-) terminal of the booster battery

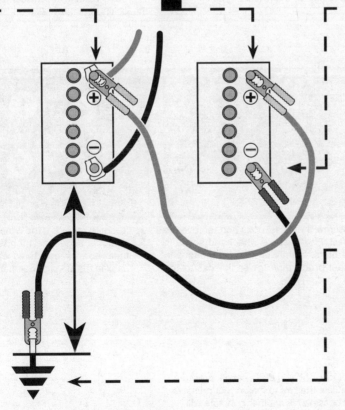

4 Connect the other end of the black jump lead to a bolt or bracket on the engine block, well away from the battery, on the vehicle to be started.

5 Make sure that the jump leads will not come into contact with the fan, drive-belts or other moving parts of the engine.

6 Start the engine using the booster battery and run it at idle speed. Switch on the lights, rear window demister and heater blower motor, then disconnect the jump leads in the reverse order of connection. Turn off the lights etc.

Wheel changing

Note: *Certain Meriva models are equipped with a puncture repair kit and do not have a spare wheel and jack. If your car has a puncture repair kit, refer to the information contained on the next page.*

 Warning: Do not change a wheel in a situation where you risk being hit by other traffic. On busy roads, try to stop in a lay-by or a gateway. Be wary of passing traffic while changing the wheel – it is easy to become distracted by the job in hand.

Preparation

☐ When a puncture occurs, stop as soon as it is safe to do so.

☐ Park on firm level ground, if possible, and well out of the way of other traffic.

☐ Use hazard warning lights if necessary.

☐ If you have one, use a warning triangle to alert other drivers of your presence.

☐ Apply the handbrake and engage first or reverse gear.

☐ Chock the wheel diagonally opposite the

one being removed – a couple of large stones will do for this.

☐ If the ground is soft, use a flat piece of wood to spread the load under the jack.

Changing the wheel

1 Lift the floor covering and unscrew the spare wheel clamp nut. Lift out the spare wheel.

2 Remove the tools from the toolbag stored beneath the spare wheel. Use the special clip to pull off the wheel trim.

3 Slacken each wheel bolt by half a turn. Locate the jack head below the jacking point nearest the wheel to be changed; the jacking point is indicated by a depression in the sill.

4 Turn the handle until the base of the jack touches the ground ensuring that the jack is vertical. Raise the vehicle until the wheel is clear of the ground. If the tyre is flat make sure that the vehicle is raised sufficiently to allow the spare wheel to be fitted.

5 Unscrew the wheel bolts and remove the wheel. Fit the spare wheel and screw in the bolts. Lightly tighten the bolts with the wheel brace then lower the car to the ground.

6 Securely tighten the wheel bolts in a diagonal sequence then refit the wheel trim. Stow the punctured wheel and tools back in the luggage compartment.

Finally . . .

☐ Remove the wheel chocks.

☐ Stow the jack and tools in the correct locations in the car.

☐ Check the tyre pressure on the wheel just fitted. If it is low, or if you don't have a pressure gauge with you, drive slowly to the next garage and inflate the tyre to the correct pressure.

☐ Have the damaged tyre or wheel repaired as soon as possible, or another puncture will leave you stranded.

Using the puncture repair kit

 Warning: Do not attempt to repair a punctured tyre in a situation where you risk being hit by other traffic. On busy roads, try to stop in a lay-by or a gateway. Be wary of passing traffic while using the kit – it is easy to become distracted by the job in hand.

 Warning: Repair of a tyre using the puncture repair kit must be regarded as a 'get you home' emergency repair only. A new tyre must be fitted as soon as possible.

Preparation

- [ ] When a puncture occurs, stop as soon as it is safe to do so.
- [ ] Park on firm level ground, if possible, and well out of the way of other traffic.
- [ ] Use hazard warning lights if necessary.
- [ ] If you have one, use a warning triangle to alert other drivers of your presence.
- [ ] Apply the handbrake and engage first or reverse gear (or Park on models with automatic transmission).

Repairing the puncture

1 Lift the luggage compartment floor covering and take out the bag containing the tyre repair kit. Remove the sealant bottle and compressor from the bag. Remove the air hose and electrical cable from the underside of the compressor.

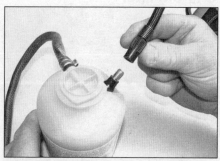

2 Screw the air hose onto the sealant bottle connection.

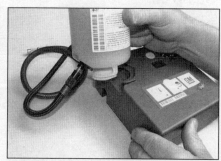

3 Fit the sealant bottle in the retainer on the compressor, then position the compressor near the punctured tyre.

4 Unscrew the dust cap from the punctured tyre, and screw the sealant bottle air hose onto the tyre valve.

5 Ensure that the switch on the compressor is set to O, then plug the compressor electrical cable into the accessory socket or cigarette lighter socket.

6 Switch on the ignition, then set the compressor switch to I to start the it. To avoid discharging the battery when the compressor is running, it is advisable to start the engine. The pump will initially pump the sealant into the tyre which will take approximately 30 seconds, and then start to inflate the tyre. During the initial 30 second period, the pressure gauge on the pump will indicate up to 6 bar (87 psi) and then drop. The correct tyre pressure (see end of *Weekly checks*) should be obtained within 10 minutes. The compressor can then be switched off by returning the switch to the O position.

7 If it is necessary to release the pressure in the tyre, press the button above the pressure gauge on the compressor.

Important notes

- [ ] If the correct tyre pressure is not obtained within 10 minutes, it is likely that the tyre is too badly damaged to be repaired with the kit.
- [ ] The maximum speed sticker attached to the sealant bottle should be placed in the driver's field of view. Do not exceed the permitted maximum speed until an undamaged wheel and tyre have been fitted.
- [ ] On completion, disconnect the tyre repair kit and connect the end of the air hose to the free connection on the sealant bottle. This will prevent any remaining sealant from leaking out.
- [ ] Continue driving immediately so that the sealant is evenly distributed around the inside of the tyre.
- [ ] After driving approximately 6 miles (but no more than 10 minutes) stop and check the tyre pressure by connecting the air hose to the tyre valve. As long as the pressure indicated on the gauge is more than 1.3 bar (19 psi) it may be adjusted to the prescribed value using the electric pump. If the pressure has fallen below 1.3 bar (19 psi) the repair has not been successful and the car should not be driven. It will therefore be necessary to seek roadside assistance.

Identifying leaks

Puddles on the garage floor or drive, or obvious wetness under the bonnet or underneath the car, suggest a leak that needs investigating. It can sometimes be difficult to decide where the leak is coming from, especially if an engine undershield is fitted. Leaking oil or fluid can also be blown rearwards by the passage of air under the car, giving a false impression of where the problem lies.

 Warning: Most automotive oils and fluids are poisonous. Wash them off skin, and change out of contaminated clothing, without delay.

 The smell of a fluid leaking from the car may provide a clue to what's leaking. Some fluids are distinctively coloured. It may help to remove the engine undershield, clean the car carefully and to park it over some clean paper overnight as an aid to locating the source of the leak.
Remember that some leaks may only occur while the engine is running.

Sump oil

Engine oil may leak from the drain plug...

Oil from filter

...or from the base of the oil filter.

Gearbox oil

Gearbox oil can leak from the seals at the inboard ends of the driveshafts.

Antifreeze

Leaking antifreeze often leaves a crystalline deposit like this.

Brake fluid

A leak occurring at a wheel is almost certainly brake fluid.

Power steering fluid

Power steering fluid may leak from the pipe connectors on the steering rack.

Towing

When all else fails, you may find yourself having to get a tow home – or of course you may be helping somebody else. Long-distance recovery should only be done by a garage or breakdown service. For shorter distances, DIY towing using another car is easy enough, but observe the following points:

☐ Use a proper tow-rope – they are not expensive. The vehicle being towed must display an ON TOW sign in its rear window.

☐ Always turn the ignition key to the 'On' position when the vehicle is being towed, so that the steering lock is released, and the direction indicator and brake lights work.

☐ A towing eye is provided with the tool kit in the luggage compartment. Only attach the tow-rope to the towing eye.

☐ To fit the towing eye, remove the circular cover from the front or rear bumper, as required, then screw in the towing eye anti-clockwise as far as it will go using the handle of the wheel brace to turn the eye. **Note that the towing eye has a left-hand thread.**

☐ Always turn the ignition key to the 'on' position when the vehicle is being towed, so that the steering lock is released, and that the direction indicator and brake lights will work.

☐ Before being towed, release the handbrake and select neutral on the transmission.

☐ Note that greater-than-usual pedal pressure will be required to operate the brakes, since the vacuum servo unit is only operational with the engine running.

☐ Greater-than-usual steering effort will also be required.

☐ The driver of the car being towed must keep the tow-rope taut at all times to avoid snatching.

☐ Make sure that both drivers know the route before setting off.

☐ Only drive at moderate speeds and keep the distance towed to a minimum. Drive smoothly and allow plenty of time for slowing down at junctions.

Introduction

There are some very simple checks which need only take a few minutes to carry out, but which could save you a lot of inconvenience and expense.

These *Weekly checks* require no great skill or special tools, and the small amount of time they take to perform could prove to be very well spent, for example:

☐ Keeping an eye on tyre condition and pressures, will not only help to stop them wearing out prematurely, but could also save your life.

☐ Many breakdowns are caused by electrical problems. Battery-related faults are particularly common, and a quick check on a regular basis will often prevent the majority of these.

☐ If your car develops a brake fluid leak, the first time you might know about it is when your brakes don't work properly. Checking the level regularly will give advance warning of this kind of problem.

☐ If the oil or coolant levels run low, the cost of repairing any engine damage will be far greater than fixing the leak, for example.

Underbonnet check points

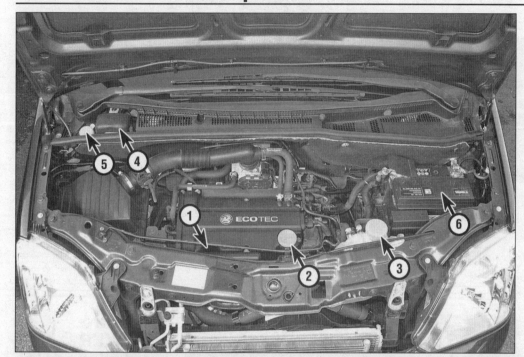

◀ 1.4 litre petrol models

1 *Engine oil level dipstick*
2 *Engine oil filler cap*
3 *Coolant reservoir (expansion tank)*
4 *Brake and clutch fluid reservoir*
5 *Washer fluid reservoir*
6 *Battery*

◀ 1.6 litre Z16SE petrol models

1 *Engine oil level dipstick*
2 *Engine oil filler cap*
3 *Coolant reservoir (expansion tank)*
4 *Brake and clutch fluid reservoir*
5 *Washer fluid reservoir*
6 *Battery*

◀ **1.6 litre Z16XE petrol models**

1 Engine oil level dipstick

2 Engine oil filler cap

3 Coolant reservoir (expansion tank)

4 Brake and clutch fluid reservoir

5 Washer fluid reservoir

6 Battery

◀ **1.6 litre Z16XEP petrol models**

1 Engine oil level dipstick

2 Engine oil filler cap

3 Coolant reservoir (expansion tank)

4 Brake and clutch fluid reservoir

5 Washer fluid reservoir

6 Battery

1 *Engine oil level dipstick*

2 *Engine oil filler cap*

3 *Coolant reservoir (expansion tank)*

4 *Brake and clutch fluid reservoir*

5 *Washer fluid reservoir*

6 *Battery*

1 *Engine oil level dipstick*

2 *Engine oil filler cap*

3 *Coolant reservoir (expansion tank)*

4 *Brake and clutch fluid reservoir*

5 *Washer fluid reservoir*

6 *Battery*

**◄ 1.7 litre
diesel models**

1 *Engine oil level dipstick*

2 *Engine oil filler cap*

3 *Coolant reservoir
(expansion tank)*

4 *Brake and clutch fluid
reservoir*

5 *Washer fluid reservoir*

6 *Battery*

Engine oil level

Before you start

✔ Make sure that the car is on level ground.
✔ The oil level must be checked with the engine at normal operating temperature, however, wait at least 5 minutes after the engine has been switched off.

 If the oil is checked immediately after driving the vehicle, some of the oil will remain in the upper engine components, resulting in an inaccurate reading on the dipstick.

The correct oil

Modern engines place great demands on their oil. It is very important that the correct oil for your car is used (see *Lubricants and fluids*).

Car care

● If you have to add oil frequently, you should check whether you have any oil leaks. Place some clean paper under the car overnight, and check for stains in the morning. If there are no leaks, then the engine may be burning oil.
● Always maintain the level between the upper and lower dipstick marks (see photo 3). If the level is too low, severe engine damage may occur. Oil seal failure may result if the engine is overfilled by adding too much oil.

1 The dipstick is brightly-coloured for easy identification (see *Underbonnet check points* for exact location). Withdraw the dipstick.

2 Using a clean rag or paper towel remove all oil from the dipstick. Insert the clean dipstick into the tube as far as it will go, then withdraw it again.

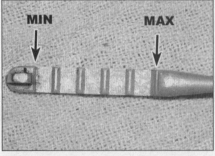

3 Note the level on the end of the dipstick, which should be between the upper (MAX) mark and lower (MIN) mark. Approximately 1.0 litre of oil will raise the level from the lower mark to the upper mark.

4 Oil is added through the filler cap. Unscrew the cap and top-up the level. A funnel may help to reduce spillage. Add the oil slowly, checking the level on the dipstick frequently. Avoid overfilling (see *Car care*).

Coolant level

 Warning: Do not attempt to remove the expansion tank pressure cap when the engine is hot, as there is a very great risk of scalding. Do not leave open containers of coolant about, as it is poisonous.

Car care

● Adding coolant should not be necessary on a regular basis. If frequent topping-up is required, it is likely there is a leak. Check the radiator, all hoses and joint faces for signs of staining or wetness, and rectify as necessary.

● It is important that antifreeze is used in the cooling system all year round, not just during the winter months. Don't top-up with water alone, as the antifreeze will become too diluted.

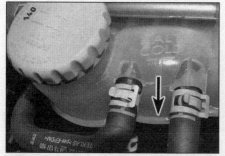

1 The coolant level varies with the temperature of the engine. When the engine is cold, the coolant level should be slightly above the KALT/COLD mark (arrowed) on the side of the tank. When the engine is hot, the level will rise.

2 If topping-up is necessary, **wait until the engine is cold**. Slowly unscrew the expansion tank cap, to release any pressure present in the cooling system, and remove it.

3 Add a mixture of water and antifreeze to the expansion tank until the coolant is up to the KALT/COLD level mark. Refit the cap and tighten it securely.

Brake and clutch fluid level

Note: *The clutch fluid on models with Easytronic is checked every 20 000 miles (see Chapter 1A).*

 Warning:
• *Hydraulic fluid can harm your eyes and damage painted surfaces, so use extreme caution when handling and pouring it.*
• *Do not use fluid that has been standing open for some time, as it absorbs moisture from the air, which can cause a dangerous loss of braking effectiveness.*

Safety first!

● If the reservoir requires repeated topping-up this is an indication of a fluid leak somewhere in the system, which should be investigated immediately.

● If a leak is suspected, the car should not be driven until the braking system has been checked. Never take any risks where brakes are concerned.

HAYNES HiNT • *Make sure that your car is on level ground.*

• *The fluid level in the reservoir will drop slightly as the brake pads and shoes wear down, but the fluid level must never be allowed to drop below the MIN mark.*

1 The MAX and MIN marks are indicated on the side of the reservoir. The fluid level must be kept between the marks at all times.

2 If topping-up is necessary, first lift off the reservoir cover.

3 Wipe clean the area around the filler cap to prevent dirt entering the hydraulic system. Unscrew the reservoir cap.

4 Carefully add fluid, taking care not to spill it onto the surrounding components. Use only the specified fluid; mixing different types can cause damage to the system. After topping-up to the correct level, securely refit the cap and wipe off any spilt fluid.

Tyre condition and pressure

It is very important that tyres are in good condition, and at the correct pressure - having a tyre failure at any speed is highly dangerous. Tyre wear is influenced by driving style - harsh braking and acceleration, or fast cornering, will all produce more rapid tyre wear. As a general rule, the front tyres wear out faster than the rears. Interchanging the tyres from front to rear ("rotating" the tyres) may result in more even wear. However, if this is completely effective, you may have the expense of replacing all four tyres at once! Remove any nails or stones embedded in the tread before they penetrate the tyre to cause deflation. If removal of a nail does reveal that the tyre has been punctured, refit the nail so that its point of penetration is marked. Then immediately change the wheel, and have the tyre repaired by a tyre dealer.

Regularly check the tyres for damage in the form of cuts or bulges, especially in the sidewalls. Periodically remove the wheels, and clean any dirt or mud from the inside and outside surfaces. Examine the wheel rims for signs of rusting, corrosion or other damage. Light alloy wheels are easily damaged by "kerbing" whilst parking; steel wheels may also become dented or buckled. A new wheel is very often the only way to overcome severe damage.

New tyres should be balanced when they are fitted, but it may become necessary to re-balance them as they wear, or if the balance weights fitted to the wheel rim should fall off. Unbalanced tyres will wear more quickly, as will the steering and suspension components. Wheel imbalance is normally signified by vibration, particularly at a certain speed (typically around 50 mph). If this vibration is felt only through the steering, then it is likely that just the front wheels need balancing. If, however, the vibration is felt through the whole car, the rear wheels could be out of balance. Wheel balancing should be carried out by a tyre dealer or garage.

1 *Tread Depth - visual check*
The original tyres have tread wear safety bands (B), which will appear when the tread depth reaches approximately 1.6 mm. The band positions are indicated by a triangular mark on the tyre sidewall (A).

2 *Tread Depth - manual check*
Alternatively, tread wear can be monitored with a simple, inexpensive device known as a tread depth indicator gauge.

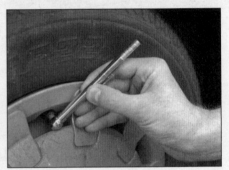

3 *Tyre Pressure Check*
Check the tyre pressures regularly with the tyres cold. Do not adjust the tyre pressures immediately after the vehicle has been used, or an inaccurate setting will result.

Tyre tread wear patterns

Shoulder Wear

Underinflation (wear on both sides)
Under-inflation will cause overheating of the tyre, because the tyre will flex too much, and the tread will not sit correctly on the road surface. This will cause a loss of grip and excessive wear, not to mention the danger of sudden tyre failure due to heat build-up.
Check and adjust pressures
Incorrect wheel camber (wear on one side)
Repair or renew suspension parts
Hard cornering
Reduce speed!

Centre Wear

Overinflation
Over-inflation will cause rapid wear of the centre part of the tyre tread, coupled with reduced grip, harsher ride, and the danger of shock damage occurring in the tyre casing.
Check and adjust pressures

If you sometimes have to inflate your car's tyres to the higher pressures specified for maximum load or sustained high speed, don't forget to reduce the pressures to normal afterwards.

Uneven Wear

Front tyres may wear unevenly as a result of wheel misalignment. Most tyre dealers and garages can check and adjust the wheel alignment (or "tracking") for a modest charge.
Incorrect camber or castor
Repair or renew suspension parts
Malfunctioning suspension
Repair or renew suspension parts
Unbalanced wheel
Balance tyres
Incorrect toe setting
Adjust front wheel alignment
Note: *The feathered edge of the tread which typifies toe wear is best checked by feel.*

Screen washer fluid level

● Screenwash additives not only keep the windscreen clean during bad weather, they also prevent the washer system freezing in cold weather – which is when you are likely to need it most. Don't top-up using plain water, as the screenwash will become diluted, and will freeze in cold weather.

 Warning: On no account use engine coolant antifreeze in the screen washer system – this may damage the paintwork.

1 The reservoir for the windscreen and rear window washer systems is located at the rear right-hand side of the engine compartment. If topping-up is necessary, open the filler cap and top up the reservoir. When topping-up the reservoir a screen wash additive should be added in the quantities recommended on the bottle.

Wiper blades

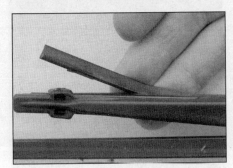

1 Check the condition of the wiper blades; if they are cracked or show any signs of deterioration, or if the glass swept area is smeared, renew them. Wiper blades should be renewed annually.

2 To remove a windscreen wiper blade, pull the arm fully away from the screen until it locks. Depress the tab at the end of the arm and slide the blade out of the arm.

3 To remove a tailgate wiper blade, pull the arm fully away from the window, then disengage the blade from the arm and lift away the blade.

Battery

Caution: Before carrying out any work on the vehicle battery, read the precautions given in 'Safety first!' at the start of this manual. If the battery is to be disconnected, refer to 'Disconnecting the battery' in the Reference Chapter, before proceeding.

✔ Make sure that the battery tray is in good condition, and that the clamp is tight. Corrosion on the tray, retaining clamp and the battery itself can be removed with a solution of water and baking soda. Thoroughly rinse all cleaned areas with water. Any metal parts damaged by corrosion should be covered with a zinc-based primer, then painted.

✔ Periodically (approximately every three months), check the charge condition of the battery as described in Chapter 5A.

✔ If the battery is flat, and you need to jump start your vehicle, see *Roadside Repairs*.

HAYNES HiNT

Battery corrosion can be kept to a minimum by applying a layer of petroleum jelly to the clamps and terminals after they are reconnected.

1 The battery is located at the front, left-hand side of the engine compartment. Lift up the plastic insulator cover over the battery positive terminal, then check the tightness of battery clamps to ensure good electrical connections. You should not be able to move them. Also check each cable for cracks and frayed conductors.

2 If corrosion (white, fluffy deposits) is evident, remove the cables from the battery terminals, clean them with a small wire brush, then refit them. Automotive stores sell a tool for cleaning the battery post . . .

3 . . . as well as the battery cable clamps

Electrical systems

✔ Check all external lights and the horn. Refer to the appropriate Sections of Chapter 12 for details if any of the circuits are found to be inoperative.

✔ Visually check all accessible wiring connectors, harnesses and retaining clips for security, and for signs of chafing or damage.

HAYNES HiNT

If you need to check your brake lights and indicators unaided, back up to a wall or garage door and operate the lights. The reflected light should show if they are working properly.

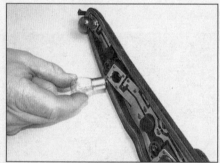

1 If a single indicator light, stop-light or headlight has failed, it is likely that a bulb has blown and will need to be renewed. Refer to Chapter 12 for details. If both stop-lights have failed, it is possible that the switch has failed (see Chapter 9).

2 If more than one indicator light or headlight has failed, it is likely that either a fuse has blown or that there is a fault in the circuit (see Chapter 12). The main fuses are located in the fusebox adjacent to the glovebox or under the lighting switch. Lift off the cover for access to the fuses.

3 To renew a blown fuse, remove it, where applicable, using the plastic tool provided. Fit a new fuse of the same rating, available from car accessory shops. It is important that you find the reason that the fuse blew (see *Electrical fault finding* in Chapter 12).

Lubricants and fluids

Engine

Petrol. . . . .   Multigrade engine oil, viscosity SAE 0W/30, 0W/40, 5W/30, 5W/40 to Vauxhall/Opel specification GM-LL-A-025

Diesel . . . .   Multigrade engine oil, viscosity SAE 0W/30, 0W/40, 5W/30, 5W/40 to Vauxhall/Opel specification GM-LL-B-025

Manual and Easytronic transmissions . . . .   Vauxhall/Opel gear oil (93 165 290)

Cooling system. . . . .   Vauxhall/Opel silicate-free coolant (93 170 402)

Brake/clutch fluid reservoir. . . . .   Hydraulic fluid to DOT 4

Tyre pressures (cold)

Note: *Pressures apply to original-equipment tyres, and may vary if any other make or type of tyre is fitted; check with the tyre manufacturer or supplier for correct pressures if necessary.*

Normal load (up to 3 passengers)	Front	Rear
All models except 1.7 litre Z17DTH diesel	2.4 bar (35 psi)	2.2 bar (32 psi)
1.7 litre Z17DTH diesel.	2.6 bar (38 psi)	2.4 bar (35 psi)
Fully laden		
All models except 1.7 litre Z17DTH diesel	2.6 bar (38 psi)	3.0 bar (44 psi)
1.7 litre Z17DTH diesel.	2.8 bar (41 psi)	3.2 bar (46 psi)

Notes

Chapter 1 Part A:
Routine maintenance and servicing – petrol models

Contents

Degrees of difficulty

| Easy, suitable for novice with little experience | Fairly easy, suitable for beginner with some experience | Fairly difficult, suitable for competent DIY mechanic | Difficult, suitable for experienced DIY mechanic | Very difficult, suitable for expert DIY or professional |

Lubricants and fluids .... Refer to the end of *Weekly checks* on page 0•19

Capacities

Engine oil (including oil filter)
1.4 litre engines	3.5 litres
1.6 litre engines	3.5 litres
1.8 litre engines	4.2 litres
Difference between MIN and MAX dipstick marks	1.0 litre

Cooling system
1.4 litre engines	5.6 litres
1.6 litre SOHC engines	6.8 litres
1.6 litre DOHC engines:	
Z16XE engines	7.1 litres
Z16XEP engines	6.3 litres
1.8 litre engines	6.4 litres

Transmission
Manual transmission	1.6 litres
Easytronic transmission	1.6 litres

Washer fluid reservoir .... 2.1 litres

Fuel tank .... 53 litres

Cooling system
Antifreeze mixture:
  50% antifreeze .... Protection down to -40°C

Ignition system
Spark plugs:
  Type:

1.4 litre engines	Bosch FQR 8 LEU2
1.6 litre engines:	
Except Z16XEP	Bosch FLR 8 LDCU
Z16XEP	Bosch FQR 8 LEU2
1.8 litre engines	Bosch FLR 8 LDCU
Electrode gap	0.9 mm

Brakes
Friction material minimum thickness (excluding backing plate) .... 2.0 mm

Torque wrench settings

	Nm	lbf ft
Oil filter housing cap-to-filter housing (paper element filter)	25	18
Roadwheel bolts	110	81
Spark plugs	25	18
Sump drain plug:		
1.4 litre engines	10	7
1.6 litre SOHC engines:		
Models without air conditioning (steel sump)	55	41
Models with air conditioning (alloy sump)	45	33
1.6 and 1.8 litre DOHC engines:		
Hexagon type (metal seal ring)	45	33
Torx type (rubber seal ring	14	10

The maintenance intervals in this manual are provided with the assumption that you, not the dealer, will be carrying out the work. These are the minimum maintenance intervals based on the standard service schedule recommended by the manufacturer for vehicles driven daily. If you wish to keep your vehicle in peak condition at all times, you may wish to perform some of these procedures more often. We encourage frequent maintenance, because it enhances the efficiency, performance and resale value of your vehicle.

If the vehicle is driven in dusty areas, used to tow a trailer, or driven frequently at slow speeds (idling in traffic) or on short journeys, more frequent maintenance intervals are recommended.

When the vehicle is new, it should be serviced by a dealer service department (or other workshop recognised by the vehicle manufacturer as providing the same standard of service) in order to preserve the warranty. The vehicle manufacturer may reject warranty claims if you are unable to prove that servicing has been carried out as and when specified, using only original equipment parts or parts certified to be of equivalent quality.

Every 250 miles or weekly

- [ ] Refer to *Weekly checks*

Every 10 000 miles or 6 months – whichever comes first

- [ ] Renew the engine oil and filter (Section 3)

Note: *Vauxhall/Opel recommend that the engine oil and filter are changed every 20 000 miles or 12 months if the vehicle is being operated under the standard service schedule. However, oil and filter changes are good for the engine and we recommend that the oil and filter are renewed more frequently, especially if the vehicle is used on a lot of short journeys.*

Every 20 000 miles or 12 months – whichever comes first

- [ ] Check all underbonnet and underbody components, pipes and hoses for leaks (Section 4)
- [ ] Check the Easytronic clutch hydraulic fluid level (Section 5)
- [ ] Check the condition of the brake pads, the calipers and discs (Section 6)
- [ ] Check the condition of all brake fluid pipes and hoses (Section 7)
- [ ] Check the condition of the front suspension and steering components, particularly the rubber gaiters and seals (Section 8)
- [ ] Check the condition of the driveshaft joint gaiters, and the driveshaft joints (Section 9)
- [ ] Check the condition of the exhaust system components (Section 10)
- [ ] Check the condition of the rear suspension components (Section 11)
- [ ] Check the bodywork and underbody for damage and corrosion, and check the condition of the underbody corrosion protection (Section 12)
- [ ] Check the tightness of the roadwheel bolts (Section 13)
- [ ] Lubricate all door, bonnet and tailgate hinges and locks (Section 14)
- [ ] Check the operation of the horn, all lights, and the wipers and washers (Section 15)
- [ ] Carry out a road test (Section 16)
- [ ] Reset the service interval indicator (Section 17)

Every 40 000 miles or 2 years – whichever comes first

- [ ] Renew the pollen filter (Section 18)
- [ ] Check the auxiliary drivebelt and tensioner (Section 19)
- [ ] Check the operation of the handbrake and adjust if necessary (Section 20)
- [ ] Check the headlight beam alignment (Section 21)

Every 2 years, regardless of mileage

- [ ] Renew the battery for the remote control handset (Section 22)
- [ ] Renew the brake and clutch fluid (Section 23)
- [ ] Renew the coolant (Section 24)*
- [ ] Exhaust emission test (Section 25)

* Note: *Vehicles using Vauxhall/Opel silicate-free coolant do not need the coolant renewed on a regular basis.*

Every 40 000 miles or 4 years – whichever comes first

- [ ] Renew the air cleaner filter element (Section 26)
- [ ] Renew the spark plugs and check the ignition system (Section 27)
- [ ] Renew the timing belt, tensioner and idler pulleys – 1.6 and 1.8 litre engines (Section 28)*
- [ ] Renew the fuel filter (Section 29)

*Note: *The normal interval for timing belt renewal is:*
- *60 000 miles or 6 years for the 1.6 litre Z16XE engines and 1.8 litre engines.*
- *80 000 miles or 8 years for the 1.6 litre Z16SE engines.*
- *90 000 miles or 10 years for the 1.6 litre Z16XEP engines.*

It is strongly recommended that the interval used is 40 000 miles on vehicles which are subjected to intensive use, ie, mainly short journeys or a lot of stop-start driving. The actual belt renewal interval is therefore very much up to the individual owner, but bear in mind that severe engine damage will result if the belt breaks.

Every 100 000 miles or 10 years whichever comes first

- [ ] Check, and if necessary adjust, the valve clearances – 1.6 litre Z16XEP engines (Section 30)

Underbonnet view of a 1.4 litre model

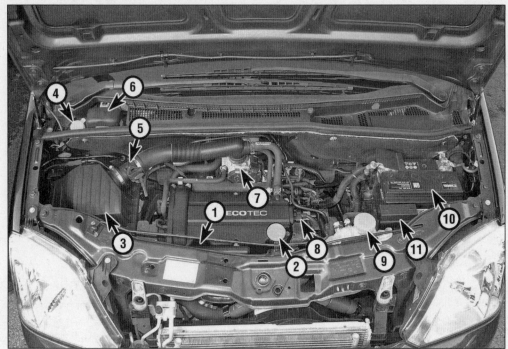

1   Engine oil level dipstick
2   Engine oil filler cap
3   Air cleaner assembly
4   Screen washer fluid
    reservoir
5   Airflow meter/inlet air
    temperature sensor
6   Brake and clutch fluid
    reservoir
7   Throttle housing
8   Ignition module
9   Coolant expansion tank
10 Battery
11 Relay box

Underbonnet view of a 1.6 litre Z16SE model

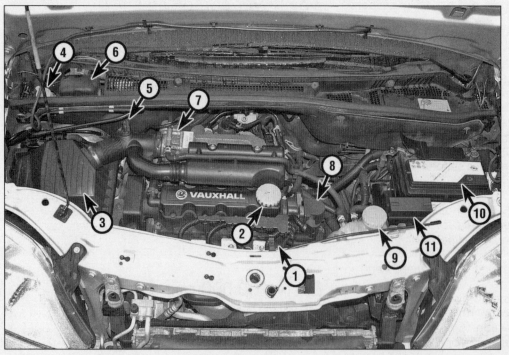

1   Engine oil level dipstick
2   Engine oil filler cap
3   Air cleaner assembly
4   Screen washer fluid
    reservoir
5   Airflow meter/inlet air
    temperature sensor
6   Brake and clutch fluid
    reservoir
7   Throttle housing
8   Ignition module
9   Coolant expansion tank
10 Battery
11 Relay box

Component location – petrol models 1A•5

Underbonnet view of a 1.6 litre Z16XE model

1 Engine oil level dipstick
2 Engine oil filler cap
3 Air cleaner assembly
4 Screen washer fluid reservoir
5 Airflow meter/inlet air temperature sensor
6 Brake and clutch fluid reservoir
7 Coolant expansion tank
8 Battery
9 Relay box

Underbonnet view of a 1.6 litre Z16XEP model

1 Engine oil level dipstick
2 Engine oil filler cap
3 Air cleaner assembly
4 Screen washer fluid reservoir
5 Airflow meter/inlet air temperature sensor
6 Brake and clutch fluid reservoir
7 Ignition module
8 Coolant expansion tank
9 Battery
10 Relay box

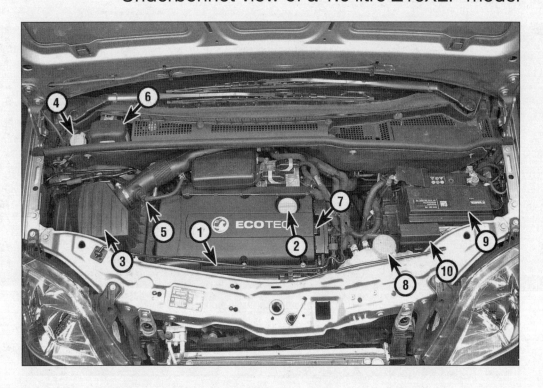

Underbonnet view of a 1.8 litre model

1   Engine oil level dipstick
2   Engine oil filler cap
3   Air cleaner assembly
4   Screen washer fluid
     reservoir
5   Airflow meter/inlet air
     temperature sensor
6   Brake and clutch fluid
     reservoir
7   Throttle housing
8   Coolant expansion tank
9   Battery
10 Relay box

Front underbody view

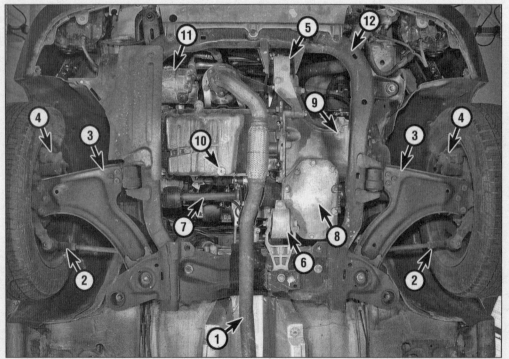

1   Exhaust front pipe
2   Steering track rods
3   Front suspension lower
     arms
4   Front brake calipers
5   Engine mounting front
     torque link
6   Engine mounting rear
     torque link
7   Right-hand driveshaft
8   Final drive cover plate
9   Manual transmission
10 Engine oil drain plug
11 Air conditioning
     compressor
12 Front subframe

Rear underbody view

1 Handbrake cable
2 Rear suspension coil springs
3 Exhaust tailpipe and silencer
4 Exhaust heat shield
5 Rear suspension trailing arms and rear axle
6 Fuel tank

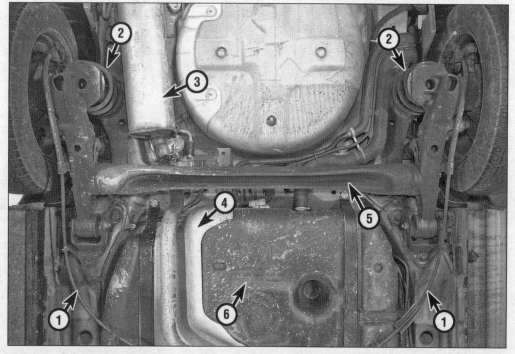

Maintenance procedures

1 General information

1 This Chapter is designed to help the home mechanic maintain his/her vehicle for safety, economy, long life and peak performance.
2 The Chapter contains a master maintenance schedule, followed by Sections dealing specifically with each task in the schedule. Visual checks, adjustments, component renewal and other helpful items are included. Refer to the accompanying illustrations of the engine compartment and the underside of the vehicle for the locations of the various components.
3 Servicing your vehicle in accordance with the mileage/time maintenance schedule and the following Sections will provide a planned maintenance programme, which should result in a long and reliable service life. This is a comprehensive plan, so maintaining some items but not others at the specified service intervals, will not produce the same results.
4 As you service your vehicle, you will discover that many of the procedures can – and should – be grouped together, because of the particular procedure being performed, or because of the proximity of two otherwise-unrelated components to one another. For example, if the vehicle is raised for any reason, the exhaust can be inspected at the same time as the suspension and steering components.
5 The first step in this maintenance programme is to prepare yourself before the actual work begins. Read through all the Sections relevant to the work to be carried out, then make a list and gather all the parts and tools required. If a problem is encountered, seek advice from a parts specialist, or a dealer service department.

2 Regular maintenance

1 If, from the time the vehicle is new, the routine maintenance schedule is followed closely, and frequent checks are made of fluid levels and high-wear items, as suggested throughout this manual, the engine will be kept in relatively good running condition, and the need for additional work will be minimised.
2 It is possible that there will be times when the engine is running poorly due to the lack of regular maintenance. This is even more likely if a used vehicle, which has not received regular and frequent maintenance checks, is purchased. In such cases, additional work may need to be carried out, outside of the regular maintenance intervals.
3 If engine wear is suspected, a compression test (refer to the relevant Part of Chapter 2) will provide valuable information regarding the overall performance of the main internal components. Such a test can be used as a basis to decide on the extent of the work to be carried out. If, for example, a compression test indicates serious internal engine wear, conventional maintenance as described in this Chapter will not greatly improve the performance of the engine, and may prove a waste of time and money, unless extensive overhaul work is carried out first.
4 The following series of operations are those most often required to improve the performance of a generally poor-running engine:

Primary operations

a) Clean, inspect and test the battery (refer to Weekly checks).
b) Check all the engine-related fluids (refer to Weekly checks).
c) Check the condition and tension of the auxiliary drivebelt (Section 19).
d) Renew the spark plugs (Section 27).
e) Check the condition of the air cleaner element, and renew if necessary (Section 26).
f) Check the condition of all hoses, and check for fluid leaks (Section 4).

5 If the above operations do not prove fully effective, carry out the following secondary operations:

Secondary operations

All items listed under Primary operations, plus the following:
a) Check the ignition system (Chapter 5B).
b) Check the charging system (Chapter 5A).
c) Check the fuel, exhaust and emission control systems (refer to the appropriate Parts of Chapter 4).

Every 10 000 miles or 6 months

3 Engine oil and filter renewal

1 Before starting this procedure, gather together all the necessary tools and materials. Also make sure that you have plenty of clean rags and newspapers handy, to mop-up any spills. Ideally, the engine oil should be warm, as it will drain more easily, and more built-up sludge will be removed with it. Take care not to touch the exhaust or any other hot parts of the engine when working under the vehicle. To avoid any possibility of scalding, and to protect yourself from possible skin irritants and other harmful contaminants in used engine oils, it is advisable to wear gloves when carrying out this work.

3.3 Removing the oil filler cap

2 Access to the underside of the vehicle will be greatly improved if it can be raised on a lift, driven onto ramps, or jacked up and supported on axle stands (see *Jacking and vehicle support*). Whichever method is chosen, make sure that the vehicle remains level, or if it is at an angle, that the drain plug is at the lowest point.
3 Remove the oil filler cap from the camshaft cover (twist it through a quarter-turn anti-clockwise and withdraw it) **(see illustration)**.
4 Using a spanner, or preferably a suitable socket and bar, slacken the drain plug about half a turn. Position the draining container under the drain plug, then remove the plug completely **(see Haynes Hint)**.
5 Allow some time for the oil to drain, noting that it may be necessary to reposition the container as the oil flow slows to a trickle.
6 Position another container under the oil

As the drain plug threads release, move it sharply away so the stream of oil issuing from the sump runs into the container, not up your sleeve.

filter, located on the front left-hand side of the cylinder block. Two different types of filter may be encountered. On 1.4 litre engines, the oil filter is of the paper element type. On 1.6 and 1.8 litre engines the oil filter is a metal canister type. Proceed as described under the following sub-Sections, according to engine.

1.4 litre engines

7 Move the container into position under the oil filter housing **(see illustration)**.
8 Unscrew the oil filter housing cap and withdraw the cap together with the filter from the oil filter housing.
9 Withdraw the filter from the oil filter housing cap.
10 Use clean rags to remove all remaining oil, dirt and sludge from the oil filter housing.
11 Remove the sealing O-ring from the oil filter housing cap.
12 Fit a new sealing O-ring to the oil filter housing cap then clip the new oil filter element to the cap **(see illustrations)**.
13 Fit the cap and filter element assembly to the oil filter housing and screw the cap into position. Finally, tighten the cap to the specified torque **(see illustrations)**.

1.6 and 1.8 litre engines

14 Move the container into position under the oil filter.
15 Use an oil filter removal tool to slacken the filter initially, then unscrew it by hand the rest of the way **(see illustration)**. Empty the oil

3.7 Oil filter (arrowed) on 1.4 litre engines

3.12a Fit a new sealing O-ring to the oil filter housing cap . . .

3.12b . . . then clip the new oil filter element to the cap – 1.4 litre engines

3.13a Fit the cap and filter element assembly to the oil filter housing . . .

3.13b . . . screw the assembly into place and tighten the cap to the specified torque – 1.4 litre engines

3.15 Using an oil filter removal tool to slacken the filter – 1.6 and 1.8 litre engines

from the old filter into the container. In order to ensure that all the old oil is removed, puncture the 'dome' of the filter in two places and allow the oil to drain from the filter completely.

16 Use a clean rag to remove all oil, dirt and sludge from the filter sealing area on the block.

17 Apply a light coating of clean engine oil to the sealing ring on the new filter, then screw the filter into position on the engine. Tighten the filter firmly by hand only – **do not** use any tools.

All engines

18 After all the oil has drained, wipe the drain plug and the sealing washer/O-ring with a clean rag. Examine the condition of the sealing washer/O-ring, and renew it if it

shows signs of damage which may prevent an oil-tight seal. Clean the area around the drain plug opening, and refit the plug complete with the washer/O-ring. Tighten the plug to the specified torque, using a torque wrench.

19 Remove the old oil and all tools from under the vehicle then lower the vehicle to the ground.

20 Fill the engine through the filler hole in the camshaft cover, using the correct grade and type of oil (refer to *Weekly checks* for details of topping-up). Pour in half the specified quantity of oil first, then wait a few minutes for the oil to drain into the sump. Continue to add oil, a small quantity at a time, until the level is up to the lower mark on the dipstick. Adding approximately a further 1.0 litre will bring the level up to the upper mark on the dipstick.

21 Start the engine and run it until it reaches normal operating temperature. While the engine is warming up, check for leaks around the oil filter and the sump drain plug.

22 Stop the engine, and wait at least five minutes for the oil to settle in the sump once more. With the new oil circulated and the filter now completely full, recheck the level on the dipstick, and add more oil as necessary.

23 Dispose of the used engine oil and filter safely, with reference to *General repair procedures* in the Reference Chapter of this manual. Do not discard the old filter with domestic household waste. The facility for waste oil disposal provided by many local council refuse tips and/or recycling centres generally has a filter receptacle alongside.

Every 20 000 miles or 12 months

4 Hose and fluid leak check

Note: *Also refer to Section 7.*

1 Visually inspect the engine joint faces, gaskets and seals for any signs of water or oil leaks. Pay particular attention to the areas around the camshaft cover, cylinder head, oil filter and sump joint faces. Similarly, check the transmission and (where applicable) the air conditioning compressor for oil leakage. Bear in mind that, over a period of time, some very slight seepage from these areas is to be expected; what you are really looking for is any indication of a serious leak. Should a leak be found, renew the offending gasket or oil seal by referring to the appropriate Chapters in this manual.

2 Also check the security and condition of all the engine-related pipes and hoses. Ensure that all cable-ties or securing clips are in place, and in good condition. Clips which are broken or missing can lead to chafing of the hoses pipes or wiring, which could cause more serious problems in the future.

3 Carefully check the radiator hoses and heater hoses along their entire length. Renew any hose which is cracked, swollen or deteriorated. Cracks will show up better if the hose is squeezed. Pay close attention to the hose clips that secure the hoses to the cooling system components. Hose clips can pinch and puncture hoses, resulting in cooling system leaks. If wire-type hose clips are used, it may be a good idea to update them with screw-type clips.

4 Inspect all the cooling system components (hoses, joint faces, etc) for leaks. Where any problems of this nature are found on system components, renew the component or gasket with reference to Chapter 3 **(see Haynes Hint)**.

5 With the vehicle raised, inspect the fuel tank and filler neck for punctures, cracks

and other damage. The connection between the filler neck and tank is especially critical. Sometimes, a rubber filler neck or connecting hose will leak due to loose retaining clamps or deteriorated rubber.

6 Carefully check all rubber hoses and metal or plastic fuel lines leading away from the fuel tank. Check for loose connections, deteriorated hoses, crimped lines and other damage. Pay particular attention to the vent pipes and hoses, which often loop up around the filler neck and can become blocked or crimped. Follow the lines to the front of the vehicle, carefully inspecting them all the way. Renew damaged sections as necessary. Similarly, whilst the vehicle is raised, take the opportunity to inspect all underbody brake fluid pipes and hoses.

7 From within the engine compartment, check the security of all fuel hose attachments and pipe unions, and inspect the fuel hoses and vacuum hoses for kinks, chafing and deterioration.

5 Clutch hydraulic fluid level check – Easytronic models

Note: *The fluid level check for manual transmission models is in 'Weekly checks'.*

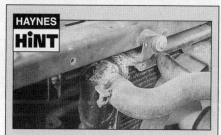

A leak in the cooling system will usually show up as white- or antifreeze-coloured deposits on the area adjoining the leak.

1 The clutch hydraulic fluid level markings are on the side of the fluid reservoir located on the front of the transmission. The use of a mirror will be helpful.

2 Check that the level of the fluid is at or near the MAX marking on the side of the reservoir **(see illustration)**.

3 If topping-up is required, unscrew the filler cap and pour in fresh fluid until the level is at the MAX marking. Retighten the cap on completion.

6 Brake pad, caliper and disc check

1 Jack up the front and rear of the vehicle and support it securely on axle stands (see *Jacking and vehicle support*). Remove the front and rear roadwheels.

2 For a quick check, the pad thickness can be carried out via the inspection hole

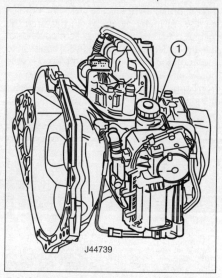

5.2 Clutch fluid reservoir (1) on Easytronic models

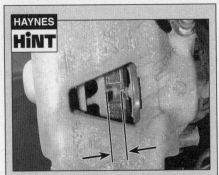

For a quick check, the thickness of friction material remaining on the inner brake pad can be measured through the aperture in the caliper body.

on the caliper **(see Haynes Hint)**. Using a steel rule, measure the thickness of the pad friction linings. This must not be less than that indicated in the Specifications.

3 The view through the caliper inspection hole gives a rough indication of the state of the brake pads. For a comprehensive check, the brake pads should be removed and cleaned. The operation of the caliper can then also be checked, and the condition of the brake disc itself can be fully examined on both sides. Chapter 9 contains a detailed description of how the brake disc should be checked for wear and/or damage.

4 If any pad's friction material is worn to the specified thickness or less, *all four pads on each axle must be renewed as a set.* Refer to Chapter 9 for details.

5 On completion, refit the roadwheels and lower the vehicle to the ground.

7 Brake fluid pipe and hose check

1 The brake hydraulic system includes a number of metal pipes, which run from the master cylinder to the hydraulic modulator of the anti-lock braking system (ABS) and then to the front and rear brake assemblies. Flexible hoses are fitted between the pipes and the front and rear brake assemblies to allow for steering and suspension movement.

8.4 Check for wear in the hub hearings by grasping the wheel and trying to rock it

2 When checking the system, first look for signs of leakage at the pipe or hose unions, then examine the flexible hoses for signs of cracking, chafing or deterioration of the rubber. Bend the hoses sharply between the fingers (but do not actually bend them double, or the casing may be damaged) and check that this does not reveal previously-hidden cracks, cuts or splits. Check that the pipes and hoses are securely fastened in their clips.

3 Carefully working along the length of the metal pipes, look for dents, kinks, damage of any sort, or corrosion. Light corrosion can be polished off, but if the depth of pitting is significant, the pipe must be renewed.

8 Front suspension and steering check

1 Firmly apply the handbrake, then jack up the front of the vehicle and support it securely on axle stands (see *Jacking and vehicle support*).

2 Inspect the balljoint dust covers and the steering gear gaiters for splits, chafing or deterioration.

3 Any wear of these components will cause loss of lubricant, and may allow water to enter the components, resulting in rapid deterioration of the balljoints or steering gear.

4 Grasp each roadwheel at the 12 o'clock and 6 o'clock positions, and try to rock it **(see illustration)**. Very slight free play may be felt, but if the movement is appreciable, further investigation is necessary to determine the source. Continue rocking the wheel while an assistant depresses the footbrake. If the movement is now eliminated or significantly reduced, it is likely that the hub bearings are at fault. If the free play is still evident with the footbrake depressed, then there is wear in the suspension joints or mountings.

5 Now grasp each wheel at the 9 o'clock and 3 o'clock positions, and try to rock it as before. Any movement felt now may again be caused by wear in the hub bearings or the steering track rod end balljoints. If the track rod end balljoint is worn, the visual movement will be obvious.

6 Using a large screwdriver or flat bar, check for wear in the suspension mounting bushes by levering between the relevant suspension component and its attachment point. Some movement is to be expected, as the mountings are made of rubber, but excessive wear should be obvious. Also check the condition of any visible rubber bushes, looking for splits, cracks or contamination of the rubber.

7 Check for any signs of fluid leakage around the suspension struts, or from the rubber gaiters around the piston rods. Should any fluid be noticed, the suspension strut is defective internally, and should be renewed. **Note:** *Suspension struts should always be renewed in pairs on the same axle.*

8 With the vehicle standing on its wheels, have an assistant turn the steering wheel

back-and-forth about an eighth of a turn each way. There should be very little, if any, lost movement between the steering wheel and roadwheels. If this is not the case, closely observe the joints and mountings previously described. In addition, check the steering column universal joints for wear, and also check the rack-and-pinion steering gear itself.

9 The efficiency of each suspension strut may be checked by bouncing the vehicle at each front corner. Generally speaking, the body will return to its normal position and stop after being depressed. If it rises and returns on a rebound, the suspension strut is probably suspect. Also examine the suspension strut upper mountings for any signs of wear.

9 Driveshaft check

1 Firmly apply the handbrake, then jack up the front of the vehicle and support it securely on axle stands (see *Jacking and vehicle support*).

2 Turn the steering onto full lock then slowly rotate the roadwheel. Inspect the condition of the outer constant velocity (CV) joint rubber gaiters while squeezing the gaiters to open out the folds **(see illustration)**. Check for signs of cracking, splits or deterioration of the rubber which may allow the grease to escape and lead to water and grit entry into the joint. Also check the security and condition of the retaining clips. Repeat these checks on the inner CV joints. If any damage or deterioration is found, the gaiters should be renewed as described in Chapter 8.

3 At the same time, check the general condition of the CV joints themselves by first holding the driveshaft and attempting to rotate the wheel. Repeat this check by holding the inner joint and attempting to rotate the driveshaft. Any appreciable movement indicates wear in the joints, wear in the driveshaft splines or loose driveshaft retaining nut.

10 Exhaust system check

1 With the engine cold (at least an hour after the

9.2 Check the condition of the driveshaft gaiters (1) and retaining clips (2)

vehicle has been driven), check the complete exhaust system from the engine to the end of the tailpipe. The exhaust system is most easily checked with the vehicle raised on a hoist, or suitably-supported on axle stands, so that the exhaust components are readily visible and accessible (see *Jacking and vehicle support*).

2 Check the exhaust pipes and connections for evidence of leaks, severe corrosion and damage. Make sure that all brackets and mountings are in good condition, and that all relevant nuts and bolts are tight. Leakage at any of the joints or in other parts of the system will usually show up as a black sooty stain in the vicinity of the leak.

3 Rattles and other noises can often be traced to the exhaust system, especially the brackets and mountings **(see illustration)**. Try to move the pipes and silencers. If the components are able to come into contact with the body or suspension parts, secure the system with new mountings. Otherwise separate the joints (if possible) and twist the pipes as necessary to provide additional clearance.

11 Rear suspension check

1 Chock the front wheels, then jack up the rear of the vehicle and support securely on axle stands (see *Jacking and vehicle support*).

2 Inspect the rear suspension components for any signs of obvious wear or damage. Pay particular attention to the rubber mounting bushes, and renew if necessary (see Chapter 10).

3 Grasp each roadwheel at the 12 o'clock and 6 o'clock positions **(see illustration 8.4)**, and try to rock it. Any excess movement indicates wear in the wheel bearings. Wear may also be accompanied by a rumbling sound when the wheel is spun, or a noticeable roughness if the wheel is turned slowly. The wheel bearing can be renewed as described in Chapter 10.

4 Check for any signs of fluid leakage around the shock absorber bodies. Should any fluid be noticed, the shock absorber is defective internally, and should be renewed. **Note:** *Shock absorbers should always be renewed in pairs on the same axle.*

5 With the vehicle standing on its wheels, the efficiency of each shock absorber may be checked by bouncing the vehicle at each rear corner. Generally speaking, the body will return to its normal position and stop after being depressed. If it rises and returns on a rebound, the shock absorber is probably suspect.

12 Bodywork and underbody condition check

Note: *This work should be carried out by a Vauxhall/Opel dealer in order to validate the vehicle warranty. The work includes a*

thorough inspection of the vehicle paintwork and underbody for damage and corrosion.

Bodywork damage and corrosion check

1 Once the car has been washed, and all tar spots and other surface blemishes have been cleaned off, carefully check all paintwork, looking closely for chips or scratches. Pay particular attention to vulnerable areas such as the front panels (bonnet and spoiler), and around the wheel arches. Any damage to the paintwork must be rectified as soon as possible, to comply with the terms of the manufacturer's anti-corrosion warranties; check with a Vauxhall/Opel dealer for details.

2 If a chip or light scratch is found which is recent and still free from rust, it can be touched-up using the appropriate touch-up stick which can be obtained from Vauxhall/Opel dealers. Any more serious damage, or rusted stone chips, can be repaired as described in Chapter 11, but if damage or corrosion is so severe that a panel must be renewed, seek professional advice as soon as possible.

3 Always check that the door and ventilation opening drain holes and pipes are completely clear, so that water can drain out.

Corrosion protection check

4 The wax-based underbody protective coating should be inspected annually, preferably just prior to Winter, when the underbody should be washed down as thoroughly as possible without disturbing the protective coating. Any damage to the coating should be repaired using a suitable wax-based sealer. If any of the body panels are disturbed for repair or renewal, do not forget to re-apply the coating. Wax should be injected into door cavities, sills and box sections, to maintain the level of protection provided by the vehicle manufacturer – seek the advice of a Vauxhall/Opel dealer.

13 Roadwheel bolt tightness check

1 Where applicable, remove the wheel trims from the wheels.

2 Using a torque wrench on each wheel bolt in turn, ensure that the bolts are tightened to the specified torque.

3 Where applicable, refit the wheel trims on completion, making sure they are fitted correctly.

14 Hinge and lock lubrication

1 Work around the vehicle and lubricate the hinges of the bonnet, doors and tailgate with a light machine oil.

2 Lightly lubricate the bonnet release mechanism and exposed section of inner cable with a smear of grease.

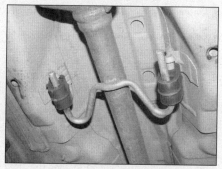

10.3 Exhaust mountings

3 Check the security and operation of all hinges, latches and locks, adjusting them where required. Check the operation of the central locking system.

4 Check the condition and operation of the tailgate support struts, renewing them both if either is leaking or no longer able to support the tailgate securely when raised.

15 Electrical systems check

1 Check the operation of all the electrical equipment, ie, lights, direction indicators, horn, etc. Refer to the appropriate sections of Chapter 12 for details if any of the circuits are found to be inoperative.

2 Note that the stop-light switch is described in Chapter 9.

3 Check all accessible wiring connectors, harnesses and retaining clips for security, and for signs of chafing or damage. Rectify any faults found.

16 Road test

Instruments and electrical equipment

1 Check the operation of all instruments, warning lights and electrical equipment.

2 Make sure that all instruments read correctly, and switch on all electrical equipment in turn, to check that it functions properly.

Steering and suspension

3 Check for any abnormalities in the steering, suspension, handling or road 'feel'.

4 Drive the vehicle, and check that there are no unusual vibrations or noises.

5 Check that the steering feels positive, with no excessive 'sloppiness', or roughness, and check for any suspension noises when cornering and driving over bumps.

Drivetrain

6 Check the performance of the engine, clutch, transmission and driveshafts.

7 Listen for any unusual noises from the engine, clutch and transmission.

8 Make sure that the engine runs smoothly when idling, and that there is no hesitation when accelerating.

9 Check that, where applicable, the clutch action is smooth and progressive, that the drive is taken up smoothly, and that the pedal travel is not excessive. Also listen for any noises when the clutch pedal is depressed.

10 Check that all gears can be engaged smoothly without noise, and that the gear lever action is smooth and not abnormally vague or 'notchy'.

11 Listen for a metallic clicking sound from the front of the vehicle, as the vehicle is driven slowly in a circle with the steering on full-lock. Carry out this check in both directions. If a clicking noise is heard, this indicates wear in a driveshaft joint (see Chapter 8).

Braking system

12 Make sure that the vehicle does not pull to one side when braking.

13 Check that there is no vibration through the steering when braking.

14 Check that the handbrake operates correctly, without excessive movement of the lever, and that it holds the vehicle stationary on a slope.

15 Test the operation of the brake servo unit as follows. Depress the footbrake four or five times to exhaust the vacuum, then start the engine. As the engine starts, there should be a noticeable 'give' in the brake pedal as vacuum builds-up. Allow the engine to run for at least two minutes, and then switch it off. If the brake pedal is now depressed again, it should be possible to detect a hiss from the servo as the pedal is depressed. After about four or five applications, no further hissing should be heard, and the pedal should feel considerably harder.

17 Service interval indicator reset

1 With the ignition switched off, the display on the instrument panel must show the trip odometer.

2 With the ignition still switched off, depress and hold the trip odometer reset button located on the instrument panel.

3 With the reset button depressed, switch on the ignition, wait until the service interval display changes (approximately 10 seconds).

4 After approximately 10 seconds the display will show the service symbol and the maximum mileage before the next required service, followed by 'InSP'. When '- - -' appears in the display, release the reset button and switch off the ignition. When the button is released, the odometer reading will appear again.

Every 40 000 miles or 2 years

18 Pollen filter renewal

1 Remove the windscreen cowl panel as described in Chapter 11.

2 Release the upper retaining catch and remove the pollen filter housing cover located at the rear left-hand side of the engine compartment **(see illustration)**.

3 Lift the lower edge of the pollen filter upwards and withdraw it from the housing **(see illustration)**.

4 Fit the new filter using a reversal of the removal procedure; make sure that the filter is fitted the correct way up as indicated on the edge of the filter.

19 Auxiliary drivebelt condition check

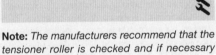

Note: *The manufacturers recommend that the tensioner roller is checked and if necessary renewed at the same time as the drivebelt.*

Checking

1 Due to their function and material make-up, drivebelts are prone to failure after a long period of time and should therefore be inspected regularly.

2 Apply the handbrake, then jack up the front of the vehicle and support it on axle stands (see *Jacking and vehicle support*). Remove the right-hand front roadwheel and the lower

wheel arch liner for access to the right-hand side of the engine.

3 With the engine stopped, inspect the full length of the drivebelt for cracks and separation of the belt plies. It will be necessary to turn the engine (using a spanner or socket and bar on the crankshaft pulley bolt) so that the belt can be inspected thoroughly. Twist the belt between the pulleys so that both sides can be viewed. Also check for fraying, and glazing which gives the belt a shiny appearance. Check the pulleys for nicks, cracks, distortion and corrosion. If the belt shows signs of wear or damage, it should be renewed as a precaution against breakage in service.

Renewal

4 If not already done, apply the handbrake, then jack up the front of the vehicle and support it on axle stands (see *Jacking and vehicle support*). Remove the right-hand front roadwheel and the lower wheel arch liner for access to the right-hand side of the engine.

5 For additional working clearance, remove the air cleaner housing as described in Chapter 4A.

6 If the drivebelt is to be re-used, mark it to indicate its normal running direction.

7 On 1.4 litre engines, support the engine and remove the right-hand engine mounting with reference to Chapter 2A. **Note:** *On these engines, the engine mounting locates within the auxiliary drivebelt.*

18.2 Release the upper retaining catch and remove the pollen filter housing cover

18.3 Lift the lower edge of the pollen filter upwards and withdraw it from the housing

8 Note the routing of the drivebelt, then, using a Torx key or spanner (as applicable) on the pulley centre bolt, or the raised projection on the tensioner arm, turn the tensioner clockwise (1.4 litre engines) or anti-clockwise (1.6 and 1.8 litre engines) against the spring tension. Hold the tensioner in this position by inserting a suitable locking pin/bolt through the special hole provided **(see illustrations)**.

9 Slip the auxiliary drivebelt off of the pulleys.

10 Locate the auxiliary drivebelt onto the pulleys in the correct routing. If the drivebelt is being re-used, make sure it is fitted the correct way around.

11 Turn back the tensioner and remove the locking bolt, then release it, making sure that the drivebelt ribs locate correctly on each of the pulley grooves.

12 On 1.4 litre engines, refit the right-hand engine mounting with reference to Chapter 2A.

13 Refit the air cleaner housing, then refit the wheel arch liner and roadwheel, and lower the vehicle to the ground.

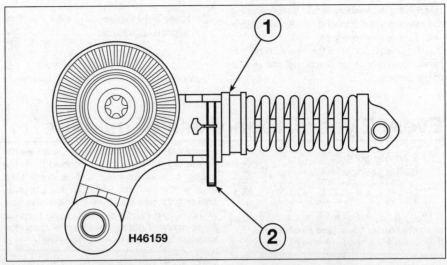

19.8a Auxiliary drivebelt tensioner on 1.4 litre engines

1 Tensioner body　　　　　　*2 Locking pin/bolt*

20 Handbrake operation and adjustment check

1 With the vehicle on a slight slope, apply the handbrake lever by up to four clicks of the ratchet, and check that it holds the vehicle stationary, then release the lever and check that there is no resistance to movement of the vehicle.

2 If necessary, adjust the handbrake as follows.

3 Chock the front wheels then jack up the rear of the car and securely support it on axle stands (see *Jacking and vehicle support*).

4 Fully depress, then release the brake pedal at least five times. Similarly, fully apply, then release the handbrake at least five times.

5 Lift out the trim panel beneath the handbrake lever, then unclip the handbrake lever gaiter from the centre console **(see illustrations)**. The handbrake cable adjuster nut is situated by the handbrake lever inside the vehicle.

6 Move the handbrake lever to the fully-released position, then turn the cable adjuster nut anti-clockwise to remove all tension from the cables **(see illustration)**.

7 With the handbrake lever set on the third

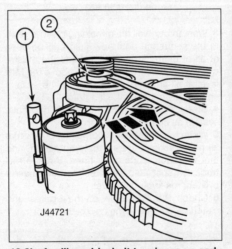

19.8b Auxiliary drivebelt tensioner on early 1.6 litre and all 1.8 litre engines

1 Locking pin/bolt
2 Turn the tensioner as indicated to release the tension

19.8c Auxiliary drivebelt tensioner on later 1.6 litre engines

1 Raised projection on tensioner arm
2 Locking pin/bolt hole

notch of the ratchet mechanism, rotate the adjuster nut clockwise until a reasonable amount of force is required to turn each wheel. **Note**: *The force required should be equal for each wheel.*

8 Now pull the handbrake lever up to the fourth notch of the ratchet mechanism and check that both rear wheels are locked. Once this is so, fully release the handbrake lever and check that the wheels rotate freely. Check the adjustment

20.5a Lift out the trim panel beneath the handbrake lever . . .

20.5b . . . then unclip the handbrake lever gaiter from the centre console

20.6 Turn the cable adjuster nut (arrowed) anti-clockwise to remove all tension from the cables

by applying the handbrake fully whilst counting the clicks emitted from the handbrake ratchet and, if necessary, re-adjust.
9 On completion of adjustment, refit the handbrake lever gaiter, then lower the vehicle to the ground.

21 Headlight beam alignment check

Accurate adjustment of the headlight beam is only possible using optical beam-setting equipment, and this work should therefore be carried out by a Vauxhall/Opel dealer or service station with the necessary facilities. Refer to Chapter 12 for further information.

Every 2 years, regardless of mileage

22 Remote control battery renewal
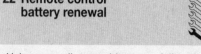

1 Using a small screwdriver, carefully prise open the battery cover (see illustration).
2 Note how the circular battery is fitted, then carefully remove it from the contacts (see illustration).
3 Fit the new battery (type CR 20 32) and refit the cover making sure that it clips fully onto the base.
4 After changing the battery, lock and unlock the driver's door with the key in the lock, then switch on the ignition to synchronise the remote control unit.

23 Hydraulic fluid renewal

Note: It is not possible for the home mechanic to bleed the clutch hydraulic system on Easytronic models. Refer to Chapter 7B for additional information.

⚠ Warning: Hydraulic fluid can harm your eyes and damage painted surfaces, so use extreme caution when handling and pouring it. Do not use fluid that has been standing open for some time, as it absorbs moisture from the air. Excess moisture can cause a dangerous loss of braking effectiveness.

1 The procedure is similar to that for the bleeding of the hydraulic system as described in Chapters 9 (brake) and 6 (clutch).
2 Working as described in Chapter 9, open the first bleed screw in the sequence, and

pump the brake pedal gently until nearly all the old fluid has been emptied from the master cylinder reservoir. Top-up to the MAX level with new fluid, and continue pumping until only the new fluid remains in the reservoir, and new fluid can be seen emerging from the bleed screw. Tighten the screw, and top the reservoir level up to the MAX level line.

> **HAYNES HiNT** Old hydraulic fluid is invariably much darker in colour than the new, making it easy to distinguish the two.

3 Work through all the remaining bleed screws in the sequence until new fluid can be seen at all of them. Be careful to keep the master cylinder reservoir topped-up to above the MIN level at all times, or air may enter the system and greatly increase the length of the task.
4 Bleed the fluid from the clutch hydraulic system as described in Chapter 6.
5 When the operation is complete, check that all bleed screws are securely tightened, and that their dust caps are refitted. Wash off all traces of spilt fluid, and recheck the master cylinder reservoir fluid level.
6 Check the operation of the brakes and clutch before taking the car on the road.

24 Coolant renewal

Note: Vauxhall/Opel do not specify renewal intervals for the antifreeze mixture, as the mixture used to fill the system when the vehicle is new is designed to last the lifetime of the vehicle. However, it is strongly recommended

that the coolant is renewed at the intervals specified in the 'Maintenance schedule', as a precaution against possible engine corrosion problems. This is particularly advisable if the coolant has been renewed using an antifreeze other than that specified by Vauxhall/Opel. With many antifreeze types, the corrosion inhibitors become progressively less effective with age. It is up to the individual owner whether or not to follow this advice.

⚠ Warning: Wait until the engine is cold before starting this procedure. Do not allow antifreeze to come in contact with your skin, or with the painted surfaces of the vehicle. Rinse off spills immediately with plenty of water. Never leave antifreeze lying around in an open container, or in a puddle in the driveway or on the garage floor. Children and pets are attracted by its sweet smell, but antifreeze can be fatal if ingested.

Cooling system draining

1 To drain the cooling system, first cover the expansion tank cap with a wad of rag, and slowly turn the cap anti-clockwise to relieve the pressure in the cooling system (a hissing sound will normally be heard). Wait until any pressure remaining in the system is released, then continue to turn the cap until it can be removed.
2 Position a suitable container beneath the right-hand side of the radiator.
3 The coolant drain plug is located at the bottom of the radiator right-hand end tank. Unscrew the drain plug and allow the coolant to drain.
4 When the flow of coolant stops, refit and tighten the drain plug.
5 As no cylinder block drain plug is fitted, it is not possible to drain all of the coolant. Due consideration must be made for this when refilling the system, in order to maintain the correct concentration of antifreeze.
6 If the coolant has been drained for a reason other than renewal, then provided it is clean and less than two years old, it can be re-used.

Cooling system flushing

7 If coolant renewal has been neglected, or if the antifreeze mixture has become diluted, then in time, the cooling system may gradually lose efficiency, as the coolant passages become restricted due to rust, scale deposits, and other sediment. The cooling system efficiency can be restored by flushing the system clean.

22.1 Using a small screwdriver, carefully prise open the remote control battery cover

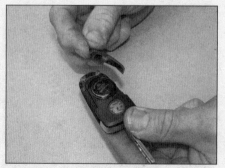
22.2 Note how the circular battery is fitted, then carefully remove it from the contacts

8 The radiator should be flushed independently of the engine, to avoid unnecessary contamination.

Radiator flushing

9 Disconnect the top and bottom hoses and any other relevant hoses from the radiator, with reference to Chapter 3.

10 Insert a garden hose into the radiator top inlet. Direct a flow of clean water through the radiator, and continue flushing until clean water emerges from the radiator bottom outlet.

11 If after a reasonable period, the water still does not run clear, the radiator can be flushed with a good proprietary cleaning agent. It is important that the manufacturer's instructions are followed carefully. If the contamination is particularly bad, remove the radiator, insert the hose in the radiator bottom outlet, and reverse-flush the radiator.

Engine flushing

12 To flush the engine, the thermostat must be removed, because it will be shut, and would otherwise prevent the flow of water around the engine. The thermostat can be removed as described in Chapter 3. Take care not to introduce dirt or debris into the system if this approach is used.

13 With the bottom hose disconnected from the radiator, insert a garden hose into the thermostat opening. Direct a clean flow of water through the engine, and continue flushing until clean water emerges from the radiator bottom hose.

14 On completion of flushing, refit the thermostat with reference to Chapter 3, and reconnect the hoses.

Cooling system filling

15 Before attempting to fill the cooling system, make sure that all hoses and clips are in good condition, and that the clips are tight. Note that an antifreeze mixture must be used all year round, to prevent corrosion of the engine components.

16 Remove the expansion tank filler cap.

17 Fill the system by slowly pouring the coolant into the expansion tank until it is up to the filler neck.

18 Refit and tighten the expansion tank filler cap.

19 Start the engine and run it at 2000 to 2500 rpm until the cooling fan switches on. Continue running the engine at between 2000 and 2500 rpm for a further 2 minutes.

20 Stop the engine, and allow it to cool, then recheck the coolant level with reference to *Weekly checks*. Top-up the level if necessary and refit the expansion tank filler cap.

Antifreeze mixture

21 Always use an ethylene-glycol based antifreeze which is suitable for use in mixed-metal cooling systems. **Note:** *Vauxhall/Opel recommend the use of silicate-free 'red' coolant (see 'Lubricants and fluids').* The quantity of antifreeze and levels of protection are given in the Specifications.

22 Before adding antifreeze, the cooling system should be completely drained, preferably flushed, and all hoses checked for condition and security.

23 After filling with antifreeze, a label should be attached to the expansion tank, stating the type and concentration of antifreeze used, and the date installed. Any subsequent topping-up should be made with the same type and concentration of antifreeze.

Caution: Do not use engine antifreeze in the windscreen/tailgate washer system, as it will cause damage to the vehicle paintwork. A screenwash additive should be added to the washer system in the quantities stated on the bottle.

25 Exhaust emission check

1 The exhaust emission check is carried out initially after 3 years, then every 2 years, however, on vehicles which are subject to intensive use (eg, taxis/hire cars/ambulances) it must be carried out annually. The check involves checking the engine management system operation by plugging an electronic tester into the system diagnostic socket to check the electronic control unit (ECU) memory for faults (see Chapter 4A).

2 In reality, if the vehicle is running correctly and the engine management warning light in the instrument panel is functioning normally, then this check need not be carried out.

Every 40 000 miles or 4 years

26 Air cleaner element renewal

1 The air cleaner is located in the front right-hand corner of the engine compartment.

2 Slacken the retaining clip and detach the air inlet duct from the air cleaner cover (see illustrations).

3 Where applicable, release the evaporative emission control vapour hoses from the clip at the rear of the air cleaner cover (see illustration).

4 Undo the screws and lift off the air cleaner cover, then lift out the filter element (see illustrations).

5 Wipe out the casing and the cover.

6 Fit the new filter element, noting that the rubber locating flange should be uppermost, and secure the cover with the screws.

26.2a Slacken the retaining clip (arrowed) . . .

26.2b . . . and detach the air inlet duct from the air cleaner cover

26.3 Where applicable, release the hoses from the clip at the rear of the air cleaner cover

26.4a **Undo the retaining screws . . .**

26.4b **. . . lift off the air cleaner cover. . .**

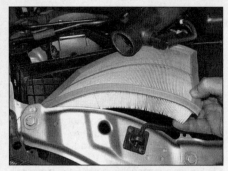

26.4c **. . . then lift out the filter element**

7 Where applicable, refit the vapour hoses to the air cleaner cover.

8 Refit the air inlet duct and secure with the retaining clip.

27 Spark plug renewal and ignition system check

Spark plug renewal

1 The correct functioning of the spark plugs is vital for the correct running and efficiency of the engine. It is essential that the plugs fitted are appropriate for the engine, the suitable type being specified at the beginning of this Chapter. If the correct type is used and the engine is in good condition, the spark plugs should not need attention between scheduled renewal intervals. Spark plug cleaning is rarely necessary, and should not be attempted

27.6a **Unscrew the spark plugs . . .**

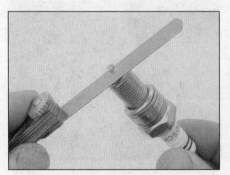

27.12a **Measuring a spark plug electrode gap using a feeler blade**

unless specialised equipment is available, as damage can easily be caused to the firing ends.

1.4, 1.6 and 1.8 litre DOHC engines

2 Where applicable, remove the engine top cover after removing the oil filler cap. Refit the cap.

3 Remove the ignition module from the spark plugs with reference to Chapter 5B.

1.6 litre SOHC engines

4 If the marks on the original-equipment spark plug (HT) leads cannot be seen, mark the leads to correspond to the cylinder the plug serves. Pull the leads from the plugs by gripping the end fitting, not the lead, otherwise the lead connection may be fractured.

All engines

5 It is advisable to remove the dirt from the spark plug recesses using a clean brush, vacuum cleaner or compressed air before

27.6b **. . . and remove them**

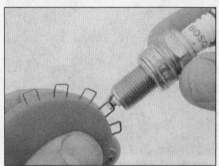

27.12b **Measuring a spark plug electrode gap using a wire gauge**

removing the plugs, to prevent dirt dropping into the cylinders.

6 Unscrew the spark plugs from the cylinder head using a spark plug spanner, suitable box spanner or a deep socket and extension bar **(see illustrations)**. Keep the socket aligned with the spark plug – if it is forcibly moved to one side, the ceramic insulator may be broken off.

7 Examination of the spark plugs will give a good indication of the condition of the engine. As each plug is removed, examine it as follows. If the insulator nose of the spark plug is clean and white, with no deposits, this is indicative of a weak mixture or too hot a plug (a hot plug transfers heat away from the electrode slowly, a cold plug transfers heat away quickly).

8 If the tip and insulator nose are covered with hard black-looking deposits, then this is indicative that the mixture is too rich. Should the plug be black and oily, then it is likely that the engine is fairly worn, as well as the mixture being too rich.

9 If the insulator nose is covered with light tan to greyish-brown deposits, then the mixture is correct and it is likely that the engine is in good condition.

10 Some engines are fitted with multi-electrode plugs as standard. On these plugs, the electrode gaps are all preset and no attempt should be made to bend the electrodes.

11 If single electrode plugs are to be installed, the spark plug electrode gap is of considerable importance. If the gap is too large or too small, the size of the spark and its efficiency will be seriously impaired and it will not perform correctly under all engine speed and load conditions. For the best results, the spark plug gap should be set in accordance with the Specifications at the beginning of this Chapter.

12 To set the gap, measure it with a feeler blade or spark plug gap gauge and then carefully bend the outer plug electrode until the correct gap is achieved. The centre electrode should never be bent, as this may crack the insulator and cause plug failure, if nothing worse. If using feeler blades, the gap is correct when the appropriate-size blade is a firm sliding fit **(see illustrations)**.

13 Special spark plug electrode gap adjusting tools are available from most motor accessory shops, or from some spark plug manufacturers.

14 Before fitting the spark plugs, check that the threaded connector sleeves on the top of the plug are tight, and that the plug exterior surfaces and threads are clean.

15 Screw in the spark plugs by hand where possible, then tighten them to the specified torque. Take extra care to enter the plug threads correctly, as the cylinder head is of light alloy construction **(see Haynes Hint)**.

16 Reconnect the HT leads to their original locations (where applicable), or refit the ignition module as described in Chapter 5B. On completion, refit the engine top cover (where applicable).

Ignition system check

Note: *The following applies to 1.6 litre SOHC engines only.*

⚠️ *Warning: Due to the high voltages produced by the electronic ignition system, extreme care must be taken when working on the system with the ignition switched on. Persons with surgically-implanted cardiac pacemaker devices should keep well clear of the ignition circuits, components and test equipment.*

17 The spark plug (HT) leads should be checked whenever new spark plugs are fitted.
18 Ensure that the leads are numbered before removing them, to avoid confusion when refitting. Pull the leads from the plugs by gripping the end fitting, not the lead, otherwise the lead connection may be fractured.
19 Check inside the end fitting for signs of corrosion, which will look like a white crusty powder. Push the end fitting back onto the spark plug, ensuring that it is a tight fit on the plug. If not, remove the lead again and use pliers to carefully crimp the metal connector inside the end fitting, until it fits securely on the end of the spark plug.
20 Using a clean rag, wipe the entire length of the lead to remove any built-up dirt and grease. Once the lead is clean, check for burns, cracks and other damage. Do not bend the lead excessively, nor pull the lead lengthwise, or the conductor inside might be damaged.
21 Disconnect the other end of the lead from the DIS module and check for corrosion and a tight fit in the same manner as the spark plug end. Refit the lead securely on completion.
22 Check the remaining leads, one at a time, in the same way.
23 If new spark plug (HT) leads are required, purchase a set for your car and engine.

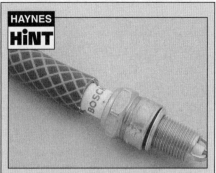

HAYNES HiNT

It's often difficult to insert spark plugs into their holes without cross-threading them. To avoid this possibility, fit a short piece of rubber hose over the end of the spark plug. The flexible hose acts as a universal joint, to help align the plug with the plug hole. Should the plug begin to cross-thread, the hose will slip on the spark plug, preventing thread damage.

24 Even with the ignition system in first-class condition, some engines may still occasionally experience poor starting attributable to damp ignition components. To disperse moisture, a water-dispersant aerosol can be very effective.

28 Timing belt, tensioner and idler pulley renewal – 1.6 and 1.8 litre engines

Refer to the procedures contained in the relevant Part of Chapter 2.

29 Fuel filter renewal

Note: *An external fuel filter is not fitted to all models.*
1 The fuel filter (where fitted) is located under the rear of the vehicle where it is clipped onto the side of the fuel tank **(see illustration)**.
2 Depressurise the fuel system as described in Chapter 4A.
3 Chock the front wheels, then jack up the rear of the vehicle and support on axle stands (see *Jacking and vehicle support*).
4 Position a suitable container below the fuel filter, to catch spilt fuel.
5 Disconnect the quick-release fittings and

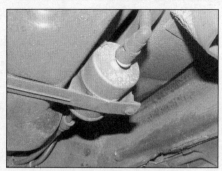

29.1 Fuel filter location

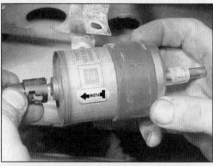

29.7 Ensure that the flow direction arrow points in the direction of the fuel flow

remove the fuel hoses from the fuel filter, noting their locations to ensure correct refitting. A Vauxhall/Opel special tool is available to disconnect the hose connectors, but provided care is taken, the connections can be released using a pair of long-nosed pliers, or a similar tool, to depress the retaining tangs. Be prepared for fuel spillage, and take adequate precautions. Vauxhall/Opel recommend that the connecting clips of the quick-release connectors are renewed whenever removed.
6 Lift the retaining tab and push the filter forwards, out of the mounting bracket. Note the orientation of the fuel flow direction arrow.
7 Fitting the new filter is a reversal of removal, bearing in mind the following points.
a) Ensure that the filter is fitted with the flow direction arrow on the filter body pointing in the direction of fuel flow **(see illustration)**.
b) Ensure that the hoses are reconnected to their correct locations, as noted before removal.
c) On completion, run the engine and check for leaks. If leakage is evident, stop the engine immediately and rectify the problem without delay.

Every 100 000 miles or 10 years

30 Valve clearance check and adjustment – 1.6 litre Z16XEP engines

Refer to the procedures contained in Chapter 2C.

Chapter 1 Part B:
Routine maintenance and servicing – diesel models

Contents

Degrees of difficulty

Easy, suitable for novice with little experience	**Fairly easy,** suitable for beginner with some experience 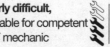	**Fairly difficult,** suitable for competent DIY mechanic	**Difficult,** suitable for experienced DIY mechanic	**Very difficult,** suitable for expert DIY or professional

Lubricants and fluids..................................   Refer to the end of *Weekly checks* on page 0•19

Capacities

Engine oil (including oil filter)

1.3 litre engines ....   3.2 litres

1.7 litre engines:

   Y17DT engines...   4.5 litres

   Z17DTH engines..   5.0 litres

Difference between MIN and MAX dipstick marks................   1.0 litre

Cooling system

1.3 litre engines ....   6.7 litres

1.7 litre engines ....   7.1 litres

Transmission

F17+ transmission ....   1.6 litres

F23 transmission ....   1.55 litres

Washer fluid reservoir ....   2.1 litres

Fuel tank ....   53 litres

Cooling system

Antifreeze mixture:

   50% antifreeze...   Protection down to -40°C

Brakes

Friction material minimum thickness (excluding backing plate).......   2.0 mm

Torque wrench settings

	Nm	lbf ft
Engine oil filter housing cover	25	18
Fuel filter housing cover retaining ring (1.3 litre engines)............	30	22
Fuel filter housing cover centre bolt (1.7 litre engines).............	6	4
Roadwheel bolts..	110	81
Sump drain plug:		
1.3 litre engines	20	15
1.7 litre engines	78	58

The maintenance intervals in this manual are provided with the assumption that you, not the dealer, will be carrying out the work. These are the minimum maintenance intervals based on the standard service schedule recommended by the manufacturer for vehicles driven daily. If you wish to keep your vehicle in peak condition at all times, you may wish to perform some of these procedures more often. We encourage frequent maintenance, because it enhances the efficiency, performance and resale value of your vehicle.

If the vehicle is driven in dusty areas, used to tow a trailer, or driven frequently at slow speeds (idling in traffic) or on short journeys, more frequent maintenance intervals are recommended.

When the vehicle is new, it should be serviced by a dealer service department (or other workshop recognised by the vehicle manufacturer as providing the same standard of service) in order to preserve the warranty. The vehicle manufacturer may reject warranty claims if you are unable to prove that servicing has been carried out as and when specified, using only original equipment parts or parts certified to be of equivalent quality.

Every 250 miles or weekly

☐ Refer to *Weekly checks*

Every 10 000 miles or 6 months – whichever comes first

☐ Renew the engine oil and filter (Section 3)

Note: *Vauxhall/Opel recommend that the engine oil and filter are changed every 20 000 miles or 12 months if the vehicle is being operated under the standard service schedule. However, oil and filter changes are good for the engine and we recommend that the oil and filter are renewed more frequently, especially if the vehicle is used on a lot of short journeys.*

Every 20 000 miles or 12 months – whichever comes first

☐ Check all underbonnet and underbody components, pipes and hoses for leaks (Section 4)
☐ Drain the water from the fuel filter (Section 5)
☐ Check the condition of the brake pads, the calipers and discs (Section 6)
☐ Check the condition of all brake fluid pipes and hoses (Section 7)
☐ Check the condition of the front suspension and steering components, particularly the rubber gaiters and seals (Section 8)
☐ Check the condition of the driveshaft joint gaiters, and the driveshaft joints (Section 9)
☐ Check the condition of the exhaust system components (Section 10)
☐ Check the condition of the rear suspension components (Section 11)
☐ Check the bodywork and underbody for damage and corrosion, and check the condition of the underbody corrosion protection (Section 12)
☐ Check the tightness of the roadwheel bolts (Section 13)
☐ Lubricate all door, bonnet and tailgate hinges and locks (Section 14)
☐ Check the operation of the horn, all lights, and the wipers and washers (Section 15)
☐ Carry out a road test (Section 16)
☐ Reset the service interval indicator (Section 17)

Every 40 000 miles or 2 years – whichever comes first

☐ Renew the pollen filter (Section 18)
☐ Renew the fuel filter (Section 19)
☐ Check the auxiliary drivebelt and tensioner (Section 20)
☐ Check the operation of the handbrake and adjust if necessary (Section 21)
☐ Check the headlight beam alignment (Section 22)

Every 2 years, regardless of mileage

☐ Renew the battery for the remote control handset (Section 23)
☐ Renew the brake and clutch fluid (Section 24)
☐ Renew the coolant (Section 25)*
☐ Exhaust emission check (Section 26)

* Note: *Vehicles using Vauxhall/Opel silicate-free coolant do not need the coolant renewed on a regular basis.*

Every 40 000 miles or 4 years – whichever comes first

☐ Renew the air cleaner filter element (Section 27)
☐ Renew the timing belt, tensioner and idler pulleys – 1.7 litre engines (Section 28)*

* Note: *The normal interval for timing belt renewal is:*
• *100 000 miles or 10 years for the Y17DT engines or 60 000 miles 10 years for the Z17DTH engines.*
It is strongly recommended that the interval used is 40 000 miles on vehicles which are subjected to intensive use, ie, mainly short journeys or a lot of stop-start driving. The actual belt renewal interval is therefore very much up to the individual owner, but bear in mind that severe engine damage will result if the belt breaks.

Every 100 000 miles or 10 years – whichever comes first

☐ Renew the auxiliary drivebelt (Section 29)
☐ Check, and if necessary adjust, the valve clearances – 1.7 litre engines (Section 30)

Underbonnet view of a 1.3 litre engine model

1 Engine oil level dipstick
2 Engine oil filler cap
3 Air cleaner assembly
4 Screen washer fluid reservoir
5 Airflow meter
6 Brake and clutch fluid reservoir
7 Fuel filter
8 Coolant expansion tank
9 Battery
10 Rrelay box

Underbonnet view of a 1.7 litre engine model

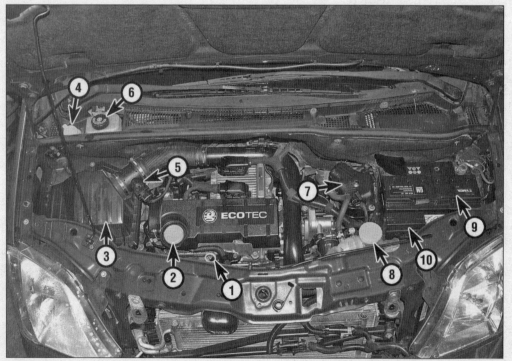

1 Engine oil level dipstick
2 Engine oil filler cap
3 Air cleaner assembly
4 Screen washer fluid reservoir
5 Airflow meter
6 Brake and clutch fluid reservoir
7 Fuel filter
8 Coolant expansion tank
9 Battery
10 Relay box

Front underbody view

1 Exhaust front pipe
2 Catalytic converter
3 Steering track rods
4 Front suspension lower arms
5 Front brake calipers
6 Engine mounting front torque link
7 Engine mounting rear torque link
8 Right-hand driveshaft
9 Final drive cover plate
10 Manual transmission
11 Engine oil drain plug
12 Air conditioning compressor
13 Front subframe

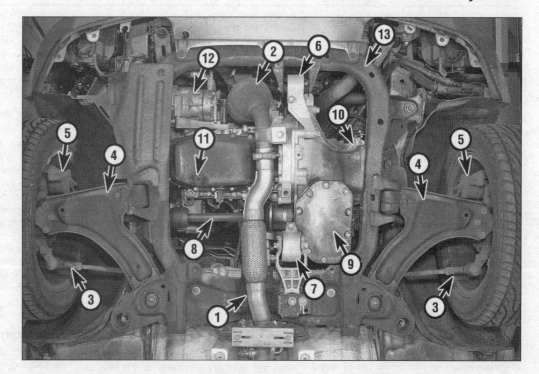

Rear underbody view

1 Handbrake cable
2 Rear suspension coil springs
3 Exhaust tailpipe and silencer
4 Exhaust heat shield
5 Rear suspension trailing arms and rear axle
6 Fuel tank

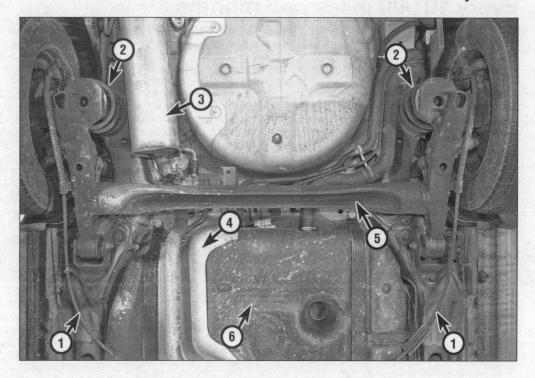

Maintenance procedures

1 General information

1 This Chapter is designed to help the home mechanic maintain his/her vehicle for safety, economy, long life and peak performance.

2 The Chapter contains a master maintenance schedule, followed by Sections dealing specifically with each task in the schedule. Visual checks, adjustments, component renewal and other helpful items are included. Refer to the accompanying illustrations of the engine compartment and the underside of the vehicle for the locations of the various components.

3 Servicing your vehicle in accordance with the mileage/time maintenance schedule and the following Sections will provide a planned maintenance programme, which should result in a long and reliable service life. This is a comprehensive plan, so maintaining some items but not others at the specified service intervals, will not produce the same results.

4 As you service your vehicle, you will discover that many of the procedures can – and should – be grouped together, because of the particular procedure being performed, or because of the proximity of two otherwise-unrelated components to one another. For example, if the vehicle is raised for any reason, the exhaust can be inspected at the same time as the suspension and steering components.

5 The first step in this maintenance programme is to prepare yourself before the actual work begins. Read through all the Sections relevant to the work to be carried out, then make a list and gather all the parts and tools required. If a problem is encountered, seek advice from a parts specialist, or a dealer service department.

2 Regular maintenance

1 If, from the time the vehicle is new, the routine maintenance schedule is followed closely, and frequent checks are made of fluid levels and high-wear items, as suggested throughout this manual, the engine will be kept in relatively good running condition, and the need for additional work will be minimised.

2 It is possible that there will be times when the engine is running poorly due to the lack of regular maintenance. This is even more likely if a used vehicle, which has not received regular and frequent maintenance checks, is purchased. In such cases, additional work may need to be carried out, outside of the regular maintenance intervals.

3 If engine wear is suspected, a compression test, or leakdown test (refer to the relevant Part of Chapter 2) will provide valuable information regarding the overall performance of the main internal components. Such a test can be used as a basis to decide on the extent of the work to be carried out. If, for example, the test indicates serious internal engine wear, conventional maintenance as described in this Chapter will not greatly improve the performance of the engine, and may prove a waste of time and money, unless extensive overhaul work is carried out first.

4 The following series of operations are those most often required to improve the performance of a generally poor-running engine:

Primary operations

a) Clean, inspect and test the battery (refer to Weekly checks).
b) Check all the engine-related fluids (refer to Weekly checks).
c) Check the condition and tension of the auxiliary drivebelt (Section 20).
d) Check the condition of the air cleaner element, and renew if necessary (Section 27).
e) Renew the fuel filter (Section 19).
f) Check the condition of all hoses, and check for fluid leaks (Section 4).

5 If the above operations do not prove fully effective, carry out the following secondary operations:

Secondary operations

All items listed under Primary operations, plus the following:

a) Check the charging system (refer to Chapter 5A).
b) Check the pre/post-heating system (refer to Chapter 5A).
c) Check the fuel, exhaust and emission control systems (refer to the appropriate Parts of Chapter 4).

Every 10 000 miles or 6 months

3 Engine oil and filter renewal

1 Before starting this procedure, gather together all the necessary tools and materials. Also make sure that you have plenty of clean rags and newspapers handy, to mop-up any spills. Ideally, the engine oil should be warm, as it will drain more easily, and more built-up sludge will be removed with it. Take care not to touch the exhaust or any other hot parts of the engine when working under the vehicle. To avoid any possibility of scalding, and to protect yourself from possible skin irritants and other harmful contaminants in used engine oils, it is advisable to wear gloves when carrying out this work.

2 Access to the underside of the vehicle will be greatly improved if it can be raised on a lift, driven onto ramps, or jacked up and supported on axle stands (see Jacking and vehicle support). Whichever method is chosen, make sure that the vehicle remains level, or if it is at an angle, that the drain plug is at the lowest point. Where fitted, remove the screws and clips and remove the engine undertray for access.

3 Remove the oil filler cap from the filler tube at the front of the engine (1.3 litre engines), or from the camshaft cover (1.7 litre engines) **(see illustration)**.

4 Using a spanner, or preferably a suitable socket and bar, slacken the drain plug about half a turn **(see illustration)**. Position the draining container under the drain plug, then remove the plug completely **(see Haynes Hint)**.

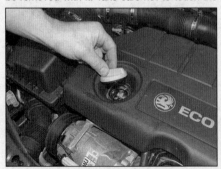

3.3 Removing the oil filler cap

3.4 Engine oil drain plug location (arrowed) – 1.3 litre engines

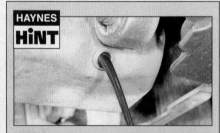

HAYNES HiNT

As the drain plug threads release, move it away quickly so that the stream of oil running out of the sump goes into the drain pan and not up your sleeve.

3.7 Undo the nut and two screws (arrowed) and remove the metal heat shield – 1.3 litre engines

3.8 Unscrew the cover and remove it from the top of the oil filter housing

5 Allow some time for the oil to drain, noting that it may be necessary to reposition the container as the oil flow slows to a trickle.

6 Position another container under the oil filter. On 1.3 litre engines the oil filter is located at the front of the engine and is accessible from above. On 1.7 litre engines the oil filter is located at the rear of the engine and is also accessible from above.

7 On 1.3 litre engines, undo the nut and two screws and remove the metal heat shield located over the filter housing **(see illustration)**.

8 Using a large socket, unscrew the cover and remove it from the top of the oil filter housing **(see illustration)**. Lift out the old filter element.

9 Wipe clean the oil filter cover and the filter housing.

10 Lubricate the sealing rings of the new filter with clean engine oil, then insert the filter into the housing or cover **(see illustrations)**.

11 Renew the sealing ring on the oil filter cover, and lubricate the new sealing ring with clean engine oil **(see illustrations)**. Refit the oil filter cover and tighten it to the specified torque. On 1.3 litre engines, refit the heat chield over the filter housing.

12 After all the oil has drained, wipe the drain plug and the sealing washer/O-ring with a clean rag. Examine the condition of the sealing washer/O-ring, and renew it if it shows signs of damage which may prevent an oil-tight seal. Clean the area around the drain plug opening, and refit the plug complete with the washer/O-ring. Tighten the plug to the specified torque, using a torque wrench.

13 Remove the old oil and all tools from under the vehicle then refit the undertray (where applicable) and lower the vehicle to the ground.

14 Fill the engine through the filler tube or filler hole in the camshaft cover, as applicable, using the correct grade and type of oil (refer to *Weekly checks* for details of topping-up). Pour in half the specified quantity of oil first, then wait a few minutes for the oil to drain into the sump. Continue to add oil, a small quantity at a time, until the level is up to the lower mark on the dipstick. Adding approximately a further 1.0 litre will bring the level up to the upper mark on the dipstick.

15 Start the engine and run it until it reaches normal operating temperature. While the engine is warming up, check for leaks around the oil filter and the sump drain plug.

16 Stop the engine, and wait at least five minutes for the oil to settle in the sump once more. With the new oil circulated and the filter now completely full, recheck the level on the dipstick, and add more oil as necessary.

17 Dispose of the used engine oil and filter safely, with reference to *General repair procedures* in the Reference Chapter of this manual. Do not discard the old filter with domestic household waste. The facility for waste oil disposal provided by many local council refuse tips and/or recycling centres generally has a filter receptacle alongside.

3.10a Lubricate the sealing rings of the new filter . . .

3.10b . . . then insert the filter into the housing – 1.3 litre engines . . .

3.10c . . . or cover – 1.7 litre engines

3.11a Renew the sealing ring on the oil filter cover . . .

3.11b . . . and lubricate the new sealing ring with clean engine oil

Every 20 000 miles or 12 months

4 Hose and fluid leak check

Note: *Also refer to Section 7.*
1 Visually inspect the engine joint faces, gaskets and seals for any signs of water or oil leaks. Pay particular attention to the areas around the camshaft cover, cylinder head, oil filter and sump joint faces. Similarly, check the transmission and (where applicable) the air conditioning compressor for oil leakage. Bear in mind that, over a period of time, some very slight seepage from these areas is to be expected; what you are really looking for is any indication of a serious leak. Should a leak be found, renew the offending gasket or oil seal by referring to the appropriate Chapters in this manual.
2 Also check the security and condition of all the engine-related pipes and hoses. Ensure that all cable-ties or securing clips are in place, and in good condition. Clips which are broken or missing can lead to chafing of the hoses pipes or wiring, which could cause more serious problems in the future.
3 Carefully check the radiator hoses and heater hoses along their entire length. Renew any hose which is cracked, swollen or deteriorated. Cracks will show up better if the hose is squeezed. Pay close attention to the hose clips that secure the hoses to the cooling system components. Hose clips can pinch and puncture hoses, resulting in cooling system leaks. If wire-type hose clips are used, it may be a good idea to update them with screw-type clips.
4 Inspect all the cooling system components (hoses, joint faces, etc) for leaks. Where any problems of this nature are found on system components, renew the component or gasket with reference to Chapter 3 **(see Haynes Hint)**.
5 With the vehicle raised, inspect the fuel tank and filler neck for punctures, cracks and other damage. The connection between the filler neck and tank is especially critical. Sometimes, a rubber filler neck or connecting hose will leak due to loose retaining clamps or deteriorated rubber.
6 Carefully check all rubber hoses and metal or plastic fuel lines leading away from the fuel tank. Check for loose connections, deteriorated hoses, crimped lines and other damage. Pay particular attention to the vent pipes and hoses, which often loop up around the filler neck and can become blocked or crimped. Follow the lines to the front of the vehicle, carefully inspecting them all the way. Renew damaged sections as necessary. Similarly, whilst the vehicle is raised, take the opportunity to inspect all underbody brake fluid pipes and hoses.
7 From within the engine compartment, check the security of all fuel hose attachments and pipe unions, and inspect the fuel hoses and vacuum hoses for kinks, chafing and deterioration.

5 Fuel filter water draining

Caution: Before starting any work on the fuel filter, wipe clean the filter assembly and the area around it; it is essential that no dirt or other foreign matter is allowed into the system. Obtain a suitable container into which the filter can be drained and place rags or similar material under the filter assembly to catch any spillages. Do not allow diesel fuel to contaminate components such as the alternator and starter motor, the coolant hoses and engine mountings, and any wiring.

Pre-2006 1.3 litre engines and all 1.7 litre engines

1 The fuel filter is located on the left-hand side of the engine compartment, adjacent to the battery.
2 Disconnect the heater element wiring connector from the fuel filter cover **(see illustration)**.
3 On 1.7 litre engines, undo the two retaining nuts and lift off the cover from the fuel filter crash box **(see illustrations)**.
4 On 1.3 litre engines, release the fuel hoses from the four support clips.
5 Carefully lift the filter housing up and out of the crash box.
6 In addition to taking the precautions noted above to catch any fuel spillages, position a suitable container beneath the filter housing.
7 Loosen the drain screw on the underside of the filter housing approximately one complete turn and allow the filter to drain until clean fuel, free of dirt or water, emerges from the tube (approximately 100 cc is usually sufficient). Note that on 1.7 litre engines, it may be necessary to slacken the filter housing cover bolt to allow the fuel to drain.
8 Remove the drain tube, then tighten the drain screw, and where necessary the housing cover screw, securely.
9 Insert the filter in the crash box making sure that the retaining clip engages.
10 Reconnect the wiring and on 1.3 litre engines, secure the fuel hoses in their support clips. On 1.7 litre engines, refit the crash box cover and secure with the two retaining nuts.
11 On completion, dispose of the drained water/fuel safely. Check all disturbed components to ensure that there are no leaks (of air or fuel) when the engine is restarted.

Post-2006 1.3 litre engines

12 The fuel filter is located on the left-hand side of the engine compartment, adjacent to the battery.
13 Release the two clips and lift open the fuel filter crash box cover **(see illustrations)**.
14 Attach a suitable length of plastic or rubber

HAYNES HINT

A leak in the cooling system will usually show up as white- or antifreeze-coloured deposits on the area adjoining the leak.

5.2 Disconnect the heater element wiring connector from the fuel filter cover

5.3a Undo the two retaining nuts (arrowed) . . .

5.3b . . . and lift off the cover from the fuel filter crash box – 1.7 litre engines

tube to the drain screw located on top of the fuel filter, ensuring that the tube is a secure fit on the drain screw **(see illustration)**. Place the other end of the tube in a suitable container.

15 Unscrew the drain screw approximately two turns.

16 Switch on the ignition for approximately 20 seconds. The in-tank fuel pump will pressurise the system and force water out of the drain screw outlet.

17 On completion, switch off the ignition and tighten the drain screw. Remove the drain tube and dispose of the drained water/fuel safely. Refit the crash box cover.

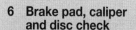

6 Brake pad, caliper and disc check

1 Jack up the front and rear of the vehicle and support it securely on axle stands (see *Jacking and vehicle support*). Remove the front and rear roadwheels.

2 For a quick check, the pad thickness can be carried out via the inspection hole on the caliper **(see Haynes Hint)**. Using a steel rule, measure the thickness of the pad friction linings. This must not be less than that indicated in the Specifications.

3 The view through the caliper inspection hole gives a rough indication of the state of the brake pads. For a comprehensive check, the brake pads should be removed and cleaned. The operation of the caliper can then also be checked, and the condition of the brake disc itself can be fully examined on both sides. Chapter 9 contains a detailed description of how the brake disc should be checked for wear and/or damage.

4 If any pad's friction material is worn to the specified thickness or less, *all four pads on each axle must be renewed as a set*. Refer to Chapter 9 for details.

5 On completion, refit the roadwheels and lower the vehicle to the ground.

7 Brake fluid pipe and hose check

1 The brake hydraulic system includes a number of metal pipes, which run from the master cylinder to the hydraulic modulator of the anti-lock braking system (ABS) and then to the front and rear brake assemblies. Flexible hoses are fitted between the pipes and the front and rear brake assemblies to allow for steering and suspension movement.

2 When checking the system, first look for signs of leakage at the pipe or hose unions, then examine the flexible hoses for signs of cracking, chafing or deterioration of the rubber. Bend the hoses sharply between the fingers (but do not actually bend them double, or the casing may be damaged) and check that this does not reveal previously-hidden

5.13a Release the two clips (arrowed) . . .

5.13b . . . and lift open the fuel filter crash box cover – post-2006 1.3 litre engines

cracks, cuts or splits. Check that the pipes and hoses are securely fastened in their clips.

3 Carefully working along the length of the metal pipes, look for dents, kinks, damage of any sort, or corrosion. Light corrosion can be polished off, but if the depth of pitting is significant, the pipe must be renewed.

8 Front suspension and steering check

1 Apply the handbrake, then raise the front of the vehicle and securely support it on axle stands (see *Jacking and vehicle support*).

2 Inspect the balljoint dust covers and the steering gear gaiters for splits, chafing or deterioration.

3 Any wear of these components will cause loss of lubricant, and may allow water to enter the components, resulting in rapid deterioration of the balljoints or steering gear.

4 Grasp each roadwheel at the 12 o'clock and 6 o'clock positions, and try to rock it **(see illustration)**. Very slight free play may be felt, but if the movement is appreciable, further investigation is necessary to determine the source. Continue rocking the wheel while an assistant depresses the footbrake. If the movement is now eliminated or significantly reduced, it is likely that the hub bearings are at fault. If the free play is still evident with the

5.14 Attach a length of plastic or rubber tube (arrowed) to the drain screw on top of the filter – post-2006 1.3 litre engines

footbrake depressed, then there is wear in the suspension joints or mountings.

5 Now grasp each wheel at the 9 o'clock and 3 o'clock positions, and try to rock it as before. Any movement felt now may again be caused by wear in the hub bearings or the steering track rod end balljoints. If the track rod end balljoint is worn, the visual movement will be obvious.

6 Using a large screwdriver or flat bar, check for wear in the suspension mounting bushes by levering between the relevant suspension component and its attachment point. Some movement is to be expected, as the mountings are made of rubber, but excessive wear should be obvious. Also check the condition of any visible rubber bushes, looking for splits, cracks or contamination of the rubber.

7 Check for any signs of fluid leakage around the suspension struts, or from the rubber

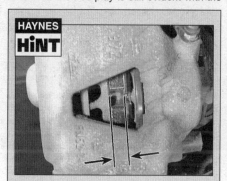
HAYNES HINT
For a quick check, the thickness of friction material remaining on the inner brake pad can be measured through the aperture in the caliper body.

8.4 Check for wear in the hub bearings by grasping the wheel and trying to rock it

9.2 Check the condition of the driveshaft gaiters (1) and the retaining clips (2)

gaiters around the piston rods. Should any fluid be noticed, the suspension strut is defective internally, and should be renewed. **Note:** *Suspension struts should always be renewed in pairs on the same axle.*

8 With the vehicle standing on its wheels, have an assistant turn the steering wheel back-and-forth about an eighth of a turn each way. There should be very little, if any, lost movement between the steering wheel and roadwheels. If this is not the case, closely observe the joints and mountings previously described. In addition, check the steering column universal joints for wear, and also check the rack-and-pinion steering gear itself.

9 The efficiency of each suspension strut may be checked by bouncing the vehicle at each front corner. Generally speaking, the body will return to its normal position and stop after being depressed. If it rises and returns on a rebound, the suspension strut is probably suspect. Also examine the suspension strut upper mountings for any signs of wear.

9 Driveshaft check

1 Firmly apply the handbrake, then jack up the front of the car and support it securely on axle stands (see *Jacking and vehicle support*).
2 Turn the steering onto full lock then slowly rotate the roadwheel. Inspect the condition of the outer constant velocity (CV) joint rubber gaiters while squeezing the gaiters to open out the folds **(see illustration)**. Check for

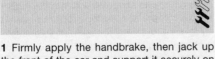

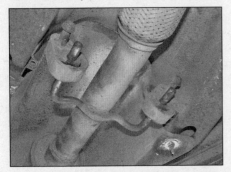

10.3 Exhaust mountings

signs of cracking, splits or deterioration of the rubber which may allow the grease to escape and lead to water and grit entry into the joint. Also check the security and condition of the retaining clips. Repeat these checks on the inner CV joints. If any damage or deterioration is found, the gaiters should be renewed as described in Chapter 8.

3 At the same time, check the general condition of the CV joints themselves by first holding the driveshaft and attempting to rotate the wheel. Repeat this check by holding the inner joint and attempting to rotate the driveshaft. Any appreciable movement indicates wear in the joints, wear in the driveshaft splines or loose driveshaft retaining nut.

10 Exhaust system check

1 With the engine cold (at least an hour after the vehicle has been driven), check the complete exhaust system from the engine to the end of the tailpipe. The exhaust system is most easily checked with the vehicle raised on a hoist, or suitably-supported on axle stands, so that the exhaust components are readily visible and accessible (see *Jacking and vehicle support*).
2 Check the exhaust pipes and connections for evidence of leaks, severe corrosion and damage. Make sure that all brackets and mountings are in good condition, and that all relevant nuts and bolts are tight. Leakage at any of the joints or in other parts of the system will usually show up as a black sooty stain in the vicinity of the leak.
3 Rattles and other noises can often be traced to the exhaust system, especially the brackets and mountings **(see illustration)**. Try to move the pipes and silencers. If the components are able to come into contact with the body or suspension parts, secure the system with new mountings. Otherwise separate the joints (if possible) and twist the pipes as necessary to provide additional clearance.

11 Rear suspension check

1 Chock the front wheels, then jack up the rear of the vehicle and support securely on axle stands (see *Jacking and vehicle support*).
2 Inspect the rear suspension components for any signs of obvious wear or damage. Pay particular attention to the rubber mounting bushes, and renew if necessary (see Chapter 10).
3 Grasp each roadwheel at the 12 o'clock and 6 o'clock positions **(see illustration 8.4)**, and try to rock it. Any excess movement indicates wear in the wheel bearings. Wear may also be accompanied by a rumbling sound when the wheel is spun, or a noticeable roughness if the

wheel is turned slowly. The wheel bearing can be renewed as described in Chapter 10.
4 Check for any signs of fluid leakage around the shock absorber bodies. Should any fluid be noticed, the shock absorber is defective internally, and should be renewed. **Note:** *Shock absorbers should always be renewed in pairs on the same axle.*
5 With the vehicle standing on its wheels, the efficiency of each shock absorber may be checked by bouncing the vehicle at each rear corner. Generally speaking, the body will return to its normal position and stop after being depressed. If it rises and returns on a rebound, the shock absorber is probably suspect.

12 Bodywork and underbody condition check

Note: *This work should be carried out by a Vauxhall/Opel dealer in order to validate the vehicle warranty. The work includes a thorough inspection of the vehicle paintwork and underbody for damage and corrosion.*

Bodywork damage and corrosion check

1 Once the car has been washed, and all tar spots and other surface blemishes have been cleaned off, carefully check all paintwork, looking closely for chips or scratches. Pay particular attention to vulnerable areas such as the front panels (bonnet and spoiler), and around the wheel arches. Any damage to the paintwork must be rectified as soon as possible, to comply with the terms of the manufacturer's anti-corrosion warranties; check with a Vauxhall/Opel dealer for details.
2 If a chip or light scratch is found which is recent and still free from rust, it can be touched-up using the appropriate touch-up stick which can be obtained from Vauxhall/Opel dealers. Any more serious damage, or rusted stone chips, can be repaired as described in Chapter 11, but if damage or corrosion is so severe that a panel must be renewed, seek professional advice as soon as possible.
3 Always check that the door and ventilation opening drain holes and pipes are completely clear, so that water can drain out.

Corrosion protection check

4 The wax-based underbody protective coating should be inspected annually, preferably just prior to Winter, when the underbody should be washed down as thoroughly as possible without disturbing the protective coating. Any damage to the coating should be repaired using a suitable wax-based sealer. If any of the body panels are disturbed for repair or renewal, do not forget to re-apply the coating. Wax should be injected into door cavities, sills and box sections, to maintain the level of protection provided by the vehicle manufacturer – seek the advice of a Vauxhall/Opel dealer.

13 Roadwheel bolt tightness check

1 Where applicable, remove the wheel trims from the wheels.
2 Using a torque wrench on each wheel bolt in turn, ensure that the bolts are tightened to the specified torque.
3 Where applicable, refit the wheel trims on completion, making sure they are fitted correctly.

14 Hinge and lock lubrication

1 Work around the vehicle and lubricate the hinges of the bonnet, doors, boot lid and tailgate with a light machine oil.
2 Lightly lubricate the bonnet release mechanism and exposed section of inner cable with a smear of grease.
3 Check the security and operation of all hinges, latches and locks, adjusting them where required. Check the operation of the central locking system.
4 Check the condition and operation of the tailgate support struts, renewing them both if either is leaking or no longer able to support the tailgate securely when raised.

15 Electrical systems check

1 Check the operation of all the electrical equipment, ie, lights, direction indicators, horn, etc. Refer to the appropriate sections of Chapter 12 for details if any of the circuits are found to be inoperative.
2 Note that the stop-light switch is described in Chapter 9.
3 Check all accessible wiring connectors, harnesses and retaining clips for security, and for signs of chafing or damage. Rectify any faults found.

16 Road test

Instruments and electrical equipment

1 Check the operation of all instruments, warning lights and electrical equipment.
2 Make sure that all instruments read correctly, and switch on all electrical equipment in turn, to check that it functions properly.

Steering and suspension

3 Check for any abnormalities in the steering, suspension, handling or road 'feel'.
4 Drive the vehicle, and check that there are no unusual vibrations or noises.
5 Check that the steering feels positive, with no excessive 'sloppiness', or roughness, and check for any suspension noises when cornering and driving over bumps.

Drivetrain

6 Check the performance of the engine, clutch, transmission and driveshafts.
7 Listen for any unusual noises from the engine, clutch and transmission.
8 Make sure that the engine runs smoothly when idling, and that there is no hesitation when accelerating.
9 Check that the clutch action is smooth and progressive, that the drive is taken up smoothly, and that the pedal travel is not excessive. Also listen for any noises when the clutch pedal is depressed.
10 Check that all gears can be engaged smoothly without noise, and that the gear lever action is smooth and not abnormally vague or 'notchy'.
11 Listen for a metallic clicking sound from the front of the vehicle, as the vehicle is driven slowly in a circle with the steering on full-lock. Carry out this check in both directions. If a clicking noise is heard, this indicates wear in a driveshaft joint (see Chapter 8).

Braking system

12 Make sure that the vehicle does not pull to one side when braking.
13 Check that there is no vibration through the steering when braking.
14 Check that the handbrake operates correctly, without excessive movement of the lever, and that it holds the vehicle stationary on a slope.
15 Test the operation of the brake servo unit as follows. Depress the footbrake four or five times to exhaust the vacuum, then start the engine. As the engine starts, there should be a noticeable 'give' in the brake pedal as vacuum builds-up. Allow the engine to run for at least two minutes, and then switch it off. If the brake pedal is now depressed again, it should be possible to detect a hiss from the servo as the pedal is depressed. After about four or five applications, no further hissing should be heard, and the pedal should feel considerably harder.

17 Service interval indicator reset

1 With the ignition switched off, the display on the instrument panel must show the trip odometer.
2 With the ignition still switched off, depress and hold the trip odometer reset button located on the instrument panel.
3 With the reset button depressed, switch on the ignition, wait until the service interval display changes (approximately 10 seconds).
4 After approximately 10 seconds the display will show the service symbol and the maximum mileage before the next required service, followed by 'InSP'. When '- - -' appears in the display, release the reset button and switch off the ignition. When the button is released, the odometer reading will appear again.

Every 40 000 miles or 2 years

18 Pollen filter renewal

1 Remove the windscreen cowl panel as described in Chapter 11.
2 Release the upper retaining catch and remove the pollen filter housing cover located at the rear left-hand side of the engine compartment (see illustration).
3 Lift the lower edge of the pollen filter upwards and withdraw it from the housing (see illustration).

18.2 Release the upper retaining catch and remove the pollen filter housing cover

18.3 Lift the lower edge of the pollen filter upwards and withdraw it from the housing

19.3a Depress the quick-release connector retaining tangs . . .

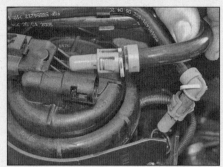

19.3b . . . and remove the hoses cover – pre-2006 1.3 litre engines

19.7 Using a home-made tool to slacken the filter housing cover retaining ring – pre-2006 1.3 litre engines

19.9a Unscrew and remove the cover retaining ring . . .

19.9b . . . then lift the cover together with the filter element . . .

19.9c . . . and recover the O-ring seal – pre-2006 1.3 litre engines

4 Fit the new filter using a reversal of the removal procedure; make sure that the filter is fitted the correct way up as indicated on the edge of the filter.

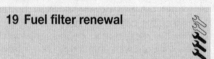

19 Fuel filter renewal

Caution: *Before starting any work on the fuel filter, wipe clean the filter assembly and the area around it; it is essential that no dirt or other foreign matter is allowed into the system. Obtain a suitable container into which the filter can be drained and place rags or similar material under the filter assembly to catch any spillages. Do not allow diesel fuel to contaminate components such as the starter motor, the coolant hoses and engine mountings, and any wiring.*

19.10 Turn the filter element approximately 50° anti-clockwise to release it from the cover – pre-2006 1.3 litre engines

Pre-2006 1.3 litre engines

Note: *Vauxhall/Opel special tool EN-46784-010, or a suitable alternative will be required to unscrew the filter housing cover retaining ring.*

1 The fuel filter is located on the left-hand side of the engine compartment, adjacent to the battery.

2 Disconnect the heater element wiring connector from the fuel filter cover (**see illustration 5.2**).

3 Detach the three fuel hose quick-release connectors and remove the hoses from the fuel filter housing and cover. A Vauxhall/ Opel special tool (KM-796-A) is available to disconnect the hose connectors, but provided care is taken, the connections can be released using two screwdrivers, a pair of long-nosed pliers, or similar, to depress the retaining tangs (**see illustrations**). Suitably

19.12a Align the arrow on the new filter element with the corresponding arrow on the cover . . .

cover or plug the open hose connections to prevent dirt entry.

4 Carefully lift the filter housing up and out of the crash box.

5 Loosen the drain screw on the base of the filter housing one complete turn and drain the fuel into a suitable container. Tighten the drain screw securely once the filter has drained.

6 Lay the filter on its side and clamp the two filter housing mounting lugs in a soft-jawed vice. Take great care not to damage the lugs and only tighten the vice sufficiently to hold the housing while the cover retaining ring is slackened.

7 Slacken the filter housing cover retaining ring using the Vauxhall/Opel special tool or a suitable alternative (**see illustration**).

8 Reposition the filter housing vertically in the vice and tighten the vice lightly.

9 Fully unscrew the cover retaining ring, then lift the cover together with the filter element from the housing. Recover the O-ring seal (**see illustrations**).

10 Turn the filter element approximately 50° anti-clockwise to release it from the cover (**see illustration**).

11 Empty the fuel from the filter housing, then thoroughly clean the housing and cover with a lint-free cloth.

12 Align the arrow on the new filter element with the corresponding arrow on the cover then push the filter onto the cover until it locks in position (**see illustrations**).

13 Locate a new O-ring seal on the filter housing, then fit the element and cover to the housing (**see illustrations**).

14 Lubricate the threads of the retaining ring

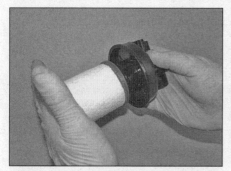

19.12b ... then push the filter onto the cover until it locks – pre-2006 1.3 litre engines

19.13a Locate a new O-ring seal on the filter housing ...

19.13b ... then fit the element and cover to the housing – pre-2006 1.3 litre engines

with a little diesel fuel then screw the ring onto the housing. Reposition the housing horizontally in the vice as before, and tighten the retaining ring to the specified torque using the special tool or alternative.

15 Insert the filter assembly into the crash box, then reconnect the fuel hoses and the wiring connectors.

16 Bleed the fuel system as described in Chapter 4B and check all disturbed components to ensure that there are no leaks (of air or fuel) when the engine is restarted.

17 On completion, safely dispose of the drained fuel.

Post-2006 1.3 litre engines

18 The fuel filter is located on the left-hand side of the engine compartment, adjacent to the battery.

19 Release the two clips and lift open the fuel filter crash box cover (see illustrations 5.13a and 5.13b).

20 Detach the fuel tank-to-filter supply hose, and filter-to-fuel pump supply hose quick-release connectors and remove the hoses from the fuel filter. A Vauxhall/Opel special tool (KM-796-A) is available to disconnect the hose connectors, but provided care is taken, the connections can be released using two screwdrivers, a pair of long-nosed pliers, or similar, to depress the retaining tangs (see illustration). Suitably cover or plug the open hose connections to prevent dirt entry.

21 Extract the fuel return hose retaining clip and remove the return hose together with the pressure relief valve from the filter (see illustration). Suitably cover or plug the open hose connection to prevent dirt entry.

22 Lift the filter out of the crash box and disconnect the heater element/water level sensor wiring connector from the base of the filter (see illustration).

23 Unscrew the heater element/water level sensor from the base of the filter and transfer it to the new filter. Tighten the element/sensor securely.

24 Connect the wiring connector to the new filter then locate the filter in the crash box. Reconnect the fuel hoses to the filter.

25 Bleed the fuel system as described in Chapter 4B and check all disturbed

components to ensure that there are no leaks (of air or fuel) when the engine is restarted.

26 On completion, refit the crash box cover and safely dispose of the drained fuel.

1.7 litre engines

27 The fuel filter is located on the left-hand side of the engine compartment, adjacent to the battery.

28 Disconnect the heater element wiring connector from the fuel filter cover (see illustration 5.2).

29 Undo the two retaining nuts and lift off the cover from the fuel filter crash box (see illustrations 5.3a and 5.3b).

30 Suitably identify the fitted position of the fuel hoses at their filter attachments to avoid confusion when refitting. Detach the two fuel hose quick-release connectors and remove the hoses from the filter housing cover. A

Vauxhall/Opel special tool (KM-796-A) is available to disconnect the hose connectors, but provided care is taken, the connections can be released using two screwdrivers, a pair of long-nosed pliers, or similar, to depress the retaining tangs (see illustration). Suitably cover or plug the open hose connections to prevent dirt entry.

31 Lift the filter housing up and out of the crash box.

32 Unscrew the centre bolt and remove the cover from the filter housing (see illustration). Collect the cover sealing ring.

33 Remove the filter element, then empty the fuel from the filter housing. Thoroughly clean the housing and cover with a lint-free cloth.

34 Fit a new sealing ring to the centre bolt and filter housing, then place the new element in the housing.

35 Fill the filter housing with fresh diesel

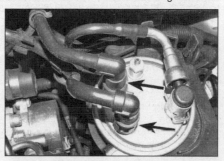

19.20 Detach the fuel hose quick-release connectors (arrowed) and remove the hoses – post-2006 1.3 litre engines

19.21 Fuel return hose retaining clip (arrowed) – post-2006 1.3 litre engines

19.22 Lift the filter out and disconnect the wiring connector from the base of the filter – post-2006 1.3 litre engines

19.30 Disconnect the fuel hoses (arrowed) from the fuel filter housing cover – 1.7 litre engines

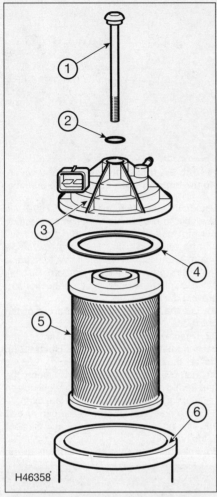

19.32 Fuel filter and housing components – 1.7 litre engines

1 Centre bolt	4 Filter housing
2 Centre bolt	cover sealing
sealing ring	ring
3 Filter housing	5 Filter element
cover	6 Filter housing

fuel until the level is just below the rim of the housing.

36 Refit the cover to the housing then refit the centre bolt, tightening it to the specified torque. **Do not** overtighten the cover screw as the housing is easily damaged.

21.5a Unclip and remove the centre console access panel

20.7 Turn the drivebelt tensioner using a spanner on the pulley centre bolt, then insert a suitable locking pin through the special hole provided – 1.3 litre engines

37 Insert the filter assembly into the crash box, then reconnect the fuel hoses in their correct locations as noted during removal. Reconnect the heater element wiring connector.

38 Bleed the fuel system as described in Chapter 4B and check all disturbed components to ensure that there are no leaks (of air or fuel) when the engine is restarted.

39 On completion, refit the crash box cover and safely dispose of the drained fuel.

20 Auxiliary drivebelt condition check

Note: *The manufacturers recommend that the tensioner roller is checked and if necessary renewed at the same time as the drivebelt.*

Checking

1 Due to their function and material make-up, drivebelts are prone to failure after a long period of time and should therefore be inspected regularly.

2 Apply the handbrake, then jack up the front of the vehicle and support it on axle stands (see *Jacking and vehicle support*). Remove the right-hand front roadwheel and the wheel arch liner cover for access to the right-hand side of the engine.

3 With the engine stopped, inspect the full length of the drivebelt for cracks and separation of the belt plies. It will be necessary to turn the engine (using a spanner or socket

21.5b Unclip the cover from around the handbrake lever . . .

and bar on the crankshaft pulley bolt) so that the belt can be inspected thoroughly. Twist the belt between the pulleys so that both sides can be viewed. Also check for fraying, and glazing which gives the belt a shiny appearance. Check the pulleys for nicks, cracks, distortion and corrosion. If the belt shows signs of wear or damage, it should be renewed as a precaution against breakage in service.

Renewal

4 If not already done, apply the handbrake, then jack up the front of the vehicle and support it on axle stands (see *Jacking and vehicle support*). Remove the right-hand front roadwheel and the wheel arch liner cover for access to the right-hand side of the engine.

5 For additional working clearance, remove the air cleaner assembly as described in Chapter 4B.

6 If the drivebelt is to be re-used, mark it to indicate its normal running direction.

7 Using a spanner on the pulley centre bolt, turn the tensioner clockwise, against the spring tension. On 1.3 litre engines, the tensioner can be held in this position by inserting a suitable locking pin or drill bit through the special hole provided **(see illustration)**.

8 Slip the drivebelt from the pulleys.

9 Locate the new drivebelt on the pulleys in the correct routing. If the drivebelt is being re-used, make sure it is fitted the correct way around.

10 Turn back the tensioner and remove the locking pin/drill bit (where applicable), then release it, making sure that the drivebelt ribs locate correctly on each of the pulley grooves.

11 Refit the air cleaner housing (if removed), then refit the wheel arch liner and roadwheel, and lower the vehicle to the ground.

21 Handbrake operation and adjustment check

1 With the vehicle on a slight slope, apply the handbrake lever by up to four clicks of the ratchet, and check that it holds the vehicle stationary, then release the lever and check that there is no resistance to movement of the vehicle.

2 If necessary, adjust the handbrake as follows.

3 Chock the front wheels then jack up the rear of the car and securely support it on axle stands (see *Jacking and vehicle support*).

4 Fully depress, then release the brake pedal at least five times. Similarly, fully apply, then release the handbrake at least five times.

5 Lift out the trim panel beneath the handbrake lever, then unclip the handbrake lever gaiter from the centre console **(see illustrations)**. The handbrake cable adjuster nut is situated by the handbrake lever inside the vehicle.

6 Move the handbrake lever to the fully released position, then turn the cable adjuster nut anti-clockwise to remove all tension from the cables **(see illustration)**.

7 With the handbrake lever set on the third notch of the ratchet mechanism, rotate the adjuster nut clockwise until a reasonable amount of force is required to turn each wheel. **Note:** *The force required should be equal for each wheel.*

8 Now pull the handbrake lever up to the fourth notch of the ratchet mechanism and check that both rear wheels are locked. Once this is so, fully release the handbrake lever and check that the wheels rotate freely. Check the adjustment by applying the handbrake fully whilst counting the clicks emitted from the handbrake ratchet and, if necessary, re-adjust.

9 On completion of adjustment, refit the handbrake lever gaiter, then lower the vehicle to the ground.

22 Headlight beam alignment check

1 Accurate adjustment of the headlight beam is only possible using optical beam-setting equipment, and this work should therefore be carried out by a Vauxhall/Opel dealer or service station with the necessary facilities. Refer to Chapter 12 for further information.

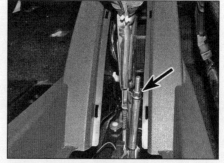

21.6 . . . for access to the handbrake cable adjuster nut (arrowed)

Every 2 years, regardless of mileage

23 Remote control battery renewal

1 Using a small screwdriver, carefully prise open the battery cover **(see illustration)**.

2 Note how the circular battery is fitted, then carefully remove it from the contacts **(see illustration)**.

3 Fit the new battery (type CR 20 32) and refit the cover making sure that it clips fully onto the base.

4 After changing the battery, lock and unlock the driver's door with the key in the lock, then switch on the ignition to synchronise the remote control unit.

24 Hydraulic fluid renewal

⚠️ **Warning: Hydraulic fluid can harm your eyes and damage painted surfaces, so use extreme caution when handling and pouring it. Do not use fluid that has been standing open for some time, as it absorbs moisture from the air. Excess moisture can cause a dangerous loss of braking effectiveness.**

1 The procedure is similar to that for the bleeding of the hydraulic system as described in Chapters 9 (brake) and 6 (clutch).

2 Working as described in Chapter 9, open the first bleed screw in the sequence, and pump the brake pedal gently until nearly all the old fluid has been emptied from the master cylinder reservoir. Top-up to the MAX level with new fluid, and continue pumping until only the new fluid remains in the reservoir, and new fluid can be seen emerging from the bleed screw. Tighten the screw, and top the reservoir level up to the MAX level line.

 HAYNES HiNT *Old hydraulic fluid is invariably much darker in colour than the new, making it easy to distinguish the two.*

3 Work through all the remaining bleed screws in the sequence until new fluid can be seen at all of them. Be careful to keep the master cylinder reservoir topped-up to above the MIN level at all times, or air may enter the system and greatly increase the length of the task.

4 Bleed the fluid from the clutch hydraulic system as described in Chapter 6.

5 When the operation is complete, check that all bleed screws are securely tightened, and that their dust caps are refitted. Wash off all traces of spilt fluid, and recheck the master cylinder reservoir fluid level.

6 Check the operation of the brakes and clutch before taking the car on the road.

25 Coolant renewal

Note: *Vauxhall/Opel do not specify renewal intervals for the antifreeze mixture, as the mixture used to fill the system when the vehicle is new is designed to last the lifetime of the vehicle. However, it is strongly recommended that the coolant is renewed at the intervals specified in the 'Maintenance schedule', as a precaution against possible engine corrosion problems. This is particularly advisable if the coolant has been renewed using an antifreeze other than that specified by Vauxhall/Opel. With many antifreeze types, the corrosion*

inhibitors become progressively less effective with age. It is up to the individual owner whether or not to follow this advice.

⚠️ *Warning: Wait until the engine is cold before starting this procedure. Do not allow antifreeze to come in contact with your skin, or with the painted surfaces of the vehicle. Rinse off spills immediately with plenty of water. Never leave antifreeze lying around in an open container, or in a puddle in the driveway or on the garage floor. Children and pets are attracted by its sweet smell, but antifreeze can be fatal if ingested.*

Cooling system draining

1 To drain the cooling system, first cover the expansion tank cap with a wad of rag, and slowly turn the cap anti-clockwise to relieve the pressure in the cooling system (a hissing sound will normally be heard). Wait until any pressure remaining in the system is released, then continue to turn the cap until it can be removed.

2 Remove the engine undertray (where fitted), then position a suitable container beneath the right-hand side of the radiator.

3 The coolant drain plug is located at the bottom of the radiator right-hand end tank. Unscrew the drain plug and allow the coolant to drain..

4 When the flow of coolant stops, refit and tighten the drain plug.

23.1 Prise off the battery cover . . .

23.2 . . . and remove the circular battery

5 As no cylinder block drain plug is fitted, it is not possible to drain all of the coolant. Due consideration must be made for this when refilling the system, in order to maintain the correct concentration of antifreeze.

6 If the coolant has been drained for a reason other than renewal, then provided it is clean and less than two years old, it can be re-used.

Cooling system flushing

7 If coolant renewal has been neglected, or if the antifreeze mixture has become diluted, then in time, the cooling system may gradually lose efficiency, as the coolant passages become restricted due to rust, scale deposits, and other sediment. The cooling system efficiency can be restored by flushing the system clean.

8 The radiator should be flushed independently of the engine, to avoid unnecessary contamination.

Radiator flushing

9 Disconnect the top and bottom hoses and any other relevant hoses from the radiator, with reference to Chapter 3.

10 Insert a garden hose into the radiator top inlet. Direct a flow of clean water through the radiator, and continue flushing until clean water emerges from the radiator bottom outlet.

11 If after a reasonable period, the water still does not run clear, the radiator can be flushed with a good proprietary cleaning agent. It is important that the manufacturer's instructions are followed carefully. If the contamination is particularly bad, remove the radiator, insert the hose in the radiator bottom outlet, and reverse-flush the radiator.

Engine flushing

12 To flush the engine, the thermostat must be removed, because it will be shut, and would otherwise prevent the flow of water around the engine. The thermostat can be removed as described in Chapter 3. Take care not to introduce dirt or debris into the system if this approach is used.

13 With the bottom hose disconnected from the radiator, insert a garden hose into the thermostat opening. Direct a clean flow of water through the engine, and continue flushing until clean water emerges from the radiator bottom hose.

14 On completion of flushing, refit the thermostat with reference to Chapter 3, and reconnect the hoses.

Cooling system filling

15 Before attempting to fill the cooling system, make sure that all hoses and clips are in good condition, and that the clips are tight. Note that an antifreeze mixture must be used all year round, to prevent corrosion of the engine components.

16 Remove the expansion tank filler cap.

17 Fill the system by slowly pouring the coolant into the expansion tank until it is up to the filler neck.

18 Refit and tighten the expansion tank filler cap.

19 Start the engine and run it at 2000 to 2500 rpm until the cooling fan switches on. Continue running the engine at between 2000 and 2500 rpm for a further 2 minutes.

20 Stop the engine, and allow it to cool, then recheck the coolant level with reference to *Weekly checks*. Top-up the level if necessary and refit the expansion tank filler cap. Refit the engine undertray (where applicable).

Antifreeze mixture

21 Always use an ethylene-glycol based antifreeze which is suitable for use in mixed-metal cooling systems. **Note:** *Vauxhall/Opel recommend the use of silicate-free 'red' coolant (see 'Lubricants and fluids').* The quantity of antifreeze and levels of protection are given in the Specifications.

22 Before adding antifreeze, the cooling system should be completely drained, preferably flushed, and all hoses checked for condition and security.

23 After filling with antifreeze, a label should be attached to the expansion tank, stating the type and concentration of antifreeze used, and the date installed. Any subsequent topping-up should be made with the same type and concentration of antifreeze.

Caution: Do not use engine antifreeze in the windscreen/tailgate washer system, as it will cause damage to the vehicle paintwork. A screenwash additive should be added to the washer system in the quantities stated on the bottle.

26 Exhaust emission check

1 The exhaust emission check is carried out initially after 3 years, then every 2 years, however, on vehicles which are subject to intensive use (eg, taxis/hire cars/ambulances) it must be carried out annually. The check involves checking the engine management system operation by plugging an electronic tester into the system diagnostic socket to check the electronic control unit (ECU) memory for faults (see Chapter 4B).

2 In reality, if the vehicle is running correctly and the engine management warning light in the instrument panel is functioning normally, then this check need not be carried out.

Every 40 000 miles or 4 years

27 Air cleaner element renewal

1 The air cleaner is located in the front right-hand corner of the engine compartment.

2 Disconnect the wiring connector from the side of the airflow meter **(see illustration)**.

3 Slacken the retaining clip and detach the airflow meter from the air cleaner cover **(see illustration)**.

4 Undo the screws and lift off the cover, then lift out the filter element **(see illustrations)**.

5 Wipe out the casing and the cover.

27.2 Disconnect the wiring connector from the airflow meter

27.3 Slacken the retaining clip and detach the airflow meter from the air cleaner cover

27.4a Undo the retaining screws . . .

6 Fit the new filter element, noting that the rubber locating flange should be uppermost, and secure the cover with the screws.

7 Where applicable, refit the vapour hoses to the air cleaner cover.

8 Refit the air inlet duct and secure with the retaining clip.

28 Timing belt, tensioner and idler pulley renewal – 1.7 litre engines

Refer to the procedures contained in Chapter 2E.

27.4b ... lift off the air cleaner cover ...

27.4c ... then lift out the filter element

Every 100 000 miles or 10 years

29 Auxiliary drivebelt renewal

Refer to the procedures contained in Section 20.

30 Valve clearance check and adjustment – 1.7 litre engines

Refer to the procedures contained in Chapter 2E.

Chapter 2 Part A:
1.4 litre petrol engine in-car repair procedures

Contents

Degrees of difficulty

Easy, suitable for novice with little experience	Fairly easy, suitable for beginner with some experience	Fairly difficult, suitable for competent DIY mechanic	Difficult, suitable for experienced DIY mechanic	Very difficult, suitable for expert DIY or professional

Specifications

General

Engine type.	Four-cylinder, in-line, water-cooled. Double overhead chain-driven camshafts, acting on rocker arms and hydraulic valve lifters
Manufacturer's engine codes*	Z14XEP
Bore	73.40 mm
Stroke.	80.60 mm
Capacity.	1364 cc
Firing order	1-3-4-2 (No 1 cylinder at timing chain end of engine)
Direction of crankshaft rotation	Clockwise (viewed from timing chain end of engine)
Compression ratio	10.5:1

For details of engine code location, see 'Vehicle identification' in the Reference Chapter.

Compression pressures

Maximum difference between any two cylinders.	1 bar

Lubrication system

Minimum oil pressure at 80°C	1.5 bars at idle speed
Oil pump type.	Gear-type, driven directly from crankshaft
Gear-to-housing clearance (endfloat).	0.020 to 0.065 mm

Torque wrench settings

	Nm	lbf ft
Air conditioning compressor to cylinder block	20	15
Auxiliary drivebelt tensioner to cylinder block:		
M8 bolt	20	15
M10 bolt	55	41
Big-end bearing cap bolts:*		
Stage 1	13	10
Stage 2	Angle-tighten a further 60°	
Stage 3	Angle-tighten a further 15°	
Camshaft bearing cap bolts	8	6
Camshaft sprocket bolt:*		
Stage 1	50	37
Stage 2	Angle-tighten a further 60°	
Coolant pump bolts	8	6
Coolant pump pulley bolts	20	15
Crankshaft pulley hub-to-crankshaft bolt:*		
Stage 1	150	111
Stage 2	Angle-tighten a further 45°	
Cylinder block baseplate to cylinder block:*		
M6 bolts:		
Stage 1	10	7
Stage 2	Angle-tighten a further 60°	
Stage 3	Angle-tighten a further 15°	
M8 bolts:		
Stage 1	25	18
Stage 2	Angle-tighten a further 60°	
Stage 3	Angle-tighten a further 15°	
Cylinder block closure bolt (for TDC setting tool)	60	44
Cylinder head bolts:*		
Stage 1	25	18
Stage 2	Angle-tighten a further 60°	
Stage 3	Angle-tighten a further 60°	
Stage 4	Angle-tighten a further 60°	
Engine/transmission mountings:		
Front mounting/torque link:		
Mounting-to-transmission bolts	95	70
Mounting to subframe	60	44
Left-hand mounting:		
Mounting-to-body bolts	25	18
Mounting to transmission bracket:*		
Stage 1	80	59
Stage 2	Angle-tighten a further 60°	
Transmission bracket to transmission	60	44
Rear mounting/torque link:		
Mounting-to-bracket bolt	80	59
Mounting-to-subframe bolt	80	59
Bracket-to-transmission bolts:*		
Stage 1	80	59
Stage 2	Angle-tighten a further 45°	
Right-hand mounting:		
Engine bracket-to-engine bolts	60	44
Mounting-to-body bolts	40	30
Mounting-to-engine bracket bolts:*		
Stage 1	60	44
Stage 2	Angle-tighten a further 30°	
Engine-to-transmission bolts	60	44
Exhaust front pipe-to-manifold nuts	20	15
Exhaust manifold securing nuts*	20	15
Exhaust manifold-to-support bracket bolts	8	6
Flywheel bolts:*		
Stage 1	35	26
Stage 2	Angle-tighten a further 30°	
Fuel hose unions	15	11
Inlet manifold support bracket to cylinder block	20	15
Oil fill channel closure plug	50	37
Oil filter housing cap to filter housing	25	18
Oil filter housing to cylinder block	20	15
Roadwheel bolts	110	81

Torque wrench settings (continued)

	Nm	lbf ft
Sump to cylinder block baseplate/timing cover..................	10	7
Sump to transmission	40	30
Timing chain tension rail pivot bolt...........................	20	15
Timing chain tensioner closure bolt (for locking pin access)	50	37
Timing cover bolts:		
M10..	35	26
M6...	8	6

* Use new fasteners.

---

1 General information

How to use this Chapter

This Part of Chapter 2 describes the repair procedures which can reasonably be carried out on the engine while it remains in the vehicle. If the engine has been removed from the vehicle and is being dismantled as described in Chapter 2F, any preliminary dismantling procedures can be ignored.

Note that, while it may be possible physically to overhaul items such as the piston/connecting rod assemblies while the engine is in the vehicle, such tasks are not usually carried out as separate operations, and usually require the execution of several additional procedures (not to mention the cleaning of components and of oilways); for this reason, all such tasks are classed as major overhaul procedures, and are described in Chapter 2F.

Chapter 2F describes the removal of the engine/transmission unit from the vehicle, and the full overhaul procedures which can then be carried out.

Engine description

The engine is of four-cylinder in-line type, with double overhead camshafts (DOHC). The engine is mounted transversely at the front of the vehicle.

The power unit is known as a 'Twinport' engine due to the design of the inlet manifold and cylinder head combustion chambers. Vacuum-operated flap valves located in the inlet manifold are opened or closed according to engine operating conditions, to create a variable venturi manifold arrangement. This system has significant advantages in terms of engine power, fuel economy and reduced exhaust emissions.

The crankshaft runs in five shell-type main bearings with crankshaft endfloat being controlled by thrustwashers which are an integral part of No 4 main bearing shells.

The connecting rods are attached to the crankshaft by horizontally-split shell- type big-end bearings. The pistons are attached to the connecting rods by gudgeon pins, which are an interference fit in the connecting rod small-end bores. The aluminium-alloy pistons are fitted with three piston rings – two compression rings and an oil control ring.

The camshafts are driven from the crankshaft by a hydraulically tensioned timing chain. Each cylinder has four valves (two inlet and two exhaust), operated via rocker arms which are supported at their pivot ends by hydraulic self-adjusting valve lifters (tappets). One camshaft operates the inlet valves, and the other operates the exhaust valves.

The inlet and exhaust valves are each closed by a single valve spring, and operate in guides pressed into the cylinder head.

A rotor-type oil pump is located in the timing cover attached to the cylinder block, and is driven directly from the crankshaft.

The coolant pump is located externally on the timing cover, and is driven by the auxiliary drivebelt.

Operations with engine in car

The following operations can be carried out without having to remove the engine from the vehicle.

a) Removal and refitting of the cylinder head.
b) Removal and refitting of the timing cover.
c) Removal and refitting of the timing chain, tensioner and sprockets.
d) Removal and refitting of the camshafts.
e) Removal and refitting of the sump.
f) Removal and refitting of the big-end bearings, connecting rods, and pistons.*
g) Removal and refitting of the oil pump.
h) Renewal of the crankshaft oil seals.
i) Renewal of the engine mountings.
j) Removal and refitting of the flywheel.

* Although the operation marked with an asterisk can be carried out with the engine in the vehicle (after removal of the sump), it is preferable for the engine to be removed, in the interests of cleanliness and improved access. For this reason, the procedure is described in Chapter 2F.

2 Compression test – general information

1 When engine performance is down, or if misfiring occurs which cannot be attributed to the ignition or fuel systems, a compression test can provide diagnostic clues as to the engine's condition. If the test is performed regularly, it can give warning of trouble before any other symptoms become apparent.

2 Due to the electronic throttle control system used on these engines, a compression test can only be carried out with the engine management electronic control unit connected to Vauxhall/Opel diagnostic test equipment, or a compatible alternative unit. Without the test equipment, the throttle valve cannot be opened (as there is no accelerator cable) and the test will be inconclusive. Note that even with the accelerator pedal fully depressed, the engine management ECU will only control the throttle valve position when the engine is running. The test equipment independently actuates the throttle valve (irrespective of ECU commands) and opens the throttle valve fully.

3 As the equipment needed for the compression test is unlikely to be available to the home mechanic, it is recommended that the test is performed by a Vauxhall/Opel dealer, or suitably-equipped garage.

3 Camshaft cover – removal and refitting

Note: A new camshaft cover rubber seal will be required for refitting, and a suitable silicone sealant will be required to seal the timing cover-to-cylinder head upper joint.

Removal

1 Disconnect the battery negative terminal (refer to Disconnecting the battery in the Reference Chapter).

2 Disconnect the wiring connectors at the airflow meter, coolant temperature sensor, camshaft position sensor and oil pressure switch **(see illustrations)**.

3.2a Disconnect the wiring connectors at the airflow meter . . .

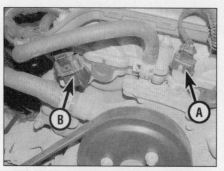

3.2b . . . coolant temperature sensor (A) and camshaft position sensor (B) . . .

3.2c . . . and at the oil pressure switch

3.3 Lift the wiring harness trough from the camshaft cover and move it to one side

3.4 Breather hoses on the rear of the camshaft cover

3 Lift the wiring harness trough from the camshaft cover and move it to one side (see illustration).

4 Disconnect the two breather hoses at the rear of the camshaft cover (see illustration).

5 Remove the ignition module from the centre of the camshaft cover as described in Chapter 5B.

6 Progressively slacken the camshaft cover retaining bolts until they are all fully unscrewed.

Note that the bolts are captive and will remain in place in the cover as it is removed.

7 Lift the camshaft cover up and off the cylinder head (see illustration).

Refitting

8 Remove the old seal from the camshaft cover, then examine the inside of the cover for a build-up of oil sludge or any other contamination, and if necessary clean the cover with paraffin, or a water-soluble solvent. Dry the cover thoroughly before refitting.

9 Check the condition of the rubber seals on the camshaft cover retaining bolts. If the seals are in any way damaged or deformed, carefully tap the bolts out of the camshaft cover using a soft-faced mallet and fit new seals to the bolts (see illustrations).

10 Fit a new rubber seal to the cover ensuring that it is correctly located in the camshaft cover groove (see illustration).

11 Inspect the joint between the timing cover and cylinder head, and cut off any projecting timing cover gasket using a sharp knife (see illustration).

12 Thoroughly clean the mating faces of the camshaft cover and cylinder head.

13 Apply a 2 mm diameter bead of silicone sealant to the joint between the timing cover and cylinder head on each side (see illustration).

14 Locate the camshaft cover on the cylinder head and screw in the retaining bolts. Progressively and evenly tighten the retaining bolts securely.

15 Refit the ignition module from the centre

3.7 Lift the camshaft cover up and off the cylinder head

3.9a If necessary, tap the bolts out of the camshaft cover . . .

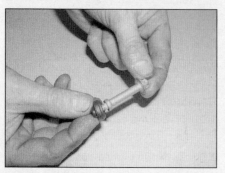

3.9b . . . and fit new seals to the bolts

3.10 Fit a new rubber seal to the camshaft cover ensuring that it is correctly located in the cover groove

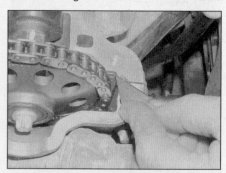

3.11 Cut off any projecting timing cover gasket using a sharp knife

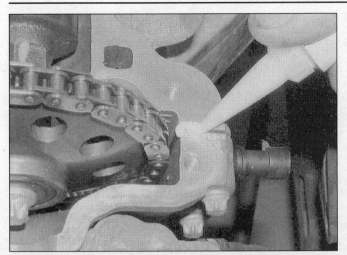

3.13 Apply a bead of silicone sealant to the joint between the timing cover and cylinder head on each side

4.6 Turn the crankshaft until the TDC notch (A) on the pulley is located just before the cast lug (B) on the timing cover

of the camshaft cover as described in Chapter 5B.

16 Reconnect the two breather hoses to the right-hand rear of the camshaft cover.

17 Locate the wiring harness trough in the camshaft cover slots then reconnect the airflow meter, coolant temperature sensor, camshaft position sensor and oil pressure switch wiring connectors.

18 Reconnect the battery negative terminal on completion.

4 Valve timing – checking and adjustment

Note: *Certain special tools will be required for this operation. Read through the entire procedure to familiarise yourself with the work involved, then either obtain the manufacturer's special tools, or use the alternatives described. New gaskets and sealing rings will also be required for all disturbed components.*

Checking

1 Disconnect the battery negative terminal (refer to *Disconnecting the battery* in the Reference Chapter).

2 Remove the air cleaner assembly as described in Chapter 4A.

3 Remove the camshaft cover as described in Section 3.

4 Firmly apply the handbrake, then jack up the front of the car and support it securely on axle stands (see *Jacking and vehicle support*). Remove the right-hand front roadwheel and the wheel arch liner lower cover for access to the crankshaft pulley.

5 On models with air conditioning, release the tension on the auxiliary drivebelt and lock the tensioner in the released position as described in the auxiliary drivebelt renewal procedure in Chapter 1A. Note that it is not necessary to completely remove the drivebelt, as this would entail removal of the right-hand engine

mounting bracket. With the drivebelt tension released, slip the belt off the compressor pulley. Unbolt the compressor from the cylinder block, release the refrigerant lines from their brackets and support the compressor clear of the engine. **Do not** disconnect the refrigerant lines from the compressor.

6 Using a socket or spanner on the crankshaft pulley hub bolt, turn the crankshaft in the normal direction of rotation (clockwise as viewed from the right-hand side of the car) until the TDC notch on the crankshaft pulley is located just before the cast lug on the timing cover **(see illustration)**.

7 Check that No 1 piston is on the compression stroke by observing No 1 cylinder camshaft lobes. All four lobes should be pointing outwards (away from the engine) **(see illustration)**. If they are not, No 1 piston is on the exhaust stroke and the crankshaft should be turned through a further full turn, stopping once again just before the TDC notch aligns with the lug on the timing cover.

8 Undo the closure bolt from the crankshaft TDC position setting hole. The plug is located on the front facing side of the cylinder block baseplate, adjacent to the timing cover joint. Note that a new closure bolt sealing ring will be required for refitting.

9 If the Vauxhall TDC positioning pin

KM-952 is available, insert the tool into the TDC position setting hole. Slowly turn the crankshaft in the normal direction of rotation until the tool engages with the TDC slot in the crankshaft, and moves fully in, up to its stop.

10 In the absence of the Vauxhall tool, a typical commercially-available clutch aligning tool of the type having interchangeable cones and collars of various diameters can be used as an alternative **(see Tool Tip 1)**. Assemble the tool so that the end collar (the part that normally engages with the crankshaft spigot bearing) is of 12 mm diameter, and the sliding cone (the part that normally engages with the clutch disc hub) is of 17.5 mm diameter. Insert the tool into the TDC position setting hole, and slowly turn the crankshaft in the normal direction of rotation until the end collar engages with the TDC slot in the crankshaft web. Push the cone fully into the setting hole as far as it will go, and the crankshaft should now be locked in the TDC position **(see illustrations)**.

11 If the Vauxhall camshaft setting tool KM-953 is available, insert the tool into the slots in the left-hand end of the camshafts. Ensure that the tool is inserted fully, up to its stop, to lock both camshafts.

12 In the absence of the Vauxhall tool, a camshaft setting tool can be made out of 5 mm

4.7 With No 1 piston on the compression stroke, the camshaft lobes for No 1 cylinder should be pointing outwards

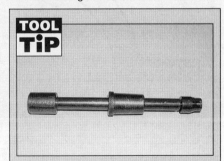

Tool Tip 1: A commercially-available clutch aligning tool can be used as a TDC positioning tool.

4.10a The end of the tool must engage with the slot in the crankshaft web (arrowed) – shown with engine partially dismantled

4.10b Clutch aligning tool in position in the TDC setting hole

4.12 Camshaft setting tool (arrowed) made from steel strip and inserted into the camshaft slots

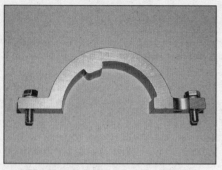

4.15a Vauxhall/Opel camshaft sensor phase disc positioning tool (KM-954)

4.15b Home-made cardboard alternative camshaft sensor phase disc positioning tool in place

thick flat steel strip, approximately 20 mm wide and long enough to engage both camshaft slots. Insert the setting tool into the camshaft slots to lock the camshafts in the TDC position **(see illustration)**. Note that a ready-made equivalent is available from tool stockists.

13 If it is not possible to insert the camshaft setting tool, then the valve timing must be adjusted as described in paragraphs 17 to 35 below.

14 If all is satisfactory so far, the position of the camshaft position sensor phase disc on the inlet camshaft should be checked. This check entails the use of Vauxhall camshaft sensor phase disc positioning tool KM-954. If this tool is not available, an alternative can be fabricated as follows.

15 The Vauxhall positioning tool (KM-954) is a relatively substantial die-casting, the purpose of which is to check the position of the phase

disc, and also to hold the phase disc in the correct position on the camshaft sprocket if adjustment is required. During the workshop procedures undertaken for the preparation of this manual, we discovered that a tool made from stiff cardboard (such that used for the cover of a Haynes manual) worked just as well as the factory tool **(see illustrations and Tool Tip 2)**.

16 Using the Vauxhall positioning tool, or the home-made alternative, check to see if the tool will engage with the phase disc on the camshaft, and also seat squarely on the timing cover surface. If it does, proceed to paragraph 31. If adjustment is required, proceed as follows.

Adjustment

Note: *New camshaft sprocket retaining bolts will be required for this operation.*

17 Remove the camshaft sensor phase disc positioning tool, and the tool used to lock the camshafts in position.

18 Unscrew the timing chain tensioner closure plug from the timing cover, located just below the heater hose union on the coolant pump. Note that a new closure bolt sealing ring will be required for refitting **(see illustration)**.

19 Using a suitable spanner engaged with the flats provided on the inlet camshaft, apply tension in a clockwise direction (as viewed from the right-hand side of the car) to the camshaft, to take up any slack in the timing chain **(see illustration)**. This will push the timing chain tensioner plunger fully into its bore.

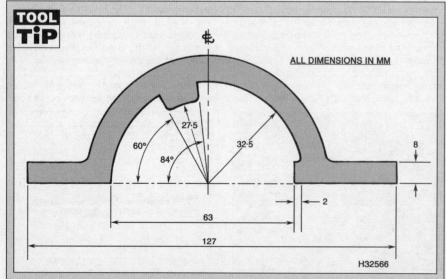

TOOL TiP

ALL DIMENSIONS IN MM

H32566

Tool Tip 2: A home-made camshaft sensor phase disc positioning tool can be fabricated using the dimensions shown.

4.18 Unscrew the timing chain tensioner closure plug from the timing cover

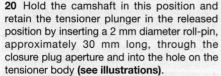

4.19 Use a spanner on the flats of the inlet camshaft to take up any slack in the timing chain

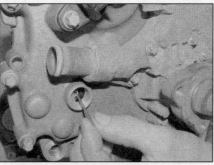
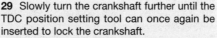

4.20a Insert a 2 mm diameter roll-pin, approximately 30 mm long, through the closure plug aperture . . .

4.20b . . . and into the hole on the tensioner body (arrowed)

20 Hold the camshaft in this position and retain the tensioner plunger in the released position by inserting a 2 mm diameter roll-pin, approximately 30 mm long, through the closure plug aperture and into the hole on the tensioner body (see illustrations).

21 Slacken and remove the sprocket retaining bolts for both camshafts, using a spanner to counterhold each camshaft as the bolts are slackened.

22 Fit the new bolts to both camshaft sprockets and tighten them finger-tight only at this stage. Check that the phase disc on the inlet camshaft can still be turned.

23 Again, using the spanner on the camshaft flats, turn the camshafts slightly, as necessary, until the camshaft setting tool can be reinserted into the slots in the ends of the camshafts.

24 Remove the roll-pin used to hold the timing chain tensioner plunger in the retracted position.

25 Turn the camshaft sensor phase disc slightly, as necessary, and locate the Vauxhall positioning tool (KM-954), or the home-made alternative over the disc and in contact with the timing cover. If the Vauxhall tool is being used, bolt it into position on the timing cover.

26 Tighten the camshaft sprocket retaining bolts to 10 Nm (7 lbf ft). The inlet camshaft sprocket bolts should be tightened first. Note that this is just an initial torque loading to hold the sprockets and the phase disc in position when the setting tools are removed.

27 Remove the crankshaft, camshaft and phase disc setting tools, then tighten the camshaft sprocket retaining bolts to the specified torque in the stages given in the Specifications. The inlet camshaft sprocket bolts should be tightened first. Counterhold the camshafts using the spanner on the camshaft flats as the sprocket bolts are tightened.

28 Turn the crankshaft through two complete revolutions, stopping just before the TDC notch on the crankshaft pulley aligns with the cast lug on the timing cover (see illustration 4.6). Check that all four lobes for No 1 cylinder are pointing outwards (away from the engine).

29 Slowly turn the crankshaft further until the TDC position setting tool can once again be inserted to lock the crankshaft.

30 It should now be possible to re-insert the camshaft setting tool into the slots in the camshafts, and to fit the camshaft sensor phase disc setting tool over the disc. If this is not possible repeat the entire adjustment procedure.

31 If all is satisfactory, remove all the setting/aligning tools and refit the timing chain tensioner and cylinder block closure bolts using new sealing rings. Tighten both closure bolts to the specified torque.

32 On models with air conditioning, refit the compressor to the cylinder block and tighten the mounting bolts to the specified torque. Refit the refrigerant lines to their relevant clips or brackets, then refit the auxiliary drivebelt as described in Chapter 1A.

33 Refit the wheel arch liner lower cover and the roadwheel. Tighten the roadwheel bolts to the specified torque, then lower the vehicle to the ground.

34 Refit the camshaft cover as described in Section 3.

35 Refit the air cleaner assembly as described in Chapter 4A, then reconnect the battery negative terminal.

5 Crankshaft pulley – removal and refitting

Removal

1 Firmly apply the handbrake, then jack up the front of the car and support it securely on axle stands (see Jacking and vehicle support). Remove the right-hand roadwheel and the wheel arch liner lower cover.

2 Release the tension on the auxiliary drivebelt and lock the tensioner in the released position as described in the auxiliary drivebelt renewal procedure in Chapter 1A. Note that it is not necessary to completely remove the drivebelt, as this would entail removal of the right-hand engine mounting bracket.

3 With the drivebelt tension released, slip the belt off the crankshaft pulley.

4 Using quick-drying paint, or similar, make

an alignment mark between the crankshaft pulley and the pulley hub. It should only be possible to refit the pulley in one position, but it is advisable to make an alignment mark anyway.

5 Unscrew the six crankshaft pulley retaining bolts and remove the pulley from the hub (see illustration). If necessary, prevent the crankshaft from turning as the pulley bolts are slackened using a spanner or socket on the pulley hub bolt.

Refitting

6 Align the marks made on removal and locate the pulley on the hub.

7 Refit the six retaining bolts and progressively tighten them securely.

8 Refit the auxiliary drivebelt over the crankshaft pulley and ensure that it is correctly seated in the other pulleys.

9 Unlock the auxiliary drivebelt tensioner as described in Chapter 1A to retension the drivebelt.

10 Refit the wheel arch liner lower cover and the roadwheel and tighten the wheel bolts to the specified torque.

11 Lower the car to the ground.

6 Timing cover and chain – removal and refitting

Note: The special tools described in Section 4 will also be required for this operation. Read through the entire procedure and also

5.5 Undo the six bolts and remove the crankshaft pulley from the pulley hub

6.9 Radiator lower hose on the coolant pump

the procedures contained in Section 4 to familiarise yourself with the work involved, then either obtain the manufacturer's special tools, or use the alternatives described. New gaskets and sealing rings will also be required for all disturbed components, together with new camshaft sprocket retaining bolts. A tube of silicone sealant will be needed to seal the joint between the cylinder block and cylinder head.

Removal

1 Disconnect the battery negative terminal (refer to *Disconnecting the battery* in the Reference Chapter).
2 Apply the handbrake, then jack up the front of the vehicle and support it on axle stands (see *Jacking and vehicle support*). Remove the right-hand roadwheel.
3 Drain the cooling system as described in Chapter 1A. Tighten the drain plug after draining the system.
4 Remove the air cleaner assembly as described in Chapter 4A.
5 At the right-hand end of the engine, loosen the clip and disconnect the throttle housing preheater hose from the thermostat housing.
6 Loosen the clip and disconnect the heater feed hose from the coolant pump.
7 Disconnect the wiring from the oil pressure switch, coolant temperature sensor and camshaft position sensor, then unclip the wiring conduit and move it to one side.
8 Loosen the clips and disconnect the radiator upper hose from the radiator and thermostat housing.
9 Loosen the clip and disconnect the radiator

6.31 Slacken the crankshaft pulley hub retaining bolt (arrowed)

6.17 The coolant pump pulley retaining bolts

lower hose from the coolant pump **(see illustration)**.
10 Remove the ignition module as described in Chapter 5B.
11 Disconnect the crankcase ventilation hose from the camshaft cover.
12 Progressively slacken the camshaft cover retaining bolts until they are all fully unscrewed. Note that the bolts are captive and will remain in place in the cover as it is removed. Lift the camshaft cover up and off the cylinder head.
13 Remove the wheel arch liner lower cover from under the right-hand wheel arch.
14 Position a container beneath the engine sump, then unscrew the drain plug and drain the engine oil. Clean, refit and tighten the drain plug on completion.
15 Refer to Chapter 4A, and disconnect the wiring from the oxygen sensor on the catalytic converter, then unbolt the exhaust front pipe from the exhaust manifold, taking care to support the flexible section. **Note:** *Angular movement in excess of 10° can cause permanent damage to the flexible section.*
16 Release the mounting rubbers and support the front of the exhaust pipe to one side.
17 Slacken, but do not remove, the three coolant pump pulley retaining bolts **(see illustration)**.
18 On models without air conditioning, turn the auxiliary drivebelt tensioner pulley bolt clockwise then insert a suitable pin through the spring centre shaft to lock the spring in its compressed state. Note the routing of the drivebelt, then remove it from the pulleys – mark the drivebelt for fitted direction. **Note:** *The drivebelt cannot be removed completely until the right-hand engine mounting has been removed.* Unscrew the auxiliary drivebelt tensioner lower mounting bolt and the tensioner roller upper pivot bolt. Remove the tensioner from the timing cover.
19 On models with air conditioning, turn the auxiliary drivebelt tensioner pulley bolt clockwise to tension the spring, then insert a suitable pin through the hole in the tensioner body and into the hole in the timing cover to lock the spring. Note the routing of the drivebelt, then remove it from the pulleys – mark the drivebelt for fitted direction. **Note:** *The drivebelt cannot be removed completely until the right-hand engine mounting has been removed.* Turn the tensioner pulley bolt

clockwise again and remove the locking pin, then gradually release the tensioner until it is fully released. Unbolt the tensioner from the timing cover.
20 Remove the alternator as described in Chapter 5A.
21 Remove the sump as described in Section 11.
22 The engine must now be supported while the right-hand engine mounting is removed. To do this, use a hoist attached to the top of the engine, or make up a wooden frame to locate on the crankcase and use a trolley jack.
23 Remove the right-hand engine mounting bracket with reference to Section 15, then remove the auxiliary drivebelt.
24 Fully unscrew the bolts and remove the coolant pump pulley from its drive flange.
25 On models with air conditioning, unbolt the compressor from the cylinder block, release the refrigerant lines from their brackets and support the compressor clear of the engine. **Do not** disconnect the refrigerant lines from the compressor.
26 Undo the three bolts securing the thermostat housing cover to the coolant pump. Remove the sealing ring from the housing cover noting that a new one will be required for refitting.
27 Using a socket or spanner on the crankshaft pulley hub bolt, turn the crankshaft in the normal direction of rotation (clockwise as viewed from the right-hand side of the car) until the TDC notch on the crankshaft pulley is located just before the cast lug on the timing cover **(see illustration 4.6)**.
28 Check that No 1 piston is on the compression stroke by observing No 1 cylinder camshaft lobes. All four lobes should be pointing outwards (away from the engine). If they are not, No 1 piston is on the exhaust stroke and the crankshaft should be turned through a further full turn, stopping once again just before the TDC notch aligns with the lug on the timing cover.
29 Using quick-drying paint, or similar, make an alignment mark between the crankshaft pulley and the pulley hub. It should only be possible to refit the pulley in one position, but it is advisable to make an alignment mark anyway.
30 Unscrew the six crankshaft pulley retaining bolts and remove the pulley from the hub. If necessary, prevent the crankshaft from turning as the pulley bolts are slackened, using a spanner or socket on the pulley hub bolt.
31 Using a suitable socket, initially slacken (but do not remove) the crankshaft pulley hub retaining bolt **(see illustration)**. The crankshaft can be prevented from turning as the bolt is slackened using Vauxhall special tool KM-956 or a similar tool which will engage with the flats on each side of the pulley hub. Alternatively, remove the starter motor, and lock the flywheel ring gear teeth using a suitable hooked tool bolted to the bellhousing.
32 Undo the closure bolt from the crankshaft

TDC position setting hole. The plug is located on the front facing side of the cylinder block baseplate, adjacent to the timing cover joint. Note that a new closure bolt sealing ring will be required for refitting.

33 Temporarily place the crankshaft pulley back on the hub and check that the TDC notch is still positioned just before the lug on the timing cover.

34 Slowly turn the crankshaft in the normal direction of rotation until the TDC positioning pin (or suitable alternative) described in Section 4, engages with the TDC slot in the crankshaft.

35 Remove the crankshaft pulley, if still in place, and check that the punch mark on the pulley hub is in the 11 o'clock position.

36 Insert the camshaft setting tool described in Section 4 into the slots in the ends of the camshafts.

37 Unscrew the coolant pump retaining bolts, noting the locations of the three short bolts. The short bolts secure the pump to the timing cover, and the long bolts secure the pump and the timing cover to the cylinder block and cylinder head.

38 Withdraw the coolant pump from the timing cover, noting that it may be necessary to tap the pump lightly with a soft-faced mallet to free it from the locating dowels.

39 Recover the pump sealing ring/gasket noting that a new one must be used for refitting.

40 Unscrew the previously-slackened crankshaft pulley hub retaining bolt and remove the hub from the crankshaft. Note that a new bolt will be required for refitting.

41 Undo the timing cover retaining bolts and remove the timing cover from the engine. The cover will be initially tight as it is located on dowels and secured by sealant. If necessary, gently tap it off using a soft-faced mallet.

42 Fully push back the timing chain tensioner plunger and secure it in the released position by inserting a 2 mm diameter roll-pin, approximately 30 mm long, in the hole on the tensioner body **(see illustration)**.

43 Undo the two bolts and remove the timing chain sliding rail from the top of the cylinder head **(see illustration)**.

44 Undo the two bolts and remove the timing

6.42 Push back the timing chain tensioner plunger and secure it in the released position with a 2 mm diameter roll-pin

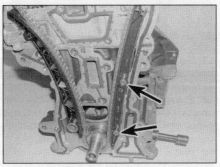

6.44 Undo the two bolts (arrowed) and remove the timing chain guide rail from the cylinder block

chain (front) guide rail from the cylinder block **(see illustration)**.

45 Undo the lower pivot bolt and remove the timing chain (rear) tension rail from the cylinder block **(see illustration)**.

46 Lift the timing chain off the sprockets and remove the chain, then remove the drive sprocket from the crankshaft **(see illustrations)**.

47 Remove the composite gasket from the cylinder block baseplate, cylinder block, and cylinder head, using a plastic spatula if necessary to release the sealant **(see illustration)**. Note that if the cylinder head has been removed previously, the gasket will be a two-piece type, with a split at the cylinder head-to-cylinder block joint. A new gasket will be required for refitting.

48 Thoroughly clean the timing cover and

6.43 Undo the two bolts (arrowed) and remove the timing chain sliding rail from the cylinder head

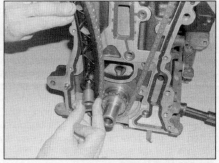

6.45 Undo the lower pivot bolt and remove the timing chain tension rail from the cylinder block

remove all traces of gasket and sealant from all the mating surfaces. Similarly clean the cylinder block baseplate, cylinder block and cylinder head mating surfaces. Ensure that all traces of old sealant are removed, particularly from the area of the cylinder head-to-cylinder block joint.

49 Inspect the timing chain, sprockets, sliding rail, guide rail and tension rail for any sign of wear or deformation, and renew any suspect components as necessary. Renew the crankshaft timing chain end oil seal in the timing cover as a matter of course using the procedures described in Section 13.

50 It is advisable to check the condition of the timing chain tensioner at this stage, as described in Section 7.

51 Obtain all new gaskets and components as necessary ready for refitting.

6.46a Lift the timing chain off the sprockets and remove the chain . . .

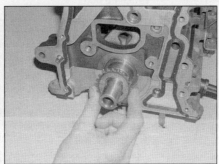

6.46b . . . then remove the drive sprocket from the crankshaft

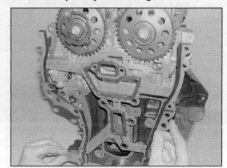

6.47 Remove the timing cover composite gasket from the cylinder block baseplate, cylinder block, and cylinder head

6.55 Apply a 2 mm diameter bead of silicone sealant to the joint between the cylinder block and cylinder head on each side

Refitting

52 Commence refitting by inserting a new coolant pump gasket or rubber seal into the timing cover.

53 Check that the locating dowels are in place, and that the mating surfaces are clean and dry, then locate the pump in position on the timing cover.

54 Refit the three coolant pump short retaining bolts, ensuring that the bolts are fitted to their correct locations (refer to Chapter 3 if necessary). Tighten the bolts to the specified torque.

55 Apply a 2 mm diameter bead of silicone sealant to the joint between the cylinder block and cylinder head on each side **(see illustration)**. The bead should be long enough to fill the joint in the area covered by the timing cover gasket. Similarly, apply silicone sealant to the joint between the cylinder block and baseplate.

6.57 Slide the timing chain drive sprocket onto the crankshaft with the markings facing outwards

56 Ensure that the locating dowels are in position, then locate the new timing cover gasket in place on the cylinder head, cylinder block and baseplate.

57 Slide the timing chain drive sprocket onto the crankshaft with the markings facing outwards **(see illustration)**.

58 Engage the timing chain with the drive sprocket then, keeping it tight on the exhaust camshaft side, feed the chain up and over the camshaft sprockets **(see illustration)**.

59 Place the timing chain tension rail in position, refit the lower pivot bolt and tighten the bolt to the specified torque.

60 Attach the timing chain guide rail to the cylinder block and secure with the two bolts tightened securely.

61 Refit the timing chain sliding rail to the cylinder head and secure with the two bolts tightened securely.

6.58 Keeping the timing chain tight on the exhaust camshaft side, locate the chain over the sprockets

62 Remove the roll-pin used to secure the timing chain tensioner plunger in the released position.

63 Locate the timing cover in position and refit all the retaining bolts, finger-tight only at this stage. Now tighten all the bolts to the specified torque, starting with the bolts around the coolant pump first, followed by the bolts around the periphery of the cover.

64 Refit the sump as described in Section 11.

65 Remove the position setting tools used to lock the crankshaft and camshafts in the TDC position.

66 Lubricate the crankshaft pulley hub with engine oil, then refit the hub to the crankshaft, ensuring that the punch mark on the hub is in the 11 o'clock position **(see illustration)**.

67 Screw in the new pulley hub retaining bolt and tighten it to the specified torque, in the stages given in the Specifications **(see illustrations)**. Prevent crankshaft rotation as the bolt is tightened, using the method employed for removal.

68 Refit the crankshaft pulley to the pulley hub, with the marks made on removal aligned, and tighten the six bolts securely.

69 Turn the crankshaft through two complete revolutions, stopping just before the TDC notch on the crankshaft pulley aligns with the cast lug on the timing cover. Check that all four lobes for No 1 cylinder are pointing outwards (away from the engine).

70 Slowly turn the crankshaft further until the TDC position setting tool can once again be inserted to lock the crankshaft.

71 It should now be possible to re-insert the camshaft setting tool into the slots in the camshafts. If the setting tool cannot be inserted, carry out the valve timing adjustment procedures contained in Section 4.

72 If all is satisfactory, remove all the setting/aligning tools and refit the closure bolt to the cylinder block using a new sealing ring. Tighten the closure bolt to the specified torque.

73 Refit the coolant pump pulley and tighten the three bolts to the specified torque. To prevent the pulley turning as the bolts are tightened, hold the pulley using a screwdriver engaged with one of the bolts and the pump centre spindle. Alternatively, wait until the auxiliary drivebelt has been refitted and tighten the bolts then.

6.66 Lubricate the crankshaft pulley hub, then refit the hub to the crankshaft

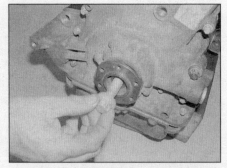

6.67a Screw in the new pulley hub retaining bolt . . .

6.67b . . . tighten it to the specified torque . . .

6.67c . . . then through the specified angle in the stages given in the Specifications

74 Ensure that the mating surfaces are clean, then fit a new sealing ring to the thermostat housing cover. Refit the cover to the coolant pump and tighten the bolts securely.

75 On models with air conditioning, refit the compressor to the cylinder block and tighten the mounting bolts to the specified torque. Refit the refrigerant lines to their relevant clips or brackets.

76 Refit the alternator as described in Chapter 5A.

77 Refit the auxiliary drivebelt tensioner and tighten the mounting bolts to the specified torque.

78 Rotate the tensioner pulley bolt clockwise as for removal, refit the auxiliary drivebelt as previously-noted and release the tensioner.

79 Refit the right-hand engine mounting bracket with reference to Section 15.

80 Refit the exhaust front pipe and oxygen sensor with reference to Chapter 4A.

81 Refill the engine with fresh oil with reference to Chapter 1A.

82 Refit the wheel arch liner lower cover.

83 Refit the camshaft cover and reconnect the crankcase ventilation hose as described in Section 3.

84 Refit the ignition module and cover.

85 Reconnect the radiator top and bottom hoses and heater hose to their respective connections.

86 Reconnect the wiring to the oil pressure switch, coolant temperature sensor and camshaft position sensor, then clip the wiring conduit in position.

87 Reconnect the throttle housing preheater hose and tighten the clip.

88 Refit the air cleaner assembly as described in Chapter 4A.

89 Refill the cooling system as described in Chapter 1A, then reconnect the battery negative terminal.

90 Refit the roadwheel and lower the vehicle to the ground.

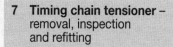

7 Timing chain tensioner – removal, inspection and refitting

Removal

1 Remove the timing cover as described in Section 6.

2 Undo the two tensioner retaining bolts and remove the tensioner from the cylinder head **(see illustration)**.

3 Extract the roll-pin used to retain the tensioner plunger in the retracted position and withdraw the tensioner plunger and spring **(see illustrations)**.

Inspection

4 Examine the components for any sign of wear, deformation or damage and, if evident, renew the complete tensioner assembly.

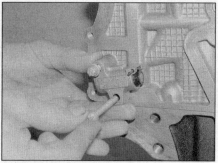

7.2 Undo the two retaining bolts and remove the timing chain tensioner from the cylinder head

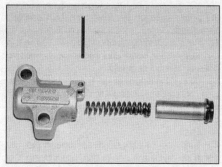

7.3b . . . and withdraw the tensioner plunger and spring

Refitting

5 Lubricate the tensioner spring and plunger, then insert the spring, followed by the plunger into the tensioner body.

6 Fully compress the tensioner plunger and reinsert the retaining roll-pin **(see illustration)**.

7 Refit the tensioner assembly to the cylinder head and tighten the retaining bolts securely.

8 Camshaft sprockets – removal and refitting

Note: *The special tools described in Section 4 will also be required for this operation. Read through the entire procedure and also the procedures contained in Section 4 to familiarise yourself with the work involved, then either obtain the manufacturer's special tools, or use the alternatives described. New gaskets and sealing rings will also be required for all disturbed components, together with new camshaft sprocket retaining bolts.*

Removal

1 Disconnect the battery negative terminal (refer to *Disconnecting the battery* in the Reference Chapter).

2 Remove the air cleaner assembly as described in Chapter 4A.

3 Disconnect the wiring from the oil pressure switch, coolant temperature sensor and camshaft position sensor, then unclip the wiring conduit and move it to one side.

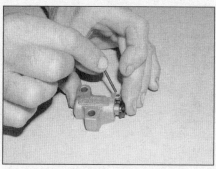

7.3a Extract the roll-pin used to retain the tensioner plunger in the retracted position . . .

7.6 Timing chain tensioner plunger fully retracted and locked with the roll-pin

4 Remove the ignition module as described in Chapter 5B.

5 Disconnect the crankcase ventilation hoses from the camshaft cover.

6 Progressively slacken the camshaft cover retaining bolts until they are all fully unscrewed. Note that the bolts are captive and will remain in place in the cover as it is removed. Lift the camshaft cover up and off the cylinder head.

7 Firmly apply the handbrake, then jack up the front of the car and support it securely on axle stands (see *Jacking and vehicle support*). Remove the right-hand front roadwheel and the wheel arch liner lower cover for access to the crankshaft pulley.

8 On models with air conditioning, release the tension on the auxiliary drivebelt and lock the tensioner in the released position as described in the auxiliary drivebelt renewal procedure in Chapter 1A. Note that it is not necessary to completely remove the drivebelt, as this entails removal of the right-hand engine mounting bracket. With the drivebelt tension released, slip the belt off the compressor pulley. Unbolt the compressor from the cylinder block, release the refrigerant lines from their brackets and support the compressor clear of the engine. **Do not** disconnect the refrigerant lines from the compressor.

9 Using a socket or spanner on the crankshaft pulley hub bolt, turn the crankshaft in the normal direction of rotation (clockwise as viewed from the right-hand side of the car) until the TDC notch on the crankshaft pulley is located just before the cast lug on the timing cover **(see illustration 4.6)**.

8.16 Slacken the camshaft sprocket retaining bolts using a spanner to counterhold each camshaft as the bolts are slackened

10 Check that No 1 piston is on the compression stroke by observing No 1 cylinder camshaft lobes. All four lobes should be pointing outwards (away from the engine). If they are not, No 1 piston is on the exhaust stroke and the crankshaft should be turned through a further full turn, stopping once again just before the TDC notch aligns with the lug on the timing cover.

11 Unscrew the timing chain tensioner closure bolt from the front of the timing cover, below the heater hose union on the coolant pump. Note that a new closure bolt sealing ring will be required for refitting.

12 Obtain a suitable roll-pin or similar of 2 mm diameter and approximately 30 mm long to use as a timing chain tensioner locking tool.

13 Using a suitable spanner engaged with the flats provided on the inlet camshaft, apply tension in a clockwise direction (as viewed from the right-hand side of the car) to the camshaft, to take up any slack in the timing chain. This will push the timing chain tensioner plunger fully into its bore.

14 Hold the camshaft in this position and retain the tensioner plunger in the released position by inserting the roll-pin through the closure plug aperture and into the hole on the tensioner body.

15 Undo the two bolts and remove the timing chain sliding rail from the top of the cylinder head.

16 Slacken the sprocket retaining bolts for both camshafts, using the spanner to counterhold each camshaft as the bolts are

9.2 Camshaft bearing cap identification numbers (arrowed)

slackened **(see illustration)**. Remove the bolt for the sprocket(s) being removed, together with the camshaft position sensor phase disc if removing the inlet camshaft. Withdraw the relevant sprocket(s) from the camshaft(s), disengage the timing chain and remove the sprocket(s) from the engine.

Refitting

17 Engage the sprocket(s) with the timing chain and locate the sprocket(s) on the camshaft(s). Fit the new retaining bolt(s) together with the phase disc, if working on the inlet camshaft. Note that new retaining bolts must be fitted to **both** sprockets, even if only one sprocket was removed. Tighten the bolts finger-tight only at this stage and check that the phase disc on the inlet camshaft can still be turned.

18 Refit the timing chain sliding rail to the top of the cylinder head and secure with the two bolts tightened securely.

19 Using the spanner on the camshaft flats, turn the camshafts slightly, as necessary, until the camshaft setting tool described in Section 4 can be inserted into the slots in the ends of the camshafts.

20 Turn the camshaft sensor phase disc as necessary until the phase disc positioning tool (or suitable alternative) described in Section 4 can be located over the phase disc. If the Vauxhall tool is being used, bolt it to the top of the timing cover. If the alternative tool described is being used, ensure that its base is in contact with the timing cover.

21 Remove the roll-pin used to hold the timing chain tensioner plunger in the retracted position.

22 Undo the closure bolt from the crankshaft TDC position setting hole. The plug is located on the front facing side of the cylinder block baseplate, adjacent to the timing cover joint. Note that a new closure bolt sealing ring will be required for refitting.

23 Slowly turn the crankshaft in the normal direction of rotation until the TDC positioning pin (or suitable alternative), described in Section 4, engages with the TDC slot in the crankshaft.

24 Tighten the camshaft sprocket retaining bolts to 10 Nm (7 lbf ft). Note that this is just an initial torque loading to hold the sprockets and the phase disc in position when the setting tools are removed.

25 Remove the crankshaft, camshaft and phase disc setting tools, then tighten the camshaft sprocket retaining bolts to the specified torque in the stages given in the Specifications. Counterhold the camshafts using the spanner on the camshaft flats as the sprocket bolts are tightened.

26 Turn the crankshaft through two complete revolutions, stopping just before the TDC notch on the crankshaft pulley aligns with the cast lug on the timing cover. Check that all four lobes for No 1 cylinder are pointing outwards (away from the engine).

27 Slowly turn the crankshaft further until the

TDC position setting tool can once again be inserted to lock the crankshaft.

28 It should now be possible to re-insert the camshaft setting tool into the slots in the camshafts, and to fit the camshaft sensor phase disc setting tool over the disc. If this is not possible carry out the valve timing adjustment procedure contained in Section 4.

29 If all is satisfactory, remove all the setting/aligning tools and refit the timing chain tensioner and cylinder block closure bolts using new sealing rings. Tighten both closure bolts to the specified torque.

30 On models with air conditioning, refit the compressor to the cylinder block and tighten the mounting bolts to the specified torque. Refit the refrigerant lines to their relevant clips or brackets, then refit the auxiliary drivebelt as described in Chapter 1A.

31 Refit the wheel arch liner lower cover and the roadwheel. Tighten the roadwheel bolts to the specified torque, then lower the vehicle to the ground.

32 Refit the camshaft cover as described in Section 3.

33 Refit the ignition module and cover, and reconnect the wiring.

34 Reconnect the wiring to the oil pressure switch, coolant temperature sensor and camshaft position sensor, then clip the wiring conduit into position.

35 Refit the air cleaner assembly as described in Chapter 4A, then reconnect the battery negative terminal.

9 Camshafts, hydraulic tappets and rocker arms – removal and refitting

Removal

1 Remove the camshaft sprocket(s) as described in Section 8.

2 Observe the identification numbers and markings on the camshaft bearing caps **(see illustration)**. On the project car used during the writing of this manual, the bearing caps with odd numbers were fitted to the exhaust camshaft, and the caps with the even numbers were fitted to the inlet camshaft. However, this may not be the case on other engines. Also, as it is possible to fit the caps either way round, it will be necessary to mark the caps with quick-drying paint, or identify them in some way, so that they can be refitted in exactly the same position. On the project car, all the numbers could be read the correct way up, when viewed from the exhaust camshaft side of the engine. Again, this may not always be the case.

3 With the bearing caps correctly identified, and working in a spiral pattern from the outside to the inside, initially slacken the bearing cap bolts, one at a time, by half a turn. When all the bolts have been initially slackened, repeat the procedure, slackening the bolts by a further half a turn. Continue until all the bolts

have been fully-slackened. The camshaft will rise up under the action of the valve springs as the bolts are slackened. Ensure that the camshaft rises uniformly and does not jam in its bearings.

4 When all the bolts have been slackened, remove the bolts and lift off the bearing caps, keeping them in order according to the identification method decided on **(see illustration)**.

5 Note the installed position of the camshafts before removal – the cam lobes for No 1 cylinder should be pointing outwards (ie, away from the centre). Carefully lift the camshafts from their locations in the cylinder head. If both camshafts are removed, identify them as exhaust and inlet **(see illustration)**.

6 Obtain sixteen small, clean plastic containers, and number them inlet 1 to 8 and exhaust 1 to 8; alternatively, divide a larger container into sixteen compartments and number each compartment accordingly. Withdraw each rocker arm and hydraulic tappet in turn, and place them in their respective container **(see illustrations)**. Do not interchange the rocker arms and tappets, or the rate of wear will be much increased.

Inspection

7 Examine the camshaft bearing surfaces and cam lobes for signs of wear ridges and scoring. Renew the camshaft if any of these conditions are apparent. Examine the condition of the bearing surfaces, both on the camshaft journals and in the cylinder head/bearing caps. If the head bearing surfaces are worn excessively, the cylinder head will need to be renewed.

8 Examine the rocker arm and hydraulic tappet bearing surfaces for wear ridges and scoring. Renew any rocker arm or tappet on which these conditions are apparent.

9 If either camshaft is being renewed, it will be necessary to renew all the rocker arms and tappets for that particular camshaft also.

Refitting

10 Before refitting, thoroughly clean all the components and the cylinder head and bearing cap journals.

11 Liberally oil the cylinder head hydraulic tappet bores and the tappets. Carefully refit the tappets to the cylinder head, ensuring that each tappet is refitted to its original bore.

12 Lay each rocker arm in position over its respective tappet.

13 Liberally oil the camshaft bearings in the cylinder head and the camshaft lobes, then place the camshafts in the cylinder head. Turn the camshafts so that the cam lobes for No 1 cylinder are pointing outwards as noted during removal.

14 Refit all the bearing caps to their respective locations ensuring they are fitted the correct way round as noted during removal.

15 Working in a spiral pattern from the inside to the outside, initially tighten the bearing cap bolts, one at a time, by half a turn. When all

9.4 Lift off the camshaft bearing caps, keeping them in order – shown with cylinder head removed

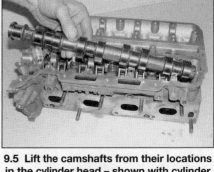

9.5 Lift the camshafts from their locations in the cylinder head – shown with cylinder head removed

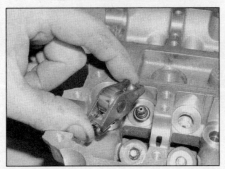

9.6a Withdraw each rocker arm . . .

9.6b . . . and hydraulic tappet in turn, and place them in their respective containers – shown with cylinder head removed

the bolts have been initially tightened, repeat the procedure, tightening the bolts by a further half a turn. Continue until all the bearing caps are in contact with the cylinder head and the bolts are lightly tightened.

16 Again, working in a spiral pattern from inside to outside, tighten all the bolts to the specified torque.

17 Refit the camshaft sprockets as described in Section 8.

10 Cylinder head
removal and refitting

Note 1: *The engine must be cold when removing the cylinder head. A new cylinder head gasket, timing cover gasket, cylinder head bolts and camshaft sprocket bolts, together with seals and sealing rings will be required for refitting. A suitable sealant will also be needed to seal the timing cover-to-cylinder block joint.*

Note 2: *The special tools described in Section 4 will also be required for this operation. Read through the entire procedure and also the procedures contained in Section 4 to familiarise yourself with the work involved, then either obtain the manufacturer's special tools, or use the alternatives described.*

Removal

1 Apply the handbrake, then jack up the front of the vehicle and support it on axle stands

(see *Jacking and vehicle support*). Remove the right-hand roadwheel.

2 Disconnect the battery negative terminal (refer to *Disconnecting the battery* in the Reference Chapter).

3 Drain the cooling system as described in Chapter 1A.

4 Remove the air cleaner assembly as described in Chapter 4A. Also remove the air inlet duct from the front of the engine compartment by unscrewing the single bolt.

5 Remove the throttle housing as described in Chapter 4A.

6 Disconnect the heater feed hose from the coolant pump and position it to one side.

7 Disconnect the brake servo vacuum line from the inlet manifold. Where applicable, also disconnect the evaporative system hose from the manifold.

8 Where applicable, undo the two bolts and remove the cover over the fuel rail. Similarly, undo the two bolts and release the wiring harness support bracket from the rear of the inlet manifold.

9 From under the car, undo the bolt securing the support bracket to the base of the inlet manifold. Slacken the bolt securing the bracket to the cylinder block and twist the bracket to one side **(see illustration)**.

10 Disconnect the heater return hose from the EGR coolant flange, and unclip the wiring harness.

11 Depressurise the fuel system as described in Chapter 4A, then disconnect the fuel feed

10.9 Undo the bolt (arrowed) securing the support bracket to the base of the inlet manifold

and return hoses from the fuel rail, noting their locations to aid refitting. Be prepared for fuel spillage, and take adequate precautions. Clamp or plug the open ends of the hoses, to minimise further fuel loss.

12 Disconnect the wiring from the following components:

 a) *Oil pressure switch.*
 b) *Coolant temperature sensor.*
 c) *Camshaft position sensor.*
 d) *Fuel injectors.*
 e) *Throttle valve adjuster.*
 f) *Engine electronic control unit (LH end of engine).*
 g) *Wiring combination plug (LH end of engine).*
 h) *EGR valve.*

13 Release the ignition module cover from the centre of the camshaft cover and remove it toward the transmission end of the engine. Disconnect the wiring plug from the left-hand end of the module.

14 Disconnect the earth cables from the electronic control unit bracket.

15 Undo the two bolts, one at each end, securing the plastic fuel injector wiring trough to the top of the fuel rail. Note that these bolts also secure the fuel rail to the inlet manifold. With the injector wiring disconnected, lift the wiring trough up and off the injectors. Place the trough to one side.

16 Remove the wheel arch liner lower cover from under the right-hand wheel arch.

17 Refer to Chapter 4A, and disconnect the wiring from the oxygen sensor in the exhaust front pipe, then unbolt the front pipe from the

10.30 Undo the three bolts and remove the oil filter housing from the cylinder block

exhaust manifold, taking care to support the flexible section. **Note:** *Angular movement in excess of 10° can cause permanent damage to the flexible section.*

18 Release the mounting rubbers and support the front of the exhaust pipe to one side.

19 Slacken, but do not remove, the three coolant pump pulley retaining bolts.

20 Unscrew the nuts and disconnect the wiring from the starter motor. Also, release the cable-ties.

21 Unbolt the two wiring harness brackets from the inlet manifold.

22 On models without air conditioning, turn the auxiliary drivebelt tensioner pulley bolt clockwise then insert a suitable pin through the spring centre shaft to lock the spring in its compressed state. Note the routing of the drivebelt, then remove it from the pulleys – mark the drivebelt for fitted direction. **Note:** *The drivebelt cannot be removed completely until the right-hand engine mounting has been removed.* Unscrew the auxiliary drivebelt tensioner lower mounting bolt and the tensioner roller upper pivot bolt. Remove the tensioner from the timing cover.

23 On models with air conditioning, turn the auxiliary drivebelt tensioner pulley bolt clockwise to tension the spring, then insert a suitable pin through the hole in the tensioner body and into the hole in the timing cover to lock the spring. Note the routing of the drivebelt, then remove it from the pulleys – mark the drivebelt for fitted direction. **Note:** *The drivebelt cannot be removed completely until the right-hand engine mounting has been removed.* Turn the tensioner pulley bolt clockwise again and remove the locking pin, then gradually release the tensioner until it is fully released. Unbolt the tensioner from the timing cover.

24 Undo the bolt securing the oil dipstick guide tube to the exhaust manifold and withdraw the dipstick and guide tube from the cylinder block baseplate. To do this, turn the guide tube forward. Suitably cover or plug the guide tube aperture in the cylinder block baseplate to prevent dirt ingress.

25 Disconnect the wiring from the oxygen sensor on the exhaust manifold at the left-hand front of the engine, then unscrew the sensor from the manifold. Refer to Chapter 4A if necessary.

26 Unbolt the left-hand engine lifting eye from the cylinder head, complete with attached wiring harness.

27 On models with air conditioning, unbolt the compressor from the cylinder block, release the refrigerant lines from their brackets and support the compressor clear of the engine. **Do not** disconnect the refrigerant lines from the compressor.

28 Unscrew the mounting nuts and lower support bracket bolts and withdraw the exhaust manifold from the cylinder head. Recover the gasket.

29 Remove the oil filter from the filter housing as described in Chapter 1A. Remove as much

of the oil remaining in the filter housing as possible using clean rags.

30 Undo the three bolts and remove the oil filter housing from the cylinder block **(see illustration)**. Place absorbent rags below the housing as it is removed to catch any remaining oil. Recover the filter housing seal noting that a new seal will be required for refitting.

31 Loosen the clips and disconnect the radiator upper hose from the radiator and thermostat housing.

32 The engine must now be supported while the right-hand engine mounting is removed. To do this, use a hoist attached to the top of the engine, or make up a wooden frame to locate beneath the sump and use a trolley jack.

33 Remove the right-hand engine mounting bracket with reference to Section 15, then remove the auxiliary drivebelt.

34 Fully unscrew the bolts and remove the coolant pump pulley from its drive flange.

35 Undo the three bolts securing the thermostat housing cover to the coolant pump. Remove the sealing ring from the housing cover noting that a new one will be required for refitting.

36 Undo the bolts securing the coolant pump and timing cover to the cylinder head **(see illustration)**. Note that it is not necessary to remove all the coolant pump bolts as three are shorter than the rest, and only secure the pump to the timing cover.

37 Remove the camshaft cover as described in Section 3.

38 Using a socket or spanner on the crankshaft pulley hub bolt, turn the crankshaft in the normal direction of rotation (clockwise as viewed from the right-hand side of the car) until the TDC notch on the crankshaft pulley is located just before the cast lug on the timing cover (see Section 4).

39 Check that No 1 piston is on the compression stroke by observing No 1 cylinder camshaft lobes. All four lobes should be pointing outwards (away from the engine). If they are not, No 1 piston is on the exhaust stroke and the crankshaft should be turned through a further full turn, stopping once again just before the TDC notch aligns with the lug on the timing cover.

40 Undo the closure bolt from the crankshaft TDC position setting hole. The plug is located on the front facing side of the cylinder block baseplate, adjacent to the timing cover joint. Note that a new closure bolt sealing ring will be required for refitting.

41 Slowly turn the crankshaft in the normal direction of rotation until the TDC positioning pin (or suitable alternative), described in Section 4, engages with the TDC slot in the crankshaft.

42 Obtain a suitable roll-pin, or similar, of 2 mm diameter and approximately 30 mm long, to use as a timing chain tensioner locking tool.

43 Using a suitable spanner engaged with the flats provided on the inlet camshaft, apply tension in a clockwise direction (as viewed from the right-hand side of the car) to the camshaft, to take up any slack in the timing chain. This will push the timing chain tensioner plunger fully into its bore.

44 Hold the camshaft in this position and retain the tensioner plunger in the released position by inserting the roll-pin through the closure plug aperture and into the hole on the tensioner body.

45 Undo the two bolts and remove the timing chain sliding rail from the top of the cylinder head.

46 Slacken the sprocket retaining bolts for both camshafts, using the spanner to counterhold each camshaft as the bolts are slackened. Remove both sprocket bolts together with the camshaft position sensor phase disc from the inlet camshaft. Ease the sprockets and chain off the camshafts and rest the sprockets on the top of the timing cover.

47 Undo the retaining bolt and remove the camshaft position sensor from the front of the timing cover.

48 Working in the specified sequence, progressively slacken the cylinder head retaining bolts half a turn at a time until all the bolts are loose **(see illustration)**. Remove the bolts from their locations noting that new bolts will be required for refitting.

49 Slightly raise the cylinder head so it just clears the cylinder block face and move the head toward the transmission end of the engine. The head will be initially tight due to the sealant on the timing cover gasket and head gasket. Note that the locating dowel holes on the cylinder head are elongated to allow the head to move sideways slightly.

50 As soon as sufficient clearance exists, lift the cylinder head up and off the cylinder block. At the same time, release the timing chain guide rail from the peg on the cylinder head, and guide the chain tensioner clear of the tensioning rail. Check that the tensioner locking pin is not dislodged as the cylinder head is lifted up. Place the cylinder head on wooden blocks after removal to avoid damage to the valves. Recover the cylinder head gasket.

Preparation for refitting

51 The mating faces of the cylinder head and cylinder block must be perfectly clean before refitting the head. Scouring agents are available for this purpose, but acceptable results can be achieved by using a hard plastic or wood scraper to remove all traces of gasket and carbon. The same method can be used to clean the piston crowns. Take particular care to avoid scoring or gouging the cylinder head mating surfaces during the cleaning operations, as aluminium alloy is easily damaged. Make sure that the carbon is not allowed to enter the oil and water passages – this is particularly important for the lubrication system, as carbon could block the oil supply to the engine's components. Using adhesive tape and paper, seal the water, oil and bolt

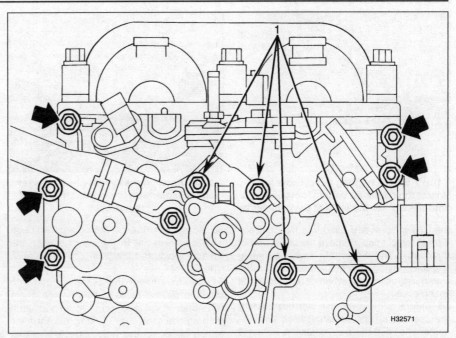

10.36 Undo the bolts (1) securing the coolant pump, and the bolts (arrowed) securing the timing cover to the cylinder head

holes in the cylinder block. To prevent carbon entering the gap between the pistons and bores, smear a little grease in the gap. After cleaning each piston, use a small brush to remove all traces of grease and carbon from the gap, then wipe away the remainder with a clean rag.

52 Check the mating surfaces of the cylinder block and the cylinder head for nicks, deep scratches and other damage. If slight, they may be removed carefully with a file, but if excessive, machining may be the only

alternative to renewal. If warpage of the cylinder head gasket surface is suspected, use a straight-edge to check it for distortion. Refer to Part F of this Chapter if necessary.

53 Thoroughly clean the threads of the cylinder head bolt holes in the cylinder block. Ensure that the bolts run freely in their threads, and that all traces of oil and water are removed from each bolt hole.

54 Using a sharp knife, partially cut through the timing cover gasket flush with the top of the cylinder block. Release the gasket from

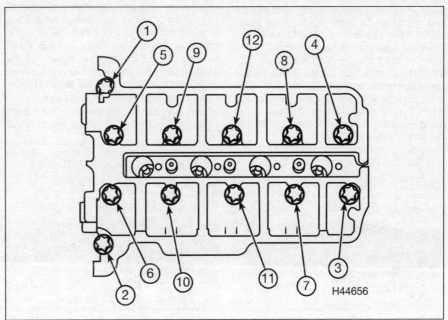

10.48 Cylinder head bolt slackening sequence

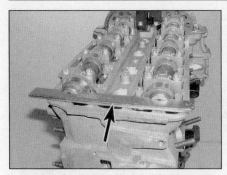

10.55 Before refitting the cylinder head, insert the camshaft setting tool (arrowed) into the slots in the ends of the camshafts

the timing cover and bend it in half to break it off at the cut line. Remove the upper part of the gasket, and thoroughly clean the mating surface, paying particular attention to the cylinder block edge where it contacts the timing cover.

55 Before refitting the cylinder head, using the spanner on the camshaft flats, turn the camshafts slightly, as necessary, until the camshaft setting tool described in Section 4 can be inserted into the slots in the ends of the camshafts **(see illustration)**. With the tool in position, the camshaft lobes for No 1 cylinder should be pointing outward.

Refitting

56 Prior to locating the cylinder head gasket on the cylinder block, cut off the two protruding tabs at the timing cover end of the gasket, flush with the gasket edge.
57 Apply a 2 mm diameter bead of silicone sealant to the joint between the cylinder block and the timing cover on each side.
58 Check that the locating dowels are in position in the cylinder block, then lay the new gasket on the block face, with the words OBEN/TOP uppermost **(see illustration)**. Push the gasket hard up against the timing cover so that it engages with the sealant.
59 Position the new timing cover gasket upper part on the timing cover, so that its lower ends engage with the sealant. Temporarily insert the left- and right-hand upper timing cover mounting bolts to locate the gasket in the correct position.

10.65a Tighten the cylinder head bolts to the Stage 1 torque setting using a torque wrench

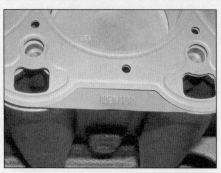

10.58 Position the cylinder head gasket on the block with the words OBEN/TOP uppermost

60 Apply a further 2 mm diameter bead of silicone sealant to the joint between the cylinder block and the timing cover on each side.
61 Carefully lower the cylinder head into position on the gasket, guiding the chain tensioner past the tensioning rail and guiding the tensioner locking pin into the timing cover access hole. Check also that the timing chain guide rail engages with cylinder head peg.
62 Once the head is seated on its dowels, tap it towards the timing cover with a rubber mallet.
63 Refit the three lower timing cover retaining bolts (one at each side, and one below the coolant pump). Tighten the three bolts to the specified torque.
64 Remove the camshaft setting tool from the camshaft slots.
65 Fit the new cylinder head retaining bolts and screw in the bolts until they contact the cylinder head. Working in the **reverse** order to the loosening sequence shown earlier in this Section, tighten the cylinder head bolts to the Stage one torque setting given in the Specifications, using a torque wrench. Again working in the correct order, tighten all the bolts through the Stage two angle using an angle measuring gauge **(see illustrations)**. Repeat for Stage three and Stage four.
66 Slacken the three previously-fitted bolts securing the timing cover to the cylinder head.

10.65b Tighten the cylinder head bolts through the Stage two, three and four angles using an angle tightening gauge

67 Refit the bolts around the coolant pump and tighten them securely.
68 Refit the remaining timing cover retaining bolts and tighten them to the specified torque.
69 Using the spanner on the camshaft flats, turn the camshafts slightly, as necessary, until the camshaft setting tool can once again be inserted into the camshaft slots.
70 Engage the camshaft sprockets with their respective camshafts, and fit the new retaining bolts together with the phase disc on the inlet camshaft. Tighten the bolts finger-tight only at this stage and check that the phase disc on the inlet camshaft can still be turned.
71 Refit the timing chain sliding rail to the top of the cylinder head and secure with the two bolts tightened securely.
72 Remove the roll-pin used to hold the timing chain tensioner plunger in the retracted position.
73 Turn the camshaft sensor phase disc as necessary until the phase disc positioning tool (or suitable alternative), described in Section 4, can be located over the phase disc. If the Vauxhall tool is being used, bolt it to the top of the timing cover. If the alternative tool described is being used, ensure that its base is in contact with the timing cover.
74 Tighten the camshaft sprocket retaining bolts to 10 Nm (7 lbf ft). Note that this is just an initial torque loading to hold the sprockets and the phase disc in position when the setting tools are removed. Tighten the inlet camshaft sprocket bolt first, followed by the exhaust camshaft sprocket bolt.
75 Remove the crankshaft, camshaft and phase disc setting tools, then tighten the camshaft sprocket retaining bolts to the specified torque in the stages given in the Specifications. Counterhold the camshafts using the spanner on the camshaft flats as the sprocket bolts are tightened.
76 Turn the crankshaft through two complete revolutions, stopping just before the TDC notch on the crankshaft pulley aligns with the cast lug on the timing cover. Check that all four lobes for No 1 cylinder are pointing outwards (away from the engine).
77 Slowly turn the crankshaft further until the TDC position setting tool can once again be inserted to lock the crankshaft.
78 It should now be possible to re-insert the camshaft setting tool into the slots in the camshafts, and to fit the camshaft sensor phase disc setting tool over the disc. If this is not possible carry out the valve timing adjustment procedure contained in Section 4.
79 If all is satisfactory, remove all the setting/aligning tools and refit the timing chain tensioner and cylinder block closure bolts using new sealing rings. Tighten both closure bolts to the specified torque.
80 Refit the camshaft position sensor using a new sealing ring and tighten the retaining bolt securely.
81 Refit the camshaft cover as described in Section 3.

82 Ensure that the mating surfaces are clean, then fit a new sealing ring to the thermostat housing cover. Refit the cover to the coolant pump and tighten the bolts securely.

83 Refit the coolant pump pulley and tighten the three bolts to the specified torque. To prevent the pulley turning as the bolts are tightened, hold the pulley using a screwdriver engaged with one of the bolts and the pump centre spindle. Alternatively, wait until the auxiliary drivebelt has been refitted and tighten the bolts then.

84 Refit the right-hand engine mounting bracket together with the auxiliary drivebelt with reference to Section 15. Remove the hoist or trolley jack supporting the engine.

85 Reconnect the radiator top hose and tighten the clips.

86 Thoroughly clean the mating surfaces of the oil filter housing and cylinder block, and refit the housing using a new seal. Refit and tighten the retaining bolts to the specified torque.

87 Fit a new sealing O-ring to the oil filter housing cap, then clip the new oil filter element to the cap.

88 Fit the cap and filter element assembly to the oil filter housing and screw the cap into position. Finally, tighten the cap to the specified torque.

89 Refit the exhaust manifold, together with a new gasket, and tighten the mounting nuts and support bracket bolts to the specified torque.

90 On models with air conditioning, refit the compressor to the cylinder block and tighten the mounting bolts to the specified torque. Refit the refrigerant lines to their relevant clips or brackets.

91 Refit the left-hand engine lifting eye to the cylinder head and tighten the bolts securely. Attach the wiring harness.

92 Refer to Chapter 4A and refit the oxygen sensor to the exhaust manifold. Reconnect the wiring.

93 Renew the oil dipstick guide tube O-rings and lubricate the O-rings with petroleum jelly. Insert the guide tube into the cylinder block baseplate then secure the tube to the exhaust manifold with the retaining bolt.

94 Refit the auxiliary drivebelt tensioner and tighten the mounting bolts to the specified torque.

95 Rotate the tensioner pulley bolt clockwise as for removal, refit the auxiliary drivebelt as previously-noted and release the tensioner.

96 Refit the wiring harness brackets to the inlet manifold.

97 Reconnect the wiring to the starter motor and tighten the nuts. Secure the cable with ties.

98 Reconnect the exhaust front pipe to the exhaust manifold using a new flange gasket. Tighten the pipe-to-manifold nuts to the specified torque. Refit the mounting rubbers, then reconnect the oxygen sensor wiring.

99 Refit the auxiliary drivebelt cover under the right-hand wheel arch.

100 Refit the injector wiring and trough to the top of the fuel rail.

101 Reconnect the earth cables to the electronic control unit bracket.

102 Refit the ignition module with reference to Chapter 5B, and reconnect the wiring.

103 Reconnect the wiring to the following components:

a) Oil pressure switch.
b) Coolant temperature sensor.
c) Camshaft position sensor.
d) Fuel injectors.
e) Throttle valve adjuster.
f) Engine electronic control unit (LH end of engine).
g) Wiring combination plug (LH end of engine).
h) EGR valve.

104 Reconnect the fuel feed and return hoses to the fuel rail.

105 Disconnect the heater return hose to the EGR coolant flange, and secure the wiring harness.

106 Refit and tighten the bolt securing the support bracket to the base of the inlet manifold.

107 Refit the wiring harness support bracket to the rear of the inlet manifold.

108 Reconnect the brake servo vacuum line to the inlet manifold.

109 Where applicable, refit the cover over the fuel rail.

110 Reconnect the heater feed hose to the coolant pump and tighten the clip.

111 Refit the throttle housing as described in Chapter 4A.

112 Refit the air cleaner assembly with reference to Chapter 4A. Also refit the air inlet duct to the front of the engine compartment.

113 Reconnect the battery negative terminal.

114 Refill the cooling system and top-up the engine oil with reference to Chapter 1A.

115 Refit the roadwheel then lower the vehicle to the ground.

11 Sump and oil pick-up pipe – removal and refitting

Note: *A new sump gasket must be used on refitting. If the oil pick-up pipe is removed, a new O-ring should be used on refitting.*

Removal

1 Firmly apply the handbrake, then jack up the front of the car and support it securely on axle stands (see *Jacking and vehicle support*). Remove the right-hand roadwheel.

2 Drain the engine oil, with reference to Chapter 1A, then refit and tighten the sump drain plug.

3 Refer to Chapter 4A, and disconnect the wiring from the oxygen sensor, then unbolt the exhaust front pipe from the exhaust manifold, taking care to support the flexible section. **Note:** *Angular movement in excess of 10° can cause permanent damage to the flexible section.* Release the mounting rubbers and support the front of the exhaust pipe to one side to allow removal of the sump.

4 Remove the wheel arch liner lower cover from under the right-hand wheel arch.

5 Undo the bolts securing the sump to the cylinder block baseplate, timing cover and transmission bellhousing, then withdraw the sump. If necessary, tap the sump with a soft-faced mallet to free it from its location – do not lever between the sump and cylinder block baseplate mating faces. Recover the gasket.

6 To remove the oil baffle plate, undo the retaining bolts and remove the baffle plate from the cylinder block baseplate.

7 If desired, the oil pick-up pipe can be removed from the sump by unscrewing the two support bracket retaining bolts and the two bolts securing the flange to the end face of the sump. Lift out the pick-up pipe and recover the O-ring from the flange **(see illustrations)**. Note that a new O-ring will be required for refitting.

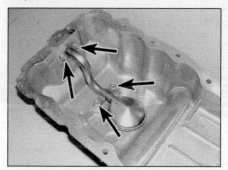
11.7a Undo the bolts (arrowed) . . .

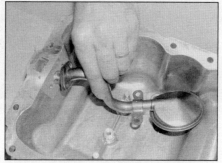
11.7b . . . remove the oil pick-up pipe . . .

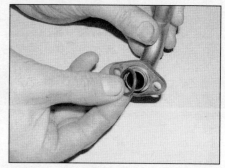
11.7c . . . and recover the O-ring from the flange

11.11a Apply a 2 mm diameter bead of silicone sealant to the joint between the timing cover and cylinder block on each side . . .

Refitting

8 Thoroughly clean the inside and outside of the sump ensuring that all traces of old gasket are removed from the mating face. Also clean the cylinder block baseplate mating face to remove all traces of old gasket.

9 If the oil pick-up pipe has been removed, fit a new O-ring to the flange, then refit the pipe to the sump. Refit the flange bolts and support bracket bolts, then tighten the flange bolts securely. Tighten the support bracket bolts securely.

10 If removed, refit the oil baffle plate and secure with the retaining bolts tightened securely.

11 Apply a 2 mm diameter bead of silicone sealant to the joint between the timing cover and cylinder block, on each side. Place a new gasket on the sump, then locate the sump on the cylinder block baseplate **(see**

11.11b . . . then place a new gasket on the sump and locate the sump on the cylinder block baseplate – shown with engine removed

illustrations). Refit the securing bolts and tighten them finger-tight at this stage.

12 If the engine has been removed from the car and separated from the transmission, use a straight-edge to check that the transmission mating face is aligned with the cylinder block baseplate mating face **(see illustration)**.

13 Tighten the bolts securing the sump to the cylinder block baseplate and timing cover progressively to the specified torque. Now tighten the bolts securing the sump to the transmission bellhousing to the specified torque.

14 Refit the lower cover under the right-hand wheel arch.

15 Reconnect the exhaust system front pipe to the manifold as described in Chapter 4A. Also, reconnect the wiring to the oxygen sensor.

16 Refit the roadwheel, then lower the car

11.12 If the engine has been separated from the transmission, use a straight-edge to check the transmission mating face alignment when refitting the sump

to the ground and refill the engine with oil as described in Chapter 1A.

12 Oil pump – removal, inspection and refitting

Note: *A new pressure relief valve cap sealing ring and new oil fill channel closure plug sealing ring will be required for refitting.*

Removal

1 Remove the timing cover and chain as described in Section 6.

2 Remove the securing screws/bolts and withdraw the oil pump cover from the rear of the timing cover **(see illustration)**.

3 Remove the inner and outer rotor from the timing cover and wipe them clean. Also clean the rotor location in the timing cover.

4 The oil pressure relief valve components can also be removed from the timing cover by unscrewing the cap. Withdraw the cap and sealing ring, the spring and plastic pin, and the plunger **(see illustrations)**.

Inspection

5 Locate the inner and outer rotor back in the timing cover, noting that the chamfer on the outer rotor outside diameter must face the timing cover.

6 Check the clearance between the end faces of the gears and the housing (endfloat) using a straight-edge and a feeler gauge **(see illustration)**.

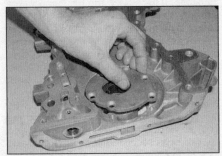

12.2 Remove the securing screws and withdraw the oil pump cover from the rear of the timing cover

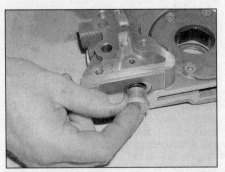

12.4a Unscrew the oil pressure relief valve cap and sealing ring . . .

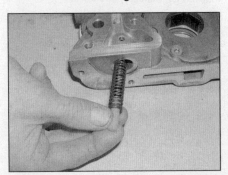

12.4b . . . then withdraw the spring and plastic pin . . .

12.4c . . . and the plunger

12.6 Check the oil pump gear endfloat using a straight-edge and feeler gauge

7 If the clearance is outside the specified limits, renew the components as necessary.

8 Examine the pressure relief valve spring and plunger, and renew if any sign of damage or wear is evident.

9 Ensure that the rotor location in the interior of the timing cover is scrupulously clean before commencing reassembly.

Refitting

10 Thoroughly clean the pressure relief valve components, and lubricate them with clean engine oil before refitting. Insert the plunger, the spring and plastic pin, then refit the cap using a new sealing ring. Tighten the cap securely.

11 Ensure that the gears are clean, then lubricate them with clean engine oil, and refit them to the pump body. Ensure that the chamfer on the outer rotor outside diameter faces the timing cover.

12 Ensure that the mating faces of the rear cover and the pump housing are clean, then refit the rear cover. Refit and tighten the securing screws securely.

13 Fit a new crankshaft oil seal to the timing cover as described in Section 13.

14 Refit the timing chain and cover to the engine as described in Section 6.

15 After refitting the timing cover, unscrew the oil fill channel closure bolt from the lower front facing side of the timing cover. Using a pump type oil can filled with clean engine oil, insert the oil can spout into the oil channel, so that the spout pushes back the internal ball valve. Prime the pump by filling it with oil until the oil runs out of the fill channel. Refit the closure plug using a new sealing ring and tighten it to the specified torque.

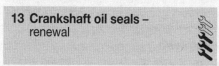

13 Crankshaft oil seals – renewal

Timing chain end oil seal

Note: *A new crankshaft pulley hub retaining bolt will be required for refitting.*

1 Disconnect the battery negative terminal (refer to *Disconnecting the battery* in the *Reference Chapter*).

2 Remove the air cleaner assembly as described in Chapter 4A.

3 Firmly apply the handbrake, then jack up the front of the car and support it securely on axle stands (see *Jacking and vehicle support*). Remove the right-hand front roadwheel and the wheel arch liner lower cover for access to the crankshaft pulley.

4 Release the tension on the auxiliary drivebelt and lock the tensioner in the released position as described in the auxiliary drivebelt renewal procedure in Chapter 1A. Note that it is not necessary to completely remove the drivebelt, as this would entail removal of the right-hand engine mounting bracket. With the drivebelt tension released, slip the belt off the crankshaft pulley.

13.10 Carefully prise out the crankshaft oil seal from the timing cover – shown with timing cover removed

5 Using a socket or spanner on the crankshaft pulley hub bolt, turn the crankshaft in the normal direction of rotation (clockwise as viewed from the right-hand side of the car) until the TDC notch on the crankshaft pulley is located just before the cast lug on the timing cover **(see illustration 4.6)**.

6 Using quick-drying paint, or similar, make an alignment mark between the crankshaft pulley and the pulley hub. It should only be possible to refit the pulley in one position, but it is advisable to make an alignment mark anyway.

7 Unscrew the six crankshaft pulley retaining bolts and remove the pulley from the hub. If necessary, prevent the crankshaft from turning as the pulley bolts are slackened, using a spanner or socket on the pulley hub bolt.

8 Using a suitable socket, slacken the crankshaft pulley hub retaining bolt. The crankshaft can be prevented from turning as the bolt is slackened, using Vauxhall special tool KM-956 or a similar tool which will engage with the flats on each side of the pulley hub. Alternatively, remove the starter motor, and lock the flywheel ring gear teeth using a suitable hooked tool bolted to the bellhousing.

9 Unscrew the slackened crankshaft pulley hub retaining bolt and remove the hub from the crankshaft. Note that a new bolt will be required for refitting.

10 The seal can now be carefully prised out with a screwdriver or similar hooked tool **(see illustration)**.

11 Clean the oil seal seat with a wooden or plastic scraper.

13.23 Locate the seal over the crankshaft and into the recess – shown with engine removed

13.12 Tap the new seal into position until it is flush with the outer face of the timing cover – shown with timing cover removed

12 Tap the new seal into position until it is flush with the outer face of the timing cover, using a suitable socket or tube, or a wooden block **(see illustration)**.

13 Refit the crankshaft pulley hub to the crankshaft, ensuring that the punch mark on the pulley hub is in the 11 o'clock position.

14 Screw in the new pulley hub retaining bolt and tighten it to the specified torque, in the stages given in the Specifications. Prevent crankshaft rotation as the bolt is tightened, using the method employed for removal.

15 Refit the crankshaft pulley to the pulley hub, with the marks made on removal aligned, and tighten the six bolts securely.

16 Refit the auxiliary drivebelt as described in Chapter 1A.

17 Refit the air cleaner assembly as described in Chapter 4A.

18 Refit the wheel arch liner lower cover and roadwheel, tightening the wheel bolts to the specified torque.

19 Lower the car to the ground, then reconnect the battery negative terminal.

Transmission end oil seal

20 Remove the flywheel as described in Section 14.

21 Carefully prise out the old seal from its location using a screwdriver or similar hooked tool.

22 Clean the oil seal seat with a wooden or plastic scraper.

23 Carefully locate the new seal over the crankshaft and into the recess in the cylinder block and baseplate **(see illustration)**.

13.24 Tap the seal into position until it is flush – shown with engine removed

14.4 If the engine is removed, lock the flywheel with a suitable tool

14.5 Unscrew the securing bolts, and remove the flywheel – shown with engine removed

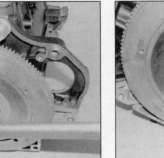

14.10a Tighten the flywheel bolts to the specified torque using a torque wrench . . .

24 Tap the seal into position using a suitable socket or tube, or a wooden block, until it is flush with the outer faces of the cylinder block and baseplate **(see illustration)**.

25 Refit the flywheel as described in Section 14.

14 Flywheel –
removal, inspection and refitting

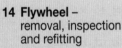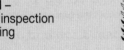

Note: *New flywheel securing bolts must be used on refitting.*

Removal

1 Remove the transmission as described in Chapter 7A or 7B, as applicable.
2 Remove the clutch assembly as described in Chapter 6.
3 Although the flywheel bolt holes are offset so that the flywheel can only be fitted in one position, it will make refitting easier if alignment marks are made between the flywheel and the end of the crankshaft.
4 Prevent the flywheel from turning by jamming the ring gear teeth using a suitable tool **(see illustration)**.
5 Unscrew the securing bolts, and remove the flywheel **(see illustration)**.
Caution: Take care, as the flywheel is heavy.

Inspection

6 Examine the flywheel for wear or chipping of the ring gear teeth. Renewal of the ring gear is possible but is not a task for the home

14.10b . . . then through the specified angle using an angle tightening gauge

mechanic; renewal requires the new ring gear to be heated (up to 180° to 230°C) to allow it to be fitted.
7 Examine the flywheel for scoring of the clutch face. If the clutch face is scored, the flywheel may be surface-ground, but renewal is preferable.
8 If there is any doubt about the condition of the flywheel, seek the advice of a Vauxhall/Opel dealer or engine reconditioning specialist. They will be able to advise if it is possible to recondition it or whether renewal is necessary.

Refitting

9 Offer the flywheel to the end of the crankshaft, and align the previously-made marks on the flywheel and crankshaft.
10 Coat the threads of the new flywheel bolts with thread-locking compound (note that new

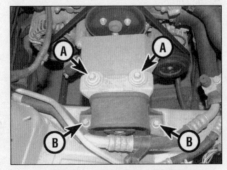

15.7 Right-hand engine mounting-to-engine bracket bolts (A) and mounting-to-body bolts (B)

bolts may be supplied ready-coated), then fit the bolts and tighten them to the specified torque, whilst preventing the flywheel from turning as during removal **(see illustrations)**.
11 Refit the clutch as described in Chapter 6, then refit the transmission as described in Chapter 7A or 7B, as applicable.

15 Engine/transmission mountings –
inspection and renewal

Inspection

1 To improve access, firmly apply the handbrake, then jack up the front of the vehicle and support it on axle stands (see *Jacking and vehicle support*).
2 Check the mounting blocks (rubbers) to see if they are cracked, hardened or separated from the metal at any point. Renew the mounting block if any such damage or deterioration is evident.
3 Check that all the mounting securing nuts and bolts are securely tightened, using a torque wrench to check if possible.
4 Using a large screwdriver, or a similar tool, check for wear in the mounting blocks by carefully levering against them to check for free play. Where this is not possible, enlist the aid of an assistant to move the engine/transmission unit back-and-forth, and from side-to-side, while you observe the mountings. While some free play is to be expected, even from new components, excessive wear should be obvious. If excessive free play is found, check first to see that the securing nuts and bolts are correctly tightened, then renew any worn components as described in the following paragraphs.

Renewal

Note: *Before slackening any of the engine mounting bolts/nuts, the relative positions of the mountings to their various brackets should be marked to ensure correct alignment upon refitting.*

Right-hand mounting

5 With reference to Chapter 4A, remove the air cleaner housing.
6 Support the weight of the engine using a trolley jack with a block of wood placed on its head.
7 Undo the bolts securing the right-hand engine mounting to the engine mounting support bracket **(see illustration)**.
8 Undo the bolts securing the mounting to the body, and withdraw the bracket with the mounting. If necessary, the engine mounting bracket may be unbolted from the cylinder block.
9 Refitting is a reversal of removal. Tighten the bolts to the specified orque.

Left-hand mounting

10 Remove the battery and battery tray as described in Chapter 5A.

15.12 Left-hand engine mounting bracket and transmission bracket bolts (arrowed)

15.17 Front engine mounting/torque link

11 Support the weight of the transmission using a trolley jack with a block of wood placed on its head.

12 Unscrew the two bolts securing the mounting bracket to the transmission bracket, and the three bolts securing the transmission bracket to the transmission **(see illustration)**.

13 Undo the four bolts securing the mounting to the body, slightly lower the engine, then remove the mounting assembly from the car.

14 Refitting is a reversal of removal. Ensure all bolts are tightened to their specified torques.

Front mounting/torque link

15 Firmly apply the handbrake, then jack up the front of the car and support it securely on axle stands (see *Jacking and vehicle support*).

16 Support the weight of the engine/transmission using a trolley jack with a block of wood placed on its head.

17 Slacken and remove the nut and washer securing the mounting to the subframe, then withdraw the bolt **(see illustration)**.

18 Undo the two bolts securing the mounting bracket to the transmission, then manoeuvre the mounting and bracket out of position.

19 Refitting is a reversal of removal. Ensure all bolts/nuts are tightened to their specified torques.

15.22 Extract the retaining spring clip (arrowed) and disconnect the gearchange linkage from the shift guide bracket

Rear mounting/torque link

20 Firmly apply the handbrake, then jack up the front of the car and support it securely on axle stands (see *Jacking and vehicle support*).

21 Support the weight of the engine/transmission using a trolley jack with a block of wood placed on its head. Position the jack underneath the transmission and raise the transmission slightly to remove all load from the rear mounting.

22 On models with conventional manual transmission (not Easytronic) extract the retaining spring clip and disconnect the gearchange linkage from the shift guide

15.23 Rear engine mounting/torque link retaining bolt (arrowed)

bracket **(see illustration)**. Move the shift guide to one side and remove the rubber damper.

23 Undo the bolt securing the torque link to the subframe, and remove the link **(see illustration)**.

24 Undo the bolts securing the torque link rubber mounting bracket to the transmission and remove the bracket and mounting.

25 Locate the new mounting bracket in position. Insert the bolts and tighten to the specified torque.

26 Refit the torque link to the subframe and mounting, insert the bolts and tighten to the specified torque.

27 On completion, reconnect the gearchange linkage and lower the vehicle to the ground.

Notes

Chapter 2 Part B:
1.6 litre SOHC petrol engine in-car repair procedures

Contents

Degrees of difficulty

Easy, suitable for novice with little experience	**Fairly easy,** suitable for beginner with some experience	**Fairly difficult,** suitable for competent DIY mechanic	**Difficult,** suitable for experienced DIY mechanic	**Very difficult,** suitable for expert DIY or professional

Specifications

General

Engine type.	Four-cylinder, in-line, water-cooled. Single overhead belt-driven camshaft, acting on hydraulic tappets
Manufacturer's engine code*	Z16SE
Bore	79.0 mm
Stroke.	81.5 mm
Capacity.	1598 cc
Firing order	1-3-4-2 (No 1 cylinder at timing belt end)
Direction of crankshaft rotation	Clockwise (viewed from timing belt end of engine)
Compression ratio	9.6:1

* For details of engine code location, see 'Vehicle identification' in the Reference Chapter.

Compression pressures

Standard.	12 to 15 bar
Maximum difference between any two cylinders.	1 bar

Camshaft

Endfloat	0.09 to 0.21 mm
Maximum permissible radial run-out	0.040 mm
Cam lift:	
Inlet valve	5.61 mm
Exhaust valve	6.12 mm

Lubrication system

Oil pump type.	Gear type, driven directly from crankshaft
Minimum permissible oil pressure at idle speed, with engine at operating temperature (oil temperature of at least 80°C).	1.5 bar
Oil pump clearances:	
Gear teeth clearance	0.08 to 0.15 mm
Gear endfloat	0.10 to 0.20 mm

Torque wrench settings

	Nm	lbf ft
Camshaft cover bolts	8	6
Camshaft sprocket bolt	45	33
Camshaft thrustplate bolts	8	6
Camshaft housing end cover bolts	8	6
Connecting rod big-end bearing cap bolt:*		
Stage 1	25	18
Stage 2	Angle-tighten a further 30°	
Coolant pump bolts	8	6
Crankshaft pulley bolt:*		
Stage 1	95	70
Stage 2	Angle-tighten a further 30°	
Stage 3	Angle-tighten a further 15°	
Crankshaft sensor mounting bracket bolt	8	6
Cylinder head bolts:*		
Stage 1	25	18
Stage 2	Angle-tighten a further 85°	
Stage 3	Angle-tighten a further 85°	
Stage 4	Angle-tighten a further 20°	
Engine/transmission mountings:		
Front mounting/torque link:		
Mounting-to-transmission bolts	95	70
Mounting to subframe	60	44
Left-hand mounting:		
Mounting-to-body bolts	25	18
Mounting to transmission bracket:		
Stage 1	80	59
Stage 2	Angle-tighten a further 60°	
Transmission bracket to transmission	60	44
Rear mounting/torque link:		
Mounting-to-bracket bolt	80	59
Mounting-to-subframe bolt	80	59
Bracket-to-transmission bolts:		
Stage 1	80	59
Stage 2	Angle-tighten a further 45°	
Right-hand mounting:		
Engine bracket-to-engine bolts:		
Stage 1	65	48
Stage 2	Angle-tighten a further 45°	
Mounting-to-body bolts	40	30
Mounting-to-engine bracket bolts:		
Stage 1	60	44
Stage 2	Angle-tighten a further 30°	
Engine-to-transmission bolts	60	44
Flywheel bolts:*		
Stage 1	35	26
Stage 2	Angle-tighten a further 30°	
Stage 3	Angle-tighten a further 15°	
Flywheel cover plate	8	6
Main bearing cap bolts:*		
Stage 1	50	37
Stage 2	Angle-tighten a further 45°	
Stage 3	Angle-tighten a further 15°	
Oil pressure switch	30	22
Oil pump:		
Retaining bolts	10	7
Pump cover screws	6	4
Oil pressure relief valve bolt	50	37
Oil pump pick-up/strainer bolts	8	6
Roadwheel bolts	110	81
Sump bolts:		
Models without air conditioning (steel sump):		
Sump-to-cylinder block/oil pump bolts	10	7
Drain plug	55	41
Models with air conditioning (alloy sump):		
Sump-to-cylinder block/oil pump bolts	10	7
Sump flange-to-transmission (M10) bolts	40	30
Drain plug	45	33

Torque wrench settings (continued)

	Nm	lbf ft
Timing belt cover bolts:		
Upper and lower covers	4	3
Rear cover	6	4
Timing belt tensioner bolt	20	15

* *Use new fasteners.*

---

1 General information

How to use this Chapter

This Part of Chapter 2 describes the repair procedures which can reasonably be carried out on the engine while it remains in the vehicle. If the engine has been removed from the vehicle and is being dismantled as described in Chapter 2F, any preliminary dismantling procedures can be ignored.

Note that, while it may be possible physically to overhaul items such as the piston/connecting rod assemblies while the engine is in the vehicle, such tasks are not usually carried out as separate operations, and usually require the execution of several additional procedures (not to mention the cleaning of components and of oilways); for this reason, all such tasks are classed as major overhaul procedures, and are described in Chapter 2F.

Chapter 2F describes the removal of the engine/transmission unit from the vehicle, and the full overhaul procedures which can then be carried out.

Engine description

The engine is a single overhead camshaft, four-cylinder, in-line unit, mounted transversely at the front of the car, with the clutch and transmission on its left-hand end.

The aluminium alloy cylinder block is of the dry-liner type. The crankshaft is supported within the cylinder block on five shell-type main bearings. Thrustwashers are fitted to number 3 main bearing, to control crankshaft endfloat.

The connecting rods are attached to the crankshaft by horizontally split shell-type big-end bearings, and to the pistons by interference-fit gudgeon pins. The aluminium alloy pistons are of the slipper type, and are fitted with three piston rings, comprising two compression rings and a scraper-type oil control ring.

The camshaft runs directly in the camshaft housing, which is mounted on top of the cylinder head, and driven by the crankshaft via a toothed rubber timing belt (which also drives the coolant pump). The camshaft operates each valve via a follower. Each follower pivots on a hydraulic self-adjusting valve lifter (tappet) which automatically adjust the valve clearances.

Lubrication is by pressure-feed from a gear-type oil pump, which is mounted on the right-hand end of the crankshaft. It draws oil through a strainer located in the sump, and then forces it through an externally-mounted full-flow cartridge-type filter. The oil flows into galleries in the main bearing cap bridge arrangement and cylinder block/crankcase, from where it is distributed to the crankshaft (main bearings) and camshaft. The big-end bearings are supplied with oil via internal drillings in the crankshaft, while the camshaft bearings also receive a pressurised supply. The camshaft lobes and valves are lubricated by splash, as are all other engine components.

A semi-closed crankcase ventilation system is employed; crankcase fumes are drawn from the cylinder head cover, and passed via a hose to the inlet manifold.

Operations with engine in car

The following operations can be carried out without having to remove the engine from the vehicle.

a) Removal and refitting of the cylinder head.
b) Removal and refitting of the timing belt and sprockets.
c) Renewal of the camshaft oil seal.
d) Removal and refitting of the camshaft housing and camshaft.
e) Removal and refitting of the sump.
f) Removal and refitting of the connecting rods and pistons.*
g) Removal and refitting of the oil pump.
h) Renewal of the crankshaft oil seals.
i) Renewal of the engine mountings.
j) Removal and refitting of the flywheel.

* *Although the operation marked with an asterisk can be carried out with the engine in the vehicle (after removal of the sump), it is preferable for the engine to be removed, in the interests of cleanliness and improved access. For this reason, the procedure is described in Chapter 2F.*

2 Compression test – description and interpretation
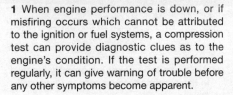

1 When engine performance is down, or if misfiring occurs which cannot be attributed to the ignition or fuel systems, a compression test can provide diagnostic clues as to the engine's condition. If the test is performed regularly, it can give warning of trouble before any other symptoms become apparent.

2 Due to the electronic throttle control system used on these engines, a compression test can only be carried out with the engine management electronic control unit connected to Vauxhall/Opel diagnostic test equipment, or a compatible alternative unit. Without the test equipment, the throttle valve cannot be opened (as there is no accelerator cable) and the test will be inconclusive. Note that even with the accelerator pedal fully depressed, the engine management ECU will only control the throttle valve position when the engine is running. The test equipment independently actuates the throttle valve (irrespective of ECU commands) and opens the throttle valve fully.

3 As the equipment needed for the compression test is unlikely to be available to the home mechanic, it is recommended that the test is performed by a Vauxhall/Opel dealer, or suitably-equipped garage.

3 Top dead centre (TDC) for No 1 piston – locating

1 In its travel up and down its cylinder bore, Top Dead Centre (TDC) is the highest point that each piston reaches as the crankshaft rotates. While each piston reaches TDC both at the top of the compression stroke, and again at the top of the exhaust stroke, for the purpose of timing the engine TDC refers to the piston position (usually number 1) at the top of its compression stroke.

2 Number 1 piston (and cylinder) is at the right-hand (timing belt) end of the engine, and its TDC position is located as follows. Note that the crankshaft rotates clockwise when viewed from the right-hand side of the car.

3 Disconnect the battery negative terminal (refer to *Disconnecting the battery* in the Reference Chapter). If necessary, remove all the spark plugs as described in Chapter 1A to enable the engine to be easily turned over.

4 To gain access to the camshaft sprocket timing mark, remove the timing belt upper cover as described in Section 6.

5 Using a socket and extension bar on the crankshaft pulley bolt, turn the crankshaft whilst keeping an eye on the camshaft sprocket. Rotate the crankshaft until the timing mark on the camshaft sprocket is correctly aligned with the cut-out on the top of the timing belt rear cover and the notch on the crankshaft pulley rim is correctly aligned with the pointer on the timing belt lower cover **(see illustrations)**.

3.5a Align the camshaft sprocket timing mark with the cut-out on the timing belt cover . . .

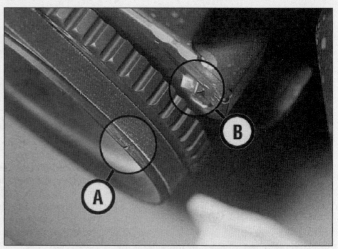

3.5b . . . and align the crankshaft pulley notch (A) with the timing mark pointer (B) to position No 1 piston at TDC on its compression stroke

6 With the crankshaft pulley and camshaft sprocket timing marks positioned as described, the engine is positioned with No 1 piston at TDC on its compression stroke.

4 Camshaft cover – removal and refitting

Removal

1 Remove the air cleaner assembly and air intake ducts as described in Chapter 4A.
2 Slacken and remove the retaining bolts, noting the correct fitted location of any clips or brackets retained by the bolts then lift the camshaft cover from the camshaft housing **(see illustration)**. If the cover is stuck, do not lever between the cover and camshaft housing mating surfaces – if necessary, gently tap the cover sideways to free it. Recover the gasket; if it shows signs of damage or deterioration it must be renewed.

Refitting

3 Prior to refitting, examine the inside of the cover for a build-up of oil sludge or any other contamination, and if necessary clean the cover with paraffin, or a water-soluble solvent.

Examine the condition of the crankcase ventilation filter inside the camshaft cover, and clean as described for the inside of the cover if clogging is evident (if desired, the filter can be removed from the cover, after removing the securing bolts). Dry the cover thoroughly before refitting.
4 Ensure the cover is clean and dry and seat the gasket in the cover recess then refit the cover to the camshaft housing, ensuring the gasket remains correctly seated **(see illustration)**.
5 Refit the retaining bolts, ensuring all relevant clips/brackets are correctly positioned, and tighten them to the specified torque working in a diagonal sequence.
6 Refit the air cleaner assembly and air intake ducts as described in Chapter 4A.

5 Crankshaft pulley – removal and refitting

Note: A new pulley retaining bolt will be required on refitting.

Removal

1 Firmly apply the handbrake, then jack up the front of the car and support it securely on

axle stands (see *Jacking and vehicle support*). Remove the right-hand roadwheel.
2 Remove the auxiliary drivebelt as described in Chapter 1A. Prior to removal, mark the direction of rotation on the belt to ensure the belt is refitted the same way around.
3 Slacken the crankshaft pulley retaining bolt. To prevent crankshaft rotation, have an assistant select top gear and apply the brakes firmly. If the engine is removed from the vehicle it will be necessary to lock the flywheel (see Section 15).
4 Unscrew the retaining bolt and washer, and remove the crankshaft pulley from the end of the crankshaft, taking care not to damage the crankshaft sensor.

Refitting

5 Refit the crankshaft pulley, aligning the pulley cut-out with the raised notch on the timing belt sprocket, then fit the washer and new retaining bolt **(see illustration)**.
6 Lock the crankshaft by the method used on removal, and tighten the pulley retaining bolt to the specified Stage 1 torque setting then angle-tighten the bolt through the specified Stage 2 angle, using a socket and extension bar, and finally through the specified Stage 3 angle. It is recommended that an angle-measuring gauge is used during the final

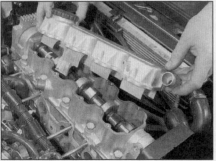

4.2 Removing the camshaft cover from the engine

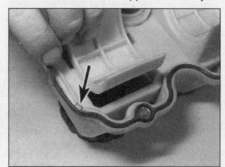

4.4 Ensure the gasket is correctly located in the camshaft cover recess (arrowed)

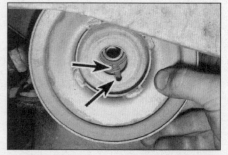

5.5 Refit the crankshaft pulley aligning the cut-out with the raised notch on the crankshaft sprocket (arrowed)

5.6 Fit the new retaining bolt and tighten it as described in the text

6.2 Timing belt upper cover retaining bolts (arrowed)

6.12 Slacken and remove the retaining bolts and remove the timing belt rear cover

stages of the tightening, to ensure accuracy **(see illustration)**. If a gauge is not available, use white paint to make alignment marks between the bolt head and pulley prior to tightening; the marks can then be used to check that the bolt has been rotated through the correct angle.

7 Refit the auxiliary drivebelt as described in Chapter 1A using the mark made prior to removal to ensure the belt is fitted the correct way around.

8 Refit the roadwheel then lower the car to the ground and tighten the wheel bolts to the specified torque.

6 Timing belt covers –
removal and refitting

Upper cover

Removal

1 Remove the air cleaner assembly and air intake ducts as described in Chapter 4A.
2 Undo the retaining bolts then unclip the timing belt upper cover and remove it from the engine **(see illustration)**.

Refitting

3 Refitting is the reverse of removal. Tighten the cover retaining bolts to the specified torque.

Lower cover

Removal

4 Remove the crankshaft pulley (see Section 5).
5 With reference to Chapter 5A, remove the auxiliary drivebelt tensioner.
6 Remove the upper cover (see paragraphs 1 and 2) then undo the retaining bolts and remove the lower cover from the engine.

Refitting

7 Refitting is the reverse of removal, using a new crankshaft pulley retaining bolt. Tighten all bolts to the specified torques.

Rear cover

Removal

8 Remove the camshaft and crankshaft timing

belt sprockets and the timing belt tensioner as described in Section 8.
9 Support the weight of the engine using a trolley jack with a block of wood placed on its head.
10 Undo the three bolts securing the right-hand engine mounting bracket to the cylinder block and remove the bracket.
11 Note the cable routing, and unclip the crankshaft position sensor cable from the rear cover.
12 Slacken and remove the bolts securing the rear cover to the camshaft housing and oil pump housing, and remove the cover from the engine **(see illustration)**.

Refitting

13 Refitting is the reverse of removal, tightening the cover retaining bolts and engine mounting bolts to the specified torque.

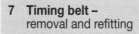

7 Timing belt –
removal and refitting

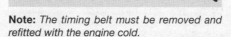

Note: *The timing belt must be removed and refitted with the engine cold.*

Removal

1 Remove the timing belt upper cover as described in Section 6.
2 Position No 1 cylinder at TDC on its compression stroke as described in Section 3.
3 Remove the crankshaft pulley as described in Section 5.
4 Support the weight of the engine using a

trolley jack with a block of wood placed on its head.
5 Remove the two bolts securing the right-hand engine mounting to the bracket on the cylinder block.
6 Undo the remaining two bolts securing the mounting to the body, and remove the mounting.
7 Unbolt the timing belt lower cover and remove it from the engine (see Section 6).
8 Insert a suitable tool (such as a pin punch) into the hole in the timing belt tensioner arm, then lever the arm clockwise to its stop, and lock it in position by inserting the tool into the corresponding hole in the tensioner backplate **(see illustrations)**. Leave the tool in position to lock the tensioner in position until the belt is refitted.
9 Check the camshaft and crankshaft sprocket timing marks are correctly aligned with the marks on the belt rear cover and oil pump housing.
10 Slacken the coolant pump retaining bolts then, using an open-ended spanner, carefully rotate the pump to relieve the tension in the timing belt. Adapters to fit the pump are available from most tool shops and allow the pump to be easily turned using a ratchet or extension bar **(see illustrations)**.
11 Slide the timing belt off its sprockets and remove it from the engine **(see illustration)**. If the belt is to be re-used, use white paint or similar to mark the direction of rotation on the belt. **Do not** rotate the crankshaft until the timing belt has been refitted.
12 Check the timing belt carefully for

7.8a Insert a tool (such as a punch) into the hole (arrowed) in the tensioner arm . . .

7.8b . . . then lever the arm clockwise and lock the tensioner in the position by locating the tool in the backplate hole

7.10a Slacken the coolant pump bolts . . .

7.10b . . . and relieve the timing belt tension by rotating the pump with a suitable adapter

7.11 Slip the timing belt from the sprockets and remove it from the engine

7.13 Ensure the timing mark on the crankshaft sprocket is correctly aligned with the mark on the oil pump housing

any signs of uneven wear, splitting or oil contamination, and renew it if there is the slightest doubt about its condition. If the engine is undergoing an overhaul and/or the vehicle is approaching 40 000 miles (see Chapter 1A) renew the belt as a matter of course, regardless of its apparent condition. If signs of oil contamination are found, trace the source of the oil leak and rectify it, then wash down the engine timing belt area and all related components to remove all traces of oil.

Refitting

13 On reassembly, thoroughly clean the timing belt sprockets then check that the camshaft sprocket timing mark is still correctly aligned

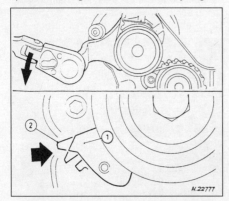

7.20 Rotate the coolant pump until the tensioner arm pointer (1) is correctly aligned with the cut-out (2) on the backplate

with the cover cut-out, and the crankshaft sprocket mark is still aligned with the mark on the oil pump housing **(see illustration)**.
14 Fit the timing belt over the crankshaft and camshaft sprockets, ensuring that the belt front run is taut (ie, all slack is on the tensioner pulley side of the belt), then fit the belt over the coolant pump sprocket and tensioner pulley. Do not twist the belt sharply while refitting it. Ensure that the belt teeth are correctly seated centrally in the sprockets, and that the timing marks remain in alignment. If a used belt is being refitted, ensure that the arrow mark made on removal points in the normal direction of rotation, as before.
15 Carefully remove the punch from the timing belt tensioner to release the tensioner spring.
16 Refit the engine mounting to the body and cylinder block bracket, tightening the securing bolts to the specified torque.
17 Check the sprocket timing marks are still correctly aligned. If adjustment is necessary, lock the tensioner in position again then disengage the belt from the sprockets and make any necessary adjustments.
18 If the marks are still correctly positioned, tension the timing belt by rotating the coolant pump whilst observing the movement of the tensioner arm. Position the pump so that the tensioner arm is fully over against its stop, without exerting any excess strain on the belt, then tighten the coolant pump retaining bolts.
19 Temporarily refit the crankshaft pulley bolt then rotate the crankshaft smoothly through two complete turns (720°) in the normal

direction of rotation to settle the timing belt in position.
20 Check that both the camshaft and crankshaft sprocket timing marks are realigned then slacken the coolant pump bolts. Adjust the pump so that the tensioner arm pointer is aligned with the cut-out on the backplate then tighten the coolant pump bolts to the specified torque **(see illustration)**. Rotate the crankshaft smoothly through another two complete turns in the normal direction of rotation, to bring the sprocket timing marks back into alignment. Check that the tensioner arm pointer is still aligned with the backplate cut-out.
21 If the tensioner arm is not correctly aligned with the backplate, repeat the procedure.
22 Once the tensioner arm and backplate remain correctly aligned, ensure the coolant pump bolts are tightened to the specified torque, then refit the timing belt covers and crankshaft pulley as described in Sections 5 and 6.

8 Timing belt tensioner and sprockets – removal and refitting

Camshaft sprocket

Removal

1 Remove the timing belt as described in Section 7.
2 The camshaft must be prevented from turning as the sprocket bolt is unscrewed, and this can be achieved in one of two ways as follows.
  a) *Make up a sprocket-holding tool using two lengths of steel strip (one long, the other short), and three nuts and bolts; one nut and bolt forms the pivot of a forked tool, with the remaining two nuts and bolts at the tips of the 'forks' to engage with the sprocket spokes (see illustration).*
  b) *Remove the camshaft cover as described in Section 4 and hold the camshaft with an open-ended spanner on the flats provided.*
3 Unscrew the retaining bolt and washer

8.2 Using a home-made sprocket holding tool to retain the camshaft whilst the bolt is slackened

8.5 Refit the camshaft sprocket making sure the locating pin (1) engages with the sprocket hole (2)

8.6 Using an open-ended spanner to retain the camshaft whilst the sprocket retaining bolt is tightened to the specified torque

and remove the sprocket from the end of the camshaft.

Refitting

4 Prior to refitting check the oil seal for signs of damage or leakage, if necessary, renewing it as described in Section 9.

5 Refit the sprocket to the end of the camshaft, aligning its cut-out with the camshaft locating pin, then refit the retaining bolt and washer **(see illustration)**.

6 Tighten the sprocket retaining bolt to the specified torque whilst preventing rotation using the method employed on removal **(see illustration)**.

7 Refit the timing belt as described in Section 7 then (where necessary) refit the camshaft cover as described in Section 4.

Crankshaft sprocket

Removal

8 Remove the timing belt (see Section 7).

9 Slide the sprocket off the end of the crankshaft, noting which way around it is fitted.

Refitting

10 Ensure the Woodruff key is correctly fitted to the crankshaft.

11 Align the sprocket with the crankshaft groove then slide the sprocket into position, making sure its timing mark is facing outwards **(see illustration)**.

12 Refit the timing belt (see Section 7).

Tensioner assembly

Removal

13 Remove the timing belt (see Section 7).

14 Slacken and remove the retaining bolt and remove the tensioner assembly from the oil pump **(see illustration)**.

Refitting

15 Fit the tensioner to the oil pump housing, making sure that the lug on the backplate is correctly located in the oil pump housing hole **(see illustration)**. Ensure the tensioner is correctly seated then refit the retaining bolt and tighten it to the specified torque.

8.11 Refit the crankshaft sprocket, making sure its timing marks are facing outwards

9 Camshaft oil seal – renewal

1 Remove the camshaft sprocket as described in Section 8.

2 Carefully punch or drill two small holes opposite each other in the oil seal. Screw a

8.14 Slacken and remove the retaining bolt and remove the timing belt tensioner assembly

8.15 On refitting, ensure the tensioner backplate lug (1) is correctly located in the oil pump housing hole (2)

9.2 Removing the camshaft oil seal

9.4 Fitting a new camshaft oil seal

self-tapping screw into each, and pull on the screws with pliers to extract the seal **(see illustration)**.

3 Clean the seal housing, and polish off any burrs or raised edges which may have caused the seal to fail in the first place.

4 Lubricate the lips of the new seal with clean engine oil, and press it into position using a suitable tubular drift (such as a socket) which bears only on the hard outer edge of the seal **(see illustration)**. Take care not to damage the seal lips during fitting; note that the seal lips should face inwards.

5 Refit the camshaft sprocket as described in Section 8.

10 Camshaft housing and camshaft – removal, inspection and refitting

Removal

Using Vauxhall tool MKM 891

Caution: Prior to fitting the special tool, rotate the crankshaft clockwise 90° past the TDC position (see Section 3). This will position the pistons approximately mid-way in the bores and prevent the valves contacting them when the tool is fitted.

1 If access to the special service tool can be gained, the camshaft can be removed from the engine without disturbing the camshaft housing. The tool is fitted to the top of the camshaft housing, once the cover has been removed (see Section 4), and depresses the

cam followers. This allows the camshaft to be withdrawn from the left-hand end of the housing once the timing belt sprocket has been removed (see Section 8) and the cover and thrustplate have been unbolted (see paragraphs 3 to 5).

Without the Vauxhall tool

2 Assuming that such a tool is not available, the camshaft can only be removed once the camshaft housing has been removed from the engine. Since the camshaft housing is secured in position by the cylinder head bolts, it is not possible to remove the camshaft without removing the cylinder head (see Section 12). **Note:** *In theory it is possible to remove the camshaft housing once the cylinder head bolts have been removed, and leave the head in position. However, this procedure carries a high risk of disturbing the head gasket, resulting in the head gasket 'blowing' once the camshaft and housing are refitted. If you wish to attempt this, remove the camshaft housing, as described in Section 12, noting that it will not be necessary to remove the manifolds, etc. Be warned though that, after refitting, you may find the head gasket will need renewing, meaning that the cylinder head will have to be removed after all and need another set of bolts. The decision is yours as to whether this is a chance worth taking.*

3 With the camshaft housing removed, unbolt the ignition module and remove it from the end of the housing.

4 Undo the retaining bolts and remove the end cover from the left-hand end of the

housing **(see illustration)**. Remove the sealing ring from the cover and discard it, a new one should be used on refitting.

5 Measure the camshaft endfloat by inserting feeler gauges between the thrustplate and the camshaft; if the endfloat is not within the limits given in the Specifications then the thrustplate will need to be renewed. Unscrew the two retaining bolts then slide out the camshaft thrustplate, noting which way round it is fitted **(see illustration)**.

6 Carefully withdraw the camshaft from the left-hand end of the housing, taking care not to damage the bearing journals **(see illustration)**.

Inspection

7 With the camshaft removed, examine the bearings in the camshaft housing for signs of obvious wear or pitting. If evident, a new camshaft housing will probably be required. Also check that the oil supply holes in the camshaft housing are free from obstructions.

8 The camshaft itself should show no marks or scoring on the journal or cam lobe surfaces. If evident, renew the camshaft. If the camshaft lobes show signs of wear also examine the followers (see Section 11).

9 Check the camshaft thrustplate for signs of wear or grooves, and renew if necessary.

Refitting

10 Carefully prise the old seal out of from the camshaft housing, using a suitable screwdriver. Ensure the housing is clean then press the in new seal, ensuring its sealing lip is facing inwards, until it is flush with the housing.

11 Liberally lubricate the camshaft and housing bearings and the oil seal lip with fresh engine oil.

12 Carefully insert the camshaft into the housing, taking care not to mark the bearing surfaces or damage the oil seal lip.

13 Slide the thrustplate into position, engaging it with the camshaft slot, and tighten its retaining bolts to the specified torque. Check the camshaft endfloat (see paragraph 5).

14 Fit a new sealing ring to the end cover recess then refit the cover to the camshaft housing and tighten its retaining bolts to the

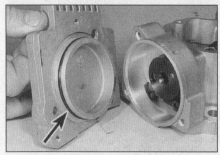

10.4 Remove the cover from the left-hand end of the camshaft housing (sealing ring arrowed)

10.5 Undo the retaining bolts then remove the thrustplate (arrowed) . . .

10.6 . . . and slide the camshaft out from the housing

11.9a Remove each follower . . .

11.9b . . . thrust pad . . .

11.9c . . . and hydraulic tappet from the cylinder head

specified torque. Refit the ignition module to the housing cover.

15 If work is being carried out using the special service tool, remove the tool and refit the camshaft sprocket. Return the crankshaft to TDC and refit the timing belt (see Sections 7 and 8).

16 If the tool is not being used, refit the camshaft housing as described in Section 12.

11 Camshaft followers and hydraulic tappets – removal, inspection and refitting

Using Vauxhall tool KM-565

Removal

1 If access to the special tool (KM-565) or a suitable equivalent can be gained, the cam followers and tappets can be removed as follows, without disturbing the camshaft.

2 Firmly apply the handbrake then jack up the front of the vehicle and support it on axle stands. Remove the right-hand front roadwheel.

3 Remove the camshaft cover (see Section 4).

4 Using a socket and extension bar, rotate the crankshaft in the normal direction of rotation until the camshaft lobe of the first follower/tappet to be removed is pointing straight upwards.

5 Fit the service tool to the top of the camshaft housing, making sure the tool end is correctly engaged with the top of the valve. Screw the tool stud into one of the housing bolt holes until the valve is sufficiently depressed to allow the follower to be slid out from underneath the camshaft. The hydraulic tappet can then also be removed, as can the thrust pad from the top of the valve. Inspect the components (see paragraphs 10 and 11) and renew if worn or damaged.

Refitting

6 Lubricate the tappet and follower with fresh engine oil then slide the tappet into its bore in the cylinder head. Manoeuvre the follower into position, ensuring it is correctly engaged with the tappet and valve stem, then carefully remove the service tool.

7 Repeat the operation on the remaining followers and tappets.

Without the Vauxhall tool

Removal

8 Without the use of the special tool, it will be necessary to remove the camshaft housing to allow the followers and tappets to be removed (see Section 10, paragraph 2).

9 With the housing removed, obtain eight small, clean plastic containers, and number them 1 to 8; alternatively, divide a larger container into eight compartments. Lift out each follower, thrust pad and hydraulic tappet in turn, and place them in their respective container. Do not interchange the cam followers, or the rate of wear will be much-increased **(see illustrations)**.

Inspection

10 Examine the cam follower bearing surfaces which contact the camshaft lobes for wear ridges and scoring. Renew any follower on which these conditions are apparent. If a follower bearing surface is badly scored, also examine the corresponding lobe on the camshaft for wear, as it is likely that both will be worn. Also check the thrust pad for signs of wear or damage. Renew worn components as necessary.

11 If the hydraulic tappets are thought to be faulty they should be renewed; testing of the tappets is not possible.

Refitting

12 Lubricate the hydraulic tappets and their cylinder head bores with clean engine oil. Refit the tappets to the cylinder head, making sure they are fitted in their original locations.

13 Fit the thrust pads to the top of its respective valves.

14 Lubricate the followers with clean engine oil. Fit each follower, making sure it is correctly located with both the tappet and thrust pad, then refit the camshaft housing (see Section 12).

12 Cylinder head – removal and refitting

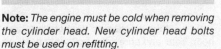

Note: *The engine must be cold when removing the cylinder head. New cylinder head bolts must be used on refitting.*

Removal

1 Depressurise the fuel system as described in Chapter 4A, then disconnect the battery negative terminal (refer to *Disconnecting the battery* in the Reference Chapter).

2 Drain the cooling system and remove the spark plugs as described in Chapter 1A.

3 Remove the timing belt as described in Section 7.

4 Unscrew the retaining bolts, and remove the engine mounting bracket from the right-hand end of the cylinder head.

5 Remove the inlet and exhaust manifolds as described in Chapter 4A. If no work is to be carried out on the cylinder head, the head can be removed complete with manifolds once the following operations have been carried out.

   a) *Disconnect the various wiring connectors from the throttle housing and manifold.*
   b) *Disconnect the fuel hoses from the throttle housing and the various vacuum and coolant hoses from the inlet manifold.*
   c) *Unbolt the inlet manifold support bracket and the alternator upper bracket.*
   d) *Unbolt the exhaust front pipe from manifold and disconnect the oxygen sensor wiring connector.*

6 Remove the camshaft cover as described in Section 4.

7 Remove the camshaft sprocket as described in Section 8.

8 Undo the retaining bolts securing the timing belt rear cover to the camshaft housing.

9 Disconnect the wiring connectors from the ignition module, purge valve and the coolant temperature sensor on the left-hand end of the cylinder head. Remove the cable guide from the camshaft cover, and position it clear of the cylinder head.

10 Slacken the retaining clip and disconnect the coolant hose from the thermostat housing.

11 Make a final check to ensure that all relevant hoses, pipes and wires, etc, have been disconnected.

12 Working in the **reverse** of the tightening sequence **(see illustration 12.30a)**, progressively slacken the cylinder head bolts by a third of a turn at a time until all bolts can be unscrewed by hand. Remove each bolt in turn, along with its washer.

13 Lift the camshaft housing from the cylinder

12.13 Removing the camshaft housing

12.14 Removing the cylinder head

head **(see illustration)**. If necessary, tap the housing gently with a soft-faced mallet to free it from the cylinder head, but **do not** lever at the mating faces. Note the fitted positions of the two locating dowels, and remove them for safe-keeping if they are loose.

14 Lift the cylinder head from the cylinder block, taking care not to dislodge the cam followers or thrust pads **(see illustration)**. If necessary, tap the cylinder head gently with a soft-faced mallet to free it from the block, but **do not** lever at the mating faces. Note the fitted positions of the two locating dowels, and remove them for safe-keeping if they are loose.

15 Recover the cylinder head gasket, and discard it.

Preparation for refitting

16 The mating faces of the cylinder head and block must be perfectly clean before refitting the head. Use a scraper to remove all traces of gasket and carbon, and also clean the tops of the pistons. Take particular care with the aluminium surfaces, as the soft metal is damaged easily. Also, make sure that debris is not allowed to enter the oil and water channels – this is particularly important for the oil circuit, as carbon could block the oil supply to the camshaft or crankshaft bearings. Using adhesive tape and paper, seal the water, oil and bolt holes in the cylinder block. To prevent carbon entering the gap between the pistons and bores, smear a little grease in the gap. After cleaning the piston, rotate the crankshaft so that the piston moves down the bore, then wipe out the grease and carbon with a cloth rag. Clean the other piston crowns in the same way.

17 Check the block and head for nicks, deep scratches and other damage. If slight,

they may be removed carefully with a file. More serious damage may be repaired by machining, but this is a specialist job.

18 If warpage of the cylinder head is suspected, use a straight-edge to check it for distortion. Refer to Chapter 2F if necessary.

19 Ensure that the cylinder head bolt holes in the crankcase are clean and free of oil. Syringe or soak up any oil left in the bolt holes. This is most important in order that the correct bolt tightening torque can be applied and to prevent the possibility of the block being cracked by hydraulic pressure when the bolts are tightened.

20 Renew the cylinder head bolts regardless of their apparent condition.

Refitting

21 Position number 1 piston at TDC, and wipe clean the mating faces of the head and block.

22 Ensure that the two locating dowels are in position at each end of the cylinder block/ crankcase surface.

23 Fit the new cylinder head gasket to the block, making sure it is fitted with the correct way up with its OBEN/TOP mark uppermost **(see illustrations)**.

24 Carefully refit the cylinder head, locating it on the dowels.

25 Ensure the mating surfaces of the cylinder head and camshaft housing are clean and dry. Check the camshaft is still correctly positioned by temporarily fitting the camshaft sprocket and checking that the sprocket timing mark is still uppermost.

26 Apply a bead of suitable sealant to the cylinder head upper mating surface **(see illustration)**.

27 Ensure the two locating dowels are in position then lubricate the camshaft followers with clean engine oil.

28 Carefully lower the camshaft housing assembly into position, locating it on the dowels.

29 Fit the washers to the new cylinder head bolts then carefully insert them into position **(do not drop)**, tightening them finger-tight only at this stage **(see illustration)**.

30 Working progressively and in sequence, first tighten all the cylinder head bolts to the Stage 1 torque setting **(see illustrations)**.

12.23a Fit the new gasket to the cylinder block, engaging it with the locating dowels (arrowed) . . .

12.23b . . . making sure its OBEN/TOP marking is uppermost

12.26 Apply sealant to the cylinder head upper mating surface then refit the camshaft housing

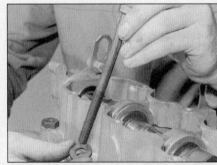

12.29 Fit the washers to the new cylinder head bolts and screw the bolts into position

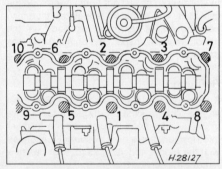

12.30a Cylinder head bolts tightening sequence

31 Once all bolts have been tightened to the Stage 1 torque, again working in sequence, tighten each bolt through its specified Stage 2 angle, using a socket and extension bar. It is recommended that an angle-measuring gauge is used during this stage of the tightening, to ensure accuracy **(see illustration)**.

32 Working in the specified sequence, go around again and tighten all bolts through the specified Stage 3 angle.

33 Finally go around in the specified sequence again and tighten all bolts through the specified Stage 4 angle.

34 Refit the bolts securing the timing belt rear cover to the camshaft housing and tighten them to the specified torque.

35 Ensure the right-hand engine mounting bracket is correctly positioned, and tighten the retaining bolts to the specified torque.

36 Refit the camshaft sprocket as described in Section 8 then fit the timing belt as described in Section 7.

37 Reconnect the wiring connectors to the cylinder head components, ensuring all wiring is correctly routed, and secure it in position with the necessary clips.

38 Reconnect the coolant hose to the thermostat housing and securely tighten its retaining clip.

39 Refit/reconnect the manifolds as described in Chapter 4A (as applicable).

40 Refit the roadwheel then lower the vehicle to the floor and tighten the wheel bolts to the specified torque.

41 Ensure all pipes and hoses are securely reconnected then refit the spark plugs and refill the cooling system (Chapter 1A).

42 Reconnect the battery then start the engine and check for signs of leaks.

13 Sump – removal and refitting

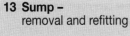

Removal

1 Disconnect the battery negative terminal (refer to *Disconnecting the battery* in the Reference Chapter).

2 Firmly apply the handbrake, then jack up the front of the car and support it securely on axle stands (see *Jacking and vehicle support*).

12.30b Working in the specified sequence, tighten the cylinder head bolts to the specified Stage 1 torque setting . . .

3 Drain the engine oil as described in Chapter 1A, then fit a new sealing washer and refit the drain plug, tightening it to the specified torque.

4 Remove the complete exhaust system as described in Chapter 4A.

5 Disconnect the wiring connector from the oil level sender unit on the sump.

Models without air conditioning

6 Slacken and remove the flywheel lower cover retaining bolts and remove the cover from the base of the transmission unit **(see illustration)**.

7 Progressively slacken and remove the bolts securing the sump to the base of the cylinder block/oil pump. Break the sump joint by striking the sump with the palm of the hand, then lower the sump from the engine and withdraw it **(see illustration)**. Remove the gasket and discard it.

8 While the sump is removed, take the opportunity to check the oil pump pick-up/strainer for signs of clogging or splitting. If necessary, unbolt the pick-up/strainer and remove it from the base of the oil pump housing along with its sealing ring. The strainer can then be cleaned easily in solvent or renewed.

Models with air conditioning

9 Slacken and remove the bolts securing the sump flange to the transmission housing.

10 Progressively slacken and remove the bolts securing the sump to the base of the cylinder block/oil pump. Note that the bolts securing the transmission end of the sump to

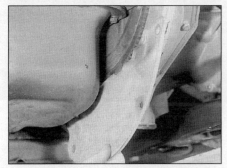

13.6 Removing the flywheel lower cover plate – models without air conditioning

13.7 Removing the pressed steel sump – models without air conditioning

12.31 . . . and then through the various specified angles (see text)

the cylinder block are accessed through the cut-outs in the sump flange, once the rubber plugs have been removed **(see illustration)**. Break the sump joint by striking the sump with the palm of the hand, then lower the sump from the engine and withdraw it. Remove the gasket and discard it. While the sump is removed, take the opportunity to check the oil pump pick-up/strainer for signs of clogging or splitting. If necessary, unbolt the pick-up/strainer and remove it from the base of the oil pump housing along with its sealing ring. The strainer can then be cleaned easily in solvent or renewed.

Refitting

Models without air conditioning

11 Remove all traces of dirt and oil from the mating surfaces of the sump and cylinder block and (where removed) the pick-up/strainer and oil pump housing. Also remove all traces of locking compound from the pick-up bolts (where removed).

12 Where necessary, position a new sealing ring on top of the oil pump pick-up/strainer and fit the strainer **(see illustration)**. Apply locking compound to the threads of the retaining bolts then fit the bolts and tighten to the specified torque.

13 Apply a smear of suitable sealant to the areas of the cylinder block mating surface around the areas of the of the oil housing and rear main bearing cap joints **(see illustration)**.

14 Fit a new gasket to the sump then offer up the sump to the cylinder block and refit the retaining bolts. Working out from the centre in

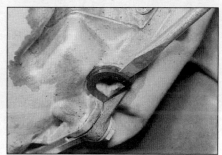

13.10 On models with air conditioning remove the rubber plugs from the sump flange to access the remaining bolts

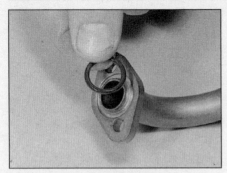

13.12 Fit a new sealing ring to the oil pump pick-up/strainer

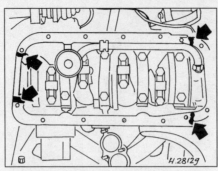

13.13 Apply sealant to the oil pump and rear main bearing cap joints (arrowed) before the sump is refitted

25 Lower the vehicle to the ground then fill the engine with fresh oil, with reference to Chapter 1A.

14 Oil pump –
removal, overhaul and refitting

Note: *The pressure relief valve can be removed with pump in position on the engine.*

Removal

1 Remove the timing belt (see Section 7).
2 Remove the camshaft and crankshaft timing belt sprockets and the tensioner as described in Section 8.
3 Unbolt the timing belt rear cover from the camshaft housing and oil pump and remove it from the engine.
4 Remove the sump and oil pump pick-up/strainer as described in Section 13.
5 Disconnect the wiring connector from the oil pressure switch.
6 Unbolt the crankshaft sensor mounting bracket and position it clear of the oil pump.
7 Slacken and remove the retaining bolts then slide the oil pump housing assembly off the end of the crankshaft, taking great care not to lose the locating dowels. Remove the housing gasket and discard it.

Overhaul

8 Undo the retaining screws and lift off the pump cover from the rear of the housing (see illustration).
9 Using a suitable marker pen, mark the surface of both the pump inner and outer gears; the marks can then be used to ensure the rotors are refitted the correct way around.
10 Lift out the inner and outer gears from the pump housing (see illustration).
11 Unscrew the oil pressure relief valve bolt from the front of the housing and withdraw the spring and plunger from the housing, noting which way around the plunger is fitted (see illustration). Remove the sealing washer from the valve bolt.
12 Clean the components, and carefully examine the gears, pump body and relief valve plunger for any signs of scoring or wear. Renew any component which shows signs of wear or damage; if the gears or pump housing are marked then the complete pump assembly should be renewed.
13 If the components appear serviceable, measure the clearance between the inner gear and outer gear using feeler blades. Also measure the gear endfloat, and check the flatness of the end cover (see illustrations). If the clearances exceed the specified tolerances, the pump must be renewed.
14 If the pump is satisfactory, reassemble the components in the reverse order of removal, noting the following.
  a) Ensure both gears are fitted the correct way around.
  b) Fit a new sealing washer to the pressure

14.8 Undo the retaining screws and remove the oil pump cover

a diagonal sequence, progressively tighten the sump retaining bolts to their specified torque setting.
15 Refit the cover plate to the transmission housing, tightening its retaining bolts to the specified torque.
16 Refit the exhaust system (see Chapter 4A) and reconnect the oil level sender wiring connector.
17 Lower the vehicle to the ground then fill the engine with fresh oil, with reference to Chapter 1A.

Models with air conditioning

18 Where necessary, refit the oil pump pick-up/strainer as described in paragraphs 11 and 12.
19 Ensure the sump and cylinder block mating surfaces are clean and dry and remove all traces of locking compound from the sump bolts.

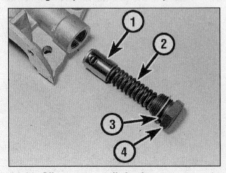

14.11 Oil pressure relief valve components

  1 *Plunger*   3 *Sealing washer*
  2 *Spring*   4 *Valve bolt*

14.10 Removal of pump outer gear – outer face identification punch mark arrowed

20 Apply a smear of suitable sealant to the areas of the cylinder block mating surface around the areas of the of the oil housing and rear main bearing cap joints.
21 Fit a new gasket to the sump and apply a few drops of locking compound to the threads of the sump-to-cylinder block/oil pump bolts.
22 Offer up the sump, ensuring the gasket remains correctly positioned, and loosely refit all the retaining bolts. Working out from the centre in a diagonal sequence, progressively tighten the bolts securing the sump to the cylinder block/oil pump to their specified torque setting.
23 Tighten the bolts securing the sump flange to the transmission housing to their specified torque setting. Refit the rubber plugs to the sump flange cut-outs.
24 Refit the exhaust system (see Chapter 4A) and reconnect the oil level sender wiring connector.

14.13a Using a feeler blade to check gear clearance

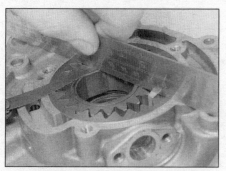

14.13b Using a straight-edge and feeler blade to measure gear endfloat

relief valve bolt and tighten the bolt to the specified torque.
c) *Remove all traces of locking compound from the cover screws. Apply a drop of fresh locking compound to each screw and tighten the screws to the specified torque.*
d) *On completion prime the oil pump by filling it with clean engine oil whilst rotating the inner gear.*

Refitting

15 Prior to refitting, carefully lever out the crankshaft oil seal using a flat-bladed screwdriver. Fit the new oil seal, ensuring its sealing lip is facing inwards, and press it squarely into the housing using a tubular drift which bears only on the hard outer edge of the seal **(see illustration)**. Press the seal into position so that it is flush with the housing and lubricate the oil seal lip with clean engine oil.

16 Ensure the mating surfaces of the oil pump and cylinder block are clean and dry and the locating dowels are in position.

17 Fit a new gasket to the cylinder block.

18 Carefully manoeuvre the oil pump into position and engage the inner gear with the crankshaft end **(see illustration)**. Locate the pump on the dowels, taking great care not damage the oil seal lip.

19 Refit the pump housing retaining bolts in their original locations and tighten them to the specified torque.

20 Refit the crankshaft sensor bracket to the pump housing and tighten its mounting bolt to the specified torque. Reconnect the oil pressure sensor wiring connector.

14.15 Fitting a new crankshaft oil seal to the oil pump housing

21 Refit the oil pump pick-up/strainer and sump as described in Section 13.

22 Refit the rear timing belt cover to the engine, tightening its retaining bolts to the specified torque.

23 Refit the timing belt sprockets and tensioner then refit the belt as described in Sections 7 and 8.

24 On completion refill the engine with clean oil as described in Chapter 1A.

15 Flywheel – removal, inspection and refitting

Note: *New flywheel retaining bolts will be required on refitting.*

Removal

1 Remove the transmission as described in Chapter 7A then remove the clutch assembly as described in Chapter 6.

2 Prevent the flywheel from turning by locking the ring gear teeth **(see illustration)**. Alternatively, bolt a strap between the flywheel and the cylinder block/crankcase. Make alignment marks between the flywheel and crankshaft using paint or a suitable marker pen.

3 Slacken and remove the retaining bolts and remove the flywheel.

Caution: Take care, as the flywheel is heavy.

Inspection

4 Examine the flywheel for wear or chipping

14.18 Take care not to damage the oil seal on the crankshaft lip (1) and engage the inner gear with the crankshaft flats (2)

of the ring gear teeth. Renewal of the ring gear is possible but is not a task for the home mechanic; renewal requires the new ring gear to be heated (up to 180° to 230ºC) to allow it to be fitted.

5 Examine the flywheel for scoring of the clutch face. If the clutch face is scored, the flywheel may be surface-ground, but renewal is preferable.

6 If there is any doubt about the condition of the flywheel, seek the advice of a Vauxhall/Opel dealer or engine reconditioning specialist. They will be able to advise if it is possible to recondition it or whether renewal is necessary.

Refitting

7 Clean the mating surfaces of the flywheel and crankshaft.

8 Offer up the flywheel and fit the new retaining bolts with a little locking compound. If the original is being refitted, align the marks made prior to removal.

9 Lock the flywheel by the method used on removal, and tighten the retaining bolts to the specified Stage 1 torque setting then angle-tighten the bolts through the specified Stage 2 angle, using a socket and extension bar, and finally through the specified Stage 3 angle **(see illustrations)**. It is recommended that an angle-measuring gauge is used during the final stages of the tightening, to ensure accuracy. If a gauge is not available, use white paint to make alignment marks between the bolt head and flywheel prior to tightening; the marks can then be used to check that the bolt has been rotated through the correct angle.

15.2 Lock the flywheel ring gear with a suitable tool

15.9a Tighten the flywheel bolts to the specified Stage 1 torque setting . . .

15.9b . . . then tighten them through the specified Stage 2 and 3 angles

10 Refit the clutch as described in Chapter 6 then remove the locking tool, and refit the transmission as described in Chapter 7A.

16 Crankshaft oil seals – renewal

Timing belt end oil seal

1 Remove the crankshaft sprocket as described in Section 8.
2 Carefully punch or drill two small holes opposite each other in the oil seal. Screw a self-tapping screw into each and pull on the screws with pliers to extract the seal (see illustration).
Caution: Great care must be taken to avoid damage to the oil pump
3 Clean the seal housing and polish off any burrs or raised edges which may have caused the seal to fail in the first place.
4 Lubricate the lips of the new seal with clean engine oil and ease it into position on the end of the shaft. Press the seal squarely into position until it is flush with the housing.

16.2 Removing the crankshaft right-hand oil seal

If necessary, a suitable tubular drift, such as a socket, which bears only on the hard outer edge of the seal can be used to tap the seal into position (see illustration). Take great care not to damage the seal lips during fitting and ensure that the seal lips face inwards.
5 Wash off any traces of oil, then refit the crankshaft sprocket as described in Section 8.

Transmission end oil seal

6 Remove the flywheel as described in Section 15.

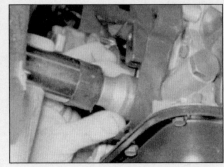

16.4 Fitting a new crankshaft right-hand oil seal

7 Renew the seal as described in paragraphs 2 to 4.
8 Refit the flywheel as described in Section 15.

17 Engine/transmission mountings – inspection and renewal

Refer to Chapter 2A, Section 15.

Chapter 2 Part C:
1.6 and 1.8 litre DOHC petrol engine in-car repair procedures

Contents

Degrees of difficulty

Easy, suitable for novice with little experience	**Fairly easy,** suitable for beginner with some experience	**Fairly difficult,** suitable for competent DIY mechanic	**Difficult,** suitable for experienced DIY mechanic	**Very difficult,** suitable for expert DIY or professional

Specifications

General

Engine type	Four-cylinder, in-line, water-cooled. Double overhead belt-driven camshafts
Manufacturer's engine code:*	
1.6 litre engines	Z16XE, Z16XEP
1.8 litre engines	Z18XE
Bore:	
1.6 litre engines	79.0 mm
1.8 litre engines	80.5 mm
Stroke:	
1.6 litre engines	81.5 mm
1.8 litre engines	88.2 mm
Capacity:	
1.6 litre engines	1598 cc
1.8 litre engines	1796 cc
Compression ratio	10.5:1
Firing order	1-3-4-2 (No 1 cylinder at timing belt end)
Direction of crankshaft rotation	Clockwise (viewed from timing belt end of engine)

* For details of engine code location, see 'Vehicle identification' in the Reference Chapter.

Compression pressures

Maximum difference between any two cylinders	1 bar

Valve clearances (Z16XEP engines)

Engine cold:	
Inlet	0.21 to 0.29 mm
Exhaust	0.26 to 0.35 mm

Lubrication system

Minimum oil pressure at 80°C	1.3 bar at idle speed
Oil pump type	Rotor-type, driven directly from crankshaft
Rotor-to-housing clearance (endfloat):	
Z16XE and Z18XE engines	0.03 to 0.10 mm
Z16XEP engines	0.02 to 0.058 mm

Torque wrench settings

	Nm	lbf ft
Z16XE and Z18XE engines		
Auxiliary drivebelt tensioner bolt	35	26
Camshaft bearing cap bolts	8	6
Camshaft cover bolts	8	6
Camshaft sprocket bolt:*		
Stage 1	50	37
Stage 2	Angle-tighten a further 60°	
Stage 3	Angle-tighten a further 15°	
Connecting rod big-end bearing cap bolt:*		
Stage 1	25	18
Stage 2	Angle-tighten a further 30°	
Crankshaft pulley bolt:*		
Stage 1	95	70
Stage 2	Angle-tighten a further 30°	
Stage 3	Angle-tighten a further 15°	
Crankshaft sensor mounting bracket bolt	8	6
Cylinder head bolts:*		
Stage 1	25	18
Stage 2	Angle-tighten a further 90°	
Stage 3	Angle-tighten a further 90°	
Stage 4	Angle-tighten a further 90°	
Stage 5	Angle-tighten a further 45°	
Engine/transmission mountings:		
Front mounting/torque link:		
Mounting-to-transmission bolts	95	70
Mounting to subframe	60	44
Left-hand mounting:		
Mounting-to-body bolts	25	18
Mounting to transmission bracket:*		
Stage 1	80	59
Stage 2	Angle-tighten a further 60°	
Transmission bracket to transmission	60	44
Rear mounting/torque link:		
Mounting-to-bracket bolt	80	59
Mounting-to-subframe bolt	80	59
Bracket-to-transmission bolts:*		
Stage 1	80	59
Stage 2	Angle-tighten a further 45°	
Right-hand mounting:		
Engine bracket-to-engine bolts	60	44
Mounting-to-body bolts	40	30
Mounting-to-engine bracket bolts:*		
Stage 1	60	44
Stage 2	Angle-tighten a further 30°	
Engine-to-transmission bolts	60	44
Flywheel bolts:*		
Stage 1	35	26
Stage 2	Angle-tighten a further 30°	
Stage 3	Angle-tighten a further 15°	
Main bearing cap bolts:*		
Stage 1	50	37
Stage 2	Angle-tighten a further 45°	
Stage 3	Angle-tighten a further 15°	
Oil pump:		
Retaining bolts	10	17
Pump cover screws	6	4
Oil pressure relief valve bolt	50	37
Oil pump pick-up/strainer and baffle plate bolts	8	6
Roadwheel bolts	110	81
Sump bolts:		
Sump-to-cylinder block/oil pump bolts	10	7
Sump flange-to-transmission bolts	40	30
Timing belt cover bolts	6	4
Timing belt idler pulley bolt	25	18
Timing belt tensioner bolt	20	15

* Use new fasteners

Torque wrench settings (continued)

	Nm	lbf ft
Z16XEP engines		
Auxiliary drivebelt tensioner retaining bolt	50	37
Camshaft bearing cap bolts	8	6
Camshaft cover bolts	8	6
Camshaft sprocket bolt:*		
Stage 1	50	37
Stage 2	Angle-tighten a further 60°	
Stage 3	Angle-tighten a further 15°	
Connecting rod big-end bearing cap bolt:*		
Stage 1	25	18
Stage 2	Angle-tighten a further 30°	
Stage 3	Angle-tighten a further 15°	
Coolant pipe flange to coolant pump	10	7
Crankshaft pulley bolt:*		
Stage 1	95	70
Stage 2	Angle-tighten a further 30°	
Stage 3	Angle-tighten a further 15°	
Cylinder head bolts:*		
Stage 1	25	18
Stage 2	Angle-tighten a further 90°	
Stage 3	Angle-tighten a further 90°	
Stage 4	Angle-tighten a further 90°	
Stage 5	Angle-tighten a further 45°	
Engine/transmission mountings:		
Front mounting/torque link:		
Mounting-to-transmission bolts	80	59
Mounting to subframe	55	41
Left-hand mounting:		
Mounting-to-body bolts	20	15
Mounting bracket to transmission bracket	55	41
Transmission bracket to transmission	35	26
Rear mounting/torque link:		
Mounting-to-bracket bolts	55	41
Mounting-to-subframe bolts	55	41
Bracket-to-transmission bolts	80	59
Right-hand mounting:		
Engine bracket-to-engine bolts	50	37
Mounting-to-body bolts	35	26
Mounting-to-engine bracket bolts	55	41
Engine-to-transmission bolts	60	44
Flywheel bolts:*		
Stage 1	35	26
Stage 2	Angle-tighten a further 30°	
Stage 3	Angle-tighten a further 15°	
Main bearing cap bolts:*		
Stage 1	50	37
Stage 2	Angle-tighten a further 45°	
Stage 3	Angle-tighten a further 15°	
Oil pump:		
Retaining bolts	20	15
Pump cover screws	8	6
Oil pressure relief valve cap	15	11
Oil pump pick-up/strainer and baffle plate bolts	8	6
Roadwheel bolts	110	81
Sump bolts:		
Sump-to-cylinder block/oil pump bolts	10	7
Sump flange-to-transmission bolts	40	30
Timing belt cover bolts	6	4
Timing belt idler pulley bolt	25	18
Timing belt tensioner bolt*	20	15

Use new fasteners

1 General information

How to use this Chapter

This Part of Chapter 2 describes the repair procedures which can reasonably be carried out on the engine while it remains in the vehicle. If the engine has been removed from the vehicle and is being dismantled as described in Chapter 2F, any preliminary dismantling procedures can be ignored.

Note that, while it may be possible physically to overhaul items such as the piston/connecting rod assemblies while the engine is in the vehicle, such tasks are not usually carried out as separate operations, and usually require the execution of several additional procedures (not to mention the cleaning of components and of oilways); for this reason, all such tasks are classed as major overhaul procedures, and are described in Chapter 2F.

Chapter 2F describes the removal of the engine/transmission unit from the vehicle, and the full overhaul procedures which can then be carried out.

Engine description

The engine is a double overhead camshaft, four-cylinder, in-line unit, mounted transversely at the front of the car, with the transmission attached to its left-hand end.

The Z16XEP and Z18XE power units are known as 'Twinport' engines due to the design of the inlet manifold and cylinder head combustion chambers. Vacuum-operated flap valves located in the inlet manifold are opened or closed according to engine operating conditions, to create a variable venturi manifold arrangement. This system has significant advantages in terms of engine power, fuel economy and reduced exhaust emissions.

The crankshaft is supported within the cylinder block on five shell-type main bearings. Thrustwashers are fitted to number 3 main bearing, to control crankshaft endfloat.

The connecting rods are attached to the crankshaft by horizontally-split shell-type big-end bearings, and to the pistons by interference-fit gudgeon pins. The aluminium alloy pistons are of the slipper type, and are fitted with three piston rings, comprising two compression rings and a scraper-type oil control ring.

The camshafts run directly in the cylinder head, and are driven by the crankshaft via a toothed composite rubber timing belt. One camshaft operates the inlet valves, and the other operates the exhaust valves.

On Z16XE and Z18XE engines, the camshafts operate each valve via a hydraulic self-adjusting camshaft follower. On Z16XEP engines, the camshafts operate each valve via a solid camshaft follower. The camshaft followers are available in various thicknesses to facilitate valve clearance adjustment.

Lubrication is by pressure-feed from a rotor-type oil pump, which is mounted on the right-hand end of the crankshaft. The pump draws oil through a strainer located in the sump, and then forces it through an externally mounted full-flow oil filter. The oil flows into galleries in the cylinder block/crankcase, from where it is distributed to the crankshaft (main bearings) and camshafts. The big-end bearings are supplied with oil via internal drillings in the crankshaft, while the camshaft bearings also receive a pressurised supply. The camshaft lobes and valves are lubricated by splash, as are all other engine components.

A semi-closed crankcase ventilation system is employed; crankcase fumes are drawn from camshaft cover, and passed via a hose to the inlet manifold.

On Z16XE and Z18XE engines, the coolant pump is situated within the cylinder block and is driven by the timing belt. On Z16XEP engines, the coolant pump is located externally on the engine, and is driven by the auxiliary drivebelt.

Operations with engine in car

The following operations can be carried out without having to remove the engine from the car.
a) Removal and refitting of the camshaft cover.
b) Adjustment of the valve clearances (Z16XEP engines).
c) Removal and refitting of the cylinder head.
d) Removal and refitting of the timing belt, tensioner and sprockets.
e) Renewal of the camshaft oil seals.
f) Removal and refitting of the camshafts and followers.
g) Removal and refitting of the sump.
h) Removal and refitting of the connecting rods and pistons.*
i) Removal and refitting of the oil pump.
j) Renewal of the crankshaft oil seals.
k) Renewal of the engine mountings.
l) Removal and refitting of the flywheel.
* Although the operation marked with an asterisk can be carried out with the engine in the car (after removal of the sump), it is preferable for the engine to be removed, in the interests of cleanliness and improved access. For this reason, the procedure is described in Chapter 2F.

2 Compression test – general information

1 When engine performance is down, or if misfiring occurs which cannot be attributed to the ignition or fuel systems, a compression test can provide diagnostic clues as to the engine's condition. If the test is performed regularly, it can give warning of trouble before any other symptoms become apparent.
2 Due to the electronic throttle control system used on these engines, a compression test can only be carried out with the engine management electronic control unit connected to Vauxhall/Opel diagnostic test equipment, or a compatible alternative unit. Without the test equipment, the throttle valve cannot be opened (as there is no accelerator cable) and the test will be inconclusive. Note that even with the accelerator pedal fully depressed, the engine management ECU will only control the throttle valve position when the engine is running. The test equipment independently actuates the throttle valve (irrespective of ECU commands) and opens the throttle valve fully.
3 As the equipment needed for the compression test is unlikely to be available to the home mechanic, it is recommended that the test is performed by a Vauxhall/Opel dealer, or suitably-equipped garage.

3 Top dead centre (TDC) for No 1 piston – locating

1 Top dead centre (TDC) is the highest point in the cylinder that a piston reaches as the crankshaft turns. Each piston reaches TDC at the end of the compression stroke, and again at the end of the exhaust stroke. For the purpose of timing the engine, TDC refers to the position of No 1 piston at the end of its compression stroke. No 1 piston and cylinder are at the timing belt end of the engine.
2 Disconnect the battery negative terminal (refer to *Disconnecting the battery* in the Reference Chapter). If necessary, remove all the spark plugs as described in Chapter 1A to enable the engine to be easily turned over.
3 Remove the timing belt upper cover as described in Section 6.
4 Apply the handbrake, then jack up the front of the vehicle and support it on axle stands (see *Jacking and vehicle support*). Remove the right-hand front roadwheel, then remove the wheel arch liner inner cover for access to the crankshaft pulley.
5 Using a socket and extension bar on the crankshaft pulley bolt, rotate the crankshaft until the timing marks on the camshaft sprockets are facing towards each other, and an imaginary straight line can be drawn through the camshaft sprocket bolts and the timing marks. With the camshaft sprocket marks correctly positioned, align the notch on the crankshaft pulley rim with the mark on the timing belt lower cover **(see illustrations)**. The engine is now positioned with No 1 piston at TDC on its compression stroke.

3.5a Camshaft timing marks

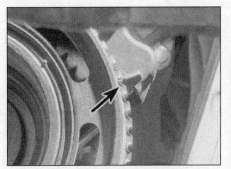

3.5b Crankshaft timing mark (arrowed) on Z16XE and Z18XE engines

3.5c Crankshaft timing marks (arrowed) on Z16XEP engines

4 Camshaft cover – removal and refitting

Z16XE engines

Removal

1 Remove the oil filler cap and undo the two engine cover retaining screws. Unclip the coolant hose, disengage the engine cover from the locating lugs at the front of the camshaft cover, and remove the cover from the engine compartment. Refit the oil filler cap.

2 Disconnect the wiring connector at the inlet air temperature sensor, then slacken the retaining clips securing the air intake duct to the air cleaner lid and throttle housing. Release the retaining clip and disconnect the breather hose, then remove the intake duct from the engine.

3 Remove the ignition module from the spark plugs as described in Chapter 5B.

4 Release the retaining clips and disconnect the remaining breather hoses from the camshaft cover **(see illustration)**.

5 Unclip the oxygen sensor and coolant temperature sensor wiring harnesses.

6 Slacken the retaining clip and disconnect the throttle housing heater hose from the thermostat housing. Be prepared for coolant loss.

7 Evenly and progressively slacken and remove the ten camshaft cover retaining bolts.

8 Lift the camshaft cover away from the cylinder head and recover the rubber seal

(see illustration). Examine the seal for signs of wear or damage and renew if necessary.

Refitting

9 Ensure the cover and cylinder head surfaces are clean and dry then fit the camshaft seal securely to the cover grooves **(see illustration)**.

10 Apply a smear of suitable sealant to areas of the cylinder head surface around the right-hand end inlet and exhaust camshaft bearing caps and also to the semi-circular cut-outs on the left-hand end of the head.

11 Carefully manoeuvre the camshaft cover into position, taking great care to ensure the seal remains correctly seated. Refit the cover retaining bolts and tighten the retaining bolts to the specified torque, working in a spiral pattern from the centre outwards.

12 Reconnect the breather hoses and throttle housing heater hose securing them in position with the retaining clips.

13 Clip the oxygen sensor and coolant temperature sensor wiring harnesses back into position.

14 Refit the ignition module with reference to Chapter 5B.

15 Refit the air intake duct and the engine cover.

16 Check, and if necessary top-up, the cooling system as described in *Weekly checks*.

Z16XEP engines

Removal

17 Remove the air cleaner assembly and intake ducts as described in Chapter 4A.

18 Remove the ignition module from the spark plugs as described in Chapter 5B.

19 Remove the timing belt upper cover as described in Section 6.

20 Release the fitting and disconnect the breather hose from the camshaft cover.

21 Unclip the wiring harness trough from the vicinity of the camshaft cover and move it to one side.

22 Unscrew the three camshaft cover retaining bolts at the timing belt end of the cover. Pull the captive bolts upward from the cover as far as possible and retain them in this position with adhesive tape.

23 Unscrew the remaining six bolts securing the camshaft cover to the cylinder head.

24 Lift the camshaft cover away from the cylinder head and recover the rubber seal. Examine the seal for signs of wear or damage and renew if necessary.

Refitting

25 Ensure that the camshaft cover grove and rubber seal are clean and dry with all traces of oil removed. If necessary, de-grease the seal and cover groove with brake cleaner or a similar product.

26 Clean the mating surface of the cylinder head and the area around the camshaft bearing caps at the timing belt end, ensuring that all traces of oil are removed.

27 Locate the rubber seal into the grooves of the camshaft cover, ensuring that it is fully seated, with no chance of it falling out as the cover is fitted **(see illustration 4.9)**.

28 Carefully manoeuvre the camshaft cover into position, taking great care to ensure the

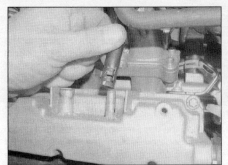

4.4 Disconnect the breather hose – Z16XE engines

4.8 Lift the camshaft cover away from the engine – Z16XE engines

4.9 Ensure the seals are correctly seated in the cover recesses – Z16XE engines

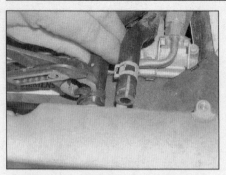

4.36 Disconnect the breather hoses – Z18XE engines

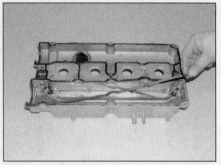

4.42 Carefully fit the camshaft cover seal – Z18XE engines

seal remains correctly seated. Locate the flywheel end of the camshaft cover on the cylinder head, then carefully bring the timing belt end of the cover down onto the head.

29 Remove the adhesive tape from the three timing belt end retaining bolts. Screw in all the cover retaining bolts and tighten them to the specified torque, working in a spiral pattern from the centre outwards.

30 Clip the wiring harness trough back into position, then reconnect the engine breather hose.

31 Refit the timing belt upper cover as described in Section 6.

32 Refit the ignition module to the spark plugs as described in Chapter 5B.

33 Refit the air cleaner assembly and intake ducts as described in Chapter 4A.

Z18XE engines

Removal

34 Remove the oil filler cap, then undo the retaining screws, and remove the plastic cover from the top of the engine. Refit the oil filler cap.

35 Remove the ignition module from the spark plugs with reference to Chapter 5B.

36 Slacken the retaining clips and disconnect the breather hoses from the left-hand rear of the cover **(see illustration)**.

37 Disconnect the wiring plug from the coolant temperature sensor and camshaft sensor, then release the wiring harness from the camshaft cover.

38 Disconnect the coolant pipe from the thermostat housing. Unbolt the retaining bracket from the camshaft cover and inlet manifold, release the retaining clips and move the pipe to one side. Be prepared for coolant spillage.

39 Unclip the oxygen sensor wiring from the camshaft cover.

40 Evenly and progressively slacken and remove the camshaft cover retaining bolts.

41 Lift the camshaft cover away from the cylinder head and recover the rubber seal. Examine the seal for signs of wear or damage and renew if necessary.

Refitting

42 Ensure the cover and cylinder head surfaces are clean and dry then fit the rubber seal securely to the cover groove **(see illustration)**.

43 Apply a smear of suitable sealant to areas of the cylinder head surface around the right-hand end inlet and exhaust camshaft bearing caps.

44 Carefully manoeuvre the camshaft cover into position, taking great care to ensure the seal remains correctly seated. Refit the cover retaining bolts and tighten the retaining bolts to the specified torque, working in a spiral pattern from the centre outwards.

45 Reconnect the coolant pipe to the thermostat housing, making sure it is secured by the retaining bracket on the camshaft cover and inlet manifold.

46 Refit the wiring plugs to the coolant temperature sensor and camshaft sensor. Clip the oxygen sensor wiring back into position in the camshaft cover.

47 Reconnect the breather hoses, securing them in position with the retaining clips.

48 Refit the ignition module with reference to Chapter 5B.

49 Refit the engine cover, then top-up the cooling system as described in *Weekly checks*.

5 Crankshaft pulley – removal and refitting

Note: *A new pulley retaining bolt will be required on refitting.*

Removal

1 Firmly apply the handbrake, then jack up the front of the car and support it securely on

5.5 Align the pulley cut-out with the raised notch

axle stands (see *Jacking and vehicle support*). Remove the right-hand roadwheel, then remove the wheel arch liner inner cover for access to the crankshaft pulley.

2 Remove the auxiliary drivebelt as described in Chapter 1A. Prior to removal, mark the direction of rotation on the belt to ensure the belt is refitted the same way around.

3 Slacken the crankshaft pulley retaining bolt. To prevent crankshaft rotation, have an assistant select top gear and apply the brakes firmly. If the engine has been removed from the vehicle, it will be necessary to lock the flywheel (see Section 16).

4 Unscrew the retaining bolt and washer and remove the crankshaft pulley from the end of the crankshaft.

Refitting

5 Refit the crankshaft pulley, aligning the pulley cut-out with the raised notch on the timing belt sprocket, then fit the washer and new retaining bolt **(see illustration)**.

6 Lock the crankshaft by the method used on removal, and tighten the pulley retaining bolt to the specified Stage 1 torque setting, then angle-tighten the bolt through the specified Stage 2 angle, using a socket and extension bar, and finally through the specified Stage 3 angle. It is recommended that an angle-measuring gauge is used during the final stages of the tightening, to ensure accuracy. If a gauge is not available, use white paint to make alignment marks between the bolt head and pulley prior to tightening; the marks can then be used to check that the bolt has been rotated through the correct angle.

7 Refit the auxiliary drivebelt as described in Chapter 1A using the mark made prior to removal to ensure it is fitted the correct way around.

8 Refit the wheel arch liner inner cover and the roadwheel. Lower the car to the ground and tighten the wheel bolts to the specified torque.

6 Timing belt covers – removal and refitting

Z16XE and Z18XE engines

Upper cover

1 Remove the oil filler cap and undo the two engine cover retaining screws. Unclip the coolant hose, disengage the engine cover from the locating lugs at the front of the camshaft cover, and remove the cover from the engine compartment. Refit the oil filler cap.

2 Remove the air cleaner assembly and intake ducts as described in Chapter 4A.

3 Undo the three retaining screws then unclip the upper cover from the rear cover and remove it from the engine compartment **(see illustration)**.

4 Refitting is the reverse of removal, tightening the retaining screws to the specified torque.

6.3 Undo the three upper cover screws –
Z16XE and Z18XE engines

Lower cover

5 Remove the upper cover as described in paragraphs 1 to 3.
6 Remove the crankshaft pulley as described in Section 5.
7 Undo the retaining bolt and remove the auxiliary drivebelt tensioner **(see illustration)**.
8 Undo the retaining bolt then unclip the cover from the rear cover and manoeuvre it out of position **(see illustration)**.
9 Refitting is the reverse of removal, clip the cover into position and tighten the cover bolts to the specified torque.

Rear cover

10 Remove the timing belt as described in Section 7.
11 Remove the camshaft cover as described in Section 4.
12 Remove the camshaft sprockets, crankshaft sprocket, timing belt tensioner, front idler pulley and the rear idler pulley as described in Section 8.
13 Slacken and remove the three retaining bolts, and withdraw the engine mounting bracket bolted to the cylinder block **(see illustration)**.
14 Undo the four retaining bolts and remove the rear cover upwards and away from the engine **(see illustration)**.
15 Refitting is the reverse of removal. Refit and tighten the cover bolts and auxiliary drivebelt tensioner bolt to the specified torque.

Z16XEP engines

Upper cover

16 Remove the air cleaner assembly and intake ducts as described in Chapter 4A.
17 Undo the two retaining bolts then unclip the upper cover from the rear cover and remove it from the engine compartment **(see illustration)**.
18 Refitting is the reverse of removal, tightening the cover retaining bolts to the specified torque.

Lower cover

19 Remove the upper cover as described in paragraphs 16 and 17.
20 Remove the crankshaft pulley as described in Section 5.

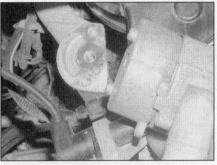

6.7 Remove the auxiliary drivebelt
tensioner – Z16XE and Z18XE engines

21 Undo the retaining bolt and remove the auxiliary drivebelt tensioner **(see illustration)**.
22 Undo the four retaining bolts then manoeuvre the lower cover off the engine.
23 Refitting is the reverse of removal, tightening the cover retaining bolts and auxiliary drivebelt tensioner bolt to the specified torque.

Rear cover

24 Remove the timing belt as described in Section 7.
25 Remove the camshaft sprockets, crankshaft sprocket, timing belt tensioner and idler pulley as described in Section 8.
26 Unclip the wiring harness from the cover, then undo the four bolts securing the cover to the cylinder head. Remove the camshaft sensor from the cover by turning it slightly, then remove the cover from the cylinder head.

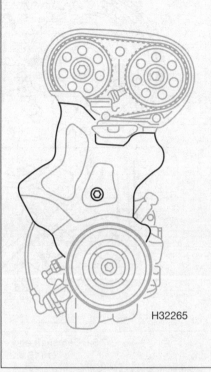

6.8 Lower timing belt cover centre
retaining bolt – Z16XE and Z18XE engines

27 Refitting is the reverse of removal, tightening the cover retaining bolts to the specified torque.

6.13 Engine mounting-to-cylinder block
bracket retaining bolts – Z16XE and
Z18XE engines

6.14 Lift the rear cover away –
Z16XE and Z18XE engines

6.17 Timing belt upper cover retaining
bolts (arrowed) – Z16XEP engines

6.21 Auxiliary drivebelt tensioner retaining
bolt (arrowed) – Z16XEP engines

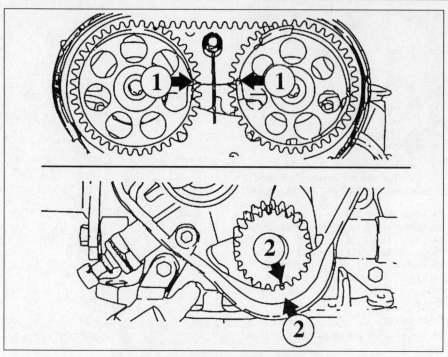

**7.3b Unbolt the camshaft sensor –
Z16XE and Z18XE engines**

**7.3a Camshaft and crankshaft timing marks –
Z16XE and Z18XE engines**

1 *Camshaft and crankshaft timing marks
aligned with the cylinder head upper surface*

2 *Crankshaft timing mark aligned with mark
on oil pump housing*

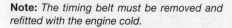

7 Timing belt –
removal and refitting

Note: *The timing belt must be removed and
refitted with the engine cold.*

Z16XE and Z18XE engines

Removal

1 Position No 1 cylinder at TDC on its compression stroke as described in Section 3.

2 Remove the timing belt lower cover as
described in Section 6.
3 Check that the timing marks on the
camshaft sprockets are still correctly aligned
and facing towards each other and the
crankshaft sprocket timing mark is aligned
with the mark on the rear timing belt cover.
Undo the two bolts securing the camshaft
sensor to the cylinder head and position it
clear of the engine **(see illustrations)**.
4 Remove the right-hand engine mounting as
described in Section 17.
5 Slacken the timing belt tensioner bolt.

Using an Allen key, rotate the tensioner arm
clockwise to its stop, to relieve the tension in
the timing belt, hold it in position and securely
tighten the retaining bolt **(see illustration)**.
6 Slide the timing belt from its sprockets and
remove it from the engine **(see illustration)**.
If the belt is to be re-used, use white paint or
similar to mark the direction of rotation on the
belt. **Do not** rotate the crankshaft or camshafts
until the timing belt has been refitted.
7 Check the timing belt carefully for any signs
of uneven wear, splitting or oil contamination,
and renew it if there is the slightest
doubt about its condition. If the engine is
undergoing an overhaul and is approaching
the manufacturer's specified interval for belt
renewal (see Chapter 1A) renew the belt as a
matter of course, regardless of its apparent
condition. If signs of oil contamination are
found, trace the source of the oil leak and
rectify it, then wash down the engine timing
belt area and all related components to
remove all traces of oil.

Refitting

8 On reassembly, thoroughly clean the timing
belt sprockets and tensioner/idler pulleys.
9 Check that the camshaft and crankshaft
sprocket timing marks are still correctly
aligned **(see illustration 7.3a)**.

**7.5 Slacken the timing belt tensioner bolt (1) and rotate the
tensioner clockwise using an Allen key in the arm cut-out (2) –
Z16XE and Z18XE engines**

**7.6 Removing the timing belt –
Z16XE and Z18XE engines**

10 Fit the timing belt over the crankshaft and camshaft sprockets and around the idler pulleys, ensuring that the belt front run is taut (ie, all slack is on the tensioner side of the belt), then fit the belt over the coolant pump sprocket and tensioner pulley **(see illustration)**. Do not twist the belt sharply while refitting it. Ensure that the belt teeth are correctly seated centrally in the sprockets, and that the timing marks remain in alignment. If a used belt is being refitted, ensure that the arrow mark made on removal points in the normal direction of rotation, as before.

11 Slacken the timing belt tensioner bolt to release the tensioner spring. Rotate the tensioner arm anti-clockwise until the tensioner pointer is positioned just before the left stop, without exerting any excess strain on the belt. Hold the tensioner in position and securely tighten its retaining bolt.

12 Check the sprocket timing marks are still correctly aligned. If adjustment is necessary, release the tensioner again then disengage the belt from the sprockets and make any necessary adjustments.

13 Using a socket on the crankshaft pulley bolt, rotate the crankshaft smoothly through two complete turns (720°) in the normal direction of rotation to settle the timing belt in position.

14 Check that both the camshaft and crankshaft sprocket timing marks are correctly realigned then slacken the tensioner bolt again.

15 If a new timing belt is being fitted, adjust the tensioner so that the pointer is aligned with the cut-out on the backplate **(see illustration)**. Hold the tensioner in the correct position and tighten its retaining bolt to the specified torque. Rotate the crankshaft smoothly through another two complete turns in the normal direction of rotation, to bring the sprocket timing marks back into alignment. Check that the tensioner pointer is still aligned with the backplate cut-out.

16 If the original belt is being refitted on Z16XE engines, adjust the tensioner so that the pointer is positioned 4 mm to the left of the cut-out on the backplate. On Z18XE engines, adjust the tensioner so that the pointer is positioned in line with the USED mark on the backplate **(see illustration)**. Hold the tensioner in the correct position and tighten its retaining bolt to the specified torque. Rotate the crankshaft smoothly through another two complete turns in the normal direction of rotation, to bring the sprocket timing marks back into alignment. Check that the tensioner pointer is still correctly positioned in relation to the backplate cut-out.

17 If the tensioner pointer is not correctly positioned in relation to the backplate, repeat the procedure in paragraph 15 (new belt) or 16 (original belt) (as applicable).

18 Once the tensioner pointer and backplate remain correctly aligned, refit the camshaft sensor, then refit the timing belt covers as described in Section 6.

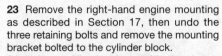

7.10 Timing belt routing – Z18XE engines

19 Refit the right-hand engine mounting as described in Section 18, then refit the crankshaft pulley as described in Section 5.

Z16XEP engines

Removal

20 Position No 1 cylinder at TDC on its compression stroke as described in Section 3.
21 Remove the timing belt lower cover as described in Section 6.
22 Check that the timing marks on the camshaft sprockets are still correctly aligned and facing towards each other, and the timing mark on the crankshaft sprocket is aligned with the corresponding mark on the oil pump housing **(see illustration 7.3a)**.

23 Remove the right-hand engine mounting as described in Section 17, then undo the three retaining bolts and remove the mounting bracket bolted to the cylinder block.
24 Using an Allen key inserted in the slot on the face of the timing belt tensioner, rotate the tensioner clockwise to relieve the tension in the timing belt. Insert a small drill bit or similar into the slot on the inner edge of the tensioner body to lock the tensioner in the released position.
25 Slide the timing belt from its sprockets and remove it from the engine. If the belt is to be re-used, use white paint or similar to mark the direction of rotation on the belt. **Do not** rotate the crankshaft or camshafts until the timing belt has been refitted.
26 Check the timing belt carefully for any signs of uneven wear, splitting or oil contamination, and renew it if there is the slightest doubt about its condition. If the engine is undergoing an overhaul and is approaching the manufacturer's specified interval for belt renewal (see Chapter 1A) renew the belt as a matter of course, regardless of its apparent condition. If signs of oil contamination are found, trace the source of the oil leak and rectify it, then wash down the engine timing belt area and all related components to remove all traces of oil.

Refitting

27 On reassembly, thoroughly clean the timing belt sprockets and tensioner/idler pulleys.

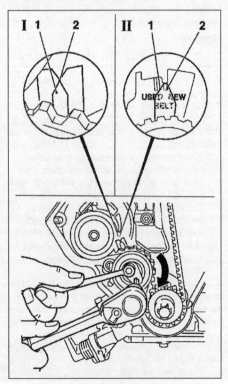

7.15 Timing belt tensioner pointer positions

I Z16XE engines:
Pointer (1) and backplate (2) for new belts
II Z18XE engines:
Pointer (1) and backplate (2) for new belts

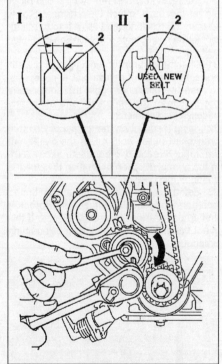

7.16 Timing belt tensioner pointer positions

I Z16XE engines:
Pointer (1) and backplate (2) for used belts
II Z18XE engines:
Pointer (1) and backplate (2) for used belts

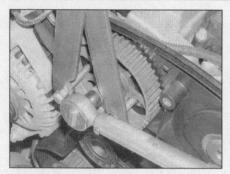

8.3a Hold the camshaft sprocket using a home-made tool . . .

8.3b . . . or use an open-ended spanner to hold the camshaft whilst the sprocket bolt is slackened

8.8 Ensure that the camshaft sprocket cut-out (arrowed) is correctly engaged with the locating pin

28 Check that the camshaft and crankshaft sprocket timing marks are still correctly aligned **(see illustration 7.3a)**.

29 Fit the timing belt over the crankshaft and camshaft sprockets and around the idler pulley, ensuring that the belt front run is taut (ie, all slack is on the tensioner side of the belt), then fit the belt over the tensioner pulley. Do not twist the belt sharply while refitting it. Ensure that the belt teeth are correctly seated centrally in the sprockets, and that the timing marks remain in alignment. If a used belt is being refitted, ensure that the arrow mark made on removal points in the normal direction of rotation, as before.

30 Using the Allen key, turn the tensioner clockwise slightly and remove the drill bit or similar tool used to lock the tensioner. Slowly release the tensioner and allow it to turn anti-clockwise and automatically tension the timing belt.

31 Check the sprocket timing marks are still correctly aligned. If adjustment is necessary, release the tensioner again then disengage the belt from the sprockets and make any necessary adjustments.

32 Using a socket on the temporarily refitted crankshaft pulley bolt, rotate the crankshaft smoothly through two complete turns (720°) in the normal direction of rotation to settle the timing belt in position.

33 Set the crankshaft back in the timing position and check that all the sprocket timing marks are still correctly aligned. If this is not the case, repeat the timing belt refitting procedure.

8.13 Refit the crankshaft sprocket with the timing mark facing outwards

34 If everything is satisfactory, refit the engine mounting bracket, tightening the three retaining bolts to the specified torque.

35 Refit the right-hand engine mounting as described in Section 17, then refit the timing belt covers as described in Section 6.

36 Refit the crankshaft pulley as described in Section 5.

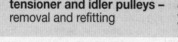

8 Timing belt sprockets, tensioner and idler pulleys – removal and refitting

Camshaft sprockets

Note: *New sprocket retaining bolt(s) will be required for refitting.*

Removal

1 Remove the camshaft cover as described in Section 4.

2 Remove the timing belt as described in Section 7.

3 The camshaft must be prevented from turning as the sprocket bolt is unscrewed, and this can be achieved in one of two ways as follows.

a) *Make up a sprocket-holding tool using two lengths of steel strip (one long, the other short), and three nuts and bolts; one nut and bolt forms the pivot of a forked tool, with the remaining two nuts and bolts at the tips of the 'forks' to engage with the sprocket holes* **(see illustration)**.

b) *Hold the camshaft with an open-ended spanner on the flats provided* **(see illustration)**.

4 Unscrew the retaining bolt and washer and remove the sprocket from the end of the camshaft. If the sprocket locating pin is a loose fit in the camshaft end, remove it and store it with the sprocket for safe-keeping.

5 If necessary, remove the remaining sprocket using the same method. The inlet and exhaust sprockets are different; the exhaust camshaft sprocket can be easily identified by the lugs which activate the camshaft position sensor.

Refitting

6 Prior to refitting check the oil seal(s) for signs of damage or leakage. If necessary, renew as described in Section 9.

7 Ensure the locating pin is in position in the camshaft end.

8 Refit the sprocket to the camshaft end, aligning its cut-out with the locating pin, and fit the washer and new retaining bolt **(see illustration)**. If both sprockets have been removed, ensure each sprocket is fitted to the correct shaft; the exhaust camshaft sprocket can be identified by the lugs on the sprocket outer face which trigger the camshaft position sensor.

9 Retain the sprocket by the method used on removal, and tighten the sprocket retaining bolt to the specified Stage 1 torque setting then angle-tighten the bolt through the specified Stage 2 angle, using a socket and extension bar, and finally through the specified Stage 3 angle. It is recommended that an angle-measuring gauge is used during the final stages of the tightening, to ensure accuracy. If a gauge is not available, use white paint to make alignment marks between the bolt head and sprocket prior to tightening; the marks can then be used to check that the bolt has been rotated through the correct angle.

10 Refit the timing belt as described in Section 7, then refit the camshaft cover as described in Section 4.

Crankshaft sprocket

Removal

11 Remove the timing belt as described in Section 7.

12 Slide the sprocket off from the end of the crankshaft, noting which way around it is fitted.

Refitting

13 Align the sprocket locating key with the crankshaft groove then slide the sprocket into position, making sure its timing mark is facing outwards **(see illustration)**.

14 Refit the timing belt as described in Section 7.

Tensioner assembly

Removal

15 Remove the timing belt as described in Section 7.

16 Slacken and remove the retaining bolt and remove the tensioner assembly from the engine.

Refitting

17 Fit the tensioner to the engine, making sure that the lug on the backplate is correctly located in the oil pump housing hole **(see illustration)**. On Z16XEP engines, also ensure that the projecting end of the tensioner spring engages with the slot on the oil pump housing. Ensure the tensioner is correctly seated then refit the retaining bolt. Using an Allen key, rotate the tensioner arm clockwise to its stop (where applicable) then securely tighten the retaining bolt.

18 Refit the timing belt as described in Section 7.

Idler pulleys

Removal

19 Remove the timing belt as described in Section 7.

20 Slacken and remove the retaining bolt(s) and remove the idler pulley(s) from the engine **(see illustration)**.

Refitting

21 Refit the idler pulley(s) and tighten the retaining bolt(s) to the specified torque.

22 Refit the timing belt as described in Section 7.

9 Camshaft oil seals – renewal

1 Remove the relevant camshaft sprocket as described in Section 8.

2 Carefully punch or drill two small holes opposite each other in the oil seal. Screw a self-tapping screw into each, and pull on the screws with pliers to extract the seal **(see illustration)**.

3 Clean the seal housing, and polish off any burrs or raised edges which may have caused the seal to fail in the first place.

4 Press the new seal into position using a suitable tubular drift (such as a socket) which bears only on the hard outer edge of the seal **(see illustration)**. Take care not to damage the seal lips during fitting; note that the seal lips should face inwards.

5 Refit the camshaft sprocket as described in Section 8.

10 Valve clearances (Z16XEP engines) – checking and adjustment

Note: *All other engines are equipped with hydraulic self-adjusting camshaft followers and valve clearance adjustment is not required.*

Checking

1 The importance of having the valve clearances correctly adjusted cannot be over-stressed, as they vitally affect the performance of the engine. The engine must be cold for the check to be accurate. The clearances are checked as follows.

8.17 Engage the tensioner backplate lug with the locating hole in the oil pump housing

8.20 Idler pulley retaining bolt

9.2 Camshaft oil seal removal method

9.4 Refit the camshaft oil seal with a tool which bears only on the hard outer edge of the seal

2 Firmly apply the handbrake, then jack up the front of the car and support it securely on axle stands (see *Jacking and vehicle support*). Remove the right-hand front roadwheel then remove the wheel arch liner inner cover for access to the crankshaft pulley.

3 Remove the camshaft cover as described in Section 4.

4 Position No 1 cylinder at TDC on its compression stroke as described in Section 3.

5 With the engine at TDC on compression for No 1 cylinder, the inlet camshaft lobes for No 2 cylinder and the exhaust camshaft lobes for No 3 cylinder are pointing upwards and slightly towards the centre. This indicates that these valves are completely closed, and the clearances can be checked.

6 On a piece of paper, draw the outline of the engine with the cylinders numbered from the timing belt end. Show the position of

each valve, together with the specified valve clearance.

7 With the cam lobes positioned as described in paragraph 5, using feeler blades, measure the clearance between the base of both No 2 cylinder inlet cam lobes and No 3 cylinder exhaust cam lobes and their followers. Record the clearances on the paper **(see illustrations)**.

8 Rotate the crankshaft pulley in the normal direction of rotation through a half a turn (180°) to position No 1 cylinder inlet camshaft lobes and No 4 cylinder exhaust camshaft lobes pointing upwards and slightly towards the centre. Measure the clearance between the base of the camshaft lobes and their followers and record the clearances on the paper.

9 Rotate the crankshaft pulley through a half a turn (180°) to position No 3 cylinder inlet camshaft lobes and No 2 cylinder exhaust

10.7a Using feeler blades, measure the inlet valve clearances . . .

10.7b . . . and the exhaust valve clearances

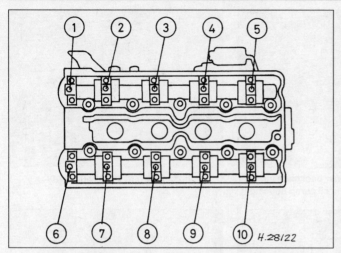

11.4a Camshaft bearing cap numbering sequence

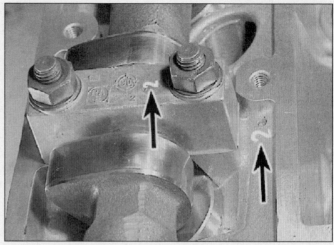

11.4b The identification numbers should be marked on both the bearing caps and the cylinder head (arrowed)

camshaft lobes pointing upwards and slightly towards the centre. Measure the clearance between the base of the camshaft lobes and their followers and record the clearances on the paper.

10 Rotate the crankshaft pulley through a half a turn (180°) to position No 4 cylinder inlet camshaft lobes and No 1 cylinder exhaust camshaft lobes pointing upwards and slightly towards the centre. Measure the clearance between the base of the camshaft lobes and their followers and record the clearances on the paper.

11 If all the clearances are correct, refit the camshaft cover (see Section 4), then refit the wheel arch liner inner cover and the roadwheel. Lower the vehicle to the ground and tighten the wheel bolts to the specified torque. If any clearance measured is not correct, adjustment must be carried out as described in the following paragraphs.

Adjustment

12 If adjustment is necessary, remove the relevant camshaft(s) and camshaft followers as described in Section 11.

13 Clean the followers of the valves that require clearance adjustment and note the thickness marking on the follower. The thickness marking is stamped on the under-side of each follower. For example, a 3.20 mm

11.7 Use a valve lapping tool to remove the cam followers

thick follower will have a 20 thickness marking, a 3.21 mm thick follower will have a 21 thickness marking, etc.

14 Add the measured clearance of the valve to the thickness of the original follower then subtract the specified valve clearance from this figure. This will give you the thickness of the follower required. For example:

Clearance measured of inlet valve   0.31 mm
Plus thickness of the original follower 3.20 mm
Equals   3.51 mm
Minus clearance required   0.25 mm
Thickness of follower required   3.26 mm

15 Repeat this procedure on the remaining valves which require adjustment, then obtain the correct thickness of follower(s) required.

16 Refit the camshaft followers and the relevant camshaft(s) as described in Section 11. Rotate the crankshaft a few times to settle all the components, then recheck the valve clearances before refitting the camshaft cover (Section 4).

17 Refit the wheel arch liner inner cover and roadwheel then lower the vehicle to the ground and tighten the wheel bolts to the specified torque.

11 Camshaft and followers – removal, inspection and refitting

Note: New timing belt end oil seals, and a tube of suitable sealant will be required when refitting.

Removal

1 Remove the timing belt as described in Section 7.

2 Remove the camshaft sprockets as described in Section 8.

3 Remove the timing belt rear cover as described in Section 6.

4 Starting on the inlet camshaft, working in a spiral pattern from the outside inwards, slacken the camshaft bearing cap retaining bolts by half a turn at a time, to relieve the pressure of the valve springs on the bearing

caps gradually and evenly (the reverse of illustration 11.16). Once the valve spring pressure has been relieved, the bolts can be fully unscrewed and removed along with the caps; the bearing caps and the cylinder head locations are numbered (inlet camshaft 1 to 5, exhaust camshaft 6 to 10) to ensure the caps are correctly positioned on refitting (see illustrations). Take care not to loose the locating dowels (where fitted).

Caution: If the bearing cap bolts are carelessly slackened, the bearing caps might break. If any bearing cap breaks then the complete cylinder head assembly must be renewed; the bearing caps are matched to the head and are not available separately.

5 Lift the camshaft out of the cylinder head and slide off the oil seal.

6 Repeat the operations described in paragraphs 4 and 5 and remove the exhaust camshaft.

7 Obtain sixteen small, clean plastic containers, and label them for identification. Alternatively, divide a larger container into compartments. Using a rubber sucker tool, lift the followers out from the top of the cylinder head and store each one in its respective fitted position (see illustration). Note: On engines with hydraulic followers, store all the followers the correct way up, with the oil groove at the bottom, to prevent the oil draining from the hydraulic valve adjustment mechanisms.

Inspection

8 Examine the camshaft bearing surfaces and cam lobes for signs of wear ridges and scoring. Renew the camshaft if any of these conditions are apparent. Examine the condition of the bearing surfaces both on the camshaft journals and in the cylinder head. If the head bearing surfaces are worn excessively, the cylinder head will need to be renewed.

9 Examine the follower bearing surfaces which contact the camshaft lobes for wear ridges and scoring. Check the followers and

11.14 Apply sealant to the right-hand bearing caps

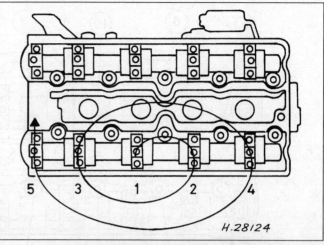

11.16 Camshaft bearing cap tightening sequence (exhaust camshaft shown – inlet the same)

their bores in the cylinder head for signs of wear or damage. If any follower is thought to be faulty or is visibly worn it should be renewed.

Refitting

10 Commence refitting by turning the crankshaft anti-clockwise by 60º. This will position Nos 1 and 4 pistons a third of the way down the bore, and prevent any chance of the valves touching the piston crowns as the camshafts are being fitted. This could happen if any of the hydraulic cam followers have excessive oil in them before the pressure of the valve springs forces it out.

11 Where removed, lubricate the followers with clean engine oil and carefully insert each one into its original location in the cylinder head.

12 Lubricate the camshaft followers with molybdenum disulphide paste (or clean engine oil) then lay the camshafts in position.

13 Ensure the mating surfaces of the bearing caps and cylinder head are clean and dry and lubricate the camshaft journals and lobes with clean engine oil.

14 Apply a smear of sealant to the mating surfaces of both the inlet (No 1) and exhaust (No 6) camshaft right-hand bearing caps **(see illustration)**.

15 Ensure the locating dowels (where fitted) are in position then refit the camshaft bearing caps and the retaining bolts in their original locations on the cylinder head. The caps are numbered (inlet camshaft 1 to 5, exhaust camshaft 6 to 10) from the timing belt end, and the corresponding numbers are marked on the cylinder head upper surface. All bearing cap numbers should be the right way up when viewed from the front of the engine.

16 Working on the inlet camshaft, tighten the bearing cap bolts by hand only then, working in a spiral pattern from the centre outwards, tighten the bolts by half a turn at a time to gradually impose the pressure of the valve springs on the bearing caps **(see illustration)**.

Repeat this sequence until all bearing caps are in contact with the cylinder head then go around and tighten the camshaft bearing cap bolts to the specified torque.

Caution: If the bearing cap bolts are carelessly tightened, the bearing caps might break. If any bearing cap breaks then the complete cylinder head assembly must be renewed; the bearing caps are matched to the head and are not available separately.

17 Tighten the exhaust camshaft bearing cap bolts as described in paragraph 16.

18 Fit new camshaft oil seals as described in Section 9.

19 Refit and tighten the timing belt rear cover bolts.

20 Refit the camshaft sprockets as described in Section 8.

21 Align all the sprocket timing marks to bring the camshafts and crankshaft back to TDC then refit the timing belt as described in Section 7.

12 Cylinder head – removal and refitting

Note: *The engine must be cold when removing the cylinder head. A new cylinder head gasket and new cylinder head bolts must be used on refitting.*

Removal

1 Depressurise the fuel system as described in Chapter 4A.

2 Disconnect the battery negative terminal (refer to *Disconnecting the battery* in the Reference Chapter).

3 Apply the handbrake, then jack up the front of the vehicle and support it on axle stands (see *Jacking and vehicle support*). Remove the right-hand front roadwheel and the wheel arch liner inner cover for access to the right-hand side of the engine.

4 Drain the cooling system as described in Chapter 1A.

5 Remove the spark plugs as described in Chapter 1A.

6 Remove the camshaft cover as described in Section 4.

7 Remove the timing belt as described in Section 7.

8 Remove the camshaft sprockets, timing belt tensioner, and the timing belt idler pulleys, as described in Section 8.

9 Remove the rear timing belt cover with reference to Section 6.

10 Refer to Chapter 4A and unbolt the exhaust front pipe from the exhaust manifold, taking care to support the flexible section. **Note:** *Angular movement in excess of 10º can cause permanent damage to the flexible section.* Release the mounting rubbers and support the front of the exhaust pipe to one side.

11 Disconnect the engine management wiring loom from the following, noting its routing:
a) *Crankshaft speed/position sensor.*
b) *Oil pressure switch.*
c) *Oil level sensor.*
d) *Camshaft sensor (Z16XEP engines).*
e) *Thermostat (Z16XEP engines).*
f) *Coolant temperature sensor (Z16XEP engines).*
g) *EGR valve (Z16XEP engines).*

12 Release the cable-ties and place the wiring loom to one side.

13 On Z16XE and Z18XE engines, unscrew the securing bolts, and remove the upper alternator mounting bracket. Pivot the alternator rearwards away from the manifold as far as it will go.

14 Remove the inlet and exhaust manifolds as described in Chapter 4A.

15 On Z16XEP engines, undo the five bolts and remove the metal coolant pipe from the coolant pump and thermostat housing.

16 Referring to Chapter 3, unclip the coolant hoses from the heater matrix unions on the engine compartment bulkhead to drain the coolant from the cylinder block. Once the flow of coolant has stopped, reconnect both hoses and mop-up any spilt coolant.

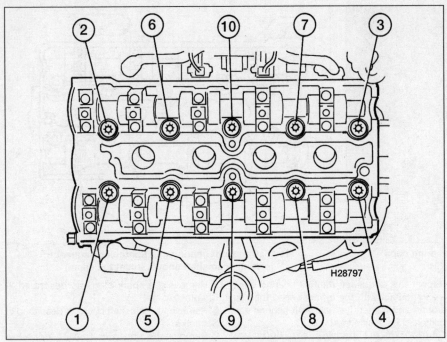

12.21 Cylinder head bolt loosening sequence

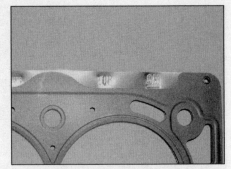

12.30 Fit the new cylinder head gasket with the OBEN/TOP marking uppermost

23 Recover the cylinder head gasket, and discard it.

Preparation for refitting

24 The mating faces of the cylinder head and block must be perfectly clean before refitting the head. Use a scraper to remove all traces of gasket and carbon, and also clean the tops of the pistons. Take particular care with the aluminium surfaces, as the soft metal is damaged easily. Also, make sure that debris is not allowed to enter the oil and water channels – this is particularly important for the oil circuit, as carbon could block the oil supply to the camshaft or crankshaft bearings. Using adhesive tape and paper, seal the water, oil and bolt holes in the cylinder block. To prevent carbon entering the gap between the pistons and bores, smear a little grease in the gap. After cleaning the piston, rotate the crankshaft so that the piston moves down the bore, then wipe out the grease and carbon with a cloth rag. Clean the other piston crowns in the same way.

25 Check the block and head for nicks, deep scratches and other damage. If slight, they may be removed carefully with a file. More serious damage may be repaired by machining, but this is a specialist job.

26 If warpage of the cylinder head is suspected, use a straight-edge to check it for distortion. Refer to Chapter 2F if necessary.

27 Ensure that the cylinder head bolt holes in the crankcase are clean and free of oil. Syringe or soak up any oil left in the bolt holes. This is most important in order that the correct bolt tightening torque can be applied and to prevent the possibility of the block being cracked by hydraulic pressure when the bolts are tightened.

28 Renew the cylinder head bolts regardless of their apparent condition.

Refitting

29 Ensure that the two locating dowels are in position at each end of the cylinder block/crankcase surface.

30 Fit the new cylinder head gasket to the block, making sure it is fitted with the correct way up with its OBEN/TOP mark uppermost (see illustration).

31 Carefully refit the cylinder head, locating it on the dowels.

17 Loosen the clips and remove the coolant hose from the radiator and thermostat housing.

18 Loosen the clips and disconnect the heater hoses from the left-hand end of the cylinder head or thermostat housing.

19 Where applicable, undo the bolt and free the oil dipstick guide tube from the cylinder head.

20 Make a final check to ensure that all relevant hoses, pipes and wires have been disconnected.

21 Working in sequence, progressively loosen the cylinder head bolts (see illustration). First loosen all the bolts by quarter of a turn, then loosen all the bolts by half a turn, then finally slacken all the bolts fully and withdraw them from the cylinder head. Recover the washers.

22 Lift the cylinder head from the cylinder block. If necessary, tap the cylinder head gently with a soft-faced mallet to free it from the block, but **do not** lever at the mating faces. Note that the cylinder head is located on dowels.

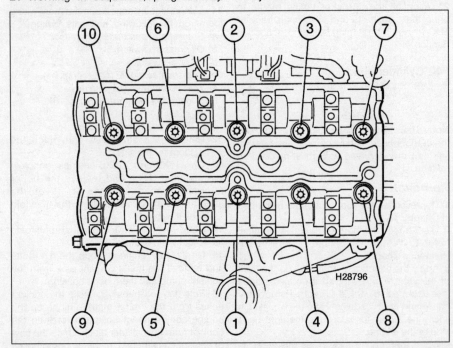

12.33 Cylinder head bolt tightening sequence

32 Fit the washers to the new cylinder head bolts then carefully insert them into position (**do not drop**), tightening them finger-tight only at this stage.

33 Working progressively and in the sequence shown, first tighten all the cylinder head bolts to the Stage 1 torque setting (**see illustration**).

34 Once all bolts have been tightened to the Stage 1 torque, again working in sequence, tighten each bolt through its specified Stage 2 angle, using a socket and extension bar. It is recommended that an angle-measuring gauge is used during this stage of the tightening, to ensure accuracy (**see illustration**).

35 Working in the specified sequence, go around again and tighten all bolts through the specified Stage 3 angle.

36 Working again in the specified sequence, go around and tighten all bolts through the specified Stage 4 angle.

37 Finally go around in the specified sequence again and tighten all bolts through the specified Stage 5 angle.

38 Refit the exhaust manifold as described in Chapter 4A.

39 On Z16XEP engines, using new gaskets, refit the metal coolant pipe to the coolant pump and thermostat housing, tightening the bolts securely.

40 Reconnect the heater hoses to the left-hand end of the cylinder head or thermostat housing and tighten the clips.

41 Refit the coolant hose to the radiator and thermostat housing and tighten the clips.

42 Refit the inlet manifold as described in Chapter 4A.

43 Where applicable, refit the alternator upper mounting bracket and tighten the bolts.

44 Reconnect the wiring to the components listed in paragraph 11, then secure the wiring with cable-ties.

45 Refer to Chapter 4A and refit the exhaust front pipe to the exhaust manifold. Refit the mounting rubbers.

46 Refit the rear timing belt cover with reference to Section 6.

47 Refit the camshaft sprockets, timing belt tensioner, and the timing belt idler pulleys, with reference to Section 8.

48 Refit the timing belt as described in Section 7.

49 Refit the camshaft cover as described in Section 4.

50 Refit the spark plugs as described in Chapter 1A.

51 Refit the wheel arch liner inner cover and front roadwheel, then lower the vehicle to the ground.

52 Reconnect the battery negative terminal.

53 Check that all relevant hoses, pipes and wires, etc, have been reconnected. Check the security of the fuel hose connections.

54 Refill and bleed the cooling system with reference to Chapter 1A.

55 When the engine is started, check for signs of oil or coolant leakage.

13 Sump –
removal and refitting

Removal

1 Disconnect the battery negative terminal (refer to *Disconnecting the battery* in the Reference Chapter).

2 Apply the handbrake, then jack up the front of the vehicle and support it on axle stands (see *Jacking and vehicle support*). Remove the right-hand front roadwheel and the wheel arch liner inner cover for access to the right-hand side of the engine.

3 Drain the engine oil as described in Chapter 1A, then fit a new sealing washer and refit the drain plug, tightening it to the specified torque.

4 Remove the exhaust system as described in Chapter 4A.

5 Disconnect the wiring connector from the oil level sensor.

6 On Z16XEP engines, undo the retaining bolt and remove the oil dipstick guide tube.

7 Slacken and remove the bolts securing the sump flange to the transmission housing.

8 Remove the rubber plugs from the transmission end of the sump flange to gain access to the sump end retaining bolts.

9 Progressively slacken and remove the bolts securing the sump to the base of the cylinder block/oil pump. Using a wide-bladed scraper or similar tool inserted between the sump and cylinder block, carefully break the joint, then remove the sump from under the car.

10 While the sump is removed, take the opportunity to check the oil pump pick-up/strainer for signs of clogging or splitting. On Z16XEP engines, undo the two bolts and remove the baffle plate from the sump. On all engines, unbolt the pick-up/strainer flange and, where applicable, the strainer base and remove it from the sump along with its sealing ring. The strainer can then be cleaned easily in solvent or renewed.

Refitting

11 Thoroughly clean the sump, baffle plate and pick-up/strainer, then remove all traces of sealer and oil from the mating surfaces of the sump and cylinder block and (where removed) the pick-up/strainer. Also remove all traces of locking compound from the pick-up bolts (where removed).

12 On Z16XEP engines, where necessary, position a new gasket/seal on the oil pump pick-up/strainer flange and fit the strainer. Refit the flange and base retaining bolts and tighten to the specified torque.

13 On all other engines, where necessary, position a new gasket/seal on top of the oil pump pick-up/strainer and fit the strainer. Apply locking compound to the threads of the retaining bolts then fit the bolts and tighten to the specified torque.

14 Ensure the sump and cylinder block mating surfaces are clean and dry and remove all traces of locking compound from the sump bolts.

15 Apply a smear of suitable sealant (available from Vauxhall/Opel dealers) to the areas of the cylinder block mating surface around the areas of the of the oil pump housing and main bearing cap joints (**see illustration**).

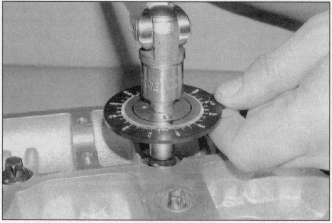

12.34 Tighten the cylinder head bolts through the various angle-tightening sequences

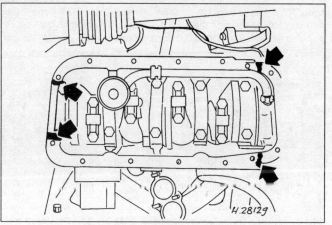

13.15 Apply sealant to the oil pump and main bearing cap joints (arrowed) before the sump is refitted

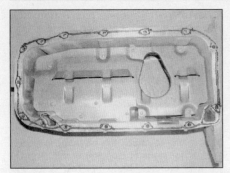

13.16 Apply a 2.5 mm thick bead of sealant to the sump sealing surface – increase the thickness to 3.5 mm around the No 5 main bearing cap area

16 Apply a bead of suitable sealant (available from Vauxhall/Opel dealers) approximately 2.5 mm thick to the sealing surface of the sump. Around the No 5 main bearing cap area, increase the thickness of the bead to 3.5 mm **(see illustration)**.

17 Offer up the sump, and loosely refit all the retaining bolts. Working out from the centre in a diagonal sequence, progressively tighten the bolts securing the sump to the cylinder block/oil pump to their specified torque setting.

18 Tighten the bolts securing the sump flange to the transmission housing to their specified torque settings. Where fitted, refit the rubber plugs to the sump flange cut-outs.

19 Refit the exhaust system (see Chapter 4A) and reconnect the oil level sensor wiring connector.

20 On Z16XEP engines, refit the oil dipstick guide tube.

21 Refit the wheel arch liner inner cover and front roadwheel, then lower the vehicle to the ground. Fill the engine with fresh oil, with reference to Chapter 1A.

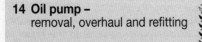

14 Oil pump –
removal, overhaul and refitting

Z16XE and Z18XE engines

Note: *The pressure relief valve can be removed with pump in position on the engine, although on some models it will be necessary to unbolt*

14.12a Using a feeler gauge to check gear clearance – Z16XE and Z18XE engines

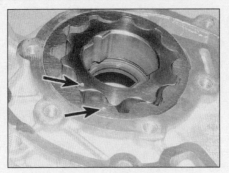

14.8 Oil pump gears identifying marks – Z16XE and Z18XE engines

the mounting bracket assembly from the block to allow the valve to be removed.

Removal

1 Remove the timing belt as described in Section 7.

2 Remove the rear timing belt cover as described in Section 6.

3 Remove the sump and oil pump pick-up/strainer as described in Section 13.

4 Disconnect the wiring connector from the oil pressure switch.

6 Slacken and remove the retaining bolts then slide the oil pump housing assembly off of the end of the crankshaft, taking great care not to lose the locating dowels. Remove the housing gasket and discard it.

Overhaul

7 Undo the retaining screws and lift off the pump cover from the rear of the housing.

8 Check the inner and outer rotors for identification dots indicating which way round they are fitted **(see illustration)**. If no marks are visible, use a suitable marker pen to mark the surface of both the pump inner and outer rotors.

9 Lift out the inner and outer rotors from the pump housing.

10 Unscrew the oil pressure relief valve bolt from the front of the housing and withdraw the spring and plunger from the housing, noting which way around the plunger is fitted. Remove the sealing washer from the valve bolt **(see illustration)**.

11 Clean the components, and carefully examine the rotors, pump body and relief valve plunger for any signs of scoring or wear.

14.12b Using a straight-edge and feeler gauge to measure gear endfloat – Z16XE and Z18XE engines

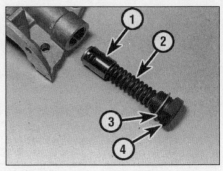

14.10 Oil pressure relief valve components – Z16XE and Z18XE engines

1 Plunger	*3 Sealing washer*
2 Spring	*4 Valve bolt*

Renew any component which shows signs of wear or damage; if the rotors or pump housing are marked then the complete pump assembly should be renewed.

12 If the components appear serviceable, measure the rotor endfloat using feeler blades, and check the flatness of the end cover **(see illustrations)**. If the clearances exceed the specified tolerances the pump must be renewed.

13 If the pump is satisfactory, reassemble the components in the reverse order of removal, noting the following.

a) *Ensure both rotors are fitted the correct way around.*

b) *Fit a new sealing ring to the pressure relief valve bolt and tighten the bolt to the specified torque.*

c) *Apply a little locking compound to the threads, and tighten the pump cover screws to the specified torque.*

d) *On completion prime the oil pump by filling it with clean engine oil whilst rotating the inner rotor.*

Refitting

14 Prior to refitting, carefully lever out the crankshaft oil seal using a flat-bladed screwdriver. Fit the new oil seal, ensuring its sealing lip is facing inwards, and press it squarely into the housing using a tubular drift which bears only on the hard outer edge of the seal **(see illustration)**. Press the seal into position so that it is flush with the housing.

15 Ensure the mating surfaces of the oil pump

14.14 Fitting a new crankshaft oil seal to the oil pump housing – Z16XE and Z18XE engines

and cylinder block are clean and dry and the locating dowels are in position.

16 Fit a new gasket to the cylinder block.

17 Carefully manoeuvre the oil pump into position and engage the inner rotor with the crankshaft end **(see illustration)**. Locate the pump on the dowels, taking great care not damage the oil seal lip.

18 Refit the pump housing retaining bolts in their original locations and tighten them to the specified torque.

19 Reconnect the oil pressure sensor wiring connector.

20 Refit the oil pump pick-up/strainer and sump as described in Section 13.

21 Refit the rear timing belt cover to the engine, tightening its retaining bolts to the specified torque.

22 Refit the timing belt sprockets, idler pulleys and tensioner then refit the belt as described in Sections 8 and 7.

23 On completion, fit a new oil filter and fill the engine with clean oil as described in Chapter 1A.

Z16XEP engines

Removal

24 Remove the alternator as described in Chapter 5A.

25 Remove the timing belt as described in Section 7.

26 Remove the timing belt tensioner and Idler pulley as described in Section 8.

27 Remove the sump as described in Section 13.

28 Undo the two bolts securing the metal coolant pipe to the rear of the coolant pump.

29 Slacken and remove the eight retaining bolts (noting their different lengths) then slide the oil pump housing assembly off of the end of the crankshaft, taking great care not to lose the locating dowels. Remove the housing gasket and discard it.

Overhaul

30 Remove the securing screws/bolts and withdraw the oil pump cover from the rear of the oil pump housing **(see illustration)**.

31 Remove the inner and outer rotor from the pump housing, noting which way round they are fitted, and wipe them clean. Also clean the rotor location in the oil pump housing.

32 The oil pressure relief valve components can also be removed from the oil pump housing by unscrewing the cap. Withdraw the cap, spring and plunger **(see illustrations)**.

33 Locate the inner and outer rotor back in the oil pump housing, ensuring they are fitted the right way round as noted during removal.

34 Check the clearance between the end faces of the rotors and the housing (endfloat) using a straight-edge and a feeler gauge **(see illustration)**.

35 If the clearance is outside the specified limits, renew the components as necessary.

36 Examine the pressure relief valve spring and plunger, and renew if any sign of damage or wear is evident.

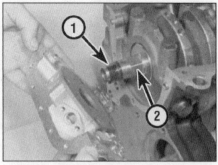

14.17 On refitting take care not to damage the oil seal on the crankshaft lip (1) and engage the inner gear with the crankshaft flats (2) – Z16XE and Z18XE engines

37 Ensure that the rotor location in the interior of the oil pump housing is scrupulously clean before commencing reassembly.

38 Thoroughly clean the pressure relief valve components, and lubricate them with clean engine oil before refitting. Insert the plunger and spring, then refit the cap and tighten to the specified torque.

39 Ensure that the rotors are clean, then lubricate them with clean engine oil, and refit them to the pump body ensuring they are fitted the right way round as noted during removal.

40 Wipe clean the mating faces of the rear cover and the pump housing, then refit the rear cover. Refit and tighten the securing screws securely. Prime the oil pump by filling it with clean engine oil whilst rotating the inner rotor

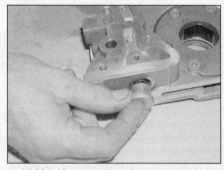

14.32a Unscrew the oil pressure relief valve cap . . .

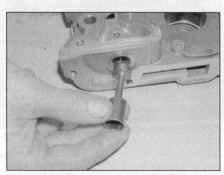

14.32c . . . and the plunger – Z16XEP engines

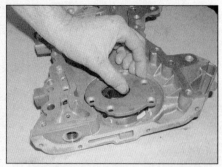

14.30 Remove the securing screws and withdraw the oil pump cover from the rear of the housing – Z16XEP engines

Refitting

41 Prior to refitting, carefully lever out the crankshaft oil seal using a flat-bladed screwdriver. Fit the new oil seal, ensuring its sealing lip is facing inwards, and press it squarely into the housing using a tubular drift which bears only on the hard outer edge of the seal. Press the seal into position so that it is flush with the housing.

42 Ensure the mating surfaces of the oil pump housing and cylinder block are clean and dry and the locating dowels are in position.

43 Fit a new gasket to the cylinder block.

44 Carefully manoeuvre the oil pump into position and engage the inner rotor with the crankshaft end. Locate the pump on the dowels, taking great care not damage the oil seal lip.

45 Refit the pump housing retaining bolts in

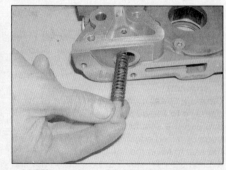

14.32b . . . then withdraw the spring . . .

14.34 Check the oil pump rotor endfloat using a straight-edge and feeler gauge – Z16XEP engines

15.2 Removing the crankshaft right-hand oil seal

15.4 Fitting a new crankshaft right-hand oil seal

15.7 Left-hand crankshaft oil seal

their original locations and tighten them to the specified torque.

46 Using a new gasket, refit the metal coolant pipe flange to the coolant pump and tighten the retaining bolts to the specified torque.

47 Refit the sump as described in Section 13.

48 Refit the timing belt tensioner and idler pulley, then refit the timing belt as described in Sections 8 and 7.

49 Refit the alternator as described in Chapter 5A.

50 On completion, fit a new oil filter and fill the engine with clean oil as described in Chapter 1A.

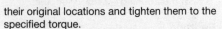

15 Crankshaft oil seals – renewal

Timing belt end oil seal

1 Remove the crankshaft sprocket as described in Section 8.

2 Carefully punch or drill two small holes opposite each other in the oil seal. Screw a self-tapping screw into each and pull on the screws with pliers to extract the seal **(see illustration)**.

Caution: Great care must be taken to avoid damage to the oil pump.

3 Clean the seal housing and polish off any burrs or raised edges which may have caused the seal to fail in the first place.

4 Ease the new seal into position on the end of the crankshaft. Press the seal squarely

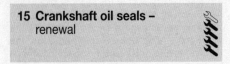

into position until it is flush with the housing. If necessary, a suitable tubular drift, such as a socket, which bears only on the hard outer edge of the seal can be used to tap the seal into position **(see illustration)**. Take great care not to damage the seal lips during fitting and ensure that the seal lips face inwards.

5 Wash off any traces of oil, then refit the crankshaft sprocket as described in Section 8.

Transmission end oil seal

6 Remove the flywheel as described in Section 16.

7 Renew the seal as described in paragraphs 2 to 4 **(see illustration)**.

8 Refit the flywheel as described in Section 16.

16 Flywheel – removal, inspection and refitting

Note: *New flywheel retaining bolts will be required on refitting.*

Removal

1 Remove the transmission as described in Chapter 7A or 7B then remove the clutch assembly as described in Chapter 6.

2 Prevent the flywheel from turning by locking the ring gear teeth with a similar arrangement to that shown **(see illustration)**. Alternatively, bolt a strap between the flywheel and the cylinder block/crankcase. Make alignment marks between the flywheel and crankshaft using paint or a suitable marker pen.

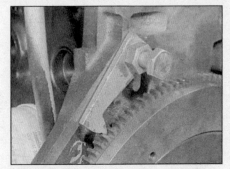

16.2 Lock the flywheel ring gear with a suitable tool

16.8 Use an angle-gauge to tighten the flywheel bolts accurately

3 Slacken and remove the retaining bolts and remove the flywheel. Do not drop it, as it is very heavy.

Inspection

4 Examine the flywheel for scoring of the clutch face. If the clutch face is scored, the flywheel may be surface-ground, but renewal is preferable.

5 If there is any doubt about the condition of the flywheel, seek the advice of a Vauxhall/Opel dealer or engine reconditioning specialist. They will be able to advise if it is possible to recondition it or whether renewal is necessary.

Refitting

6 Clean the mating surfaces of the flywheel and crankshaft.

7 Apply a drop of locking compound to each of the new retaining bolt threads then offer up the flywheel, if the original is being refitted, align the marks made prior to removal. Screw in the retaining bolts.

8 Lock the flywheel by the method used on removal, and tighten the retaining bolts to the specified Stage 1 torque setting then angle-tighten the bolts through the specified Stage 2 angle, using a socket and extension bar, and finally through the specified Stage 3 angle. It is recommended that an angle-measuring gauge is used during the final stages of the tightening, to ensure accuracy **(see illustration)**. If a gauge is not available, use white paint to make alignment marks between the bolt head and flywheel prior to tightening; the marks can then be used to check that the bolt has been rotated through the correct angle.

9 Refit the clutch as described in Chapter 6 then remove the locking tool, and refit the transmission as described in Chapter 7A or 7B.

17 Engine/transmission mountings – inspection and renewal

Refer to Chapter 2A, Section 15, but observe the different torque wrench settings given in the Specifications of this Chapter.

Chapter 2 Part D:
1.3 litre diesel engine in-car repair procedures

Contents

Section number

Degrees of difficulty

Easy, suitable for novice with little experience	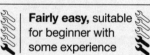 Fairly easy, suitable for beginner with some experience	Fairly difficult, suitable for competent DIY mechanic	Difficult, suitable for experienced DIY mechanic	Very difficult, suitable for expert DIY or professional

Specifications

General

Engine type.	Four-cylinder, in-line, water-cooled. Double overhead chain-driven camshafts, 16 valves
Manufacturer's engine code*	Z13DTJ
Bore	69.6 mm
Stroke	82.0 mm
Capacity	1248 cc
Firing order	1-3-4-2 (No 1 cylinder at timing chain end)
Direction of crankshaft rotation	Clockwise (viewed from timing chain end of engine)
Compression ratio	18.0:1

* For details of engine code location, see 'Vehicle identification' in the Reference Chapter.

Compression pressures

Maximum difference between any two cylinders	1.5 bar

Lubrication system

Oil pump type	Gear-type, driven directly from crankshaft
Oil pressure at 80ºC (approximate)	1.4 bars at idle speed
Oil pump clearances:	
Outer rotor-to-body clearance	0.10 to 0.23 mm
Rotor endfloat	0.050 to 0.075 mm

Torque wrench settings

	Nm	lbf ft
Auxiliary drivebelt tensioner to cylinder block	50	37
Big-end bearing cap nuts:*		
Stage 1.	20	15
Stage 2.	Angle-tighten a further 40°	
Camshaft drivegear bolts.	150	111
Camshaft housing closure bolts.	15	11
Camshaft housing to cylinder head:		
M8 stud bolts.	25	18
M7 bolts	18	13
Camshaft position sensor retaining bolt.	7	5
Camshaft sprocket bolt	150	111
Catalytic converter support bracket to sump reinforcement bracket . .	25	18
Catalytic converter-to-turbocharger bolts	25	18
Coolant pipe-to-heat exchanger bolts	9	7
Coolant pump nuts.	9	7
Crankshaft pulley hub to crankshaft:†*		
Stage 1.	50	37
Stage 2.	Angle-tighten a further 90°	
Crankshaft pulley to pulley hub	25	18
Cylinder block baseplate bolts:*		
M10 bolts:		
Stage 1	20	15
Stage 2	Angle-tighten a further 90°	
M8 bolts	30	22
Cylinder head bolts:*		
Stage 1.	40	30
Stage 2.	Angle-tighten a further 90°	
Stage 3.	Angle-tighten a further 90°	
Engine/transmission mountings:		
Front mounting/torque link:		
Mounting-to-transmission bolts	95	70
Mounting to subframe	60	44
Left-hand mounting:		
Mounting-to-body bolts	25	18
Mounting to transmission bracket:*		
Stage 1	80	59
Stage 2	Angle-tighten a further 60°	
Transmission bracket to transmission	60	44
Rear mounting/torque link:		
Mounting-to-bracket bolt	80	59
Mounting-to-subframe bolt	80	59
Bracket-to-transmission bolts:*		
Stage 1	80	59
Stage 2	Angle-tighten a further 45°	
Right-hand mounting:		
Engine bracket-to-engine bolts	60	44
Mounting-to-body bolts	40	30
Mounting-to-engine bracket bolts:*		
Stage 1	60	44
Stage 2	Angle-tighten a further 30°	
Engine-to-transmission bolts	60	44
Flywheel bolts*	44	32
Fuel rail mounting bracket to camshaft housing	25	18
Fuel rail-to-mounting bracket bolts	25	18
Oil cooler/heat exchanger to oil filter housing	9	7
Oil filter housing cover	25	18
Oil filter housing to cylinder block	9	7
Roadwheel bolts.	110	81
Sump drain plug.	20	15
Sump reinforcement bracket bolts.	30	22
Sump to cylinder block baseplate	9	7
Timing chain guide rail bolts.	9	7
Timing chain tensioner bolts	9	7
Timing chain tensioner rail pivot bolt	9	7
Timing cover retaining nuts/bolts.	9	7
Turbocharger oil supply pipe banjo union bolts	12	9

* Use new fasteners

† Left-hand thread

1 General information

How to use this Chapter

This Part of Chapter 2 describes the repair procedures which can reasonably be carried out on the engine while it remains in the vehicle. If the engine has been removed from the vehicle and is being dismantled as described in Chapter 2F, any preliminary dismantling procedures can be ignored.

Note that, while it may be possible physically to overhaul items such as the piston/connecting rod assemblies while the engine is in the vehicle, such tasks are not usually carried out as separate operations, and usually require the execution of several additional procedures (not to mention the cleaning of components and of oilways); for this reason, all such tasks are classed as major overhaul procedures, and are described in Chapter 2F.

Chapter 2F describes the removal of the engine/transmission unit from the vehicle, and the full overhaul procedures which can then be carried out.

Engine description

The 1.3 litre common-rail diesel engine is of sixteen-valve, in-line four-cylinder, double overhead camshaft (DOHC) type, mounted transversely at the front of the car with the transmission attached to its left-hand end.

The crankshaft runs in five main bearings. Thrustwashers are fitted to No 3 main bearing shell (upper half) to control crankshaft endfloat.

The cylinder block is made of cast iron and the cylinder bores are an integral part of the block. On this type of engine the cylinder bores are sometimes referred to as having dry liners. An aluminium baseplate is bolted to the cylinder block and forms the lower half of the crankcase.

The connecting rods rotate on horizontally-split bearing shells at their big-ends. The pistons are attached to the connecting rods by gudgeon pins, which are a sliding fit in the connecting rod small-end eyes and retained by circlips. The aluminium-alloy pistons are fitted with three piston rings – two compression rings and an oil control ring.

The camshafts are situated in a separate housing bolted to the top of the cylinder head. The exhaust camshaft is driven by the crankshaft by a hydraulically-tensioned timing chain and drives the inlet camshaft via a spur gear. Each cylinder has four valves (two inlet and two exhaust), operated via rocker arms which are supported at their pivot ends by hydraulic self-adjusting valve lifters (tappets). One camshaft operates the inlet valves, and the other operates the exhaust valves.

The inlet and exhaust valves are each closed by a single valve spring, and operate in guides pressed into the cylinder head.

A rotor-type oil pump is located in the timing cover attached to the cylinder block, and is driven directly from the crankshaft. An oil cooler (heat exchanger) is fitted to keep the oil temperature stable under arduous operating conditions.

The coolant pump is located externally on the timing cover, and is driven by the auxiliary drivebelt.

Operations with engine in place

The following operations can be carried out without having to remove the engine from the vehicle.
a) Removal and refitting of the cylinder head.
b) Removal and refitting of the timing cover.
c) Removal and refitting of the timing chain, tensioner, sprockets and guide rails.
d) Removal and refitting of the camshaft housing.
e) Removal and refitting of the hydraulic tappets and rocker arms.
f) Removal and refitting of the camshafts.
g) Removal and refitting of the sump.
h) Removal and refitting of the big-end bearings, connecting rods, and pistons.*
i) Removal and refitting of the oil pump.
j) Removal and refitting of the oil cooler/ heat exchanger.
k) Renewal of the crankshaft oil seals.
l) Renewal of the engine mountings.
m) Removal and refitting of the flywheel.

Although the operation marked with an asterisk can be carried out with the engine in the vehicle (after removal of the sump), it is preferable for the engine to be removed, in the interests of cleanliness and improved access. For this reason, the procedure is described in Chapter 2F.

2 Compression test – description and interpretation

Compression test

Note: *A compression tester specifically designed for diesel engines must be used for this test.*

1 When engine performance is down, or if misfiring occurs which cannot be attributed to the fuel system, a compression test can provide diagnostic clues as to the engine's condition. If the test is performed regularly, it can give warning of trouble before any other symptoms become apparent.

2 A compression tester specifically intended for diesel engines must be used, because of the higher pressures involved. The tester is connected to an adapter which screws into the glow plug or injector hole. On these models, an adapter suitable for use in the

injector holes will be required. It is unlikely to be worthwhile buying such a tester for occasional use, but it may be possible to borrow or hire one – if not, have the test performed by a garage.

3 Before carrying out the test, ensure that the battery is in a good state of charge, that the air filter is clean, and that preferably the engine is at normal operating temperature.

4 Unless specific instructions to the contrary are supplied with the tester, observe the following points:
a) *The battery must be in a good state of charge, the air filter must be clean, and the engine should be at normal operating temperature.*
b) *All the fuel injectors must be removed before starting the test (see Chapter 4B).*
c) *Refer to Chapter 12 and remove the fuel pump relay from the engine compartment relay box.*

5 Screw the compression tester and adapter in to the fuel injector hole of No 1 cylinder.

6 With the help of an assistant, crank the engine on the starter motor; after one or two revolutions, the compression pressure should build-up to a maximum figure, and then stabilise. Record the highest reading obtained.

7 Repeat the test on the remaining cylinders, recording the pressure in each.

8 All cylinders should produce very similar pressures; any difference greater than that specified indicates the existence of a fault. Note that the compression should build-up quickly in a healthy engine; low compression on the first stroke, followed by gradually-increasing pressure on successive strokes, indicates worn piston rings. A low compression reading on the first stroke, which does not build-up during successive strokes, indicates leaking valves or a blown head gasket (a cracked head could also be the cause). **Note:** *The cause of poor compression is less easy to establish on a diesel engine than on a petrol one. The effect of introducing oil into the cylinders ('wet' testing) is not conclusive, because there is a risk that the oil will sit in the recess on the piston crown instead of passing to the rings.*

9 On completion of the test, refit the fuel pump relay, then refit the fuel injectors as described in Chapter 4B.

Leakdown test

10 A leakdown test measures the rate at which compressed air fed into the cylinder is lost. It is an alternative to a compression test, and in many ways it is better, since the escaping air provides easy identification of where pressure loss is occurring (piston rings, valves or head gasket).

11 The equipment needed for leakdown testing is unlikely to be available to the home mechanic. If poor compression is suspected, have the test performed by a dealership.

3.2 Camshaft timing slot (arrowed) for use with the camshaft locking tools

3.3a Inserting the Vauxhall/Opel crankshaft locking tool through the timing hole in the bellhousing

3 Engine assembly/ valve timing holes – general information and usage

Note: *Do not attempt to rotate the engine whilst the camshafts are locked in position. If the engine is to be left in this state for a long period of time, it is a good idea to place suitable warning notices inside the car, and in the engine compartment. This will reduce the possibility of the engine being accidentally cranked on the starter motor, which is likely to cause damage with the locking tools in place.*

1 To accurately set the valve timing for all operations requiring removal and refitting of the timing chain, timing slots are machined in the camshafts and corresponding holes are drilled in the camshaft housing. Timing holes are also drilled in the flywheel, and transmission bellhousing. The holes are used in conjunction with camshaft and crankshaft locking tools to lock the camshafts and crankshaft when all the pistons are positioned at the mid-point of their stroke. This arrangement prevents the possibility of the valves contacting the pistons when refitting

the cylinder head or timing chain, and also ensures that the correct valve timing can be obtained. The design of the engine is such that there are no conventional timing marks on the crankshaft or camshaft sprockets to indicate the normal TDC position. Therefore, for any work on the timing chain, camshafts or cylinder head, the locking tools must be used.

2 The Vauxhall/Opel special tool for locking the camshafts comprises a spring loaded plunger free to slide in the bore of the tool body. The tool body is screwed into the camshaft housing timing hole (after removal of a closure plug) so that the sliding plunger contacts the exhaust camshaft. The plunger is retained in contact with the camshaft by the spring. The crankshaft is then rotated by means of the crankshaft pulley bolt until a machined slot in the camshaft aligns with the tool plunger **(see illustration)**. The spring then forces the plunger into engagement with the slot, locking the camshaft in the timing position. To accurately check the valve timing, or for any work that entails removal of the camshafts or their drivegears, two of these tools will be required, one for each camshaft.

3 The Vauxhall/Opel special tool for locking the crankshaft is simply a 6 mm diameter pin which is inserted through a hole in the bellhousing to engage with a corresponding hole in the rim of the flywheel. An additional hole is provided in the inner face of the flywheel with a corresponding hole in the cylinder block, for use when the transmission has been removed **(see illustrations)**.

4 The Vauxhall/Opel tool numbers are as follows:

Camshaft locking tools – EN-46781
Crankshaft locking tool (bellhousing into flywheel) – EN-46785
Crankshaft locking tool (flywheel into cylinder block) – EN-46778

5 Although the Vauxhall/Opel camshaft locking tools (or aftermarket equivalents) are relatively inexpensive and should be readily available, it is possible to fabricate suitable alternatives, with the help of a local machine shop, as described below. Once the tools have been made up, their usage is described in the relevant Sections of this Chapter where the tools are required.

Camshaft locking tool

6 Lift off the plastic cover over the top of the engine.

7 Unscrew the three bolts securing the plastic wiring harness guide to the top of the camshaft housing.

8 Release the locking catches securing the wiring connectors to the four injectors, then disconnect the injector wiring, while at the same time moving the wiring harness guide forward **(see illustration)**.

9 Unscrew the closure bolt from the valve timing checking hole on the front face of the camshaft housing. The bolt is located above, and just between, Nos 2 and 3 glow plugs.

10 Using the closure bolt as a pattern, obtain a length of threaded dowel rod, or suitable bolt to screw into the closure bolt hole. With

3.3b Using a drill bit (arrowed) to lock the crankshaft through the additional timing hole provided in the flywheel

3.8 Disconnect the injector wiring then move the wiring harness guide forward

the help of a machine shop or engineering works, make up the camshaft locking tool by having the dowel rod or bolt machined **(see illustrations)**. Note that for some of the procedures described in this Chapter, two locking tools will be needed, one for each camshaft.

11 To refit the closure bolt, thoroughly clean the bolt threads and apply suitable thread-locking compound. Screw the bolt into the camshaft housing and tighten to the specified torque.

12 Securely reconnect the injector wiring connectors, then refit and tighten the three wiring harness guide retaining bolts. Refit the engine cover on completion.

Crankshaft locking tools

13 Suitable drill bits or dowel rods can be used as alternatives for the Vauxhall/Opel special tools described previously. Their respective diameters are as follows:

Crankshaft locking tool (bellhousing
into flywheel)   6.0 mm diameter
Crankshaft locking tool (flywheel
into cylinder block)   9.0 mm diameter

4 Valve timing – checking and adjustment

Note: *Certain special tools will be required for this operation. Read through the entire procedure to familiarise yourself with the work involved, then either obtain the manufacturer's special tools, or use the alternatives described. New gaskets and sealing rings will also be required for all disturbed components.*

Checking

1 Disconnect the battery negative terminal (refer to *Disconnecting the battery* in the Reference Chapter).
2 Remove the turbocharger charge air pipe as described in Chapter 4B.
3 Disconnect the wiring connector at the camshaft position sensor on the top of the camshaft housing.
4 Disconnect the wiring connectors at the four glow plugs.

4.8 Undo the three bolts and remove the engine lifting bracket and fuel rail mounting bracket from the camshaft housing

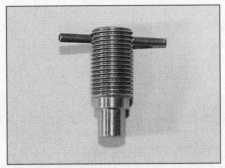

3.10a To make an alternative camshaft locking tool . . .

5 Unscrew the three bolts securing the plastic wiring harness guide to the top of the camshaft housing.
6 Release the locking catches securing the wiring connectors to the four injectors, then disconnect the injector wiring, while at the same time moving the wiring harness guide forward **(see illustration 3.8)**.
7 Undo the two retaining bolts securing the fuel rail to the mounting bracket.
8 Undo the three bolts and remove the engine lifting bracket and fuel rail mounting bracket from the camshaft housing **(see illustration)**. After removal of the mounting bracket, take care not to apply any force to the fuel rail otherwise damage could be caused to the high-pressure fuel pipes.
9 Unscrew the closure bolt from the valve timing checking hole on each side of the camshaft housing **(see illustration)**.
10 The camshafts must now be set to the timing position, to enable a camshaft locking tool to be inserted (see Section 3).

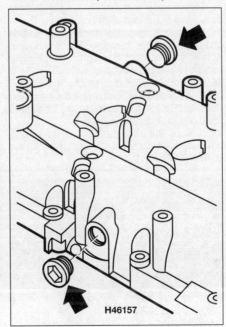

4.9 Unscrew the closure bolt from valve timing checking hole on each side of the camshaft housing

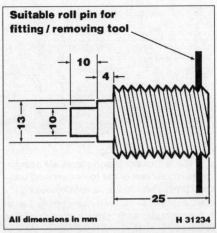

3.10b . . . have suitable dowel rods or bolts machined to the dimensions shown

11 If the Vauxhall/Opel camshaft locking tools or similar alternatives are available, screw one of the tools into each of the valve timing checking holes. Ensure that the mark on the tool plunger is facing upwards **(see illustration)**. Using a socket or spanner on the

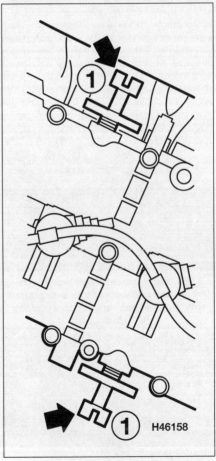

4.11 If the Vauxhall/Opel camshaft locking tools (1) are being used, screw the tools into the valve timing checking holes. Ensure that the mark on the tool plunger (arrowed) is facing upwards

4.12a If the home-made tools are being used, screw one of the tools (arrowed) into each timing hole in the camshaft housing . . .

crankshaft pulley hub bolt, turn the crankshaft in the normal direction of rotation (clockwise as viewed from the right-hand side of the car) until the spring-loaded plungers of the locking tools slide into engagement with the slot on each camshaft. There will be an audible click from each tool when this happens and the plungers will be seen to move in, towards the camshafts.

12 If the home-made locking tools described in Section 3 are being used, insert a screwdriver through the valve timing checking hole on the front of the camshaft housing, and into contact with the exhaust camshaft. Using a socket or spanner on the crankshaft pulley hub bolt, turn the crankshaft in the normal direction of rotation (clockwise as viewed from the right-hand side of the car) until the screwdriver can be felt to engage with the slot in the camshaft. Screw the tool into the

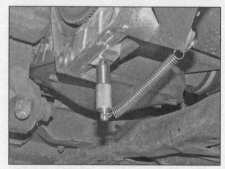

4.14a Insert the camshaft locking tool through the bellhousing into engagement with the flywheel. Hold the tool in place with the spring

4.14b Alternatively, use a suitable drill bit . . .

4.12b . . . so the end of the tool engages with the slot in the camshaft (shown with camshaft removed)

camshaft housing until resistance is felt, then turn the crankshaft slightly until the camshaft slot is correctly aligned, and the tool can be screwed fully in **(see illustrations)**. Repeat this procedure for the inlet camshaft.

13 Firmly apply the handbrake, then jack up the front of the car and support it securely on axle stands (see *Jacking and vehicle support*).

14 Insert the Vauxhall/Opel crankshaft locking tool or suitable alternative (see Section 3) into the timing hole at the base of the transmission bellhousing and into engagement with the flywheel **(see illustrations)**. It may be necessary to turn the crankshaft very slightly one way or the other (within the limits of any slack afforded by the timing chain/tensioner) to allow the tool to fully engage.

15 If the crankshaft locking tool has engaged fully, then the valve timing is correct. Refit the disturbed components as described in the following paragraphs. If it is not possible to fully insert the crankshaft locking tool, then it will be necessary to adjust the valve timing as described in paragraphs 24 to 33.

16 Remove the camshaft locking tools from both sides of the camshaft housing.

17 Thoroughly clean the closure bolt threads and apply suitable thread-locking compound. Screw the bolts into the camshaft housing and tighten to the specified torque.

18 Place the engine lifting bracket and fuel rail mounting bracket in position on the camshaft housing. Refit the three retaining bolts and tighten to the specified torque.

19 Locate the fuel rail on the mounting bracket, insert the two bolts and tighten to the specified torque.

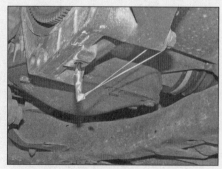

4.14c . . . and hold it in place with an elastic band

20 Reconnect the fuel injector wiring connectors and secure with the locking catches.

21 Refit the three bolts securing the plastic wiring harness guide to the top of the camshaft housing.

22 Reconnect the wiring connectors at the four glow plugs and at the camshaft position sensor.

23 Refit the turbocharger charge air pipe as described in Chapter 4B, then reconnect the battery and lower the car to the ground.

Adjustment

24 Remove the crankshaft pulley as described in Section 5.

25 It will now be necessary to hold the crankshaft pulley hub to enable the retaining bolt to be removed. Vauxhall/Opel special tool KM-662-C is available for this purpose, however, a home-made tool can easily be fabricated **(see Tool Tip)**.

26 Using the Vauxhall/Opel tool or the home-made alternative, hold the pulley hub stationary and unscrew the retaining bolt. **Note:** *The pulley hub retaining bolt has a **left-hand** thread and is unscrewed by turning it clockwise.*

27 Withdraw the pulley hub from the crankshaft and refit the retaining bolt sufficiently tight to allow the crankshaft to be turned.

28 Using a socket or spanner on the crankshaft pulley hub bolt, turn the crankshaft as necessary, until it is possible to fully insert the crankshaft locking tool into engagement with the flywheel.

29 Undo the bolt, refit the crankshaft pulley hub, and refit the bolt.

30 Hold the pulley hub using the holding tool and tighten the bolt to the specified torque.

31 Remove the crankshaft locking tool.

32 Refit the crankshaft pulley as described in Section 5.

33 Refit the disturbed components as described in paragraphs 16 to 23.

TOOL TiP

To make a sprocket holding tool, obtain two lengths of steel strip about 6 mm thick by about 30 mm wide or similar, one 600 mm long, the other 200 mm long (all dimensions are approximate). Bolt the two strips together to form a forked end, leaving the bolt slack so that the shorter strip can pivot freely. At the other end of each 'prong' of the fork, drill a suitable hole and fit a nut and bolt to allow the tool to be bolted to the crankshaft pulley hub.

5 Crankshaft pulley – removal and refitting

Removal

1 Apply the handbrake, then jack up the front of the vehicle and support it on axle stands (see *Jacking and vehicle support*). Remove the right-hand front roadwheel and the inner wheel arch liner for access to the crankshaft pulley.

2 Remove the auxiliary drivebelt as described in Chapter 1B. Prior to removal, mark the direction of rotation on the belt to ensure the belt is refitted the same way around.

3 Slacken and remove the four retaining bolts securing the pulley to the pulley hub. If necessary, prevent the crankshaft from turning by holding the pulley hub retaining bolt with a socket.

Refitting

4 Refit the crankshaft pulley to the pulley hub. Refit the pulley retaining bolts, tightening them to the specified torque.

5 Refit the auxiliary drivebelt as described in Chapter 1B using the mark made prior to removal to ensure the belt is fitted the correct way around.

6 Refit the wheel arch liner and roadwheel, then lower the car to the ground and tighten the wheel bolts to the specified torque.

6 Timing cover – removal and refitting

Note: *The special tools described in Section 3, together with additional tools will be required for this operation. Read through the entire procedure and also the procedures contained in Section 3 to familiarise yourself with the work involved, then either obtain the manufacturer's special tools, or use the alternatives described, where applicable. New gaskets and sealing rings will be needed for all disturbed components, together with a tube of suitable gasket sealant.*

Removal

1 Disconnect the battery negative terminal (refer to *Disconnecting the battery* in the Reference Chapter).

2 Referring to the procedures contained in Chapter 1B, drain the engine oil and the cooling system. Refit the drain plug, using a new seal, when the oil has drained. Close the cooling system when the coolant has drained.

3 Remove the crankshaft pulley as described in Section 5.

4 Remove the air cleaner assembly and the turbocharger charge air pipe and charge air hose as described in Chapter 4B.

5 Disconnect the wiring connector at the camshaft position sensor on the top of the camshaft housing.

6.13 Undo nut and two bolts (arrowed) and remove the oil filter heat shield

6 Disconnect the wiring connectors at the four glow plugs.

7 Unscrew the three bolts securing the plastic wiring harness guide to the top of the camshaft housing.

8 Release the locking catches securing the wiring connectors to the four injectors, then disconnect the injector wiring, while at the same time moving the wiring harness guide forward (see illustration 3.8).

9 Unscrew the closure bolt from the valve timing checking hole on the exhaust camshaft side of the camshaft housing (see illustration 4.9).

10 If the Vauxhall/Opel camshaft locking tool or similar alternative is available (see Section 3), screw the tool into the valve timing checking hole. Ensure that the mark on the tool plunger is facing upwards. Using a socket or spanner on the crankshaft pulley hub bolt, turn the crankshaft in the normal direction of rotation (clockwise as viewed from the right-hand side of the car) until the spring-loaded plunger of the locking tool slides into engagement with the slot on the camshaft. There will be an audible click from the tool when this happens, and the plunger will be seen to move in, towards the camshaft.

11 If the home-made locking tool described in Section 3 is being used, insert a screwdriver through the valve timing checking hole on the front of the camshaft housing, and into contact with the exhaust camshaft. Using a socket or spanner on the crankshaft pulley hub bolt, turn the crankshaft in the normal direction of rotation (clockwise as viewed from the right-hand side of the car) until the screwdriver can be felt to

6.15 Unscrew the turbocharger oil supply pipe banjo union bolt (arrowed) from the oil filter housing

6.14 Undo the two bolts (arrowed) securing the coolant pipe to the heat exchanger

engage with the slot in the camshaft. Screw the tool into the camshaft housing until resistance is felt, then turn the crankshaft slightly until the camshaft slot is correctly aligned, and the tool can be screwed fully in (see illustrations 4.12a and 4.12b).

12 Referring to the procedures contained in Chapter 4B, separate the exhaust system front section from the catalytic converter.

13 Undo the upper nut and two lower bolts and remove the oil filter heat shield (see illustration).

14 Undo the two bolts securing the coolant pipe to the heat exchanger on the oil filter housing (see illustration). Release the retaining clip securing the other end of the pipe to the hose on the thermostat housing. Undo the pipe support bracket bolt, release the wiring harness from the retaining clip and remove the coolant pipe from the engine. Recover the gasket noting that a new one will be required for refitting.

15 Unscrew the banjo union bolt and release the turbocharger oil supply pipe from the oil filter housing (see illustration). Recover the two copper washers from the banjo union, and suitably cover the end of the pipe to prevent dirt entry. Note that new copper washers will be required for refitting.

16 Slacken the retaining clip and disconnect the radiator bottom hose from the outlet at the base of the oil filter housing.

17 Undo the three bolts securing the heat shield support bracket to the heat exchanger on the oil filter housing (see illustration).

18 Undo the remaining bolt and remove the

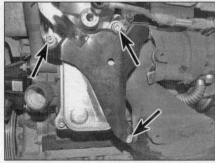

6.17 Undo the three bolts (arrowed) securing the heat shield support bracket to the heat exchanger

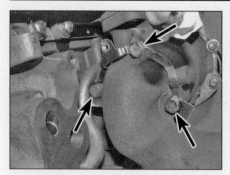

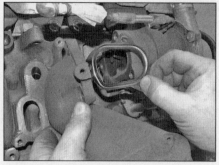

6.20 Unscrew the three bolts (arrowed) securing the catalytic converter to the turbocharger

6.21 Separate the catalytic converter from the turbocharger and recover the gasket

6.26 Remove the sump reinforcement bracket from the cylinder block baseplate and transmission bellhousing

oil filter housing and heat exchanger assembly from the cylinder block. Recover the rubber seal from the rear of the housing. Note that a new seal will be required for refitting.

19 From under the car, undo the bolt securing the catalytic converter support bracket to the sump reinforcement bracket.

20 Suitably support the weight of the catalytic converter on blocks or on a jack. Bend back the locking plate tabs and unscrew the three bolts securing the catalytic converter flange to the turbocharger **(see illustration)**. Remove the bolts and locking plate, noting that a new locking plate will be required for refitting.

21 Separate the catalytic converter from the turbocharger and recover the gasket **(see illustration)**. Carefully lower the converter and remove it from under the car. Note that a new gasket will be required for refitting.

22 It will now be necessary to hold the crankshaft pulley hub to enable the retaining bolt to be removed. Vauxhall/Opel special tool KM-662-C is available for this purpose, however, a home-made tool can easily be fabricated. Refer to the Tool Tip in Section 4.

23 Using the Vauxhall/Opel tool or the home-made alternative, hold the pulley hub stationary and unscrew the retaining bolt. **Note:** *The pulley hub retaining bolt has a left-hand thread and is unscrewed by turning it clockwise.*

24 Withdraw the pulley hub from the crankshaft and refit the retaining bolt sufficiently tight to allow the crankshaft to be turned.

25 Insert the Vauxhall/Opel crankshaft locking tool or suitable alternative (see Section 3) into

the timing hole in the base of the transmission bellhousing and into engagement with the flywheel **(see illustrations 4.14a, 4.14b and 4.14c)**. It may be necessary to turn the crankshaft very slightly one way or the other, by means of the pulley retaining bolt, to allow the tool to fully engage.

26 Undo the five bolts securing the sump reinforcement bracket to the cylinder block baseplate and transmission bellhousing, and remove the bracket **(see illustration)**. Note the locations of the different length bolts to aid refitting.

27 Disconnect the oil level sensor wiring connector at the rear of the sump **(see illustration)**.

28 Undo the thirteen bolts and two nuts securing the sump to the cylinder block baseplate and timing cover. Using a wide-bladed scraper or similar tool inserted between the sump and baseplate, carefully break the joint, then remove the sump from under the car.

29 Connect a suitable hoist and lifting tackle to the right-hand end of the engine and support its weight. If available, the type of support bar which locates in the engine compartment side channels is to be preferred. Alternatively, support the engine on a jack with a block of wood positioned between the jack head and cylinder block baseplate.

30 Mark the bolt positions for correct refitting, then undo the two bolts securing the right-hand engine mounting to the body, and the two bolts securing the mounting to the engine bracket **(see illustration 17.8)**. Remove the mounting.

31 Undo the four bolts securing the engine bracket to the cylinder block and cylinder head, and remove the engine bracket **(see illustration)**.

32 Undo the centre retaining bolt and remove the auxiliary drivebelt tensioner from the timing cover.

33 Release the wiring harness from the support clips on the timing cover and move the harness to one side **(see illustration)**.

34 Undo the retaining bolt and detach the crankcase ventilation hose attachment at the timing cover **(see illustration)**.

6.27 Disconnect the oil level sensor wiring connector

6.31 Undo the four bolts (arrowed) and remove the engine bracket

6.33 Release the wiring harness from the timing cover support clips

6.34 Undo the retaining bolt and detach the crankcase ventilation hose attachment

35 Working through the apertures in the pulley, unscrew and remove the four coolant pump retaining nuts **(see illustration)**.
36 Withdraw the coolant pump from the cylinder block studs. **Note:** *Coolant which is trapped in the cylinder block will leak out when the pump is removed.*
37 Recover the pump sealing ring, and discard it; a new one must be used on refitting.
38 Undo the retaining bolt and remove the wiring harness support clip bracket from the top of the timing cover **(see illustration)**.
39 Undo the fourteen bolts and three nuts securing the timing cover to the cylinder block, cylinder block baseplate, cylinder head and camshaft housing. Using a flat-bladed screwdriver inserted behind the lugs on the edge of the timing cover, carefully prise the cover free and remove it from the engine **(see illustrations)**. Recover the timing cover gasket, a new gasket will be required for refitting.
40 Thoroughly clean the timing cover and remove all traces of gasket and sealant from all the mating surfaces. Similarly clean the cylinder block baseplate, cylinder block, cylinder head and camshaft housing mating surfaces. Ensure that all traces of old sealant are removed, particularly from the joint areas between these components.
41 Obtain all new gaskets and components as necessary ready for refitting. In addition, a new crankshaft oil seal will be required together with a tube of Loctite 5900 sealant, or equivalent. Vauxhall/Opel special tool EN-46775, or a suitable alternative, will be required to centralise the timing cover during refitting.

Refitting

42 Prior to refitting the timing cover, ensure that the face of the timing chain sprocket on the crankshaft is free from oil or grease.
43 Apply a 2 mm bead of Loctite 5900 across the camshaft housing-to-cylinder head joint, the cylinder head-to-cylinder block joint and the cylinder block-to-baseplate joint **(see illustration)**.
44 Place the new gasket in position on the engine then locate the timing cover over the gasket. Insert the Vauxhall/Opel tool (EN-46775) or a suitable equivalent, over the crankshaft and into engagement with the timing cover.
45 Refit the fourteen bolts and three nuts securing the timing cover to the engine, and tighten them to the specified torque, in sequence **(see illustration)**.
46 Remove the centering tool and carefully prise out the old crankshaft oil seal with a screwdriver or similar hooked tool. Clean the oil seal seat with a wooden or plastic scraper.
47 Tap a new crankshaft oil seal into position until it is flush with the outer face of the timing cover, using a suitable socket or tube, or a wooden block.
48 Refit the wiring harness support clip bracket to the top of the timing cover.

49 Ensure that the coolant pump and cylinder block mating surfaces are clean and dry. Fit a new sealing ring to the pump, and install the pump in the cylinder block.
50 Refit the pump retaining nuts, tightening them to the specified torque.
51 Insert the crankcase ventilation hose attachment to the timing cover and secure with the retaining bolt.
52 Refit the wiring harness to the support clips on the timing cover.
53 Thoroughly clean the crankshaft pulley hub, ensuring that the timing chain sprocket contact face is free from oil or grease.
54 Refit the pulley hub to the crankshaft, then fit the new retaining bolt. Using the method employed on removal to hold the pulley hub stationary, tighten the retaining bolt to the specified torque.
55 Refit the auxiliary drivebelt tensioner

6.35 Working through the pulley apertures, unscrew and remove the coolant pump retaining nuts

6.39a Using a flat-bladed screwdriver inserted behind the lugs on the edge of the timing cover . . .

6.43 Apply a bead of sealant across the housing joints

6.38 Undo the retaining bolt (arrowed) and remove the wiring harness support clip bracket

6.39b . . . carefully prise the cover free and remove it from the engine

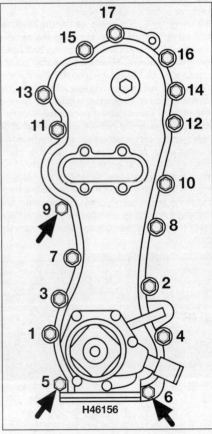
6.45 Timing cover tightening sequence. Arrows indicate the location of the three nuts

6.55 Refit the auxiliary drivebelt tensioner ensuring that the lug (arrowed) engages with the hole in the cylinder block

ensuring that the lug on the tensioner body engages with the hole in the cylinder block **(see illustration)**. Refit the retaining bolt and tighten the bolt to the specified torque.

56 Locate the engine bracket in position, refit the four retaining bolts and tighten to the specified torque.

57 Refit the right-hand engine mounting and secure the mounting to the body and engine bracket with the four retaining bolts. Tighten the bolts to the specified torque. Remove the hoist or jack used to support the engine.

58 Thoroughly clean the inside and outside of the sump ensuring that all traces of old sealant are removed from the mating face. Also clean the cylinder block baseplate mating face to remove all traces of old sealant.

59 Apply a 2 mm bead of Loctite 5900 to the sump mating face, ensuring the sealant bead runs around the inside of the bolt holes **(see illustration)**. Position the sump on the cylinder block baseplate, then refit the thirteen bolts and two nuts. Progressively tighten the bolts/nuts to the specified torque. Reconnect the oil level sensor wiring connector.

60 Refit the sump reinforcement bracket to the cylinder block baseplate and transmission bellhousing, and secure with the five bolts, tightened to the specified torque.

61 Using a new gasket, position the catalytic converter on the turbocharger. Insert the three retaining bolts, with a new locking plate and tighten the bolts to the specified torque. Bend over the tabs of the locking plate to retain the bolts.

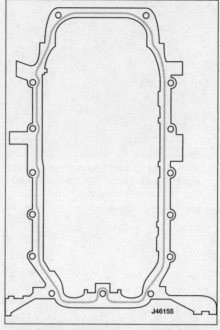

6.59 Apply a bead of sealant to the sump mating face, ensuring the bead runs around the inside of the bolt holes

62 From under the car, refit the bolt securing the catalytic converter support bracket to the sump reinforcement bracket and tighten the bolt to the specified torque.

63 Place a new rubber seal on the oil filter housing, ensuring the seal is fully engaged with the housing grooves **(see illustration)**.

64 Position the oil filter housing on the cylinder block and fit the lower left retaining bolt finger-tight. Place the heat shield support bracket in position and fit the remaining three retaining bolts. Tighten the four bolts to the specified torque.

65 Connect the radiator bottom hose to the outlet at the base of the oil filter housing and secure with the retaining clip.

66 Using a new copper washer on each side of the banjo union, refit the turbocharger oil supply pipe and screw in the banjo union bolt. Tighten the bolt to the specified torque.

67 Locate a new gasket over the heat exchanger coolant pipe and bend over the tabs of the gasket to retain it on the flange **(see illustration)**.

68 Engage the coolant pipe with the hose on the thermostat housing, then position the pipe flange on the heat exchanger. Refit the two bolts and tighten them to the specified torque. At the other end of the pipe, tighten the hose retaining clip, refit and tighten the pipe support bracket bolt and secure the wiring harness with the retaining clip.

69 Place the heat shield over the oil filter, refit the two lower bolts and tighten them finger-tight. Refit the two upper nuts securing the heat shield(s), then tighten the engine lifting bracket bolt, the manifold heat shield upper nuts and the oil filter heat shield lower bolts securely.

70 Refit the exhaust system components with reference to Chapter 4B.

71 Refit the crankshaft pulley as described in Section 5.

72 Remove the camshaft and crankshaft locking tools. Turn the engine through two complete revolutions, then check that the locking tools can be reinserted. Remove the locking tools.

73 Thoroughly clean the threads of the closure bolt and apply suitable thread-locking compound. Screw the bolt into the camshaft housing and tighten to the specified torque.

74 Reconnect the fuel injector wiring connectors and secure with the locking catches.

75 Refit the three bolts securing the plastic wiring harness guide to the top of the camshaft housing.

76 Reconnect the camshaft position sensor wiring connector.

77 Reconnect the glow plug wiring connectors.

78 Refit the air cleaner assembly, and the turbocharger charge air pipe and charge air hose as described in Chapter 4B.

79 Refill the engine with fresh oil with reference to Chapter 1B.

80 Refill the cooling system as described in Chapter 1B, then reconnect the battery negative terminal.

81 Refit the wheel arch liner and roadwheel, then lower the car to the ground and tighten the wheel bolts to the specified torque.

6.63 Place a new rubber seal on the oil filter housing, ensuring it fully engages with the housing grooves

6.67 Locate a new gasket over the heat exchanger coolant pipe and bend over the tabs to retain it on the flange

7.2 Push the timing chain tensioner plunger back into its bore and retain it using a suitable drill bit (arrowed)

7.3 Undo the two bolts and remove the tensioner from the cylinder head

7.4a Undo the lower pivot bolt . . .

7.4b . . . and remove the chain tensioner rail

7.5 Slip the chain off the camshaft sprocket and remove it together with the crankshaft sprocket

TOOL TiP

To make a sprocket holding tool, obtain two lengths of steel strip about 6 mm thick by about 30 mm wide or similar, one 600 mm long, the other 200 mm long (all dimensions are approximate). Bolt the two strips together to form a forked end, leaving the bolt slack so that the shorter strip can pivot freely. At the other end of each 'prong' of the fork, drill a suitable hole and fit a nut and bolt. The bolts can be engaged with the holes in the sprocket to hold the sprocket stationary.

7 Timing chain, sprockets, tensioner and guide rails – removal and refitting

Removal

1 Remove the timing cover as described in Section 6.

2 Push the timing chain tensioner plunger back into its bore and insert a suitable drill bit or similar tool to retain it in the released position **(see illustration)**.

3 Undo the two retaining bolts and remove the tensioner from the cylinder head **(see illustration)**.

4 Undo the lower pivot bolt and remove the chain tensioner rail **(see illustrations)**.

5 Slide the crankshaft sprocket off the end of the crankshaft. Slip the chain off the camshaft

sprocket and remove it together with the crankshaft sprocket **(see illustration)**.

6 It will now be necessary to hold the camshaft sprocket to enable the retaining bolt to be removed. Vauxhall/Opel special tools KM-956-1 and KM-6347 are available for this purpose, however, a home-made tool can easily be fabricated **(see Tool Tip)**.

7 Using the holding tool to prevent rotation of the camshaft, slacken the sprocket retaining bolt. Remove the holding tool, unscrew the retaining bolt and remove the sprocket **(see illustrations)**.

8 Undo the two retaining bolts and remove the timing chain guide rail **(see illustration)**.

9 Inspect the timing chain, sprockets, tensioner rail and guide rail for any sign of wear or deformation, and renew any suspect components as necessary.

10 Push the timing chain tensioner plunger

into the tensioner body and remove the locking drill bit. Check that the tensioner plunger is free to move in out of the tensioner body with no trace of binding. If any binding or sticking of the plunger is felt, renew the tensioner assembly. On completion of the check, or if a new tensioner is being fitted, Compress the plunger and refit the locking drill bit.

7.7a Using the holding tool to prevent rotation, slacken the camshaft sprocket retaining bolt . . .

7.7b . . . then unscrew the bolt and remove the sprocket

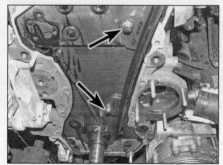

7.8 Undo the two retaining bolts (arrowed) and remove the timing chain guide rail

8.13a Place a new gasket on the cylinder head . . .

Refitting

11 Locate the timing chain guide rail in position, refit the two retaining bolts and tighten the bolts to the specified torque.

12 Fit the sprocket to the camshaft and screw in the retaining bolt. Using the method employed on removal to hold the sprocket, tighten the retaining bolt to the specified torque.

13 Thoroughly clean the crankshaft and crankshaft sprocket, ensuring that there is no oil or grease on the contact faces.

14 Place the sprocket in the timing chain, then engage the chain over the camshaft sprocket. Slide the crankshaft sprocket over the end of the crankshaft.

15 Refit the timing chain tensioner rail, screw in the lower pivot bolt and tighten the bolt to the specified torque.

16 Refit the timing chain tensioner and tighten the two retaining bolts to the specified torque. Depress the tensioner plunger, withdraw the locking drill bit and release the plunger.

17 Refit the timing cover as described in Section 6.

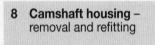

8 Camshaft housing –
removal and refitting

Removal

1 Remove the battery and battery tray as described in Chapter 5A.

2 Remove the braking system vacuum pump as described in Chapter 9.

8.17 Camshaft housing retaining bolt tightening sequence

3 Refer to the procedures contained in Chapter 4B, and remove the following components:
a) High-pressure fuel pump.
b) Fuel rail.
c) Fuel injectors.

4 Disconnect the engine wiring harness at the following connectors, if not already done:
a) Crankshaft speed/position sensor.
b) Manifold pressure sensor.
c) EGR valve.
d) Starter/alternator.
e) Injection system electronic control unit.

5 Move the disconnected wiring harness to one side.

6 Remove the timing cover as described in Section 6.

7 Remove the timing chain, sprockets and tensioner as described in Section 7.

8 Undo the three bolts and remove the engine lifting bracket and fuel rail mounting bracket from the camshaft housing.

9 Undo the sixteen bolts, and two stud bolts, securing the camshaft housing to the cylinder head.

10 Lift the camshaft housing off the cylinder head and recover the gasket.

11 Thoroughly clean the mating faces of the cylinder head and camshaft housing and obtain a new gasket for refitting.

Refitting

12 Check that all the hydraulic tappets and rocker arms are correctly positioned in the cylinder head and none have been disturbed.

13 Place a new gasket on the cylinder head, then locate the camshaft housing in position. Refit the two stud bolts to align the assembly but only tighten them finger-tight at this stage **(see illustrations)**.

14 Using a straight-edge, align the front face of the camshaft housing with the front face of the cylinder head. Lightly tighten the two stud bolts to retain the housing and maintain the alignment.

15 Refit the sixteen camshaft housing retaining bolts, noting that the longer bolt is fitted at the flywheel end of the housing between the high-pressure fuel pump and vacuum pump locations. Progressively screw in the retaining bolts to gradually draw the housing down and into contact with the cylinder head.

16 Using the straight-edge, check the alignment of the camshaft housing and cylinder head once more and correct if necessary.

8.13b . . . locate the camshaft housing in position . . .

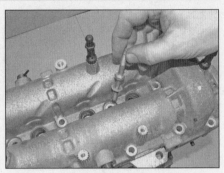

8.13c . . . then refit the two stud bolts to align the assembly

17 Working in sequence, tighten the camshaft housing retaining bolts to the specified torque **(see illustration)**. Note that the torque setting for the two stud bolts is different from the other bolts.

18 Refit the engine lifting bracket and fuel rail mounting bracket to the camshaft housing. Refit the three retaining bolts and tighten to the specified torque.

19 Refit the timing chain, sprockets and tensioner as described in Section 7.

20 Refit the timing cover as described in Section 6.

21 Reconnect the engine wiring harness to the connectors listed in paragraph 4.

22 Refit the fuel injectors, fuel rail and high-pressure fuel pump as described in Chapter 4B.

23 Refit the braking system vacuum pump as described in Chapter 9.

24 Refit the battery tray and battery as described in Chapter 5A.

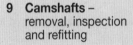

9 Camshafts –
removal, inspection and refitting

Note: An additional camshaft locking tool (two in total) will be required for this operation (see Section 3).

Removal

1 Carry out the operations described in Section 8, paragraphs 1 to 6.

2 Before removing the camshaft housing completely, the retaining bolts for the camshaft drivegears and sprocket should be slackened as follows.

3 It will be necessary to hold the camshaft sprocket to enable the drivegear and sprocket retaining bolts to be slackened. Vauxhall/Opel special tools KM-956-1 and KM-6347 are available for this purpose, however, a home-made tool can easily be fabricated **(see Tool Tip in Section 7)**.

4 Working through the vacuum pump aperture, and using the holding tool to prevent rotation of the camshaft, slacken the inlet camshaft drivegear retaining bolt. Working through the high-pressure fuel pump aperture, slacken the exhaust camshaft drivegear retaining bolt in the same way.

9.9a Unscrew the previously-slackened retaining bolt . . .

9.9b . . . lift off the drivegear . . .

9.9c . . . and carefully withdraw the inlet camshaft from the camshaft housing

5 Again, using the holding tool, slacken the camshaft sprocket retaining bolt.

6 Continue with the camshaft housing removal procedure as described in Section 8, paragraphs 7 to 11.

7 With the camshaft housing removed, unscrew the retaining bolt and withdraw the camshaft position sensor from the top of the housing.

8 Turn the housing over and remove the camshaft locking tool.

9 Unscrew the previously-slackened retaining bolt, lift off the drivegear and carefully withdraw the inlet camshaft from the camshaft housing **(see illustrations)**. Using quick-drying paint, correction fluid or a label, suitably mark the sprocket and camshaft to identify them as the inlet components.

10 At the exhaust camshaft, unscrew the previously-slackened retaining bolt and lift off the camshaft sprocket. Unscrew the retaining bolt, lift off the drivegear and carefully withdraw the exhaust camshaft from the camshaft housing **(see illustrations)**. Using quick-drying paint, correction fluid or a label, suitably mark the sprocket and camshaft to identify them as the exhaust components.

Inspection

11 Examine the camshaft bearing surfaces and cam lobes for signs of wear ridges and scoring. Renew the camshaft if any of these conditions are apparent. Examine the condition of the bearing surfaces in the camshaft housing. If the any wear or scoring is evident, the camshaft housing will need to be renewed.

12 If either camshaft is being renewed, it will be necessary to renew all the rocker arms and

tappets for that particular camshaft also (see Section 10).

13 Check the condition of the camshaft drivegears and sprocket for chipped or damaged teeth, wear ridges and scoring. Renew any components as necessary.

Refitting

14 Prior to refitting, thoroughly clean all components and dry with a lint-free cloth. Ensure that all traces of oil and grease are removed from the contact faces of the drivegears, sprocket and camshafts.

15 Lubricate the exhaust camshaft bearing journals in the camshaft housing and carefully insert the exhaust camshaft. Ensuring that the contact faces are clean and dry, refit the drivegear to the camshaft and insert the retaining bolt. Screw in the bolt two or three turns at this stage.

16 Locate the sprocket on the exhaust

9.10a Unscrew the previously-slackened retaining bolt and lift off the exhaust camshaft sprocket

camshaft with the writing on the sprocket facing away from the camshaft housing. Insert the retaining bolt and screw in the bolt two or three turns at this stage.

17 Lubricate the inlet camshaft bearing journals in the camshaft housing and carefully insert the inlet camshaft. Ensuring that the contact faces are clean and dry, refit the drivegear to the camshaft and insert the retaining bolt. Screw in the bolt two or three turns at this stage.

18 Turn each camshaft to align the timing slot with the valve timing checking hole in the camshaft housing. Insert the camshaft locking tools (either the Vauxhall/Opel tool or the home-made equivalent described in Section 3) ensuring that the tools fully engage with the camshaft slots **(see illustration)**.

19 With the camshafts locked in the timing position, tighten the drivegear retaining bolts and the sprocket retaining bolt to 20 Nm (15 lbf ft). Note that this is only an initial setting to retain the

9.10b Unscrew the retaining bolt . . .

9.10c . . . lift off the drivegear . . .

9.10d . . . and carefully withdraw the exhaust camshaft from the camshaft housing

9.18 Insert the locking tools (arrowed) to lock the camshafts in the timing position

9.23 Hold the sprocket with the tool and tighten the retaining bolt to the specified torque

9.24 While still holding the sprocket with the tool, tighten the drivegear retaining bolt on each camshaft

10.3a Withdraw each rocker arm and hydraulic tappet in turn . . .

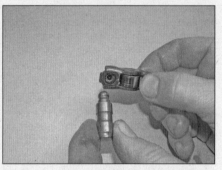

10.3b . . . then unclip the rocker arm from the tappet

components. Final tightening is carried out after the camshaft housing has been refitted to the cylinder head.

20 Refit the camshaft position sensor to the camshaft housing and tighten the retaining bolt securely.

21 Refit the camshaft housing to the cylinder head as described in Section 8, paragraphs 12 to 17.

22 With the camshaft housing installed, final tightening of the drivegear and sprocket retaining bolts can be carried out.

23 Using the method employed on removal to hold the sprocket, tighten the sprocket retaining bolt to the specified torque **(see illustration)**.

24 While still holding the sprocket with the tool, tighten the exhaust camshaft drivegear retaining bolt to the specified torque followed by the inlet camshaft drivegear retaining bolt **(see illustration)**.

25 Remove the locking tool from the inlet camshaft, but leave the exhaust camshaft locking tool in place.

26 Continue with the camshaft housing refitting procedure as described in Section 8, paragraphs 18 to 24.

10 Hydraulic tappets and rocker arms – removal, inspection and refitting

Removal

1 Remove the camshaft housing as described in Section 8.

2 Obtain sixteen small, oil tight clean plastic

containers, and number them inlet 1 to 8 and exhaust 1 to 8; alternatively, divide a larger container into sixteen compartments and number each compartment accordingly.

3 Withdraw each rocker arm and hydraulic tappet in turn, unclip the rocker arm from the tappet, and place them in their respective container **(see illustrations)**. Do not interchange the rocker arms and tappets, or the rate of wear will be much increased. Fill each container with clean engine oil and ensure that the tappet is submerged.

Inspection

4 Examine the rocker arm and hydraulic tappet bearing surfaces for wear ridges and scoring. Renew any rocker arm or tappet on which these conditions are apparent.

5 If any new hydraulic tappets are obtained, they should be immersed in a container of clean engine oil prior to refitting.

11.6 Undo the two bolts (arrowed) and free the oil separator from the inlet manifold

Refitting

6 Liberally oil the cylinder head hydraulic tappet bores and the tappets. Working on one assembly at a time, clip the rocker arm back onto the tappet, then refit the tappet to the cylinder head, ensuring that it is refitted to its original bore. Lay the rocker arm over its respective valve.

7 Refit the remaining tappets and rocker arms in the same way.

8 With all the tappets and rocker arms in place, refit the camshaft housing as described in Section 8.

11 Cylinder head – removal and refitting

Note: *New cylinder head retaining bolts will be required for refitting.*

Removal

1 Remove the camshaft housing as described in Section 8, and the hydraulic tappets and rocker arms as described in Section 10.

2 Remove the turbocharger charge air pipe as described in Chapter 4B.

3 Remove the exhaust gas recirculation (EGR) valve as described in Chapter 4C.

4 Withdraw the engine oil dipstick, then undo the retaining bolt securing the dipstick guide tube to the inlet manifold.

5 Using a small screwdriver, lift up the locking catch and disconnect the manifold pressure sensor wiring connector.

6 Undo the two bolts and free the crankcase ventilation system oil separator from the inlet manifold **(see illustration)**.

7 Working in the **reverse** of the tightening sequence **(see illustration 11.27b)**, progressively slacken the cylinder head bolts by half a turn at a time, until all bolts can be unscrewed by hand. Note that an M12 RIBE socket bit will be required to unscrew the bolts. Remove the cylinder head bolts and recover the washers.

8 Engage the help of an assistant and lift the cylinder head from the cylinder block. Take care as it is a bulky and heavy assembly.

9 Remove the gasket and keep it for identification purposes (see paragraph 16).

10 If the cylinder head is to be dismantled for overhaul, then refer to Part F of this Chapter.

Preparation for refitting

11 The mating faces of the cylinder head and cylinder block/crankcase must be perfectly clean before refitting the head. Use a hard plastic or wood scraper to remove all traces of gasket and carbon; also clean the piston crowns. Take particular care, as the surfaces are damaged easily. Also, make sure that the carbon is not allowed to enter the oil and water passages – this is particularly important for the lubrication system, as carbon could block the oil supply to any of the engine's components. Using adhesive tape and paper, seal the water, oil and bolt holes in the cylinder block/crankcase. To prevent

carbon entering the gap between the pistons and bores, smear a little grease in the gap. After cleaning each piston, use a small brush to remove all traces of grease and carbon from the gap, then wipe away the remainder with a clean rag. Clean all the pistons in the same way.

12 Check the mating surfaces of the cylinder block/crankcase and the cylinder head for nicks, deep scratches and other damage. If slight, they may be removed carefully with a file, but if excessive, machining may be the only alternative to renewal.

13 Ensure that the cylinder head bolt holes in the crankcase are clean and free of oil. Syringe or soak up any oil left in the bolt holes. This is most important in order that the correct bolt tightening torque can be applied and to prevent the possibility of the block being cracked by hydraulic pressure when the bolts are tightened.

14 The cylinder head bolts must be discarded and renewed, regardless of their apparent condition.

15 If warpage of the cylinder head gasket surface is suspected, use a straight-edge to check it for distortion. Refer to Part F of this Chapter if necessary.

16 On this engine, the cylinder head-to-piston clearance is controlled by fitting different thickness head gaskets. The gasket thickness can be determined by looking at the left-hand front corner of the gasket and checking on the number of holes **(see illustration)**.

Holes in gasket	Gasket thickness
No holes	0.67 to 0.77 mm
One hole	0.77 to 0.87 mm
Two holes	0.87 to 0.97 mm

The correct thickness of gasket required is selected by measuring the piston protrusions as follows.

17 Remove the crankshaft locking tool from the base of the bellhousing and temporarily refit the crankshaft pulley retaining bolt to enable the crankshaft to be turned.

18 Mount a dial test indicator securely on the block so that its pointer can be easily pivoted between the piston crown and block mating surface. Turn the crankshaft to bring No 1 piston roughly to the TDC position. Move the dial test indicator probe over and in contact with No 1 piston. Turn the crankshaft back-and-forth slightly until the highest reading is shown on the gauge, indicating that the piston is at TDC.

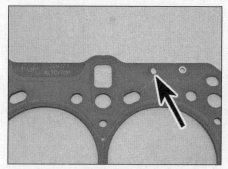

11.16 Cylinder head gasket thickness identification hole (arrowed)

19 Zero the dial test indicator on the gasket surface of the cylinder block then carefully move the indicator over No 1 piston. Measure its protrusion at the highest point between the valve cut-outs, and then again at its highest point between the valve cut-outs at 90° to the first measurement **(see illustration)**. Repeat this procedure with No 4 piston.

20 Rotate the crankshaft half a turn (180°) to bring No 2 and 3 pistons to TDC. Ensure the crankshaft is accurately positioned then measure the protrusions of No 2 and 3 pistons at the specified points. Once all pistons have been measured, rotate the crankshaft to position all the pistons at their mid-stroke and refit the crankshaft locking tool. If the tool will not engage the hole in the flywheel, turn the crankshaft one complete turn and try again.

21 Select the correct thickness of head gasket required by determining the largest amount of piston protrusion, and using the following table.

Piston protrusion measurement	Gasket thickness required
0.028 to 0.127 mm	0.67 to 0.77 mm (no holes)
0.128 to 0.227 mm	0.77 to 0.87 mm (one hole)
0.228 to 0.327 mm	0.87 to 0.97 mm (two holes)

Refitting

22 Wipe clean the mating surfaces of the cylinder head and cylinder block/crankcase. Place the new gasket in position with the words ALTO/TOP uppermost.

23 If not already done, rotate the crankshaft to position all the pistons at their mid-stroke

11.19 Using a dial test indicator to measure piston protrusion

11.26 Using a straight-edge, align the front face of the cylinder head with the front face of the cylinder block

and refit the crankshaft locking tool. If the tool will not engage the hole in the flywheel, turn the crankshaft one complete turn and try again. Once the tool is in place, remove the crankshaft pulley hub retaining bolt.

24 With the aid of an assistant, carefully refit the cylinder head assembly to the block, aligning it with the locating dowels.

25 Apply a thin film of engine oil to the bolt threads and the underside of the bolt heads. Carefully enter each new cylinder head bolt into its relevant hole (*do not drop them in*). Screw all bolts in, by hand only, until finger-tight.

26 Using a straight-edge, align the front face of the cylinder head with the front face of the cylinder block **(see illustration)**. Lightly tighten the cylinder head bolts to retain the head and maintain the alignment.

27 Working progressively in sequence, tighten the cylinder head bolts to their Stage 1 torque setting, using a torque wrench and suitable socket **(see illustrations)**.

11.27a Working in sequence, tighten the cylinder head bolts to their Stage 1 torque, using a torque wrench

11.27b Cylinder head bolt tightening sequence

28 Once all bolts have been tightened to the Stage 1 torque, working again in the same sequence, go around and tighten all bolts through the specified Stage 2 angle, then through the specified Stage 3 angle using an angle-measuring gauge **(see illustration)**.

29 Refit the crankcase ventilation system oil separator to the inlet manifold and secure with the two bolts

30 Reconnect the manifold pressure sensor wiring connector.

31 Refit the dipstick guide tube to the inlet manifold, refit and tighten the retaining bolt, then insert the dipstick.

32 Refit the exhaust gas recirculation (EGR) valve as described in Chapter 4C.

33 Refit the turbocharger charge air pipe as described in Chapter 4B.

34 Refit the hydraulic tappets and rocker arms as described in Section 10 and the camshaft housing as described in Section 8.

12 Sump –
removal and refitting

Removal

1 Disconnect the battery negative terminal (refer to *Disconnecting the battery* in the Reference Chapter).

2 Apply the handbrake, then jack up the front of the vehicle and support it on axle stands (see *Jacking and vehicle support*).

3 Drain the engine oil as described in Chapter 1B, then fit a new sealing ring and refit

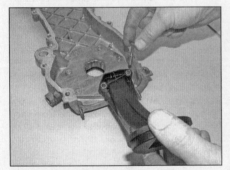

13.2a Remove the oil pick-up pipe from the oil pump cover . . .

13.3 Remove the screws and withdraw the oil pump cover from the rear of the timing cover

11.28 Tighten the bolts through the Stage 2 and Stage 3 angle using an angle-measuring gauge

the drain plug, tightening it to the specified torque. It is also recommended that the oil filter is renewed at the same time.

4 Referring to the relevant procedures contained in Chapter 4B, remove the catalytic converter from the turbocharger.

5 Undo the five bolts securing the sump reinforcement bracket to the cylinder block baseplate and transmission bellhousing, and remove the bracket **(see illustration 6.26)**. Note the locations of the different length bolts to aid refitting.

6 Disconnect the oil level sensor wiring connector at the rear of the sump **(see illustration 6.27)**.

7 Undo the thirteen bolts and two nuts securing the sump to the cylinder block baseplate and timing cover. Using a wide-bladed scraper or similar tool inserted between the sump and baseplate, carefully

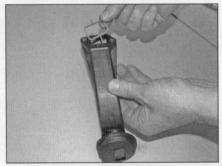

13.4a Remove the oil pump inner rotor . . .

break the joint, then remove the sump from under the car.

Refitting

8 Thoroughly clean the inside and outside of the sump ensuring that all traces of old sealant are removed from the mating face. Also clean the cylinder block baseplate mating face to remove all traces of old sealant.

9 Apply a 2 mm bead of Loctite 5900 to the sump mating face, ensuring the sealant bead runs around the inside of the bolt holes **(see illustration 6.59)**. Position the sump on the cylinder block baseplate, then refit the thirteen bolts and two nuts. Progressively tighten the bolts/nuts to the specified torque. Reconnect the oil level sensor wiring connector.

10 Refit the sump reinforcement bracket to the cylinder block baseplate and transmission bellhousing, and secure with the five bolts, tightened to the specified torque.

11 Refit the catalytic converter to the turbocharger as described in the relevant procedures contained in Chapter 4B.

12 Lower the vehicle to the ground then fill the engine with fresh oil, with reference to Chapter 1B.

13 Refill the cooling system as described in Chapter 1B, then reconnect the battery negative terminal.

13 Oil pump –
removal, inspection and refitting

Removal

1 Remove the timing cover as described in Section 6.

2 Undo the two retaining bolts and remove the oil pick-up pipe from the oil pump cover on the rear of the timing cover. Remove the rubber seal from the pick-up pipe, noting that a new seal will be required for refitting **(see illustrations)**.

3 Remove the securing screws and withdraw the oil pump cover from the rear of the timing cover **(see illustration)**.

4 Remove the inner and outer rotor from the timing cover and wipe them clean. Also clean the rotor location in the timing cover **(see illustrations)**.

13.2b . . . then remove the rubber seal from the pick-up pipe

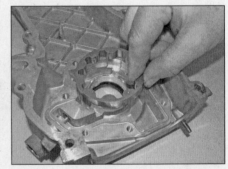

13.4b . . . and outer rotor from the timing cover

5 The oil pressure relief valve components can also be removed from the timing cover by unscrewing the cap. Withdraw the cap, the spring and the plunger **(see illustrations)**.

Inspection

6 Check for any signs of scoring, pitting, scuffing or general wear on the rotors or their location in the timing cover. Renew any components as necessary. If the pump components are satisfactory, check the rotor clearances as follows.

7 Locate the inner and outer rotor back in the timing cover. Check the clearance between the end faces of the gears and the housing (endfloat) using a straight-edge and a feeler gauge **(see illustration)**.

8 Check the outer rotor-to-body clearance using a feeler gauge **(see illustration)**.

9 If the clearances are outside the specified limits, renew the components as necessary.

10 Examine the pressure relief valve spring and plunger, and renew if any sign of damage or wear is evident.

11 Ensure that the rotor location in the interior of the timing cover is scrupulously clean before commencing reassembly.

Refitting

12 Thoroughly clean the pressure relief valve components, and lubricate them with clean engine oil before refitting. Insert the plunger and spring, then apply thread-locking compound to the cap threads and refit the cap. Tighten the cap securely.

13 Ensure that the rotors are clean, then lubricate them with clean engine oil. Locate the inner and outer rotor back in the timing cover, with the dot marks aligned and facing away from the timing cover **(see illustration)**.

14 Ensure that the mating faces of the rear cover and the pump housing are clean, then refit the rear cover. Refit and tighten the securing screws securely.

15 Fit a new rubber seal to the oil pick-up pipe and locate the pipe on the oil pump cover. Refit the two retaining bolts and tighten securely.

16 Refit the timing cover as described in Section 6.

14 Crankshaft oil seals – renewal

Timing cover end oil seal

Note 1: *The design of the engine is such, that once the crankshaft pulley hub bolt is undone the valve timing will be lost unless suitable locking tools are used to retain the camshafts and crankshaft in the timing position. Refer to the information contained in Section 3 for further details and obtain the tools described.*

Note 2: *A new crankshaft pulley hub retaining bolt will be required for refitting.*

1 Remove the crankshaft pulley as described in Section 5.

2 Disconnect the wiring connector at the

13.5a Unscrew the oil pressure relief valve cap . . .

13.5b . . . then withdraw the spring . . .

13.5c . . . and the plunger

13.7 Checking the oil pump rotor endfloat

camshaft position sensor on the top of the camshaft housing.

3 Disconnect the wiring connectors at the four glow plugs.

4 Unscrew the three bolts securing the plastic wiring harness guide to the top of the camshaft housing.

5 Release the locking catches securing the wiring connectors to the four injectors, then disconnect the injector wiring, while at the same time moving the wiring harness guide forward **(see illustration 3.8)**.

6 Unscrew the closure bolt from the valve timing checking hole on the exhaust camshaft side of the camshaft housing **(see illustration 4.9)**.

7 If the Vauxhall/Opel camshaft locking tool or similar alternative is available (see Section 3), screw the tool into the valve timing checking hole. Ensure that the mark on the tool plunger is facing upwards. Using a socket or spanner

on the crankshaft pulley hub bolt, turn the crankshaft in the normal direction of rotation (clockwise as viewed from the right-hand side of the car) until the spring-loaded plunger of the locking tool slides into engagement with the slot on the camshaft. There will be an audible click from the tool when this happens, and the plunger will be seen to move in, towards the camshaft.

8 If the home-made locking tool described in Section 3 is being used, insert a screwdriver through the valve timing checking hole on the front of the camshaft housing, and into contact with the exhaust camshaft. Using a socket or spanner on the crankshaft pulley hub bolt, turn the crankshaft in the normal direction of rotation (clockwise as viewed from the right-hand side of the car) until the screwdriver can be felt to engage with the slot in the camshaft. Screw the tool into the camshaft housing until resistance is felt, then turn the crankshaft slightly until the

13.8 Checking the oil pump outer rotor-to-body clearance

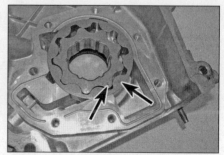

13.13 Locate the rotors in the timing cover with the dot marks (arrowed) aligned and facing away from the timing cover

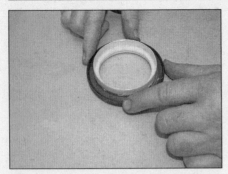

14.29 Fit the oil seal to the fitting tool, so that the seal lip is spread open toward the crankshaft side

camshaft slot is correctly aligned, and the tool can be screwed fully in **(see illustrations 4.12a and 4.12b)**.

9 Once the camshaft is locked in position, insert the Vauxhall/Opel crankshaft locking tool or suitable alternative (see Section 3) into the timing hole at the base of the transmission bellhousing and into engagement with the flywheel **(see illustrations 4.14a, 4.14b and 4.14c)**. It may be necessary to turn the crankshaft very slightly one way or the other (within the limits of any slack afforded by the timing chain/tensioner) to allow the tool to fully engage.

10 It will now be necessary to hold the crankshaft pulley hub to enable the retaining bolt to be removed. Vauxhall/Opel special tool KM-662-C is available for this purpose, however, a home-made tool can easily be fabricated **(see Tool Tip in Section 4)**.

11 Using the Vauxhall/Opel tool or the home-made alternative, hold the pulley hub stationary and unscrew the retaining bolt. **Note:** *The pulley hub retaining bolt has a left-hand thread and is unscrewed by turning it clockwise.*

12 Withdraw the pulley hub from the crankshaft.

13 Carefully prise out the old crankshaft oil seal with a screwdriver or similar hooked tool. Clean the oil seal seat with a wooden or plastic scraper.

14 Tap the new oil seal into position until it is flush with the outer face of the timing cover, using a suitable socket or tube, or a wooden block.

15 Thoroughly clean the crankshaft pulley hub, ensuring that the timing chain sprocket contact face is free from oil or grease.

16 Refit the pulley hub to the crankshaft, then fit the new retaining bolt. Using the method employed on removal to hold the pulley hub stationary, tighten the retaining bolt to the specified torque.

17 Refit the crankshaft pulley to the pulley hub. Refit the pulley retaining bolts, tightening them to the specified torque.

18 Remove the camshaft and crankshaft locking tools.

19 Thoroughly clean the threads of the closure bolt and apply suitable thread-locking compound. Screw the bolt into the camshaft housing and tighten to the specified torque.

20 Reconnect the fuel injector wiring connectors and secure with the locking catches.

21 Reconnect the wiring connector at the camshaft position sensor.

22 Reconnect the wiring connectors at the four glow plugs.

23 Refit the three bolts securing the plastic wiring harness guide to the top of the camshaft housing.

24 Refit the auxiliary drivebelt as described in Chapter 1B using the mark made prior to removal to ensure the belt is fitted the correct way around.

25 Refit the wheel arch liner and roadwheel, then lower the car to the ground and tighten the wheel bolts to the specified torque.

Transmission end oil seal

Note: *Vauxhall/Opel special tools EN-4677-10 and EN-4677-20 or a suitable equivalent oil seal fitting tool will be required for this operation.*

26 Remove the flywheel as described in Section 16.

27 Carefully prise out the old seal from its location using a screwdriver or similar hooked tool.

28 Clean the oil seal seat with a wooden or plastic scraper.

29 Fit the new seal to the Vauxhall/Opel tool, or equivalent fitting tool, so that the seal lip is spread open toward the crankshaft side **(see illustration)**.

30 Position the seal, together with the fitting

tool over the end of the crankshaft, then tap the seal into position using a suitable socket or tube, or a wooden block, until it is flush with the outer faces of the cylinder block and baseplate **(see illustrations)**.

31 Once the seal is in position, remove the fitting tool **(see illustration)**.

32 Refit the flywheel as described in Section 16.

15 Oil cooler/heat exchanger – removal and refitting

Removal

1 Disconnect the battery negative terminal (refer to *Disconnecting the battery* in the Reference Chapter).

2 Referring to the procedures contained in Chapter 4B, separate the exhaust system front section from the catalytic converter.

3 Drain the cooling system as described in Chapter 1B.

4 Remove the turbocharger charge air hose as described in Chapter 4B.

5 Undo the upper nut and two lower bolts and remove the oil filter heat shield **(see illustration 6.13)**.

6 Undo the two bolts securing the coolant pipe to the oil filter housing **(see illustration 6.14)**. Recover the gasket noting that a new one will be required for refitting.

7 Unscrew the banjo union bolt and release the turbocharger oil supply pipe from the oil filter housing **(see illustration 6.15)**. Recover the two copper washers from the banjo union, and suitable cover the end of the pipe to prevent dirt entry. Note that new copper washers will be required for refitting.

8 Slacken the retaining clip and disconnect the radiator bottom hose from the outlet at the base of the oil filter housing.

9 Undo the three bolts securing the heat shield support bracket to the heat exchanger on the oil filter housing **(see illustration 6.17)**.

10 Undo the remaining bolt and remove the oil filter housing and heat exchanger assembly from the cylinder block. Recover the rubber seal from the rear of the housing. Note that a new seal will be required for refitting.

11 Undo the three retaining bolts and withdraw the heat exchanger from the oil filter

14.30a Position the seal, together with the fitting tool over the end of the crankshaft . . .

14.30b . . . then tap the seal into position using a suitable wooden block or similar

14.31 Once the seal is in position, remove the fitting tool

housing **(see illustration)**. Recover the four sealing rings, noting that new sealing rings will be required for refitting.

Refitting

12 Thoroughly clean the heat exchanger and oil filter housing, then fit the four new sealing rings to the filter housing.
13 Place the heat exchanger in position and secure with the three retaining bolts, securely tightened.
14 Place a new rubber seal on the oil filter housing, ensuring the seal is fully engaged with the housing grooves **(see illustration 6.63)**.
15 Position the oil filter housing on the cylinder block and fit the lower left retaining bolt finger-tight. Place the heat shield support bracket in position and fit the remaining three retaining bolts. Tighten the four bolts to the specified torque.
16 Connect the radiator bottom hose to the outlet at the base of the oil filter housing and secure with the retaining clip.
17 Using a new copper washer on each side of the banjo union, refit the turbocharger oil supply pipe and screw in the banjo union bolt. Tighten the bolt to the specified torque.
18 Locate a new gasket over the coolant pipe and bend over the tabs of the gasket to retain it on the flange.
19 Position the pipe flange on the oil filter housing. Refit the two bolts and tighten them to the specified torque.
20 Place the heat shield over the oil filter and secure with the two lower bolts and upper nut.
21 Refit the turbocharger charge air hose as described in Chapter 4B.
22 Refit the exhaust system components with reference to Chapter 4B.
23 Lower the vehicle to the ground, then reconnect the battery negative terminal.
24 Refill the cooling system as described in Chapter 1B.

16 Flywheel –
removal, inspection and refitting

Note: *New flywheel retaining bolts will be required on refitting.*

Removal

1 Remove the transmission as described in Chapter 7A, then remove the clutch assembly as described in Chapter 6.
2 Prevent the flywheel from turning by inserting one of the bellhousing-to-engine retaining bolts. Rest a large screwdriver against the bolt with its end in contact with the flywheel ring gear teeth.
3 Slacken and remove the retaining bolts and remove the flywheel **(see illustration)**. Do not drop it, as it is very heavy.

Inspection

4 Examine the flywheel for wear or chipping

of the ring gear teeth. Renewal of the ring gear is possible but is not a task for the home mechanic; renewal requires the new ring gear to be heated (up to 180° to 230°C) to allow it to be fitted.
5 Examine the flywheel for scoring of the clutch face. If the clutch face is scored, the flywheel may be surface-ground, but renewal is preferable.
6 If there is any doubt about the condition of the flywheel, seek the advice of a Vauxhall/ Opel dealer or engine reconditioning specialist. They will be able to advise if it is possible to recondition it or whether renewal is necessary.

Refitting

7 Clean the mating surfaces of the flywheel and crankshaft.
8 Apply a drop of locking compound to the threads of each of the new flywheel retaining bolts (unless they are already pre-coated) then refit the flywheel and install the new bolts.
9 Lock the flywheel using the method employed on removal then, working in a diagonal sequence, evenly and progressively tighten the retaining bolts to the specified torque setting.
10 Refit the clutch as described in Chapter 6, then refit the transmission as described in Chapter 7A.

17 Engine/transmission mountings –
inspection and renewal

Inspection

1 To improve access, firmly apply the handbrake, then jack up the front of the vehicle and support it on axle stands (see *Jacking and vehicle support*).
2 Check the mounting blocks (rubbers) to see if they are cracked, hardened or separated from the metal at any point. Renew the mounting block if any such damage or deterioration is evident.
3 Check that all the mounting securing nuts and bolts are securely tightened, using a torque wrench to check if possible.
4 Using a large screwdriver, or a similar tool, check for wear in the mounting blocks by

15.11 Undo the three bolts (arrowed) and withdraw the heat exchanger from the oil filter housing

carefully levering against them to check for free play. Where this is not possible, enlist the aid of an assistant to move the engine/gearbox unit back-and-forth, and from side-to-side, while you observe the mountings. While some free play is to be expected, even from new components, excessive wear should be obvious. If excessive free play is found, check first to see that the securing nuts and bolts are correctly tightened, then renew any worn components as described in the following paragraphs.

Renewal

Note: *Before slackening any of the engine mounting bolts/nuts, the relative positions of the mountings to their various brackets should be marked to ensure correct alignment upon refitting.*

Right-hand mounting

5 Apply the handbrake, then jack up the front of the vehicle and support it on axle stands (see *Jacking and vehicle support*).
6 Remove the air cleaner assembly as described in Chapter 4B.
7 Attach a suitable hoist and lifting tackle to the engine lifting brackets on the cylinder head, and support the weight of the engine.
8 Mark the position of the four mounting bracket bolts, then undo the two bolts securing the mounting to the body and the two bolts securing the mounting to the engine bracket **(see illustration)**. Remove the mounting.
9 If necessary, undo the four bolts securing the engine bracket to the cylinder block and cylinder head and remove the engine bracket **(see illustration 6.31)**.

16.3 Flywheel retaining bolts (arrowed)

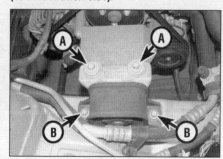
17.8 Right-hand engine mounting-to-engine bracket bolts (A) and mounting-to-body bolts (B)

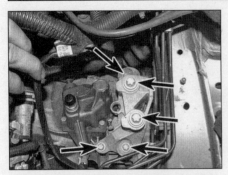

17.16 Left-hand engine mounting bracket and transmission bracket bolts (arrowed)

17.21 Front engine mounting/torque link

17.26 Extract the retaining spring clip (arrowed) and disconnect the gearchange linkage from the shift guide bracket

17.27 Rear engine mounting/torque link retaining bolt (arrowed)

10 If removed, refit the engine mounting bracket and tighten the bolts to the specified torque.

11 Place the engine mounting in position and refit the four retaining bolts. Align the mounting in its original position, then tighten the bolts to the specified torque.

12 Remove the hoist, then refit the air cleaner as described in Chapter 4B.

13 On completion, lower the vehicle to the ground.

Left-hand mounting

14 Remove the battery and battery tray as described in Chapter 5A.

15 Support the weight of the transmission using a trolley jack with a block of wood placed on its head.

16 Unscrew the two bolts securing the mounting bracket to the transmission bracket, and the three bolts securing the transmission bracket to the transmission **(see illustration)**.

17 Undo the four bolts securing the mounting to the body, slightly lower the engine, then remove the mounting assembly from the car.

18 Refitting is a reversal of removal. Ensure all bolts are tightened to their specified torques.

Front mounting/torque link

19 Firmly apply the handbrake, then jack up the front of the car and support it securely on axle stands (see *Jacking and vehicle support*).

20 Support the weight of the engine/transmission using a trolley jack with a block of wood placed on its head.

21 Slacken and remove the nut and washer securing the mounting to the subframe, then withdraw the bolt **(see illustration)**.

22 Undo the two bolts securing the mounting bracket to the transmission, then manoeuvre the mounting and bracket out of position.

23 Refitting is a reversal of removal. Ensure all bolts/nuts are tightened to their specified torques.

Rear mounting/torque link

24 Firmly apply the handbrake, then jack up the front of the car and support it securely on axle stands (see *Jacking and vehicle support*).

25 Support the weight of the engine/transmission using a trolley jack with a block of wood placed on its head. Position the jack underneath the transmission and raise the transmission slightly to remove all load from the rear mounting.

26 Extract the retaining spring clip and disconnect the gearchange linkage from the shift guide bracket **(see illustration)**. Move the shift guide to one side and remove the rubber damper.

27 Undo the bolt securing the torque link to the subframe, and remove the link **(see illustration)**.

28 Undo the bolts securing the torque link rubber mounting bracket to the transmission and remove the bracket and mounting.

29 Locate the new mounting bracket in position. Insert the bolts and tighten to the specified torque.

30 Refit the torque link to the subframe and mounting, insert the bolts and tighten to the specified torque.

31 On completion, reconnect the gearchange linkage and lower the vehicle to the ground.

Chapter 2 Part E:
1.7 litre diesel engine in-car repair procedures

Contents

Degrees of difficulty

Easy, suitable for novice with little experience 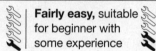 | **Fairly easy,** suitable for beginner with some experience | **Fairly difficult,** suitable for competent DIY mechanic | **Difficult,** suitable for experienced DIY mechanic | **Very difficult,** suitable for expert DIY or professional

Specifications

General

Engine type...	Four-cylinder, in-line, water-cooled. Double overhead belt-driven camshaft, 16 valves
Manufacturer's engine codes:*	
Engines with distributor fuel injection pump	Y17DT
Engines with common rail high-pressure diesel injection	Z17DTH
Bore..	79.0 mm
Stroke..	86.0 mm
Capacity..	1686 cc
Firing order..	1-3-4-2 (No 1 cylinder at timing belt end)
Direction of crankshaft rotation	Clockwise (viewed from timing belt end of engine)
Compression ratio	18.4:1

* For details of engine code location, see 'Vehicle identification' in the Reference Chapter.

Compression pressures

Maximum difference between any two cylinders.................	1.5 bar

Valve clearances

Engine cold:	
Inlet and exhaust	0.4 ± 0.05 mm

Lubrication system

Oil pump type..	Rotor-type, driven by timing belt	
Oil pressure at 80ºC (approximate)	1.3 bars at idle speed	
Oil pump clearances:	**Standard**	**Service limit**
Outer rotor-to-body clearance	0.24 to 0.36 mm	0.40 mm
Inner-to-outer rotor clearance	0.13 to 0.15 mm	0.20 mm
Rotor endfloat..	0.035 to 0.100 mm	0.150 mm

Torque wrench settings

	Nm	lbf ft
Auxiliary belt tensioner to alternator support	50	37
Auxiliary belt guide roller to alternator support	38	28
Baffle plate-to-cylinder block bolts	19	14
Camshaft bearing cap bolts/nuts:		
Y17DT engines:		
M8 nuts	21	15
M10 nuts	43	32
Z17DTH engines:		
Nuts	22	16
Bolts	27	20
Camshaft cover bolts	10	7
Camshaft housing to cylinder head:		
Y17DT engines	22	16
Z17DTH engines:		
M8 bolts	21	15
M10 bolts	27	20
Camshaft sprocket bolt:		
Y17DT engines	64	47
Z17DTH engines:		
Sprocket part number 97320335	64	47
Sprocket part number 98021306	111	82
Charge air pipe to throttle housing and inlet manifold	25	18
Coolant pump pulley bolts	12	9
Coolant pipe to cylinder block	95	70
Connecting rod big-end bearing cap nuts:*		
Stage 1	25	18
Stage 2	Angle-tighten a further 100°	
Stage 3	Angle-tighten a further 15°	
Crankshaft pulley bolts	20	15
Crankshaft oil seal housing bolts	10	7
Crankshaft sprocket bolt	196	145
Cylinder head bolts:*		
Stage 1	40	30
Stage 2	Angle-tighten a further 60°	
Stage 3	Angle-tighten a further 60°	
Engine electronic control unit bracket bolts/nuts:		
Y17DT engines:		
Bolts	25	18
Nuts	10	7
Z17DTH engines	25	18
Engine electronic control unit to bracket:		
Y17DT engines	6	4
Z17DTH engines	10	7
Engine/transmission mountings:		
Front mounting/torque link:		
Mounting-to-transmission bolts	95	70
Mounting to subframe	60	44
Left-hand mounting:		
Mounting-to-body bolts	25	18
Mounting to transmission bracket	55	41
Transmission bracket to transmission	60	44
Rear mounting/torque link:		
Mounting-to-bracket bolt	80	59
Mounting-to-subframe bolt	80	59
Bracket-to-transmission bolts:*		
Stage 1	80	59
Stage 2	Angle-tighten a further 45°	
Right-hand mounting:		
Engine bracket-to-engine bolts	40	30
Mounting-to-body bolts	40	30
Mounting-to-engine bracket bolts:*		
Stage 1	60	44
Stage 2	Angle-tighten a further 30°	
Engine-to-transmission unit bolts:		
M10 bolts	40	30
M12 bolts	60	44
Engine transport shackles	25	18

Torque wrench settings (continued)

	Nm	lbf ft
Flywheel bolts:*		
Stage 1	30	22
Stage 2	Angle-tighten a further 60°	
Stage 3	Angle-tighten a further 15°	
Fuel injector outer seal plate bolts	10	7
Fuel injector upper seal plate bolts:		
Stage 1	10	7
Stage 2	20	15
Fuel pipe union nuts	25	18
High-pressure fuel pump sprocket nut	68	50
Injection pump sprocket nut	68	50
Main bearing cap bolts*	88	65
Oil dipstick guide tube bolts	10	7
Oil cooler/filter housing to cylinder block	25	18
Oil pressure relief valve bolt	30	22
Oil pump cover retaining bolts	10	7
Oil pump sprocket nut:		
Y17DT engines	44	32
Z17DTH engines	60	44
Oil pump pick-up/strainer bolts	19	14
Sump bolts:		
Main casting-to-block bolts	10	7
Sump pan-to-main casting bolts	10	7
Drain plug	78	58
Roadwheel bolts	110	81
Timing belt cover bolts	10	7
Timing belt idler pulley bolt	80	59
Timing belt tensioner pulley bolt	38	28

* Use new fasteners

1 General information

How to use this Chapter

This Part of Chapter 2 describes the repair procedures which can reasonably be carried out on the engine while it remains in the vehicle. If the engine has been removed from the vehicle and is being dismantled as described in Chapter 2F, any preliminary dismantling procedures can be ignored.

Note that, while it may be possible physically to overhaul items such as the piston/connecting rod assemblies while the engine is in the vehicle, such tasks are not usually carried out as separate operations, and usually require the execution of several additional procedures (not to mention the cleaning of components and of oilways); for this reason, all such tasks are classed as major overhaul procedures, and are described in Chapter 2F.

Chapter 2F describes the removal of the engine/transmission unit from the vehicle, and the full overhaul procedures which can then be carried out.

Engine description

The 1.7 litre diesel engine is of the sixteen-valve, in-line four-cylinder, double overhead camshaft (DOHC) type, mounted transversely at the front of the car with the transmission attached to its left-hand side.

The crankshaft runs in five main bearings. Thrustwashers are fitted to No 2 main bearing shell (upper half) to control crankshaft endfloat.

The connecting rods rotate on horizontally-split bearing shells at their big-ends. The pistons are attached to the connecting rods by gudgeon pins, which are a sliding fit in the connecting rod small-end eyes and retained by circlips. The aluminium-alloy pistons are fitted with three piston rings – two compression rings and an oil control ring.

The cylinder block is made of cast iron and the cylinder bores are an integral part of the block. On this type of engine the cylinder bores are sometimes referred to as having dry liners.

The inlet and exhaust valves are each closed by coil springs, and operate in guides pressed into the cylinder head.

The inlet camshaft is driven by the crankshaft by a timing belt and rotates directly in the camshaft housing. The exhaust camshaft is driven by the inlet camshaft via a spur gear. The camshafts operate the valves via followers, which are situated directly below the camshafts. Valve clearances are adjusted using camshaft followers of different thickness.

Lubrication is by means of an oil pump, which is driven by the timing belt. It draws oil through a strainer located in the sump, and then forces it through an externally-mounted filter into galleries in the cylinder block/crankcase. From there, the oil is distributed to the crankshaft (main bearings) and camshaft. The big-end bearings are supplied with oil via internal drillings in the crankshaft, while the camshaft bearings also receive a pressurised supply. The camshaft lobes and valves are lubricated by splash, as are all other engine components. An oil cooler is fitted to keep the oil temperature stable under arduous operating conditions.

Operations with engine in place

The following operations can be carried out without having to remove the engine from the vehicle.

a) Compression pressure testing.
b) Camshaft cover – removal and refitting.
c) Timing belt cover – removal and refitting.
d) Timing belt – removal and refitting.
e) Timing belt tensioner and sprockets – removal and refitting.
f) Valve clearances – checking and adjustment.
g) Camshaft and followers – removal, inspection and refitting.
h) Cylinder head – removal and refitting.
i) Connecting rods and pistons – removal and refitting.*
j) Sump – removal and refitting.
k) Oil pump – removal, overhaul and refitting.
l) Oil cooler – removal and refitting.
m) Crankshaft oil seals – renewal.
n) Engine/transmission mountings – inspection and renewal.
o) Flywheel – removal, inspection and refitting.
p) Camshaft housing – removal and refitting.

* Although the operation marked with an asterisk can be carried out with the engine in the car after removal of the sump, it is better for the engine to be removed, in the interests of cleanliness and improved access. For this reason, the procedure is described in Chapter 2F.

3.6 Align the timing mark on the crankshaft pulley with the pointer on the oil pump cover to bring No 1 piston to TDC

2 Compression and leakdown tests – general information

Compression test

1 When engine performance is down, or if misfiring occurs which cannot be attributed to the fuel system, a compression test can provide diagnostic clues as to the engine's condition. If the test is performed regularly, it can give warning of trouble before any other symptoms become apparent.

2 A compression tester specifically intended for diesel engines must be used, because of the higher pressures involved. The tester is connected to an adapter which screws into the glow plug or injector hole. On these models, an adapter suitable for use in the glow plug holes will be required, due to the design of the injectors. It is unlikely to be worthwhile buying such a tester for occasional use, but it may be possible to borrow or hire one – if not, have the test performed by a garage.

3 Unless specific instructions to the contrary are supplied with the tester, observe the following points:

a) *The battery must be in a good state of charge, the air filter must be clean, and the engine should be at normal operating temperature.*

b) *Remove the air cleaner assembly and intake air ducts as described in Chapter 4B.*

c) *On Y17DT engines, release the retaining clip and disconnect the wiring connector from the fuel injection pump control unit (see Chapter 4B) to prevent the engine from running or fuel from being discharged.*

d) *Remove the glow plugs as described in Chapter 5A.*

4 There is no need to hold the accelerator pedal down during the test, because the diesel engine air intake is not throttled.

5 Crank the engine on the starter motor; after one or two revolutions, the compression pressure should build up to a maximum figure, and then stabilise. Record the highest reading obtained.

6 Repeat the test on the remaining cylinders, recording the pressure in each.

7 All cylinders should produce very similar pressures; any difference greater than that specified indicates the existence of a fault. Note that the compression should build-up quickly in a healthy engine; low compression on the first stroke, followed by gradually-increasing pressure on successive strokes, indicates worn piston rings. A low compression reading on the first stroke, which does not build-up during successive strokes, indicates leaking valves or a blown head gasket (a cracked head could also be the cause). Deposits on the undersides of the valve heads can also cause low compression.

Note: *The cause of poor compression is less easy to establish on a diesel engine than on a petrol one. The effect of introducing oil into the cylinders ('wet' testing) is not conclusive, because there is a risk that the oil will sit in the recess on the piston crown instead of passing to the rings.*

8 On completion of the test, reconnect/refit the components listed in paragraph 3, with reference to the Chapters indicated.

Leakdown test

9 A leakdown test measures the rate at which compressed air fed into the cylinder is lost. It is an alternative to a compression test, and in many ways it is better, since the escaping air provides easy identification of where pressure loss is occurring (piston rings, valves or head gasket).

10 As the equipment needed for the compression test is also unlikely to be available to the home mechanic, it is recommended that the test is performed by a Vauxhall/Opel dealer, or suitably-equipped garage.

3 Top dead centre (TDC) for No 1 piston – locating

Note: *If the engine is to be locked in position with No 1 piston at TDC on its compression stroke then a M6 and M8 bolt will be required.*

1 In its travel up and down its cylinder bore, Top Dead Centre (TDC) is the highest point that each piston reaches as the crankshaft rotates. While each piston reaches TDC both at the top of the compression stroke and again at the top of the exhaust stroke, for the purpose of timing the engine, TDC refers to the piston position (usually number 1) at the top of its compression stroke.

2 Number 1 piston (and cylinder) is at the right-hand (timing belt) end of the engine, and its TDC position is located as follows. Note that the crankshaft rotates clockwise when viewed from the right-hand side of the car.

3 Disconnect the battery negative terminal (refer to *Disconnecting the battery* in the Reference Chapter).

4 Firmly apply the handbrake, then jack up the front of the car and support it securely on axle stands (see *Jacking and vehicle support*). Remove the right-hand front roadwheel.

5 Remove the timing belt upper cover as described in Section 6.

6 Using a socket and extension bar on the crankshaft sprocket bolt, rotate the crankshaft until the notch on the crankshaft pulley rim is aligned with the pointer on the base of the oil pump cover **(see illustration)**. Once the mark is correctly aligned, No 1 and 4 pistons are at TDC.

7 To determine which piston is at TDC on its compression stroke, check the position of the timing holes in the camshaft and high-pressure fuel pump/injection pump sprockets. When No 1 piston is at TDC on its compression stroke, both sprocket holes will be aligned with the threaded holes in the cylinder head/block, and both exhaust camshaft lobes for cylinder No 1 are pointing upwards if viewed through the oil filler hole. If the timing holes are out of alignment, continue rotating the crankshaft until they align. Note that because the sprockets are of different diameters, it may take up to six revolutions of the crankshaft to achieve alignment.

8 With No 1 piston at TDC on its compression stroke, if necessary, the camshaft and high-pressure fuel pump/injection pump sprockets can be locked in position. Secure the camshaft sprocket in position by screwing a M6 bolt into the hole in the cylinder head and lock the pump sprocket in position by screwing a M8 bolt into the cylinder block **(see illustrations)**.

3.8a The camshaft sprocket can be locked using a 6 mm bolt (arrowed) . . .

3.8b . . . and the fuel pump/injection pump sprocket by an 8 mm bolt (arrowed)

4 Camshaft cover –
removal and refitting

Y17DT engines

Removal

1 Disconnect the battery negative terminal (refer to *Disconnecting the battery* in the Reference Chapter).
2 Remove the air cleaner assembly and intake duct as described in Chapter 4B.
3 Remove the engine management electronic control unit from above the camshaft cover, as described in Chapter 4B.
4 Unclip the wiring loom cable-tie, undo the retaining screws/nut and remove the engine management electronic control unit bracket.
5 Slacken the retaining clips securing the charge air pipe to the turbocharger.
6 Release the retaining clip and disconnect the crankcase ventilation hose from the camshaft cover.
7 Undo the two charge air pipe retaining bolts, disengage the pipe from the turbocharger, then remove the pipe from the top of the engine.
8 Undo the bolt, release the wiring loom retaining clip, and remove the engine transport shackle from the right-hand rear of the cylinder head. Slacken the bolt securing the left-hand rear shackle.
9 Slacken the fuel injector pipe unions located at the fuel injection pump **(see illustration)**. Access to the unions on the pump is limited. We found it necessary to remove the oil cooler/filter housing retaining bolt, and prise the foam filling from between the injection pump and filter housing.
10 Undo the injector pipe unions at the injectors.
11 Remove the retaining bolts, and lift away the injector outer seal plates.
12 Undo the wiring tray retaining bolt from the end of the cylinder head, release the two

4.9 Slacken the fuel injector pipe unions

retaining clips, and lift the tray out of the way **(see illustration 6.7)**.
13 Unscrew the bolts securing the timing belt upper cover to the camshaft housing.
14 Unscrew the two nuts and one bolt and detach the oil dipstick guide tube holder.
15 Disconnect the wiring from the glow plugs by squeezing the connectors with thumb and forefinger, and pulling them from the plugs.
16 Remove the retaining bolts and lift away the camshaft cover, complete with seal.
17 Examine the cover seal for signs of damage or deterioration and renew if necessary.
18 Prior to refitting, obtain four new injector outer seal plates, a new camshaft cover rubber seal (if necessary) and a tube of Vauxhall/Opel sealant compound (white), part No 90 511 124.

Refitting

19 Ensure the cover and cylinder head surfaces are clean and dry then fit the seal to the cover groove. Check the condition of the O-ring seal on the underside of the cover and renew if necessary **(see illustration)**.
20 Apply Vauxhall/Opel sealant compound to the camshaft housing mating surfaces at the end of each camshaft. Ensure that the oil borehole at the right-hand end of the exhaust camshaft is not covered in sealant **(see illustrations)**.
21 Carefully lower the cover into position, ensuring the seal remains correctly seated. Refit the timing belt upper cover and camshaft cover retaining bolts and tighten them to the specified torque.
22 The remainder of the reassembly procedure is a reversal of removal, noting the following points:

4.19 Check the O-ring on the underside of the cover

a) Ensure all bolts are tightened to the correct torque setting where specified.
b) The injector outer seal plates are marked 'upper' and 'outer'. Fit the seal plates and make sure that the centre of the seal is pushed over the injector taper **(see illustration)**.
c) After starting the engine, check for leaks.

Z17DTH engines

 Warning: Refer to the information contained in Chapter 4B, Section 2 before proceeding.

Removal

23 Disconnect the battery negative terminal (refer to *Disconnecting the battery* in the Reference Chapter).
24 Remove the engine oil filler cap, then lift off the plastic cover over the top of the engine. Refit the oil filler cap.
25 Remove the front bumper as described in Chapter 11.
26 Using cable-ties, string or wire, suitably secure the radiator to the upper crossmember on each side.
27 Undo the two bolts securing the radiator upper mounting brackets to the upper cross-member.
28 Undo the two bolts each side securing the radiator left-hand and right-hand lower mounting brackets to the front subframe. Disengage and remove the brackets from the radiator.
29 Carefully move the radiator forwards to gain access to the charge air pipe connection on the turbocharger. Slacken the retaining clamp and detach the charge air pipe from the turbocharger.

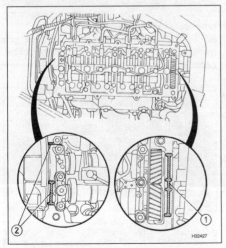

4.20a Apply sealant to areas (1) and (2)

4.20b Ensure the borehole (arrowed) is not covered in sealant

4.22 The injector seals are marked 'upper' and 'outside'

4.31 Disconnect the rear wiring connector (arrowed) from the electronic control unit

4.32 Release the clips and cable-ties (arrowed) securing the wiring harness to the charge air pipe

4.33 Charge air pipe front retaining bolt (arrowed)

4.34 Release the retaining clip (arrowed) and disconnect the crankcase breather hose

4.35 Slacken the retaining clip and disconnect the air cleaner intake duct from the charge air pipe

30 Remove the windscreen cowl panel and the bulkhead closure panel as described in Chapter 11.
31 Lift the locking bar and disconnect the rear wiring connector from the engine management electronic control unit **(see illustration)**. Also disconnect the wiring multiplug located behind the ECU, then undo the nut and disconnect the earth lead from the control unit stud.
32 Release the clips and cable-ties securing the wiring harness to the charge air pipe and move the harness to one side **(see illustration)**.
33 Undo the two charge air pipe retaining bolts. One bolt is located adjacent to the crankcase breather hose connection at the front of the camshaft cover and the other bolt is located centrally at the rear of the charge air pipe **(see illustration)**.
34 Release the retaining clip and disconnect

the crankcase breather hose at the front of the camshaft cover **(see illustration)**.
35 Slacken the retaining clip and disconnect the air cleaner intake duct from the charge air pipe **(see illustration)**.
36 Turn the charge air pipe and manipulate it out of position and off the engine.
37 Drain the engine oil and remove the oil filter as described in Chapter 1B.
38 Remove the complete exhaust system as described in Chapter 4B.
39 Slacken the two retaining clips and remove the oil filter housing oil return hose.
40 At the rear of the engine, disconnect the two vacuum hoses and six wiring connectors at the solenoid mounting brackets. Unscrew the bolt and detach the earth cable, then unscrew the two nuts and one bolt, and remove the solenoid mounting bracket assembly.

41 Unscrew the three bolts, unclip the coolant hose and detach the oil dipstick guide tube holder from the camshaft cover.
42 Lift the locking bar and disconnect the remaining wiring connector from the engine management electronic control unit. Undo the two nuts and two bolts and lift the control unit off the mounting bracket.
43 Unscrew the four bolts and remove the electronic control unit mounting bracket from the camshaft cover and support frame, then undo the two bolts and remove the support frame.
44 Release the locking catches securing the wiring connectors to the four fuel injectors then disconnect the injector wiring.
45 Thoroughly clean the fuel pipe unions on the fuel injectors and fuel rail. Using an open-ended spanner, unscrew the union nuts securing the high pressure fuel pipes to the injectors and fuel rail. Withdraw the high-pressure fuel pipes and plug or cover the open unions to prevent dirt entry.
46 Disconnect the wiring from the glow plugs by squeezing the connectors with thumb and forefinger, and pulling them from the plugs **(see illustration)**.
47 Unscrew the two bolts and remove the left-hand engine lifting bracket from the rear of the camshaft cover. Similarly, release the wiring harness support clip, undo the retaining bolt and remove the right-hand engine lifting bracket **(see illustrations)**.
48 Undo the bolt securing the exhaust gas recirculation heat exchanger to the front of the camshaft cover.

4.46 Squeeze the connectors and disconnect the wiring at the four glow plugs

4.47a Unscrew the bolts and remove the left-hand engine lifting bracket . . .

4.47b . . . and right-hand engine lifting bracket

4.49 Push in the locking clip and lift out the leak-off hose fitting on each injector

4.50a Undo the two bolts . . .

4.50b . . . and remove the outer seal plate from each fuel injector

4.51 Undo the two bolts and remove the upper seal plate from each fuel injector

4.53 Unscrew the retaining bolts and lift away the camshaft cover, complete with rubber seal

4.56 Fit the new rubber seal to the camshaft cover ensuring it is fully seated in the cover groove

49 Disconnect the fuel leak-off hose connection at each injector by pushing in the locking clip and lifting out the hose fitting **(see illustration)**. Move the hose assembly to one side and suitably plug or cover the open unions to prevent dirt entry.
50 Undo the two bolts and remove the outer seal plate from each fuel injector **(see illustrations)**. Note that new seal plates will be required for refitting.
51 Undo the two bolts and remove the upper seal plate from each fuel injector **(see illustration)**. Note that new seal plates will be required for refitting.
52 Unscrew the two bolts securing the timing belt upper cover to the camshaft cover.
53 Unscrew the nut and the retaining bolts, noting the different bolt lengths, and lift away the camshaft cover, complete with rubber seal **(see illustration)**. Note that a new rubber seal will be required for refitting.
54 Prior to refitting, obtain four new injector upper seal plates, four new injector outer seal plates, a new camshaft cover rubber seal and a tube of Vauxhall/Opel sealant compound (white), part No 90 511 124.

Refitting

55 Thoroughly clean the camshaft cover and the mating surfaces of the cover and camshaft housing ensuring that all traces of oil are removed from the mating surfaces.
56 Fit the new rubber seal to the camshaft cover ensuring it is fully seated in the cover groove **(see illustration)**.
57 Apply Vauxhall/Opel sealant compound to the camshaft housing mating surfaces at

the end of each camshaft. Ensure that the oil borehole at the right-hand end of the exhaust camshaft is not covered in sealant **(see illustrations 4.20a and 4.20b)**.
58 Carefully lower the cover into position, ensuring the seal remains correctly seated. Refit the timing belt upper cover and camshaft cover retaining bolts and tighten them progressively to the specified torque.
59 Locate the injector upper seal plates in position on the camshaft cover ensuring they are centralised over each injector. Apply Vauxhall/Opel sealant compound to the underside of the bolt heads and screw in the bolts finger-tight.
60 Hold the upper seal plates in position by hand, while tightening the retaining bolts to the specified torque in the two stages given in the Specifications.
61 The remainder of the reassembly

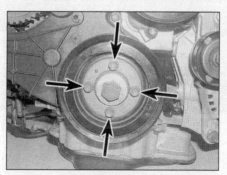

5.3 Remove the bolts (arrowed) securing the crankshaft pulley to the sprocket

procedure is a reversal of removal, noting the following points:
a) Ensure all nuts, bolts and pipe unions are tightened to the correct torque setting where specified.
b) The injector outer seal plates are marked 'up' or 'upper' and 'outside' on their outer surface. Fit the seal plates and make sure that the centre of the seal is pushed over the injector taper **(see illustration 4.22)**.
c) Fit a new oil filter and fill the engine with fresh oil as described in Chapter 1B.
d) After starting the engine, check for leaks.

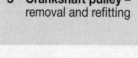

5 Crankshaft pulley –
removal and refitting

Removal

1 Firmly apply the handbrake, then jack up the front of the car and support it securely on axle stands (see Jacking and vehicle support). Remove the right-hand roadwheel.
2 Remove the auxiliary drivebelt as described in Chapter 1B. Prior to removal, mark the direction of rotation on the belt to ensure the belt is refitted the same way around.
3 Slacken and remove the small retaining bolts securing the pulley to the crankshaft sprocket and remove the pulley from the engine **(see illustration)**. If necessary, prevent crankshaft rotation by holding the sprocket retaining bolt with a suitable socket.

5.4a Refit the pulley to the crankshaft sprocket, aligning the pulley hole (arrowed) . . .

5.4b . . . with the sprocket locating pin (arrowed)

6.5 Undo the bolts and separate the engine mounting support bracket from the mounting adapter

6.7 Undo the Torx bolt and release the wiring tray retaining clips (arrowed)

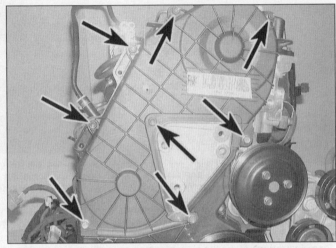

6.8 Remove the eight upper timing belt cover retaining bolts (arrowed)

Refitting

4 Refit the pulley to the crankshaft sprocket, aligning the pulley hole with the sprocket locating pin **(see illustrations)**. Refit the pulley retaining bolts, tightening them to the specified torque.

5 Refit the auxiliary drivebelt as described in Chapter 1B using the mark made prior to removal to ensure the belt is fitted the correct way around.

6 Refit the roadwheel, then lower the car to the ground and tighten the wheel bolts to the specified torque.

---

6 Timing belt covers –
removal and refitting

Y17DT engines

Upper cover removal

1 Disconnect the battery negative terminal (refer to *Disconnecting the battery* in the Reference Chapter).

2 Remove the air cleaner assembly and intake duct as described in Chapter 4B.

3 Support the weight of the engine using a trolley jack with a block of wood placed on its head.

4 Mark the position of the right-hand engine mounting to the support bracket, then undo the four securing bolts and remove the mounting.

5 Undo the retaining bolts and separate the engine mounting support bracket from the engine block mounting adapter **(see illustration)**.

6 With reference to Chapter 5A if necessary, disconnect the wiring plug and connection from the alternator.

7 Undo the Torx retaining bolt, release the wiring tray and loom retaining clips by squeezing the tangs of the retaining clips, and remove the wiring tray from the right-hand end of the cylinder head **(see illustration)**.

6.15a Lower cover retaining bolts (arrowed)

8 Release the hoses from the upper cover clips, remove the eight upper cover retaining bolts and withdraw the cover. Note the cover bolts are of different lengths **(see illustration)**.

Lower cover removal

9 Disconnect the battery negative terminal (refer to *Disconnecting the battery* in the Reference Chapter).

10 Firmly apply the handbrake, then jack up the front of the vehicle and support it securely on axle stands (see *Jacking and vehicle support*). Remove the right-hand roadwheel.

11 Remove the auxiliary drivebelt as described in Chapter 1B

12 Remove the upper cover as described in paragraphs 2 to 8.

13 Undo the three retaining bolts and remove the coolant pump pulley.

14 With reference to Section 5, remove the crankshaft pulley.

15 Undo the three retaining bolts, and remove the lower cover from the oil pump housing, then manoeuvre the engine mounting adapter out from the timing belt area **(see illustrations)**.

Rear cover removal

16 Remove the timing belt as described in Section 7.

17 With reference to Section 8, remove the

6.15b Manoeuvre the engine mounting adapter from the timing belt area (arrowed)

6.18 Rear timing belt cover bolts

6.26a Disconnect the camshaft sensor wiring connector . . .

6.26b . . . then undo the sensor bracket retaining bolt (arrowed) . . .

6.26c . . . and remove the sensor

6.27a Undo the bolt (arrowed) securing the wiring trough to the camshaft housing . . .

timing belt tension and guide rollers, camshaft sprocket and injection pump sprocket.

18 Undo the four retaining bolts, and remove the rear timing belt cover **(see illustration)**.

Upper, lower and rear cover refitting

19 Refitting is the reverse of removal, ensuring all retaining bolts are tightened to the specified torque.

Z17DTH engines

Upper cover removal

20 Disconnect the battery negative terminal (refer to *Disconnecting the battery* in the Reference Chapter).

21 Remove the engine oil filler cap, then lift off the plastic cover over the top of the engine. Refit the oil filler cap.

22 Remove the air cleaner assembly and intake duct as described in Chapter 4B.

23 Support the weight of the engine using a trolley jack with a block of wood placed on its head.

24 Mark the position of the right-hand engine mounting to the support bracket, then undo the four securing bolts and remove the mounting.

25 Undo the retaining bolts and separate the engine mounting support bracket from the engine block mounting adapter **(see illustration 6.5)**.

26 Disconnect the camshaft sensor wiring connector, then undo the sensor bracket retaining bolt and remove the sensor **(see illustrations)**.

27 Undo the bolt securing the wiring trough to the camshaft housing, and release the trough, wiring harness and vacuum pipe from the timing belt cover **(see illustrations)**.

28 Release the lower vacuum pipe from the

clips at the base of the timing belt cover **(see illustration)**.

29 Undo the eight upper cover retaining bolts and withdraw the cover **(see illustration)**. Note the cover bolts are of different lengths.

Lower cover removal

30 Disconnect the battery negative terminal (refer to *Disconnecting the battery* in the Reference Chapter).

31 Firmly apply the handbrake, then jack up the front of the car and support it securely on axle stands (see *Jacking and vehicle support*). Remove the right-hand roadwheel.

32 Remove the auxiliary drivebelt as described in Chapter 1B.

33 Remove the upper cover as described in paragraphs 21 to 29.

34 With reference to Section 5, remove the crankshaft pulley.

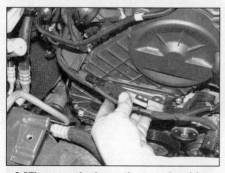

6.27b . . . and release the trough, wiring harness and vacuum pipe from the timing belt cover

6.28 Release the lower vacuum pipe from the clips at the base of the timing belt cover

6.29 Undo the eight upper cover retaining bolts and withdraw the cover

6.36a Undo the three retaining bolts, and remove the lower cover from the oil pump housing . . .

35 Undo the three retaining bolts and remove the coolant pump pulley.

36 Undo the three retaining bolts, and remove the lower cover from the oil pump housing, then manoeuvre the engine mounting adapter out from the timing belt area **(see illustrations)**.

Rear cover removal

37 Remove the timing belt as described in Section 7.

38 With reference to Section 8, remove the timing belt guide roller, camshaft sprocket and high-pressure fuel pump sprocket.

39 Undo the five retaining bolts, and remove the rear timing belt cover.

Upper, lower and rear cover refitting

40 Refitting is the reverse of removal, ensuring all retaining bolts are tightened to the specified torque.

---

7 Timing belt – removal and refitting

Note: *The timing belt must be removed and refitted with the engine cold.*

Removal

1 Position No 1 cylinder at TDC on its com-

6.36b . . . then manoeuvre the engine mounting adapter out from the timing belt area

pression stroke as described in Section 3. Lock the camshaft and high-pressure fuel pump/injection pump sprockets in position by screwing the bolts into the threaded holes in the cylinder head/block.

2 Remove the crankshaft pulley as described in Section 5.

3 Unbolt and remove the timing belt upper and lower covers with reference to Section 6.

4 Slacken the timing belt tensioner retaining bolt, then turn the tensioner anti-clockwise to relieve the belt tension, using a suitable hexagon bit or Allen key engaged with the hole provided in the tensioner front plate **(see illustration)**. Hold the tensioner in this position and tighten the retaining bolt.

5 Slide the timing belt off its sprockets and remove it from the engine. If the belt is to be re-used, use white paint or similar to mark the direction of rotation on the belt. **Do not** rotate the crankshaft until the timing belt has been refitted.

6 Check the timing belt carefully for any signs of uneven wear, splitting or oil contamination, and renew it if there is the slightest doubt about its condition. If the engine is undergoing an overhaul and is approaching the specified interval for belt renewal (see Chapter 1B) renew the belt as a matter of course, regardless of its apparent condition. If signs of

---

oil contamination are found, trace the source of the oil leak and rectify it, then wash down the engine timing belt area and all related components to remove all traces of oil.

Refitting

7 On reassembly, thoroughly clean the timing belt sprockets and ensure the camshaft and high-pressure fuel pump/injection pump sprockets are locked correctly in position. Temporarily refit the crankshaft pulley to the sprocket and check that the pulley cut-out is still aligned with the pointer on the oil pump cover; the mark on the crankshaft sprocket should also be aligned with the mark on the oil pump cover **(see illustration)**.

8 Remove the pulley and fit the timing belt over the crankshaft, oil pump, high-pressure fuel pump/injection pump and camshaft sprockets, ensuring that the belt rear run is taut (ie, all slack is on the tensioner pulley side of the belt). Do not twist the belt sharply while refitting it. Ensure that the belt teeth are correctly seated centrally in the sprockets, and that the timing marks remain in alignment. If a used belt is being refitted, ensure that the arrow mark made on removal points in the normal direction of rotation, as before.

9 Tension the belt by slackening the tensioner retaining bolt and allowing the tensioner to automatically take up the slack in the belt.

10 Check that the crankshaft sprocket timing mark is still correctly positioned then unscrew the locking bolts from the high-pressure fuel pump/injection pump and camshaft sprockets.

11 With the tensioner pulley retaining bolt still slackened, rotate the crankshaft pulley approximately 60° **backwards** (anti-clockwise) to automatically adjust the timing belt tension. Hold the crankshaft pulley stationary and tighten the tensioner pulley retaining bolt to the specified torque.

12 Rotate the crankshaft through two complete turns (720°) in the normal direction of rotation to settle the timing belt in position.

7.4 Slacken the timing belt tensioner retaining bolt (arrowed) then turn the tensioner anti-clockwise to relieve the belt tension

7.7 Align the notch on the crankshaft sprocket with the pointer on the oil pump cover (arrowed)

To make a sprocket holding tool, obtain two lengths of steel strip about 6 mm thick by about 30 mm wide or similar, one 600 mm long, the other 200 mm long (all dimensions are approximate). Bolt the two strips together to form a forked end, leaving the bolt slack so that the shorter strip can pivot freely. At the other end of each 'prong' of the fork, drill a suitable hole and fit a nut and bolt to allow the tool to engage with the spokes in the sprocket.

Realign the crankshaft sprocket timing mark and check that the camshaft and high-pressure fuel pump/injection pump sprocket locking bolts can be refitted. If it is not possible to fit the locking bolts with the crankshaft sprocket timing mark aligned, repeat the belt refitting procedure.

13 Refit the timing belt covers and the crankshaft pulley as described in Sections 5 and 6.

8 Timing belt tensioner and sprockets – removal and refitting

Camshaft sprocket

Removal

1 Remove the timing belt as described in Section 7. Prior to attempting to unscrew the sprocket retaining bolt, turn the crankshaft 60° **backwards** (anti-clockwise) to prevent any accidental piston-to-valve contact.

2 Remove the locking bolt securing the camshaft sprocket in the TDC position.

3 It will now be necessary to hold the camshaft sprocket to enable the retaining bolt to be removed. Vauxhall/Opel special tools KM-956-1 and KM-6347 are available for this purpose, however, a home-made tool can easily be fabricated **(see Tool Tip)**.

4 Using the holding tool to prevent rotation of the camshaft, slacken the sprocket retaining bolt. Remove the holding tool, unscrew the retaining bolt and remove the sprocket, noting which way round it is fitted **(see illustration)**. If the sprocket locating pin is a loose fit, remove it from the camshaft end and store it with the sprocket for safe-keeping.

8.4 Using the holding tool to prevent rotation of the camshaft, slacken the sprocket retaining bolt

Refitting

5 Ensure the locating pin is in position then refit the sprocket to the camshaft end aligning its locating hole with the pin.

6 Refit the sprocket retaining bolt, then tighten the bolt to the specified torque using the holding tool to prevent rotation. Note that on Z17DTH engines, there are two different torque settings for the sprocket retaining bolt, depending on the part number of the sprocket. Refer to the Specifications at the start of this Chapter.

7 Turn the camshaft sprocket slightly, as necessary, then refit the locking bolt to secure the sprocket in the TDC position.

8 Rotate the crankshaft 60° **forwards** (clockwise) until the groove in the crankshaft timing belt sprocket is at '12 o'clock' and aligns with the cast-in mark on the oil pump cover.

9 Refit the timing belt as described in Section 7.

High-pressure fuel pump/injection pump sprocket

Removal

10 Remove the timing belt as described in Section 7.

11 Remove the locking bolt securing the high-pressure fuel pump/injection pump sprocket in the TDC position.

12 Refer to the information contained in paragraph 3 and suitably hold the sprocket, then slacken and remove the sprocket retaining nut **(see illustration)**.

8.13 Using a puller to remove the high-pressure fuel pump/injection pump sprocket

8.12 Using a sprocket holding tool to prevent rotation as the high-pressure fuel pump/injection pump sprocket nut is slackened

13 Remove the sprocket from the pump shaft, noting which way around it is fitted. If the Woodruff key is a loose fit in the pump shaft, remove it and store it with the sprocket for safe-keeping. **Note:** *The sprocket is a tapered-fit on the pump shaft and in some cases a suitable puller may be needed to free it from the shaft* **(see illustration)**.

Refitting

14 Ensure the Woodruff key is correctly fitted to the pump shaft then refit the sprocket, aligning the sprocket groove with the key **(see illustration)**.

15 Refit the retaining nut and tighten it to the specified torque whilst using the holding tool to prevent rotation.

16 If not already done, align the sprocket timing hole with the threaded hole in the cylinder block and screw in the locking bolt.

17 Refit the timing belt as described in Section 7.

Crankshaft sprocket

Removal

18 Remove the timing belt as described in Section 7.

19 Slacken the crankshaft sprocket retaining bolt. To prevent crankshaft rotation, have an assistant select top gear and apply the brakes firmly. If the engine is removed from the vehicle it will be necessary to lock the flywheel (see Section 18).

20 Unscrew the retaining bolt and washer and remove the crankshaft sprocket from the end of the crankshaft **(see illustration)**.

8.14 Align the keyway in the sprocket with the Woodruff key in the shaft

8.20 Slide the sprocket from the shaft

8.22 Fit the flanged spacer with the convex side away from the oil pump cover

8.24 Refit the sprocket retaining bolt and washer

8.29 Use a socket and extension bar on one of the oil pump cover bolts to prevent the sprocket from turning

If the sprocket is a tight fit, draw it off of the crankshaft using a suitable puller. If the Woodruff key is a loose fit in the crankshaft, remove it and store it with the sprocket for safe-keeping.

21 Slide the flanged spacer off of the crankshaft, noting which way around it is fitted.

Refitting

22 Refit the flanged spacer to the crankshaft with its convex surface facing away from the oil pump housing (see illustration).

23 Ensure the Woodruff key is correctly fitted then slide on the crankshaft sprocket aligning its groove with the key.

24 Refit the retaining bolt and washer then lock the crankshaft by the method used on removal, and tighten the sprocket retaining bolt to the specified torque setting (see illustration).

25 Refit the timing belt as described in Section 7.

8.36 Timing belt idler pulley retaining bolt

Oil pump sprocket

Removal

26 Remove the timing belt as described in Section 7.

27 Prevent the oil pump sprocket from rotating using a socket and extension bar fitted to one of the oil pump cover bolts then slacken and remove the sprocket retaining nut.

28 Remove the sprocket from the oil pump shaft, noting which way around it is fitted.

Refitting

29 Refit the sprocket, aligning it with the flat on the pump shaft, and fit the retaining nut. Tighten the sprocket retaining nut to the specified torque, using the socket and extension bar to prevent rotation (see illustration).

30 Refit the timing belt as described in Section 7.

Tensioner assembly

Removal

31 Remove the timing belt as described in Section 7.

32 Unscrew the retaining bolt and remove the tensioner assembly from the engine. Disengage the tension spring from its locating stud as the tensioner is removed.

Refitting

33 Fit the tensioner assembly to the engine, engaging the tension spring over the stud. Screw in the tensioner retaining bolt, then turn the tensioner anti-clockwise using a suitable hexagon bit or Allen key engaged with the hole provided in the tensioner front plate. Hold the tensioner in this position and tighten the retaining bolt.

34 Refit the timing belt as described in Section 7.

Idler pulley

Removal

35 Remove the timing belt as described in Section 7.

36 Slacken and remove the retaining bolt and remove the idler pulley from the engine (see illustration).

Refitting

37 Refit the idler pulley and tighten the retaining bolt to the specified torque.

38 Refit the timing belt as described in Section 7.

9 Camshaft oil seal – renewal

1 Remove the camshaft sprocket as described in Section 8.

2 Carefully punch or drill a small hole in the oil seal. Screw in a self-tapping screw, and pull on the screw with pliers to extract the seal (see illustration).

3 Clean the seal housing, and polish off any burrs or raised edges which may have caused the seal to fail in the first place.

4 Press the new seal into position using a suitable tubular drift (such as a socket) which bears only on the hard outer edge of the seal.

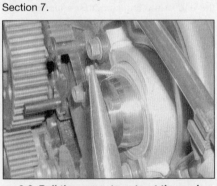

9.2 Pull the screw to extract the seal

9.4 Press the oil seal into position using a tubular drift such as a socket

10.7 With the camshaft lobe pointing away from the follower measure the clearance

10.14 Carefully depress the follower and slide the shim out

10.15 The thickness of each shim should be stamped on one of its surfaces

Take care not to damage the seal lips during fitting; note that the seal lips should face inwards **(see illustration)**.

5 Refit the camshaft sprocket as described in Section 8.

10 Valve clearances – checking and adjustment

Checking

1 The importance of having the valve clearances correctly adjusted cannot be overstressed, as they vitally affect the performance of the engine. The engine must be cold for the check to be accurate. The clearances are checked as follows.

2 Firmly apply the handbrake, then jack up the front of the car and support it securely on axle stands (see *Jacking and vehicle support*). Remove the right-hand roadwheel to gain access to the crankshaft pulley.

3 Remove the camshaft cover as described in Section 4, and with reference to Chapter 4B, remove the fuel injectors.

4 Using a socket and extension on the crankshaft sprocket bolt, rotate the crankshaft in the normal direction of rotation (clockwise when viewed from the right-hand end of the engine) until the notch on the crankshaft pulley is correctly aligned with the pointer on the base of the oil pump cover.

5 Now rotate the crankshaft in the normal direction (clockwise) until the inlet camshaft lobes for No 1 cylinder (nearest the timing belt end of the engine) and the exhaust camshaft lobes for No 3 cylinder are pointing away from the followers. This indicates that these valves are completely closed, and the clearances can be checked.

6 On a piece of paper, draw the outline of the engine with the cylinders numbered from the timing belt end. Show the position of each valve, together with the specified valve clearance. Note that the clearance for both the inlet and exhaust valves is the same.

7 With the cam lobes positioned as described in paragraph 5, using feeler blades, measure the clearance between the base of both No 1 cylinder inlet cam lobes and No 3 cylinder exhaust cam lobes and their followers. Record

the clearances on the paper **(see illustration)**.

8 Rotate the crankshaft pulley through a half a turn (180°) to position No 3 cylinder inlet camshaft lobes and No 4 cylinder exhaust camshaft lobes pointing away from their followers. Measure the clearance between the base of the camshaft lobes and their followers and record the clearances on the paper.

9 Rotate the crankshaft pulley through a half a turn (180°) to position No 2 cylinder exhaust camshaft lobes and No 4 cylinder inlet camshaft lobes pointing away from their followers. Measure the clearance between the base of the camshaft lobes and their followers and record the clearances on the paper.

10 Rotate the crankshaft pulley through a half a turn (180°) to position No 1 cylinder exhaust camshaft lobes and No 2 cylinder inlet camshaft lobes pointing away from their followers. Measure the clearance between the base of the camshaft lobes and their followers and record the clearances on the paper.

11 If all the clearances are correct, refit the cylinder head cover (see Section 4), and injectors (see Chapter 4B), then refit the roadwheel, lower the vehicle to the ground and tighten the wheel bolts to the specified torque. If any clearance measured is not correct, adjustment must be carried out as described in the following paragraphs.

Adjustment

12 Rotate the crankshaft pulley until the lobe of the valve to be adjusted is pointing directly away from the follower. **Note:** *Ensure that the crankshaft is **not** positioned at TDC, as when a valve follower is depressed to remove the shim, the valve will strike the piston.*

13 Rotate the follower until the groove on its upper edge is facing towards the front of the engine (exhaust followers), or rear of the engine (inlet followers).

14 In the absence of the special Vauxhall/Opel tool (KM-6090), position a large flat-bladed screwdriver between the edge of the follower and the base of the camshaft. Use the screwdriver to carefully depress the follower until there is enough clearance to allow the shim to be slid out from between the follower and camshaft (a magnetic tool is particularly useful for this task) **(see illustration)**.

15 Clean the shim, and measure its thickness with a micrometer. The shims carry thickness

markings, but wear may have reduced the original thickness, so be sure to check **(see illustration)**.

16 Add the measured clearance of the valve to the thickness of the original shim then subtract the specified valve clearance from this figure. This will give you the thickness of the shim required. For example:

Clearance measured of valve	0.35 mm
Plus thickness of the original shim	2.70 mm
Equals	3.05 mm
Minus clearance required	0.40 mm
Thickness of shim required	2.65 mm

17 Obtain the correct thickness of shim required and lubricate it with clean engine oil. Carefully depress the follower and slide the shim into position, with the thickness number downwards, ensuring it is correctly located.

> **HAYNES HINT** *It may be possible to correct the clearances by moving the shims around between the valves, but the engine must not be rotated with any shims missing. Keep a note of all the shim thicknesses to assist valve clearance adjustment when they need to be done again.*

18 Repeat the procedure given in paragraphs 12 to 17 on the remaining valves which require adjustment.

19 Rotate the crankshaft a few times to settle all shims in position then recheck the valve clearances before refitting the fuel injectors (Chapter 4B) and the camshaft cover (Section 4).

20 Refit the roadwheel then lower the vehicle to the ground and tighten the wheel bolts to the specified torque.

11 Camshaft and followers – removal, inspection and refitting

Removal

1 Remove the camshaft cover as described in Section 4.

2 Remove the fuel injectors as described in Chapter 4B.

3 Remove the camshaft sprocket as described in Section 8.

11.5 Insert a screw through the fixed gear and into the backlash compensating gear (arrowed)

4 Undo the nuts and remove the No 5 bearing cap from the left-hand (gearbox) end of the camshafts.

5 The exhaust camshaft gear incorporates a backlash compensating gear. This must now be locked to the fixed exhaust camshaft gear by inserting a suitably-sized bolt/rod into the hole on the inboard face of the fixed gear, and through into the backlash compensating gear. This prevents the spring preload of the compensating gear being lost when either camshaft is removed **(see illustration)**.

6 Working in a spiral pattern from the outside in, slacken the remaining camshaft bearing cap retaining nuts by one turn at a time, to relieve the pressure of the valve springs on the bearing caps gradually and evenly. Once the valve spring pressure has been relieved, the nuts can be fully unscrewed and removed.
Caution: If the bearing cap nuts are carelessly

11.13 Ensure each shim is correctly located

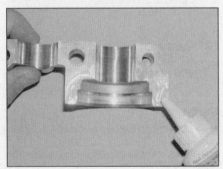

11.16 Apply a smear of sealant to the No 1 camshaft-bearing cap

11.9 Lift out the cam followers and shims

slackened, the bearing caps might break. If any bearing cap breaks then the complete cylinder head assembly must be renewed; the bearing caps are matched to the head and are not available separately.

7 Remove the bearing caps, noting each caps correct fitted location. The bearing caps are numbered 1 to 5 and the arrow on each cap points towards the timing belt end of the engine.

8 Lift the camshafts out of the cylinder head.

9 Obtain sixteen small, clean plastic containers, and label them for identification. Alternatively, divide a larger container into compartments. Lift the followers and shims out from the top of the cylinder head and store each one in its respective fitted position. Make sure the followers and shims are not mixed to ensure the valve clearances remain correctly adjusted on refitting **(see illustration)**.

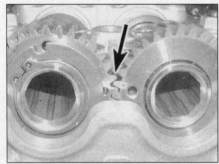

11.14 Align the camshaft gear marks (arrowed)

11.17 The arrows on the camshaft bearing caps should point towards the timing belt end of the engine

Inspection

10 Examine the camshaft bearing surfaces and camshaft lobes for signs of wear ridges and scoring. Renew the camshaft if any of these conditions are apparent.

11 Examine the condition of the bearing surfaces both on the camshaft journals and in the cylinder head. If the head bearing surfaces are worn excessively, the cylinder head will need to be renewed.

12 Examine the followers and their bores in the cylinder head for signs of wear or damage. If any follower is visibly worn it should be renewed.

Refitting

13 Where removed, lubricate the followers with clean engine oil and carefully insert each one into its original location in the cylinder head. Ensure each shim is correctly located in the top of the its relevant follower **(see illustration)**.

14 Rotate the crankshaft approximately 60° **backwards** (anti-clockwise) as a precaution against accidental piston-to-valve contact. Lubricate the camshaft followers with clean engine oil then lay the camshafts in position. Check that the exhaust camshaft backlash compensating gear is still locked to the fixed gear. Ensure that the mark on the outer face exhaust camshaft gear lies between the two marks on the outer face of the inlet camshaft gear, and that the marks are approximately level with the upper edge of the camshaft housing **(see illustration)**. Note: *If the exhaust camshaft is being renewed, it will be necessary to obtain Vauxhall/Opel tool No KM 6092, and pretension the backlash compensating gear prior to installation.*

15 Ensure the mating surfaces of the bearing caps and camshaft housing are clean and dry and lubricate the camshaft journals and lobes with clean engine oil.

16 Apply a smear of suitable sealant (available from Vauxhall/Opel dealers) to the areas of the camshaft housing No 1 bearing cap mating surface **(see illustration)**.

17 Refit the No 1 to 4 camshaft bearing caps in their original locations on the cylinder head. The caps are numbered 1 to 5 (No 1 cap being at the timing belt end of the engine) and the arrow cast onto the top of each cap should point towards the timing belt end of the engine **(see illustration)**.

18 Refit the No 1 to 4 bearing cap nuts, tightening them by hand only.

19 Remove the bolt/rod locking the backlash compensating gear to the exhaust camshaft fixed gear, and refit the No 5 camshaft bearing cap.

20 Working in the specified sequence, tighten the nuts by one turn at a time to gradually impose the pressure of the valve springs evenly on the bearing caps **(see illustration)**. Repeat this sequence until all bearing caps are in contact with the cylinder head then go around in the specified sequence and tighten them to the specified torque.

Caution: If the bearing cap bolts are carelessly tightened, the bearing caps might break. If any bearing cap breaks then the complete cylinder head assembly must be renewed; the bearing caps are matched to the head and are not available separately.

21 Fit a new camshaft oil seal as described in Section 9.

22 Refit the camshaft sprocket and timing belt as described in Sections 7 and 8.

23 Check the valve clearances as described in Section 10, then refit the fuel injectors as described in Chapter 4B and the camshaft cover as described in Section 4.

12 Camshaft housing –
removal and refitting

Y17DT engines

Removal

1 Remove the camshafts and followers as described in Section 11.

2 Remove the two bolts securing the rear timing belt cover to the camshaft housing **(see illustration)**.

3 Disconnect the wiring connectors at the coolant temperature sensor, oil pressure switch, charge pressure sensor, injection pump and glow plugs. Release the wiring harness from the retaining clips.

4 Remove the bolts securing the charge air pipe and bracket to the left-hand end of the camshaft housing and inlet manifold. Undo the retaining clips and release the pipe from the inlet trunking.

5 Undo the bolts and remove the left-hand rear transport shackle.

6 On models with air conditioning, without undoing the refrigerant pipes, disconnect the wiring plug, unbolt the air conditioning compressor from its support bracket (3 bolts), and position it clear of the engine. Use a cable-tie or similar to tie the compressor to the upper crossmember out of the way. Undo the three bolts and remove the air conditioning support bracket **(see illustrations)**.

7 Slacken the camshaft housing retaining bolts 1/2 turn at a time in the **reverse** of the sequence shown in illustration 12.12.

8 Undo the bolts completely and remove the camshaft housing. Remove and discard the gasket **(see illustration)**.

9 Unscrew the oil leak line banjo union bolt and mounting bolt and remove the line. Recover the sealing rings.

Refitting

10 Refit the oil leak line using new sealing rings and tighten the banjo union bolt and mounting bolt securely.

11 Ensure all mating surfaces are clean and free from any gasket or sealant residue.

12 With a new gasket in place, position the camshaft housing on to the cylinder head, and tighten the housing bolts evenly and gradually

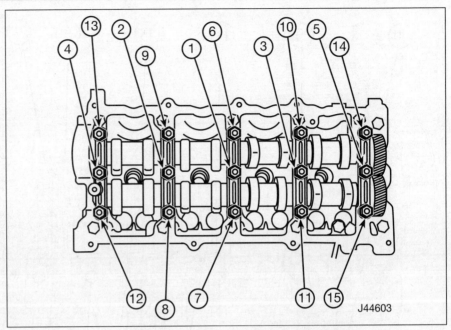

11.20 Camshaft bearing cap tightening sequence

to the specified torque, in sequence **(see illustration)**.

13 The remainder of refitting is a reversal of removal.

Z17DTH engines

Removal

14 Drain the cooling system as described in Chapter 1B.

15 Remove the camshafts and followers as described in Section 11.

16 Remove the two bolts securing the rear timing belt cover to the camshaft housing **(see illustration 12.2)**.

17 With reference to Chapter 4B, remove the throttle housing.

18 Undo the retaining bolt(s) and remove the throttle housing mounting bracket.

19 Release the retaining clips and disconnect

12.2 Remove the two bolts securing the rear timing belt cover to the camshaft housing

12.6a Tie the compressor to the upper crossmember . . .

12.6b . . . and remove the compressor mounting bracket

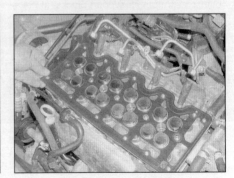

12.8 Remove the gasket

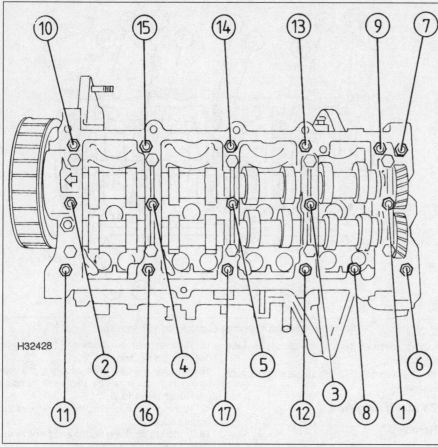

12.12 Camshaft housing bolts tightening sequence

the two lower coolant hoses from the EGR valve heat exchanger. Undo the two bolts at each end of the metal EGR pipe, securing the pipe flanges to the exhaust manifold and EGR valve housing. Undo the retaining bolt and detach the EGR valve heat exchanger bracket from the front of the camshaft housing. Remove the EGR valve heat exchanger/pipe assembly from the engine and collect the two flange gaskets.

20 Undo the retaining bolt and remove the engine lifting bracket from the front of the camshaft housing.

21 On models with air conditioning, without undoing the refrigerant pipes, disconnect the wiring plug, unbolt the air conditioning compressor from its support bracket (3 bolts),

13.10 Lift the cylinder head off the block

and position it clear of the engine. Use a cable-tie or similar to tie the compressor to the upper crossmember out of the way. Undo the three bolts and remove the air conditioning support bracket (see illustrations 12.6a and 12.6b).

22 Slacken the camshaft housing retaining bolts 1/2 turn at a time in the **reverse** of the sequence shown in illustration 12.12.

23 Undo the bolts completely and remove the camshaft housing. Remove and discard the gasket.

Refitting

24 Ensure all mating surfaces are clean and free from any gasket or sealant residue.

25 With a new gasket in place, position the camshaft housing on to the cylinder head, and tighten the housing bolts evenly and gradually to the specified torque, in sequence (see illustration 12.12).

26 The remainder of refitting is a reversal of removal. On completion refill the cooling system as described in Chapter 1B.

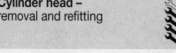

13 Cylinder head –
removal and refitting

Caution: Be careful not to allow dirt into the fuel injection pump or injector pipes during this procedure.

Note: *New cylinder head bolts will be required on refitting.*

Removal

1 Remove the battery and battery tray as described in Chapter 5A.

2 Drain the cooling system as described in Chapter 1B.

3 Remove the camshaft housing as described in Section 12.

4 Remove the exhaust manifold as described in Chapter 4B.

5 Remove the exhaust gas recirculation (EGR) valve as described in Chapter 4C.

6 Slacken the retaining clips and disconnect the remaining coolant hoses from the cylinder head, thermostat housing, oil cooler and coolant pipe.

7 On Z17DTH engines, disconnect the wiring connectors at the charge pressure sensor and inlet manifold switch-over valve solenoid. Disconnect the vacuum hose at the switch-over valve vacuum unit.

8 Working in the **reverse** of the tightening sequence given in paragraph 26, progressively slacken the cylinder head bolts by half a turn at a time, until all bolts can be unscrewed by hand.

9 Lift out the cylinder head bolts and recover the washers.

10 Lift the cylinder head away; seek assistance if possible, as it is a heavy assembly **(see illustration)**. Remove the gasket, noting the two locating dowels fitted to the top of the cylinder block. If they are a loose fit, remove the locating dowels and store them with the head for safe-keeping. Keep the head gasket for identification purposes (see paragraph 17).

11 If the cylinder head is to be dismantled for overhaul, then refer to Part F of this Chapter.

Preparation for refitting

12 The mating faces of the cylinder head and cylinder block/crankcase must be perfectly clean before refitting the head. Use a hard plastic or wood scraper to remove all traces of gasket and carbon; also clean the piston crowns. Take particular care, as the surfaces are damaged easily. Also, make sure that the carbon is not allowed to enter the oil and water passages – this is particularly important for the lubrication system, as carbon could block the oil supply to any of the engine's components. Using adhesive tape and paper, seal the water, oil and bolt holes in the cylinder block/crankcase. To prevent carbon entering the gap between the pistons and bores, smear a little grease in the gap. After cleaning each piston, use a small brush to remove all traces of grease and carbon from the gap, then wipe away the remainder with a clean rag. Clean all the pistons in the same way.

13 Check the mating surfaces of the cylinder block/crankcase and the cylinder head for nicks, deep scratches and other damage. If slight, they may be removed carefully with a file, but if excessive, machining may be the only alternative to renewal.

14 Ensure that the cylinder head bolt holes in the crankcase are clean and free of oil. Syringe or soak up any oil left in the bolt holes. This is most important in order that the correct bolt tightening torque can be applied and to prevent the possibility of the block being cracked by hydraulic pressure when the bolts are tightened.

15 The cylinder head bolts must be discarded and renewed, regardless of their apparent condition.

16 If warpage of the cylinder head gasket surface is suspected, use a straight-edge to check it for distortion. Refer to Part F of this Chapter if necessary.

17 On this engine, the cylinder head-to-piston clearance is controlled by fitting different thickness head gaskets. The gasket thickness can be determined by looking at the left-hand front corner of the gasket and checking on the number of holes **(see illustration)**.

Y17DT engines

Holes in gasket	Gasket thickness
No holes	1.45 mm
One hole	1.50 mm
Two holes	1.55 mm

Z17DTH engines

Holes in gasket	Gasket thickness
No holes	1.35 mm
One hole	1.40 mm
Two holes	1.45 mm

The correct thickness of gasket required is selected by measuring the piston protrusions as follows.

18 Ensure that the crankshaft is still correctly positioned in the TDC position. Mount a dial test indicator securely on the block so that its pointer can be easily pivoted between the piston crown and block mating surface. Zero the dial test indicator on the gasket surface of the cylinder block then carefully move the indicator over No 1 piston and measure the its protrusion at its highest point between the valve cut-outs, and then again at its highest point between the valve cut-outs at 90° to the first measurement **(see illustration)**.

19 Rotate the crankshaft half a turn (180°) to bring No 2 and 3 pistons to TDC. Ensure the crankshaft is accurately positioned then measure the protrusions of No 2 and 3 pistons at the specified points. Once both pistons

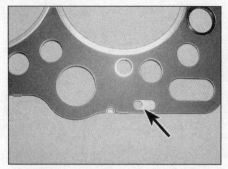

13.17 Cylinder head gasket identification hole (arrowed)

have been measured, rotate the crankshaft through a further one and a half turns (540°) to bring No 1 and 4 pistons back to TDC.

20 Select the correct thickness of head gasket required by determining the largest amount of piston protrusion, and using the following table.

Y17DT engines

Piston protrusion measurement	Gasket thickness required
0.630 to 0.696 mm	1.45 mm
0.697 to 0.763 mm	1.50 mm
0.764 to 0.830 mm	1.55 mm

Z17DTH engines

Piston protrusion measurement	Gasket thickness required
0.630 to 0.696 mm	1.35 mm
0.697 to 0.763 mm	1.40 mm
0.764 to 0.830 mm	1.45 mm

Refitting

21 Wipe clean the mating surfaces of the cylinder head and cylinder block/crankcase.

22 Check that the two locating dowels are in position then fit a new gasket to the cylinder block **(see illustration)**.

23 If not already positioned at TDC, rotate the crankshaft so that No 1 piston is at its highest point in the cylinder. Now turn the crankshaft 60° **backwards** (anti-clockwise). This is to ensure that whist the cylinder head and camshafts are being refitted, there is little chance of accidental piston-to-valve contact.

24 With the aid of an assistant, carefully

13.18 Measure the piston projection at the highest points between the valve cut-outs

refit the cylinder head assembly to the block, aligning it with the locating dowels.

25 Carefully enter each new cylinder head bolt into its relevant hole (*do not drop them in*). Screw all bolts in, by hand only, until finger-tight.

26 Working progressively in a spiral sequence starting at the centre and working outwards, tighten the cylinder head bolts to their Stage 1 torque setting, using a torque wrench and suitable socket **(see illustration)**.

27 Once all bolts have been tightened to the Stage 1 torque, working again in sequence, go around and tighten all bolts through the specified Stage 2 and Stage 3 angles. It is recommended that an angle-measuring gauge is used to ensure accuracy **(see illustration)**. If a gauge is not available, use white paint to make alignment marks prior to tightening; the marks can then be used to check that the bolt has been rotated through the correct angle.

28 The remainder of refitting is a reversal of removal. On completion, refill the engine with fresh oil and coolant as described in Chapter 1B.

14 Sump – removal and refitting

Removal

1 Disconnect the battery negative terminal (refer to *Disconnecting the battery* in the Reference Chapter).

2 Firmly apply the handbrake, then jack up

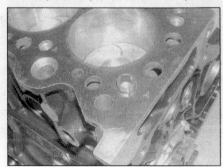

13.22 Check the locating dowels are in place

13.26 Tighten the bolts to the Stage 1 torque setting . . .

13.27 . . . then through the Stage 2 and 3 angles

14.4 If the lower pan is stuck to the main casting, carefully ease it away using a wide-bladed scraper

the front of the car and support it securely on axle stands (see *Jacking and vehicle support*).
3 Drain the engine oil as described in Chapter 1B, then fit a new sealing washer and refit the drain plug, tightening it to the specified torque.
4 Slacken and remove the bolts securing the sump lower pan to the main casting then remove the sump pan from underneath the vehicle **(see illustration)**.
5 To remove the main casting from the engine, remove the exhaust system front pipe as described in Chapter 4B.
6 Undo the two bolts securing the oil dipstick guide tube to the main sump casting.
7 Progressively slacken and remove the nuts and bolts securing the main casting to the base of the cylinder block/oil pump cover and transmission. Break the joint by striking the casting with the palm of the hand, or using a wide plastic spatula carefully inserted in the

14.10 Fit a new oil pick-up pipe sealing ring

14.13 Refit the sump main casting

14.8 Remove the oil pick-up pipe and strainer

joint between the sump and cylinder block. Lower the casting away from the engine and withdraw it from underneath the vehicle.
8 While the sump main casting is removed, take the opportunity to check the oil pump pick-up/strainer for signs of clogging or splitting. If necessary, unbolt the pick-up/strainer and remove it from the engine along with its sealing ring **(see illustration)**. The strainer can then be cleaned easily in solvent or renewed.

Refitting

9 Remove all traces of dirt, oil and sealant from the mating surfaces of the sump main casting and pan, the cylinder block and (where removed) the pick-up/strainer.
10 Where necessary, fit a new sealing ring to the oil pump pick-up/strainer and fit the strainer to the base of the cylinder block **(see illustration)**. Refit the strainer retaining bolt and tighten it to the specified torque.

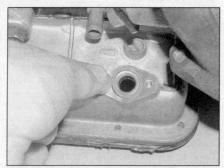

14.12 Position a new oil dipstick guide tube sealing ring

14.17 Apply a bead of sealant and refit the pan to the sump main casting

11 Ensure the main casting and cylinder block mating surfaces are clean and dry, and apply a coat of suitable sealant (available from Vauxhall/Opel dealers) to the upper mating surface of the casting.
12 Position a new dipstick guide tube rubber seal on the main casting **(see illustration)**.
13 Offer up the main casting and loosely refit all the retaining nuts and bolts **(see illustration)**. Note that the four long bolts correspond with the bolts holes at the rear of the casting. If the sump is being fitted with the engine removed from the vehicle and separated from the transmission, ensure that the face of the casting is flush with the transmission mounting face of the cylinder block. Working out from the centre in a diagonal sequence, progressively tighten the main casting retaining bolts to the specified torque setting.
14 Refit the bolts securing the main casting to the transmission housing and tighten them to the specified torque.
15 Ensure that the oil dipstick guide tube is correctly positioned, refit the retaining bolts, and tighten to the specified torque.
16 Refit the exhaust front pipe as described in Chapter 4B.
17 Ensure the main casting and sump pan mating surfaces are clean and dry and apply a coat of suitable sealant (available from Vauxhall/Opel dealers) to the upper mating surface of the pan. Refit the pan to the base of the main casting and tighten its retaining bolts to the specified torque **(see illustration)**.
18 Lower the vehicle to the ground then fill the engine with fresh oil, with reference to Chapter 1B.

15 Oil pump – removal, inspection and refitting

Removal

1 Remove the timing belt as described in Section 7.
2 Remove the oil pump and crankshaft timing belt sprockets as described in Section 8.
3 Remove the sump main casting as described in Section 14.
4 Slacken and remove the retaining bolts then slide the oil pump cover off of the end of the crankshaft, taking great care not to lose the locating dowels. Remove the sealing ring, which is fitted around the oil pump housing section of the cover, and discard it.
5 Using a suitable marker pen, mark the surface of the pump outer rotor; the mark can then be used to ensure the rotor is refitted the correct way around.
6 Remove the oil pump inner and outer rotors from the cylinder block **(see illustrations)**.
7 If necessary, unscrew the oil pressure relief valve assembly from the rear of the cylinder block. Remove the sealing ring.

Inspection

8 Clean the components, and carefully examine the rotors, pump housing and cover for any signs of scoring or wear. Renew any component which shows signs of wear or damage. If the pump housing in the cylinder block is marked then seek the advice of a Vauxhall/Opel dealer on the best course of action.

9 If the components appear serviceable, fit the rotors into the housing and measure the clearance between the outer rotor and pump housing, and the inner rotor tip-to-outer rotor clearance using feeler blades **(see illustration)**. Also measure the rotor endfloat, and check the flatness of the end cover. If the clearances exceed the specified tolerances, renew the worn components.

10 If the relief valve has been removed, check that the valve piston is free to move easily and return smoothly under spring pressure. If not renew the valve assembly.

Refitting

11 Where removed, fit a new sealing ring to the oil pressure relief valve then refit the valve assembly to the cylinder block and tighten it to the specified torque setting.

12 Lubricate the pump rotors with clean engine oil and refit them to the pump housing, using the mark made prior to removal to ensure the outer rotor is fitted the correct way around.

13 Prior to refitting, carefully lever out the crankshaft and oil pump oil seals using a flat-bladed screwdriver. Fit the new oil seals, ensuring that each seals sealing lip is facing inwards, and press them squarely into the housing using a tubular drift which bears only on the hard outer edge of the seal. Press each seal into position so that it is flush with the housing **(see illustration)**.

14 Ensure the mating surfaces of the oil pump and cylinder block are clean and dry and the locating dowels are in position. Remove all traces of sealant from the threads of the pump cover bolts.

15 Fit a new seal into the groove around the oil pump housing section of the cover, and apply a bead of suitable sealant (available from Vauxhall/Opel dealers) to the pump cover mating surface **(see illustration)**.

16 Carefully manoeuvre the oil pump cover into position, taking great care not to damage the oil seal lips on the crankshaft and inner rotor shaft. Locate the cover on the dowels making sure the pump sealing ring remains correctly positioned.

17 Apply a smear of sealant to the threads of each cover retaining bolt then refit all bolts and tighten them to the specified torque. Note that the longer bolt corresponds to the lower left-hand bolt hole in the cover.

18 Refit the timing belt sprockets and belt as described in Sections 7 and 8 then refit the sump as described in Section 13.

19 On completion refill the engine with fresh oil as described in Chapter 1B.

15.6a Remove the oil pump inner rotor . . .

15.6b . . . and outer rotor

15.9 Measure the inner rotor tip-to-outer rotor clearance

16 Oil pump seal – renewal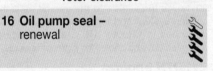

1 Remove the oil pump sprocket as described in Section 8.

2 Carefully punch or drill a small hole in the oil seal. Screw a self-tapping screw into the seal, and pull on the screw with pliers to extract the seal **(see illustration)**.
Caution: Great care must be taken to avoid damage to the oil pump.

3 Clean the seal housing, and polish off any burrs or raised edges which may have caused the seal to fail in the first place.

4 Press the new seal into position using a suitable tubular drift (such as a socket) which bears only on the hard outer edge of the seal. Take care not to damage the seal lips during fitting; note that the seal lips should face inwards.

15.15 Fit a new seal to the oil pump cover

15.13 The seal fits flush with the housing

5 Refit the oil pump sprocket as described in Section 8.

17 Oil cooler – removal and refitting

Y17DT engines

Removal

1 The oil cooler and integral oil filter housing is situated on the rear left-hand side of the cylinder block. Firmly apply the handbrake, then jack up the front of the car and support it securely on axle stands (see *Jacking and vehicle support*).

2 Remove the battery and battery tray as described in Chapter 5A.

3 Remove the air cleaner assembly and intake duct as described in Chapter 4B.

16.2 Pull the screw to extract the seal

17.14 Fit a new sealing ring to the recess in the oil cooler

4 Remove the engine management electronic control unit from above the camshaft cover, as described in Chapter 4B.
5 Unclip the wiring loom cable-tie, undo the retaining screws/nut and remove the engine management electronic control unit bracket.
6 Slacken the retaining clips securing the charge air pipe to the turbocharger.
7 Release the retaining clip and disconnect the crankcase ventilation hose from the camshaft cover.
8 Undo the two upper charge air pipe retaining bolts, disengage the pipe from the turbocharger, then remove the pipe from the top of the engine.
9 Unclip the wiring harness, undo the retaining bolts and retaining nut and remove the lower charge air pipe from the rear of the engine. Recover the gaskets.
10 Drain the cooling system as described in Chapter 1B.
11 Position a suitable container beneath the oil filter. Undo the oil cooler return hose union, release the retaining clip and disconnect the return hose.
12 Release the clips and disconnect the coolant hoses from the oil cooler, and release the wiring loom retaining clip.
13 Remove the single bolt securing the oil filter housing to the cylinder block. Discard the sealing ring; a new one must be used on refitting.

Refitting

14 Fit a new sealing ring to the recess in the rear of the cooler, then offer the cooler to the cylinder block **(see illustration)**.

18.2 Fabricate a locking tool to retain the flywheel

17.15 Ensure that the lug of the oil filter housing engages, then refit the centre bolt

15 Ensure that the oil cooler return hose union is correctly positioned, ensure that the lug of the oil filter housing engages correctly, then refit the centre bolt and tighten it to the specified torque **(see illustration)**.
16 Reconnect the coolant hoses to the cooler and secure them in position with the retaining clips.
17 Refit the charge air pipes and electronic control unit bracket.
18 Refit the electronic control unit, air cleaner assembly and intake duct as described in Chapter 4B.
19 Refit the battery tray and battery as described in Chapter 5A.
20 Lower the vehicle to the ground, refill the cooling system and top-up the engine oil as described in Chapter 1B. Start the engine, and check the oil cooler for signs of leakage.

Z17DTH engines

Removal

21 The oil cooler and integral oil filter housing is situated on the rear left-hand side of the cylinder block. Firmly apply the handbrake, then jack up the front of the car and support it securely on axle stands (see *Jacking and vehicle support*).
22 Remove the battery and battery tray as described in Chapter 5A.
23 Drain the cooling system as described in Chapter 1B.
24 Remove the starter motor as described in Chapter 5A.
25 Release the clips and disconnect the coolant hoses from the oil cooler.

18.3 Remove the flywheel bolts and recover the plate

26 Position a suitable container beneath the oil filter. Slacken the retaining clip and disconnect the oil cooler return hose at the cylinder block connection.
27 Remove the single bolt securing the oil filter housing to the cylinder block. Discard the sealing ring; a new one must be used on refitting.

Refitting

28 Fit a new sealing ring to the recess in the rear of the cooler, then offer the cooler to the cylinder block. Refit the centre bolt and tighten it to the specified torque.
29 Reconnect the coolant hoses to the cooler and secure them in position with the retaining clips.
30 Reconnect the oil cooler return hose to the cylinder block and secure in position with the retaining clip.
31 Refit the starter motor as described in Chapter 5A.
32 Refit the battery tray and battery as described in Chapter 5A.
33 Lower the vehicle to the ground, refill the cooling system and top-up the engine oil as described in Chapter 1B. Start the engine, and check the oil cooler for signs of leakage.

18 Flywheel –
removal, inspection and refitting

Note: *New flywheel retaining bolts will be required on refitting.*

Removal

1 Remove the transmission as described in Chapter 7A then remove the clutch assembly as described in Chapter 6.
2 Prevent the flywheel from turning by locking the ring gear teeth **(see illustration)**. Alternatively, bolt a strap between the flywheel and the cylinder block/crankcase. Make alignment marks between the flywheel and crankshaft using paint or a suitable marker pen.
3 Slacken and remove the retaining bolts and plate, then remove the flywheel **(see illustration)**. Do not drop it, as it is very heavy.

Inspection

4 Examine the flywheel for wear or chipping of the ring gear teeth. Renewal of the ring gear is possible but is not a task for the home mechanic; renewal requires the new ring gear to be heated (up to 180° to 230°C) to allow it to be fitted.
5 Examine the flywheel for scoring of the clutch face. If the clutch face is scored, the flywheel may be surface-ground, but renewal is preferable.
6 If there is any doubt about the condition of the flywheel, seek the advice of a Vauxhall/Opel dealer or engine reconditioning specialist. They will be able to advise if it is possible to recondition it or whether renewal is necessary.

Refitting

7 Clean the mating surfaces of the flywheel and crankshaft.
8 Apply a drop of locking compound to the threads of each of the new flywheel retaining bolts then refit the flywheel and retaining plate and install the new bolts. If the original is being refitted align the marks made prior to removal.
9 Lock the flywheel using the method employed on dismantling then, working in a diagonal sequence, evenly and progressively tighten the retaining bolts to the specified Stage 1 torque setting.
10 Once all bolts have been tightened to the Stage 1 torque, go around and tighten all bolts through the specified Stage 2 angle, then the Stage 3 angle. It is recommended that an angle-measuring gauge is used during the final stages of the tightening, to ensure accuracy. If a gauge is not available, use white paint to make alignment marks prior to tightening; the marks can then be used to check that the bolt has been rotated through the correct angle.
11 Refit the clutch as described in Chapter 6 then remove the locking tool and refit the transmission as described in Chapter 7A.

19 Crankshaft oil seals – renewal

Timing belt end oil seal

1 Remove the crankshaft sprocket as described in Section 8.
2 Carefully punch or drill two small holes opposite each other in the oil seal. Screw a self-tapping screw into each and pull on the screws with pliers to extract the seal.
3 Clean the seal housing and polish off any burrs or raised edges which may have caused the seal to fail in the first place.
4 Ease the new seal into position on the end of the crankshaft. Press the seal squarely into position until it is flush with the housing. If

19.7 The seal fits flush with the housing

necessary, a suitable tubular drift which bears only on the hard outer edge of the seal can be used to tap the seal into position. Take great care not to damage the seal lips during fitting and ensure that the seal lips face inwards.
5 Wash off any traces of oil, then refit the crankshaft sprocket as described in Section 8.

Flywheel end oil seal

6 Remove the flywheel as described in Section 18.
7 Renew the seal as described in paragraphs 2 to 4 (see illustration).
8 Refit the flywheel as described in Section 18.

20 Engine/transmission mountings – inspection and renewal

Inspection

1 If improved access is required, raise the front of the car and support it securely on axle stands. Where necessary, undo the retaining bolts and remove the undertray from beneath the engine/transmission unit.
2 Check the mounting rubber to see if it is cracked, hardened or separated from the metal at any point; renew the mounting if any such damage or deterioration is evident.
3 Check that all the mountings' fasteners are

securely tightened; use a torque wrench to check if possible.
4 Using a large screwdriver or a pry bar, check for wear in the mounting by carefully levering against it to check for free-play; where this is not possible, enlist the aid of an assistant to move the engine/transmission unit back-and-forth, or from side-to-side, while you watch the mounting. While some free play is to be expected even from new components, excessive wear should be obvious. If excessive free play is found, check first that the fasteners are correctly secured, then renew any worn components as described below.

Renewal

Note: Before slackening any of the engine mounting bolts/nuts, the relative positions of the mountings to their various brackets should be marked to ensure correct alignment upon refitting.

Right-hand mounting

5 With reference to Chapter 4B, remove the air cleaner housing.
6 Support the weight of the engine using a trolley jack with a block of wood placed on its head.
7 Undo the two bolts securing the right-hand engine mounting to the engine mounting support bracket (see illustration).
8 Undo the two bolts securing the mounting to the body, and withdraw the bracket with the mounting.
9 Refitting is a reversal of removal. Tighten the bolts to the specified torque.

Front mounting/torque link

10 Firmly apply the handbrake, then jack up the front of the car and support it securely on axle stands (see Jacking and vehicle support).
11 Support the weight of the engine/transmission using a trolley jack with a block of wood placed on its head.
12 Slacken and remove the nut and washer securing the mounting to the subframe. Withdraw the bolt (see illustration).

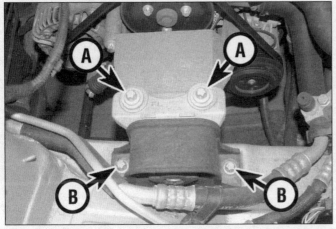

20.7 Right-hand engine mounting-to-engine bracket bolts (A) and mounting-to-body bolts (B)

20.12 Front engine mounting/torque link

20.21 Extract the retaining spring clip (arrowed) and disconnect the gearchange linkage from the shift guide bracket

20.22 Rear engine mounting/torque link retaining bolt (arrowed)

20.29 Left-hand engine mounting bracket and transmission bracket bolts (arrowed)

13 Undo the bolts securing the mounting bracket to the transmission, then manoeuvre the mounting and bracket out of position.

14 Check all components for signs of wear or damage, and renew as necessary.

15 On reassembly, refit the mounting bracket (aligning the previously-made marks) and tighten its bolts to the specified torque.

16 Locate the mounting in the subframe, ensuring it is fitted the correct way up, and manoeuvre the engine/transmission into position. Refit the mounting bolt and nut. Tighten the nut to the specified torque.

17 Lower the vehicle to the ground.

Rear mounting/torque link

18 Firmly apply the handbrake, then jack up the front of the car and support it securely on axle stands (see *Jacking and vehicle support*).

19 Remove the complete exhaust system as described in Chapter 4B.

20 Support the weight of the engine/transmission using a trolley jack with a block of wood placed on its head. Position the jack underneath the transmission and raise the transmission slightly to remove all load from the rear mounting.

21 Extract the retaining spring clip and disconnect the gearchange linkage from the shift guide bracket **(see illustration)**. Move the shift guide to one side and remove the rubber damper.

22 Undo the bolt securing the torque link to the subframe, and remove the link **(see illustration)**.

23 Undo the bolts securing the torque link rubber mounting bracket to the transmission and remove the bracket and mounting.

24 Locate the new mounting bracket in position. Insert the bolts and tighten to the specified torque.

25 Refit the torque link to the subframe and

mounting, insert the bolts and tighten to the specified torque.

26 Reconnect the gearchange linkage, then refit the exhaust system as described in Chapter 4B. On completion, lower the vehicle to the ground.

Left-hand mounting

27 Remove the battery and battery tray as described in Chapter 5A.

28 Support the weight of the transmission using a trolley jack with a block of wood placed on its head.

29 Unscrew the two bolts securing the mounting bracket to the transmission bracket, and the three bolts securing the transmission bracket to the transmission **(see illustration)**.

30 Undo the four bolts securing the mounting to the body, slightly lower the engine, then remove the mounting assembly from the car.

31 Refitting is a reversal of removal. Ensure all bolts are tightened to their specified torques.

Chapter 2 Part F:
Engine removal and overhaul procedures

Contents

Degrees of difficulty

Easy, suitable for novice with little experience	**Fairly easy,** suitable for beginner with some experience	**Fairly difficult,** suitable for competent DIY mechanic	**Difficult,** suitable for experienced DIY mechanic	**Very difficult,** suitable for expert DIY or professional

Specifications

Engine identification

Engine type	Manufacturer's engine code*
Petrol engines:	
1.4 litre (1364 cc) DOHC 16-valve	Z14XEP
1.6 litre (1598 cc):	
SOHC 8-valve.	Z16SE
DOHC 16-valve.	Z16XE and Z16XEP
1.8 litre (1796 cc) DOHC 16-valve	Z18XE
Diesel engines:	
1.3 litre (1248 cc) DOHC 16-valve	Z13DTJ
1.7 litre (1686 cc) DOHC 16-valve	Y17DT and Z17DTH

* For details of engine code location, see 'Vehicle identification' in the Reference Chapter.

1.4 litre petrol engines (Z14XEP)

Cylinder head

Maximum gasket face distortion	0.02 mm
Cylinder head height	126.0 mm
Valve seat angle in cylinder head	90° 30'
Valve seat width in cylinder head:	
Inlet valve	1.0 to 1.4 mm
Exhaust valve	1.4 to 1.8 mm

Valves and guides

Stem diameter:	
Inlet valve	4.955 to 4.970 mm
Exhaust valve	4.945 to 4.960 mm
Valve head diameter:	
Inlet valve	27.90 to 28.10 mm
Exhaust valve	24.90 to 25.10 mm
Valve length:	
Inlet valve	93.65 to 94.05 mm
Exhaust valve	93.65 to 94.05 mm
Maximum permissible valve stem play in guide:	
Inlet valve	0.021 to 0.052 mm.
Exhaust valve	0.031 to 0.062 mm.
Valve clearances	Automatic adjustment by hydraulic cam followers

Cylinder block

Maximum gasket face distortion	0.05 mm
Cylinder bore diameter	73.385 to 73.415 mm (nominal)
Maximum cylinder bore ovality and taper	0.013 mm

Crankshaft and bearings

Number of main bearings	5
Main bearing journal diameter	50.004 to 50.017 mm (nominal)
Big-end bearing journal diameter	42.971 to 42.987 mm (nominal)
Crankshaft endfloat	0.100 to 0.200 mm

Pistons

Piston diameter	73.345 to 73.375 mm (nominal)

Piston rings

Number of rings (per piston)	2 compression, 1 oil control
Ring end gap:	
Compression	0.30 to 0.45 mm
Oil control	0.25 to 0.75 mm

Torque wrench settings

Refer to Chapter 2A Specifications

1.6 litre SOHC petrol engines (Z16SE)

Cylinder head

Maximum gasket face distortion	0.05 mm
Cylinder head height	95.90 to 96.10 mm
Valve seat angle in cylinder head	90°
Valve seat width in cylinder head:	
Inlet valve	1.3 to 1.5 mm
Exhaust valve	1.6 to 1.8 mm

Valves and guides

Stem diameter:	
Inlet valve	6.998 to 7.012 mm
Exhaust valve	6.978 to 6.992 mm
Valve head diameter:	
Inlet valve	38.0 mm
Exhaust valve	31.0 mm
Valve length:	
Inlet valve	93.35 mm
Exhaust valve	99.65 mm
Maximum permissible valve stem play in guide:	
Inlet valve	0.018 to 0.052 mm.
Exhaust valve	0.038 to 0.072 mm.
Valve clearances	Automatic adjustment by hydraulic cam followers

1.6 litre SOHC petrol engines (Z16SE) (continued)

Cylinder block
Maximum gasket face distortion . . . . 0.05 mm
Cylinder bore diameter. . . . . 78.975 to 79.025 mm (nominal)
Maximum cylinder bore ovality and taper . . . . 0.013 mm

Crankshaft and bearings
Number of main bearings. 5
Main bearing journal diameter . . . . 54.980 to 54.997 mm
Big-end bearing journal diameter. . . . . 42.971 to 42.987 mm
Crankshaft endfloat . . . . 0.100 to 0.200 mm

Pistons
Piston diameter . . . . 78.955 to 79.005 mm (nominal)

Piston rings
Number of rings (per piston). . . . . 2 compression, 1 oil control
Ring end gap:
   Compression . . . . 0.30 to 0.50 mm
   Oil control . . . . 0.40 to 1.40 mm

Torque wrench settings
Refer to Chapter 2B Specifications

1.6 litre DOHC petrol engines (Z16XE)
Note: *Where specifications are given as N/A, no information was available at the time of writing. Refer to your Vauxhall/Opel dealer for the latest information available.*

Cylinder head
Maximum gasket face distortion . . . . 0.05 mm
Cylinder head height . . . . 134.9 to 135.1 mm
Valve seat angle in cylinder head. . . . . 90° 30'
Valve seat width in cylinder head:
   Inlet valve . . . . 1.0 to 1.4 mm
   Exhaust valve . . . . 1.4 to 1.8 mm

Valves and guides
Stem diameter:
   Inlet valve . . . . 5.955 to 5.970 mm
   Exhaust valve . . . . 5.935 to 5.950 mm
Valve head diameter:
   Inlet valve . . . . 31.0 mm
   Exhaust valve . . . . 27.50 mm
Valve length:
   Inlet valve . . . . 101.50 to 101.93 mm
   Exhaust valve . . . . 100.55 to 100.97 mm
Maximum permissible valve stem play in guide. . . . . N/A
Valve clearances. . . . . Automatic adjustment by hydraulic cam followers

Cylinder block
Maximum gasket face distortion . . . . 0.05 mm
Cylinder bore diameter. . . . . 78.975 to 79.025 mm (nominal)
Maximum cylinder bore ovality and taper . . . . 0.013 mm

Crankshaft and bearings
Number of main bearings. 5
Main bearing journal diameter . . . . 54.980 to 54.997 mm (nominal)
Big-end bearing journal diameter. . . . . 42.971 to 42.987 mm (nominal)
Crankshaft endfloat . . . . 0.100 to 0.202 mm

Pistons
Piston diameter . . . . 78.955 to 79.005 mm (nominal)

Piston rings
Number of rings (per piston). . . . . 2 compression, 1 oil control
Ring end gap:
   Compression . . . . 0.30 to 0.50 mm
   Oil control . . . . 0.40 to 1.40 mm

Torque wrench settings
Refer to Chapter 2C Specifications

1.6 litre DOHC petrol engines (Z16XEP)

Note: *Where specifications are given as N/A, no information was available at the time of writing. Refer to your Vauxhall/Opel dealer for the latest information available.*

Cylinder head

Maximum gasket face distortion	0.05 mm
Cylinder head height	N/A
Valve seat angle in cylinder head	90° 30'
Valve seat width in cylinder head:	
Inlet valve	1.0 to 1.4 mm
Exhaust valve	1.4 to 1.8 mm

Valves and guides

Stem diameter:	
Inlet valve	4.955 to 4.970 mm
Exhaust valve	4.935 to 4.950 mm
Valve head diameter:	
Inlet valve	30.70 to 30.80 mm
Exhaust valve	27.10 to 27.20 mm
Valve length:	
Inlet valve	117.10 to 117.30 mm
Exhaust valve	116.16 to 116.36 mm
Maximum permissible valve stem play in guide:	
Inlet valve	0.030 to 0.061 mm
Exhaust valve	0.050 to 0.081 mm
Valve clearances (cold):	
Inlet valve	0.21 to 0.29 mm
Exhaust valve	0.26 to 0.35 mm

Cylinder block

Maximum gasket face distortion	0.05 mm
Cylinder bore diameter	78.992 to 79.058 mm (nominal)
Maximum cylinder bore ovality and taper	0.013 mm

Crankshaft and bearings

Number of main bearings	5
Main bearing journal diameter	54.980 to 54.997 mm (nominal)
Big-end bearing journal diameter	42.971 to 42.987 mm (nominal)
Crankshaft endfloat	0.100 to 0.202 mm

Pistons

Piston diameter	78.833 to 78.847 mm (nominal)

Piston rings

Number of rings (per piston)	2 compression, 1 oil control
Ring end gap:	
Compression	0.25 to 0.50 mm
Oil control	0.25 to 0.75 mm

Torque wrench settings

Refer to Chapter 2C Specifications

1.8 litre DOHC petrol engines (Z18XE)

Cylinder head

Maximum gasket face distortion	0.05 mm
Cylinder head height	135.85 to 136.00 mm
Valve seat angle in cylinder head	90° 30'
Valve seat width in cylinder head:	
Inlet valve	1.0 to 1.4 mm
Exhaust valve	1.4 to 1.8 mm

Valves and guides

Stem diameter:	
Inlet valve	4.955 to 4.970 mm
Exhaust valve	4.935 to 4.950 mm
Valve head diameter:	
Inlet valve	31.10 to 31.30 mm
Exhaust valve	27.40 to 27.60 mm
Valve length:	
Inlet valve	101.20 to 101.60 mm
Exhaust valve	100.56 to 100.96 mm

1.8 litre DOHC petrol engines (Z18XE) (continued)

Valves and guides (continued)

Maximum permissible valve stem play in guide:

    Inlet valve . . . . 0.030 to 0.057 mm

    Exhaust valve . . . . 0.050 to 0.077 mm

Valve clearances. . . . . Automatic adjustment by hydraulic cam followers

Cylinder block

Maximum gasket face distortion . . . . 0.05 mm

Cylinder bore diameter. . . . . 80.485 to 80.555 mm (nominal)

Maximum cylinder bore ovality and taper . . . . 0.013 mm

Crankshaft and bearings

Number of main bearings. 5

Main bearing journal diameter . . . . 54.980 to 54.997 mm (nominal)

Big-end bearing journal diameter. . . . . 42.971 to 42.987 mm (nominal)

Crankshaft endfloat . . . . 0.100 to 0.202 mm

Pistons

Piston diameter . . . . 80.455 to 80.525 mm (nominal)

Piston rings

Number of rings (per piston). . . . . 2 compression, 1 oil control

Ring end gap:

    Compression . . . . 0.30 to 0.50 mm

    Oil control . . . . 0.40 to 1.40 mm

Torque wrench settings

Refer to Chapter 2C Specifications

1.3 litre DOHC diesel engines (Z13DTJ)

Note: *Where specifications are given as N/A, no information was available at the time of writing.*
Refer to your Vauxhall/Opel dealer for the latest information available.

Cylinder head

Maximum gasket face distortion . . . . 0.10 mm

Cylinder head height . . . . 105.45 to 105.55 mm

Valve seat angle in cylinder head . . . . 90°

Valve seat width in cylinder head (inlet and exhaust). . . . . 1.5 to 1.7 mm

Valves and guides

Stem diameter (inlet and exhaust) . . . . 5.90 to 5.94 mm

Valve head diameter (inlet and exhaust). . . . . 22.0 mm

Valve length (inlet and exhaust) . . . . 107.95 mm

Maximum permissible valve stem play in guide. . . . . 0.028 to 0.064 mm

Valve clearances. . . . . Automatic adjustment by hydraulic cam followers

Cylinder block

Maximum gasket face distortion . . . . N/A

Cylinder bore diameter. . . . . 69.600 to 69.630 mm (nominal)

Maximum cylinder bore ovality. . . . . 0.005 mm

Maximum cylinder bore taper. . . . . 0.001 mm

Crankshaft and bearings

Number of main bearings. 5

Main bearing journal diameter . . . . 50.855 to 51.000 mm (nominal)

Big-end bearing journal diameter. . . . . 42.455 to 42.600 mm (nominal)

Crankshaft endfloat . . . . 0.055 to 0.265 mm

Pistons

Piston diameter . . . . 69.520 to 69.550 mm (nominal)

Piston rings

Number of rings (per piston). . . . . 2 compression, 1 oil control

Ring end gap:

    Top compression ring. . . . . 0.20 to 0.30 mm

    Second compression ring. . . . . 1.00 to 1.50 mm

    Oil control ring . . . . 0.25 to 0.50 mm

Torque wrench settings

Refer to Chapter 2D Specifications

1.7 litre DOHC diesel engines (Y17DT and Z17DTH)

Note: *Where specifications are given as N/A, no information was available at the time of writing. Refer to your Vauxhall/Opel dealer for the latest information available.*

Cylinder head

Maximum gasket face distortion	0.10 mm
Cylinder head height	94.95 to 95.05 mm
Valve seat angle in cylinder head	89.5°
Valve seat width in cylinder head:	
Inlet valve	1.6 to 1.8 mm
Exhaust valve	1.4 to 1.6 mm

Valves and guides

Stem diameter (inlet and exhaust)	5.96 to 5.97 mm
Valve head diameter:	
Inlet valve	27.50 mm
Exhaust valve	26.50 mm
Valve length:	
Inlet valve	98.45 mm
Exhaust valve	98.10 mm
Maximum permissible valve stem play in guide	
Inlet valve	0.019 mm
Exhaust valve	0.021 mm
Valve clearances (cold):	
Inlet and exhaust	0.4 ± 0.05 mm

Cylinder block

Maximum gasket face distortion	N/A
Cylinder bore diameter	79.000 to 79.030 mm (nominal)
Maximum cylinder bore ovality and taper	0.015 mm

Crankshaft and bearings

Number of main bearings	5
Main bearing journal diameter	51.918 to 51.938 mm (nominal)
Big-end bearing journal diameter	N/A
Crankshaft endfloat	0.030 to 0.120 mm

Pistons

Piston diameter	78.930 to 78.959 mm (nominal)

Piston rings

Number of rings (per piston)	2 compression, 1 oil control
Ring end gap:	
Top compression	0.25 to 0.35 mm
Second compression	0.20 to 0.30 mm
Oil control	0.20 to 0.40 mm

Torque wrench settings

Refer to Chapter 2E Specifications

1 General information

Included in this Part of Chapter 2 are details of removing the engine/transmission from the car and general overhaul procedures for the cylinder head, cylinder block/crankcase and all other engine internal components.

The information given ranges from advice concerning preparation for an overhaul and the purchase of parts, to detailed step-by-step procedures covering removal, inspection, renovation and refitting of engine internal components.

After Section 6, all instructions are based on the assumption that the engine has been removed from the car. For information concerning in-car engine repair, as well as the removal and refitting of those external components necessary for full overhaul, refer to Parts A to E of this Chapter (as applicable) and to Section 6. Ignore any preliminary dismantling operations described in Parts A to E that are no longer relevant once the engine has been removed from the car.

Apart from torque wrench settings, which are given at the beginning of Parts A to E (as applicable), all specifications relating to engine overhaul are at the beginning of this Part of Chapter 2.

2 Engine overhaul – general information

It is not always easy to determine when, or if, an engine should be completely overhauled, as a number of factors must be considered.

High mileage is not necessarily an indication that an overhaul is needed, while low mileage does not preclude the need for an overhaul. Frequency of servicing is probably the most important consideration. An engine which has had regular and frequent oil and filter changes, as well as other required maintenance, should give many thousands of miles of reliable service. Conversely, a neglected engine may require an overhaul very early in its life.

Excessive oil consumption is an indication that piston rings, valve seals and/or valve guides are in need of attention. Make sure that oil leaks are not responsible before deciding that the rings and/or guides are worn. Have a compression test performed (refer to Parts A to E of this Chapter, to determine the likely cause of the problem.

Check the oil pressure with a gauge fitted in place of the oil pressure switch, and compare it with that specified. If it is extremely low, the main and big-end bearings, and/or the oil pump, are probably worn out.

Loss of power, rough running, knocking or metallic engine noises, excessive valve gear noise, and high fuel consumption may also point to the need for an overhaul, especially if they are all present at the same time. If a complete service does not cure the situation, major mechanical work is the only solution.

A full engine overhaul involves restoring all internal parts to the specification of a new engine. During a complete overhaul, the pistons and the piston rings are renewed, and the cylinder bores are reconditioned. New main and big-end bearings are generally fitted; if necessary, the crankshaft may be reground, to compensate for wear in the journals. The valves are also serviced as well, since they are usually in less-than-perfect condition at this point. Always pay careful attention to the condition of the oil pump when overhauling the engine, and renew it if there is any doubt as to its serviceability. The end result should be an as-new engine that will give many trouble-free miles.

Critical cooling system components such as the hoses, thermostat and coolant pump should be renewed when an engine is overhauled. The radiator should also be checked carefully, to ensure that it is not clogged or leaking.

Before beginning the engine overhaul, read through the entire procedure, to familiarise yourself with the scope and requirements of the job. Check on the availability of parts and make sure that any necessary special tools and equipment are obtained in advance. Most work can be done with typical hand tools, although a number of precision measuring tools are required for inspecting parts to determine if they must be renewed.

The services provided by an engineering machine shop or engine reconditioning specialist will almost certainly be required, particularly if major repairs such as crankshaft regrinding or cylinder reboring are necessary. Apart from carrying out machining operations, these establishments will normally handle the inspection of parts, offer advice concerning reconditioning or renewal and supply new components such as pistons, piston rings and bearing shells. It is recommended that the establishment used is a member of the Federation of Engine Re-Manufacturers, or a similar society.

Always wait until the engine has been completely dismantled, and until all components (especially the cylinder block/ crankcase and the crankshaft) have been inspected, before deciding what service and repair operations must be performed by an engineering works. The condition of these components will be the major factor to consider when determining whether to overhaul the original engine, or to buy a reconditioned unit. Do not, therefore, purchase parts or have overhaul work done

on other components until they have been thoroughly inspected. As a general rule, time is the primary cost of an overhaul, so it does not pay to fit worn or sub-standard parts.

As a final note, to ensure maximum life and minimum trouble from a reconditioned engine, everything must be assembled with care, in a spotlessly-clean environment.

3 Engine removal – methods and precautions

If you have decided that the engine must be removed for overhaul or major repair work, several preliminary steps should be taken.

Engine/transmission removal is extremely complicated and involved on these vehicles. It must be stated, that unless the vehicle can be positioned on a ramp, or raised and supported on axle stands over an inspection pit, it will be very difficult to carry out the work involved.

Cleaning the engine compartment and engine/transmission before beginning the removal procedure will help keep tools clean and organised.

An engine hoist will also be necessary. Make sure the equipment is rated in excess of the combined weight of the engine and transmission. Safety is of primary importance, considering the potential hazards involved in removing the engine/transmission from the car.

The help of an assistant is essential. Apart from the safety aspects involved, there are many instances when one person cannot simultaneously perform all of the operations required during engine/transmission removal.

Plan the operation ahead of time. Before starting work, arrange for the hire of or obtain all of the tools and equipment you will need. Some of the equipment necessary to perform engine/transmission removal and installation safely (in addition to an engine hoist) is as follows: a heavy duty trolley jack, complete sets of spanners and sockets as described in the rear of this manual, wooden blocks, and plenty of rags and cleaning solvent for mopping-up spilled oil, coolant and fuel. If the hoist must be hired, make sure that you arrange for it in advance, and perform all of the operations possible without it beforehand. This will save you money and time.

Plan for the car to be out of use for quite a while. An engineering machine shop or engine reconditioning specialist will be required to perform some of the work which cannot be accomplished without special equipment. These places often have a busy schedule, so it would be a good idea to consult them before removing the engine, in order to accurately estimate the amount of time required to rebuild or repair components that may need work.

During the engine/transmission removal procedure, it is advisable to make notes of the locations of all brackets, cable-ties,

earthing points, etc, as well as how the wiring harnesses, hoses and electrical connections are attached and routed around the engine and engine compartment. An effective way of doing this is to take a series of photographs of the various components before they are disconnected or removed; the resulting photographs will prove invaluable when the engine/transmission is refitted.

Always be extremely careful when removing and refitting the engine/transmission. Serious injury can result from careless actions. Plan ahead and take your time, and a job of this nature, although major, can be accomplished successfully.

On all Meriva models, the engine must be removed complete with the transmission as an assembly. There is insufficient clearance in the engine compartment to remove the engine leaving the transmission in the vehicle. The assembly is removed by raising the front of the vehicle, and lowering the assembly from the engine compartment.

4 Petrol engine and transmission unit – removal, separation and refitting

Note 1: *The engine can be removed from the car only as a complete unit with the transmission; the two are then separated for overhaul. The engine/transmission unit is lowered out of position, and withdrawn from under the vehicle. Bearing this in mind, and also bearing in mind the information contained in Section 3, ensure the vehicle is raised sufficiently so that there is enough clearance between the front of the vehicle and the floor to allow the engine/transmission unit to be slid out once it has been lowered out of position.*

Note 2: *Such is the complexity of the power unit arrangement on these vehicles, and the variations that may be encountered according to model and optional equipment fitted, that the following should be regarded as a guide to the work involved, rather than a step-by-step procedure. Where differences are encountered, or additional component disconnection or removal is necessary, make notes of the work involved as an aid to refitting.*

Removal

1 Position the vehicle as described in Section 3, paragraph 2, and remove both front road-wheels. Also remove the right-hand wheel arch liner inner cover.

2 Remove the bonnet and the front bumper as described in Chapter 11.

3 Where fitted, remove the plastic cover from the top of the engine.

4 Remove the battery and battery tray as described in Chapter 5A.

5 Undo the retaining nuts, remove the bolts and disconnect the positive and negative secondary leads from the main battery positive and negative terminals.

4.10a Undo the retaining screw (arrowed) . . .

4.10b . . . extract the plastic rivet . . .

4.10c . . . squeeze together the legs of the guide clip . . .

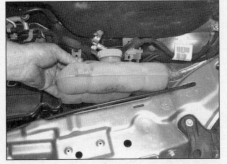

4.10d . . . and withdraw the expansion tank from the crossmember

6 Carry out the following operations as described in Chapter 1A:
  a) *Drain the engine oil.*
  b) *Drain the cooling system.*
  c) *Remove the auxiliary drivebelt.*

7 Remove the air cleaner assembly and intake ducts as described in Chapter 4A.

8 Disconnect the main wiring harness connector situated adjacent to the battery location.

9 Disconnect the wiring connector(s) from the engine management ECU and release the wiring harness from the cable-ties.

10 Undo the retaining screw and extract the plastic rivet securing the cooling system expansion tank to the front upper cross-member. Squeeze together the legs of the guide clip and withdraw the expansion tank from the crossmember **(see illustrations)**.

11 Disconnect the wiring block connector from the cooling fan module. Release the

wiring harness from the retaining clips so that it is free to be removed with the engine.

12 On models with Easytronic transmission, disconnect the transmission wiring harness connectors, and release the harness from the transmission.

13 Disconnect the wiring connector from the reversing light switch on the transmission.

14 Unbolt the air conditioning compressor from the engine **without disconnecting the refrigerant lines** and support the compressor to one side.

15 Depressurise the fuel system with reference to Chapter 4A, then disconnect the fuel supply pipe from the fuel rail and support bracket. Be prepared for fuel spillage, and take adequate precautions. Clamp or plug the open unions, to minimise further fuel loss.

16 Disconnect the brake vacuum servo hose, and fuel evaporation purge hose.

17 Loosen the clips and remove the upper and lower radiator hoses.

18 Release the quick-release connectors by sliding them forward, and disconnect the two heater hoses from the heater matrix pipe stubs.

19 Where applicable, release the clip and disconnect the coolant hose at the throttle housing.

20 Drain the transmission oil as described in Chapter 7A or 7B, as applicable.

21 Remove both driveshafts as described in Chapter 8.

22 On standard manual transmission models (not Easytronic), remove the filler cap from the brake/clutch fluid reservoir on the bulkhead, then tighten it onto a piece of polythene. This will reduce the loss of fluid when the clutch hydraulic hose is disconnected. Alternatively, fit a hose clamp to the flexible hose next to the clutch hydraulic connection on the transmission housing.

23 Place some cloth rags beneath the hose, then prise out the retaining clip securing the clutch hydraulic hose to the end fitting on top of the transmission bellhousing. Detach the hose from the end fitting **(see illustrations)**. Gently squeeze the two legs of the retaining clip together and re-insert the retaining clip back into position in the end fitting. Discard the sealing ring from the hose end; a new sealing ring must be used on refitting. Plug/cover both the end fitting and hose end to minimise fluid loss and prevent the entry of dirt into the hydraulic system. **Note:** *Whilst the hose is disconnected, do not depress the clutch pedal.*

24 Attach a suitable hoist and lifting tackle to the engine lifting brackets on the cylinder head, and support the weight of the engine/transmission.

25 Remove the front subframe as described in Chapter 10.

26 Mark the position of the two bolts securing the right-hand engine mounting bracket to the engine bracket and undo the bolts **(see illustration)**. **Note:** *There is no need to remove the mounting, since the engine/transmission is lowered from the engine compartment.*

27 Mark the position of the two bolts

4.23a Prise out the clip securing the clutch hydraulic hose to the end fitting on the transmission bellhousing . . .

4.23b . . . then detach the hose from the end fitting

4.26 Undo the two bolts (arrowed) securing the right-hand engine mounting bracket to the engine bracket

securing the left-hand engine mounting to the transmission bracket **(see illustration)**.

28 Make a final check to ensure that all relevant pipes, hoses, wires, etc, have been disconnected, and that they are positioned clear of the engine and transmission.

29 With the help of an assistant, carefully lower the engine/transmission assembly to the ground. Make sure that the surrounding components in the engine compartment are not damaged. Ideally, the assembly should be lowered onto a trolley jack or low platform with castors, so that it can easily be withdrawn from under the car.

30 Ensure that the assembly is adequately supported, then disconnect the engine hoist and lifting tackle, and withdraw the engine/transmission assembly from under the front of the vehicle.

Separation

31 Clean away any external dirt using paraffin or a water-soluble solvent and a stiff brush.

32 Refer to the procedures contained in Chapter 7A or 7B, and unbolt the transmission from the engine. Carefully withdraw the transmission from the engine. Ensure that the weight of the transmission is not allowed to hang on the input shaft while engaged with the clutch friction disc. Note that the transmission locates on dowels positioned in the rear of the cylinder block.

Refitting

33 With reference to Chapter 7A or 7B, refit the transmission to the engine and tighten the bolts to the specified torque.

34 With the front of the vehicle raised and supported on axle stands, move the engine/transmission assembly under the vehicle, ensuring that the assembly is adequately supported.

35 Reconnect the hoist and lifting tackle to the engine lifting brackets, and carefully raise the engine/transmission assembly up into the engine compartment with the help of an assistant.

36 Reconnect the right- and left-hand engine/transmission mountings and tighten the bolts to the specified torque given in Chapter 2A, 2B or 2C, as applicable. Ensure that the marks made on removal are correctly aligned when tightening the retaining bolts.

37 Refit the front subframe as described in Chapter 10.

38 Disconnect the hoist and lifting tackle from the engine lifting brackets.

39 Refit the driveshafts as described in Chapter 8.

40 Refill the transmission with correct quantity and type of oil, as described in Chapter 7A or 7B.

41 Reconnect and bleed the clutch hydraulic connection at the transmission with reference to Chapter 6.

42 Push the heater hoses back onto the matrix pipe stubs. Ensure that the quick- release connectors securely lock the hoses in position.

43 Refit the cooling system expansion tank.

44 Reconnect the upper and lower radiator hoses and all other disconnected hoses.

45 Reconnect the brake vacuum servo hose, and fuel evaporation purge hose and fuel supply pipe.

46 Refit the air conditioning system compressor as described in Chapter 3, then refit the auxiliary drivebelt as described in Chapter 1A.

47 Reconnect the wiring block connector to the cooling fan module.

48 Reconnect the main wiring harness connector situated adjacent to the battery location.

49 Reconnect the wiring connector(s) from the engine management ECU.

50 On models with Easytronic transmission, reconnect the transmission wiring harness connectors, and secure the harness to the transmission.

51 Reconnect the reversing light switch wiring connector.

52 Refit the air cleaner assembly and intake ducts as described in Chapter 4A.

53 Refit the battery tray and battery as described in Chapter 5A.

54 Reconnect the positive and negative secondary leads to the main battery positive and negative terminals.

55 Refit the bonnet and the front bumper as described in Chapter 11.

56 Refit the right-hand wheel arch liner inner cover and both front roadwheels, then lower the vehicle to the ground.

57 Make a final check to ensure that all relevant hoses, pipes and wires have been correctly reconnected.

58 Refill the engine with oil with reference to Chapter 1A.

59 Refill and bleed the cooling system with reference to Chapter 1A.

---

5   Diesel engine and transmission unit – removal, separation and refitting

Note 1: *The engine can be removed from the car only as a complete unit with the transmission; the two are then separated for overhaul. The engine/transmission unit is lowered out of position, and withdrawn from under the vehicle. Bearing this in mind, and also bearing in mind the information contained in Section 3, ensure the vehicle is raised sufficiently so that there is enough clearance between the front of the vehicle and the floor to allow the engine/transmission unit to be slid out once it has been lowered out of position.*

Note 2: *Such is the complexity of the power unit arrangement on these vehicles, and the variations that may be encountered according to model and optional equipment fitted, that the following should be regarded as a guide to the work involved, rather than a step-by-step procedure. Where differences are encountered,*

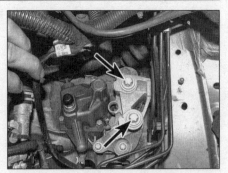

4.27 Undo the two bolts (arrowed) securing the left-hand engine mounting to the transmission bracket

or additional component disconnection or removal is necessary, make notes of the work involved as an aid to refitting.

Removal

1 On models equipped with air conditioning, have the air conditioning system fully discharged by an air conditioning specialist.

2 Position the vehicle as described in Section 3, paragraph 2, and remove both front roadwheels.

3 Remove the bonnet and the front bumper as described in Chapter 11.

4 Where fitted, remove the plastic cover from the top of the engine.

5 Remove the fuel filter or fuel filter housing as described in Chapter 1B.

6 Remove the battery and battery tray as described in Chapter 5A.

7 Carry out the following operations as described in Chapter 1B:
   a) *Drain the engine oil.*
   b) *Drain the cooling system.*
   c) *Remove the auxiliary drivebelt.*

8 Remove the air cleaner assembly, intake ducts and charge air pipes/hoses as described in Chapter 4B.

9 On models equipped with air conditioning, remove the air conditioning compressor as described in Chapter 3.

10 Undo the retaining screw and extract the plastic rivet securing the cooling system expansion tank to the front upper cross-member. Squeeze together the legs of the guide clip and withdraw the expansion tank from the crossmember **(see illustrations 4.10a to 4.10d)**.

11 Disconnect the wiring connector from the reversing light switch on the transmission.

12 Undo the retaining nuts, remove the bolts and disconnect the positive and negative secondary leads from the main battery positive and negative terminals.

13 On 1.3 litre engines, disconnect the two main wiring harness connectors located rear left-hand side of the engine compartment. Release the harness from the cable-ties so that it is free to be removed with the engine.

14 Disconnect the wiring block connector from the cooling fan module adjacent to the cooling fan. Release the wiring harness from the retaining bolt and clips.

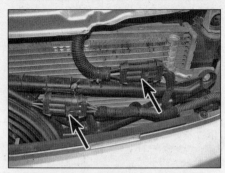

5.15 On 1.3 litre engines with air conditioning, disconnect the two wiring harness connectors (arrowed) at the auxiliary cooling fan shroud

15 On 1.3 litre engines equipped with air conditioning, disconnect the two wiring harness connectors at the auxiliary cooling fan shroud and release the wiring harness from the cable-ties **(see illustration)**.

16 On 1.3 litre engines, working under the front, left-hand side of the car, release the locking lever catch, then lift the locking lever and disconnect the wiring connector from the engine management system ECU. Free the wiring harness from the retaining clips and cable-ties.

17 On 1.7 litre engines, release the locking lever catches and disconnect the three wiring connectors at the engine management system ECU. Where applicable, disconnect the two adjacent engine management wiring harness connectors and free the wiring harness from the retaining clips and cable-ties.

18 Disconnect the brake vacuum servo hose from the vacuum pump.

19 On 1.3 litre engines, detach the fuel return hose quick-release connector and remove the hose from the fuel rail. A Vauxhall/Opel special tool (KM-796-A) is available to disconnect the hose connector, but provided care is taken, the connection can be released using two screwdrivers, a pair of long-nosed pliers, or similar, to depress the retaining tangs. Suitably cover or plug the open hose connections to prevent dirt entry.

20 On 1.7 litre Y17DT engines, release the retaining clip and detach the fuel return hose. Suitably cover or plug the open hose connection to prevent dirt entry.

21 On all engines, disconnect any remaining fuel supply and return hoses likely to impede removal of the engine.

22 Loosen the clips and remove the upper and lower radiator hoses.

23 Extract the retaining spring clips and disconnect the two heater hoses from the heater matrix pipe stubs.

24 On models with a cable-operated gear-change mechanism, using a suitable forked tool, release the gearchange selector cable end fittings from the transmission selector levers. Pull back the retaining sleeves and detach the outer cables from the mounting bracket on the transmission **(see illustrations)**.

25 Drain the transmission oil as described in Chapter 7A.

26 Remove both driveshafts as described in Chapter 8.

27 Remove the filler cap from the brake/clutch fluid reservoir on the bulkhead, then tighten it onto a piece of polythene. This will reduce the loss of fluid when the clutch hydraulic hose is disconnected. Alternatively, fit a hose clamp to the flexible hose next to the clutch hydraulic connection on the transmission housing.

28 Place some cloth rags beneath the hose, then prise out the retaining clip securing the clutch hydraulic hose to the end fitting on top of the transmission bellhousing. Detach the hose from the end fitting **(see illustrations 4.23a and 4.23b)**. Gently squeeze the two legs of the retaining clip together and re-insert the retaining clip back into position in the end fitting. Discard the sealing ring from the hose end; a new sealing ring must be used on refitting. Plug/cover both the end fitting and hose end to minimise fluid loss and prevent the entry of dirt into the hydraulic system. **Note:** *Whilst the hose is disconnected, do not depress the clutch pedal.*

29 Attach a suitable hoist and lifting tackle to the engine lifting brackets on the cylinder head, and support the weight of the engine/transmission.

30 Remove the front subframe as described in Chapter 10.

31 Mark the position of the two bolts securing the right-hand engine mounting bracket to the engine bracket and undo the bolts **(see illustration 4.26)**. **Note:** *There is no need to remove the mounting, since the engine/*

transmission is lowered from the engine compartment.

32 Mark the position of the two bolts securing the left-hand engine mounting to the transmission bracket **(see illustration 4.27)**.

33 Make a final check to ensure that all relevant pipes and hoses have been disconnected, and that they are positioned clear of the engine and transmission. Check that all wiring connectors have been disconnected and that the main engine harness is free to be removed with the engine.

34 With the help of an assistant, carefully lower the engine/transmission assembly to the ground. Make sure that the surrounding components in the engine compartment are not damaged. Ideally, the assembly should be lowered onto a trolley jack or low platform with castors, so that it can easily be withdrawn from under the car.

35 Ensure that the assembly is adequately supported, then disconnect the engine hoist and lifting tackle, and withdraw the engine/transmission assembly from under the front of the vehicle.

Separation

36 Clean away any external dirt using paraffin or a water-soluble solvent and a stiff brush.

37 With reference to Chapter 7A, unbolt the transmission from the engine. Carefully withdraw the transmission from the engine. Ensure that the weight of the transmission is not allowed to hang on the input shaft while engaged with the clutch friction disc. Note that the transmission locates on dowels positioned in the rear of the cylinder block.

Refitting

38 With reference to Chapter 7A, refit the transmission to the engine and tighten the bolts to the specified torque.

39 With the front of the vehicle raised and supported on axle stands, move the engine/transmission assembly under the vehicle, ensuring that the assembly is adequately supported.

40 Reconnect the hoist and lifting tackle to the engine lifting brackets, and carefully raise the engine/transmission assembly up into the engine compartment with the help of an assistant.

41 Reconnect the right- and left-hand engine/transmission mountings and tighten the bolts to the specified torque given in Chapter 2D or 2E, as applicable. Ensure that the marks made on removal are correctly aligned when tightening the retaining bolts.

42 Refit the front subframe as described in Chapter 10.

43 Disconnect the hoist and lifting tackle from the engine lifting brackets.

44 Refit the driveshafts as described in Chapter 8.

45 Refill the transmission with correct quantity and type of oil, as described in Chapter 7A.

46 Reconnect and bleed the clutch hydraulic connection at the transmission with reference to Chapter 6.

5.24a Release the selector inner cable end fittings from the transmission selector levers . . .

5.24b . . . then pull back the retaining sleeves and detach the outer cables from the transmission mounting bracket

47 On models with a cable-operated gearchange mechanism, refit the gearchange/selector outer cables to the mounting bracket on the transmission. Engage the inner cable end fittings with the selector lever balljoints, squeezing them together with pliers if necessary.

48 Push the heater hoses back onto the matrix pipe stubs. Ensure that the quick-release connectors securely lock the hoses in position.

49 Reconnect the upper and lower radiator hoses.

50 Reconnect the brake vacuum servo hose to the vacuum pump, and the disconnected fuel supply and return hoses.

51 Reconnect the wiring connectors to the engine management system ECU.

52 Refit the air conditioning system compressor as described in Chapter 3, then refit the auxiliary drivebelt as described in Chapter 1B.

53 Reconnect the wiring connectors at the cooling fan module and auxiliary cooling fan shroud, and secure the harness with the clips and cable-ties.

54 Refit the cooling system expansion tank to the front upper crossmember.

55 Reconnect the positive and negative wiring terminals to the battery positive and negative terminal clamps.

56 Reconnect all remaining wiring connectors and secure the wiring and harness with the cable clips or new cable-ties.

57 Refit the air cleaner assembly, intake ducts and charge air pipes/hoses as described in Chapter 4B.

58 Refit the battery tray and battery as described in Chapter 5A.

59 Refit the fuel filter or fuel filter housing as described in Chapter 1B

60 Refit the bonnet and the front bumper as described in Chapter 11.

61 Refit both front roadwheels, then lower the vehicle to the ground.

62 Make a final check to ensure that all relevant hoses, pipes and wires have been correctly reconnected.

63 Refill the engine with oil with reference to Chapter 1B.

64 Refill and bleed the cooling system with reference to Chapter 1B.

65 On models equipped with air conditioning, have the air conditioning system evacuated, charged and leak-tested by the specialist who discharged it.

6 Engine overhaul – dismantling sequence

1 It is much easier to dismantle and work on the engine if it is mounted on a portable engine stand. These stands can often be hired from a tool hire shop. Before the engine is mounted on a stand, the flywheel should be removed, so that the stand bolts can be tightened into the end of the cylinder block/crankcase.

2 If a stand is not available, it is possible to dismantle the engine with it blocked up on a sturdy workbench, or on the floor. Be extra careful not to tip or drop the engine when working without a stand.

3 If you are going to obtain a reconditioned engine, all the external components must be removed first, to be transferred to the replacement engine (just as they will if you are doing a complete engine overhaul yourself). These components include the following:

a) Engine wiring harness and supports.

b) Alternator and air conditioning compressor mounting brackets (as applicable).

c) Coolant pump (where applicable) and inlet/outlet housings.

d) Dipstick tube.

e) Fuel system components.

f) All electrical switches and sensors.

g) Inlet and exhaust manifolds.

h) Oil filter and oil cooler/heat exchanger.

i) Flywheel.

Note: *When removing the external components from the engine, pay close attention to details that may be helpful or important during refitting. Note the fitted position of gaskets, seals, spacers, pins, washers, bolts, and other small items.*

4 If you are obtaining a 'short' engine (which consists of the engine cylinder block/crankcase, crankshaft, pistons and connecting rods all assembled), then the cylinder head, sump, oil pump, and timing belt/chains (as applicable) will have to be removed also.

5 If you are planning a complete overhaul, the engine can be dismantled, and the internal components removed, in the order given below.

1.4 litre petrol engines

a) Inlet and exhaust manifolds (see Chapter 4A).

b) Sump (see Chapter 2A).

c) Coolant pump (see Chapter 3).

d) Timing chain and sprockets (see Chapter 2A).

e) Oil pump (see Chapter 2A).

f) Cylinder head (see Chapter 2A).

g) Flywheel (see Chapter 2A).

h) Pistons/connecting rod assemblies (see Section 10).

i) Crankshaft (see Section 11).

1.6 and 1.8 litre petrol engines

a) Inlet and exhaust manifolds (see Chapter 4A).

b) Timing belt, sprockets, tensioner and idler pulleys (see Chapter 2B or 2C).

c) Coolant pump (see Chapter 3).

d) Cylinder head (see Chapter 2B or 2C).

e) Flywheel (see Chapter 2B or 2C).

f) Sump (see Chapter 2B or 2C).

g) Oil pump (see Chapter 2B or 2C).

h) Pistons/connecting rod assemblies (see Section 10).

i) Crankshaft (see Section 11).

1.3 litre diesel engines

a) Inlet and exhaust manifolds (see Chapter 4B).

b) Coolant pump (see Chapter 3).

c) Sump (see Chapter 2D).

d) Timing chains and sprockets (see Chapter 2D).

e) Oil pump (see Chapter 2D).

f) Cylinder head (see Chapter 2D).

g) Flywheel (see Chapter 2D).

h) Piston/connecting rod assemblies (see Section 10).

i) Crankshaft (see Section 11).

1.7 litre diesel engines

a) Inlet and exhaust manifolds (see Chapter 4B).

b) Timing belt, sprockets, tensioner and idler pulleys (see Chapter 2E).

c) Coolant pump (see Chapter 3).

d) Cylinder head (see Chapter 2E).

e) Flywheel (see Chapter 2E).

f) Sump (see Chapter 2E).

g) Oil pump (see Chapter 2E).

h) Piston/connecting rod assemblies (see Section 10).

i) Crankshaft (see Section 11).

6 Before beginning the dismantling and overhaul procedures, make sure that you have all of the correct tools necessary. See *Tools and working facilities* for further information.

7 Cylinder head – dismantling

Note: *New and reconditioned cylinder heads are available from the manufacturer, and from engine overhaul specialists. Due to the fact that some specialist tools are required for the dismantling and inspection procedures, and new components may not be readily available, it may be more practical and economical for the home mechanic to purchase a reconditioned head rather than to dismantle, inspect and recondition the original head. A valve spring compressor tool will be required for this operation.*

1 With the cylinder head removed as described in the relevant Part of this Chapter, clean away all external dirt, and remove the following components as applicable, if not already done:

a) Manifolds (see Chapter 4A or 4B).

b) Spark plugs (petrol engines – see Chapter 1A).

c) Glow plugs (diesel engines – see Chapter 5A).

d) Fuel injectors (diesel engines – see Chapter 4B).

e) Camshafts and and associated valve train components (see the relevant Part of Chapter 2).

f) Cooling system components (see Chapter 3).

g) Engine lifting brackets.

2 To remove a valve, fit a valve spring

7.2 Using a valve spring compressor, compress the valve spring to relieve the pressure on the collets

7.4 Extract the two split collets by hooking them out using a small screwdriver

7.5a Remove the valve spring cap . . .

7.5b . . . and the spring . . .

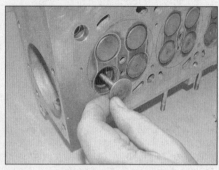

7.5c . . . then withdraw the valve through the combustion chamber

7.5d Using pliers, remove the valve stem oil seal, which also incorporates the spring seat on most engines

compressor tool. Ensure that the arms of the compressor tool are securely positioned on the head of the valve and the spring cap **(see illustration)**. The valves are deeply-recessed on most engines, and a suitable extension piece may be required for the spring compressor.

3 Compress the valve spring to relieve the pressure of the spring cap acting on the collets.

> **HAYNES HiNT** *If the spring cap sticks to the valve stem, support the compressor tool, and give the end a light tap with a soft-faced mallet to help free the spring cap.*

4 Extract the two split collets by hooking them out using a small screwdriver, then slowly release the compressor tool **(see illustration)**.

5 Remove the valve spring cap and the

7.6 Place each valve assembly in a labelled polythene bag or similar container

spring, then withdraw the valve through the combustion chamber. Using pliers, remove the valve stem oil seal which also incorporates the spring seat on most engines **(see illustrations)**. If the spring seat is not part of the valve stem oil seal, hook it out using a small screwdriver.

6 Repeat the procedure for the remaining valves, keeping all components in strict order so that they can be refitted in their original positions, unless all the components are to be renewed. If the components are to be kept and used again, place each valve assembly in a labelled polythene bag or a similar small container **(see illustration)**. Note that as with cylinder numbering, the valves are normally numbered from the timing chain (or timing belt) end of the engine. Make sure that the valve components are identified as inlet and exhaust, as well as numbered.

8 Cylinder head and valves – cleaning and inspection

1 Thorough cleaning of the cylinder head and valve components, followed by a detailed inspection, will enable you to decide how much valve service work must be carried out during the engine overhaul. **Note:** *If the engine has been severely overheated, it is best to assume that the cylinder head is warped – check carefully for signs of this.*

Cleaning

2 Scrape away all traces of old gasket material from the cylinder head.

3 Scrape away the carbon from the combustion chambers and ports, then wash the cylinder head thoroughly with paraffin or a suitable solvent.

4 Scrape off any heavy carbon deposits that may have formed on the valves, then use a power-operated wire brush to remove deposits from the valve heads and stems.

Inspection

Note: *Be sure to perform all the following inspection procedures before concluding that the services of a machine shop or engine overhaul specialist are required. Make a list of all items that require attention.*

Cylinder head

5 Inspect the head very carefully for cracks, evidence of coolant leakage, and other damage. If cracks are found, a new cylinder head should be obtained.

6 Use a straight-edge and feeler gauge blade

8.6 Using a straight-edge and feeler gauge to check cylinder head surface distortion

to check that the cylinder head surface is not distorted **(see illustration)**. If it is, it may be possible to resurface it, provided that the cylinder head is not reduced to less than the minimum specified height.

7 Examine the valve seats in each of the combustion chambers. If they are severely pitted, cracked or burned, then they will need to be recut by an engine overhaul specialist. If they are only slightly pitted, this can be removed by grinding-in the valve heads and seats with fine valve-grinding compound, as described below.

8 If the valve guides are worn, indicated by a side-to-side motion of the valve, oversize valve guides are available, and valves with oversize stems can be fitted. This work is best carried out by an engine overhaul specialist. A dial gauge may be used to determine whether the amount of side play of a valve exceeds the specified maximum.

9 Check the tappet bores in the cylinder head for wear. If excessive wear is evident, the cylinder head must be renewed. Also check the tappet oil holes in the cylinder head for obstructions.

Valves

10 Examine the head of each valve for pitting, burning, cracks and general wear, and check the valve stem for scoring and wear ridges. Rotate the valve, and check for any obvious indication that it is bent. Look for pitting and excessive wear on the tip of each valve stem. Renew any valve that shows any such signs of wear or damage.

11 If the valve appears satisfactory at this stage, measure the valve stem diameter at several points using a micrometer **(see illustration)**. Any significant difference in the readings obtained indicates wear of the valve stem. Should any of these conditions be apparent, the valve(s) must be renewed.

12 If the valves are in satisfactory condition, they should be ground (lapped) into their respective seats, to ensure a smooth gas-tight seal. If the seat is only lightly pitted, or if it has been recut, fine grinding compound **only** should be used to produce the required finish. Coarse valve-grinding compound should **not** be used unless a seat is badly burned or deeply pitted; if this is the case, the cylinder head and valves should be inspected by an

8.11 Using a micrometer to measure valve stem diameter

expert to decide whether seat recutting, or even the renewal of the valve or seat insert, is required.

13 Valve grinding is carried out as follows. Place the cylinder head upside-down on a bench, with a block of wood at each end to give clearance for the valve stems.

14 Smear a trace of the appropriate grade of valve-grinding compound on the seat face, and press a suction grinding tool onto the valve head. With a semi-rotary action, grind the valve head to its seat, lifting the valve occasionally to redistribute the grinding compound **(see illustration)**. A light spring placed under the valve head will greatly ease this operation.

15 If coarse grinding compound is being used, work only until a dull, matt even surface is produced on both the valve seat and the valve, then wipe off the used compound and repeat the process with fine compound. When a smooth unbroken ring of light grey matt finish is produced on both the valve and seat, the grinding operation is complete. **Do not** grind in the valves any further than absolutely necessary, or the seat will be prematurely sunk into the cylinder head.

16 When all the valves have been ground-in, carefully wash off all traces of grinding compound using paraffin or a suitable solvent before reassembly of the cylinder head.

Valve components

17 Examine the valve springs for signs of damage and discoloration; if possible; also compare the existing spring free length with new components.

8.14 Grinding-in a valve

18 Stand each spring on a flat surface, and check it for squareness. If any of the springs are damaged, distorted or have lost their tension, obtain a complete new set of springs.

9 Cylinder head –
reassembly

1 Lubricate the stems of the valves, and insert them into their original locations **(see illustration)**. If new valves are being fitted, insert them into the locations to which they have been ground.

2 Working on the first valve, refit the spring seat if it is not an integral part of the valve stem oil seal. Dip the new valve stem seal in fresh engine oil, then carefully locate it over the valve and onto the guide. Take care not to damage the seal as it is passed over the valve stem. Use a suitable socket or metal tube to press the seal firmly onto the guide. **Note:** *If genuine seals are being fitted, use the oil seal protector which is supplied with the seals; the protector fits over the valve stem and prevents the oil seal lip being damaged on the valve* **(see illustrations)**.

3 Locate the spring on the seat and fit the spring cap **(see illustration)**.

4 Compress the valve spring, and locate the split collets in the recess in the valve stem **(see illustration and Haynes Hint)**. Release the compressor, then repeat the procedure on the remaining valves.

5 With all the valves installed, support the

9.1 Lubricate the valve stem with engine oil and insert the valve into the correct guide

9.2a Fit the spring seat . . .

9.2b . . . then fit the seal protector (where supplied) to the valve . . .

9.2c . . . and install the new valve stem oil seal . . .

9.2d . . . pressing it onto the valve guide with a suitable socket

9.3 Refit the valve spring and fit the spring cap

9.4 Compress the valve and locate the collets in the recess on the valve stem

HAYNES HiNT

Use a little dab of grease to hold the collets in position on the valve stem while the spring compressor is released.

cylinder head on blocks on the bench and, using a hammer and interposed block of wood, tap the end of each valve stem to settle the components.

6 Refit the components removed in Section 7, paragraph 1.

10 Pistons/connecting rods – removal

Note : *New connecting rod big-end cap bolts will be needed on refitting.*

1 Referring to the relevant Part of Chapter 2, remove the cylinder head and sump. Where fitted, unbolt the pick-up/strainer from the base of the oil pump and the oil baffle plate from the cylinder block baseplate **(see illustration)**.

2 If there is a pronounced wear ridge at the top of any bore, it may be necessary to remove it with a scraper or ridge reamer, to avoid piston damage during removal. Such a ridge indicates excessive wear of the cylinder bore.

3 If the connecting rods and big-end caps are not marked to indicate their positions in the cylinder block (ie, marked with cylinder numbers), suitably mark both the rod and cap with quick-drying paint or similar. Note which side of the engine the marks face and accurately record this also. There may not be any other way of identifying which way round the cap fits on the rod, when refitting.

4 Turn the crankshaft to bring pistons 1 and 4 to BDC (bottom dead centre).

5 Unscrew the bolts from No 1 piston big-end bearing cap, then take off the cap and recover the bottom half-bearing shell **(see illustration)**. If the bearing shells are to be re-used, tape the cap and the shell together.

Caution: On some engines, the connecting rod/bearing cap mating surfaces are not machined flat; the big-end bearing caps are 'cracked' off from the rod during production and left untouched to ensure the cap and rod mate perfectly. Where this type of connecting rod is fitted, great care must be taken to ensure the mating surfaces of the cap and rod are not marked or damaged in anyway. Any damage to the mating surfaces will adversely affect the strength of the connecting rod and could lead to premature failure.

6 Using a hammer handle, push the piston up through the bore, and remove it from the top of the cylinder block **(see illustration)**. Recover the bearing shell, and tape it to the connecting rod for safe-keeping.

7 Loosely refit the big-end cap to the connecting rod, and secure with the nuts/bolts – this will help to keep the components in their correct order.

8 Remove No 4 piston assembly in the same way.

9 Turn the crankshaft through 180° to bring pistons 2 and 3 to BDC, and remove them in the same way.

11 Crankshaft – removal

1.4 litre petrol engines

Note: *New cylinder block baseplate retaining bolts will be required for refitting.*

10.1 Undo the bolts and remove the oil baffle plate from the cylinder block baseplate

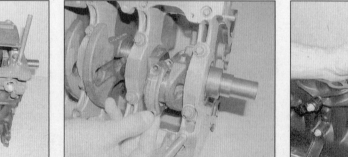

10.5 Unscrew the big-end cap bolts from the first connecting rod, and remove the cap

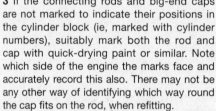
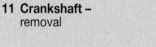
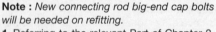

10.6 Push the piston/rod assembly up and out of the top of the cylinder bore

11.4 Check the crankshaft endfloat using a dial gauge . . .

11.5 . . . or a feeler gauge

11.8 Lift the cylinder block baseplate off the cylinder block – 1.4 litre petrol engines

1 Remove the flywheel as described in Chapter 2A.

2 Remove the pistons and connecting rods, as described in Section 10. If no work is to be done on the pistons and connecting rods, unbolt the caps and push the pistons far enough up the bores that the connecting rods are positioned clear of the crankshaft journals.

3 Invert the engine so that the crankshaft is uppermost.

4 Before removing the crankshaft, check the endfloat using a dial gauge in contact with the end of the crankshaft. Push the crankshaft fully one way, and then zero the gauge. Push the crankshaft fully the other way, and check the endfloat **(see illustration)**. The result should be compared with the specified limit, and will give an indication as to the size of the main bearing shell thrust journal width which will be required for reassembly.

5 If a dial gauge is not available, a feeler gauge can be used to measure crankshaft endfloat. Push the crankshaft fully towards one end of the crankcase, and insert a feeler gauge between the thrust flange of the main bearing shell and the machined surface of the crankshaft web **(see illustration)**. Before measuring, ensure that the crankshaft is fully forced towards one end of the crankcase, to give the widest possible gap at the measuring location. **Note:** *Measure at the bearing with the thrustwasher (see Section 18).*

6 Working in a diagonal sequence, progressively slacken the outer (M6) bolts securing the cylinder block baseplate to the cylinder block.

7 When all the outer bolts have been slackened, repeat the procedure on the inner (M8) retaining bolts.

8 Remove all the bolts and lift the cylinder block baseplate off the cylinder block **(see illustration)**. If the baseplate is initially tight to remove, carefully tap it free using a soft-faced mallet.

9 As the baseplate is withdrawn check that the lower main bearing shells come away with the baseplate. If they remain on the crankshaft journals, lift them off and refit them to their respective locations in the baseplate.

10 Lift the crankshaft from the cylinder block and remove the crankshaft oil seal.

11 Extract the upper bearing shells, and identify them for position if they are to be re-used.

1.6 and 1.8 litre petrol engines

Note: *New main bearing cap bolts will be required on refitting.*

12 Working as described in Part B or C of this Chapter, remove the flywheel and the oil pump.

13 Remove the piston and connecting rod assemblies as described in Section 10.

14 Before removing the crankshaft, check the endfloat as described previously in paragraphs 4 and 5.

15 The main bearing caps should be numbered 1 to 5 from the timing belt end of the engine and all identification numbers should be the right way up when read from the rear of the cylinder block **(see illustration)**. If the bearing caps are not marked, using a hammer and punch or a suitable marker pen, number the caps from 1 to 5 from the timing belt end of the engine and mark each cap to indicate its correct fitted direction to avoid confusion on refitting.

16 Working in a diagonal sequence, evenly and progressively slacken the ten main bearing cap retaining bolts by half a turn at a time until all bolts are loose. Remove all the bolts.

17 Carefully remove each cap from the cylinder block, ensuring that the lower main bearing shell remains in position in the cap.

18 Carefully lift out the crankshaft, taking care not to displace the upper main bearing

shells **(see illustration)**. Remove the oil seal and discard it.

19 Recover the upper bearing shells from the cylinder block, and tape them to their respective caps for safe-keeping.

1.3 litre diesel engines

Note: *New cylinder block baseplate retaining bolts will be required for refitting.*

20 Working as described in Part D of this Chapter, remove the flywheel.

21 Remove the piston and connecting rod assemblies as described in Section 10. If no work is to be done on the pistons and connecting rods, unbolt the caps and push the pistons far enough up the bores that the connecting rods are positioned clear of the crankshaft journals.

22 Before removing the crankshaft, check the endfloat as described previously in paragraphs 4 and 5.

23 Working in a diagonal sequence, progressively slacken the outer (M8) bolts securing the cylinder block baseplate to the cylinder block.

24 When all the outer bolts have been slackened, repeat the procedure on the inner (M10) retaining bolts.

25 Remove all the bolts and lift the cylinder block baseplate off the cylinder block **(see illustration)**. If the baseplate is initially tight to remove, carefully tap it free using a soft-faced mallet. Alternatively, use a spatula to break the seal between the baseplate and cylinder block.

26 As the baseplate is withdrawn check that

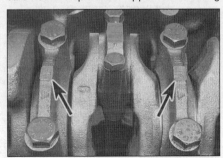

11.15 Main bearing cap identification markings (arrowed) – 1.6 and 1.8 litre petrol engines

11.18 Removing the crankshaft – 1.6 and 1.8 litre petrol engines

11.25 Lift the cylinder block baseplate off the cylinder block – 1.3 litre diesel engines

the lower main bearing shells come away with the baseplate. If they remain on the crankshaft journals, lift them off and refit them to their respective locations in the baseplate.

27 Lift the crankshaft from the cylinder block and remove the crankshaft oil seal.

28 Extract the upper bearing shells, and identify them for position if they are to be re-used.

1.7 litre diesel engines

Note: *New main bearing cap bolts will be required on refitting.*

29 Working as described in Part E of this Chapter, remove the flywheel, main sump casting, oil pump cover and oil pick-up pipe.

30 Unbolt the crankshaft oil seal housing and remove it from the cylinder block. If the housing locating dowels are a loose fit, remove them and store them with the housing for safe-keeping.

31 Remove the piston and connecting rod assemblies as described in Section 10. If no work is to be done on the pistons and connecting rods, unbolt the caps and push the pistons far enough up the bores that the connecting rods are positioned clear of the crankshaft journals.

32 Before removing the crankshaft, check the endfloat as described in paragraphs 4 and 5.

33 Unscrew the main bearing cap bolts and remove the bearing caps. Note that the caps should are numbered 1 to 5, Number 1 cap being at the timing belt end, and the arrow on each cap should point towards the timing belt end of the engine. Ensure that the lower main bearing shell remains in position in the cap.

12.4 Unscrew the retaining bolts and remove the piston oil spray nozzles from the cylinder block – 1.3 litre diesel engines

34 Carefully remove the crankshaft, and recover the thrustwasher halves from the sides of Number 2 main bearing.

35 Recover the upper bearing shells and tape them to their respective caps for safe-keeping.

12 Cylinder block – cleaning and inspection

Cleaning

1 For complete cleaning, remove all external components (senders, sensors, brackets, oil pipes, coolant pipes, etc) from the cylinder block.

2 Scrape all traces of gasket and/or sealant from the cylinder block and lower baseplate (where applicable), taking particular care not to damage the cylinder head and sump mating faces.

3 Remove all oil gallery plugs, where fitted. The plugs are usually very tight – they may have to be drilled out and the holes retapped. Use new plugs when the engine is reassembled.

4 On 1.3 litre diesel engines undo the retaining bolts and remove the piston oil spray nozzles from inside the cylinder block **(see illustration)**. On 1.7 litre diesel engines, the oil spray nozzles are a push-fit in the block and a Vauxhall/Opel special tool is required for removal.

5 On 1.3 litre diesel engines, remove the timing chain oil spray pipe from the front face of the cylinder block.

6 If the block and baseplate (where applicable) are extremely dirty, they should be steam-cleaned.

7 If the components have been steam-cleaned, clean all oil holes and oil galleries one more time on completion. Flush all internal passages with warm water until the water runs clear. Dry the block and, where necessary, the baseplate thoroughly and wipe all machined surfaces with a light oil. If you have access to compressed air, use it to speed-up the drying process, and to blow out all the oil holes and galleries.

 Warning: Wear eye protection when using compressed air.

8 If the block and baseplate are relatively clean, an adequate cleaning job can be achieved with hot soapy water and a stiff brush. Take plenty of time, and do a thorough job. Regardless of the cleaning method used, be sure to clean all oil holes and galleries very thoroughly, dry everything completely, and coat all cast-iron machined surfaces with light oil.

9 The threaded holes in the cylinder block must be clean, to ensure accurate torque readings during reassembly. Run the correct-size tap (which can be determined from the size of the relevant bolt) into each of the holes to

remove rust, corrosion, thread sealant or other contamination, and to restore damaged threads. If possible, use compressed air to clear the holes of debris produced by this operation. Do not forget to clean the threads of all bolts and nuts which are to be re-used, as well.

10 Where applicable, apply suitable sealant to the new oil gallery plugs, and insert them into the relevant holes in the cylinder block. Tighten the plugs securely.

11 If the engine is to be left dismantled for some time, cover the cylinder block with a large plastic bag to keep it clean and prevent corrosion. Where applicable, refit the baseplate and tighten the bolts finger-tight.

Inspection

12 Visually check the block for cracks, rust and corrosion. Look for stripped threads in the threaded holes. It's also a good idea to have the block checked for hidden cracks by an engine reconditioning specialist that has the equipment to do this type of work, especially if the vehicle had a history of overheating or using coolant. If defects are found, have the block repaired, if possible, or renewed.

13 If in any doubt as to the condition of the cylinder block, have it inspected and measured by an engine reconditioning specialist. If the bores are worn or damaged, they will be able to carry out any necessary reboring (where possible), and supply appropriate oversized pistons, etc.

13 Pistons/connecting rods – inspection

1 Before the inspection process can begin, the piston/connecting rod assemblies must be cleaned, and the original piston rings removed from the pistons. **Note:** *Always use new piston rings when the engine is reassembled.*

2 Carefully expand the old rings over the top of the pistons. The use of two or three old feeler gauges will be helpful in preventing the rings dropping into empty grooves **(see illustration)**. Take care, however, as piston rings are sharp.

3 Scrape away all traces of carbon from the

13.2 Using a feeler blade to remove a piston ring

top of the piston. A hand-held wire brush, or a piece of fine emery cloth, can be used once the majority of the deposits have been scraped away.

4 Remove the carbon from the ring grooves in the piston, using an old ring. Break the ring in half to do this (be careful not to cut your fingers – piston rings are sharp). Be very careful to remove only the carbon deposits – do not remove any metal, and do not nick or scratch the sides of the ring grooves.

5 Once the deposits have been removed, clean the piston/connecting rod assembly with paraffin or a suitable solvent, and dry thoroughly. Make sure that the oil return holes in the ring grooves are clear.

6 If the pistons and cylinder bores are not damaged or worn excessively, and if the cylinder block does not need to be rebored, the original pistons can be refitted. Normal piston wear shows up as even vertical wear on the piston thrust surfaces, and slight looseness of the top ring in its groove. New piston rings should always be used when the engine is reassembled.

7 Carefully inspect each piston for cracks around the skirt, at the gudgeon pin bosses, and at the piston ring lands (between the ring grooves).

8 Look for scoring and scuffing on the thrust faces of the piston skirt, holes in the piston crown, and burned areas at the edge of the crown. If the skirt is scored or scuffed, the engine may have been suffering from overheating, and/or abnormal combustion ('pinking') which caused excessively-high operating temperatures. The cooling and lubrication systems should be checked thoroughly. A hole in the piston crown, or burned areas at the edge of the piston crown indicates that abnormal combustion (pre-ignition, 'pinking', knocking or detonation) has been occurring. If any of the above problems exist, the causes must be investigated and corrected, or the damage will occur again.

9 Corrosion of the piston, in the form of pitting, indicates that coolant has been leaking into the combustion chamber and/or the crankcase. Again, the cause must be corrected, or the problem may persist in the rebuilt engine.

10 If in any doubt as to the condition of the pistons and connecting rods, have them inspected and measured by an engine reconditioning specialist. If new parts are required, they will be able to supply and fit appropriate-sized pistons/rings, and rebore (where possible) or hone the cylinder block.

14 Crankshaft – inspection
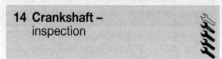

1 Clean the crankshaft using paraffin or a suitable solvent, and dry it, preferably with compressed air if available. Be sure to clean the oil holes with a pipe cleaner or

14.8 Transfer the crankshaft speed/position sensor pulse pick-up ring to the new crankshaft

similar probe, to ensure that they are not obstructed.

 Warning: Wear eye protection when using compressed air.

2 Check the main and big-end bearing journals for uneven wear, scoring, pitting and cracking.

3 Big-end bearing wear is accompanied by distinct metallic knocking when the engine is running (particularly noticeable when the engine is pulling from low revs), and some loss of oil pressure.

4 Main bearing wear is accompanied by severe engine vibration and rumble – getting progressively worse as engine revs increase – and again by loss of oil pressure.

5 Check the bearing journal for roughness by running a finger lightly over the bearing surface. Any roughness (which will be accompanied by obvious bearing wear) indicates that the crankshaft requires regrinding.

6 Have the crankshaft journals measured by an engine reconditioning specialist. If the crankshaft is worn or damaged, they may be able to regrind the journals and supply suitable

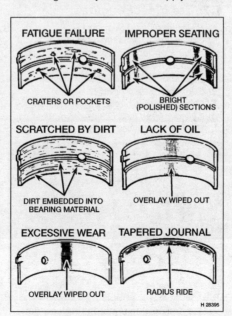

FATIGUE FAILURE — CRATERS OR POCKETS

IMPROPER SEATING — BRIGHT (POLISHED) SECTIONS

SCRATCHED BY DIRT — DIRT EMBEDDED INTO BEARING MATERIAL

LACK OF OIL — OVERLAY WIPED OUT

EXCESSIVE WEAR — OVERLAY WIPED OUT

TAPERED JOURNAL — RADIUS RIDE

H.28395

15.2 Typical bearing failures

undersize bearing shells. If no undersize shells are available and the crankshaft has worn beyond the specified limits, it will have to be renewed. Consult your Vauxhall/Opel dealer or engine reconditioning specialist for further information on parts availability.

7 If the crankshaft has been reground, check for burrs around the crankshaft oil holes (the holes are usually chamfered, so burrs should not be a problem unless regrinding has been carried out carelessly). Remove any burrs with a fine file or scraper, and thoroughly clean the oil holes as described previously.

8 If a new crankshaft is to be fitted, undo the screws securing the crankshaft speed/position sensor pulse pick-up ring to the crankshaft, and transfer the ring to the new crankshaft **(see illustration)**.

15 Main and big-end bearings – inspection

1 Even though the main and big-end bearings should be renewed during the engine overhaul, the old bearings should be retained for close examination, as they may reveal valuable information about the condition of the engine.

2 Bearing failure occurs because of lack of lubrication, the presence of dirt or other foreign particles, overloading the engine, or corrosion **(see illustration)**. If a bearing fails, the cause must be found and eliminated before the engine is reassembled, to prevent the failure from happening again.

3 To examine the bearing shells, remove them from the cylinder block, the main bearing caps or cylinder block lower casing, the connecting rods and the big-end bearing caps, and lay them out on a clean surface in the same order as they were fitted to the engine. This will enable any bearing problems to be matched with the corresponding crankshaft journal.

4 Dirt and other foreign particles can enter the engine in a variety of ways. Contamination may be left in the engine during assembly, or it may pass through filters or the crankcase ventilation system. Normal engine wear produces small particles of metal, which can eventually cause problems. If particles find their way into the lubrication system, it is likely that they will eventually be carried to the bearings. Whatever the source, these foreign particles often end up embedded in the soft bearing material, and are easily recognised. Large particles will not embed in the bearing, and will score or gouge the bearing and journal. To prevent possible contamination, clean all parts thoroughly, and keep everything spotlessly-clean during engine assembly. Once the engine has been installed in the vehicle, ensure that engine oil and filter changes are carried out at the recommended intervals.

5 Lack of lubrication (or lubrication breakdown) has a number of interrelated causes. Excessive heat (which thins the oil), overloading (which squeezes the oil from the bearing face), and oil leakage (from excessive bearing clearances, worn oil pump or high engine speeds) all contribute to lubrication breakdown. Blocked oil passages, which may be the result of misaligned oil holes in a bearing shell, will also starve a bearing of oil and destroy it. When lack of lubrication is the cause of bearing failure, the bearing material is wiped or extruded from the steel backing of the bearing. Temperatures may increase to the point where the steel backing turns blue from overheating.

6 Driving habits can have a definite effect on bearing life. Full-throttle, low-speed operation (labouring the engine) puts very high loads on bearings, which tends to squeeze out the oil film. These loads cause the bearings to flex, which produces fine cracks in the bearing face (fatigue failure). Eventually the bearing material will loosen in places, and tear away from the steel backing. Regular short journeys can lead to corrosion of bearings, because insufficient engine heat is produced to drive off the condensed water and corrosive gases which form inside the engine. These products collect in the engine oil, forming acid and sludge. As the oil is carried to the bearings, the acid attacks and corrodes the bearing material.

7 Incorrect bearing installation during engine assembly will also lead to bearing failure. Tight-fitting bearings leave insufficient bearing lubrication clearance, and will result in oil starvation. Dirt or foreign particles trapped behind a bearing shell results in high spots on the bearing which can lead to failure.

8 *Do not* touch any shell's bearing surface with your fingers during reassembly; there is a risk of scratching the delicate surface, or of depositing particles of dirt on it.

9 As mentioned at the beginning of this Section, the bearing shells should be renewed as a matter of course during engine overhaul; to do otherwise is false economy.

16 Engine overhaul – reassembly sequence

1 Before reassembly begins, ensure that all necessary new parts have been obtained (particularly gaskets, and various bolts which must be renewed), and that all the tools required are available. Read through the entire procedure to familiarise yourself with the work involved, and to ensure that all items necessary for reassembly of the engine are to hand. In addition to all normal tools and materials, a thread-locking compound will be required. A tube of suitable sealant will be required to seal certain joint faces which are not fitted with gaskets.

2 In order to save time and avoid problems, engine reassembly can be carried out in the following order:

1.4 litre petrol engines

a) *Piston rings (see Section 17).*

b) *Crankshaft (see Section 18).*
c) *Piston/connecting rod assemblies (see Section 19).*
d) *Flywheel (see Chapter 2A).*
e) *Cylinder head (see Chapter 2A).*
f) *Oil pump (see Chapter 2A).*
g) *Timing chain and sprockets (see Chapter 2A).*
h) *Coolant pump (see Chapter 3).*
i) *Sump (see Chapter 2A).*
j) *Inlet and exhaust manifolds (see Chapter 4A).*

1.6 and 1.8 litre petrol engines

a) *Piston rings (see Section 17).*
b) *Crankshaft (see Section 18).*
c) *Piston/connecting rod assemblies (see Section 19).*
d) *Oil pump (see Chapter 2B or 2C).*
e) *Sump (see Chapter 2B or 2C).*
f) *Flywheel (see Chapter 2B or 2C).*
g) *Cylinder head (see Chapter 2B or 2C).*
h) *Coolant pump (see Chapter 3).*
i) *Timing belt, sprockets and tensioner (see Chapter 2B or 2C).*
j) *Inlet and exhaust manifolds (see Chapter 4A).*

1.3 litre diesel engines

a) *Piston rings (see Section 17).*
b) *Crankshaft (see Section 18).*
c) *Piston/connecting rod assemblies (see Section 19).*
d) *Flywheel (see Chapter 2D).*
e) *Cylinder head (see Chapter 2D).*
f) *Oil pump (see Chapter 2D).*
g) *Timing chain and sprockets (see Chapter 2D).*
h) *Sump (see Chapter 2D).*
i) *Coolant pump (see Chapter 3).*
j) *Inlet and exhaust manifolds (see Chapter 4B).*

1.7 litre diesel engines

a) *Piston rings (see Section 17).*
b) *Crankshaft (see Section 18).*
c) *Piston/connecting rod assemblies (see Section 19).*
d) *Oil pump (see Chapter 2E).*
e) *Sump (see Chapter 2E).*
f) *Flywheel (see Chapter 2E).*
g) *Cylinder head (see Chapter 2E).*
h) *Coolant pump (see Chapter 3).*

17.4 Measuring a piston ring end gap using a feeler gauge

i) *Timing belt, sprockets and tensioner (see Chapter 2E).*
j) *Inlet and exhaust manifolds (see Chapter 4B).*

3 At this stage, all engine components should be absolutely clean and dry, with all faults repaired. The components should be laid out (or in individual containers) on a completely clean work surface.

17 Piston rings – refitting

1 Before refitting the new piston rings, the ring end gaps must be checked as follows.

2 Lay out the piston/connecting rod assemblies and the new piston ring sets, so that the ring sets will be matched with the same piston and cylinder during the end gap measurement and subsequent engine reassembly.

3 Insert the top ring into the first cylinder, and push it down the bore slightly using the top of the piston. This will ensure that the ring remains square with the cylinder walls. Push the ring down into the bore until it is positioned 15 to 20 mm down from the top edge of the bore, then withdraw the piston.

4 Measure the end gap using feeler gauges, and compare the measurements with the figures given in the Specifications **(see illustration)**.

5 If the gap is too small (unlikely if genuine Vauxhall/Opel parts are used), it must be enlarged or the ring ends may contact each other during engine operation, causing serious damage. Ideally, new piston rings providing the correct end gap should be fitted, but as a last resort, the end gap can be increased by filing the ring ends very carefully with a fine file. Mount the file in a vice equipped with soft jaws, slip the ring over the file with the ends contacting the file face, and slowly move the ring to remove material from the ends – take care, as piston rings are sharp, and are easily broken.

6 With new piston rings, it is unlikely that the end gap will be too large. If they are too large, check that you have the correct rings for your engine and for the particular cylinder bore size.

7 Repeat the checking procedure for each ring in the first cylinder, and then for the rings in the remaining cylinders. Remember to keep rings, pistons and cylinders matched up.

8 Once the ring end gaps have been checked and if necessary corrected, the rings can be fitted to the pistons.

9 The oil control ring (lowest one on the piston) is composed of three sections, and should be installed first. Fit the lower steel ring, then the spreader ring, followed by the upper steel ring **(see illustration)**.

10 With the oil control ring components installed, the second (middle) ring can be fitted. It is usually stamped with a mark (TOP) which must face up, towards the top of the piston. **Note:** *Always follow the instructions supplied with the new piston ring sets – different manufacturers may specify different procedures. Do not mix up the top and middle rings, as they have different cross-sections.* Using two or three old feeler blades, as for removal of the old rings, carefully slip the ring into place in the middle groove.

11 Fit the top ring in the same manner, ensuring that, where applicable, the mark on the ring is facing up. If a stepped ring is being fitted, fit the ring with the smaller diameter of the step uppermost.

12 Repeat the procedure for the remaining pistons and rings.

18 Crankshaft – refitting

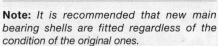

Note: *It is recommended that new main bearing shells are fitted regardless of the condition of the original ones.*

1 Refitting the crankshaft is the first step in the engine reassembly procedure. It is assumed at this point that the cylinder block, baseplate (where applicable) and crankshaft have been cleaned, inspected and repaired or reconditioned as necessary.

2 Position the cylinder block with the sump/baseplate mating face uppermost.

3 Clean the bearing shells and the bearing recesses in both the cylinder block and the baseplate/caps. If new shells are being fitted, ensure that all traces of the protective grease are cleaned off using paraffin. Wipe the shells dry with a clean lint-free cloth.

4 Note that the crankshaft endfloat is controlled by thrustwashers located on one of the main bearing shells. The thrustwashers may be separate, incorporated into, or attached to, the bearing shells themselves.

5 If the original bearing shells are being re-used, they must be refitted to their original

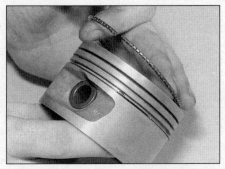

17.9 Fitting the oil control spreader ring

locations in the block and baseplate, or caps.

6 Fit the upper main bearing shells in place in the cylinder block, ensuring that the tab on each shell engages in the notch in the cylinder block **(see illustration)**. Where separate thrustwashers are fitted, use a little grease to stick them to each side of their respective bearing upper location; ensure that the oilway grooves on each thrustwasher face outwards (away from the block).

1.4 litre petrol engines

Note: *New cylinder block baseplate bolts*

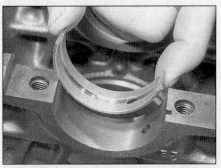

18.6 Fitting a main bearing shell to the cylinder block

must be used when refitting the crankshaft. A tube of sealant (Loctite 5900 or equivalent) will be required when fitting the baseplate to the cylinder block.

7 Liberally lubricate each bearing shell in the cylinder block, and lower the crankshaft into position **(see illustration)**.

8 If necessary, seat the crankshaft using light taps from a soft-faced mallet on the crankshaft balance webs.

9 Fit the bearing shells in the baseplate.

10 Lubricate the crankshaft journals, and the bearing shells in the baseplate **(see illustration)**.

11 Ensure that the cylinder block and baseplate mating surfaces are clean and dry, then apply a 2 mm diameter bead of sealant to the outside of the groove (not in the groove itself) in the baseplate **(see illustration)**.

12 Locate the baseplate over the crankshaft and onto the cylinder block.

13 Fit the new baseplate retaining bolts, then working progressively and in a diagonal sequence, tighten the inner (M8) bolts to the specified torque, then through the specified angle, in the two stages given in the Specifications. Now similarly tighten the outer (M6) retaining bolts **(see illustrations)**.

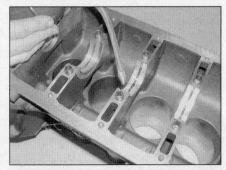

18.7 Liberally lubricate each bearing shell in the cylinder block then lower the crankshaft into position – 1.4 litre petrol engines

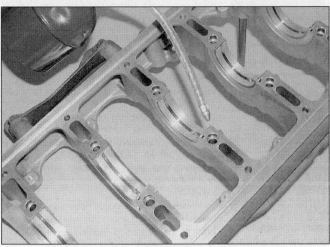

18.10 Lubricate the bearing shells in the baseplate – 1.4 litre petrol engines

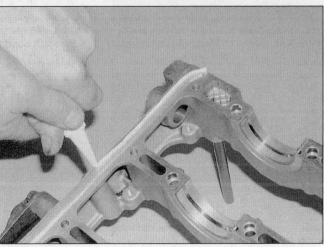

18.11 Apply a 2 mm diameter bead of silicone sealant to the outside of the groove in the baseplate – 1.4 litre petrol engines

18.13a Fit the new baseplate inner bolts . . .

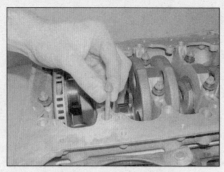

18.13b . . . and outer bolts – 1.4 litre petrol engines

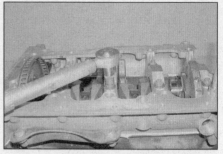

18.13c Tighten the inner bolts to the specified Stage 1 torque setting using a torque wrench . . .

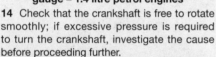

18.13d . . . then through the specified Stage 2 angle using an angle tightening gauge – 1.4 litre petrol engines

18.13e Similarly tighten the outer bolts to the specified torque . . .

18.13f . . . and through the specified angle – 1.4 litre petrol engines

14 Check that the crankshaft is free to rotate smoothly; if excessive pressure is required to turn the crankshaft, investigate the cause before proceeding further.

15 Check the crankshaft endfloat with reference to Section 11.

16 Refit the pistons and connecting rods as described in Section 19.

17 Continue with engine reassembly following the sequence given in Section 16.

1.6 and 1.8 litre petrol engines

Note: *New main bearing cap bolts must be used when refitting the crankshaft. A tube of suitable sealant will be required when fitting the rear main bearing cap to the cylinder block.*

18 Liberally lubricate each bearing shell in the cylinder block, and lower the crankshaft into position **(see illustration)**.

19 If necessary, seat the crankshaft using light taps from a soft-faced mallet on the crankshaft balance webs.

20 Fit the bearing shells into the bearing caps.

18.18 Lubricate the upper bearing shells with clean engine oil then fit the crankshaft – 1.6 and 1.8 litre petrol engines

18.21 Lubricate the crankshaft journals then refit bearing caps Nos 1 to 4 – 1.6 and 1.8 litre petrol engines

21 Lubricate the bearing shells in the bearing caps, and the crankshaft journals, then fit Nos 2, 3 and 4 bearing caps, and tighten the new bolts as far as possible by hand **(see illustration)**.

22 Ensure the No 5 bearing cap is clean and dry then fill the groove on each side of the cap with sealing compound (Vauxhall/Opel recommend the use of sealant, part No 90485251, available from your dealer) **(see illustration)**. Fit the bearing cap to the engine, ensuring it is fitted the correct way around, and tighten the new bolts as far as possible by hand.

23 Working in a diagonal sequence from the centre outwards, tighten the main bearing cap bolts to the specified Stage 1 torque setting **(see illustration)**.

24 Once all bolts are tightened to the specified Stage 1 torque, go around again

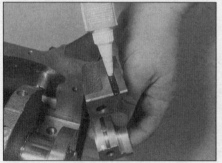

18.22 Fill the side grooves of the No 5 bearing cap with sealant prior to refitting it to the engine – 1.6 and 1.8 litre petrol engines

18.23 Tighten the bolts to the specified Stage 1 torque setting . . .

18.24 . . . and then through the specified Stages 2 and 3 angles – 1.6 and 1.8 litre petrol engines

18.30a Liberally lubricate each bearing shell in the cylinder block . . .

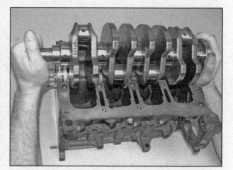

18.30b . . . and lower the crankshaft into position – 1.3 litre diesel engines

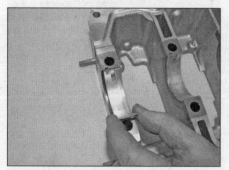

18.32 Fit the bearing shells in the baseplate . . .

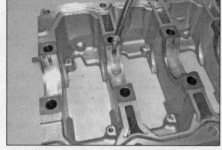
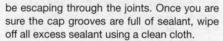
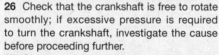

18.33 . . . then lubricate the crankshaft journals, and the bearing shells – 1.3 litre diesel engines

18.34a Apply a bead of sealant to the cylinder block mating face . . .

and tighten all bolts through the specified Stage 2 angle then go around for once more and tighten all bolts through the specified Stage 3 angle. It is recommended that an angle-measuring gauge is used during the final stages of the tightening, to ensure accuracy **(see illustration)**. If a gauge is not available, use white paint to make alignment marks between the bolt head and cap prior to tightening; the marks can then be used to check that the bolt has been rotated through the correct angle.

25 Once all the bolts have been tightened, inject more sealant down the grooves in the rear main bearing cap until sealant is seen to

be escaping through the joints. Once you are sure the cap grooves are full of sealant, wipe off all excess sealant using a clean cloth.

26 Check that the crankshaft is free to rotate smoothly; if excessive pressure is required to turn the crankshaft, investigate the cause before proceeding further.

27 Check the crankshaft endfloat with reference to Section 11.

28 Refit the piston connecting rod assemblies to the crankshaft as described in Section 19.

29 Continue with engine reassembly following the sequence given in Section 16.

1.3 litre diesel engines

Note: *New cylinder block baseplate bolts must be used when refitting the crankshaft. A tube of sealant (Loctite 5900 or equivalent) will be required when fitting the baseplate to the cylinder block.*

30 Liberally lubricate each bearing shell in

the cylinder block, and lower the crankshaft into position **(see illustrations)**.

31 If necessary, seat the crankshaft using light taps from a soft-faced mallet on the crankshaft balance webs.

32 Fit the bearing shells in the baseplate **(see illustration)**.

33 Lubricate the crankshaft journals, and the bearing shells in the baseplate **(see illustration)**.

34 Ensure that the cylinder block and baseplate mating surfaces are clean and dry, then apply a 2.5 mm diameter bead of sealant to the cylinder block face **(see illustrations)**.

35 Locate the baseplate over the crankshaft and onto the cylinder block.

36 Fit the new baseplate retaining bolts, then working progressively and in the sequence shown, tighten the inner (M10) bolts to the specified torque, then through the specified angle, in the two stages given in the

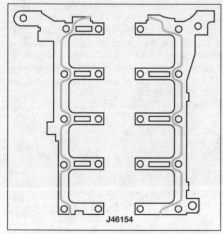

J46154

18.34b . . . ensuring the sealant is applied around the inside of the bolt holes as shown – 1.3 litre diesel engines

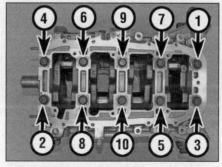

18.36a Tightening sequence for cylinder block baseplate inner (M10) bolts . . .

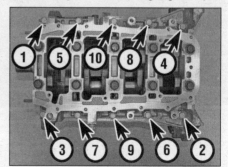

18.36b . . . and outer (M8) bolts – 1.3 litre diesel engines

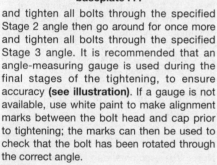

18.36c Tighten the M10 bolts to the specified torque . . .

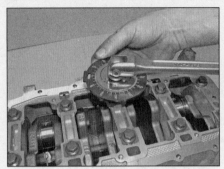

18.36d . . . then through the specified angle . . .

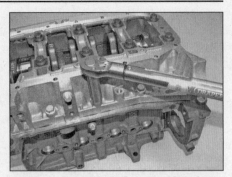

18.36e . . . and tighten the outer M8 bolts to the specified torque – 1.3 litre diesel engines

Specifications. Now similarly tighten the outer (M8) retaining bolts to the specified torque in the sequence shown **(see illustrations)**.

37 Check that the crankshaft is free to rotate smoothly; if excessive force is required to turn the crankshaft, investigate the cause before proceeding further.

38 Check the crankshaft endfloat with reference to Section 11.

39 Refit the piston connecting rod assemblies to the crankshaft as described in Section 19.

40 Continue with engine reassembly following the sequence given in Section 16.

1.7 litre diesel engines

41 Lubricate the upper shells with clean engine oil then lower the crankshaft into position **(see illustration)**.

42 Ensure the crankshaft is correctly seated.

43 Fit the bearing shells to the bearing caps, then lubricate the crankshaft journals and

bearing shells in the caps. Refit the caps to the cylinder block **(see illustration)**. Ensure the caps are fitted in their correct locations, with Number 1 cap at the timing belt end, and are fitted the correct way around so that the arrows all point towards the timing belt end of the engine. Prior to refitting Number 1 cap, apply a smear of sealant to its mating surface.

44 Apply a smear of clean engine to oil to the threads and underneath the heads of the new main bearing cap bolts. Fit the bolts tightening them all by hand then working in a diagonal sequence from the centre outwards, evenly and progressively tighten them to the specified torque setting **(see illustration)**.

45 Check that the crankshaft is free to rotate smoothly; if excessive force is required to turn the crankshaft, investigate the cause before proceeding further.

46 Check the crankshaft endfloat with reference to Section 11.

47 Ensure that the mating surfaces of the oil seal housing and cylinder block are clean and dry. Note the correct fitted depth of the oil seal then tap/lever the seal out of the housing.

48 Apply a smear of sealant to the oil seal housing mating surface, and make sure that the locating dowels are in position **(see illustration)**. Slide the housing over the end of the crankshaft, and into position on the cylinder block. Put a drop of locking compound on the threads, then tighten the retaining bolts to the specified torque setting.

49 Referring to Part E of this Chapter, fit a new transmission end crankshaft oil seal.

50 Fit the transmission input shaft guide into the end of the crankshaft **(see illustration)**.

51 Refit/reconnect the piston connecting rod assemblies to the crankshaft as described in Section 19.

52 Continue with engine reassembly following the sequence given in Section 16.

19 Pistons/connecting rods – refitting

Note: *It is recommended that new big-end bearing shells are fitted regardless of the condition of the original ones. New big-end bearing cap bolts/nuts will also be required.*

1 Prior to refitting, where applicable, carefully tap the original bolts out from the connecting rod and install the new bolts **(see illustration)**.

2 Clean the backs of the big-end bearing shells and the recesses in the connecting rods and big-end caps. If new shells are being

18.41 Lower the crankshaft into position – 1.7 litre diesel engines

18.43 Fit the bearing caps with the arrows towards the timing belt end of the engine – 1.7 litre diesel engines

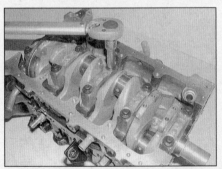

18.44 Tighten the main bearing cap bolts to the specified torque – 1.7 litre diesel engines

18.48 Apply sealant to the oil seal housing mating surface – 1.7 litre diesel engines

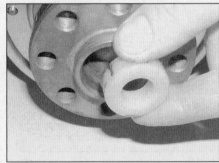

18.50 Fit the input shaft guide into the end of the crankshaft – 1.7 litre diesel engines

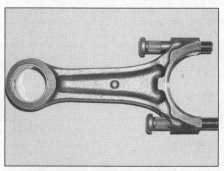

19.1 Renew the big-end bolts –
1.7 litre diesel engines

19.3 Fit the bearing shells, making sure
their tabs are correctly located in the
connecting rod/cap groove (arrowed)

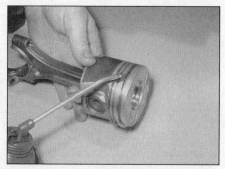

19.4 Lubricate the piston rings with clean
engine oil

19.7a Ensure the piston ring end gaps
are correctly spaced then fit the ring
compressor

19.7b Ensuring the arrow on the piston
crown (circled) is pointing towards the
timing belt/chain end of the engine

19.7c Tap the piston gently into the bore
using handle of a hammer

fitted, ensure that all traces of the protective grease are cleaned off using paraffin. Wipe the shells, caps and connecting rods dry with a lint-free cloth.

3 Press the bearing shells into their locations, ensuring that the tab on each shell engages in the notch in the connecting rod and cap (see illustration). If there is no tab on the bearing shell (and no notch in the rod or cap) position the shell equidistant from each side of the rod and cap. If the original bearing shells are being used ensure they are refitted in their original locations.

4 Lubricate the bores, the pistons and piston rings then lay out each piston/connecting rod assembly in its respective position (see illustration).

5 Lubricate No 1 piston and piston rings, and check that the ring gaps are correctly positioned. On petrol engines and 1.3 litre diesel engines, the gaps in the upper and lower steel rings of the oil control ring should be offset by 25 to 50 mm to the right and left of the spreader ring gap. The two upper compression ring gaps should be offset by 180° to each other. On 1.7 litre diesel engines, space the ring gaps uniformly around the piston at 120° intervals.

6 Liberally lubricate the cylinder bore with clean engine oil.

7 Fit a ring compressor to No 1 piston, then

insert the piston and connecting rod into the cylinder bore so that the base of the compressor stands on the block. With the crankshaft big-end bearing journal positioned at its lowest point, tap the piston carefully into the cylinder bore with the wooden handle of a hammer, and at the same time guide the connecting rod onto the bearing journal. Note that the arrow, notch or dot on the piston crown must point towards the timing chain/belt end of the engine (see illustrations).

8 Liberally lubricate the bearing journals and bearing shells, and fit the bearing cap in its original location.

9 Screw in the new bearing cap retaining bolts/nuts then tighten the bolts/nuts to the Stage 1 torque setting, then through the specified angles.

10 Refit the remaining three piston and connecting rod assemblies in the same way.

11 Rotate the crankshaft, and check that it turns freely, with no signs of binding or tight spots.

12 Continue with engine reassembly following the sequence given in Section 16.

20 Engine –
initial start-up after overhaul

1 With the engine refitted in the vehicle,

double-check the engine oil and coolant levels. Make a final check that everything has been reconnected, and that there are no tools or rags left in the engine compartment.

2 On diesel engines, prime and bleed the fuel system as described in Chapter 4B.

3 Start the engine, noting that this may take a little longer than usual. Make sure that the oil pressure warning light goes out.

4 While the engine is idling, check for fuel, water and oil leaks. Don't be alarmed if there are some odd smells and smoke from parts getting hot and burning off oil deposits.

5 Assuming all is well, run the engine until it reaches normal operating temperature, then switch off the engine.

6 After a few minutes, recheck the oil and coolant levels as described in Weekly checks, and top-up as necessary.

7 Note that there is no need to retighten the cylinder head bolts once the engine has first run after reassembly.

8 If new pistons, rings or crankshaft bearings have been fitted, the engine must be treated as new, and run-in for the first 600 miles. Do not operate the engine at full-throttle, or allow it to labour at low engine speeds in any gear. It is recommended that the oil and filter be changed at the end of this period.

Chapter 3
Cooling, heating and air conditioning systems

Contents

Degrees of difficulty

Easy, suitable for novice with little experience	Fairly easy, suitable for beginner with some experience	Fairly difficult, suitable for competent DIY mechanic	Difficult, suitable for experienced DIY mechanic	Very difficult, suitable for expert DIY or professional

Specifications

Engine identification

Engine type	Manufacturer's engine code*
Petrol engines:	
1.4 litre (1364 cc) DOHC 16-valve	Z14XEP
1.6 litre (1598 cc):	
SOHC 8-valve	Z16SE
DOHC 16-valve	Z16XE and Z16XEP
1.8 litre (1796 cc) DOHC 16-valve	Z18XE
Diesel engines:	
1.3 litre (1248 cc) DOHC 16-valve	Z13DTJ
1.7 litre (1686 cc) DOHC 16-valve	Y17DT and Z17DTH

* For details of engine code location, see 'Vehicle identification' in the Reference Chapter.

Thermostat

Opening temperature:	
Petrol engines:	
1.4 litre engines	92°C
1.6 and 1.8 litre engines:	
With wax thermostat (except Z16XEP engines)	92°C
With wax thermostat (Z16XEP engines)	90°C
With electric thermostat	105°C
Diesel engines	
1.3 litre engines	80°C
1.7 litre engines	92°C

Air conditioning compressor

Lubricant capacity:	
Petrol engines	150 cc
Diesel engines	120 cc
Lubricant type (synthetic PAG fluid)	Vauxhall part number 90 509 933/19 49 873

Torque wrench settings

	Nm	lbf ft
Petrol engine models		
Air conditioning compressor mounting bolts	22	16
Air conditioning refrigerant pipe block connections.	20	15
Coolant pump cover retaining bolts.	8	6
Coolant pump pulley retaining bolts	20	15
Coolant pump retaining bolts.	8	6
Thermostat housing/cover bolts:		
1.4 and 1.6 litre engines	8	6
1.8 litre engines	20	15
Diesel engine models		
Air conditioning compressor mounting bolts:		
1.3 litre engines	25	18
1.7 litre engines	20	15
Air conditioning refrigerant pipe block connections.	20	15
Coolant pump pulley retaining bolts	16	12
Coolant pump retaining bolts/nuts:		
1.3 litre engines	9	7
1.7 litre engines	24	18
Thermostat housing/cover bolts	25	18

1 General information and precautions

General information

The cooling system is of pressurised type, comprising a coolant pump, a crossflow radiator, electric cooling fan, and thermostat. On 1.6 litre Z16SE and Z16XE, and 1.8 litre petrol engines, the coolant pump is driven by the timing belt. On all other engines the coolant pump is driven by the auxiliary drivebelt.

The system functions as follows. Cold coolant from the radiator passes through the hose to the coolant pump, where it is pumped around the cylinder block and head passages. After cooling the cylinder bores, combustion surfaces and valve seats, the coolant reaches the underside of the thermostat, which is initially closed. The coolant passes through the heater, and is returned to the coolant pump.

When the engine is cold, the coolant circulates only through the cylinder block, cylinder head, expansion tank and heater. When the coolant reaches a predetermined temperature, the thermostat opens and the coolant passes through to the radiator. As the coolant circulates through the radiator, it is cooled by the inrush of air when the car is in forward motion. Airflow is supplemented by the action of the electric cooling fan when necessary. Once the coolant has passed through the radiator, and has cooled, the cycle is repeated.

On 1.6 litre Z16XEP engines, an electrically-assisted thermostat is fitted. Engine coolant temperature is monitored by the engine management system electronic control unit, via the coolant temperature sensor. In conjunction with information received from various other engine sensors, the thermostat opening temperature can be controlled according to engine speed and load. During normal engine operation the thermostat operates conventionally. Under conditions of high engine speed and load, an electric heating element within the thermostat is energised, to cause the thermostat to open at a lower temperature (typically 90°).

The electric cooling fan, mounted on the rear of the radiator, is controlled by the engine management system electronic control unit, in conjunction with a cooling fan module. At a predetermined coolant temperature, the fan is actuated. On certain models equipped with air conditioning, an auxiliary cooling fan, mounted at the front of the radiator is used to provide additional cooling for the air conditioning condenser.

An expansion tank is fitted to the front, left-hand side of the engine compartment to accommodate expansion of the coolant when hot. The expansion tank is connected to the top of the radiator and to the thermostat housing.

Precautions

⚠️ *Warning: Do not attempt to remove the expansion tank filler cap, or disturb any part of the cooling system, while the engine is hot; there is a high risk of scalding. If the expansion tank filler cap must be removed before the engine and radiator have fully cooled (even though this is not recommended) the pressure in the cooling system must first be relieved. Cover the cap with a thick layer of cloth, to avoid scalding, and slowly unscrew the filler cap until a hissing sound can be heard. When the hissing has stopped, indicating that the pressure has reduced, slowly unscrew the filler cap until it can be removed; if more hissing sounds are heard, wait until they have stopped before unscrewing the cap completely. At all times, keep well away from the filler cap opening.*

⚠️ *Warning: Do not allow antifreeze to come into contact with skin, or with the painted surfaces of the vehicle. Rinse off spills immediately, with plenty of water. Never leave antifreeze lying around in an open container, or in a puddle on the driveway or garage floor. Children and pets are attracted by its sweet smell, but antifreeze can be fatal if ingested.*

⚠️ *Warning: If the engine is hot, the electric cooling fan may start rotating even if the engine is not running; be careful to keep hands, hair and loose clothing well clear when working in the engine compartment.*

⚠️ *Warning: Refer to Section 10 for precautions to be observed when working on models equipped with air conditioning.*

2 Cooling system hoses – disconnection and renewal

Note: *Refer to the warnings given in Section 1 of this Chapter before proceeding. Do not attempt to disconnect any hose while the system is still hot.*

1 If the checks described in Chapter 1A or 1B reveal a faulty hose, it must be renewed as follows.

2 First drain the cooling system (see Chapter 1A or 1B). If the coolant is not due for renewal, it may be re-used if it is collected in a clean container.

3 Before disconnecting a hose, first note its routing in the engine compartment, and whether it is secured by any additional retaining clips or cable-ties. Use a pair of pliers to release the clamp-type clips, or a screwdriver to slacken the screw-type clips, then move the clips along the hose, clear of the relevant inlet/outlet union. Carefully work the hose free.

4 Depending on engine, some of the hose attachments may be of the quick-release type. Where this type of hose is encountered, lift the ends of the wire retaining clip, to spread the clip, then withdraw the hose from the inlet/outlet union **(see illustrations)**.
5 Note that the radiator inlet and outlet unions are fragile; do not use excessive force when attempting to remove the hoses. If a hose proves to be difficult to remove, try to release it by rotating the hose ends before attempting to free it.

HAYNES HiNT *If all else fails, cut the coolant hose with a sharp knife, then slit it so that it can be peeled off in two pieces. Although this may prove expensive if the hose is otherwise undamaged, it is preferable to buying a new radiator.*

6 When fitting a hose, first slide the clips onto the hose, then work the hose into position. If clamp-type clips were originally fitted, it is a good idea to use screw-type clips when refitting the hose. If the hose is stiff, use a little soapy water (washing-up liquid is ideal) as a lubricant, or soften the hose by soaking it in hot water.
7 Work the hose into position, checking that it is correctly routed and secured. Slide each clip along the hose until it passes over the flared end of the relevant inlet/outlet union, before tightening the clips securely.
8 Refill the cooling system with reference to Chapter 1A or 1B.
9 Check thoroughly for leaks as soon as possible after disturbing any part of the cooling system.

3 Radiator –
removal, inspection
and refitting

Removal

Petrol engines

1 Disconnect the battery negative terminal (refer to *Disconnecting the battery* in the Reference Chapter).

3.9b . . . and fan resistor wiring connectors located on the cooling fan shroud

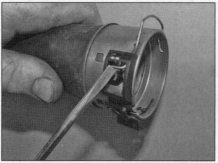
2.4a To disconnect quick-release hose fittings, lift the ends of the wire retaining clip, to spread the clip . . .

2 Firmly apply the handbrake, then jack up the front of the car and support it securely on axle stands (see *Jacking and vehicle support*).
3 Where fitted, remove the plastic cover over the top of the engine.
4 Remove the front bumper as described in Chapter 11.
5 Drain the cooling system as described in Chapter 1A.
6 Slacken the retaining clips, and disconnect the coolant top and bottom hoses from the radiator.
7 Release the retaining clip and disconnect the expansion tank hose from the radiator or expansion tank.
8 Where applicable, unclip the coolant hoses from the cooling fan shroud **(see illustration)**.
9 Disconnect the cooling fan and fan resistor wiring connectors located on the cooling fan

3.8 Unclip the coolant hoses from the cooling fan shroud

3.10 Where fitted, disconnect the wiring connector at the second coolant temperature sensor

2.4b . . . then withdraw the hose from the inlet/outlet union

shroud, and release the wiring harness from the cable-ties and clips **(see illustrations)**.
10 Where fitted, disconnect the wiring connector at the second coolant temperature sensor located at the base of the radiator right-hand tank **(see illustration)**.
11 On models with the horn mounted above the radiator, disconnect the horn wiring connector, undo the retaining bolt and remove the horn.
12 On all except 1.6 litre Z16XEP engine models, undo the bolt securing the air intake resonator to the upper front crossmember. Slide the resonator sideways to disengage the three locating lugs, and remove the resonator from the crossmember **(see illustrations)**.
13 On models equipped with air conditioning, undo the bolt securing the refrigerant pipe connector block to the mounting bracket

3.9a Disconnect the cooling fan wiring connector . . .

3.12a Undo the intake resonator retaining bolt (arrowed) . . .

3.12b . . . then slide the resonator sideways and remove it from the crossmember

3.13 Undo the bolt (arrowed) securing the refrigerant pipe connector block to the mounting bracket above the condenser

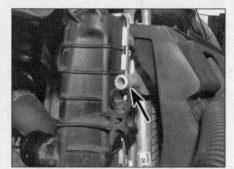

3.14a Lift the condenser upwards to disengage the upper (arrowed) . . .

3.14b . . . and lower (arrowed) mounting each side

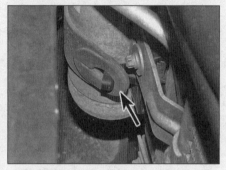

3.15 Release the rubber strap (arrowed) securing the receiver/dryer to the right-hand side of the radiator

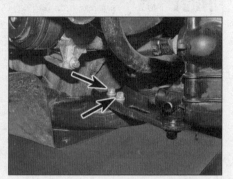

3.16 Undo the two bolts each side (arrowed) securing the radiator mounting brackets to the subframe

above the right-hand end of the condenser (see illustration). On all except 1.6 litre Z16XEP engine models, undo the radiator upper right-hand side mounting bracket bolt and remove the refrigerant pipe connector block mounting bracket.

14 On models equipped with air conditioning, undo the bolt each side (where fitted) securing the condenser lower mounting brackets to the radiator. Lift the condenser upwards to disengage the upper and lower mounting each side and suitably suspend the condenser from the upper front crossmember using cable-ties, to avoid straining the refrigerant lines (see illustrations).

15 Also on models equipped with air conditioning, where applicable, release the rubber strap securing the receiver/dryer

to the right-hand side of the radiator (see illustration).

16 Engage the help of an assistant to support the radiator, then undo the two bolts each side securing the radiator left-hand and right-hand mounting brackets to the subframe (see illustration).

17 Carefully lower the radiator out through the bottom of the vehicle, disengaging it from its upper mountings (see illustration).

18 If required, the electric cooling fan can be detached after releasing the wiring harness.

Diesel engines

19 Disconnect the battery negative terminal (refer to Disconnecting the battery in the Reference Chapter).

20 Firmly apply the handbrake, then jack up

the front of the car and support it securely on axle stands (see Jacking and vehicle support).

21 Remove the front bumper as described in Chapter 11.

22 Drain the cooling system as described in Chapter 1B.

23 Slacken the retaining clips and disconnect the two charge air hoses from the intercooler. Where applicable release the wiring harness from the cable-ties.

24 On models with air conditioning, suitably suspend the condenser from the upper front crossmember using cable-ties, to avoid straining the refrigerant lines.

25 On models with air conditioning but without an auxiliary cooling fan, disconnect the two wiring harness connectors located in front of the condenser (see illustration). Release the wiring harness from the cable-ties on the support bracket, then undo the two bolts and remove the support bracket.

26 On models with the horn mounted above the radiator, disconnect the horn wiring connector, undo the retaining bolt and remove the horn.

27 On 1.7 litre Y17DT engine models equipped with air conditioning, undo the bolt securing the refrigerant pipe connector block to the mounting bracket above the right-hand end of the condenser. Undo the radiator upper right-hand side mounting bracket bolt and remove the refrigerant pipe connector block mounting bracket. Release the rubber strap securing the receiver/dryer to the right-hand side of the radiator, then lift the condenser

3.17 Carefully lower the radiator out through the bottom of the vehicle, disengaging it from its upper mountings

3.25 Disconnect the two wiring harness connectors (arrowed) located in front of the condenser

upwards to disengage the upper and lower mounting each side.

28 On models with air conditioning with an auxiliary cooling fan, disconnect the cooling fan wiring connectors and release the wiring harness cable-ties. Undo the four fan housing retaining bolts and remove the auxiliary cooling fan and housing **(see illustrations)**.

29 On models with air conditioning (except 1.7 litre Y17DT engine models) undo the two bolts securing the condenser to the radiator. Release the rubber strap securing the receiver/dryer to the right-hand side of the radiator then carefully pull the refrigerant pipe connector block forward out of the radiator bracket.

30 Slacken the retaining clips, and disconnect the coolant top and bottom hoses from the radiator.

31 Undo the radiator left-hand upper mounting bracket retaining bolt and remove the bracket. Release the retaining clip and disconnect the expansion tank hose from the left-hand side of the radiator.

32 Where applicable, unclip the coolant hoses from cooling fan shroud.

33 Engage the help of an assistant to support the radiator, then undo the two bolts each side securing the radiator left-hand and right-hand mounting brackets to the subframe **(see illustration 3.16)**.

34 Carefully lower the radiator out through the bottom of the vehicle, disengaging it from its upper mountings.

35 If required, the electric cooling fan can be detached after undoing the retaining bolts and releasing the wiring harness.

36 On Y17DT engine models, if required, the intercooler can be removed by unclipping it from the fan housing and lifting it upward out of the guide. On all other models, undo the two retaining bolts and detach the intercooler from the guide.

Inspection

37 If the radiator has been removed due to suspected blockage, reverse-flush it as described in Chapter 1A or 1B. Clean dirt and debris from the radiator fins, using an airline (in which case, wear eye protection) or a soft brush.

3.28a Undo the auxiliary cooling fan left-hand retaining bolts (upper bolt arrowed) . . .

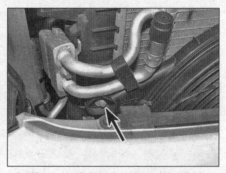
3.28b . . . and right-hand retaining bolts (upper bolt arrowed)

Caution: Be careful, as the fins are easily damaged, and are sharp.

38 If necessary, a radiator specialist can perform a 'flow test' on the radiator, to establish whether an internal blockage exists.

39 A leaking radiator must be referred to a specialist for permanent repair. Do not attempt DIY repairs to a leaking radiator, as damage may result.

40 In an emergency, minor leaks from the radiator can be cured by using a suitable radiator sealant (in accordance with its manufacturer's instructions) with the radiator *in situ*.

41 Inspect the radiator mounting rubbers, and renew them if necessary.

Refitting

42 Refitting is a reversal of removal, bearing in mind the following points:
 a) *Ensure that all hoses are correctly reconnected, and their retaining clips securely tightened.*
 b) *On completion, refill the cooling system as described in Chapter 1A or 1B.*

4 Thermostat –
removal, testing and refitting

Removal

1.4 litre petrol engines

1 Drain the cooling system (see Chapter 1A).

2 Slacken the retaining clip, and disconnect the coolant hose from the thermostat housing cover **(see illustration)**.

3 Slacken and remove the three retaining bolts, and remove the thermostat housing cover **(see illustration)**. Remove the thermostat from the housing cover.

4 Remove the sealing ring from the housing cover and discard it; a new one should be used on refitting **(see illustration)**. Thoroughly clean the housing contact surfaces.

1.6 litre Z16SE petrol engines

5 Drain the cooling system (see Chapter 1A).

6 Remove the timing belt rear cover as described in Chapter 2B.

7 Loosen the clip and disconnect the radiator hose from the thermostat cover on the right-hand side of the engine.

8 Slacken and remove the two retaining bolts, and remove the thermostat cover. Carefully prise the thermostat from the cylinder head.

9 Remove the sealing ring from the thermostat and discard it; a new one should be used on refitting. Thoroughly clean the thermostat cover contact surfaces.

1.6 litre Z16XE litre petrol engines

10 Drain the cooling system (see Chapter 1A).

11 Remove the plastic cover over the top of the engine.

12 Loosen the clips and disconnect the radiator hose and throttle housing coolant hose from the thermostat housing cover.

13 Undo the three bolts and remove the housing cover from the cylinder head, then

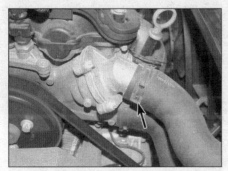
4.2 Release the clip (arrowed) and disconnect the hose from the thermostat housing cover – 1.4 litre petrol engines

4.3 Remove the thermostat housing cover from the coolant pump – 1.4 litre petrol engines

4.4 Remove the sealing ring from the thermostat cover – 1.4 litre petrol engines

4.34 Undo the two retaining bolts (arrowed) and remove the thermostat housing – 1.3 litre diesel engines

remove the gasket and discard it; a new one should be used on refitting. Note that the thermostat is an integral part of the housing cover, and cannot be renewed separately. Thoroughly clean the housing contact surfaces.

1.6 litre Z16XEP petrol engines

14 Drain the cooling system (see Chapter 1A).
15 Undo the two bolts and detach the wiring harness bracket from the side of the thermostat housing.
16 Loosen the clip and disconnect the radiator hose from the thermostat housing cover.
17 Undo the three bolts and free the heat shield from the exhaust manifold.
18 Disconnect the thermostat wiring connector.
19 Unscrew the four bolts and remove the thermostat cover from the housing. Note that

4.39a Undo the retaining screw (arrowed) . . .

4.39c . . . squeeze together the legs of the guide clip . . .

4.35 Remove the sealing ring from the thermostat housing – 1.3 litre diesel engines

the thermostat is an integral part of the housing cover, and cannot be renewed separately.
20 Remove the sealing ring from the housing cover and discard it; a new one should be used on refitting. Thoroughly clean the housing contact surfaces.

1.8 litre petrol engines

21 Drain the cooling system (see Chapter 1A).
22 Remove the plastic cover over the top of the engine.
23 Undo the bolt securing the air intake resonator to the upper front crossmember **(see illustration 3.12a)**. Slide the resonator sideways to disengage the three locating lugs, and remove the resonator from the crossmember.
24 Loosen the clips and disconnect the radiator hose and throttle housing coolant hose from the thermostat housing cover.
25 Disconnect the wiring connector from the coolant temperature sensor on the housing.

4.39b . . . extract the plastic rivet . . .

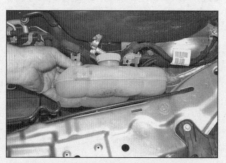

4.39d . . . and withdraw the expansion tank from the crossmember – 1.7 litre diesel engines

26 Unbolt and remove the housing cover from the cylinder head, then unclip and remove the thermostat from the cover.
27 Remove the gasket and discard it; a new one should be used on refitting. Thoroughly clean the housing contact surfaces.

1.3 litre diesel engines

28 Drain the cooling system (see Chapter 1B).
29 Remove the plastic cover over the top of the engine.
30 Remove the battery and battery tray as described in Chapter 5A.
31 Undo the four bolts securing the charge air pipe to the throttle housing. Undo the bolt securing the charge air pipe to the thermostat housing, release the charge air hose retaining clip and remove the charge air pipe.
32 Slacken the retaining clips, and disconnect the four coolant hoses from the thermostat housing.
33 Disconnect the coolant temperature sensor wiring connector.
34 Undo and remove the two retaining bolts, unclip the wiring harness and remove the thermostat housing from the engine **(see illustration)**. Note that the thermostat is an integral part of the housing, and cannot be renewed separately.
35 Remove the sealing ring from the housing and discard it; a new one should be used on refitting **(see illustration)**.

1.7 litre diesel engines

36 Drain the cooling system (see Chapter 1B).
37 Remove the plastic cover over the top of the engine.
38 Remove the battery and battery tray as described in Chapter 5A.
39 Undo the retaining screw and extract the plastic rivet securing the cooling system expansion tank to the front upper crossmember. Squeeze together the legs of the guide clip and withdraw the expansion tank from the crossmember **(see illustrations)**.
40 Loosen the clip and disconnect the top hose from the thermostat housing cover located on the left-hand end of the cylinder head.
41 Undo the two bolts and remove the wiring harness support bracket from the thermostat cover.
42 Undo the two bolts and remove the thermostat cover from the housing **(see illustration)**.

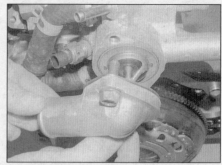

4.42 Remove the thermostat housing cover . . .

43 Lift the thermostat from the housing **(see illustration)**.
44 Remove the gasket and discard it; a new one should be used on refitting. Thoroughly clean the housing contact surfaces.

Testing

45 Where it is possible to separate the thermostat from the cover, a rough test of the thermostat's operation may be made by suspending it with a piece of string in a container full of water. Heat the water to bring it to the boil – the thermostat must open by the time the water boils. If not, renew it **(see illustration)**.
46 The opening temperature is marked on the thermostat. If a thermometer is available, the precise opening temperature of the thermostat may be determined, and compared with the value marked on the thermostat.
47 A thermostat which fails to close as the water cools must also be renewed.

Refitting

48 Refitting is a reversal of removal, bearing in mind the following points:
a) Fit the new sealing rings/gaskets to all applicable mating faces.
b) Tighten the thermostat housing/cover bolts to the specified torque.
c) On 1.6 litre Z16SE engines, refit the timing belt rear cover as described in Chapter 2B.
d) On completion, refill the cooling system as described in Chapter 1A or 1B.

5 Electric cooling fan – removal and refitting

Warning: If the engine is hot, the cooling fan may start up at any time. Take extra precautions when working in the vicinity of the fan.

Removal

Petrol engines

1 Disconnect the battery negative terminal (refer to *Disconnecting the battery* in the Reference Chapter).
2 Firmly apply the handbrake, then jack up the front of the car and support it securely on axle stands (see *Jacking and vehicle support*).
3 On 1.6 litre Z16XEP engine models, drain the cooling system as described in Chapter 1A, then release the retaining clip and disconnect the left-hand coolant hose from the radiator.
4 Remove the front bumper as described in Chapter 11.
5 Where applicable, unclip the coolant hoses from the cooling fan shroud **(see illustration 3.8)**.
6 Disconnect the cooling fan and fan resistor wiring connectors located on the cooling fan shroud, and release the wiring harness from the cable-ties and clips **(see illustrations 3.9a and 3.9b)**.
7 On all except 1.6 litre Z16XEP engine models, undo the bolt securing the air intake resonator

4.43 . . . and withdraw the thermostat from the housing – 1.7 litre diesel engines

to the upper front crossmember **(see illustration 3.12a)**. Slide the resonator sideways to disengage the three locating lugs, and remove the resonator from the crossmember.
8 Suitably suspend the radiator from the upper front crossmember using cable-ties.
9 Undo the two bolts each side securing the radiator left-hand and right-hand mounting brackets to the subframe **(see illustration 3.16)**.
10 On 1.6 litre Z16XEP engine models, undo the two bolts securing the cooling fan shroud to the radiator.
11 Unclip the cooling fan shroud from the radiator, then lower the fan and shroud assembly and remove it from under the vehicle.
12 To remove the fan motor, disconnect the motor wiring connector, then unscrew the three retaining bolts/nuts and remove the motor from the shroud **(see illustration)**.

Diesel engines

13 Remove the radiator as described in Section 3.
14 Unclip the cooling fan shroud from the radiator, or undo the four retaining bolts, as applicable, and remove the cooling fan shroud from the radiator.
15 To remove the fan motor, disconnect the motor wiring connector (where applicable) unscrew the three retaining bolts/nuts and remove the motor from the shroud.

Refitting

16 Refitting is a reversal of removal, bearing in mind the following points:
a) Ensure that the shroud is correctly located on the radiator.

5.12 Undo the three bolts (arrowed) and remove the motor from the shroud

4.45 Testing the thermostat opening temperature

b) Use new cable-ties to secure all disturbed wiring harnesses.
c) On diesel engines, refit the radiator as described in Section 3.
d) Refit the front bumper as described in Chapter 11.
e) On completion, start the engine and run it until it reaches normal operating temperature; continue to run the engine, and check that the cooling fan cuts in and functions correctly.

6 Coolant temperature sensor – testing, removal and refitting

Testing

1 Testing of the coolant temperature sensor circuit is best entrusted to a Vauxhall/Opel dealer, who will have the necessary specialist diagnostic equipment.

Removal

2 Partially drain the cooling system with reference to Chapter 1A or 1B. Alternatively, it is possible to change the sensor quickly with minimal loss of coolant by first releasing any pressure from the cooling system. With the engine cold, temporarily remove the expansion tank cap.
3 Where fitted, remove the plastic cover over the top of the engine.

1.4 litre petrol engines

4 The coolant temperature sensor is located at the top of the coolant pump housing **(see illustration)**.

6.4 Coolant temperature sensor location (arrowed) – 1.4 litre petrol engines

6.17a Coolant temperature sensor location (arrowed) on 1.3 litre diesel engines . . .

5 Disconnect the wiring from the temperature sensor, then unscrew and remove it from the coolant pump. If the cooling system has not been drained, either insert the new sensor or fit a blanking plug to prevent further loss of coolant.

1.6 litre Z16SE petrol engines

6 The coolant temperature sensor is located at the left-hand end of the cylinder head.
7 Disconnect the wiring from the temperature sensor, then unscrew and remove it from the cylinder head. If the cooling system has not been drained, either insert the new sensor or fit a blanking plug to prevent further loss of coolant.

1.6 litre Z16XE petrol engines

8 The coolant temperature sensor is located in the thermostat housing at the front right-hand end of the engine.
9 Disconnect the wiring from the temperature sensor, then unscrew and remove it from the cylinder head. If the cooling system has not been drained, either insert the new sensor or fit a blanking plug to prevent further loss of coolant.

1.6 litre Z16XEP petrol engines

10 The coolant temperature sensor is located in the thermostat housing at the left-hand end of the cylinder head.
11 Remove the battery and battery tray as described in Chapter 5A.
12 Disconnect the wiring from the temperature sensor, then unscrew and remove it from the thermostat housing. If the cooling system has not been drained, either insert the new sensor

6.17b . . . and 1.7 litre diesel engines

or fit a blanking plug to prevent further loss of coolant.

1.8 litre petrol engines

13 Remove the thermostat housing cover as described in Section 4.
14 Unscrew the sensor and remove it from the thermostat housing cover.

Diesel engines

15 Remove the battery and battery tray as described in Chapter 5A.
16 On 1.7 litre Z17DTH engines carry out the following:
a) Drain the cooling system as described in Chapter 1B.
b) Slacken the clips and disconnect the radiator hose from the thermostat housing and the two coolant hoses from the expansion tank.
c) Undo the retaining screw and extract the plastic rivet securing the cooling system expansion tank to the front upper crossmember. Squeeze together the legs of the guide clip and withdraw the expansion tank from the crossmember (see illustrations 4.39a to 4.39d).
17 Disconnect the wiring connector from the sensor located on the thermostat housing on the left-hand end of the cylinder head (see illustrations).
18 Unscrew and remove the sensor.

Refitting

19 Refitting is a reversal of removal, bearing in mind the following points:
a) Where applicable fit a new sealing O-ring to the sensor. Where the sensor is fitted

without an O-ring, ensure the sensor threads are clean, and apply a smear of suitable sealant to them.
b) *On completion, top-up/refill the cooling system as described in Chapter 1A or 1B.*

7 Coolant pump – removal and refitting

Removal

1.4 litre petrol engines

1 Disconnect the battery negative terminal (refer to *Disconnecting the battery* in the Reference Chapter).
2 Remove the air cleaner assembly and air intake ducts as described in Chapter 4A.
3 Remove the auxiliary drivebelt as described in Chapter 1A.
4 Drain the cooling system as described in Chapter 1A.
5 Support the engine and remove the right-hand engine mounting and engine mounting bracket as described in Chapter 2A.
6 Unscrew the three coolant pump pulley bolts and withdraw the pulley from the pump.
7 Disconnect the coolant temperature sensor wiring connector.
8 Release the retaining clips and disconnect the hoses from the coolant pump and thermostat housing (see illustrations).
9 Unscrew the coolant pump retaining bolts, noting the locations of the three short bolts (see illustration). The short bolts secure the pump to the timing cover, and the long bolts secure the pump and the timing cover to the cylinder block and cylinder head.
10 Withdraw the coolant pump from the timing cover, noting that it may be necessary to tap the pump lightly with a soft-faced hammer to free it from the locating dowels. **Note:** *Coolant which is trapped in the cylinder block will leak out when the pump is removed.*
11 Recover the pump sealing ring/gasket, and discard it; a new one must be used on refitting (see illustration).
12 Note that it is not possible to overhaul the pump. If it is faulty, the unit must be renewed complete.
13 If the pump is being renewed, remove

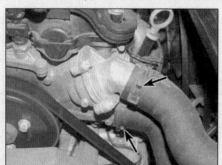

7.8a Release the clips (arrowed) and disconnect the hoses from the front . . .

7.8b . . . and rear (arrowed) of the coolant pump housing – 1.4 litre petrol engines

7.9 Coolant pump short retaining bolt locations (arrowed) – 1.4 litre petrol engines shown with timing cover removed

the thermostat (referring to the procedures in Section 4) and coolant temperature sensor then transfer them to the new pump.

14 Similarly, unscrew the two bolts and withdraw the coolant pump top cover from the old pump and fit the cover to the new pump using a new seal. Tighten the cover bolts to the specified torque. Note that later engines have a modified coolant pump without a detachable top cover.

1.6 litre Z16SE and Z16XE, and 1.8 litre petrol engines

15 Disconnect the battery negative terminal (refer to *Disconnecting the battery* in the Reference Chapter).
16 Remove the plastic cover from the top of the engine.
17 Drain the cooling system as described in Chapter 1A.
18 Remove the timing belt and tensioner as described in the relevant Part of Chapter 2.
19 Unscrew and remove the three coolant pump securing bolts **(see illustration)**.
20 Withdraw the coolant pump from the cylinder block, noting that it may be necessary to tap the pump lightly with a soft-faced mallet to free it from the cylinder block.
21 Recover the pump sealing ring, and discard it; a new one must be used on refitting.
22 Note that it is not possible to overhaul the pump. If it is faulty, the unit must be renewed complete.

1.6 litre Z16XEP petrol engines

23 Disconnect the battery negative terminal (refer to *Disconnecting the battery* in the Reference Chapter).
24 Remove the air cleaner assembly and air intake ducts as described in Chapter 4A.
25 Slacken the three coolant pump pulley retaining bolts.
26 Remove the auxiliary drivebelt as described in Chapter 1A.
27 Drain the cooling system as described in Chapter 1A.
28 Unscrew the previously-slackened coolant pump pulley retaining bolts and remove the pulley from the pump flange.
29 Undo the five retaining bolts and remove the pump from the oil pump housing.
30 Note that it is not possible to overhaul the pump. If it is faulty, the unit must be renewed complete.

1.3 litre diesel engines

31 Disconnect the battery negative terminal (refer to *Disconnecting the battery* in the Reference Chapter).
32 Drain the cooling system with reference to Chapter 1B.
33 Remove the auxiliary drivebelt as described in Chapter 1B.
34 Working through the apertures in the pulley, unscrew and remove the four coolant pump retaining nuts **(see illustration)**.
35 Withdraw the coolant pump from the cylinder block studs. **Note:** *Coolant which is*

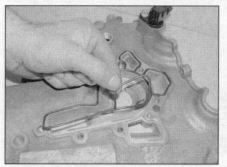

7.11 Remove the sealing ring or gasket from the timing cover – 1.4 litre petrol engines shown with timing cover removed

trapped in the cylinder block will leak out when the pump is removed.
36 Recover the pump sealing ring, and discard it; a new one must be used on refitting **(see illustration)**.
37 Note that it is not possible to overhaul the pump. If it is faulty, the unit must be renewed complete.

1.7 litre diesel engines

38 Disconnect the battery negative terminal (refer to *Disconnecting the battery* in the Reference Chapter).
39 Drain the cooling system and remove the auxiliary drivebelt as described in Chapter 1B.
40 Remove the air cleaner assembly and intake duct as described in Chapter 4B.

7.34 Working through the pulley apertures, unscrew and remove the four coolant pump retaining nuts – 1.3 litre diesel engines

7.41 Remove the pulley from the drive flange on the coolant pump – 1.7 litre diesel engines

7.19 Unscrew and remove the three coolant pump securing bolts – 1.6 litre Z16SE and Z16XE, and 1.8 litre petrol engines

41 Hold the pump pulley stationary (if necessary using an old auxiliary drivebelt or an oil filter strap wrench), then unscrew and remove the bolts and remove the pulley from the drive flange on the coolant pump **(see illustration)**.
42 Unscrew and remove the coolant pump retaining bolts **(see illustration)**.
43 Withdraw the coolant pump from the cylinder block, noting that it may be necessary to tap the pump lightly with a soft-faced mallet to free it.
44 Recover the gasket and discard it; a new one must be used on refitting **(see illustration)**.
45 Note that it is not possible to overhaul the pump. If it is faulty, the unit must be renewed complete.

7.36 Remove the sealing ring from the coolant pump – 1.3 litre diesel engines

7.42 Unscrew and remove the coolant pump retaining bolts (arrowed) – 1.7 litre diesel engines

Refitting

1.4 litre petrol engines

46 Ensure that the pump and timing cover mating faces are clean and dry and locate a new seal in the timing cover groove.

47 Check that the locating dowels are in place and locate the pump in position on the timing cover.

48 Refit the pump retaining bolts, ensuring that the short bolts are fitted to their correct locations **(see illustration 7.9)**. Tighten the bolts to the specified torque.

49 Refit the coolant pump pulley and tighten the three bolts to the specified torque. To prevent the pulley turning as the bolts are tightened, hold the pulley using a screwdriver engaged with one of the bolts and the pump centre spindle.

50 Reconnect the coolant hoses and the coolant temperature sensor wiring connector.

51 Refit the auxiliary drivebelt as described in Chapter 1A.

52 Refit the right-hand engine mounting bracket and engine mounting with reference to Chapter 2A.

53 Refit the air cleaner assembly and air intake ducts as described in Chapter 4A, then reconnect the battery.

54 Refill the cooling system as described in Chapter 1A.

1.6 litre Z16SE and Z16XE, and 1.8 litre petrol engines

55 Ensure that the pump and cylinder block mating surfaces are clean and dry, and apply a smear of silicone grease to the pump mating surface in the cylinder block.

56 Fit a new sealing ring to the pump, and locate the pump in the cylinder block. On Z16SE engines, align the mark on the edge of the pump flange with the mark on the cylinder block. On 1.8 litre engines, make sure that the lug on the oil pump housing engages in the groove of the pump.

57 Insert the securing bolts and tighten to the specified torque.

58 Refit the timing belt tensioner and timing belt as described in the relevant Part of Chapter 2.

59 Refit the plastic cover to the top of the engine.

60 Reconnect the battery negative terminal, then refill the cooling system as described in Chapter 1A.

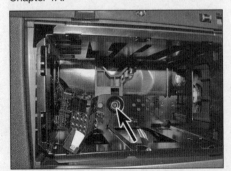

9.2a Undo the retaining screw (arrowed) . . .

7.44 Withdraw the coolant pump and remove the gasket – 1.7 litre diesel engines

1.6 litre Z16XEP petrol engines

61 Ensure that the pump and oil pump housing mating faces are clean and dry and locate the pump in position.

62 Refit the pump retaining bolts and tighten the bolts to the specified torque.

63 Refit the coolant pump pulley and tighten the three bolts to the specified torque. To prevent the pulley turning as the bolts are tightened, hold the pulley using a screwdriver engaged with one of the bolts and the pump centre spindle.

64 Refit the auxiliary drivebelt as described in Chapter 1A.

65 Refit the air cleaner assembly and air intake ducts as described in Chapter 4A, then reconnect the battery.

66 Refill the cooling system as described in Chapter 1A.

1.3 litre diesel engines

67 Ensure that the pump and cylinder block mating surfaces are clean and dry.

68 Fit a new sealing ring to the pump, and install the pump in the cylinder block.

69 Refit the pump retaining nuts, tightening them to the specified torque setting.

70 Refit the auxiliary drivebelt as described in Chapter 1B.

71 Reconnect the battery then refill the cooling system as described in Chapter 1B.

1.7 litre diesel engines

72 Ensure that the pump and cylinder block mating faces are clean and dry.

73 Refit the pump to the cylinder block together with a new gasket.

9.2b . . . and withdraw the radio/cassette/ CD player housing

74 Refit the pump retaining bolts, tightening them to the specified torque setting.

75 Refit the coolant pump pulley and tighten the three bolts to the specified torque while holding the pulley stationary using the method used on removal.

76 Refit the auxiliary drivebelt as described in Chapter 1B.

77 Refit the air cleaner assembly and air intake ducts as described in Chapter 4B, then reconnect the battery.

78 Refill the cooling system as described in Chapter 1B.

8 Heater/ventilation system – general information

The heater/ventilation system consists of a four-speed blower motor which is inside the vehicle behind the facia to the left-hand side of the heater housing, face-level vents in the centre and at each end of the facia, and air ducts to the front/rear footwells and windscreen.

The heater controls are located in the centre of the facia, and the controls operate flap valves to deflect and mix the air flowing through the various parts of the heater/ventilation system. The flap valves are contained in the air distribution housing, which acts as a central distribution unit, passing air to the various ducts and vents.

Cold air enters the system through the grille at the rear of the engine compartment. A pollen filter is fitted to the ventilation intake, to filter out dust, soot, pollen and spores from the air entering the vehicle.

The air (boosted by the blower fan if required) then flows through the various ducts, according to the settings of the controls. Stale air is expelled through ducts at the rear of the vehicle. If warm air is required, the cold air is passed through the heater matrix, which is heated by the engine coolant.

A recirculation switch enables the outside air supply to be closed off, while the air inside the vehicle is recirculated. This can be useful to prevent unpleasant odours entering from outside the vehicle, but should only be used briefly, as the recirculated air inside the vehicle will soon deteriorate.

9 Heater/ventilation system components – removal and refitting

Heater control assembly

Removal

1 Disconnect the battery negative terminal (refer to *Disconnecting the battery* in the Reference Chapter).

2 Remove the radio/cassette/CD player as described in Chapter 12, then undo the retaining screw and withdraw the radio/cassette/CD player housing **(see illustrations)**.

9.3 Carefully prise the trim from the heater control assembly, starting at the top then working down each side

9.4 Undo the two retaining screws (arrowed) from the top of the heater control assembly

9.5 Unclip the direction control cable from the rear of the control assembly

9.6a Push the control assembly forward to release the upper and lower central locating lugs . . .

9.6b . . . until access can be gained to release the temperature control outer cable . . .

9.6c . . . and inner cable from the rear of the control assembly

3 Carefully prise the trim from the heater control assembly, starting at the top then working down each side, withdrawing the trim from the control assembly, taking great care not to damage the trim **(see illustration)**.
4 From inside the radio aperture undo the two retaining screws from the top of the heater control assembly **(see illustration)**.
5 From inside the radio aperture, unclip the direction control cable from the rear of the control assembly **(see illustration)**.
6 Push the control assembly forward to release the upper and lower central locating lugs until access can be gained to release the temperature control cable from the rear of the control assembly **(see illustrations)**.
7 Turn the control assembly over and

disconnect the wiring connectors at the rear, noting the wiring's correct fitted location and routing **(see illustration)**.
8 Manipulate the control assembly out through the facia aperture **(see illustration)**.
9 If necessary, the control knobs can be removed by carefully prising them from the control assembly **(see illustration)**.

Refitting

10 Refitting is reversal of removal. Ensure that the wiring connectors and control cables are correctly routed and reconnected to the control assembly, as noted before removal. Clip the outer cable(s) in position, and check the operation of each knob before refitting the radio/cassette/CD player housing.

Temperature control cable

Removal

11 Remove the heater control assembly from the facia, as described above in paragraphs 1 to 9.
12 Remove the driver's side lower trim panel and lower centre trim panel from beneath the facia as described in Chapter 11.
13 Extract the expanding rivet and remove the footwell air duct on the driver's side **(see illustrations)**.
14 Release the temperature control outer cable support clip from the side of the air distribution housing.
15 Detach the linkage lever from the operating lever then disengage temperature control inner cable end from the operating lever.

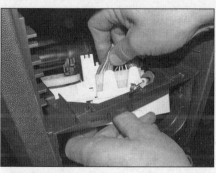

9.7 Turn the control assembly over and disconnect the wiring connectors at the rear

9.8 Manipulate the control assembly out through the facia aperture

9.9 If necessary, the control knobs can be removed by carefully prising them from the control assembly

9.13a Extract the expanding rivet . . .

16 Follow the run of the cable behind the facia, taking note of its routing, and withdraw it out from the heater control panel aperture.

Refitting

17 Refitting is reversal of removal. Ensure that the wiring connectors and control cables are correctly routed and reconnected to the control assembly, as noted before removal.

Direction control cable and drive assembly

Removal

18 Remove the heater control assembly from the facia, as described above in paragraphs 1 to 9.
19 Remove the driver's side lower trim panel and lower centre trim panel from beneath the facia as described in Chapter 11.
20 Extract the expanding rivet and remove

9.29 Carefully cut through the lower portion of the air distribution housing around the edge of the heater matrix

9.31b . . . withdraw the pipes from the matrix . . .

9.13b . . . and remove the footwell air duct on the driver's side

the footwell air duct on the driver's side **(see illustrations 9.13a and 9.13b)**.
21 Undo the screw securing the drive assembly to the air distribution housing.
22 Unclip the rear of the drive assembly from the two guides on the air distribution housing.
23 Detach the three linkage arms from the air flap levers and remove the control cable and drive assembly from the air distribution housing.

Refitting

24 Refitting is reversal of removal. Ensure that the wiring connectors and control cables are correctly routed and reconnected to the control assembly, as noted before removal.

Heater matrix

Removal

25 Disconnect the battery negative terminal

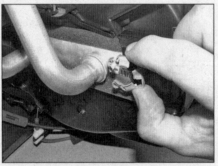

9.31a Remove the two spring clips securing the coolant pipes to the heater matrix . . .

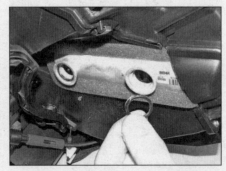

9.31c . . . and collect the two seals

(refer to *Disconnecting the battery* in the Reference Chapter).
26 Drain the cooling system as described in Chapter 1A or 1B.
27 Remove the following components as described in Chapter 11:
  a) Centre console.
  b) Driver's side lower trim panel.
  c) Driver's side lower centre trim panel.
28 Extract the expanding rivet and remove the footwell air duct on the driver's side **(see illustrations 9.13a and 9.13b)**.
29 Using a sharp knife, carefully cut through the lower portion of the air distribution housing around the edge of the heater matrix **(see illustration)**. Remove the cut off section. Note that a substitute section, known as a 'service cover' is available from Vauxhall/Opel parts stockists, together with a tube of adhesive.
30 Cover the carpet directly underneath the air distribution housing, to catch any coolant which may be spilt from the matrix as it is removed.
31 Remove the two spring clips securing the coolant pipes to the heater matrix. Withdraw the pipes from the matrix and collect the two seals **(see illustrations)**.
32 Slide the matrix out from the air distribution housing, then remove the matrix from the vehicle. **Note:** *Keep the matrix unions uppermost as the matrix is removed, to prevent coolant spillage.* Mop-up any spilt coolant immediately, and wipe the affected area with a damp cloth to prevent staining.
33 Obtain new coolant pipe seals, a service cover and a tube of suitable adhesive (Vauxhall/Opel part No 93 160 953) for refitting.

Refitting

34 Thoroughly clean the air distribution housing around the cut area and also clean the new service flap.
35 Slide the matrix into the housing, then refit the coolant pipes, together with the new seals. Secure the pipes with the spring clips.
36 Apply a uniform bead of adhesive to the seating area of the service cover. Locate the service cover on the air distribution housing and retain it in position until the adhesive sets using tape. Note that, depending on ambient temperature, the setting time for the adhesive is approximately eight hours.
37 Once the adhesive has set, remove the tape securing the service cover in position.
38 Refit the footwell air duct and secure with the expanding rivet.
39 Refit the components removed in paragraph 27 with reference to Chapter 11.
40 On completion, reconnect the battery and refill the cooling system as described in Chapter 1A or 1B.

Heater blower motor

Removal

41 Disconnect the battery negative terminal (refer to *Disconnecting the battery* in the Reference Chapter).
42 Remove the glovebox and the passenger's

Cooling, heating and air conditioning systems 3•13

side lower trim panel as described in Chapter 11.

43 Extract the expanding rivet and remove the footwell air duct on the passenger's side **(see illustrations)**.

44 Disconnect the wiring connector from the heater blower motor, then reach up behind the blower motor and disconnect the wiring connector from the underside of the blower motor resistor **(see illustration)**.

45 Undo the screw, situated behind the blower motor resistor, securing the blower motor housing to the air distribution housing.

46 Working around the periphery of the blower motor-to-air distribution housing joint, release the six retaining clips (or four clips and two screws) and withdraw the motor from the housing **(see illustration)**. If the motor has been previously-removed, the two clips nearest to the bulkhead may be screws.

Refitting

47 Refitting is a reversal of the removal procedure. Note that due to the limited clearance between the motor housing and the bulkhead, two holes are provided to allow two self-tapping screws to be used instead of the two clips.

Heater blower motor resistor

Removal

48 Disconnect the battery negative terminal (refer to *Disconnecting the battery* in the Reference Chapter).

49 Remove the glovebox and the passenger's side lower trim panel as described in Chapter 11.

50 Extract the expanding rivet and remove the footwell air duct on the passenger's side **(see illustrations 9.43a and 9.43b)**.

51 Reach up behind the blower motor and disconnect the wiring connector from the underside of the blower motor resistor **(see illustration 9.44)**.

52 Undo the two retaining screws and withdraw the resistor from the blower motor housing.

Refitting

53 Refitting is the reverse of removal.

Recirculating air valve servo motor

Removal

54 Disconnect the battery negative terminal

9.43a Extract the expanding rivet . . .

9.43b . . . and remove the footwell air duct on the passenger's side

9.44 Reach up behind the blower motor and disconnect the wiring connector from the underside of the blower motor resistor

9.46 Withdraw the blower motor from the housing

(refer to *Disconnecting the battery* in the Reference Chapter).

55 Remove the glovebox as described in Chapter 11.

56 Disconnect the wiring connector, then undo the three screws and remove the recirculating air valve servo motor located above the heater blower motor.

Refitting

57 Refitting is the reverse of removal.

Air distribution housing

Note: *On models with air conditioning, it is not possible to remove the air distribution housing without opening the refrigerant circuit (see Sections 10 and 11). Have the refrigerant discharged at a dealer service department or an automotive air conditioning repair facility before proceeding.*

Removal

58 Drain the cooling system as described in Chapter 1A or 1B.

59 Remove the windscreen cowl panel and the bulkhead closure panel as described in Chapter 11.

60 Remove the centre console and the complete facia assembly as described in Chapter 11.

61 Working in the engine compartment, release the retaining spring clips, and disconnect both hoses from the heater matrix unions **(see illustrations)**.

62 On models with air conditioning, working in the engine compartment, undo the bolt securing the refrigerant pipe block connection to the expansion valve and withdraw the refrigerant pipes from the valve **(see illustration)**. Note that new seals for the refrigerant pipes will be required for refitting.

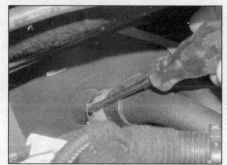
9.61a Working in the engine compartment, release the retaining spring clips . . .

9.61b . . . and disconnect both coolant hoses from the heater matrix pipe unions

9.62 Undo the bolt (arrowed) securing the refrigerant pipe block connection to the expansion valve

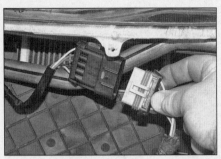

9.63 Disconnect the windscreen wiper motor wiring connector and release the wiring harness from its location

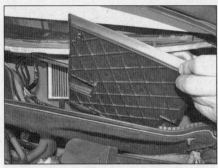

9.64 Release the upper retaining catch and remove the pollen filter housing cover

9.65 Lift the lower edge of the pollen filter upwards and withdraw it from the housing

Suitably plug or cover the disconnected pipes.

63 Disconnect the windscreen wiper motor wiring connector and release the wiring harness from its location **(see illustration)**.

64 Release the upper retaining catch and remove the pollen filter housing cover located at the rear left-hand side of the engine compartment **(see illustration)**.

65 Lift the lower edge of the pollen filter upwards and withdraw it from the housing **(see illustration)**.

66 Undo the two screws each side and remove the pollen filter housing from the bulkhead **(see illustrations)**.

67 Undo the two lower mounting bolts, and remove the facia and centre console central mounting bracket.

68 Undo the two lower mounting bolts and upper mounting nut, and remove the facia crossmember central support strut.

69 Disconnect the wiring connectors at the heater blower motor, blower motor resistor and recirculating air valve servo motor. Release the wiring harness from the clips and cable-ties.

70 Firmly apply the handbrake, then jack up the front of the vehicle and support it securely on axle stands (see *Jacking and vehicle support*).

71 From under the vehicle undo the air distribution housing lower retaining screw located just above the steering gear rack and pinion housing **(see illustration)**. Also detach the rubber cover over the heater matrix condensation drain tube, adjacent to the housing lower retaining screw.

72 From within the engine compartment, undo the screw adjacent to the expansion valve and the screw just below the heater matrix unions, securing the air distribution housing to the bulkhead **(see illustrations)**.

73 Undo the remaining retaining screw located just behind the windscreen wiper motor **(see illustration)**.

74 From inside the car extract the cable-ties or retaining clips and release the wiring harness from the air distribution housing.

75 Cover the carpet directly underneath the air distribution housing, to catch any coolant which may be spilt from the matrix as the housing assembly is removed.

76 Withdraw the air distribution housing from the bulkhead. Rotate the recirculating air valve housing clockwise and lift it off the top of the blower motor housing.

77 Manoeuvre the air distribution housing out from its location and remove it from inside the vehicle. **Note:** *Keep the matrix unions uppermost as the housing is removed, to prevent coolant spillage.* Mop-up any spilt coolant immediately, and wipe the affected area with a damp cloth to prevent staining.

9.66a Undo the two right-hand retaining screws (arrowed) . . .

9.66b . . . and two left-hand retaining screws (arrowed) and remove the pollen filter housing from the bulkhead

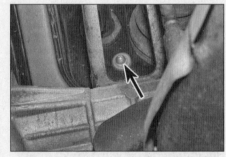

9.71 From under the vehicle undo the air distribution housing lower retaining screw (arrowed)

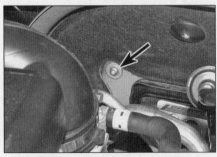

9.72a From within the engine compartment, undo the screw adjacent to the expansion valve (arrowed) . . .

9.72b . . . and the screw below the heater matrix unions (arrowed), securing the air distribution housing to the bulkhead

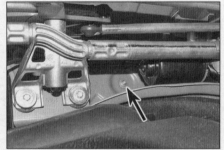

9.73 Undo the remaining screw (arrowed) located just behind the windscreen wiper motor

Refitting

78 Refitting is the reverse of removal. On completion, refill the cooling system as described in Chapter 1A or 1B. On models with air conditioning, have the system evacuated, charged and leak-tested by the specialist who discharged it.

10 Air conditioning system – general information and precautions

General information

1 Air conditioning is available on certain models. It enables the temperature of incoming air to be lowered, and also dehumidifies the air, which makes for rapid demisting and increased comfort.

2 The cooling side of the system works in the same way as a domestic refrigerator. Refrigerant gas is drawn into a belt-driven compressor, and passes into a condenser mounted in front of the radiator, where it loses heat and becomes liquid. The liquid passes through an expansion valve to an evaporator, where it changes from liquid under high pressure to gas under low pressure. This change is accompanied by a drop in temperature, which cools the evaporator. The refrigerant returns to the compressor, and the cycle begins again.

3 Air blown through the evaporator passes to the air distribution unit, where it is mixed with hot air blown through the heater matrix, to achieve the desired temperature in the passenger compartment.

4 The heating side of the system works in the same way as on models without air conditioning (see Section 8).

5 The operation of the system is controlled electronically. Any problems with the system should be referred to a Vauxhall/Opel dealer.

Air conditioning service ports

6 The low-pressure service port is located at the front right-hand side of the engine compartment, in front of the air conditioning condenser **(see illustration)**.

7 The high-pressure service port is located on the right-hand side of the engine compartment, behind the air cleaner housing **(see illustration)**. It may be necessary to remove the air cleaner assembly for improved access (see the relevant Part of Chapter 4).

Precautions

8 It is necessary to observe special precautions whenever dealing with any part of the system, its associated components, and any items which necessitate disconnection of the system.

⚠️ *Warning: The refrigeration circuit contains a liquid refrigerant. This refrigerant is potentially dangerous, and should only be handled by qualified persons. If it is splashed onto the*

10.6 Air conditioning system low-pressure service port (arrowed) . . .

skin, it can cause frostbite. It is not itself poisonous, but in the presence of a naked flame it forms a poisonous gas; inhalation of the vapour through a lighted cigarette could prove fatal. Uncontrolled discharging of the refrigerant is dangerous, and potentially damaging to the environment. It is therefore dangerous to disconnect any part of the system without specialised knowledge and equipment. If for any reason the system must be disconnected, entrust this task to your Vauxhall/Opel dealer or air conditioning specialist.
Caution: Do not operate the air conditioning system if it is known to be short of refrigerant, as this may damage the compressor.

11 Air conditioning system components – removal and refitting

⚠️ *Warning: The air conditioning system is under high pressure. Do not loosen any fittings or remove any components until after the system has been discharged. Air conditioning refrigerant should be properly discharged into an approved type of container at a dealer service department or an automotive air conditioning repair facility capable of handling R134a refrigerant. Cap or plug the pipe lines as soon as they are disconnected, to prevent the entry of moisture. Always wear eye protection when disconnecting air conditioning system fittings.*

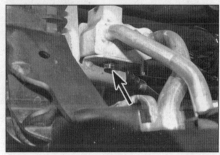

11.6a Undo the bolt (arrowed) securing the refrigerant pipe connector block to the mounting bracket . . .

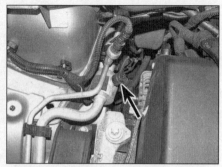

10.7 . . . and high-pressure service port (arrowed)

Note: *This Section refers to the components of the air conditioning system itself – refer to Sections 8 and 9 for details of components common to the heating/ventilation system.*

Condenser

Petrol engines

1 Have the refrigerant discharged at a dealer service department or an automotive air conditioning repair facility.

2 Disconnect the battery negative terminal (refer to *Disconnecting the battery* in the Reference Chapter).

3 Firmly apply the handbrake, then jack up the front of the car and support it securely on axle stands (see *Jacking and vehicle support*).

4 Remove the front bumper as described in Chapter 11.

5 On models with the horn mounted above the radiator, disconnect the horn wiring connector, undo the retaining bolt and remove the horn.

6 Undo the bolt securing the refrigerant pipe connector block to the mounting bracket above, or adjacent to, the right-hand end of the condenser. Now undo the retaining bolt and separate the refrigerant pipe connector block **(see illustrations)**. Discard the O-ring seals – new ones must be used when refitting. Suitably cap the open fittings immediately to keep moisture and contamination out of the system

7 On all except certain 1.6 litre Z16XEP engine models, undo the radiator upper right-hand side mounting bracket bolt and remove the refrigerant pipe connector block mounting bracket.

11.6b . . . then undo the retaining bolt (arrowed) and separate the refrigerant pipe connector block

11.17 Undo the retaining bolt (arrowed) and disconnect the refrigerant pipe connector block from the receiver/dryer

8 On all except certain 1.6 litre Z16XEP engine models, undo the retaining bolt and disconnect the refrigerant pipe connector block from the receiver/dryer. Discard the O-ring seals – new ones must be used when refitting. Suitably cap the open fittings immediately to keep moisture and contamination out of the system.

9 On all except certain 1.6 litre Z16XEP engine models, disengage the rubber retaining strap and remove the receiver/dryer.

10 Lift the condenser upwards to disengage the upper and lower mounting each side, then turn the condenser and lift it up and out of the engine compartment **(see illustrations 3.14a and 3.14b)**. Take care not to damage the condenser fins.

11 Refitting is the reverse of removal. Renew the O-rings and lubricate with refrigerant oil.

12 Have the system evacuated, charged and leak-tested by the specialist who discharged it.

1.3 litre diesel engines

13 Have the refrigerant discharged at a dealer service department or an automotive air conditioning repair facility.

14 Disconnect the battery negative terminal (refer to *Disconnecting the battery* in the Reference Chapter).

15 Firmly apply the handbrake, then jack up the front of the car and support it securely on axle stands (see *Jacking and vehicle support*).

16 Remove the front bumper as described in Chapter 11.

17 Undo the retaining bolt and disconnect the refrigerant pipe connector block from

11.19 Undo the retaining bolt (arrowed) and separate the refrigerant pipe connector block

11.18 Disengage the rubber retaining strap (arrowed) and remove the receiver/dryer

the receiver/dryer **(see illustration)**. Discard the O-ring seals – new ones must be used when refitting. Suitably cap the open fittings immediately to keep moisture and contamination out of the system.

18 Disengage the rubber retaining strap and remove the receiver/dryer **(see illustration)**.

19 Undo the retaining bolt and separate the refrigerant pipe connector block adjacent to the right-hand end of the condenser **(see illustration)**.

20 Disconnect the two wiring harness connectors located in front of the condenser **(see illustration)**. Release the wiring harness from the cable-ties on the support bracket.

21 Suitably support the condenser then undo the two bolts each side securing the auxiliary cooling fan and condenser to the radiator. Lift the cooling fan and condenser up and out of the engine compartment. Take care not to damage the condenser fins.

22 Refitting is the reverse of removal. Renew the O-rings and lubricate with refrigerant oil.

23 Have the system evacuated, charged and leak-tested by the specialist who discharged it.

1.7 litre diesel engines

24 Have the refrigerant discharged at a dealer service department or an automotive air conditioning repair facility.

25 Disconnect the battery negative terminal (refer to *Disconnecting the battery* in the Reference Chapter).

26 Firmly apply the handbrake, then jack up the front of the car and support it securely

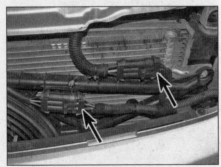

11.20 Disconnect the two wiring harness connectors (arrowed) located in front of the condenser

on axle stands (see *Jacking and vehicle support*).

27 Remove the front bumper as described in Chapter 11.

28 On models with the horn mounted above the radiator, disconnect the horn wiring connector, undo the retaining bolt and remove the horn.

29 On Y17DT engine models, undo the bolt securing the refrigerant pipe connector block to the mounting bracket above the right-hand end of the condenser. On all models, undo the retaining bolt and separate the refrigerant pipe connector block **(see illustration 11.19)**. Discard the O-ring seals – new ones must be used when refitting. Suitably cap the open fittings immediately to keep moisture and contamination out of the system.

30 Undo the radiator upper right-hand side mounting bracket bolt and remove the refrigerant pipe connector block mounting bracket.

31 Undo the retaining bolt and disconnect the refrigerant pipe connector block from the receiver/dryer. Discard the O-ring seals – new ones must be used when refitting. Suitably cap the open fittings immediately to keep moisture and contamination out of the system.

32 Disengage the rubber retaining strap and remove the receiver/dryer.

33 On Y17DT engine models, lift the condenser upwards to disengage the upper and lower mounting each side, then turn the condenser and lift it up and out of the engine compartment **(see illustrations 3.14a and 3.14b)**. Take care not to damage the condenser fins.

34 On Z17DTH engine models, disconnect the two wiring harness connectors located in front of the condenser **(see illustration 11.20)**. Release the wiring harness from the cable-ties.

35 On Z17DTH engine models without an auxiliary cooling fan, undo the two bolts and remove the support brace located in front of the condenser.

36 On Z17DTH engine models, suitably support the condenser then undo the two bolts each side securing the condenser, or auxiliary cooling fan and condenser, to the radiator. Lift the cooling fan (if fitted) and/or condenser up and out of the engine compartment. Take care not to damage the condenser fins.

37 Refitting is the reverse of removal. Renew the O-rings and lubricate with refrigerant oil.

38 Have the system evacuated, charged and leak-tested by the specialist who discharged it.

Evaporator

39 Have the refrigerant discharged at a dealer service department or an automotive air conditioning repair facility.

40 Remove the air distribution housing as described in Section 9.

41 Undo the retaining bolt and detach the rear air duct from the air distribution housing **(see illustrations)**.

11.41a Undo the retaining bolt . . .

11.41b . . . and detach the rear air duct from the air distribution housing

11.42a Undo the front retaining screw (arrowed . . .

42 Undo the three retaining screws and detach the blower motor and housing from the air distribution housing **(see illustrations)**.
43 On models with electronic climate control, disconnect the two wiring harness connectors, then release and remove the wiring harness.
44 Remove the two spring clips securing the coolant pipes to the heater matrix. Withdraw the pipes from the matrix and collect the two seals **(see illustrations)**.
45 Undo the two screws securing the bulkhead seal plate to the air distribution housing. Lift off the seal plate and remove the two coolant pipes **(see illustrations)**.
46 Working around the periphery of the service cover, undo the retaining screws, extract the retaining clips and remove the service cover from the air distribution housing **(see illustration)**.

11.42b . . . two rear retaining screws (arrowed) . . .

47 Carefully remove the heater matrix from the air distribution housing **(see illustration)**.
48 Using a sharp knife, carefully cut the foam

11.42c . . . and detach the blower motor and housing from the air distribution housing

seal at the join of the two halves of the air distribution housing **(see illustration)**.
49 Extract the seven retaining clips securing

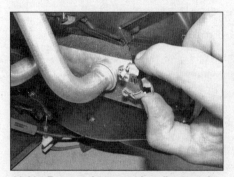

11.44a Remove the two spring clips securing the coolant pipes to the heater matrix . . .

11.44b . . . withdraw the pipes from the matrix . . .

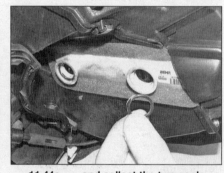

11.44c . . . and collect the two seals

11.45a Undo the two screws (arrowed) securing the bulkhead seal plate to the air distribution housing . . .

11.45b . . . then lift off the seal plate and remove the two coolant pipes

11.46 Undo the retaining screws, extract the retaining clips and remove the service cover from the air distribution housing

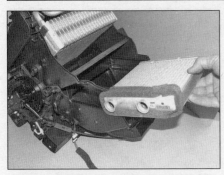

11.47 Carefully remove the heater matrix from the air distribution housing

11.48 Using a sharp knife, carefully cut the foam seal at the join of the two halves of the air distribution housing

11.50a Separate the two halves of the air distribution housing . . .

11.50b . . . and take out the evaporator

the two halves of the air distribution housing together.

50 Separate the two halves of the air distribution housing and take out the evaporator **(see illustrations)**.

51 Refitting is the reverse of removal, bearing in mind the following points:

a) When reassembling the two halves of the air distribution, ensure that the air distribution valves are correctly seated in the housing guides

b) Ensure that all disturbed seals are renewed.

c) Refit the air distribution housing as described in Section 9.

Compressor

Petrol engines

52 Have the refrigerant discharged at a dealer service department or an automotive air conditioning repair facility.

53 Disconnect the battery negative terminal (refer to *Disconnecting the battery* in the Reference Chapter).

54 Firmly apply the handbrake, then jack up the front of the car and support it securely on axle stands (see *Jacking and vehicle support*).

55 Remove the auxiliary drivebelt as described in Chapter 1A.

56 On models with the horn mounted above the radiator disconnect the horn wiring connector, undo the retaining bolt and remove the horn.

57 With the system discharged, undo the retaining bolt and disconnect the refrigerant pipes from the compressor. Discard the O-ring

seals – new ones must be used when refitting. Suitably cap the open fittings immediately to keep moisture and contamination out of the system.

58 Disconnect the compressor wiring connector.

59 Unbolt the compressor from the cylinder block/crankcase, then withdraw the compressor downwards from under the vehicle **(see illustration)**.

60 Refit the compressor in the reverse order of removal; renew all seals disturbed.

61 If you are installing a new compressor, refer to the compressor manufacturer's instructions for adding refrigerant oil to the system.

62 Have the system evacuated, charged and leak-tested by the specialist that discharged it.

63 After installing a new compressor, always observe the following running-in procedure:

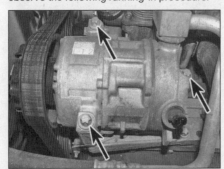

11.59 Compressor mounting bolts (arrowed)

1) Open all instrument panel air outlet flaps.

2) Start vehicle engine and stabilise idle speed for approximately 5 seconds.

3) Switch fan to maximum speed.

4) Switch on the air conditioning and let it run for at least 2 minutes without interruption at engine speed under 1500 rpm.

1.3 litre diesel engines

64 Have the refrigerant discharged at a dealer service department or an automotive air conditioning repair facility.

65 Disconnect the battery negative terminal (refer to *Disconnecting the battery* in the Reference Chapter).

66 Firmly apply the handbrake, then jack up the front of the car and support it securely on axle stands (see *Jacking and vehicle support*).

67 Remove the auxiliary drivebelt as described in Chapter 1B.

68 On models with the horn mounted above the radiator, disconnect the horn wiring connector, undo the retaining bolt and remove the horn.

69 With the system discharged, undo the retaining bolt(s) and disconnect the refrigerant pipes from the compressor. Discard the O-ring seals – new ones must be used when refitting. Suitably cap the open fittings immediately to keep moisture and contamination out of the system.

70 Disconnect the compressor wiring connector.

71 Unbolt the compressor from the cylinder block/crankcase, then withdraw the compressor downwards from under the vehicle **(see illustration 11.59)**.

72 Refit the compressor in the reverse order of removal; renew all seals disturbed.

73 If you are installing a new compressor, refer to the compressor manufacturer's instructions for adding refrigerant oil to the system.

74 Have the system evacuated, charged and leak-tested by the specialist that discharged it.

75 After installing a new compressor, always observe the following running-in procedure:

1) Open all instrument panel air outlet flaps.

2) Start vehicle engine and stabilise idle speed for approximately 5 seconds.

3) Switch fan to maximum speed.

4) Switch on the air conditioning and let it run for at least 2 minutes without interruption at engine speed under 1500 rpm.

1.7 litre Y17DT diesel engines

76 Have the refrigerant discharged at a dealer service department or an automotive air conditioning repair facility.

77 Disconnect the battery negative terminal (refer to *Disconnecting the battery* in the Reference Chapter).

78 Firmly apply the handbrake, then jack up the front of the car and support it securely on axle stands (see *Jacking and vehicle support*).

79 Remove the auxiliary drivebelt as described in Chapter 1B.

80 On models with the horn mounted above

the radiator, disconnect the horn wiring connector, undo the retaining bolt and remove the horn.

81 Undo the bolt securing the air intake resonator to the upper front crossmember. Slide the resonator sideways to disengage the three locating lugs, and remove the resonator from the crossmember.

82 With the system discharged, undo the retaining bolt and disconnect the refrigerant pipes from the compressor. Discard the O-ring seals – new ones must be used when refitting. Suitably cap the open fittings immediately to keep moisture and contamination out of the system.

83 Disconnect the compressor wiring connector.

84 Undo the two nuts and one bolt and remove the oil dipstick guide tube bracket from the engine.

85 Release the vacuum hose from the retaining clip on the compressor.

86 Unbolt the compressor from the cylinder block/crankcase, lift it up at the rear and remove it upwards from the engine compartment.

87 Refit the compressor in the reverse order of removal; renew all seals disturbed.

88 If you are installing a new compressor, refer to the compressor manufacturer's instructions for adding refrigerant oil to the system.

89 Have the system evacuated, charged and leak-tested by the specialist that discharged it.

90 After installing a new compressor, always observe the following running-in procedure:
  1) Open all instrument panel air outlet flaps.
  2) Start vehicle engine and stabilise idle speed for approximately 5 seconds.
  3) Switch fan to maximum speed.
  4) Switch on the air conditioning and let it run for at least 2 minutes without interruption at engine speed under 1500 rpm.

1.7 litre Z17DTH diesel engines

91 Have the refrigerant discharged at a dealer service department or an automotive air conditioning repair facility.

92 Disconnect the battery negative terminal (refer to *Disconnecting the battery* in the Reference Chapter).

93 Drain the cooling system as described in Chapter 1B.

94 Remove the condenser as described previously in this Section.

95 Remove the radiator as described in Section 3.

96 Remove the auxiliary drivebelt as described in Chapter 1B.

97 Undo the retaining bolt and disconnect the refrigerant pipes from the compressor. Discard the O-ring seals – new ones must be used when refitting. Suitably cap the open fittings immediately to keep moisture and contamination out of the system.

98 Disconnect the compressor wiring connector.

99 Unbolt the compressor from the cylinder block/crankcase and remove the compressor from the engine compartment.

100 Refit the compressor in the reverse order of removal; renew all seals disturbed.

101 If you are installing a new compressor, refer to the compressor manufacturer's instructions for adding refrigerant oil to the system.

102 Have the system evacuated, charged and leak-tested by the specialist that discharged it.

103 After installing a new compressor, always observe the following running-in procedure:
  1) *Open all instrument panel air outlet flaps.*
  2) *Start vehicle engine and stabilise idle speed for approximately 5 seconds.*
  3) *Switch fan to maximum speed.*
  4) *Switch on the air conditioning and let it run for at least 2 minutes without interruption at engine speed under 1500 rpm.*

Receiver/dryer

Note: *On certain 1.6 litre Z16XEP petrol engines, the receiver/dryer is an integral part of the condenser and cannot be individually removed.*

104 Have the refrigerant discharged at a dealer service department or an automotive air conditioning repair facility.

105 Disconnect the battery negative terminal (refer to *Disconnecting the battery* in the Reference Chapter).

106 Firmly apply the handbrake, then jack up the front of the car and support it securely on axle stands (see *Jacking and vehicle support*).

107 Remove the front bumper as described in Chapter 11.

108 Undo the retaining bolt and disconnect the refrigerant pipe connector block from the receiver/dryer **(see illustration 11.17)**. Discard the O-ring seals – new ones must be used when refitting. Suitably cap the open fittings immediately to keep moisture and contamination out of the system.

109 Disengage the rubber retaining strap and remove the receiver/dryer **(see illustration 11.18)**.

110 Refitting is the reverse of removal. Renew the O-rings and lubricate with refrigerant oil.

111 Have the system evacuated, charged and leak-tested by the specialist who discharged it.

Auxiliary fan

Note: *An auxiliary fan is only fitted to certain diesel engine models.*

112 Disconnect the battery negative terminal (refer to *Disconnecting the battery* in the Reference Chapter).

113 Firmly apply the handbrake, then jack up the front of the car and support it securely on axle stands (see *Jacking and vehicle support*).

114 Remove the front bumper as described in Chapter 11.

115 Suitably suspend the condenser from the upper front crossmember using cable-ties or similar.

116 Disconnect the two wiring harness connectors located in front of the condenser **(see illustration 11.20)**. Release the wiring harness from the cable-ties on the auxiliary fan housing.

117 Undo the four fan housing retaining bolts and remove the auxiliary cooling fan and housing from below.

118 To separate the fan from the housing, undo the four retaining bolts and lift off the fan guard.

119 If required, undo the two bolts and remove the series resistor from the housing.

120 Undo the three bolts and remove the fan motor and fan from the housing.

121 Refitting is the reverse of removal. Renew the O-rings and lubricate with refrigerant oil.

Chapter 4 Part A:
Fuel and exhaust systems – petrol engines

Contents

Degrees of difficulty

Easy, suitable for novice with little experience	**Fairly easy,** suitable for beginner with some experience	**Fairly difficult,** suitable for competent DIY mechanic	**Difficult,** suitable for experienced DIY mechanic	**Very difficult,** suitable for expert DIY or professional

Specifications

Engine identification

Engine type	**Manufacturer's engine code***
1.4 litre (1364 cc) DOHC 16-valve	Z14XEP
1.6 litre (1598 cc):	
SOHC 8-valve.	Z16SE
DOHC 16-valve.	Z16XE and Z16XEP
1.8 litre (1796 cc) DOHC 16-valve	Z18XE

* For details of engine code location, see 'Vehicle identification' in the Reference Chapter.

System type

1.4 litre engines	Bosch Motronic ME 7.6.1/2 sequential multipoint fuel injection
1.6 litre engines	Multec-S sequential multipoint fuel injection
1.8 litre engines	Simtec 71.5 sequential multipoint fuel injection

Fuel system data

Fuel supply pump type.	Electric, immersed in tank
Fuel pump regulated constant pressure.	3.8 bar
Specified idle speed.	Not adjustable – controlled by ECU
Idle mixture CO content	Not adjustable – controlled by ECU

Torque wrench settings

	Nm	lbf ft
Accelerator pedal position sensor nuts	12	9
Camshaft sensor retaining bolt:		
1.4 litre engines	6	4
1.6 litre engines:		
Z16SE	16	12
Z16XE	10	7
Z16XEP	6	4
1.8 litre engines	8	6
Crankshaft speed/position sensor retaining bolt	10	7
Exhaust front pipe to manifold*	20	15
Exhaust manifold securing nuts:*		
1.4 litre engines	20	15
1.6 litre engines:		
Z16SE and Z16XE . . . . :	22	16
Z16XEP	15	11
1.8 litre engines	12	9
Exhaust system clamp bolt	50	37
Fuel tank retaining strap bolts	23	17
Inlet manifold retaining bolts/nuts:		
1.4 litre engines	10	7
1.6 litre engines:		
Z16SE* and Z16XE	22	16
Z16XEP	8	6
1.8 litre engines	22	16
Knock sensor	20	15
Manifold pressure sensor bolt	8	6
Throttle housing retaining bolts	8	6

* Use new fasteners

---

1 General information and precautions

General information

The fuel supply system consists of a fuel tank (which is mounted under the rear of the car, with an electric fuel pump immersed in it), and fuel feed lines. The fuel pump supplies fuel to the fuel rail, which acts as a reservoir for the fuel injectors which inject fuel into the inlet tracts. The fuel pressure regulator is located on the fuel pump module in the fuel tank.

The electronic control unit controls both the fuel injection system and the ignition system, integrating the two into a complete engine management system. Refer to Section 10 for further information on the operation of the fuel system and to Chapter 5B for details of the ignition side of the system.

1.4, 1.6 Z16XEP and 1.8 litre engines utilise a 'Twinport' inlet manifold configuration. Vacuum-operated flap valves located in the inlet manifold are opened or closed according to engine operating conditions, to create a variable venturi manifold arrangement. This layout has significant advantages in terms of engine power, fuel economy and reduced exhaust emissions.

The exhaust manifold on all engines incorporates an integral catalytic converter to reduce harmful exhaust gas emissions. The remaining exhaust system is in two sections.

Further details can be found in Section 23 and in Part C of this Chapter, along with details of the other emission control systems and components.

Precautions

Note: *Refer to Part C of this Chapter for general information and precautions relating to the catalytic converter.*

Before disconnecting any fuel lines, or working on any part of the fuel system, the system must be depressurised as described in Section 5.

Care must be taken when disconnecting the fuel lines. When disconnecting a fuel union or hose, loosen the union or clamp screw slowly, to avoid sudden uncontrolled fuel spillage. Take adequate fire precautions.

When working on fuel system components, scrupulous cleanliness must be observed, and care must be taken not to introduce any foreign matter into fuel lines or components.

After carrying out any work involving disconnection of fuel lines, it is advisable to check the connections for leaks; pressurise the system by switching the ignition on and off several times.

Electronic control units are very sensitive components, and certain precautions must be taken to avoid damage to these units as follows:

a) *When carrying out welding operations on the vehicle using electric welding equipment, the battery and alternator should be disconnected.*

b) *Although the underbonnet-mounted control units will tolerate normal underbonnet conditions, they can be adversely affected by excess heat or moisture. If using welding equipment or pressure-washing equipment in the vicinity of an electronic control unit, take care not to direct heat, or jets of water or steam, at the unit. If this cannot be avoided, remove the control unit from the vehicle, and protect its wiring plug with a plastic bag.*

c) *Before disconnecting any wiring, or removing components, always ensure that the ignition is switched off.*

d) *After working on fuel injection/engine management system components, ensure that all wiring is correctly reconnected before reconnecting the battery or switching on the ignition.*

 Warning: Many of the procedures in this Chapter require the removal of fuel lines and connections, which may result in some fuel spillage. Before carrying out any operation on the fuel system, refer to the precautions given in 'Safety first!' at the beginning of this manual, and follow them implicitly. Petrol is a highly-dangerous and volatile liquid, and the precautions necessary when handling it cannot be overstressed.

Note: *Residual pressure will remain in the fuel lines long after the vehicle was last used. Before disconnecting any fuel line, first depressurise the fuel system as described in Section 5.*

2.1a Disconnect the wiring connector from the intake air temperature sensor . . .

2.1b . . . and unclip the wiring harness (arrowed) from the air duct

2.3a Slacken the air intake duct retaining clamp at the throttle housing (arrowed) . . .

2 Air cleaner assembly and intake ducts – removal and refitting

Removal

1 Disconnect the wiring connector from the intake air temperature sensor or airflow meter and unclip or release the wiring harness from the air duct **(see illustrations)**.

2 On 1.6 litre Z16SE engines, undo the two bolts securing the resonator to the inlet manifold. Release the throttle housing coolant hose from the retaining clip, then lift the hose from the guides on the resonator.

3 Slacken the retaining clamps securing the air intake duct to the throttle housing and air cleaner. Where applicable, release the clip and disconnect the crankcase ventilation hose from the duct or cylinder head cover, then remove the duct from the engine **(see illustration)**.

4 Unclip the evaporative emission system hoses or the purge valve from the rear of the air cleaner **(see illustration)**.

5 Undo the retaining bolt and release the mounting bracket at the rear of the air cleaner housing **(see illustration)**.

6 Detach the air intake duct at the front of the air cleaner housing **(see illustration)**.

7 Lift the housing upwards at the rear, then disengage the front mounting rubber from the body bracket **(see illustrations)**.

8 When sufficient clearance exists, release the retaining clip and disconnect the water

2.3b . . . and air cleaner (arrowed) . . .

drain tube (where fitted) from the base of the air cleaner housing. Remove the assembly from the engine compartment.

9 To remove the intake pipe/resonator from

2.3c . . . then remove the duct from the engine

the front crossmember, undo the retaining screw, and slide the intake pipe to one side to release it from the crossmember **(see illustrations)**.

2.4 Unclip the evaporative emission system hoses or the purge valve from the rear of the air cleaner

2.5 Undo the retaining bolt (arrowed) and release the air cleaner housing mounting bracket

2.6 Detach the air intake duct at the front of the air cleaner housing

2.7a Lift the housing upwards at the rear . . .

2.7b . . . then disengage the front mounting rubber (arrowed) from the body bracket

2.9a To remove the intake pipe/resonator from the front crossmember, undo the retaining screw (arrowed) . . .

Refitting

10 Refitting is the reverse of removal, making sure all the air intake ducts are securely reconnected.

3 Accelerator pedal/position sensor – removal and refitting

Removal

1 Disconnect the battery negative terminal (refer to *Disconnecting the battery* in the Reference Chapter).
2 Working in the driver's footwell under the facia, disconnect the wiring connector from the top of the accelerator pedal/position sensor **(see illustration)**.
3 Unscrew the three mounting nuts, and withdraw the sensor from the bulkhead.

Refitting

4 Refitting is a reversal of removal.

4 Unleaded petrol – general information and usage

Note: *The information given in this Chapter is correct at the time of writing. If updated information is thought to be required, check with a Vauxhall/Opel dealer. If travelling abroad, consult one of the motoring organisations*

3.2 Disconnect the wiring connector (arrowed) from the accelerator pedal/position sensor

2.9b . . . and slide the intake pipe to one side to release it from the crossmember

(or a similar authority) for advice on the fuel available.

All models are designed to run on fuel with a minimum octane rating of 95 RON. However, if unavailable, 91 octane may be used although a reduction in engine power and torque will be noticed.

All models have a catalytic converter, and so must be run on unleaded fuel only. Under no circumstances should leaded fuel or LRP be used, as this will damage the converter.

Super unleaded petrol (97 to 99 octane) can also be used in all models if wished, though there is no advantage in doing so.

5 Fuel injection system – depressurisation

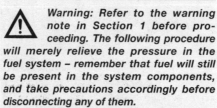

⚠️ **Warning: Refer to the warning note in Section 1 before proceeding. The following procedure will merely relieve the pressure in the fuel system – remember that fuel will still be present in the system components, and take precautions accordingly before disconnecting any of them.**

1 The fuel system referred to in this Section is defined as the tank-mounted fuel pump, the fuel injectors, and the metal pipes and flexible hoses of the fuel lines between these components. All these contain fuel which will be under pressure while the engine is running, and/or while the ignition is switched on. The

5.3 Fuel pressure connection valve (arrowed) on the fuel rail

pressure will remain for some time after the ignition has been switched off, and it must be relieved in a controlled fashion when any of these components are disturbed for servicing work.

2 Where fitted, remove the plastic cover over the top of the engine. According to engine, it may also be necessary to remove the air cleaner and intake duct as described in Section 2, for improved access.
3 Locate the fuel pressure connection valve which is fitted to the right-hand end of the fuel rail on 1.4 litre and 1.6 litre Z16XEP engines, and to the left-hand end on all other engines **(see illustration)**.
4 Unscrew the cap from the valve and position a container beneath the valve. Hold a wad of rag over the valve and relieve the pressure in the fuel system by depressing the valve core with a suitable screwdriver. Be prepared for the squirt of fuel as the valve core is depressed and catch it with the rag. Hold the valve core down until no more fuel is expelled from the valve.
5 Once all pressure is relieved, securely refit the valve cap.

6 Fuel gauge sender unit – removal and refitting

General information

1 The fuel gauge sender unit is attached to the side of the 'in-tank module' which, as its name suggests, is located inside the fuel tank. Access is gained from inside the vehicle after removal of the centre rear seat.
2 The design of the in-tank module was changed in 2007. On early models it will be necessary to first remove the in-tank module from the fuel tank to allow removal of the sender unit. On later models the sender unit can be removed from the side of the in-tank module without having to remove the module from the tank.
3 During vehicle manufacture the in-tank module cover retaining ring is secured by a large circular clip which is crimped in position. To remove the module cover retaining ring, the clip must be prised off rendering it unsuitable for further use. A new service replacement clip is supplied by Vauxhall/Opel parts stockists, which is essentially a large worm-drive hose clip with a shear-off head at the drive end. The clip is tightened until the head shears off, ensuring that the correct tightening torque has been applied.
4 Proceed as described under the following sub-headings according to year of vehicle manufacture.

Pre-2007 model year vehicles

Note 1: *A new in-tank module cover sealing ring and cover retaining ring clip will be required on refitting.*
Note 2: *The fuel tank should be as empty as possible when carrying out this procedure.*

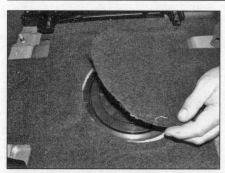

6.7 Lift up the carpet flap to reveal the fuel tank access cover

6.8 Carefully prise the plastic access cover from the floor

6.9 Lift up the tab and disconnect the wiring connector from the in-tank module cover

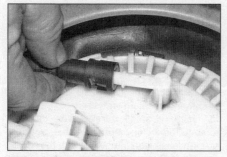

6.10 Compress the clips on each side of the fuel hose quick-release connector and ease the connector off of its union

6.12a Release the the in-tank module cover retaining ring clip using a screwdriver to prise it apart . . .

6.12b . . . then remove the clip from the top of the tank

Removal

5 Depressurise the fuel system as described in Section 5, then disconnect the battery negative terminal (refer to *Disconnecting the battery* in the Reference Chapter).

6 Remove the centre rear seat as described in Chapter 11.

7 Lift up the carpet flap to reveal the fuel tank access cover **(see illustration)**.

8 Using a large screwdriver or suitable wide-bladed tool, carefully prise the plastic access cover from the floor **(see illustration)**.

9 Lift up the tab and disconnect the wiring connector from the in-tank module cover, and tape the connector to the vehicle body, to prevent it disappearing behind the tank **(see illustration)**.

10 Compress the clips located on each side of the fuel supply hose quick-release connector and ease the connector off of its union **(see illustration)**. Be prepared for some loss of fuel. A Vauxhall/Opel special tool is available to release the fuel hose connector, but provided care is taken, the connector can be released using a pair of long-nosed pliers, or a similar tool, to depress the retaining tangs. Suitably plug the disconnected hose to prevent entry of dust and dirt.

11 Where fitted, disconnect the fuel return hose quick-release connector in the same way.

12 If the in-tank module cover retaining ring clip is the original (from the date of vehicle manufacture), release the clip using a screwdriver to prise it apart **(see illustrations)**. If the cover retaining ring clip is not the original, unscrew the clip using a small 7 mm spanner on the worm-drive hexagon.

13 With clip removed, lift off the in-tank module cover retaining ring **(see illustration)**.

14 Lift the in-tank module cover off the fuel tank and collect the sealing ring **(see illustration)**.

15 Carefully insert a screwdriver or similar tool into the fuel tank and depress the three tabs, one at a time, securing the in-tank module to the mounting plate in the tank base. As each tab is depressed, lift the in-tank module upwards until the tab releases.

16 Once all three tabs in the tank mounting plate are released, carefully lift the in-tank module up and out of the fuel tank and place it in a suitable container.

17 Unclip the protective cap over the sender unit located on the side of the in-tank module.

18 Cut off the cable-tie securing the fuel pump and fuel gauge sender unit wiring to the fuel hose, then disconnect the sender unit wiring connector from the underside of the in-tank module cover **(see illustrations)**.

6.13 Lift off the in-tank module cover retaining ring

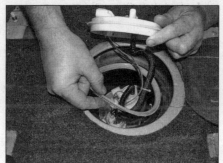

6.14 Lift the in-tank module cover off the fuel tank and collect the sealing ring

6.18a Cut off the cable-tie securing the wiring to the fuel hose . . .

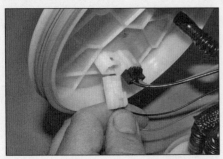

6.18b . . . then disconnect the sender unit wiring connector from the underside of the in-tank module cover

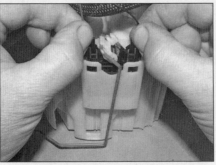

6.19a Release the two retaining tabs . . .

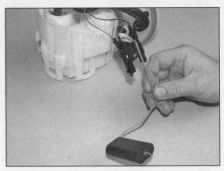

6.19b . . . and lift the fuel gauge sender unit up and out of the in-tank module

19 Release the two retaining tabs and lift the fuel gauge sender unit up and out of the in-tank module **(see illustrations)**.

Refitting

20 Refit the gauge sender unit to the in-tank module ensuring that the retaining tabs positively engage.

21 Reconnect the wiring connector and secure the wiring to the fuel hose using a new cable-tie. Refit the protective cap over the sender unit.

22 Manoeuvre the in-tank module carefully in through the tank aperture and push it down onto the retaining tabs of the tank mounting plate. Ensure that the retaining tabs audibly engage with the module.

23 Lubricate the inner surface of a new in-tank module sealing ring and locate the ring in the fuel tank aperture. Make sure the ring seats squarely on the tank aperture.

24 Position the in-tank module cover so that the arrow on the cover is towards the front of the vehicle and carefully push the cover down into the sealing ring **(see illustration)**. Take care not to dislodge the sealing ring and check that, with the cover fully in place, the outer edge of the sealing ring is visible equally, all around the cover periphery.

25 Place the in-tank module cover retaining ring over the module cover and position it so that the small cut-out is toward the front of the vehicle and aligned with the arrow on the module cover **(see illustrations)**.

26 Locate the new retaining ring clip over the ring and position it so that the worm-drive screw head is situated centrally within the large cut-out in the retaining ring **(see illustration)**. Ensure that the clip sits squarely in the retaining ring groove.

27 Using a 7 mm spanner, tighten the clip

until the head shears off. Note that this is a lengthy process as the limited working clearance only allows the clip to be tightened one flat at a time.

28 Once the clip is fully-tightened, tap off the collar remaining on the worm-drive screw head using a screwdriver **(see illustration)**. This will allow the clip to be unscrewed, if necessary, for future removal.

29 Using a small screwdriver, carefully remove the locking portion of the fuel hose quick-release fitting, together with the locking ring, from the fuel pipe stub on the in-tank module cover **(see illustration)**.

30 Place the locking ring over the end of the locking portion, then insert the locking portion into the fuel hose end fitting. Push the hose back onto the pipe stub until it clicks into place and the locking portion pops out **(see illustrations)**.

6.24 With the arrow on the in-tank module cover towards the front of the vehicle, push the cover down into the sealing ring

6.25a Place the in-tank module cover retaining ring over the module cover . . .

6.25b . . . and position it so that the small cut-out (arrowed) is aligned with the arrow on the module cover

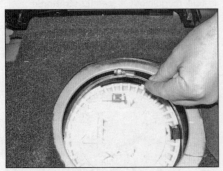

6.26 Position the new clip over the retaining ring with the screw head situated centrally within the large cut-out in the ring

6.28 With the clip fully-tightened, tap off the collar remaining on the worm-drive screw head using a screwdriver

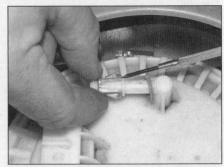

6.29 Carefully remove the locking portion of the fuel hose quick-release fitting, together with the locking ring, from the pipe stub

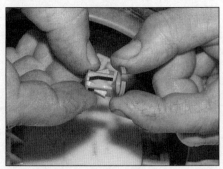

6.30a Place the locking ring over the end of the locking portion . . .

6.30b . . . then insert the locking portion into the fuel hose end fitting

6.30c Push the hose back onto the pipe stub until it clicks into place and the locking portion pops out

31 Reconnect the wiring connector to the in-tank module cover.

32 Reconnect the battery then start the engine and check for fuel leaks. If all is well, refit the access cover and carpet flap, then refit the centre rear seat.

Post-2007 model year vehicles

Note 1: *A new in-tank module cover sealing ring and cover retaining ring clip will be required on refitting.*

Note 2: *The fuel tank should be as empty as possible when carrying out this procedure.*

Removal

33 Carry out the operations described previously in paragraphs 5 to 14.

34 Using a small screwdriver inserted down through the tank aperture, release the two retaining tabs and lift the fuel gauge sender unit up and out of the in-tank module **(see illustrations)**.

35 Cut off the cable-tie securing the fuel pump and fuel gauge sender unit wiring to the fuel hose, then disconnect the sender unit wiring connector from the underside of the in-tank module cover **(see illustrations)**. Remove the sender unit from the vehicle.

Refitting

36 Refit the gauge sender unit to the in-tank module ensuring that the retaining tabs positively engage.

37 Reconnect the wiring connector and secure the wiring to the fuel hose using a new cable-tie. Refit the protective cap over the sender unit.

38 Carry out the operations described previously in paragraphs 23 to 32.

7 Fuel pump –
removal and refitting

General information

1 The fuel pump is located in the 'in-tank module' which, as its name suggests, is located inside the fuel tank. The pump is integral with the in-tank module and cannot be renewed separately.

2 To remove the in-tank module on models

produced from 2007 onwards, Vauxhall/Opel special tool KM-6391 (or suitable alternative) will be required to remove the in-tank module from the fuel tank.

3 Proceed as described under the following sub-headings according to year of vehicle manufacture.

Pre-2007 model year vehicles

Removal

4 Refer to the information contained in Section 6, paragraphs 1 to 16. If, necessary, transfer the fuel gauge sender unit to the new in-tank module as described in the relevant paragraphs of Section 6.

Refitting

5 Refit the in-tank module as described in Section 6, paragraphs 20 to 32.

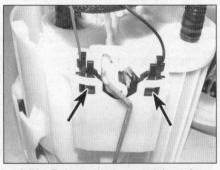

6.34a Release the two retaining tabs (arrowed) . . .

6.35a Cut off the cable-tie securing the wiring to the fuel hose . . .

Post-2007 model year vehicles

Note: *Vauxhall/Opel special tool KM-6391 (or suitable alternative) will be required to remove the in-tank module from the fuel tank.*

Removal

6 Carry out the operations described in Section 6, paragraphs 5 to 14.

7 To remove the in-tank module Vauxhall/ Opel special tool KM-6391, or a suitable alternative will be required. The special tool consists of four metal strips that are inserted down the sides of the in-tank module, to release the module from the four tabs of the mounting plate, which remains in the tank. In the absence of the special tool a suitable alternative can be easily made **(see Tool Tip)**.

8 To allow clearance for one of the tools to be inserted, it will be necessary to release the fuel

6.34b . . . and lift the fuel gauge sender unit up and out of the in-tank module

6.35b . . . then disconnect the sender unit wiring connector from the underside of the in-tank module cover

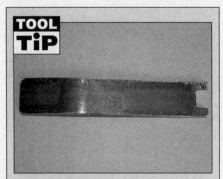

An in-tank module removal tool can be made from 3 mm thick steel strip, approximately 150 mm long and 26 mm wide. Cut or file a 12 mm slot in one end of the tool and put a slight bend in the tool at the other end, approximately 100 mm from the slotted end. Note that 4 of these tools will be required to remove the module.

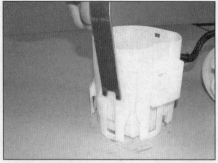

7.9a Carefully insert the removal tools down through the slots on the side of the in-tank module . . .

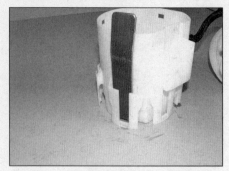

7.9b . . . push the tools down into the slots . . .

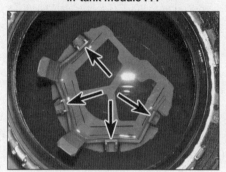

7.9c . . . until they release the four retaining tabs (arrowed) in the tank mounting bracket (shown with in-tank module removed)

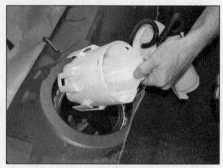

7.10 With the tabs in the mounting bracket released, lift the in-tank module up and out of the fuel tank

gauge sender unit from the side of the in-tank module Using a small screwdriver inserted down through the tank aperture, release the two retaining tabs and lift the fuel gauge sender unit up and out of the in-tank module **(see illustrations 6.34a and 6.34b)**.

9 Carefully insert the four tools down through the slots on the side of the in-tank module until they engage and release the four retaining tabs in the tank mounting plate **(see illustrations)**.

10 Once the tabs in the tank mounting plate are released, carefully lift the in-tank module up and out of the fuel tank and place it in a suitable container **(see illustration)**.

11 If necessary, cut off the cable-tie securing the fuel pump and fuel gauge sender unit wiring to the fuel hose, then disconnect the sender unit wiring connector from the underside of the in-tank module cover and remove the sender unit **(see illustrations 6.18a and 6.18b)**.

Refitting

12 Where removed, refit the fuel gauge sender unit to the in-tank module ensuring that the retaining tabs positively engage.

13 Reconnect the wiring connector and secure the wiring to the fuel hose using a new cable-tie.

14 Manoeuvre the in-tank module carefully

in through the tank aperture and push it down onto the retaining tabs of the tank mounting plate. Ensure that the retaining tabs audibly engage with the module.

15 Refit the in-tank module cover as described in Section 6, paragraphs 23 to 32.

8 Fuel tank – removal and refitting

Note 1: *Refer to the information contained in Section 1 before proceeding.*
Note 2: *The fuel tank should be as empty as possible when carrying out this procedure.*

Removal

1 Depressurise the fuel system as described

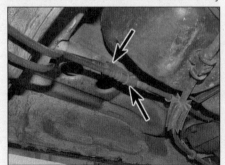

8.5 Disconnect the fuel lines at the underbody quick-release connectors (arrowed)

8.7 Fuel tank securing strap retaining bolt (arrowed)

in Section 5, then disconnect the battery negative terminal (refer to *Disconnecting the battery* in the Reference Chapter).

2 Before removing the fuel tank, all fuel must be drained from the tank. Since a fuel tank drain plug is not provided, it is therefore preferable to carry out the removal operation when the tank is nearly empty. The remaining fuel can then be siphoned or hand-pumped from the tank.

3 Remove the complete exhaust system and relevant heat shield(s) as described in Section 23.

4 Unclip the handbrake cables from the underside of the fuel tank.

5 Disconnect the fuel lines at the underbody quick-release connectors (or on early models at the fuel filter) on the side of the tank **(see illustration)**. Be prepared for some loss of fuel. A Vauxhall/Opel special tool is available to release the fuel line connectors, but provided care is taken, the connectors can be released using a pair of long-nosed pliers, or a similar tool, to depress the retaining tangs. Suitably plug the disconnected fuel and vent hoses to prevent entry of dust and dirt.

6 Support the weight of the fuel tank on a jack with interposed block of wood.

7 Undo the four bolts and remove the two securing straps from the fuel tank **(see illustration)**.

8 Place a suitable container under the tank, then release the retaining clamp and disconnect the fuel filler pipe connection hose from the fuel tank **(see illustration)**. Collect the escaping fuel in the container.

9 Slowly lower the fuel tank, and when sufficient clearance exists, disconnect the wiring for the gauge sender unit and fuel pump at the underbody connector adjacent to the fuel tank. Unclip the wiring harness from the retaining clips.

10 Disconnect the remaining fuel and vent hoses from the tank and underbody connectors.

11 Continue to lower the tank until it can be removed from under the vehicle.

12 If the tank contains sediment or water, it may cleaned out with two or three rinses of clean fuel. Remove the in-tank module as described in Sections 6. Shake the tank vigorously, and change the fuel as necessary to remove all contamination from the tank.

13 Any repairs to the fuel tank should be carried out by a professional. Do not under any circumstances attempt any form of DIY repair to a fuel tank.

Refitting

14 Refitting is the reverse of the removal procedure, noting the following points:

a) *When lifting the tank back into position, take care to ensure that none of the hoses become trapped between the tank and vehicle body. Refit the retaining straps and tighten the bolts securely.*

b) *Ensure all pipes and hoses are correctly routed and all hoses unions are securely joined.*

c) *Refit the exhaust system as described in Section 23.*

d) *On completion, refill the tank with a small amount of fuel, and check for signs of leakage prior to taking the vehicle out on the road.*

9 Throttle housing – removal and refitting

Removal

1 Disconnect the battery negative terminal (refer to *Disconnecting the battery* in the Reference Chapter).

2 Where fitted, remove the plastic cover over the top of the engine.

3 Remove the air cleaner assembly and intake ducts as described in Section 2.

4 Disconnect the wiring connector from the throttle housing **(see illustration)**.

5 Partially drain the cooling system as described in Chapter 1A (drain sufficient coolant to empty the coolant expansion tank).

6 Release the retaining clips and disconnect the two coolant hoses from the rear of the throttle housing.

7 Where applicable, release the retaining clips and disconnect the crankcase ventilation hose and, where fitted, the evaporative emission system hose from the throttle housing.

8.8 Release the retaining clamp (arrowed) and disconnect the fuel filler pipe connection hose

8 Undo the four bolts and lift the throttle housing off the inlet manifold **(see illustration)**. Recover the gasket.

9 It is not possible to obtain the throttle valve control motor or throttle valve position sensor separately, so if either is faulty, the complete throttle housing must be renewed.

Refitting

10 Refitting is a reversal of removal, but thoroughly clean the mating faces and use a new gasket. Tighten the bolts progressively to the specified torque. Top-up the coolant level as described in *Weekly checks*. Finally, switch on the ignition for 30 seconds without starting the engine to allow ECU matching.

10 Fuel injection systems – general information

The fuel injection system is integrated with the emissions control system and ignition system to form a combined engine management system under the control of one electronic control unit (ECU).

All the systems operate in a similar manner and comply with the latest emission control standards. The fuel injection side of the systems operate as follows. Refer to Chapter 4C for information on the emissions control systems, and to Chapter 5B for information on the ignition system.

Fuel is supplied from the rear-mounted tank, via a pressure regulator to the fuel rail. The fuel

9.4 Disconnect the wiring connector from the throttle housing

rail acts as a reservoir for the fuel injectors, which inject fuel into the cylinder inlet tracts, upstream of the inlet valves. The systems are of the 'sequential' injection type, which means that each of the four fuel injectors is triggered individually, just before the inlet valve on the relevant cylinder opens.

The duration of the electrical pulses to the fuel injectors determines the quantity of fuel injected. The pulse duration is computed by the ECU on the basis of information received from the following sensors:

a) *Accelerator pedal position sensor – informs the ECU of accelerator pedal position, and the rate of throttle opening/closing.*

b) *Throttle potentiometer (integral with the throttle housing) – informs the ECU of the throttle position, and confirms the signals received from the accelerator pedal position sensor.*

c) *Coolant temperature sensor – informs the ECU of engine temperature.*

d) *Airflow meter (1.4 and 1.8 litre engines) – informs the ECU of the load on the engine (expressed in terms of the mass of air passing from the air cleaner to the throttle housing).*

e) *Inlet air temperature sensor (1.6 litre engines) – informs the ECU of the temperature of the air passing from the air cleaner to the throttle housing.*

f) *Oxygen sensors (two) – inform the ECU of the oxygen content of the exhaust gases (explained in greater detail in Part C of this Chapter).*

g) *Manifold pressure sensor (1.6 litre engines) – informs the ECU of the engine load by monitoring the pressure in the inlet manifold.*

h) *Crankshaft speed/position sensor – informs the ECU of the crankshaft speed and position.*

i) *Camshaft sensor – inform the ECU of speed and position of the camshaft(s).*

j) *Knock sensor – informs the ECU when pre-ignition ('pinking') is occurring.*

The signals from the various sensors are processed by the ECU, and the optimum fuelling and ignition settings are selected for the prevailing engine operating conditions.

Idle speed and throttle position is controlled by the throttle valve control motor, which is an

9.8 Throttle housing retaining bolts (arrowed)

11.3a Unclip and remove the trim panel beneath the handbrake lever . . .

11.3b . . . for access to the diagnostic socket (arrowed)

integral part of the throttle housing. The motor is controlled by the ECU, in conjunction with signals received from the accelerator pedal position sensor.

A catalytic converter is incorporated in the exhaust manifold, to reduce harmful exhaust gas emissions. Details of this and other emissions control system equipment are given in Chapter 4C.

If certain sensors fail, and send abnormal signals to the ECU, the ECU has a back-up programme. In this event, the abnormal signals are ignored, and a pre-programmed value is substituted for the sensor signal, allowing the engine to continue running, albeit at reduced efficiency. If the ECU enters its back-up mode, a warning light on the instrument panel will illuminate, and a fault code will be stored in the ECU memory. This fault code can be read using suitable specialist test equipment.

11 Fuel injection system components – testing

1 If a fault appears in the engine management system, first ensure that all the system wiring connectors are securely connected and free of corrosion. Ensure that the fault is not due to poor maintenance; ie, check that the air cleaner filter element is clean, the spark plugs are in good condition and correctly gapped, the cylinder compression pressures are correct and that the engine breather hoses are clear and undamaged, referring to Chapters 1A, 2A, 2B and 2C for further information.

2 If these checks fail to reveal the cause of the problem, the vehicle should be taken to a Vauxhall/Opel dealer or suitably-equipped engine management diagnostic specialist for testing.
3 A diagnostic socket is located in the centre console, to which a fault code reader or other suitable test equipment can be connected. Lift out the trim panel beneath the handbrake lever for access (see illustrations). By using the code reader or test equipment, the engine management ECU (and the various other vehicle system ECUs) can be interrogated, and any stored fault codes can be retrieved. This will allow the fault to be quickly and simply traced, alleviating the need to test all the system components individually, which is a time-consuming operation that carries a risk of damaging the ECU.

12 Fuel injection system components (1.4 litre engine) – removal and refitting

Airflow meter

Removal

1 Disconnect the wiring connector from the airflow meter at the right-hand rear corner of the engine compartment (see illustration).
2 Slacken the retaining clamps and remove the airflow meter from the air intake ducts.

Refitting

3 Refitting is a reversal of removal, but ensure that the arrow on the airflow meter body points toward the throttle housing when fitted.

Fuel injectors and fuel rail

Note: Refer to the precautions given in Section 1 before proceeding. The seals at both ends of the fuel injectors must be renewed on refitting.

Removal

4 Disconnect the battery negative terminal (refer to Disconnecting the battery in the Reference Chapter).
5 Depressurise the fuel system as described in Section 5.
6 Remove the throttle housing as described in Section 9, however, it is not necessary to drain the cooling system, as the housing can be placed to one side with the hoses still attached.
7 Loosen the clip and disconnect the engine breather hose from the camshaft cover.
8 Undo the two screws and remove the cover over the fuel rail (where fitted).
9 Disconnect the wiring connector from each fuel injector (see illustration).
10 Disconnect the fuel feed hose quick-release connector at the fuel rail. Be prepared for some loss of fuel. A Vauxhall/Opel special tool is available to release the connector, but provided care is taken, it can be released using a pair of long-nosed pliers, or a similar tool, to depress the retaining tangs. Clamp or plug the open end of the hose, to prevent dirt ingress and further fuel spillage.
11 Unscrew the mounting bolts, then lift the fuel rail complete with the injectors off of the inlet manifold.
12 To remove an injector from the fuel rail, prise out the metal securing clip using a screwdriver or a pair of pliers, and pull the injector from the fuel rail. Remove and discard the injector sealing rings; new ones must be fitted on refitting.
13 Overhaul of the fuel injectors is not possible, as no spares are available. If faulty, an injector must be renewed.

Refitting

14 Before refitting, clean thoroughly the mating surfaces of the throttle housing and inlet manifold.
15 Commence refitting by fitting new O-ring seals to both ends of the fuel injectors (see illustration). Coat the seals with a thin layer of petroleum jelly before fitting.

12.1 Disconnect the wiring connector from the airflow meter

12.9 Fuel injector wiring connectors (arrowed)

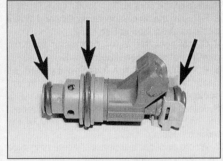

12.15 Fit new O-rings (arrowed) to the fuel injectors before refitting

16 Refitting is a reversal of removal, bearing in mind the following points:

a) *When refitting the injectors to the fuel rail, note that the groove in the metal securing clip must engage with the lug on the injector body.*

b) *Make sure that the quick-release connector audibly engages on the fuel rail.*

c) *Refit the throttle housing as described in Section 9.*

d) *Ensure that all wiring connectors are securely reconnected, and that the wiring is secured in the relevant clips and brackets.*

Crankshaft speed/position sensor

Note: *A new O-ring seal must be used on refitting.*

Removal

17 The crankshaft speed/position sensor is located at the rear left-hand end of the cylinder block baseplate, below the starter motor **(see illustration)**.

18 Apply the handbrake, then jack up the front of the vehicle and support it on axle stands (see *Jacking and vehicle support*).

19 Disconnect the sensor wiring connector, then undo the retaining bolt and withdraw the sensor from the cylinder block baseplate.

Refitting

20 Refitting is a reversal of removal, but ensure that the mating surfaces of the sensor and baseplate are clean and fit a new O-ring seal to the sensor before refitting. Tighten the bolt to the specified torque.

Camshaft sensor

Removal

21 The camshaft position sensor is located on the timing cover, on the inlet camshaft side.

22 Disconnect the sensor wiring connector.

23 Undo the retaining bolt and withdraw the sensor from the timing cover.

Refitting

24 Refitting is a reversal of removal, but ensure that the mating surfaces of the sensor and timing cover are clean before fitting.

Coolant temperature sensor

25 Refer to Chapter 3 for removal and refitting details.

Knock sensor

Removal

26 The knock sensor is located on the rear of the cylinder block, just above the starter motor.

27 Apply the handbrake, then jack up the front of the vehicle and support it on axle stands (see *Jacking and vehicle support*).

28 On the left-hand side of the engine, disconnect the wiring connectors for the

engine ECU by releasing them in the direction of the arrow marked on the connector.

29 Unscrew the bolt securing the earth wire to the cylinder head, then unbolt and remove the ECU.

30 Reach up behind the engine and disconnect the wiring from the knock sensor.

31 Note its position, then unscrew the bolt and remove the knock sensor from the block.

Refitting

32 Clean the contact surfaces of the sensor and block. Also clean the threads of the sensor mounting bolt.

33 Locate the sensor on the block and insert the mounting bolt. Position the sensor as previously-noted, then tighten the bolt to the specified torque. Note that the torque setting is critical for the sensor to function correctly.

34 Reconnect the wiring, then refit the engine ECU together with its wiring and earth wire.

35 Lower the vehicle to the ground and reconnect the battery.

Electronic control unit (ECU)

Note: *If a new ECU is to be fitted, this work must be entrusted to a Vauxhall/Opel dealer or suitably-equipped specialist as it is necessary to programme the new ECU after installation. This work requires the use of dedicated Vauxhall/Opel diagnostic equipment or a compatible alternative.*

Removal

36 The engine management ECU is located on the rear, left-hand side of the engine.

37 Disconnect the battery negative terminal (refer to *Disconnecting the battery* in the Reference Chapter).

38 Lift up the locking bars and disconnect the two wiring connectors at the ECU by releasing them in the direction of the arrow marked on the connector **(see illustration)**.

39 Unscrew the bolt securing the earth wire to the cylinder head, then unbolt and remove the unit.

Refitting

40 Refitting is a reversal of removal.

Oxygen sensors

41 Refer to Chapter 4C for removal and refitting details.

---

13 Fuel injection system components (1.6 litre Z16SE engine) – removal and refitting

---

Inlet air temperature sensor

Removal

1 The inlet air temperature sensor is mounted in the intake duct which connects the air cleaner housing to the throttle housing.

2 Ensure the ignition is switched off, then disconnect the wiring connector from the sensor.

3 Carefully ease the sensor out of position

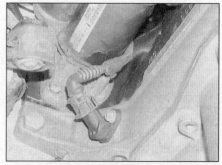

12.17 Crankshaft speed/position sensor location

and remove its sealing grommet from the intake duct. If the sealing grommet shows signs of damage or deterioration it should be renewed.

Refitting

4 Refitting is the reverse of removal, ensuring the sensor and grommet are correctly located in the duct.

Fuel injectors and fuel rail

Note: *Refer to the precautions given in Section 1 before proceeding. The seals at both ends of the fuel injectors must be renewed on refitting.*

Removal

5 Disconnect the battery negative terminal (refer to *Disconnecting the battery* in the Reference Chapter).

6 Remove the air cleaner assembly and intake ducts as described in Section 2.

7 Depressurise the fuel system as described in Section 5.

8 Disconnect the fuel feed hose quick-release connector at the fuel rail. Be prepared for some loss of fuel. A Vauxhall/Opel special tool is available to release the connector, but provided care is taken, it can be released using a pair of long-nosed pliers, or a similar tool, to depress the retaining tangs. Clamp or plug the open end of the hose, to prevent dirt ingress and further fuel spillage.

9 Remove the throttle housing as described in Section 9, however, it is not necessary to drain the cooling system, as the housing can be placed to one side with the hoses still attached.

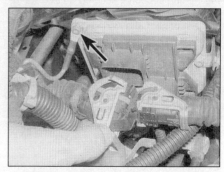

12.38 Disconnect the wiring connectors from the electronic control unit. Note the location of the earth lead (arrowed)

10 Disconnect the wiring connector at the camshaft sensor.

11 Disconnect the wiring connector at each fuel injector, then move the wiring harness to one side.

12 Unscrew the two retaining bolts and remove the fuel rail with the injectors from the inlet manifold.

13 To remove an injector from the fuel rail, prise out the metal securing clip using a screwdriver or a pair of pliers, and pull the injector from the fuel rail. Remove and discard the injector sealing rings; new ones must be fitted on refitting.

14 Overhaul of the fuel injectors is not possible, as no spares are available. If faulty, an injector must be renewed.

Refitting

15 Before refitting, clean thoroughly the mating surfaces of the throttle housing and inlet manifold.

16 Commence refitting by fitting new O-ring seals to both ends of the fuel injectors (**see illustration 12.15**). Coat the seals with a thin layer of petroleum jelly before fitting.

17 Refitting is a reversal of removal, bearing in mind the following points:

a) *When refitting the injectors to the fuel rail, note that the groove in the metal securing clip must engage with the lug on the injector body.*

b) *Make sure that the quick-release connector audibly engages on the fuel rail.*

c) *Refit the throttle housing as described in Section 9.*

d) *Ensure that all wiring connectors are securely reconnected, and that the wiring is secured in the relevant clips and brackets.*

Crankshaft speed/ position sensor

Note: *A new O-ring seal must be used on refitting.*

Removal

18 The sensor is mounted on the front of the cylinder block at the left-hand end and is accessible from underneath the vehicle. Firmly apply the handbrake, then jack up the front of the car and support it securely on axle stands (see *Jacking and vehicle support*).

19 Disconnect the wiring connector, then unscrew the retaining bolt and remove the sensor from underneath the vehicle.

Refitting

20 Refitting is a reversal of removal using a new sealing ring. Tighten the sensor retaining bolt to the specified torque.

Camshaft sensor

Removal

21 Remove the air cleaner assembly and intake ducts as described in Section 2.

22 Disconnect the sensor wiring connector, unscrew the retaining bolt and remove the sensor from the right-hand end of the cylinder head.

Refitting

23 Refitting is a reversal of removal tightening the sensor retaining bolt to the specified torque.

Coolant temperature sensor

24 Refer to Chapter 3 for removal and refitting details.

Manifold pressure sensor

Removal

25 The manifold pressure sensor is located on the left-hand side of the inlet manifold.

26 Disconnect the battery negative terminal (refer to *Disconnecting the battery* in the Reference Chapter).

27 Undo the two bolts securing the air intake resonator to the inlet manifold. Release the throttle housing coolant hose from the retaining clip, then lift the hose from the guides on the resonator.

28 Release the locking catch, then disconnect the upper wiring connector from the engine management ECU.

29 Undo the two upper ECU mounting bolts.

30 Release the pressure sensor wiring harness from the bracket on the ECU, then disconnect the wiring connector from the sensor.

31 Turn the sensor 1/4 turn clockwise and carefully pull it out of the inlet manifold.

Refitting

32 Refitting is a reversal of removal using a new sealing ring.

Knock sensor

Removal

33 The knock sensor is mounted on the rear of the cylinder block and is accessible from underneath the vehicle. Firmly apply the handbrake, then jack up the front of the car and support it securely on axle stands (see *Jacking and vehicle support*).

34 Trace the wiring back from the sensor, noting its correct routing, and disconnect it at the connector.

35 Slacken and remove the retaining bolt and remove the sensor from the engine.

Refitting

36 On refitting ensure the mating surfaces are clean and dry then fit the sensor and tighten its retaining bolt to the specified torque. Ensure the wiring is correctly routed and securely reconnected then lower the vehicle to the ground.

Electronic control unit (ECU)

Note: *If a new ECU is to be fitted, this work must be entrusted to a Vauxhall/Opel dealer or suitably-equipped specialist as it is necessary to programme the new ECU after installation. This work requires the use of dedicated Vauxhall/Opel diagnostic equipment or a compatible alternative.*

Removal

37 The ECU is located on the left-hand end of the inlet manifold.

38 Disconnect the battery negative terminal (refer to *Disconnecting the battery* in the Reference Chapter).

39 Release the locking catches, then disconnect the wiring connectors from the ECU.

40 Release the manifold pressure sensor wiring harness from the bracket on the ECU.

Refitting

41 Refitting is the reverse of removal, ensuring the wiring connectors are securely reconnected.

Oxygen sensors

42 Refer to Chapter 4C for removal and refitting details.

---

14 Fuel injection system components (1.6 litre Z16XE engine) – removal and refitting

---

Inlet air temperature sensor

Removal

1 The inlet air temperature sensor is mounted in the intake duct which connects the air cleaner housing to the inlet manifold.

2 Ensure the ignition is switched off, then disconnect the wiring connector from the sensor.

3 Carefully ease the sensor out of position and remove its sealing grommet from the intake duct. If the sealing grommet shows signs of damage or deterioration it should be renewed.

Refitting

4 Refitting is a reversal of removal, ensuring the sensor and grommet are correctly located in the duct.

Fuel injectors and fuel rail

Note: *Refer to the precautions given in Section 1 before proceeding. The seals at both ends of the fuel injectors must be renewed on refitting.*

Removal

5 Disconnect the battery negative terminal (refer to *Disconnecting the battery* in the Reference Chapter).

6 Remove the oil filler cap, undo the retaining screws, and remove the engine cover.

7 Remove the air cleaner assembly and intake ducts as described in Section 2.

8 Depressurise the fuel system as described in Section 5.

9 Disconnect the engine breather hose from the camshaft cover and unclip the throttle housing coolant hose.

10 Firmly apply the handbrake, then jack up the front of the vehicle and support it securely on axle stands (see *Jacking and vehicle support*).

11 From under the car, disconnect the wiring connectors at the oil pressure switch and oxygen sensor, then release the wiring harness from the cable clips and ties.

12 Lower the car to the ground then, working in the engine compartment, unscrew the union nut and disconnect the fuel supply hose from the fuel rail.

13 Detach all of the wiring connectors which are associated with the wiring harness plastic tray which runs above the fuel rail. Note the cable routing. The items to disconnect are:

  a) *Throttle housing.*
  b) *Camshaft sensor.*
  c) *Manifold pressure sensor.*
  d) *EGR valve.*
  e) *Knock sensor.*

14 Release the wiring harness from the clips and cable-ties.

15 Undo the two bolts and detach the camshaft sensor wiring harness bracket.

16 Unscrew the two retaining bolts and remove the fuel rail with the injectors, complete with the plastic wiring tray **(see illustration)**.

17 To remove an injector from the fuel rail, prise out the metal securing clip using a screwdriver or a pair of pliers, and pull the injector from the fuel rail. Remove and discard the injector sealing rings; new ones must be fitted on refitting.

18 Overhaul of the fuel injectors is not possible, as no spares are available. If faulty, an injector must be renewed.

19 Commence refitting by fitting new O-ring seals to both ends of the fuel injectors **(see illustration 12.15)**. Coat the seals with a thin layer of petroleum jelly before fitting.

Refitting

20 Refitting is a reversal of removal, noting the following points.

  a) *When refitting the injectors to the fuel rail, note that the groove in the metal securing clip must engage with the lug on the injector body.*
  b) *Ensure that all wiring connectors are securely reconnected, and that the wiring is secured in the relevant clips and brackets.*

Crankshaft speed/ position sensor

Note: *A new O-ring seal must be used on refitting.*

Removal

21 The sensor is mounted on the front of the cylinder block below the oil filter.

22 Trace the wiring back from the sensor, releasing it from all the relevant clips and ties whilst noting its correct routing. Disconnect the wiring connector so the wiring is free to be removed with the sensor.

23 Unscrew the retaining bolt and remove the sensor from underneath the vehicle.

Refitting

24 Refitting is a reversal of removal using a new sealing ring. Tighten the sensor retaining bolt to the specified torque.

Camshaft sensor

Removal

25 Remove the timing belt upper cover as described in Chapter 2C.

26 Trace the wiring back from the sensor, releasing it from all the relevant clips and ties whilst noting its correct routing. Disconnect the wiring connector so the wiring is free to be removed with the sensor.

27 Unscrew the retaining bolts and remove the sensor from the end of the cylinder head **(see illustration)**.

Refitting

28 Refitting is a reversal of removal, apply a little locking compound, and tighten the retaining bolts to the specified torque. Ensure the wiring is correctly routed and retained by all the necessary clips and ties.

Coolant temperature sensor

29 Refer to Chapter 3 for removal and refitting details.

Manifold pressure sensor

Removal

30 The manifold pressure sensor is located on the left-hand side of the inlet manifold.

31 Undo the two retaining screws and the oil filler cap, and remove the engine cover. Ensure the ignition is switched off then disconnect the wiring connector from the sensor. The sensor can then be unbolted and removed from the manifold.

Refitting

32 Refitting is a reversal of removal.

Knock sensor

Removal

33 The knock sensor is mounted onto the rear of the cylinder block, just to the right of the starter motor.

34 Undo the two retaining screws and the oil filler cap, and remove the engine cover.

35 Remove the air intake duct between the throttle housing and air cleaner, with reference to Section 2.

36 Trace the wiring back from the sensor, noting its correct routing, and disconnect it at the connector.

37 Firmly apply the handbrake, then jack up the front of the vehicle and support it securely on axle stands (see *Jacking and vehicle support*).

38 From under the car, undo the two bolts and remove the inlet manifold support bracket.

39 Slacken and remove the retaining bolt and remove the sensor from the engine.

Refitting

40 Refitting is a reversal of removal. Ensure the mating surfaces are clean and dry and tighten the sensor retaining bolt to the specified torque. Ensure the wiring is correctly routed and securely reconnected.

Electronic control unit (ECU)

Note: *If a new ECU is to be fitted, this work*

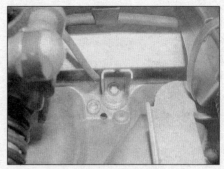

14.16 Fuel rail retaining bolt

must be entrusted to a Vauxhall/Opel dealer or suitably-equipped specialist as it is necessary to programme the new ECU after installation. This work requires the use of dedicated Vauxhall/Opel diagnostic equipment or a compatible alternative.

Removal

41 Disconnect the battery negative terminal (refer to *Disconnecting the battery* in the Reference Chapter).

42 Undo the two retaining screws and the oil filler cap, and remove the engine cover.

43 Release the retaining clips then disconnect the wiring connectors from the ECU. Undo the three retaining bolts and remove the ECU from the vehicle.

Refitting

44 Refitting is a reversal of removal, ensuring the wiring connectors are securely reconnected.

Oxygen sensors

45 Refer to Chapter 4C for removal and refitting details.

---

15 Fuel injection system components (1.6 litre Z16XEP engine) – removal and refitting

---

Inlet air temperature sensor

Removal

1 The inlet air temperature sensor is mounted in the intake duct which connects the air cleaner housing to the inlet manifold.

14.27 Undo the two retaining bolts and remove the sensor from the cylinder head

15.2 Disconnect the wiring connector from the inlet air temperature sensor

2 Ensure the ignition is switched off, then disconnect the wiring connector from the sensor (see illustration).

3 Carefully ease the sensor out of position and remove its sealing grommet from the intake duct. If the sealing grommet shows signs of damage or deterioration it should be renewed.

Refitting

4 Refitting is a reversal of removal, ensuring the sensor and grommet are correctly located in the duct.

Fuel injectors and fuel rail

Note: *Refer to the precautions given in Section 1 before proceeding. The seals at both ends of the fuel injectors must be renewed on refitting.*

Removal

5 Disconnect the battery negative terminal (refer to *Disconnecting the battery* in the Reference Chapter).

6 Remove the air cleaner assembly and air intake duct as described in Section 2.

7 Depressurise the fuel system as described in Section 5.

8 Disconnect the fuel feed hose quick-release connector at the fuel rail (see illustration). Be prepared for some loss of fuel. A Vauxhall/Opel special tool is available to release the connector, but provided care is taken, it can be released using a pair of long-nosed pliers, or a similar tool, to depress the retaining tangs. Clamp or plug the open end of the hose, to prevent dirt ingress and further fuel spillage.

9 Remove the engine management ECU as described later in this Section.

15.11 Disconnect the wiring connector from the manifold pressure sensor

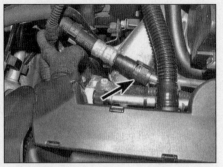

15.8 Disconnect the fuel feed hose quick-release connector (arrowed) at the fuel rail

10 Disconnect the wiring connector from the throttle housing.

11 Disconnect the wiring connector from the manifold pressure sensor on the side of the inlet manifold (see illustration).

12 Release the two clips and move the wiring harness clear of the fuel rail.

13 Disconnect the wiring connector from each fuel injector.

14 Unscrew the two mounting bolts, then lift the fuel rail complete with the injectors off of the inlet manifold.

15 To remove an injector from the fuel rail, prise out the metal securing clip using a screwdriver or a pair of pliers, and pull the injector from the fuel rail. Remove and discard the injector sealing rings; new ones must be fitted on refitting.

16 Overhaul of the fuel injectors is not possible, as no spares are available. If faulty, an injector must be renewed.

Refitting

17 Before refitting, clean thoroughly the mating surfaces of the throttle housing and inlet manifold.

18 Commence refitting by fitting new O-ring seals to both ends of the fuel injectors. Coat the seals with a thin layer of petroleum jelly before fitting.

19 Refitting is a reversal of removal, bearing in mind the following points:

a) *When refitting the injectors to the fuel rail, note that the groove in the metal securing clip must engage with the lug on the injector body.*

b) *Make sure that the quick-release connector audibly engages on the fuel rail.*

c) *Ensure that all wiring connectors are securely reconnected, and that the wiring is secured in the relevant clips and brackets.*

Crankshaft speed/position sensor

Note: *A new O-ring seal must be used on refitting.*

Removal

20 The crankshaft sensor is mounted on the front of the cylinder block below the oil filter.

21 Firmly apply the handbrake, then jack up the front of the car and support it securely on

axle stands (see *Jacking and vehicle support*).

22 Disconnect the wiring connector, then unscrew the retaining bolt and remove the sensor from the front of the cylinder block. Discard the sealing ring, a new one should be used on refitting.

Refitting

23 Refitting is a reversal of removal using a new sealing ring and tightening the sensor bolt to the specified torque.

Camshaft sensor

Removal

24 The camshaft position sensor is located behind the timing belt rear cover, on the exhaust camshaft side.

25 Remove the air cleaner assembly and intake duct as described in Section 2.

26 Undo the two retaining bolts then unclip and remove the timing belt upper cover from the rear cover.

27 Disconnect the camshaft sensor wiring connector.

28 Using a spanner or socket on the crankshaft pulley retaining bolt, turn the crankshaft until the camshaft sensor retaining bolt is accessible through the spokes in the exhaust camshaft sprocket.

29 Undo the sensor retaining bolt, then turn the sensor and remove it from the rear of the timing belt cover.

Refitting

30 Refitting is a reversal of removal, tightening the sensor retaining bolt to the specified torque.

Coolant temperature sensor

31 Refer to Chapter 3 for removal and refitting details.

Manifold pressure sensor

Removal

32 Remove the engine management ECU as described later in this Section.

33 Disconnect the pressure sensor wiring connector (see illustration 15.11).

34 Undo the sensor retaining bolt, then remove the sensor from the inlet manifold.

Refitting

35 Refitting is a reversal of removal, tightening the sensor retaining bolt to the specified torque.

Knock sensor

Removal

36 The knock sensor is located on the rear of the cylinder block, just above the starter motor.

37 Apply the handbrake, then jack up the front of the vehicle and support it on axle stands (see *Jacking and vehicle support*).

38 Release the vacuum hose from the inlet manifold support bracket, then undo the two bolts and remove the support from the cylinder block and manifold.

39 Disconnect the wiring connector from the knock sensor.
40 Note its position, then unscrew the bolt and remove the knock sensor from the block.

Refitting

41 Clean the contact surfaces of the sensor and block. Also clean the threads of the sensor mounting bolt.
42 Locate the sensor on the block and insert the mounting bolt. Position the sensor as previously-noted, then tighten the bolt to the specified torque.
43 Refit the inlet manifold support bracket and attach the vacuum hose, then lower the vehicle to the ground.

Electronic control unit (ECU)

Note: *If a new ECU is to be fitted, this work must be entrusted to a Vauxhall/Opel dealer or suitably-equipped specialist as it is necessary to programme the new ECU after installation. This work requires the use of dedicated Vauxhall/Opel diagnostic equipment or a compatible alternative.*

Removal

44 The engine management ECU is located on the left-hand side of the inlet manifold.
45 Disconnect the battery negative terminal (refer to *Disconnecting the battery* in the Reference Chapter).
46 Lift up the locking bars and disconnect the two wiring connectors from the ECU **(see illustration)**.
47 Undo the bolt securing the earth lead to the top of the ECU, then undo the three retaining bolts and remove the ECU from the inlet manifold **(see illustration)**.

Refitting

48 Refitting is a reversal of removal.

Oxygen sensors

49 Refer to Chapter 4C for removal and refitting details.

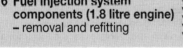

16 Fuel injection system components (1.8 litre engine) – removal and refitting

Airflow meter

Removal

1 Disconnect the wiring from the airflow meter at the right-hand rear corner of the engine compartment **(see illustration 12.1)**.
2 Slacken the retaining clamps and remove the airflow meter from the air intake ducts.

Refitting

3 Refitting is a reversal of removal, but ensure that the arrow on the airflow meter body points toward the throttle housing when fitted.

Fuel injectors and fuel rail

Note: *Refer to the precautions given in Section 1 before proceeding. The seals at both ends of the fuel injectors must be renewed on refitting.*

15.46 Disconnect the two wiring connectors from the ECU

Removal

4 Disconnect the battery negative terminal (refer to *Disconnecting the battery* in the Reference Chapter).
5 Remove the plastic cover over the top of the engine.
6 Depressurise the fuel system as described in Section 5.
7 Remove the air cleaner assembly and intake duct as described in Section 2.
8 Firmly apply the handbrake, then jack up the front of the car and support it securely on axle stands (see *Jacking and vehicle support*).
9 From under the rear of the engine, disconnect the wiring connectors for the oxygen sensor and oil pressure switch. Release the wiring harness from its clips.
10 From under the front of the engine disconnect the wiring connectors at the oil level sensor and crankshaft sensor. Release the wiring harness from its clips.
11 Working from above, disconnect the camshaft sensor wiring connector, then undo the nut and disconnect the earth lead from the alternator.
12 Release the clip and disconnect the remaining crankcase ventilation hose from the camshaft cover.
13 Undo the union nut securing the fuel feed hose to the pipe on the fuel rail. Be prepared for some loss of fuel. Suitably cover or plug the open unions, to prevent dirt ingress and further fuel spillage.
14 Disconnect the wiring connectors from the following components, labelling each connector to avoid confusion when refitting:
  a) Fuel injectors.
  b) Coolant temperature sensor.
  c) Throttle housing.
  d) Engine management ECU.
  e) Knock sensor.
15 Detach the knock sensor wiring harness plug bracket and the earth lead.
16 Release the wiring harness cable clips and ties.
17 Unscrew the two mounting bolts, then lift the fuel rail complete with the injectors off of the inlet manifold.
18 To remove an injector from the fuel rail, prise out the metal securing clip using a screwdriver or a pair of pliers, and pull the injector from the fuel rail. Remove and discard

15.47 Undo the three retaining bolts and remove the ECU from the inlet manifold

the injector sealing rings; new ones must be fitted on refitting.
19 Overhaul of the fuel injectors is not possible, as no spares are available. If faulty, an injector must be renewed.

Refitting

20 Commence refitting by fitting new O-ring seals to both ends of the fuel injectors. Coat the seals with a thin layer of petroleum jelly before fitting.
21 Refitting is a reversal of removal, bearing in mind the following points:
  a) *When refitting the injectors to the fuel rail, note that the groove in the metal securing clip must engage with the lug on the injector body.*
  b) *Make sure that the quick-release connector audibly engages on the fuel rail.*
  c) *Ensure that all wiring connectors are securely reconnected, and that the wiring is secured in the relevant clips and brackets.*

Crankshaft speed/ position sensor

Note: *A new O-ring seal must be used on refitting.*

Removal

22 The crankshaft sensor is mounted on the front of the cylinder block below the oil filter.
23 Firmly apply the handbrake, then jack up the front of the car and support it securely on axle stands (see *Jacking and vehicle support*).
24 Disconnect the wiring connector, then unscrew the retaining bolt and remove the sensor from the front of the cylinder block. Discard the sealing ring, a new one should be used on refitting.

Refitting

25 Refitting is a reversal of removal using a new sealing ring and tightening the sensor bolt to the specified torque.

Camshaft sensor

Removal

26 Remove the plastic cover over the top of the engine.
27 Remove the air cleaner assembly and intake duct as described in Section 2.

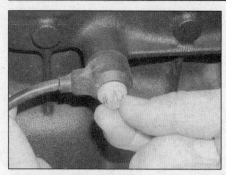

16.36 Undo the retaining bolt and release the knock sensor from the cylinder block

28 Undo the three retaining screws, then unclip the timing belt upper cover from the rear cover and remove it from the engine compartment.

29 Disconnect the camshaft sensor wiring connector, then unclip the wiring harness.

30 Undo the two retaining bolts and remove the sensor from the cylinder head **(see illustration 14.27)**.

Refitting

31 Refitting is the reverse of removal, tightening the sensor retaining bolts to the specified torque.

Coolant temperature sensor

32 Refer to Chapter 3 for removal and refitting details.

Knock sensor

Removal

33 The knock sensor is located on the rear of the cylinder block, just above the starter motor.

34 Apply the handbrake, then jack up the front of the vehicle and support it on axle stands (see *Jacking and vehicle support*).

35 Undo the two bolts and remove the inlet manifold support bracket from the cylinder block and manifold.

36 Undo the retaining bolt securing the knock sensor to the cylinder block and release the sensor from its location **(see illustration)**.

37 Trace the wiring back to the knock sensor wiring connector. Disconnect the connector, release the wiring harness and remove the sensor.

17.14 Fit new individual rubber seals to the grooves in the inlet manifold

Refitting

38 On refitting, ensure the mating surfaces are clean and dry then fit the sensor and tighten its retaining bolt to the specified torque. Note that the torque setting is critical for the sensor to function correctly. Ensure the wiring is correctly routed and securely reconnected.

Electronic control unit (ECU)

Note: *If a new ECU is to be fitted, this work must be entrusted to a Vauxhall/Opel dealer or suitably-equipped specialist as it is necessary to programme the new ECU after installation. This work requires the use of dedicated Vauxhall/Opel diagnostic equipment or a compatible alternative.*

Removal

39 The ECU is located on the left-hand side of the inlet manifold.

40 Disconnect the battery negative terminal (refer to *Disconnecting the battery* in the Reference Chapter).

41 Remove the plastic cover over the top of the engine.

42 Lift up the locking bars and disconnect the two ECU wiring connectors.

43 Disconnect the knock sensor wiring connector and unclip the connector from the support bracket.

44 Undo the retaining bolt and detach the earth lead and knock sensor wiring support bracket from the ECU.

45 Undo the three retaining bolts and remove the ECU from the engine.

Refitting

46 Refitting is a reversal of removal.

Oxygen sensors

47 Refer to Chapter 4C for removal and refitting details.

17 Inlet manifold (1.4 litre engines) – removal and refitting

Removal

1 Apply the handbrake, then jack up the front of the vehicle and support it on axle stands (see *Jacking and vehicle support*).

2 Disconnect the battery negative terminal (refer to *Disconnecting the battery* in the Reference Chapter).

3 Drain the cooling system as described in Chapter 1A.

4 Remove the throttle housing as described in Section 9.

5 Disconnect the evaporative emission control system hose from the inlet manifold.

6 Depressurise the fuel system as described in Section 5.

7 Disconnect the fuel supply line from the fuel rail and release it from the support clip. A quick-release connector is fitted and Vauxhall/Opel technicians use a special tool to release it, however, provided care is taken,

the connector can be released using a pair of long-nosed pliers, or a similar tool, to depress the retaining tangs.

8 Disconnect the crankcase ventilation hose from the camshaft cover, and the brake servo vacuum line from the inlet manifold.

9 Undo the two screws and remove the cover over the fuel rail.

10 Disconnect the wiring from the injectors and engine ECU, also unbolt the earth cable and unclip the wiring conduit. Place the wiring harness to one side.

11 Unbolt the EGR valve pipe from the EGR valve housing and position to one side. Discard the gasket; a new one must be used for refitting.

12 Disconnect the wiring connector from the evaporative emission control system purge valve.

13 Unscrew the six bolts and withdraw the inlet manifold from the cylinder head. Discard the seals; new ones must be used for refitting.

Refitting

14 Thoroughly clean the mating face of the inlet manifold and cylinder head, then locate the new rubber seals in the grooves in the manifold mating face **(see illustration)**.

15 Locate the inlet manifold on the cylinder head, refit the bolts and tighten progressively to the specified torque.

16 Refit the EGR valve pipe together with a new gasket, and tighten the bolts securely.

17 Reconnect the wiring connector to the evaporative emission control system purge valve.

18 Reconnect the wiring to the injectors and engine ECU, and tighten the earth cable bolt.

19 Reconnect the brake servo vacuum line and crankcase ventilation hose.

20 Reconnect the fuel supply line to the fuel rail, making sure that an audible click is heard as it engages.

21 Reconnect the fuel evaporation system hose to the inlet manifold.

22 Refit the throttle housing with reference to Section 9.

23 Refit the cover over the fuel rail.

24 Lower the vehicle to the ground and reconnect the battery negative terminal.

25 Refill the cooling system with reference to Chapter 1A.

18 Inlet manifold (1.6 litre Z16SE engines) – removal and refitting

Note: *New manifold retaining nuts will be required on refitting.*

Removal

1 Apply the handbrake, then jack up the front of the vehicle and support it on axle stands (see *Jacking and vehicle support*).

2 Disconnect the battery negative terminal (refer to *Disconnecting the battery* in the Reference Chapter).

3 Drain the cooling system as described in Chapter 1A.

4 Remove the throttle housing as described in Section 9.

5 Remove the alternator as described in Chapter 5A.

6 Depressurise the fuel system as described in Section 5.

7 Disconnect the fuel feed hose quick-release connector at the fuel rail. Be prepared for some loss of fuel. A Vauxhall/Opel special tool is available to release the connector, but provided care is taken, it can be released using a pair of long-nosed pliers, or a similar tool, to depress the retaining tangs. Clamp or plug the open end of the hose, to prevent dirt ingress and further fuel spillage.

8 Release the retaining spring clips, and disconnect both coolant hoses from the heater matrix pipe unions on the engine compartment bulkhead.

9 Release the retaining clip and disconnect the coolant hose from the inlet manifold.

10 From under the rear of the engine, disconnect the wiring connectors for the oxygen sensor and oil pressure switch. Release the wiring harness from its clips.

11 Undo and remove the two lower nuts securing the inlet manifold to the cylinder head.

12 Remove the engine management ECU as described in Section 13.

13 Disconnect the wiring connectors from the following components, labelling each connector to avoid confusion when refitting:
  a) Manifold pressure sensor.
  b) EGR valve.
  c) Knock sensor.
  d) Camshaft sensor.
  e) Fuel injectors.

14 Depress the retaining clip and disconnect the braking system servo unit hose from the manifold.

15 Undo the retaining bolt and detach the engine wiring harness support bracket. Move the wiring harness to one side.

16 Remove the EGR valve as described in Chapter 4C.

17 Unscrew the remaining seven nuts securing the inlet manifold to the cylinder head.

18 Attach a suitable hoist and lifting tackle to the engine lifting brackets on the cylinder head, and support the weight of the engine/transmission.

19 Remove the engine/transmission front mounting/torque link, rear mounting/torque link and right-hand mounting, as described in Chapter 2B.

20 Carefully lower the engine at the timing belt end approximately 30 mm, taking care not to damage any components or attachments.

21 When sufficient clearance exists, remove the inlet manifold and recover the gasket.

Refitting

22 Refitting is a reversal of removal bearing in mind the following points.

a) Prior to refitting, check the manifold studs and renew any that are worn or damaged. New manifold retaining nuts must be used.
b) Ensure the manifold and cylinder mating surfaces are clean and dry and fit the new gasket. Refit the manifold and tighten the retaining nuts evenly and progressively to the specified torque.
c) Ensure that all relevant hoses are reconnected to their original positions, and are securely held (where necessary) by their retaining clips.
d) Refit the engine mountings as described in Chapter 2B.
e) Refit the EGR valve as described in Chapter 4C.
f) Refit the engine management ECU as described in Section 13.
g) Refit the alternator as described in Chapter 5A.
h) Refit the throttle housing as described in Section 9.
i) Refit the auxiliary drivebelt and refill the cooling system as described in Chapter 1A.

19 Inlet manifold (1.6 litre Z16XE engines) – removal and refitting

Note: If only the upper section of the manifold is to be removed carry out the operations described in paragraphs 1 to 13.

Removal

1 Apply the handbrake, then jack up the front of the vehicle and support it on axle stands (see *Jacking and vehicle support*).

2 Disconnect the battery negative terminal (refer to *Disconnecting the battery* in the Reference Chapter).

3 Drain the cooling system as described in Chapter 1A.

4 Remove the oil filler cap then undo the retaining screws and lift off the cover from the top of the engine. Refit the oil filler cap.

5 Remove the air cleaner assembly and intake ducting as described in Section 2.

6 Depressurise the fuel system as described in Section 5.

7 Remove the throttle housing as described in Section 9.

8 Remove the alternator as described in Chapter 5A.

9 Disconnect the wiring connectors from the following components, labelling each connector to avoid confusion when refitting:
  a) Oxygen sensor.
  b) Oil pressure switch.
  c) Crankshaft sensor.
  d) Oil level sensor.

10 Remove the support bracket between the inlet manifold and the cylinder block **(see illustration)**.

11 Remove the fuel injectors and fuel rail assembly, as described in Section 14.

19.10 Remove the support bracket between the inlet manifold and the cylinder block

12 Release the retaining clip and disconnect the braking system vacuum servo hose from the manifold.

13 Undo the five manifold-to-flange retaining bolts and remove the manifold **(see illustration)**. No further dismantling of the manifold is recommended.

14 To remove the manifold flange, first undo the retaining bolt and detach the coolant pipe.

15 Slacken and remove the nine retaining nuts then manoeuvre the manifold flange away from the cylinder head and out of the engine compartment. It will be necessary to gently push the coolant pipe at the rear of the cylinder head downwards a little, to allow the manifold flange to clear the mounting studs.

Refitting

16 Refitting is a reversal of removal bearing in mind the following points.

a) Prior to refitting, check the manifold studs and renew any that are worn or damaged.
b) Ensure the manifold flange and cylinder mating surfaces are clean and dry and fit the new gasket. Fit the manifold flange and tighten the retaining nuts and bolts evenly and progressively to the specified torque.
c) Fit the rear section of the manifold using a new gasket and tighten its retaining bolts to the specified torque.
d) Refit the fuel injectors and fuel rail as described in Section 14.
e) Refit the alternator as described in Chapter 5A.

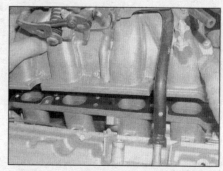

19.13 Undo the five manifold-to-flange retaining bolts and remove the manifold

f) Refit the throttle housing as described in Section 9.

g) Ensure that all relevant hoses are reconnected to their original positions, and are securely held (where necessary) by their retaining clips.

h) Refill the cooling system as described in Chapter 1A.

20 Inlet manifold (1.6 litre Z16XEP engines) – removal and refitting

Removal

1 Apply the handbrake, then jack up the front of the vehicle and support it on axle stands (see Jacking and vehicle support).

2 Disconnect the battery negative terminal (refer to Disconnecting the battery in the Reference Chapter).

3 Drain the cooling system as described in Chapter 1A.

4 Release the vacuum hose from the inlet manifold support bracket, then undo the two bolts and remove the support from the cylinder block and manifold.

5 Disconnect the wiring connector from the evaporative emission control system purge valve. Release the quick-release connector and disconnect the hose from the valve.

6 Remove the air cleaner assembly and air intake duct as described in Section 2.

7 Depressurise the fuel system as described in Section 5.

8 Disconnect the fuel supply line from the fuel rail and release it from the support clip. A quick-release connector is fitted and Vauxhall/Opel technicians use a special tool to release it, however, provided care is taken, the connector can be released using a pair of long-nosed pliers, or a similar tool, to depress the retaining tangs.

9 Release the clips and disconnect the coolant hose from the throttle housing and thermostat housing.

10 Remove the engine management ECU from the inlet manifold as described in Section 15.

11 Disconnect the wiring connectors from the inlet manifold pressure sensor and throttle housing.

12 Disconnect the brake servo vacuum hose from the inlet manifold.

13 Unclip the wiring harness trough from the rear of the camshaft cover. Release the harness from the two support clips and move the harness to one side.

14 Pull out the retaining wire clip and disconnect the breather hose from the camshaft cover.

15 Unscrew the five bolts and withdraw the inlet manifold from the cylinder head. Discard the seals; new ones must be used for refitting.

Refitting

16 Thoroughly clean the mating face of the inlet manifold and cylinder head, then locate the new rubber seals in the grooves in the manifold mating face.

17 Locate the inlet manifold in position on the cylinder head and secure with the bolts tightened progressively and securely.

18 Reconnect the breather hose to the camshaft cover, then clip the wiring harness trough back in position. Secure the harness with the support clips.

19 Reconnect the brake servo vacuum hose to the inlet manifold.

20 Reconnect the wiring connectors to the inlet manifold pressure sensor and throttle housing.

21 Refit the engine management ECU as described in Section 15.

22 Reconnect the coolant hose to the throttle housing and thermostat housing.

23 Reconnect the fuel supply line to the fuel rail, making sure that an audible click is heard as it engages.

24 Refit the air cleaner assembly and air intake duct as described in Section 2.

25 Reconnect the wiring connector and vapour hose to the emission control system purge valve.

26 Refit the inlet manifold support bracket and attach the vacuum hose.

27 Lower the vehicle to the ground and reconnect the battery negative terminal.

28 Refill the cooling system with reference to Chapter 1A.

21 Inlet manifold (1.8 litre engines) – removal and refitting

Removal

1 Disconnect the battery negative terminal (refer to Disconnecting the battery in the Reference Chapter).

2 Remove the windscreen cowl panel and bulkhead closure panel as described in Chapter 11.

3 Remove the plastic cover over the top of the engine.

4 Drain the cooling system as described in Chapter 1A.

5 Remove the air cleaner assembly and air intake duct as described in Section 2.

6 Depressurise the fuel system as described in Section 5.

7 Remove the auxiliary drivebelt as described in Chapter 1A.

8 Remove the alternator as described in Chapter 5A.

9 Undo the two bolts and remove the inlet manifold support bracket.

10 Disconnect the engine breather hose from the camshaft cover.

11 Release the quick-release connector and disconnect the evaporative emission control system hose from the throttle housing.

12 Release the retaining clips and disconnect the two coolant hoses from the throttle housing. Undo the two bolts securing the throttle housing coolant pipe to the inlet manifold and camshaft cover.

13 Disconnect the brake servo vacuum hose from the inlet manifold.

14 Disconnect the wiring connectors from the following components, labelling each connector to avoid confusion when refitting:

a) Throttle housing.

b) Evaporative emission control system purge valve.

c) Camshaft sensor.

d) Manifold switchover flap solenoid valve.

e) Oxygen sensor.

f) Coolant temperature sensor.

g) Knock sensor.

15 Lift up the locking bars and disconnect the two ECU wiring connectors.

16 Disconnect the knock sensor wiring connector and unclip the connector from the support bracket.

17 Undo the retaining bolt and detach the earth lead and knock sensor wiring support bracket from the ECU.

18 Undo the retaining bolts and remove the left-hand and right-hand engine lifting brackets from the cylinder head.

19 Disconnect the wiring connectors from the four fuel injectors, then move the wiring harness trough to one side.

20 Undo the union nut securing the fuel feed hose to the pipe on the fuel rail. Be prepared for some loss of fuel. Suitably cover or plug the open unions, to prevent dirt ingress and further fuel spillage.

21 Release the retaining spring clip and disconnect the upper coolant hose from the heater matrix union on the engine compartment bulkhead.

22 Slacken and remove the seven retaining nuts, and manoeuvre the manifold assembly away from the cylinder head. Remove the gasket and discard it. Note: The manifold assembly must be treated as a sealed unit; do not attempt to dismantle it as no components, other than the switchover diaphragm and solenoid, are available separately.

Refitting

23 Refitting is the reverse of removal noting the following.

a) Prior to refitting, check the manifold studs and renew any that are worn or damaged.

b) Ensure the manifold and cylinder head mating surfaces are clean and dry and fit the new gasket. Refit the manifold and tighten the retaining nuts evenly and progressively to the specified torque.

c) Ensure that all relevant hoses are reconnected to their original positions, and are securely held (where necessary) by their retaining clips.

d) Refit the windscreen cowl panel and bulkhead closure panel as described in Chapter 11.

e) On completion, refill the cooling system as described in Chapter 1A.

22 Exhaust manifold – removal and refitting

1.4 litre and 1.6 litre Z16XEP engines

Note: *New manifold and exhaust front pipe retaining nuts, a new manifold gasket, exhaust front pipe gasket and oil dipstick guide tube O-rings must be used on refitting.*

Removal

1 Apply the handbrake, then jack up the front of the vehicle and support it on axle stands (see *Jacking and vehicle support*).
2 Disconnect the battery negative lead (refer to *Disconnecting the battery* in the Reference Chapter).
3 Disconnect the wiring from the oxygen sensor, then unbolt the exhaust front pipe from the exhaust manifold, taking care to support the flexible section. **Note:** *Angular movement in excess of 10° can cause permanent damage to the flexible section.* Recover the gasket.
4 Release the mounting rubbers and support the front of the exhaust pipe to one side.
5 Undo the two lower exhaust manifold support bolts.
6 Remove the oxygen sensor from the exhaust manifold as described in Chapter 4C.
7 Unbolt the engine lifting brackets from the cylinder head.
8 Unbolt and remove the oil dipstick guide tube, and withdraw it from the baseplate. Remove and discard the O-ring seals.
9 Where applicable, undo the two bolts and remove the heat shield from the exhaust manifold.
10 Undo the retaining nuts, withdraw the exhaust manifold from the cylinder head studs and remove it from under the car. Recover the gasket.

Refitting

11 Thoroughly clean the mating face of the exhaust manifold and cylinder head, then locate a new gasket over the studs.
12 Locate the exhaust manifold over the cylinder head studs and secure with the (new) nuts tightened progressively to the specified torque.
13 Where applicable, refit the heat shield to the manifold and tighten the retaining bolts securely.
14 Refit the engine lifting brackets and securely tighten the bolts.
15 Fit the new O-ring seals to the oil dipstick guide tube, then insert the tube in the baseplate. Insert and tighten the retaining bolt.
16 Refer to Chapter 4C and refit the oxygen sensor to the manifold.
17 Refit and tighten the two lower exhaust manifold support bolts.
18 Refit the exhaust front pipe to the manifold together with a new gasket, then tighten the (new) nuts to the specified torque. Reconnect the oxygen sensor wiring connector.

19 Lower the vehicle to the ground, then reconnect the battery negative lead.

1.6 litre Z16SE engines

Note: *New manifold and exhaust front pipe retaining nuts, a new manifold gasket and exhaust front pipe gasket must be used on refitting.*

Removal

20 Apply the handbrake, then jack up the front of the vehicle and support it on axle stands (see *Jacking and vehicle support*).
21 Disconnect the battery negative lead (refer to *Disconnecting the battery* in the Reference Chapter).
22 Remove the complete exhaust system as described in Section 23.
23 Remove the oxygen sensor from the exhaust manifold as described in Chapter 4C.
24 Undo the five bolts and remove the exhaust manifold heat shield and the engine lifting bracket.
25 Disconnect the oil level sensor wiring connector.
26 Undo the eight retaining nuts and withdraw the exhaust manifold from the cylinder head studs and remove it from under the car. Recover the gasket.

Refitting

27 Thoroughly clean the mating face of the exhaust manifold and cylinder head, then locate a new gasket over the studs.
28 Locate the exhaust manifold over the cylinder head studs and secure with the (new) nuts tightened progressively to the specified torque.
29 Reconnect the oil level sensor wiring connector.
30 Refit the exhaust manifold heat shield and engine lifting bracket.
31 Refer to Chapter 4C and refit the oxygen sensor to the manifold.
32 Refit the exhaust system as described in Section 23.
33 Lower the vehicle to the ground, then reconnect the battery negative lead.

1.6 litre Z16XE and 1.8 litre engines

Note: *New manifold and exhaust front pipe retaining nuts, a new manifold gasket and exhaust front pipe gasket must be used on refitting.*

Removal

34 Apply the handbrake, then jack up the front of the vehicle and support it on axle stands (see *Jacking and vehicle support*).
35 Disconnect the battery negative lead (refer to *Disconnecting the battery* in the Reference Chapter).
36 Remove the plastic cover over the top of the engine.
37 Drain the cooling system as described in Chapter 1A.
38 Remove the complete exhaust system as described in Section 23.

39 Undo the retaining screw, and slide the air intake pipe/resonator to one side to release it from the front crossmember.
40 Remove the oxygen sensor from the exhaust manifold as described in Chapter 4C.
41 Release the retaining clips and disconnect the top hose from the radiator and thermostat housing.
42 Undo the three bolts and remove the exhaust manifold heat shield.
43 Disconnect the oil level sensor and crankshaft speed/position sensor wiring connectors.
44 Undo the nine exhaust manifold retaining nuts and collect the engine lifting bracket. Withdraw the manifold from the cylinder head studs and remove it from under the car. Recover the gasket.

Refitting

45 Thoroughly clean the mating face of the exhaust manifold and cylinder head, then locate a new gasket over the studs.
46 Locate the exhaust manifold over the cylinder head studs, refit the engine lifting bracket and secure with the (new) nuts tightened progressively to the specified torque.
47 Reconnect the oil level sensor and crankshaft speed/position sensor wiring connector.
48 Refit the exhaust manifold heat shield.
49 Refit the top hose the radiator and thermostat housing.
50 Refer to Chapter 4C and refit the oxygen sensor to the manifold.
51 Refit the air intake pipe/resonator to the front crossmember and secure with the retaining screw.
52 Refit the exhaust system as described in Section 23.
53 Lower the vehicle to the ground, then reconnect the battery negative lead.
54 Refill the cooling system as described in Chapter 1A, then refit the cover over the top of the engine.

23 Exhaust system – general information, removal and refitting

General information

1 The exhaust system consists of two main sections comprising a front pipe including the oxygen sensor (catalytic converter control) and front silencer, and a tailpipe incorporating the rear silencer. The catalytic converter is integral with the exhaust manifold.
2 The front pipe is attached to the exhaust manifold (catalytic converter) by a flange joint secured by nuts. The tailpipe is attached to the front pipe by an overlap joint which is secured by a clamp.
3 The front pipe is fitted with a flexible section to allow for exhaust system movement and the system is suspended throughout its entire length by rubber mountings.

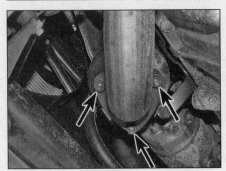

23.7 Undo the three nuts (arrowed) securing the front pipe to the exhaust manifold

23.9 Exhaust front pipe rubber mountings

23.10 Exhaust tailpipe retaining clamp

Removal

4 To remove the various parts of the system, first jack up the front or rear of the car, and support it on axle stands. Alternatively, position the car over an inspection pit, or on car ramps.

Front pipe

5 Remove the tailpipe as described later in this Section.

6 Trace the wiring back from the oxygen sensor, noting its correct routing, and disconnect its wiring connector. Free the wiring from its retaining clips so the sensor is free to be removed with the front pipe.

7 Undo the three nuts securing the front pipe to the exhaust manifold, then free the front pipe from the manifold and recover the gasket **(see illustration)**. While doing this, take care to support the flexible section. **Note:** *Angular movement in excess of 10° can cause permanent damage to the flexible section.*

8 Spray some penetrating oil over the exhaust rubber mounting blocks so that the mounting blocks will slide easily on the exhaust and underbody hangers.

9 Slide the front pipe rubber mounting blocks as far forward as possible **(see illustration)**. Move the exhaust system to the rear and disengage the front pipe hangers from the mounting blocks. Lower the front pipe to the ground and slide it out from under the car.

Tailpipe

10 Loosen the clamp securing the tail pipe to the front pipe **(see illustration)**.

11 Unhook the tailpipe from its rubber mountings and slide the tailpipe from the front pipe. If the tailpipe is rusted onto the front pipe, apply liberal amounts of penetrating oil and tap around the joint with a hammer to free it. Twist the tailpipe in both directions until free.

Heat shield(s)

12 The heat shields are secured to the underside of the body by various nuts and bolts. Each shield can be removed once the relevant exhaust section has been removed. If a shield is being removed to gain access to a component located behind it, it may prove sufficient in some cases to remove the retaining nuts and/or bolts, and simply lower the shield, without disturbing the exhaust system.

Refitting

13 Each section is refitted by reversing the removal sequence, noting the following points:
 a) *Ensure that all traces of corrosion have been removed from the system joints.*
 b) *When refitting the front pipe to the exhaust manifold flange joint, use a new gasket and new retaining nuts, and tighten the nuts to the specified torque.*
 c) *Inspect the rubber mountings for signs of damage or deterioration, and renew as necessary.*
 d) *Prior to tightening the exhaust system fasteners, ensure that all rubber mountings are correctly located, and that there is adequate clearance between the exhaust system and vehicle underbody.*

Chapter 4 Part B:
Fuel and exhaust systems – diesel engines

Contents

Degrees of difficulty

Easy, suitable for novice with little experience	Fairly easy, suitable for beginner with some experience	Fairly difficult, suitable for competent DIY mechanic	Difficult, suitable for experienced DIY mechanic	Very difficult, suitable for expert DIY or professional

Specifications

Engine identification

Engine type	Manufacturer's engine code*
1.3 litre (1248 cc) DOHC 16-valve	Z13DTJ
1.7 litre (1686 cc) DOHC 16-valve	Y17DT and Z17DTH

For details of engine code location, see 'Vehicle identification' in the Reference Chapter.

System type

1.3 litre engines	Magneti-Marelli 6JO2 high-pressure direct injection 'common-rail' system electronically-controlled
1.7 litre engines:	
Y17DT.	ECD V5 direct injection system incorporating an electronically-controlled Nippon Denso V5 distributor fuel injection pump
Z17DTH	Nippon Denso DECe01 high-pressure direct injection 'common-rail' system, electronically-controlled

Fuel system data

1.3 litre engines

Firing order.	1–3–4–2 (No 1 at timing chain end of engine)
Fuel system operating pressure.	1600 bar at 2200 rpm
Idle speed.	Controlled by ECU
Maximum speed.	Controlled by ECU
High-pressure fuel pump:	
Type	Bosch CP1
Fuel supply pump:	
Type	Electric, mounted in fuel tank
Delivery pressure	3.3 bar (maximum)
Injectors:	
Type	Bosch CRIP 1-MI

1.7 litre engines

Y17DT engines:	
Firing order	1–3–4–2 (No 1 at timing belt end of engine)
Idle speed.	Controlled by ECU
Maximum speed.	Controlled by ECU
Injection pump timing (static).	0.28 to 0.33 mm pump piston travel @ TDC
Injectors:	
Opening pressure	175 bar (1st stage) to 335 bar (2nd stage)
Z17DTH engines:	
Firing order	1–3–4–2 (No 1 at timing belt end of engine)
Fuel system operating pressure	1400 to 1600 bar at 2200 rpm
Idle speed.	Controlled by ECU
Maximum speed.	Controlled by ECU
High-pressure fuel pump:	
Type	Denso - HP - 3
Injectors:	
Type	Denso - DLL - P

Torque wrench settings

	Nm	lbf ft
1.3 litre engines		
Catalytic converter-to-turbocharger nuts.	25	18
Catalytic converter support bracket to sump reinforcement bracket . .	25	18
Camshaft position sensor retaining bolt.	7	5
Coolant pipe-to-heat exchanger bolts.	9	7
Crankshaft speed/position sensor retaining bolt	9	7
EGR valve bolts	22	16
Exhaust manifold nuts:*		
Stage 1.	15	11
Stage 2.	Angle-tighten a further 30°	
Exhaust system clamp nuts.	50	37
Fuel injector clamp bracket nuts	20	15
Fuel pressure regulator to fuel rail	60	44
Fuel pressure sensor to fuel rail	70	52
Fuel rail-to-mounting bracket bolts	25	18
Fuel rail mounting bracket-to-camshaft housing bolts	25	18
High-pressure fuel pipe unions:		
M12 union nuts.	25	18
M14 union nuts.	28	21
High-pressure fuel pump mounting bolts.	15	11
Inlet manifold bolts.	25	18
Injector retaining clamp nut	20	15
Oil filter housing to cylinder block	9	7
Turbocharger oil return pipe bolts	9	7
Turbocharger oil supply pipe banjo union bolts	12	9
Turbocharger-to-exhaust manifold.	25	18

Torque wrench settings (continued)

	Nm	lbf ft
1.7 litre Y17DT engines		
Atmospheric pressure sensor	10	7
Charge (boost) pressure sensor	10	7
Crankshaft speed/position sensor retaining bolt	9	7
Engine electronic control unit	6	4
Engine electronic control unit bracket:		
Bolts	25	18
Nut	10	7
Exhaust gas recirculation pipe bolts	28	21
Exhaust front pipe-to-turbocharger nuts	65	48
Exhaust manifold nuts and bolts*	25	18
Exhaust system clamp nuts	50	37
Fuel injector inner leak-off pipe unions	15	11
Fuel injector clamp nuts	22	16
Fuel pipe union nuts	25	18
Inlet manifold nuts and bolts*	24	18
Injection pump:		
Pump to pump bracket	18	13
Pump to cylinder block	20	15
Pump bracket to cylinder block	54	40
Injection pump control unit	10	7
Turbocharger:		
Exhaust connection flange nuts	27	20
Oil feed pipe unions	10	7
Turbocharger-to-manifold nuts	27	20
1.7 litre Z17DTH engines		
Catalytic converter heat shield bolts	12	9
Catalytic converter-to-turbocharger nuts	25	18
Crankshaft speed/position sensor retaining bolt	9	7
EGR valve heat exchanger pipe flange bolts	28	21
EGR valve heat exchanger to camshaft housing	25	18
Exhaust manifold nuts/bolts	70	52
Exhaust system clamp nuts	50	37
Exhaust system front pipe to catalytic converter	25	18
Fuel injector clamp bracket bolt:		
Stage 1	40	30
Stage 2	Slacken bolt	
Stage 3	32	24
Fuel leak-off pipe banjo union	15	11
High-pressure fuel pipe unions:		
6.00 mm diameter pipes	30	22
6.35 mm diameter pipes	25	18
High-pressure fuel pump mounting nuts	20	15
Inlet manifold nuts/bolts	26	18
Throttle housing mounting bracket bolts	25	18
Throttle housing to charge air pipe elbow	10	7
Turbocharger oil supply pipe banjo union bolts:		
Cylinder block union	28	21
Turbocharger union	20	15
Turbocharger to exhaust manifold:*		
Stage 1	24	18
Stage 2	48	35

* Use new fasteners

1 General information and precautions

General information

1.3 litre and 1.7 litre Z17DTH engines

These engines are fitted with a high-pressure direct injection common-rail system which incorporates the very latest in diesel injection technology. On this system, a high-pressure fuel pump is used purely to provide the pressure required for the injection system and has no control over the injection timing (unlike conventional diesel injection systems). The injection timing is controlled by the electronic control unit (ECU) via the electrically-operated injectors. The system operates as follows.

The fuel system consists of a fuel tank (which is mounted under the rear of the car), a fuel filter with integral water separator, a high-pressure fuel pump, injectors and associated components. 1.3 litre engines also contain an electric fuel supply pump mounted inside the fuel tank.

Fuel is supplied to the fuel filter housing which is located in the engine compartment. The fuel filter removes all foreign matter and water, and ensures that the fuel supplied to the pump is clean.

The high-pressure fuel pump is driven at half-crankshaft speed by the timing chain/belt. The high-pressure required in the system (up to 1600 bar) is produced by the three pistons in the pump. The high-pressure pump supplies high-pressure fuel to the fuel rail, which acts as a reservoir for the four injectors.

The electrical control system consists of the ECU, along with the following sensors:

a) *Accelerator pedal position sensor – informs the ECU of the accelerator pedal position, and the rate of throttle opening/closing.*

b) *Coolant temperature sensor – informs the ECU of engine temperature.*

c) *Airflow meter – informs the ECU of the amount of air passing through the intake duct.*

d) *Crankshaft sensor – informs the ECU of the crankshaft position and speed of rotation.*

e) *Camshaft sensor – informs the ECU of the positions of the pistons.*

f) *Charge (boost) pressure sensor – informs ECU of the pressure in the inlet manifold.*

g) *Fuel pressure sensor – informs the ECU of the fuel pressure present in the fuel rail.*

All the above signals are analysed by the ECU which selects the fuelling response appropriate to those values. The ECU controls the fuel injectors (varying the pulse width – the length of time the injectors are held open – to provide a richer or weaker mixture, as appropriate). The mixture is constantly varied by the ECU, to provide the best setting for cranking, starting (with either a hot or cold engine), warm-up, idle, cruising and acceleration.

The ECU also has full control over the fuel pressure present in the fuel rail via the high-pressure fuel regulator and third piston deactivator solenoid valve which are fitted to the high-pressure pump. To reduce the pressure, the ECU opens the high-pressure fuel regulator which allows the excess fuel to return direct to the tank from the pump. The third piston deactivator is used mainly to reduce the load on the engine, but can also be used to lower the fuel pressure. The deactivator solenoid valve relieves the fuel pressure from the third piston of the pump which results in only two of the pistons pressurising the fuel system.

The ECU also controls the exhaust gas recirculation (EGR) system, described in detail in Part C of this Chapter, the pre/post-heating system (see Chapter 5A), and the engine cooling fan.

On 1.7 litre engines, the inlet manifold is fitted with a butterfly valve (changeover flap) arrangement to improve efficiency at low engine speeds. Each cylinder has two inlet tracts in the manifold, one of which is fitted with a valve; the operation of the valve is controlled by the ECU via a vacuum solenoid. At low engine speeds (below approximately 1500 rpm) the valves remain closed, meaning that air entering each cylinder is passing through only one of the two manifold tracts. At higher engine speeds, the ECU opens up each of the four valves allowing the air passing through the manifold to pass through both inlet tracts.

A variable-vane turbocharger is fitted to increases engine efficiency. It does this by raising the pressure in the inlet manifold above atmospheric pressure. Instead of the air simply being sucked into the cylinders, it is forced in.

Between the turbocharger and the inlet manifold, the compressed air passes through an intercooler. This is an air-to-air heat exchanger mounted on the radiator, and supplied with cooling air from the front of the vehicle. The purpose of the intercooler is to remove some of the heat gained in being compressed from the inlet air. Because cooler air is denser, removal of this heat further increases engine efficiency.

Energy for the operation of the turbocharger comes from the exhaust gas. The gas flows through a specially-shaped housing (the turbine housing) and in so doing, spins the turbine wheel. The turbine wheel is attached to a shaft, at the end of which is another vaned wheel known as the compressor wheel. The compressor wheel spins in its own housing, and compresses the inlet air on the way to the inlet manifold. The turbo shaft is pressure-lubricated by an oil feed pipe from the main oil gallery. The shaft 'floats' on a cushion of oil. A drain pipe returns the oil to the sump. Boost pressure (the pressure in the inlet manifold) is limited by a wastegate, which diverts the exhaust gas away from the turbine wheel in response to a pressure-sensitive actuator.

If certain sensors fail, and send abnormal signals to the ECU, the ECU has a back-up programme. In this event, the abnormal signals are ignored, and a pre-programmed value is substituted for the sensor signal, allowing the engine to continue running, albeit at reduced efficiency. If the ECU enters its back-up mode, a warning light on the instrument panel will illuminate, and a fault code will be stored in the ECU memory. This fault code can be read using suitable specialist test equipment plugged into the system's diagnostic socket.

1.7 litre Y17DT engines

The fuel system consists of a rear-mounted fuel tank, a fuel filter with integral water separator and fuel heater, a fuel injection pump, injectors and associated components.

Fuel is drawn from the fuel tank by the fuel injection pump. Before reaching the pump, the fuel passes through a fuel filter, where foreign matter and water are removed. Excess fuel lubricates the moving components of the pump, and is then returned to the tank.

The fuel injection pump is driven at half-crankshaft speed by the timing belt. The high pressure required to inject the fuel into the compressed air in the cylinder is achieved by a radial piston pump.

The injection pump is electronically-controlled to meet the latest emission standards. The system consists of the engine electronic control unit, the injection electronic control unit, and the following sensors:

a) *Accelerator pedal position sensor –*

informs the ECUs of the accelerator pedal position.

b) *Coolant temperature sensor – informs the ECUs of engine temperature.*

c) *Airflow meter – informs the ECUs of the amount of air passing through the intake duct.*

d) *Crankshaft speed/position sensor – informs the ECUs of engine speed and crankshaft position.*

e) *Charge (boost) pressure sensor – informs ECUs of the pressure in the inlet manifold.*

f) *Atmospheric pressure sensor – informs the ECUs of the atmospheric pressure.*

g) *Fuel temperature sensor – informs the ECUs of the fuel temperature.*

h) *Injection pump shaft sensor – used by the ECUs to determine the exact injection timing.*

All the above information is analysed by the ECUs and, based on this, the ECUs determine the appropriate injection requirements for the engine. The engine ECU controls the injection pump timing, via the pump control unit, to provide the best setting for cranking, starting (with either a hot or cold engine), warm-up, idle, cruising, and acceleration.

Basic injection timing is determined when the pump is fitted. When the engine is running, it is varied automatically to suit the prevailing engine speed by a mechanism which turns the cam plate or ring – controlled by the ECU.

The engine ECU also controls the exhaust gas recirculation (EGR) system (see Chapter 4C) and the preheating system (see Chapter 5A).

The four fuel injectors produce a spray of fuel directly into the cylinders. The injectors are calibrated to open and close at critical pressures to provide efficient and even combustion. Each injector needle is lubricated by fuel, which accumulates in the spring chamber and is channelled to the injection pump return hose by leak-off pipes.

The inlet manifold is a two-part assembly sealed by a metal gasket. The EGR (exhaust gas recirculation) valve and charge pressure sensor are mounted to the upper part of the manifold.

A turbocharger is fitted to increase engine efficiency by raising the pressure in the inlet manifold above atmospheric pressure. Instead of the air simply being sucked into the cylinders, it is forced in. Additional fuel is supplied by the injection pump in proportion to the increased air intake.

Energy for the operation of the turbocharger comes from the exhaust gas. The gas flows through a specially-shaped housing (the turbine housing) and in so doing, spins the turbine wheel. The turbine wheel is attached to a shaft, at the end of which is another vaned wheel known as the compressor wheel. The compressor wheel spins in its own housing, and compresses the inlet air on the way to the inlet manifold.

Between the turbocharger and the inlet manifold, the compressed air passes through an intercooler. This is an air-to-air heat exchanger is mounted on the radiator, and supplied with cooling air from the front of the vehicle. The purpose of the intercooler is to remove some of the heat gained in being compressed from the inlet air. Because cooler air is denser, removal of this heat further increases engine efficiency.

Charge pressure (the pressure in the inlet manifold) is limited by a wastegate which diverts the exhaust gas away from the turbine wheel in response to a pressure-sensitive actuator. A pressure-operated switch operates a warning light on the instrument panel in the event of excessive charge pressure developing.

The turbo shaft is pressure-lubricated by an oil feed pipe from the engine main oil so that the shaft 'floats' on a cushion of oil. A drain pipe returns the oil to the sump.

The charge pressure wastegate is controlled by the ECU via a solenoid valve.

If there is an abnormality in any of the readings obtained from any sensor, the ECU enters its back-up mode. In this event, the ECU ignores the abnormal sensor signal, and assumes a pre-programmed value which will allow the engine to continue running (albeit at reduced efficiency). If the ECU enters this back-up mode, the warning light on the instrument panel will come on, and the relevant fault code will be stored in the ECU memory.

Precautions

⚠️ *Warning: It is necessary to take certain precautions when working on the fuel system components, particularly the high-pressure side of the system. Before carrying out any operations on the fuel system, refer to the precautions given in 'Safety first!' at the beginning of this manual, and to any additional warning notes at the start of the relevant Sections. Also refer to the additional information contained in Section 2.*
Caution: Do not operate the engine if any of air intake ducts are disconnected or the filter element is removed. Any debris entering the engine will cause severe damage to the turbocharger.
Caution: To prevent damage to the turbocharger, do not race the engine immediately after start-up, especially if it is cold. Allow it to idle smoothly to give the oil a few seconds to circulate around the turbocharger bearings. Always allow the engine to return to idle speed before switching it off – do not blip the throttle and switch off, as this will leave the turbo spinning without lubrication.
Caution: Observe the recommended intervals for oil and filter changing, and use a reputable oil of the specified quality. Neglect of oil changing, or use of inferior oil, can cause carbon formation on the turbo shaft, leading to subsequent failure.

2 High-pressure diesel injection system – special information

Note: *The following information is only applicable to 1.3 litre and 1.7 litre Z17DTH engines.*

Warnings and precautions

1 It is essential to observe strict precautions when working on the fuel system components, particularly the high-pressure side of the system. Before carrying out any operations on the fuel system, refer to the precautions given in *Safety first!* at the beginning of this manual, and to the following additional information.
• Do not carry out any repair work on the high-pressure fuel system unless you are competent to do so, have all the necessary tools and equipment required, and are aware of the safety implications involved.
• Before starting any repair work on the fuel system, wait at least 30 seconds after switching off the engine to allow the fuel circuit to return to atmospheric pressure.
• Never work on the high-pressure fuel system with the engine running.
• Keep well clear of any possible source of fuel leakage, particularly when starting the engine after carrying out repair work. A leak in the system could cause an extremely high-pressure jet of fuel to escape, which could result in severe personal injury.
• Never place your hands or any part of your body near to a leak in the high-pressure fuel system.
• Do not use steam cleaning equipment or compressed air to clean the engine or any of the fuel system components.

Repair procedures and general information

2 Strict cleanliness must be observed at all times when working on any part of the fuel system. This applies to the working area in general, the person doing the work, and the components being worked on.
3 Before working on the fuel system components, they must be thoroughly cleaned with a suitable degreasing fluid. Cleanliness is particularly important when working on the fuel system connections at the following components:
   a) Fuel filter.
   b) High-pressure fuel pump.
   c) Fuel rail.
   d) Fuel injectors.
   e) High-pressure fuel pipes.
4 After disconnecting any fuel pipes or components, the open union or orifice must be immediately sealed to prevent the entry of dirt or foreign material. Plastic plugs and caps in various sizes are available in packs from motor factors and accessory outlets, and are particularly suitable for this application **(see illustration)**. Fingers cut from disposable rubber gloves should be used to protect

2.4 Typical plastic plug and cap set for sealing disconnected fuel pipes and components

components such as fuel pipes, fuel injectors and wiring connectors, and can be secured in place using elastic bands. Suitable gloves of this type are available at no cost from most petrol station forecourts.
5 Whenever any of the high-pressure fuel pipes are disconnected or removed, a new pipe(s) must be obtained for refitting.
6 The torque wrench settings given in the Specifications must be strictly observed when tightening component mountings and connections. This is particularly important when tightening the high-pressure fuel pipe unions. To enable a torque wrench to be used on the fuel pipe unions, two crow-foot adapters are required. Suitable types are available from motor factors and accessory outlets **(see illustration)**.

3 Air cleaner assembly and intake ducts – removal and refitting

Removal

1 Disconnect the wiring connector from the side of the airflow meter **(see illustration)**.
2 Slacken the retaining clip and detach the flexible air intake duct from the turbocharger charge air pipe **(see illustration)**.
3 Where applicable, unclip the vacuum hose or wiring harness from the side of the air cleaner housing.
4 Undo the retaining screw and release the

2.6 Two crow-foot adapters will be necessary for tightening the fuel pipe unions

3.1 Disconnect the wiring connector from the airflow meter – 1.7 litre engine shown

3.2 Detach the flexible air intake duct from the turbocharger charge air pipe – 1.7 litre engine shown

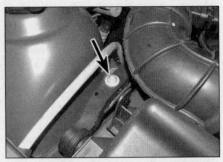

3.4 Undo the retaining screw (arrowed) and release the air cleaner housing mounting bracket

3.5 Detach the air intake duct at the front of the air cleaner housing

3.7 Release the clip and disconnect the water drain tube from the base of the air cleaner housing

mounting bracket at the rear of the air cleaner housing (see illustration).

5 Detach the air intake duct at the front of the air cleaner housing (see illustration).

6 Lift the housing upwards at the rear, then disengage the front mounting rubber from the body bracket.

7 When sufficient clearance exists, release the retaining clip and disconnect the water drain tube from the base of the air cleaner housing (see illustration). Remove the assembly from the engine compartment.

8 The various air intake ducts and charge air pipes/hoses linking the intercooler to the manifold and turbocharger can be disconnected and removed once the retaining

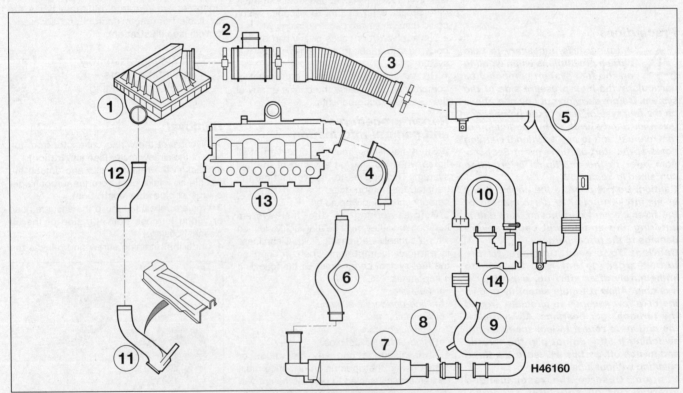

3.8 Typical air intake duct arrangement

1 Air cleaner assembly	5 Turbocharger charge air pipe	8 Intercooler charge air pipe hose connection	11 Resonator
2 Airflow meter	6 Inlet manifold charge air pipe connection hose	9 Charge air hose	12 Air cleaner intake duct
3 Upper intake duct	7 Intercooler	10 Charge air hose	13 Inlet manifold
4 Inlet manifold charge air pipe			14 Turbocharger

clips have been slackened **(see illustration)**. In some cases it will be necessary to disconnect breather hoses, vacuum pipes and wiring connectors to allow the pipe/duct to be removed; the pipe/duct may also be bolted to a support bracket.

Refitting

9 Refitting is the reverse of removal, making sure all the air intake ducts and charge air pipes/hoses are securely reconnected.

4 Accelerator pedal/ position sensor – removal and refitting

Refer to Chapter 4A, Section 3.

5 Fuel system – priming and bleeding

1 After disconnecting part of the fuel supply system or running out of fuel, it is necessary to prime the fuel system and bleed off any air which may have entered the system components, as follows.
2 On 1.3 litre engines, prime the system by switching on the ignition three times for approximately 15 seconds each time. On all engines, operate the starter for a maximum of 30 seconds. If the engine does not start within this time, wait 5 seconds and repeat the procedure.
3 When the engine starts, run it at a fast idle speed for a minute or so to purge any trapped air from the fuel lines. After this time the engine should idle smoothly at a constant speed.
4 If the engine idles roughly, then there is still some air trapped in the fuel system. Increase the engine speed again for another minute or so then allow it to idle. Repeat this procedure as necessary until the engine is idling smoothly.

6 Fuel gauge sender unit – removal and refitting

1 The fuel gauge sender unit can be removed and refitted as described in Chapter 4A, Section 6. **Note:** *On 1.7 litre engines, the in-tank module does not have the fuel pump as part of the assembly, just a fuel pick-up filter.*
2 On completion, bleed the fuel system as described in Section 5.

7 Fuel supply pump (1.3 litre engine) – removal and refitting

Note: *A fuel supply pump is not fitted to 1.7 litre engines.*
1 On 1.3 litre engines, the diesel fuel supply

9.3a Unclip and remove the trim panel beneath the handbrake lever . . .

pump is located in the in-tank module in the fuel tank. The removal and refitting procedures are as described in Chapter 4A, Section 7. The pump is integral with the in-tank module and cannot be renewed separately.
2 On completion, bleed the fuel system as described in Section 5.

8 Fuel tank – removal and refitting

1 Refer to Chapter 4A, Section 8, noting that there is no fuel filter clipped to the tank.
2 On completion, bleed the fuel system as described in Section 5.

9 Injection system electrical components – testing

1 If a fault is suspected in the electronic control side of the system, first ensure that all the wiring connectors are securely connected and free of corrosion. Ensure that the suspected problem is not of a mechanical nature, or due to poor maintenance; ie, check that the air cleaner filter element is clean, the engine breather hoses are clear and undamaged, and that the cylinder compression pressures are correct, referring to Chapter 1B and the relevant Parts of Chapter 2.
2 If these checks fail to reveal the cause of the problem, the vehicle should be taken to a Vauxhall/Opel dealer or suitably-equipped

10.1 Disconnect the airflow meter wiring connector (arrowed)

9.3b . . . for access to the diagnostic socket (arrowed)

engine management diagnostic specialist for testing.
3 A diagnostic socket is located in the centre console, to which a fault code reader or other suitable test equipment can be connected. Lift out the trim panel beneath the handbrake lever for access **(see illustrations)**. By using the code reader or test equipment, the engine management ECU (and the various other vehicle system ECUs) can be interrogated, and any stored fault codes can be retrieved. This will allow the fault to be quickly and simply traced, alleviating the need to test all the system components individually, which is a time-consuming operation that carries a risk of damaging the ECU.

10 Injection system electrical components (1.3 litre engine) – removal and refitting

Airflow meter

1 Disconnect the airflow meter wiring connector **(see illustration)**.
2 Slacken the retaining clip securing the air intake duct to the airflow meter and disconnect the duct.
3 Slacken the retaining clip and remove the airflow meter from the air cleaner housing lid.
4 Refitting is a reversal of removal, but ensure that the arrow on the airflow meter points in the direction of airflow when fitted.

Crankshaft speed/ position sensor

5 Lift off the plastic cover over the top of the engine.
6 The crankshaft speed/position sensor is located on the front of the cylinder block, in line with the flywheel.
7 Disconnect the sensor wiring connector, then undo the retaining bolt and remove the sensor from the cylinder block **(see illustration)**.
8 Refitting is a reversal of removal, tightening the retaining bolt securely.

Camshaft position sensor

9 Lift off the plastic cover over the top of the engine.
10 The camshaft position sensor is located on the front right-hand side of the camshaft

10.7 Undo the retaining bolt and remove the crankshaft speed/position sensor from the cylinder block

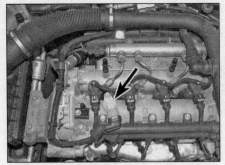

10.10 Camshaft position sensor location (arrowed)

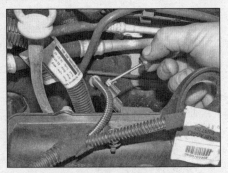

10.16 Lift up the locking catch to disconnect the charge (boost) pressure sensor wiring connector

housing, above the exhaust camshaft **(see illustration)**.

11 Disconnect the sensor wiring connector, then undo the retaining bolt and remove the sensor from the camshaft housing.

12 Refitting is a reversal of removal, tightening the retaining bolt securely.

Coolant temperature sensor

13 Refer to the procedures contained in Chapter 3.

Charge (boost) pressure sensor

14 Lift off the plastic cover over the top of the engine.

15 The charge pressure sensor is located on the upper face of the inlet manifold, near the centre. For improved access, remove the turbocharger charge air pipe.

16 Using a small screwdriver, lift up the locking catch and disconnect the sensor wiring connector **(see illustration)**.

17 Undo the retaining bolt and withdraw the sensor from the manifold. Recover the sealing O-ring.

18 Renew the sealing O-ring, then refit the sensor and tighten the retaining bolt securely. Reconnect the wiring connector and secure with the locking catch.

19 If removed, refit the charge air pipe, then refit the engine cover.

Fuel pressure regulator

20 Disconnect the battery negative terminal (refer to *Disconnecting the battery* in the Reference Chapter).

21 Lift off the plastic cover over the top of the engine.

22 Disconnect the wiring connector from the fuel pressure regulator **(see illustration)**.

23 Remove the regulator from the fuel rail by unscrewing the inner nut (nearest the fuel rail) while counterholding the regulator body with a second spanner. Be prepared for some loss of fuel.

24 Refitting is the reverse of removal, tightening the regulator to the specified torque.

Fuel pressure sensor

25 Lift off the plastic cover over the top of the engine.

26 The fuel pressure sensor is located at the right-hand end of the fuel rail.

27 Disconnect the sensor wiring connector, then unscrew the sensor from the fuel rail **(see illustration)**.

28 Refitting is a reversal of removal, tightening the sensor to the specified torque.

Electronic control unit

Note: *If a new ECU is to be fitted, this work must be entrusted to a Vauxhall/Opel dealer or suitably-equipped specialist. It is necessary to initialise the new ECU after installation, which requires the use of dedicated diagnostic equipment.*

29 Disconnect the battery negative terminal (refer to *Disconnecting the battery* in the Reference Chapter).

30 Remove the front bumper as described in Chapter 11.

31 Withdraw the locking plates, lift the

locking levers and disconnect the two wiring connectors from the ECU, located under the left-hand wheel arch.

32 Undo the four nuts securing the ECU to its mounting frame and remove the ECU from under the wheel arch.

33 Refitting is a reversal of removal, ensuring that the wiring connectors are securely connected and locked with the locking levers.

Turbocharger wastegate solenoid

34 The wastegate (charge pressure) solenoid valve is located at the front of the engine compartment above the radiator **(see illustration)**.

35 Firmly apply the handbrake, then jack up the front of the car and support it securely on axle stands (see *Jacking and vehicle support*).

36 Disconnect the wiring connector and the two vacuum hoses from the valve then undo the retaining nuts and remove the valve from its mounting bracket.

37 Refitting is the reverse of removal.

11 Injection system electrical components (1.7 litre Y17DT engine) – removal and refitting

Airflow meter

1 Disconnect the airflow meter wiring connector **(see illustration 3.1)**.

2 Slacken the retaining clip securing the air intake duct to the airflow meter and disconnect the duct.

10.22 Disconnect the wiring connector (arrowed) from the fuel pressure regulator

10.27 Disconnect the fuel pressure sensor wiring connector (arrowed)

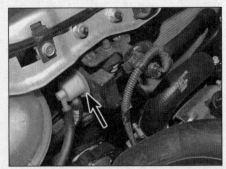

10.34 Turbocharger wastegate solenoid valve (arrowed)

3 Slacken the retaining clip and remove the airflow meter from the air cleaner housing lid.

4 Refitting is a reversal of removal, but ensure that the arrow on the airflow meter points in the direction of airflow when fitted.

Crankshaft speed/position sensor

5 Firmly apply the handbrake, then jack up the front of the vehicle and support it securely on axle stands (see *Jacking and vehicle support*).

6 The sensor is located on the rear of the cylinder block, underneath the starter motor. Working from under the vehicle, disconnect the wiring plug from the sensor.

7 Undo the retaining bolt and remove the sensor. Recover the sealing ring **(see illustration)**.

8 Refitting is a reversal of removal. If necessary renew the sealing ring and tighten the sensor retaining bolt to the specified torque.

Coolant temperature sensor

9 Refer to the procedures contained in Chapter 3.

Charge (boost) pressure sensor

10 Remove the air cleaner ducting at the rear of the engine compartment (see Section 2).

11 Disconnect the wiring plug from the sensor on the right-hand end of the inlet manifold.

12 Undo the retaining bolts and remove the sensor **(see illustration)**.

13 Refitting is a reversal of removal. Tighten the sensor retaining bolts to the specified torque.

Engine electronic control unit

Note: *If a new ECU is to be fitted, this work must be entrusted to a Vauxhall/Opel dealer or suitably-equipped specialist. It is necessary to initialise the new ECU after installation, which requires the use of dedicated diagnostic equipment.*

14 The engine control unit is located on top of the engine above the exhaust gas recirculation valve.

15 Disconnect the battery negative terminal (refer to *Disconnecting the battery* in the Reference Chapter).

16 Disconnect the two outer wiring plugs from the ECU. The plugs are unlocked by lifting up the metal levers **(see illustration)**.

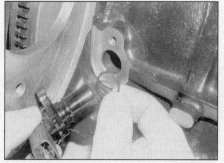

11.7 Crankshaft position sensor

Disconnect and release the third wiring plug located between the two outer plugs.

17 Undo the two retaining bolts and remove the wiring harness support bracket.

18 Undo the two retaining bolts and two retaining nuts, and remove the ECU.

19 Refitting is a reversal of removal. Tighten the ECU retaining bolts/nuts to the specified torque. The ECU wiring plugs are shaped such that each plug will only fit its correct socket. The plug from the left-hand side of the engine compartment connects to the rearmost socket. Take great care when refitting the plugs, as the terminals are very delicate and easily damaged.

Injection electronic control unit

20 The injection ECU is located at the rear of the injection pump.

21 Disconnect the battery negative terminal (refer to *Disconnecting the battery* in the Reference Chapter).

22 Firmly apply the handbrake, then jack up the front of the vehicle and support it securely on axle stands (see *Jacking and vehicle support*).

23 Working under the vehicle, disconnect the ECU wiring plug.

24 Undo the retaining bolts, and remove the ECU **(see illustration)**.

25 Refitting is a reversal of removal.

Turbocharger wastegate solenoid

26 Remove the injection ECU as described in paragraphs 20 to 24.

11.12 Undo the bolts and remove the charge pressure sensor

27 Disconnect the vacuum pipes, and wiring plug from the solenoid valve.

28 Undo the two retaining bolts and remove the solenoid valve.

29 Refitting is a reversal of removal. Tighten the solenoid valve retaining bolts securely. Note that the vacuum pipes are of two different diameters. The smaller pipe is fitted to the outer connection.

Atmospheric pressure sensor

30 The atmospheric pressure sensor is located at the rear of the cylinder block, between the injection pump and the starter motor.

31 Firmly apply the handbrake, then jack up the front of the vehicle and support it securely on axle stands (see *Jacking and vehicle support*).

32 Slacken the retaining clip and detach the oil filter housing oil return hose from the rear of the cylinder block. Be prepared for oil spillage.

33 Disconnect the wiring plug from the pressure sensor.

34 Lift the sensor up and off the retaining bracket **(see illustration)**.

35 Refitting is a reversal of removal.

Fuel temperature sensor

36 The fuel temperature sensor is fitted to the right-hand top of the injection pump **(see illustration)**.

37 To remove the sensor, disconnect the wiring plug and unscrew the sensor from the top of the injection pump.

11.16 Lift the metal levers to unplug the engine ECU wiring connectors

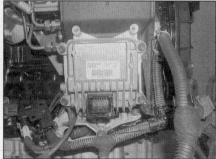

11.24 Unscrew the injection ECU retaining bolts

11.34 Slide the atmospheric pressure sensor from the bracket

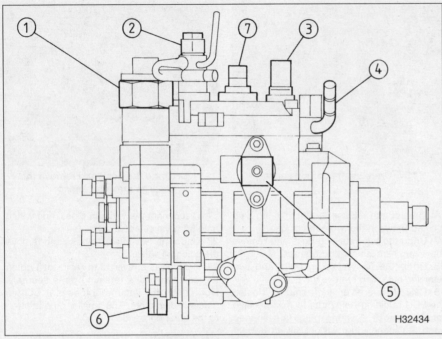

11.36 Fuel injection pump details

1 Spill valve	4 Fuel supply line
2 Fuel return line	5 Programmable read-only
3 Fuel temperature sensor	memory

6 Timing control solenoid
7 Injection pump shaft
position sensor

38 With a new seal fitted, screw the sensor into the injection pump and tighten the nut securely **(see illustration)**.

39 Reconnect the wiring plug.

12 Injection system electrical components (1.7 litre Z17DTH engine) – removal and refitting

Airflow meter

1 Disconnect the airflow meter wiring connector **(see illustration 3.1)**.

2 Slacken the retaining clip securing the air intake duct to the airflow meter and disconnect the duct.

3 Slacken the retaining clip and remove the airflow meter from the air cleaner housing lid.

4 Refitting is a reversal of removal, but ensure that the arrow on the airflow meter points toward the throttle housing when fitted.

12.7 Disconnect the throttle housing wiring connector

Throttle housing

5 Remove the plastic cover over the top of the engine.

6 Slacken the retaining clip and disconnect the charge air hose from the throttle housing.

7 Disconnect the throttle housing wiring connector **(see illustration)**.

8 Undo the bolts securing the throttle housing to the mounting bracket, and the bolts securing the mounting bracket to the camshaft housing. Remove the mounting bracket.

9 Undo the four bolts securing the throttle housing to the charge air pipe elbow and remove the housing from the engine. Recover the seal.

10 Refitting is a reversal of removal, but thoroughly clean the mating faces and use a new seal on the charge air pipe elbow. Tighten the retaining bolts to the specified torque.

Crankshaft speed/position sensor

11 The sensor is located at the rear of the

12.17a Disconnect the camshaft sensor wiring connector . . .

11.38 Screw the fuel temperature sensor into the injection pump

cylinder block, below the starter motor. To gain access, firmly apply the handbrake, then jack up the front of the car and support it securely on axle stands (see *Jacking and vehicle support*).

12 Wipe clean the area around the crankshaft sensor then disconnect the wiring connector.

13 Slacken and remove the retaining bolt and remove the sensor from the cylinder block **(see illustration 11.7)**. Recover the sealing ring.

14 Refitting is a reversal of removal, using a new sealing ring. Tighten the sensor retaining bolt to the specified torque.

Camshaft position sensor

15 Remove the plastic cover over the top of the engine.

16 The camshaft position sensor is located on the front right-hand side of the camshaft housing, adjacent to the exhaust camshaft sprocket.

17 Disconnect the camshaft sensor wiring connector, then undo the sensor retaining bolt and remove the sensor from the mounting bracket **(see illustrations)**.

18 Refitting is a reversal of removal, tightening the retaining bolt securely.

Coolant temperature sensor

19 Refer to the procedures contained in Chapter 3.

Charge (boost) pressure sensor

20 Remove the plastic cover over the top of the engine.

21 The charge pressure sensor is located on

12.17b . . . then undo the sensor retaining bolt (arrowed) and remove the sensor from the mounting bracket

the right-hand side of the inlet manifold below the changeover flap vacuum actuator.

22 Slacken the retaining clips and remove the flexible air intake hose connecting the airflow meter to the charge air pipe.

23 Unclip the engine management wiring harness from the right-hand rear engine lifting bracket.

24 Unscrew the fuel leak-off pipe bracket retaining nut, then unscrew the banjo union bolt and release the fuel leak-off pipe from the fuel rail. Recover the two copper washers from the banjo union, and suitably cover the end of the pipe and the fuel rail to prevent dirt entry. Note that new copper washers will be required for refitting.

25 Disconnect the wiring connector and unscrew the two bolts securing the changeover flap vacuum actuator to the inlet manifold. Carefully lift the actuator upwards slightly for access to the charge pressure sensor.

26 Using a small screwdriver, lift up the locking catch and disconnect the sensor wiring connector.

27 Undo the retaining bolt and withdraw the sensor from the manifold. Recover the sealing O-ring.

28 Renew the sealing O-ring, then refit the sensor and tighten the retaining bolt securely. Reconnect the wiring connector and secure with the locking catch.

29 Place the changeover flap vacuum actuator back in position, refit the two stud bolts and tighten securely.

30 The remainder of refitting is a reversal of removal.

Electronic control unit

Note: *If a new ECU is to be fitted, this work must be entrusted to a Vauxhall/Opel dealer or suitably-equipped specialist. It is necessary to initialise the new ECU after installation, which requires the use of dedicated diagnostic equipment.*

31 Disconnect the battery negative terminal (refer to *Disconnecting the battery* in the Reference Chapter).

32 Remove the plastic cover over the top of the engine.

33 Lift the locking bars and disconnect the two wiring connectors from the ECU **(see illustration)**.

34 Undo the two bolts and two nuts and remove the ECU from the mounting bracket. Note the location of the earth lead on the front mounting stud.

35 Refitting is a reversal of removal, ensuring that the wiring connectors are securely connected and locked with the locking levers.

Turbocharger wastegate solenoid

36 The wastegate (charge pressure) solenoid valve is located at the rear of the engine above the starter motor.

37 Firmly apply the handbrake, then jack up the front of the car and support it securely on axle stands (see *Jacking and vehicle support*).

38 Disconnect the wiring connector and the two vacuum hoses from the valve then undo the two retaining bolts and remove the valve from its location.

39 Refitting is a reversal of removal.

Changeover flap actuator solenoid

40 The solenoid valve controlling the inlet manifold changeover flap vacuum actuator is located at the rear right-hand side of the cylinder block.

41 Firmly apply the handbrake, then jack up the front of the car and support it securely on axle stands (see *Jacking and vehicle support*).

42 Mark the two vacuum hoses for correct refitting, then disconnect the hoses from the valve.

43 Disconnect the wiring connector then undo the two retaining bolts and remove the valve from its location.

44 Refitting is a reversal of removal.

---

13 High-pressure fuel pump (1.3 litre engine) – removal and refitting

> ⚠️ **Warning: Refer to the information contained in Section 2 before proceeding.**

Note: *A new fuel pump-to-fuel rail high-pressure fuel pipe will be required for refitting.*

Removal

1 Disconnect the battery negative terminal (refer to *Disconnecting the battery* in the Reference Chapter).

12.33 Lift the locking bars (arrowed) and disconnect the two wiring connectors from the ECU

2 Lift off the plastic cover over the top of the engine.

3 Slacken the retaining clip and detach the flexible air intake duct from the turbocharger charge air pipe **(see illustration)**.

4 Slacken the retaining clip and disconnect the turbocharger charge air pipe from the turbocharger.

5 Working along the charge air pipe, release the wiring harness retaining clips from the pipe supports and release the fuel hose from the retaining clips.

6 Release the locking clip and disconnect the crankcase breather hose at the quick-release connection on the charge air pipe.

7 Undo the two mounting bolts and remove the charge air pipe from the engine.

8 Thoroughly clean the fuel pipe unions on the fuel pump and fuel rail. Using an open-ended spanner, unscrew the union nuts securing the high-pressure fuel pipe to the fuel pump and fuel rail. Counterhold the union on the pump with a second spanner, while unscrewing the union nut. Withdraw the high-pressure fuel pipe and plug or cover the open unions to prevent dirt entry.

9 Release the retaining clips and disconnect the fuel supply and return hoses from the unions on the side of the fuel pump **(see illustration)**. Plug or cover the pump unions and hose ends to prevent dirt entry.

10 Remove the brake servo vacuum pump as described in Chapter 9.

11 Unscrew the three mounting bolts and withdraw the pump from the camshaft housing. Recover the sealing O-ring **(see illustrations)**.

13.3 Slacken the clip (arrowed) and detach the flexible air intake duct from the turbocharger charge air pipe

13.9 Release the retaining clips (arrowed) and disconnect the fuel hoses from the unions on the side of the fuel pump

13.11a Unscrew the three mounting bolts (arrowed) . . .

13.11b . . . withdraw the fuel pump from the camshaft housing . . .

Caution: The high-pressure fuel pump is manufactured to extremely close tolerances and must not be dismantled in any way. No parts for the pump are available separately and if the unit is in any way suspect, it must be renewed.

Refitting

12 Thoroughly clean the fuel pump and camshaft housing mating faces.
13 Locate a new sealing O-ring on the pump flange and lubricate the O-ring with clean diesel fuel.
14 Align the pump drive dog with the slot on the camshaft, then place the pump in position. Refit the three mounting bolts and tighten them to the specified torque.
15 Refit the brake servo vacuum pump as described in Chapter 9.
16 Reconnect the fuel supply and return hoses and secure with the retaining clips.
17 Remove the blanking plugs from the fuel pipe unions on the pump and fuel rail. Locate a new high-pressure fuel pipe over the unions and screw on the union nuts finger-tight at this stage.
18 Using a torque wrench and crow-foot adapter, tighten the fuel pipe union nuts to the specified torque. Counterhold the union on the pump with an open-ended spanner, while tightening the union nut.
19 Refit the charge air pipe, then reconnect the battery.
20 Observing the precautions listed in Section 2, prime the fuel system as described in Section 5, then start the engine and allow it to idle. Check for leaks at the high-pressure fuel pipe unions with the engine idling. If satisfactory, increase the engine speed to 4000 rpm and check again for leaks. If any leaks are detected, obtain and fit a new high-pressure fuel pipe.
21 Refit the engine cover on completion.

---

14 High-pressure fuel pump (1.7 litre Z17DTH engine) – removal and refitting

Warning: Refer to the information contained in Section 2 before proceeding.
Note: *A new fuel pump-to-fuel rail high-pressure fuel pipe will be required for refitting.*

13.11c . . . and recover the sealing O-ring

Removal

1 Disconnect the battery negative terminal (refer to *Disconnecting the battery* in the Reference Chapter).
2 Remove the plastic cover over the top of the engine.
3 Remove the timing belt and the high-pressure fuel pump sprocket as described in Chapter 2E.
4 At the rear of the engine, mark the locations of the vacuum hoses at the turbocharger wastegate solenoid and changeover flap actuator solenoid, then disconnect the four vacuum hoses.
5 Slacken the two retaining clips and remove the oil filter housing oil return hose. Be prepared for oil spillage.
6 At the solenoid mounting brackets and fuel pump, disconnect the wiring connectors at the following components:
 a) *Turbocharger wastegate solenoid.*
 b) *Changeover flap actuator solenoid.*
 c) *Fuel metering unit.*
 d) *Fuel pressure regulator.*
 e) *Fuel pressure sensor.*
 f) *Atmospheric pressure sensor.*
7 Release the disconnected wiring harness from the clips and cable-ties.
8 Unscrew the bolt and detach the earth cable, then unscrew the two nuts and one bolt and remove the solenoid mounting bracket assembly.
9 Thoroughly clean the fuel pipe unions on the fuel pump and fuel rail. Using an open-ended spanner, unscrew the union nuts securing the high-pressure fuel pipe to the fuel pump and fuel rail. Counterhold the union on the pump with a second spanner, while unscrewing the union nut. Withdraw the high-pressure fuel pipe and plug or cover the open unions to prevent dirt entry.
10 Unscrew the fuel leak-off pipe bracket retaining nut, then unscrew the banjo union bolt and release the fuel leak-off pipe from the fuel rail. Recover the two copper washers from the banjo union, and suitably cover the end of the pipe and the fuel rail to prevent dirt entry. Note that new copper washers will be required for refitting.
11 Unscrew the two nuts from the high-pressure fuel pump mounting stud bolts. Unscrew the two stud bolts and remove the pump from the engine bracket.

Caution: The high-pressure fuel pump is manufactured to extremely close tolerances and must not be dismantled in any way. No parts for the pump are available separately and if the unit is in any way suspect, it must be renewed.

Refitting

12 Refit the pump to the engine bracket and securely tighten the retaining stud bolts. Refit the retaining nuts and tighten to the specified torque.
13 Refit the fuel leak-off pipe using new copper washers at the banjo union. Tighten the banjo union to the specified torque, then refit and tighten the pipe bracket retaining nut.
14 Remove the blanking plugs from the fuel pipe unions on the pump and fuel rail. Locate a new high-pressure fuel pipe over the unions and screw on the union nuts finger-tight at this stage.
15 Using a torque wrench and crow-foot adapter, tighten the fuel pipe union nuts to the specified torque. Counterhold the union on the pump with an open-ended spanner, while tightening the union nut.
16 Refit the solenoid mounting bracket assembly and secure with the bolt and two nuts tightened securely. Refit the earth cable.
17 Reconnect the wiring to the components listed in paragraph 6, then secure the wiring harness with clips and cable-ties.
18 Refit the oil filter housing oil return hose and secure with the two retaining clips.
19 Reconnect the pump wiring connector and secure the harness to the pump stud bolt with the retaining nut.
20 Refit the fuel supply and return hoses to the fuel pump and secure with the retaining clips.
21 Reconnect the vacuum hoses to the turbocharger wastegate solenoid and changeover flap actuator solenoid.
22 Refit the high-pressure fuel pump sprocket and the timing belt as described in Chapter 2E.
23 Reconnect the battery negative terminal.
24 Observing the precautions listed in Section 2, prime the fuel system as described in Section 5, then start the engine and allow it to idle. Check for leaks at the high-pressure fuel pipe unions with the engine idling. If satisfactory, increase the engine speed to 4000 rpm and check again for leaks. If any leaks are detected, obtain and fit a new high-pressure fuel pipe.
25 Refit the engine cover on completion.

---

15 Fuel injection pump (1.7 litre Y17DT engine) – removal and refitting

Removal

1 Disconnect the battery negative terminal (refer to *Disconnecting the battery* in the Reference Chapter).

2 Remove the timing belt and the fuel injection pump sprocket as described in Chapter 2E.

3 Remove the inlet manifold as described in Section 23 of this Chapter.

4 Refer to Section 11, and remove the injection electronic control unit (ECU).

5 Disconnect the two vacuum pipes, the wiring plug, the two retaining bolts and remove the turbocharger wastegate solenoid. Refer to Section 11 if necessary.

6 Unplug the atmospheric pressure sensor (see Section 11), remove the sensor from the mounting bracket. Undo the two retaining bolts and remove the bracket. Remove the injection pump ECU bracket **(see illustration)**.

7 Disconnect the fuel supply and return pipes from the pump.

8 Pull out the injection pump insulation, disconnect the various sensor wiring plugs from the injection pump, and release the wiring harness from the various retaining clips **(see illustration)**. Note the routing of the various wiring looms.

9 Undo the bolts and remove the injection pump mounting bracket from the left-hand end of the pump **(see illustration)**.

10 Remove the two retaining nuts, and manoeuvre the injection pump from the timing case. Recover the foam insulator from between the pump and cylinder block.

Caution: Never attempt to dismantle the pump assembly. If there is a problem, take the pump to a Vauxhall/Opel dealer or diesel injection specialist for testing/repair.

Refitting

11 To refit the pump, hold the correct piece of foam insulator against the cylinder block, engage the pump shaft with the corresponding hole in the timing case, and fit the two retaining nuts. Hand-tighten the nuts at this stage.

12 Refit the pump mounting bracket to the cylinder block, and tighten the bolts to the specified torque. Fit the bolts securing the bracket to the pump, but only hand-tighten the bolts at this stage. Refit the foam insulation pieces around the pump **(see illustration)**.

Note: Reconnect the wiring plug to the PROM (Programmable read-only memory) on the side of the pump before fitting the rearmost foam insulation piece.

13 Refit the fuel injection pump sprocket and the timing belt as described in Chapter 2E.

14 Carry out the injection timing checking and adjustment procedure described in Section 16.

15 The remainder of the procedure is a reversal of the removal procedure, bearing in mind the following points:

  a) *Tighten all fixings to the correct torque setting where specified.*

  b) *Ensure all wiring plugs are securely reconnected, the wiring looms routed as noted on removal, and secured using new cable-ties where necessary.*

  c) *Prime and bleed the fuel system as described in Section 5.*

  d) *Check all fuel connections for leaks.*

15.6 Injection pump ECU bracket

15.8 Injection pump wiring plugs

15.9 Fuel injection pump mounting bracket bolts

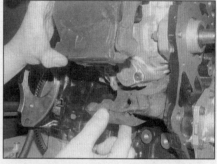

15.12 Refit the foam insulation pieces

16 Injection timing (1.7 litre Y17DT engine) – checking and adjustment

Note: A dial gauge and adapter (Vauxhall/Opel special tool No KM-798) or a suitable alternative will be required for this operation.

1 If not already done so, remove the air cleaner housing and ducting (Section 2), and the upper timing belt cover (Chapter 2E).

2 Undo the unions and remove the fuel injection delivery pipes. We found it necessary to remove the oil cooler housing retaining bolt (Chapter 2E) and push the housing to the rear, to allow sufficient access to the rear of the pump. Be prepared for fluid spillage.

3 With reference to Chapter 2E, Section 3, position the crankshaft at approximately 45° before TDC for No 1 piston.

4 Remove the central bleed screw from the

centre of the four fuel delivery unions at the left-hand end of the injection pump **(see illustration)**.

5 Screw the adapter into the rear of the pump and mount the dial gauge in the adapter **(see illustration)**. Position the dial gauge so that its plunger is at the mid-point of its travel and securely tighten the adapter locknut.

6 Slowly rotate the crankshaft back and forth whilst observing the dial gauge, to determine when the injection pump piston is at the bottom of its travel (BDC). When the piston is correctly positioned, zero the dial gauge.

7 Rotate the crankshaft slowly in the correct direction until the crankshaft pulley mark is correctly aligned with the pointer (No 1 cylinder at TDC on its compression stroke).

8 The reading obtained on the dial gauge should be equal to the specified pump timing measurement given in the Specifications at the start of this Chapter. If adjustment is necessary,

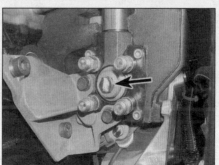

16.4 Remove the central bleed screw

16.5 Screw the adapter into the pump and mount the dial gauge

17.8a Disconnect the wiring connector at the fuel pressure sensor . . .

17.8b . . . and fuel pressure regulator

17.9a Unscrew the union nuts securing the high-pressure fuel pipes to the fuel injectors . . .

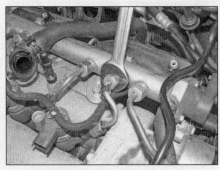

17.9b . . . and the fuel rail

slacken the pump front mounting nuts and rear mounting bolts and slowly rotate the pump body until the point is found where the specified reading is obtained. If the reading is too large turn the pump towards the engine, and if the reading is too small turn the pump away from the engine. When the pump is correctly positioned, tighten both its front and rear mounting nuts and bolts to the specified torque.

9 Rotate the crankshaft through one and three quarter rotations in the normal direction of rotation. Find the injection pump piston BDC as described in paragraph 6 and zero the dial gauge.

10 Rotate the crankshaft slowly in the correct direction of rotation until the crankshaft pulley mark is realigned with the pointer (bringing the engine back to TDC). Recheck the timing measurement.

11 If adjustment is necessary, slacken the pump sprocket bolts and repeat the operations in paragraphs 8 to 10.

12 When the pump timing is correctly set unscrew the adapter and remove the dial gauge.

13 Refit the central bleed screw.

14 Refit the fuel injection pipes, tightening the unions to the specified torque, and refit the oil cooler housing and retaining bolt (if removed).

15 Refit the upper timing belt cover, and air cleaner housing and ducting.

16 On completion, prime and bleed the fuel system as described in Section 5.

17 Fuel rail (1.3 litre engine) – removal and refitting

 Warning: Refer to the information contained in Section 2 before proceeding.

Note: *A complete new set of high-pressure fuel pipes will be required for refitting.*

Removal

1 Disconnect the battery negative terminal (refer to *Disconnecting the battery* in the Reference Chapter).

2 Lift off the plastic cover over the top of the engine.

3 Slacken the retaining clip and detach the flexible air intake duct from the turbocharger charge air pipe **(see illustration 3.2)**.

4 Slacken the retaining clip and disconnect the turbocharger charge air pipe from the turbocharger.

5 Working along the charge air pipe, release the wiring harness retaining clips from the pipe supports and release the fuel hose from the retaining clips.

6 Release the locking clip and disconnect the crankcase breather hose at the quick-release connection on the charge air pipe.

7 Undo the two mounting bolts and remove the charge air pipe from the engine.

8 Disconnect the wiring connectors at the fuel pressure sensor and fuel pressure regulator on the fuel rail **(see illustrations)**.

9 Thoroughly clean all the high-pressure fuel pipe unions on the fuel rail, fuel pump and injectors. Using two spanners, hold the unions and unscrew the union nuts securing the high-pressure fuel pipes to the fuel injectors. Unscrew the union nuts securing the high-pressure fuel pipes to the fuel rail, withdraw the pipes and plug or cover the open unions to prevent dirt entry **(see illustrations)**. It is advisable to label each fuel pipe (1 to 4) to aid identification of the new fuel pipes when refitting.

10 Using an open-ended spanner, unscrew the union nuts securing the high-pressure fuel pipe to the fuel pump and fuel rail. Counterhold the union on the pump with a second spanner, while unscrewing the union nut **(see illustrations)**. Withdraw the high-pressure fuel pipe and plug or cover the open unions to prevent dirt entry.

11 Release the retaining clips and disconnect the fuel return hoses at the fuel rail. Cover the hose ends to prevent dirt entry.

12 Undo the two retaining bolts and lift the fuel rail off the mounting bracket **(see illustrations)**.

17.10a Unscrew the union nuts securing the high-pressure fuel pipe to the fuel pump . . .

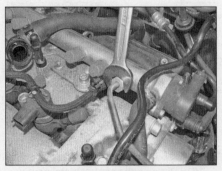

17.10b . . . and fuel rail

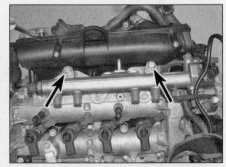

17.12a Undo the two fuel rail retaining bolts (arrowed) . . .

13 If required, the fuel pressure sensor and fuel pressure regulator can be unscrewed from the end of the fuel rail with reference to Section 10. Recover the sealing O-rings from the pressure sensor and pressure regulator.

Refitting

14 If removed, refit the fuel pressure sensor and pressure regulator to the fuel rail using new sealing O-rings lubricated with clean diesel fuel. Tighten the pressure sensor and the pressure regulator to the specified torque.
15 Locate the fuel rail on the mounting bracket, refit the two retaining bolts and tighten them to the specified torque.
16 Refit the fuel return hose and secure with the retaining clip.
17 Working on one fuel injector at a time, remove the blanking plugs from the fuel pipe unions on the fuel rail and the relevant injector. Locate the new high-pressure fuel pipe over the unions and screw on the union nuts finger-tight. Tighten the union nuts to the specified torque using a torque wrench and crow-foot adapter **(see illustration)**. Counterhold the union on the injector with an open-ended spanner, while tightening the union nut. Repeat this operation for the remaining three injectors.
18 Similarly, fit the new high-pressure fuel pipe to the fuel pump and fuel rail, and tighten the union nuts to the specified torque. Counterhold the union on the pump with an open-ended spanner, while tightening the union nut.
19 Reconnect the wiring connectors at the fuel pressure sensor and pressure regulator.
20 Refit the turbocharger charge air pipe and charge air hose.
21 Observing the precautions listed in Section 2, prime the fuel system as described in Section 5, then start the engine and allow it to idle. Check for leaks at the high-pressure fuel pipe unions with the engine idling. If satisfactory, increase the engine speed to 4000 rpm and check again for leaks. If any leaks are detected, obtain and fit a new high-pressure fuel pipe(s).
22 Refit the engine cover on completion.

18 Fuel rail (1.7 litre Z17DTH engine) – removal and refitting

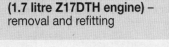

⚠️ **Warning: Refer to the information contained in Section 2 before proceeding.**
Note: *A complete new set of high-pressure fuel pipes will be required for refitting.*

Removal

1 Disconnect the battery negative terminal (refer to *Disconnecting the battery* in the Reference Chapter).
2 Remove the engine oil filler cap, then lift off the plastic cover over the top of the engine. Refit the oil filler cap.
3 Remove the front bumper as described in Chapter 11.

17.12b . . . and lift the fuel rail off the mounting bracket

4 Using cable-ties, string or wire, suitably secure the radiator to the upper crossmember on each side.
5 Undo the two bolts securing the radiator upper mounting brackets to the upper crossmember.
6 Undo the two bolts each side securing the radiator left-hand and right-hand lower mounting brackets to the front subframe. Disengage and remove the brackets from the radiator.
7 Carefully move the radiator forwards to gain access to the charge air pipe connection on the turbocharger. Slacken the retaining clamp and detach the charge air pipe from the turbocharger.
8 Remove the windscreen cowl panel and the bulkhead closure panel as described in Chapter 11.

18.9 Disconnect the rear wiring connector (arrowed) from the engine management ECU

18.11 Charge air pipe front retaining bolt (arrowed)

17.17 Tighten the fuel pipe union nuts using a torque wrench and crow-foot adapter

9 Lift the locking bar and disconnect the rear wiring connector from the engine management electronic control unit **(see illustration)**. Also disconnect the wiring multiplug located behind the ECU, then undo the nut and disconnect the earth lead from the control unit stud.
10 Release the clips and cable-ties securing the wiring harness to the charge air pipe and move the harness to one side **(see illustration)**.
11 Undo the two charge air pipe retaining bolts. One bolt is located adjacent to the crankcase breather hose connection at the front of the camshaft cover and the other bolt is located centrally at the rear of the charge air pipe **(see illustration)**.
12 Release the retaining clip and disconnect the crankcase breather hose at the front of the camshaft cover **(see illustration)**.

18.10 Release the clips and cable-ties (arrowed) securing the wiring harness to the charge air pipe

18.12 Release the retaining clip (arrowed) and disconnect the crankcase breather hose

18.13 Slacken the retaining clip and disconnect the air cleaner intake duct from the charge air pipe

18.17a Release the wiring connector locking catches . . .

18.17b . . . and disconnect the wiring connectors at the fuel injectors

13 Slacken the retaining clip and disconnect the air cleaner intake duct from the charge air pipe **(see illustration)**.
14 Turn the charge air pipe and manipulate it out of position and off the engine.
15 Lift the locking bar and disconnect the remaining wiring connector from the engine management electronic control unit. Undo the two nuts and two bolts and lift the control unit off the mounting bracket.
16 Unscrew the four bolts and remove the electronic control unit mounting bracket from the camshaft cover and support frame, then undo the two bolts and remove the support frame.
17 Release the locking catches securing the wiring connectors to the four fuel injectors then disconnect the injector wiring **(see illustrations)**.
18 Disconnect the wiring connectors from the

changeover flap vacuum actuator and charge (boost) pressure sensor.
19 Disconnect the wiring from the glow plugs by squeezing the connectors with thumb and forefinger, and pulling them from the plugs **(see illustration)**.
20 Release the wiring harness from the clips and cable-ties and move the harness to one side.
21 Undo the two nuts and detach the wiring harness bracket from the rear charge air pipe. Undo the six bolts securing the rear charge air pipe to the throttle housing and inlet manifold. Release the two clips and remove the charge air pipe. Recover the two gaskets **(see illustrations)**.
22 Unscrew the fuel leak-off pipe bracket retaining nut, then unscrew the banjo union bolt and release the fuel leak-off pipe from the fuel rail. Recover the two copper washers

from the banjo union, and suitably cover the end of the pipe and the fuel rail to prevent dirt entry. Note that new copper washers will be required for refitting.
23 Slacken the two retaining clips and remove the oil filter housing oil return hose. Be prepared for oil spillage.
24 Disconnect the two vacuum hoses and six wiring connectors at the solenoid mounting brackets. Unscrew the bolt and detach the earth cable, then unscrew the two nuts and one bolt and remove the solenoid mounting bracket assembly.
25 Thoroughly clean the fuel pipe unions on the fuel injectors and fuel rail. Using an open-ended spanner, unscrew the union nuts securing the high-pressure fuel pipes to the injectors and fuel rail. Withdraw the high-pressure fuel pipes and plug or cover the open unions to prevent dirt entry **(see illustrations)**.

18.19 Squeeze the connectors and disconnect the wiring at the four glow plugs

18.21a Undo the six bolts then remove the rear charge air pipe . . .

18.21b . . . and recover the gaskets

18.25a Unscrew the union nuts securing the high-pressure fuel pipes to the injectors and fuel rail . . .

18.25b . . . withdraw the high-pressure fuel pipes . . .

18.25c . . . and plug or cover the open unions to prevent dirt entry

26 Thoroughly clean the fuel pipe unions on the fuel pump and fuel rail. Using an open-ended spanner, unscrew the union nuts securing the high-pressure fuel pipe to the fuel pump and fuel rail. Counterhold the union on the pump with a second spanner, while unscrewing the union nut. Withdraw the high-pressure fuel pipe and plug or cover the open unions to prevent dirt entry.

27 Unscrew and remove the two fuel rail retaining stud bolts and recover the spacer sleeves. Note the different lengths of the two bolts and the two spacer sleeves. Lift away the fuel rail and remove it from the engine.

Refitting

28 Locate the spacer sleeves and fuel rail in position, refit the two retaining bolts and tighten them securely.

29 Remove the blanking plugs from the fuel pipe unions on the fuel rail and fuel injectors. Locate the new high-pressure fuel pipes over the unions and screw on the union nuts finger-tight. Tighten the union nuts to the specified torque using a torque wrench and crow-foot adapter. Counterhold the union on the injectors with an open-ended spanner, while tightening the union nuts.

30 Similarly, fit a new high-pressure fuel pipe to the fuel pump and fuel rail, and tighten the union nuts to the specified torque. Counterhold the union on the pump with an open-ended spanner, while tightening the union nut.

31 Refit the solenoid mounting brackets and secure with the bolt and two nuts. Refit the earth cable retaining bolt then reconnect the six wiring connectors and two vacuum hoses.

32 Refit the oil filter housing oil return hose and tighten the two retaining clips.

33 Refit the fuel leak-off pipe using new copper washers at the banjo union. Tighten the banjo union to the specified torque, then refit and tighten the pipe bracket retaining nut.

34 Refit the rear charge air pipe and gaskets, then refit and tighten the six retaining bolts. Refit the wiring harness bracket and tighten the two retaining nuts.

35 Reconnect the wiring connectors at the glow plugs, fuel injectors, changeover flap vacuum actuator and charge (boost) pressure sensor. Secure the wiring harness with the clips and cable-ties.

36 Refit the ECU mounting bracket support frame then refit and tighten the two retaining bolts. Refit the mounting bracket to the support frame and secure with the four retaining bolts.

37 Place the ECU on the mounting bracket then refit and tighten the two nuts and two bolts. Reconnect the front wiring connector to the ECU and secure it in position with the locking bar.

38 Locate the upper charge air pipe in position over the turbocharger and secure with the retaining clamp and two bolts. Reconnect the crankcase ventilation hose. Clip the wiring harness and fuel hose back into place on the charge air pipe.

39 Reconnect the air cleaner intake duct to the charge air pipe and secure with the retaining clip.

40 Reconnect the rear wiring connector to the ECU and secure it in position with the locking bar. Position the earth lead on the ECU stud, then refit and tighten the retaining nut.

41 Refit the bulkhead closure panel and windscreen cowl panel as described in Chapter 11.

42 Refit and tighten the two bolts each side securing the radiator lower mounting brackets to the front subframe. Locate the upper mounting brackets in position, then refit and tighten the two retaining bolts.

43 Refit the front bumper as described in Chapter 11.

44 Reconnect the battery negative terminal.

45 Observing the precautions listed in Section 2, prime the fuel system as described in Section 5, then start the engine and allow it to idle. Check for leaks at the high-pressure fuel pipe unions with the engine idling. If satisfactory, increase the engine speed to 4000 rpm and check again for leaks. If any leaks are detected, obtain and fit a new high-pressure fuel pipe(s).

46 Refit the engine cover on completion.

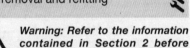

19 Fuel injectors (1.3 litre engine) – removal and refitting

⚠️ **Warning: Refer to the information contained in Section 2 before proceeding.**

Note: *The following procedure describes the removal and refitting of the injectors as a complete set, however the injectors may be removed in pairs if required. A new copper sealing washer, camshaft housing seal and high-pressure fuel pipe will be required for each disturbed injector when refitting.*

Removal

1 Disconnect the battery negative terminal (refer to *Disconnecting the battery* in the Reference Chapter).

2 Lift off the plastic cover over the top of the engine.

3 Slacken the retaining clip and detach the flexible air intake duct from the turbocharger charge air pipe (see illustration 3.2).

4 Slacken the retaining clip and disconnect the turbocharger charge air pipe from the turbocharger.

5 Working along the charge air pipe, release the wiring harness retaining clips from the pipe supports and release the fuel hose from the retaining clips.

6 Release the locking clip and disconnect the crankcase breather hose at the quick-release connection on the charge air pipe.

7 Undo the two mounting bolts and remove the charge air pipe from the engine.

19.9 Unscrew the three bolts (arrowed) securing the wiring harness guide to the camshaft housing

8 Disconnect the wiring connector at the camshaft position sensor on the top of the camshaft housing.

9 Unscrew the three bolts securing the plastic wiring harness guide to the top of the camshaft housing **(see illustration)**.

10 Release the locking catches securing the wiring connectors to the four injectors, then disconnect the injector wiring, while at the same time moving the wiring harness guide forward **(see illustration)**.

11 Thoroughly clean all the high-pressure fuel pipe unions on the fuel rail and injectors.

12 Using two spanners, hold the unions and unscrew the union nuts securing the high-pressure fuel pipes to the fuel injectors. Unscrew the union nuts securing the high-pressure fuel pipes to the fuel rail, withdraw the pipes and plug or cover the open unions to prevent dirt entry **(see illustrations 17.9a and 17.9b)**. It is advisable to label each fuel pipe (1 to 4) to avoid confusion when refitting.

13 Disconnect the fuel leak-off hose connection at each injector by pushing in the locking clip and lifting out the hose fitting. Slip a plastic bag over the disconnected leak-off hose to prevent dirt entry **(see illustrations)**.

14 Unscrew the retaining nut then remove the two washers (where fitted) from the injector clamp brackets **(see illustrations)**. There are two clamp brackets, one securing injectors one and two, and the other securing injectors three and four.

15 Working on one pair of injectors at a time (one and two, or three and four) withdraw the

19.10 Disconnect the injector wiring, while moving the wiring harness guide forward

19.13a Disconnect the fuel leak-off hose connection at each injector . . .

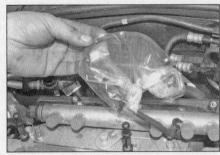

19.13b . . . and slip a plastic bag over the disconnected leak-off hose to prevent dirt entry

19.14a Unscrew the retaining nut . . .

19.14b . . . then remove the upper washer . . .

19.14c . . . and lower washer from the injector clamp brackets

two injectors, together with the clamp bracket, from the camshaft housing and cylinder head. If difficulty is experienced removing the injectors, liberally apply penetrating oil to the base of each injector and allow time for the oil to penetrate. If the injectors are still reluctant to free, it will be necessary to use a small slide hammer engaged under the flange of the injector body casting, and gently tap them free. Note that it is not possible to twist the injectors from side-to-side to free them due to the design of the clamp bracket which positively engages in slots in the injector body (see illustrations).

16 Once the injector pair has been removed, separate them from the clamp bracket and remove the copper washer from each injector (see illustration). The copper washers may have remained in place at the base of the injector orifice in the cylinder head. If so, hook them out with a length of wire. Remove the upper injector seals from the camshaft housing. Label the injectors (1 to 4) so they can be refitted in their original cylinders (unless new injectors are to be fitted).

17 Examine each injector visually for any signs of obvious damage or deterioration. If any defects are apparent, renew the injector(s).

Caution: The injectors are manufactured to extremely close tolerances and must not be dismantled in any way. Do not unscrew the fuel pipe union on the side of the injector, or separate any parts of the injector body. Do not attempt to clean carbon deposits from the injector nozzle or carry out any form of ultrasonic or pressure testing.

18 If the injectors are in a satisfactory condition, plug the fuel pipe union (if not already done) and suitably cover the electrical element and the injector nozzle.

19 Prior to refitting, obtain a new copper washer and camshaft housing seal for each removed injector.

Refitting

20 Locate a new copper washer on the base of each injector, and fit a new seal to the injector location in the camshaft housing.

21 Place the injector clamp bracket in the slot on each injector body and refit the injectors to the cylinder head in pairs. Guide the clamp bracket over the mounting stud as each injector pair is inserted.

22 Fit the two washers (where applicable) and the injector clamp bracket retaining nut to the mounting stud of each injector pair. Tighten the nuts finger-tight only at this stage.

23 Working on one fuel injector at a time, remove the blanking plugs from the fuel pipe unions on the fuel rail and the relevant injector. Locate the high-pressure fuel pipe over the unions and screw on the union nuts. Take care not to cross-thread the nuts or strain the

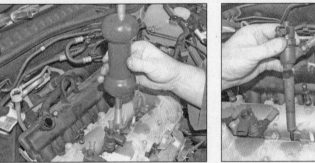

19.15a If necessary, use a slide hammer to free the injectors . . .

19.15b . . . then withdraw the two injectors, together with the clamp bracket

19.15c The clamp bracket engages with slots in the injector body

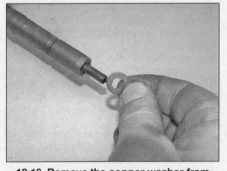

19.16 Remove the copper washer from each injector

fuel pipes as they are fitted. Once the union nut threads have started, tighten the nuts moderately tight only at this stage.

24 When all the fuel pipes are in place, tighten the injector clamp bracket retaining nuts to the specified torque.

25 Tighten the fuel pipe union nuts to the specified torque using a torque wrench and crow-foot adapter **(see illustration 17.17)**. Counterhold the union on the injector with an open-ended spanner, while tightening the union nut. Repeat this operation for the remaining three injectors.

26 Reconnect the fuel leak-off hose fittings to the injectors by pushing in the locking clip, attaching the fitting, then releasing the locking clip. Ensure that each fitting is securely connected and retained by the clip.

27 Reconnect the fuel injector wiring connectors and secure with the locking catches.

28 Refit the three bolts securing the plastic wiring harness guide to the top of the camshaft housing.

29 Reconnect the camshaft position sensor wiring connector.

30 Refit the turbocharger charge air pipe.

31 Observing the precautions listed in Section 2, prime the fuel system as described in Section 5, then start the engine and allow it to idle. Check for leaks at the high-pressure fuel pipe unions with the engine idling. If satisfactory, increase the engine speed to 4000 rpm and check again for leaks. If any leaks are detected, obtain and fit a new high-pressure fuel pipe(s).

32 Refit the engine cover on completion.

20 Fuel injectors (1.7 litre Y17DT engine) – removal and refitting

Removal

1 Remove the camshaft cover as described in Chapter 2E.

2 Undo the five bolts and remove the inner fuel leak-off pipe **(see illustrations)**. Recover the copper washers.

3 Slacken and remove the retaining nuts, and remove the injector clamps **(see illustration)**.

4 Lift the injectors out of the cylinder head. Discard the rubber seals and copper washers, new seals/washers must be fitted prior to reassembly. **Do not** attempt to dismantle the injectors any further.

5 Testing of the injectors requires the use of special equipment. If any injector is thought to be faulty have it tested and, if necessary, reconditioned by a diesel engine specialist or Vauxhall/Opel dealer.

Refitting

6 Commence refitting by ensuring that the injector and cylinder head mating faces are clean, and fitting new copper sealing washers/ rubber seals to each injector. Note the correct

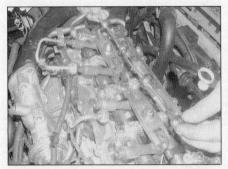

20.2a Copper washers fit either side of the fuel leak-back pipe unions on the injectors . . .

20.3 The injector clamp washer fits with the dished side facing down

orientation of the copper washers **(see illustration)**.

7 Carefully fit each injector into the cylinder head, and secure them in place by fitting the injector clamps. Tighten the clamps retaining nuts to the specified torque.

8 Refit the inner fuel leak-off pipe to the injectors and the camshaft housing. The larger diameter bolt secures the leak-off pipe to the camshaft housing. Note that new copper washers should be fitted to the top of each injector, and the underside of each bolt. Reconnect the pipe to the camshaft housing using new copper washers. Tighten the bolts to the specified torque.

9 Refit the camshaft cover as described in Chapter 2E.

10 Restart the engine and check for leaks.

21 Fuel injectors (1.7 litre Z17DTH engine) – removal and refitting

⚠️ *Warning: Refer to the information contained in Section 2 before proceeding.*

Note: *A new copper washer, O-ring seal and high-pressure fuel pipe will be required for each removed injector when refitting.*

Removal

1 Remove the camshaft cover as described in Chapter 2E.

2 Before removing the injectors it is advisable to mark their fitted position in relation to the camshaft housing. This will ensure that the

20.2b . . . and the union on the camshaft housing

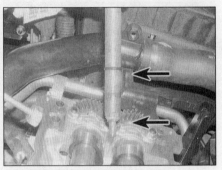

20.6 Note the rubber seal and copper washer

injector extension will fit centrally through the outer seal plates in the camshaft cover and will also prevent any difficulties when screwing on the fuel pipe union nuts. Place a square or similar tool on the camshaft housing and in contact with the injector extension. Using a permanent ink marker pen, mark the position of the edge of the square on the camshaft housing surface **(see illustration)**.

3 Starting with injector No 1, unscrew the retaining bolt then remove the injector clamp bracket **(see illustrations)**.

4 Using pointed-nose pliers, lift out the clamp bracket locating dowel from the camshaft housing **(see illustration)**.

5 Withdraw the injector from the cylinder head, twisting it from side-to-side if it is initially tight.

6 Once the injector has been withdrawn, remove the copper washer from the injector

21.2 Mark the position of the injectors on the camshaft housing surface

21.3a Unscrew the retaining bolt . . .

21.3b . . . and remove the the injector clamp bracket

21.4 Lift out the clamp bracket locating dowel from the camshaft housing

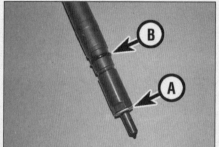

21.6 Remove the copper washer (A) from the injector base and the O-ring seal (B) from the injector body

base and the O-ring seal from the injector body **(see illustration)**. The copper washer may have remained in place at the base of the injector orifice in the cylinder head. If so, hook it out with a length of wire.

7 Remove the remaining injectors in the same way. Label the injectors (1 to 4) so they can be refitted in their original cylinders (unless new injectors are to be fitted).

8 Examine the injector visually for any signs of obvious damage or deterioration. If any defects are apparent, renew the injector.

Caution: The injectors are manufactured to extremely close tolerances and must not be dismantled in any way. Do not unscrew the fuel pipe union on the side of the injector, or separate any parts of the injector body. Do not attempt to clean carbon deposits from the injector nozzle or carry out any form of ultrasonic or pressure testing.

9 If the injectors are in a satisfactory condition, plug the fuel pipe union (if not already done) and suitably cover the electrical element and the injector nozzle.

10 Prior to refitting, obtain a new copper washer, O-ring seal and high-pressure fuel pipe for each injector.

Refitting

11 Thoroughly clean the injector seat in the cylinder head, ensuring all traces of carbon and other deposits are removed.

12 Locate a new O-ring seal on the injector body and a new copper washer on the base of the injector.

13 Place the injector in position in the cylinder head.

14 Refit the clamp bracket locating dowel to the camshaft housing, then engage the clamp bracket over the injector. Refit the clamp bracket retaining bolt finger-tight only at this stage.

15 Using the square, align the injector with the marks made on the camshaft housing during removal. To be absolutely sure that the injector is correctly aligned, temporarily refit the high-pressure fuel pipe to the injector and fuel rail and lightly tighten the union nuts.

16 Tighten the clamp bracket retaining bolt to the specified torque in the three stages given in the specifications. Remove the high-pressure fuel pipe.

17 Repeat this procedure for the remaining injectors.

18 Once all the injectors are installed, refit the camshaft cover as described in Chapter 2E.

19 Observing the precautions listed in Section 2, prime the fuel system as described in Section 5, then start the engine and allow it to idle. Check for leaks at the high-pressure fuel pipe unions with the engine idling. If satisfactory, increase the engine speed to 4000 rpm and check again for leaks. If any leaks are detected, obtain and fit a new high-pressure fuel pipe(s).

20 Refit the engine cover on completion.

22 Inlet manifold (1.3 litre engine) – removal and refitting

Removal

1 Disconnect the battery negative terminal (refer to *Disconnecting the battery* in the Reference Chapter).

2 Lift off the plastic cover over the top of the engine.

3 Remove the windscreen cowl panel and the bulkhead closure panel as described in Chapter 11.

4 Slacken the two retaining clips and disconnect the turbocharger charge air pipe from the flexible upper intake duct and turbocharger **(see illustration 13.3)**.

5 Working along the charge air pipe, release the wiring harness retaining clips from the pipe supports and release the fuel hose from the retaining clips.

6 Release the locking clip and disconnect the crankcase breather hose at the quick-release connection on the charge air pipe.

7 Undo the two mounting bolts and remove the charge air pipe from the engine.

8 Remove the exhaust gas recirculation (EGR) valve as described in Chapter 4C.

9 Withdraw the engine oil dipstick, then undo the retaining bolt securing the dipstick guide tube to the inlet manifold.

10 Disconnect the wiring connector at the charge (boost) pressure sensor.

11 Undo the retaining bolt and detach the crankcase ventilation hose attachment at the timing cover **(see illustration)**.

12 Undo the two retaining bolts and free the crankcase ventilation system oil separator from the inlet manifold **(see illustration)**.

13 Release the retaining spring clips, and disconnect both coolant hoses from the heater matrix unions.

22.11 Undo the retaining bolt and detach the crankcase ventilation hose attachment

22.12 Undo the two bolts (arrowed) and free the oil separator from the inlet manifold

14 Undo the retaining bolt and detach the wiring harness support bracket around the starter motor.

15 Undo the nine retaining bolts (noting their different lengths) and remove the inlet manifold from the cylinder head. Remove the rubber gasket from the manifold flange **(see illustrations)**.

Refitting

16 Thoroughly clean the inlet manifold and cylinder head mating faces, then locate a new rubber gasket on the inlet manifold flange.

17 Locate the manifold in position and refit the retaining bolts. Diagonally and progressively, tighten the bolts to the specified torque.

18 Refit the retaining bolt and secure the wiring harness support bracket.

19 Reconnect the coolant hoses to the heater matrix unions.

20 Refit the crankcase ventilation system oil separator to the inlet manifold.

21 Refit the crankcase ventilation hose attachment to the timing cover and secure with the retaining bolt, securely tightened.

22 Refit the wiring connector to the charge (boost) pressure sensor.

23 Refit and tighten the bolt securing the oil dipstick guide tube to the manifold, then re-insert the dipstick.

24 Refit the exhaust gas recirculation (EGR) valve as described in Chapter 4C.

25 Refit the turbocharger charge air pipe.

26 Refit the bulkhead closure panel and the windscreen cowl panel as described in Chapter 11.

27 Reconnect the battery, refit the engine cover, then refill the cooling system as described in Chapter 1B.

23 Inlet manifold (1.7 litre Y17DT engine) – removal and refitting

Note: *New manifold retaining nuts will be required on refitting*

Removal

1 Disconnect the battery negative terminal (refer to *Disconnecting the battery* in the Reference Chapter).

2 Remove the air cleaner assembly and intake duct as described in Section 3.

3 Remove the engine management electronic control unit as described in Section 11.

4 Slacken the retaining clips securing the charge air pipe to the turbocharger.

5 Release the retaining clip and disconnect the crankcase ventilation hose from the camshaft cover.

6 Undo the two charge air pipe retaining bolts, disengage the pipe from the turbocharger, then remove the pipe from the top of the engine.

7 Unclip the wiring loom cable-tie, undo the retaining screws/nut and remove the engine management electronic control unit bracket.

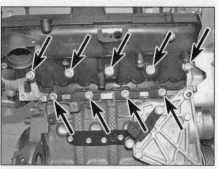

22.15a Undo the retaining bolts (arrowed) and remove the inlet manifold . . .

8 Undo the two nuts and remove the control unit bracket support frame.

9 Disconnect the wiring from the glow plugs by squeezing the connectors with thumb and forefinger, and pulling them from the plugs.

10 Undo the bolts/nuts securing the rear charge air pipe to the inlet manifold and intercooler charge air pipe. Unclip the wiring harness and remove the charge air pipe. Recover the two gaskets.

11 Undo the unions and remove the fuel injection delivery pipes. We found it necessary to remove the oil cooler housing retaining bolt and push the housing to the rear, to allow sufficient access to the rear of the pump. Be prepared for oil spillage. Due to the high injection pressures, under no circumstances should the pipes be bent.

12 Unscrew the outer fuel leak-off pipe banjo union bolt and release the fuel leak-off pipe. Recover the two copper washers from the banjo union, and suitably cover the end of the pipe and the fuel rail to prevent dirt entry. Note that new copper washers will be required for refitting. Slacken the leak-off hose retaining clip, unscrew the leak-off pipe retaining bolt and remove the leak-off pipe.

13 Disconnect the wiring plug from the charge (boost) pressure sensor on the right-hand end of the inlet manifold. Undo the retaining bolts and remove the sensor.

14 Undo the retaining bolt and remove the right-hand rear engine lifting bracket.

15 Disconnect the three wiring harness connectors from the fuel injection pump.

16 Unscrew the fastening nuts and bolts, and

23.16a Remove the rear section of the manifold . . .

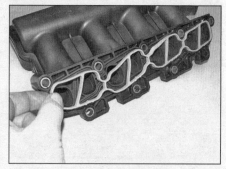

22.15b . . . then remove the rubber gasket from the manifold flange

remove the inlet manifold rear section and, if necessary, front section **(see illustrations)**.

Refitting

17 Clean the cylinder head and manifold(s) gasket faces, and fit a new gasket(s) in place.

18 The remainder of the refitting procedure is a reversal of removal, noting the following points:

a) *Tighten all nuts and bolts to the specified torque (where given).*

b) *Tighten the injector pipe unions to the specified torque, and check them for leaks after starting the engine.*

24 Inlet manifold (1.7 litre Z17DTH engine) – removal and refitting

Removal

1 Remove the fuel rail as described in Section 18.

2 Undo the seven bolts and two nuts, then remove the inlet manifold from the cylinder head. Recover the gasket.

3 The changeover flap housing can be removed by extracting the circlip and disconnecting the vacuum unit lever from changeover flap linkage. Undo the three bolts and separate the housing from the inlet manifold.

Refitting

4 Thoroughly clean the inlet manifold, cylinder head and, where applicable, the changeover flap housing mating faces.

23.16b . . . and the front section

26.4 Undo the two bolts (arrowed) securing the coolant pipe to the heat exchanger

5 If removed, apply sealant to the changeover flap housing and locate the housing on the manifold. Refit the three bolts and tighten securely. Reconnect the vacuum unit lever to changeover flap linkage.
6 Place a new gasket on the inlet manifold flange, then position the manifold over the cylinder head studs.
7 Refit the retaining bolts and nuts, then diagonally and progressively, tighten the bolts and nuts to the specified torque.
8 Refit the fuel rail as described in Section 18.

25 Intercooler – removal and refitting

Removal

1.3 litre and 1.7 litre Z17DTH engines

1 Remove the front bumper as described in Chapter 11.
2 Slacken the retaining clips and disconnect the two charge air hoses from the intercooler.
3 Undo the two retaining bolts and detach the intercooler from the radiator.

1.7 litre Y17DT engines

4 Remove the radiator as described in Chapter 3.
5 Unclip the intercooler from the fan housing and lift it upward out of the guide to remove.

Refitting

6 Refitting is the reverse of removal.

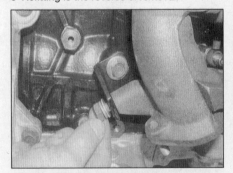

27.11 Unbolt the turbocharger from the cylinder block mounting bracket

26.7 Locate a new gasket over the heat exchanger coolant pipe and bend over the tabs to retain it on the flange

26 Exhaust manifold (1.3 litre engine) – removal and refitting

Removal

1 Remove the turbocharger as described in Section 30.
2 Remove the battery and battery tray as described in Chapter 5A.
3 Release the retaining clamp, undo the four bolts and remove the charge air pipe from the inlet manifold.
4 Undo the two bolts securing the coolant pipe to the heat exchanger on the oil filter housing **(see illustration)**. Release the retaining clip securing the other end of the pipe to the hose on the thermostat housing. Undo the pipe support bracket bolt, release the wiring harness from the retaining clip and remove the coolant pipe from the engine. Recover the gasket noting that a new one will be required for refitting.
5 Undo the ten nuts securing the exhaust manifold to the cylinder head. Withdraw the manifold from the cylinder head studs and remove it from the engine. Recover the manifold gasket, noting that a new gasket and new manifold retaining nuts will be required for refitting.

Refitting

6 Thoroughly clean the mating faces of the exhaust manifold then locate the exhaust manifold over the cylinder head studs. Secure

27.12 Disconnect the oil return hose

with the new nuts tightened progressively to the specified torque.
7 Locate a new gasket over the heat exchanger coolant pipe and bend over the tabs of the gasket to retain it on the flange **(see illustration)**.
8 Engage the coolant pipe with the hose on the thermostat housing, then position the pipe flange on the heat exchanger. Refit the two bolts and tighten them to the specified torque. At the other end of the pipe, tighten the hose retaining clip, refit and tighten the pipe support bracket bolt and secure the wiring harness with the retaining clip.
9 Refit the charge air pipe and secure with the four bolts and retaining clamp.
10 Refit the battery and battery tray as described in Chapter 5A.
11 Refit the turbocharger as described in Section 30.

27 Exhaust manifold (1.7 litre Y17DT engine) – removal and refitting

Note: *New exhaust manifold nuts and bolts, new gaskets for all disturbed joints, and new copper washers for the turbocharger oil supply pipe unions will be required for refitting.*

Removal

1 The exhaust manifold is removed together with the turbocharger.
2 On models equipped with air conditioning, have the refrigerant discharged at a dealer service department or an automotive air conditioning repair facility.
3 Firmly apply the handbrake, then jack up the front of the vehicle and support it securely on axle stands (see *Jacking and vehicle support*).
4 Disconnect the battery negative terminal (refer to *Disconnecting the battery* in the Reference Chapter).
5 Drain the cooling system as described in Chapter 1B.
6 Remove the front bumper as described in Chapter 11.
7 Remove the air cleaner assembly and intake duct as described in Section 3.
8 On models equipped with air conditioning, remove the compressor as described in Chapter 3.
9 Undo the three bolts and remove the air conditioning compressor mounting bracket.
10 Undo the two nuts and free the exhaust system front pipe from the turbocharger. While doing this, take care to support the flexible section. **Note:** *Angular movement in excess of 10° can cause permanent damage to the flexible section.* Recover the front pipe-to-turbocharger gasket.
11 Unscrew the bolt securing the turbocharger to the cylinder block mounting bracket **(see illustration)**.
12 Release the retaining clips and disconnect the oil return hose from the turbocharger **(see illustration)**.

27.13 Remove the oil feed pipe from the cylinder block

27.24 Remove the oil dipstick guide tube mounting bolt

27.25 Wastegate actuator vacuum pipe

13 Slacken and remove the turbocharger oil feed pipe nut from the cylinder block. Recover the copper sealing washers and be prepared for oil spillage **(see illustration)**.

14 Release the retaining clips and remove the turbocharger-to-intercooler charge air hose.

15 Unscrew the two bolts and release the coolant distribution pipe.

16 Disconnect the wiring connectors at the engine management electronic control unit, then disconnect the additional connector located behind the control unit. Release the wiring harness from the clips and cable-ties.

17 Slacken the retaining clips securing the charge air pipe to the turbocharger.

18 Release the retaining clip and disconnect the crankcase ventilation hose from the camshaft cover.

19 Undo the two charge air pipe retaining bolts, disengage the pipe from the turbo-charger, then remove the pipe from the top of the engine.

20 Undo the four flange bolts and one retaining bracket bolt and remove the EGR pipe from the manifold and EGR valve. Recover the two gaskets.

21 Undo the retaining bolt and remove the left-hand engine lifting bracket.

22 Undo the four retaining bolts and remove the exhaust manifold heat shield.

23 Unscrew the banjo union bolt and release the turbocharger oil supply pipe from the turbocharger. Recover the two copper washers from the banjo union, and suitably cover the end of the pipe to prevent dirt entry. Note that new copper washers will be required for refitting.

24 Unscrew the bolts securing the oil dipstick guide tube bracket to the cylinder block, and the two bolts securing the guide tube to the sump **(see illustration)**.

25 Disconnect the vacuum hose from the turbocharger wastegate actuator **(see illustration)**.

26 Undo the exhaust manifold retaining nuts/bolts, unscrew and remove the two manifold studs, and remove the exhaust manifold from above.

27 If required, the manifold can now be separated from the turbocharger as described in Section 30.

Refitting

28 Refitting is the reverse of removal, noting the following points.

a) *Ensure all mating surfaces are clean and dry and renew all gaskets/sealing washers.*

b) *Tighten the manifold nuts and bolts to their specified torque settings.*

c) *On models equipped with air conditioning, refit the compressor as described in Chapter 3.*

d) *Refit the front bumper as described in Chapter 11.*

e) *Refill the cooling system as described in Chapter 1B.*

f) *On starting the engine for the first time, allow the engine to idle for a few minutes before increasing the engine speed; this will allow oil to be circulated around the turbocharger bearings.*

g) *On models equipped with air conditioning, have the system evacuated, charged and leak-tested by the specialist that discharged it.*

28 Exhaust manifold (1.7 litre Z17DTH engine) – removal and refitting

Note: *New gaskets for all disturbed joints, and new copper washers for the turbocharger oil supply pipe unions will be required for refitting.*

Removal

1 Disconnect the battery negative terminal

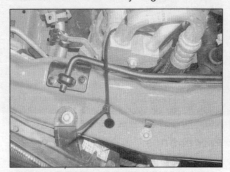

28.8a Tie the compressor to the slam panel . . .

(refer to *Disconnecting the battery* in the Reference Chapter).

2 Remove the plastic cover from the top of the engine.

3 Remove the air cleaner assembly and intake duct as described in Section 3.

4 Remove the radiator as described in Chapter 3.

5 Drain the cooling system and the engine oil as described in Chapter 1B.

6 Remove the complete exhaust system as described in Section 31.

7 On models equipped with air conditioning, remove the auxiliary drivebelt as described in Chapter 1B.

8 On models equipped with air conditioning, release the refrigerant hoses from the retaining clip on the right-hand side inner wing. Without undoing the refrigerant pipes, disconnect the wiring plug, unbolt the air conditioning compressor from its support bracket (3 bolts), and position it clear of the engine. Use a cable-tie or similar to tie the compressor to the upper front crossmember. Undo the three bolts and remove the air conditioning compressor support bracket **(see illustrations)**.

9 Slacken the retaining clamp and detach the charge air pipe from the turbocharger.

10 Lift the locking bar and disconnect the rear wiring connector from the engine management electronic control unit **(see illustration 18.9)**. Also disconnect the wiring multiplug located behind the ECU, then undo the nut and disconnect the earth lead from the control unit stud.

28.8b . . . and remove the compressor mounting bracket

11 Release the clips and cable-ties securing the wiring harness to the charge air pipe and move the harness to one side **(see illustration 18.10)**.

12 Undo the two charge air pipe retaining bolts. One bolt is located adjacent to the crankcase breather hose connection at the front of the camshaft cover and the other bolt is located centrally at the rear of the charge air pipe **(see illustration 18.11)**.

13 Release the retaining clip and disconnect the crankcase breather hose at the front of the camshaft cover **(see illustration 18.12)**.

14 Turn the charge air pipe and manipulate it out of position and off the engine.

15 Slacken the retaining clips and disconnect the charge air hose from the intercooler and throttle housing.

16 Slacken the retaining clips and disconnect the charge air hose from the turbocharger and intercooler.

17 Disconnect the vacuum pipes for the EGR solenoid valve and brake servo from the vacuum pump on the rear of the alternator.

18 Unscrew the bolts securing the oil dipstick guide tube bracket to the cylinder block, and the two bolts securing the guide tube to the sump. Remove the guide tube.

19 Release the retaining clips and disconnect the upper and lower coolant hoses from the EGR valve heat exchanger. Undo the two bolts at each end of the metal EGR pipe, securing the pipe flanges to the exhaust manifold and EGR valve housing. Undo the retaining bolts and remove the EGR valve heat exchanger/pipe assembly from the engine. Collect the two flange gaskets.

20 Unscrew the four bolts and remove the exhaust manifold heat shield.

21 Undo the two bolts securing the base of the catalytic converter to the support bracket.

22 Release the two retaining clips and remove the turbocharger oil return hose.

23 Disconnect the vacuum hose from the turbocharger wastegate actuator.

24 Unscrew the banjo union bolt and release the turbocharger oil supply pipe from the turbocharger. Recover the two copper washers from the banjo union, and suitably cover the end of the pipe to prevent dirt entry. Note that new copper washers will be required for refitting.

25 Undo the two bolts and seven nuts securing the exhaust manifold to the cylinder head. Withdraw the manifold from the cylinder head studs and remove it, complete with turbocharger and catalytic converter, from the engine. Recover the manifold gasket.

26 If required, the catalytic converter and turbocharger can now be removed from the manifold as described in Section 30.

Refitting

27 Refitting is the reverse of removal, noting the following points.

 a) *If removed, refit the turbocharger and catalytic converter to the manifold as described in Section 30.*

 b) *Ensure all mating surfaces are clean and dry and renew all gaskets, seals and copper washers.*

 c) *Tighten the manifold nuts and bolts evenly and progressively to the specified torque, working in a diagonal sequence.*

 d) *Tighten all other retaining nuts and bolts to the specified torque (where given).*

 e) *Refit the exhaust system as described in Section 31.*

 f) *On models with air conditioning, refit the auxiliary drivebelt as described in Chapter 1B.*

 g) *Refit the radiator as described in Chapter 3.*

 h) *On completion refill the cooling system and refill the engine with fresh oil as described in Chapter 1B.*

 i) *On starting the engine for the first time, allow the engine to idle for a few minutes before increasing the engine speed; this will allow oil to be circulated around the turbocharger bearings.*

29 Turbocharger – description and precautions

Description

1 The turbocharger increases engine efficiency by raising the pressure in the inlet manifold above atmospheric pressure. Instead of the air simply being sucked into the cylinders, it is forced in.

2 Energy for the operation of the turbocharger comes from the exhaust gas. The gas flows through a specially-shaped housing (the turbine housing) and, in so doing, spins the turbine wheel. The turbine wheel is attached to a shaft, at the end of which is another vaned wheel known as the compressor wheel. The compressor wheel spins in its own housing, and compresses the inlet air on the way to the inlet manifold.

3 On 1.3 litre and 1.7 litre Z17DTH engines, the turbocharger operates on the principle of variable vane geometry. At low engine speeds the vanes close to give less flow cross-section, then as the speed increases the vanes open to give an increased flow cross-section. This helps improve the efficiency of the turbocharger.

4 Boost pressure (the pressure in the inlet manifold) is limited by a wastegate, which diverts the exhaust gas away from the turbine wheel in response to a pressure-sensitive actuator.

5 The turbo shaft is pressure-lubricated by an oil feed pipe from the main oil gallery. The shaft 'floats' on a cushion of oil. A drain pipe returns the oil to the sump.

Precautions

6 The turbocharger operates at extremely high speeds and temperatures. Certain precautions must be observed, to avoid premature failure of the turbo, or injury to the operator.

7 Do not operate the turbo with any of its parts exposed, or with any of its hoses removed. Foreign objects falling onto the rotating vanes could cause excessive damage, and (if ejected) personal injury.

8 Do not race the engine immediately after start-up, especially if it is cold. Give the oil a few seconds to circulate.

9 Always allow the engine to return to idle speed before switching it off – do not blip the throttle and switch off, as this will leave the turbo spinning without lubrication.

10 Allow the engine to idle for several minutes before switching off after a high-speed run.

11 Observe the recommended intervals for oil and filter changing, and use a reputable oil of the specified quality. Neglect of oil changing, or use of inferior oil, can cause carbon formation on the turbo shaft, leading to subsequent failure.

30 Turbocharger – removal and refitting

1.3 litre engines

Removal

1 Disconnect the battery negative terminal (refer to *Disconnecting the battery* in the Reference Chapter).

2 Lift off the plastic cover over the top of the engine.

3 Drain the cooling system as described in Chapter 1B.

4 Remove the complete exhaust system as described in Section 31.

5 Release the retaining clips, undo the two nuts and remove the charge air hose and pipe assembly from the turbocharger and intercooler.

6 Slacken the two retaining clips and disconnect the turbocharger charge air pipe from the flexible upper intake duct and turbocharger.

7 Working along the charge air pipe, release the wiring harness retaining clips from the pipe supports and release the fuel hose from the retaining clips.

8 Release the locking clip and disconnect the crankcase breather hose at the quick-release connection on the charge air pipe.

9 Undo the two mounting bolts and remove the charge air pipe from the engine.

10 Disconnect the wiring from the glow plugs by squeezing the connectors with thumb and forefinger, and pulling them from the plugs.

11 Disconnect the wiring connector at the oil pressure warning light switch at the front left-hand end of the cylinder head.

12 Undo the upper nut and two lower bolts, and remove the oil filter heat shield **(see illustration)**.

13 Undo the bolt securing the engine lifting bracket to the exhaust manifold, and the central nut securing the heat shield to the manifold **(see illustration)**. Remove the lifting

30.12 Undo nut and two bolts (arrowed), and remove the oil filter heat shield

30.13 Engine lifting bracket retaining bolt (A) and heat shield centre retaining nut (B)

bracket, then manipulate the heat shield off the manifold.

14 Unscrew the two banjo union bolts and disconnect the turbocharger oil supply pipe from the oil filter housing and turbocharger **(see illustration)**. Recover the two copper washers from each banjo union, and suitably cover the ends of the pipe to prevent dirt entry. Note that new copper washers will be required for refitting.

15 Slacken the retaining clip and disconnect the radiator bottom hose from the outlet at the base of the oil filter housing.

16 Undo the two bolts securing the coolant pipe to the heat exchanger on the oil filter housing **(see illustration)**. Release the retaining clip securing the other end of the pipe to the hose on the thermostat housing. Undo the pipe support bracket bolt, release the wiring harness from the retaining clip and remove the coolant pipe from the engine. Recover the gasket noting that a new one will be required for refitting.

17 Undo the four bolts and remove the oil filter housing and heat exchanger assembly from the cylinder block. Recover the rubber seal from the rear of the housing. Note that a new seal will be required for refitting.

18 Bend back the locking plate tabs and unscrew the three bolts securing the catalytic converter flange to the turbocharger. Remove the bolts and locking plate, noting that a new

locking plate will be required for refitting.

19 From under the car, undo the bolt securing the catalytic converter support bracket to the sump reinforcement bracket.

20 Separate the catalytic converter from the turbocharger and recover the gasket. Note that a new gasket will be required for refitting.

21 Undo the four bolts securing the turbocharger oil return pipe to the cylinder block and turbocharger. Disconnect the vacuum hose from the turbocharger waste gate actuator.

22 Undo the three retaining nuts and remove the turbocharger from the exhaust manifold.

Inspection

23 With the turbocharger removed, inspect the housing for cracks or other visible damage.

24 Spin the turbine or the compressor wheel, to verify that the shaft is intact and to feel for excessive shake or roughness. Some play is normal, since in use, the shaft is 'floating' on a film of oil. Check that the wheel vanes are undamaged.

25 If oil contamination of the exhaust or induction passages is apparent, it is likely that turbo shaft oil seals have failed.

26 No DIY repair of the turbo is possible and none of the internal or external parts are available separately. If the turbocharger is suspect in any way a complete new unit must be obtained.

Refitting

27 Refitting is the reverse of removal, noting the following points.

a) Thoroughly clean the turbocharger and exhaust manifold mating faces.

b) Ensure all mating surfaces are clean and dry and renew all gaskets, seals and copper washers.

c) Tighten all retaining nuts and bolts to the specified torque (where given).

d) Refit the exhaust system as described in Section 31.

e) On completion refill the cooling system as described in Chapter 1B.

f) On starting the engine for the first time, allow the engine to idle for a few minutes before increasing the engine speed; this will allow oil to be circulated around the turbocharger bearings.

1.7 litre Y17DT engines

Removal

28 Remove the exhaust manifold as described in Section 27.

29 With the assembly on the bench, undo the bolt and remove the turbocharger heat shield.

30 Undo the retaining nuts and remove the exhaust connection flange and gasket from the turbocharger **(see illustration)**.

31 Undo the union nut and remove the oil

30.14 Unscrew the turbocharger oil supply pipe banjo union bolt (arrowed) from the oil filter housing

30.16 Undo the two bolts (arrowed) securing the coolant pipe to the heat exchanger

30.30 Exhaust flange connection nuts

30.31 Turbocharger oil feed pipe union

30.32 Turbocharger oil return union

30.34 Undo the nuts and separate the turbocharger from the exhaust manifold

feed pipe along with the sealing washers which are fitted on each side of the pipe union **(see illustration)**.

32 Unscrew the retaining bolts and remove the oil return pipe union and gasket **(see illustration)**.

33 Undo the two bolts, detach the retaining clamp and remove the wastegate unit.

34 Slacken and remove the four mounting nuts then remove the turbocharger and gasket from the manifold **(see illustration)**.

Inspection

35 Refer to the information contained in paragraphs 23 to 26.

Refitting

36 Refitting is the reverse of removal, noting the following points.
   a) *Thoroughly clean the turbocharger and exhaust manifold mating faces.*
   b) *Ensure all mating surfaces are clean and dry and renew all gaskets, seals and copper washers.*
   c) *Tighten all retaining nuts and bolts to the specified torque (where given).*
   d) *Refit the exhaust manifold as described in Section 27.*

1.7 litre Z17DTH engines

Note: *New turbocharger-to-manifold retaining nuts will be required for refitting.*

Removal

37 Remove the exhaust manifold as described in Section 28.

31.8 Undo the union nuts (arrowed) and detach the particulate filter temperature sensor and the differential pressure sensor from the front pipe

38 Undo the three bolts and remove the heat shield from the catalytic converter.

39 Undo the three bolts and separate the catalytic converter from the turbocharger. Recover the gasket.

40 Unscrew the retaining bolts and remove the oil return pipe union and gasket.

41 Undo the three nuts and remove the turbocharger from the exhaust manifold. Recover the gasket.

Inspection

42 Refer to the information contained in paragraphs 23 to 26.

Refitting

43 Refitting is the reverse of removal, noting the following points.
   a) *Thoroughly clean the turbocharger and exhaust manifold mating faces.*
   b) *Ensure all mating surfaces are clean and dry and renew all gaskets and seals.*
   c) *Tighten all retaining nuts and bolts to the specified torque (where given).*
   d) *Refit the exhaust manifold as described in Section 28.*

---

31 Exhaust system –
general information,
removal and refitting

General information

1 On 1.3 litre models, a three section exhaust system is used. The front section comprises

31.9 Undo the two nuts (arrowed) securing the rubber mountings to the front pipe bracket

the front pipe, the centre section contains the intermediate pipe and diesel particulate filter and the rear section consists of the tailpipe and silencer. A primary catalytic converter is fitted between the exhaust manifold and front pipe.

2 On 1.7 litre models, the exhaust system is in two sections. The front section comprises the front pipe incorporating an auxiliary catalytic converter and the rear section consists of the tailpipe and silencer. A primary catalytic converter is fitted between the exhaust manifold and front pipe on Z17DTH engines.

3 The front pipe is fitted with a flexible section to allow for exhaust system movement and the system is suspended throughout its entire length by rubber mountings.

4 Periodically, the exhaust system should be checked for signs of leaks or damage. Also inspect the system rubber mountings, and renew if necessary.

5 Small holes or cracks can be repaired using proprietary exhaust repair products.

6 Before renewing an individual section of the exhaust system, it is wise to inspect the remaining section(s). If corrosion or damage is evident, it may prove more economical to renew the entire system.

Removal – 1.3 litre models

Front pipe

7 Firmly apply the handbrake, then jack up the front of the vehicle and support it securely on axle stands (see *Jacking and vehicle support*).

8 Undo the two union nuts and detach the particulate filter temperature sensor and the differential pressure sensor from the front pipe **(see illustration)**.

9 Undo the two nuts securing the rubber mountings to the front pipe bracket **(see illustration)**.

10 Suitably support the intermediate pipe, then undo the three nuts and separate the front pipe flange from the intermediate pipe flange.

11 Loosen the clamp securing the exhaust front pipe to the catalytic converter and slide the front pipe from the catalytic converter **(see illustration)**. While doing this, take care to support the flexible section. **Note:** *Angular movement in excess of 10° can cause permanent damage to the flexible section.*

31.11 Removing the exhaust system front pipe from the catalytic converter

If the front pipe is rusted onto the catalytic converter, apply liberal amounts of penetrating oil and tap around the joint with a hammer to free it. Twist the front pipe in both directions until free.

Intermediate pipe

12 Jack up the front and rear of the vehicle and support it on axle stands (see *Jacking and vehicle support*). Remove the tailpipe as described in paragraphs 15 and 16.
13 Undo the three nuts and separate the front pipe flange from the intermediate pipe flange.
14 Release the rubber mountings and remove the intermediate pipe from under the car.

Tailpipe

15 Chock the front wheels then jack up the rear of the vehicle and support on axle stands (see *Jacking and vehicle support*).
16 Loosen the clamp securing the intermediate pipe to the tailpipe, then release the rubber mountings and slide the tailpipe from the intermediate pipe **(see illustration)**. If the tailpipe is rusted onto the intermediate pipe, apply liberal amounts of penetrating oil and tap around the joint with a hammer to free it. Twist the tailpipe in both directions while holding the intermediate pipe.

Primary catalytic converter

17 Refer to Section 30, paragraphs 1 to 20.

Heat shield(s)

18 The heat shields are secured to the underside of the body by various nuts and bolts. Each shield can be removed once the relevant exhaust section has been removed. If a shield is being removed to gain access to a component located behind it, it may prove sufficient in some cases to remove the retaining nuts and/or bolts, and simply lower the shield, without disturbing the exhaust system.

Removal – 1.7 litre models

Front pipe

19 Jack up the front and rear of the vehicle and support it on axle stands (see *Jacking and vehicle support*).
20 Remove the tailpipe as described in paragraphs 23 and 24.
21 Undo the nuts securing the front pipe to the catalytic converter or turbocharger, then free the front pipe and recover the gasket. While doing this, take care to support the flexible section. **Note:** *Angular movement in excess of 10° can cause permanent damage to the flexible section.*
22 Release the rubber mountings and remove the front pipe from the car.

Tailpipe

23 Chock the front wheels then jack up the rear of the vehicle and support it on axle stands (see *Jacking and vehicle support*).
24 Loosen the clamp securing the front pipe to the tailpipe, then release the rubber mountings and slide the tailpipe from the front pipe **(see illustration 31.16)**. If the tailpipe is rusted onto the front pipe, apply liberal amounts of penetrating oil and tap around the joint with a hammer to free it. Twist the tailpipe in both directions while holding the front pipe.

31.16 Loosen the clamp (arrowed), release the rubber mountings and slide the tailpipe from the intermediate pipe

Primary catalytic converter (Z17DTH engines)

25 Refer to Section 30, paragraphs 37 to 39.

Heat shield(s)

26 Refer to paragraph 18.

Refitting – all models

27 Each section is refitted by reversing the removal sequence, noting the following points:
a) Ensure that all traces of corrosion have been removed from the system joints.
b) When refitting the primary catalytic converter, refer to the Sections indicated in the removal procedures and follow the relevant refitting procedures.
c) When refitting the front pipe to the catalytic converter flange joint, use a new gasket and new retaining nuts, and tighten the nuts to the specified torque.
d) Inspect the rubber mountings for signs of damage or deterioration, and renew as necessary.
e) Prior to tightening the exhaust system fasteners, ensure that all rubber mountings are correctly located, and that there is adequate clearance between the exhaust system and vehicle underbody.

Chapter 4 Part C:
Emission control systems

Contents

Degrees of difficulty

Easy, suitable for novice with little experience	**Fairly easy,** suitable for beginner with some experience	**Fairly difficult,** suitable for competent DIY mechanic	**Difficult,** suitable for experienced DIY mechanic	**Very difficult,** suitable for expert DIY or professional

Specifications

Torque wrench settings	Nm	lbf ft
1.4 litre petrol engines		
Oxygen sensors	40	30
1.6 litre petrol engines		
Z16SE and Z16XE:		
Oxygen sensors	30	22
Z16XEP:		
Oxygen sensors	40	30
1.8 litre petrol engines		
Oxygen sensors	30	22
1.3 litre diesel engines		
EGR valve heat exchanger to EGR valve	25	18
EGR valve mounting bolts	22	16
1.7 litre Y17DT diesel engines		
EGR valve housing mounting bolts	20	15
Rear charge air pipe retaining bolts	25	18
1.7 litre Z17DTH diesel engines		
EGR valve heat exchanger pipe flange bolts	28	21
EGR valve housing mounting bolts	25	18
Rear charge air pipe to throttle housing and manifold	25	18

1 General information and precautions

1 All petrol engine models use unleaded petrol and also have various other features built into the fuel/exhaust system to help minimise harmful emissions. All models are equipped with a crankcase emission control system, a catalytic converter, an exhaust gas recirculation (EGR) system and an evaporative emission control system to keep fuel vapour/exhaust gas emissions down to a minimum.

2 Diesel engine models are also designed to meet strict emission requirements. A crankcase emission control system, a catalytic converter and on 1.3 litre engines, a diesel particulate filter are fitted to keep exhaust emissions down to a minimum. An exhaust gas recirculation (EGR) system is also used to further decrease exhaust emissions.

3 The emission control systems function as follows.

Petrol engines

Crankcase emission control

4 To reduce the emission of unburned hydro-carbons from the crankcase into the atmosphere, the engine is sealed and the blow-by gases and oil vapour are drawn from the camshaft cover into the inlet manifold to be burned by the engine during normal combustion.

5 The gases are forced out of the crankcase by the relatively higher crankcase pressure; if the engine is worn, the raised crankcase pressure (due to increased blow-by) will cause some of the flow to return under all manifold conditions.

Exhaust emission control

6 To minimise the amount of pollutants which escape into the atmosphere, all models are fitted with a catalytic converter which is integral with the exhaust manifold. The system is of the closed-loop type, in which oxygen sensors in the exhaust system provide the fuel injection/ignition system ECU with constant feedback, enabling the ECU to adjust the mixture to provide the best possible conditions for the converter to operate.

7 On all petrol engines covered by this manual, there are two heated oxygen sensors fitted to the exhaust system. The sensor on the top of the exhaust manifold/catalytic converter determines the residual oxygen content of the exhaust gases for mixture correction. The sensor in the exhaust front pipe (after the catalytic converter) monitors the function of the catalytic converter to give the driver a warning signal if there is a fault.

8 The oxygen sensor's tip is sensitive to oxygen and sends the ECU a varying voltage depending on the amount of oxygen in the exhaust gases. Peak conversion efficiency of all major pollutants occurs if the intake air/fuel mixture is maintained at the chemically-correct ratio for the complete combustion of petrol of 14.7 parts (by weight) of air to 1 part of fuel (the 'stoichiometric' ratio). The sensor output voltage alters in a large step at this point, the ECU using the signal change as a reference point and correcting the intake air/fuel mixture accordingly by altering the fuel injector pulse width.

Fuel evaporation emission control

9 To minimise the escape into the atmosphere of unburned hydrocarbons, a fuel evaporation emission control system is fitted. The fuel tank filler cap is sealed and a charcoal canister is mounted behind the wheel arch liner under the right-hand front wing. The canister collects the petrol vapours generated in the tank when the car is parked and stores them until they can be cleared from the canister (under the control of the fuel injection/ignition system ECU) via the purge valve into the inlet manifold to be burned by the engine during normal combustion.

10 To ensure that the engine runs correctly when it is cold and/or idling and to protect the catalytic converter from the effects of an over-rich mixture, the purge control valve is not opened by the ECU until the engine has warmed-up, and the engine is under load; the valve solenoid is then modulated on and off to allow the stored vapour to pass into the inlet manifold.

Exhaust gas recirculation system

11 This system is designed to recirculate small quantities of exhaust gas into the inlet manifold, and therefore into the combustion process. This reduces the level of unburnt hydrocarbons present in the exhaust gas before it reaches the catalytic converter. The system is controlled by the fuel injection/ignition ECU, using the information from its various sensors, via the electrically-operated EGR solenoid valve mounted on a housing bolted to the left-hand end of the cylinder head. A metal pipe from the EGR housing links the exhaust ports in the cylinder head to the inlet manifold on the rear of the head.

Diesel engines

Crankcase emission control

12 Refer to paragraphs 4 and 5.

Exhaust emission control

13 To minimise the level of exhaust pollutants released into the atmosphere, a catalytic converter and, on 1.3 litre engines, a diesel particulate filter are fitted in the exhaust system.

14 The catalytic converter consists of a canister containing a fine mesh impregnated with a catalyst material, over which the hot exhaust gases pass. The catalyst speeds up the oxidation of harmful carbon monoxide and unburned hydrocarbons, effectively reducing the quantity of harmful products released into the atmosphere via the exhaust gases.

Particulate filter

15 On 1.3 litre engines, a diesel particulate filter is incorporated in the exhaust system intermediate section and contains a silicon carbide honeycomb block containing microscopic channels in which the exhaust gases flow. As the gases flow through the honeycomb channels, soot particles are deposited on the channel walls. To prevent clogging of the honeycomb channels, the soot particles are burned off at regular intervals

2.3 Disconnect the charcoal canister quick-release connectors

during what is known as a 'regeneration phase'. Under the control of the injection system ECU, the injection characteristics are altered to raise the temperature of the exhaust gases to approximately 600°C. At this temperature, the soot particles are effectively burned off the honeycomb walls as the exhaust gases pass through. A differential pressure sensor and temperature sensor are used to inform the ECU of the condition of the particulate filter, and the temperature of the exhaust gases during the regeneration phase. When the ECU detects that soot build-up is reducing the efficiency of the particulate filter, it will instigate the regeneration process. This occurs at regular intervals under certain driving conditions and will normally not be detected by the driver.

Exhaust gas recirculation system

16 This system is designed to recirculate small quantities of exhaust gas into the inlet manifold, and therefore into the combustion process. This reduces the level of unburnt hydrocarbons present in the exhaust gas before it reaches the catalytic converter. The system is controlled by the injection system ECU, using the information from its various sensors, via the electrically-operated EGR valve.

2 Petrol engine emission control systems – testing and component renewal

Crankcase emission control

1 The components of this system require no attention other than to check that the hose(s) are clear and undamaged at regular intervals.

Evaporative emission control

Testing

2 If the system is thought to be faulty, disconnect the hoses from the charcoal canister and purge control valve, and check that they are clear by blowing through them. Full testing of the system can only be carried out using specialist electronic equipment which is connected to the engine management system diagnostic wiring connector. If the purge control valve or charcoal canister are thought to be faulty, they must be renewed.

Charcoal canister renewal

3 At the right-hand rear corner of the engine compartment, disconnect the quick-release connector(s) connecting the charcoal canister to the inlet manifold and fuel vapour hose **(see illustration)**. A Vauxhall/Opel special tool is available to release the connector(s), but provided care is taken, the connector(s) can be released using a pair of long-nosed pliers, or a similar tool, to depress the retaining tangs.

4 Apply the handbrake, then jack up the front of the vehicle and support it on axle stands (see *Jacking and vehicle support*). Remove the right-hand front roadwheel.

5 Remove the wheel arch liner for access to the charcoal canister which is located on the inner wing.

6 Undo the charcoal canister lower retaining nut **(see illustration)**.

7 Disconnect the scavenging air hose from the connector at the top of the canister.

8 Withdraw the canister, together with the vapour hoses from the inner wing **(see illustration)**.

9 Refitting is a reversal of the removal procedure. Make sure the hoses are correctly and securely reconnected.

Purge valve renewal

10 On 1.6 litre Z16SE and Z16XE engines, and 1.8 litre engines the purge valve is mounted on the rear of the air cleaner housing. On 1.4 litre and 1.6 litre Z16XEP engines, the purge valve is mounted on the top of the inlet manifold **(see illustrations)**.

11 To gain access to the purge valve mounted on the inlet manifold, remove the air cleaner intake ducting as necessary, with reference to Chapter 4A.

12 Disconnect the wiring from the purge valve and release the valve from its mounting bracket. Disconnect the vapour hoses and remove the purge valve.

13 Refitting is a reversal of the removal procedure, ensuring the valve is fitted the correct way around and the hoses are securely connected. Check the hoses carefully for cracking and damage, and where evident, renew them. **Note:** *A cracked ventilation hose is potentially a fire hazard.*

Exhaust emission control

Testing

14 The performance of the catalytic converter can be checked only by measuring the exhaust gases using a good-quality, carefully-calibrated exhaust gas analyser.

15 If the CO level at the tailpipe is too high, the vehicle should be taken to a Vauxhall/Opel dealer so that the complete fuel injection and ignition systems, including the oxygen sensors, can be thoroughly checked using the special diagnostic equipment. Once these have been checked and are known to be free from faults, the fault must be in the catalytic converter, which must be renewed.

Catalytic converter renewal

16 The catalytic converter is welded to the exhaust manifold, and the removal and refitting procedure is described in Chapter 4A.

Oxygen sensor (mixture regulation) renewal

Caution: The sensor will be very hot if the engine has been running.

17 The mixture regulation oxygen sensor is located on the exhaust manifold **(see illustration)**. First, trace the wiring back from the sensor to the connector on the left-hand side of the cylinder head and disconnect it. Release the wiring from the clip.

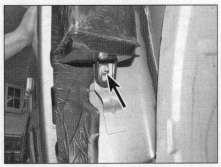

2.6 Undo the charcoal canister lower retaining nut (arrowed)

18 Unscrew the sensor from the exhaust manifold. Ideally, a special 'split' socket should be used, as this will locate over the sensor wiring.

19 Clean the threads of the sensor then coat them with Vauxhall/Opel special grease for oxygen sensors. If a new sensor is being fitted, it will be supplied with the threads already coated with the special grease to prevent it seizing in the manifold.

20 Screw the sensor into the exhaust manifold and tighten to the specified torque.

21 Reconnect the wiring and clip it in place.

Oxygen sensor (catalytic converter control) renewal

Caution: The sensor will be very hot if the engine has been running.

22 The catalytic converter control oxygen sensor is located in the exhaust front pipe, just behind the flexible section **(see illustration)**.

2.8 Withdraw the canister, together with the vapour hoses from the inner wing

First, apply the handbrake, then jack up the front of the vehicle and support it on axle stands (see *Jacking and vehicle support*).

23 Trace the wiring back from the sensor to the connector above the right-hand driveshaft, and disconnect it. Release the wiring from the clips.

24 Unscrew the sensor from the exhaust front pipe. Ideally, a special 'split' socket should be used, as this will locate over the sensor wiring.

25 Clean the threads of the sensor then coat them with Vauxhall/Opel special grease for oxygen sensors. If a new sensor is being fitted, it will be supplied with the threads already coated with the special grease to prevent it seizing in the pipe.

26 Screw the sensor into the exhaust front pipe and tighten to the specified torque.

27 Reconnect the wiring and clip it in place.

2.10a Purge valve location on the rear of the air cleaner housing

2.10b Purge valve location on the top of the inlet manifold

2.17 Mixture regulation oxygen sensor (arrowed)

2.22 Catalytic converter control oxygen sensor (arrowed)

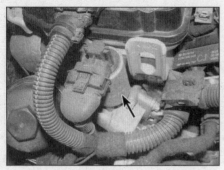

2.29 EGR valve location (arrowed) –
1.4 litre engines

Exhaust gas recirculation system

Testing

28 Comprehensive testing of the system can only be carried out using specialist electronic equipment which is connected to the engine management system diagnostic wiring connector (see Chapter 4A). If the EGR valve is thought to be faulty, it must be renewed.

EGR valve renewal – 1.4 litre engines

29 The exhaust gas recirculation valve is bolted to the left-hand end of the cylinder head (see illustration). First drain the cooling system as described in Chapter 1A.
30 Undo the retaining screw, remove the plastic rivet, then depress the locating catches and withdraw the coolant expansion tank from the crossmember.
31 Disconnect the wiring connector from the EGR valve and ignition module (see illustration).
32 Undo the retaining bolt and remove the left-hand engine lifting bracket.
33 Disconnect the oxygen sensor wiring connector.
34 Undo the two retaining bolts and detach the wiring harness support bracket.
35 Disconnect the two wiring harness connectors from the engine management ECU.
36 Release the clip and disconnect the coolant hose from the EGR valve (see illustration).
37 Unscrew the bolts securing the EGR pipe to the EGR valve (see illustration). Recover the gasket and seal.
38 Unbolt the EGR valve/housing from the cylinder block and recover the gasket (see illustration).

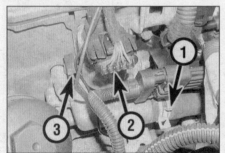

2.36 EGR valve coolant hose (1), wiring plug (2) and coolant temperature sensor wiring connector (3) – 1.4 litre engines

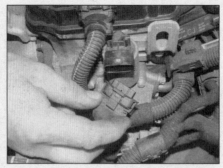

2.31 Disconnecting the wiring from the EGR valve – 1.4 litre engines

39 Refitting is a reversal of removal, but clean the mating surfaces, fit new gaskets, and tighten all bolts securely. Refill the cooling system with reference to Chapter 1A.

EGR valve renewal – 1.6 litre Z16SE and Z16XE engines

40 The exhaust gas recirculation valve is bolted to the top of the inlet manifold.
41 Where applicable remove the plastic cover over the top of the engine.
42 Disconnect the wiring connector from the top of the EGR valve.
43 Undo the two bolts and remove the valve from the manifold.
44 Refitting is a reversal of removal, but clean the mating surfaces, fit a new gasket, and tighten the retaining bolts securely.

EGR valve renewal – 1.6 litre Z16XEP engines

45 The exhaust gas recirculation valve is an integral part of the coolant housing attached to the left-hand end of the cylinder head. First drain the cooling system as described in Chapter 1A.
46 Remove the battery and battery tray as described in Chapter 5A.
47 Disconnect the wiring connectors at the thermostat, coolant temperature sensor and EGR valve.
48 Release the retaining clips and disconnect the four coolant hoses from the coolant housing.
49 Undo the two bolts and detach the oxygen sensor wiring harness support bracket.
50 Undo the two bolts and remove the coolant pipe from the front of the coolant housing.

2.37 EGR pipe-to-EGR valve housing securing bolts (arrowed) – 1.4 litre engines

51 Undo the four bolts and remove the coolant housing from the cylinder head. Recover the gasket.
52 Refitting is a reversal of removal, but clean the mating surfaces, fit new gaskets, and tighten all bolts securely. Refill the cooling system with reference to Chapter 1A.

EGR valve renewal – 1.8 litre engines

53 Disconnect the wiring connector from the EGR valve which mounted at the left-hand end of the cylinder head.
54 Undo the mounting bolts and remove the valve from its location. Recover the gasket.
55 Refitting is the reverse of removal using a new gasket and tightening the valve bolts securely.

<table>
<tr><td>3</td><td>Diesel engine emission control systems – testing and component renewal</td><td></td></tr>
</table>

Crankcase emission control

1 The components of this system require no attention other than to check that the hose(s) are clear and undamaged at regular intervals.

Exhaust emission control

Testing

2 The performance of the catalytic converter and diesel particulate filter can only be checked using special diagnostic equipment. If a system fault is suspected, the vehicle should be taken to a Vauxhall/Opel dealer so that the complete fuel injection system can be thoroughly checked.

Catalytic converter/ diesel particulate filter renewal

3 Refer to Chapter 4B, for removal and refitting details.

Exhaust gas recirculation system

Testing

4 Comprehensive testing of the system can only be carried out using specialist electronic equipment which is connected to the injection system diagnostic wiring connector (see Chapter 4B). If the EGR valve or solenoid valve are thought to be faulty, they must be renewed.

2.38 EGR valve housing securing bolts (arrowed) – 1.4 litre engines

EGR valve renewal – 1.3 litre engines

5 The exhaust gas recirculation valve is bolted to the rear, left-hand side of the cylinder head.
6 Remove the battery and battery tray as described in Chapter 5A.
7 Drain the cooling system as described in Chapter 1B.
8 Remove the windscreen cowl panel and the bulkhead closure panel as described in Chapter 11.
9 Working below the thermostat housing, slacken the retaining clip and disconnect the air hose connecting the intercooler to the inlet manifold charge air pipe.
10 Undo the bolts securing the charge air pipe to the inlet manifold flange, and the bolt securing the pipe support to the thermostat housing. Manipulate the charge air pipe out from its location and recover the sealing ring.
11 Slacken the retaining clips, or disconnect the quick-release fittings and detach the two coolant hoses for the EGR valve heat exchanger.
12 Slacken clip and detach coolant hose from thermostat housing.
13 Release the quick-release fittings and disconnect the brake servo vacuum hose from vacuum pump.
14 Undo the bolt and detach the wiring harness bracket located above the starter motor.
15 Disconnect the wiring connector from the top of the EGR valve.
16 Slacken the retaining screw and release the clamp securing the EGR pipe to the inlet manifold **(see illustration)**.
17 Undo the two mounting bolts and one support bracket bolt, then remove the EGR valve and heat exchanger assembly from the engine **(see illustration)**. Recover the gasket.
18 Refit the EGR valve assembly using the reversal of removal, but bearing in mind the following points:
a) *Thoroughly clean the mating faces and use a new gasket. It will be necessary to insert the mounting bolts into the valve prior to refitting, to retain the gasket in position.*
b) *Tighten the mounting bolts to the specified torque.*
c) *Refit the bulkhead closure panel and windscreen cowl panel as described in Chapter 11.*
d) *Refill the cooling system as described in Chapter 1B.*

EGR valve renewal – 1.7 litre Y17DT engines

19 The exhaust gas recirculation valve is bolted to the rear, left-hand side of the cylinder head.
20 Drain the cooling system as described in Chapter 1B.
21 Remove the battery and battery tray as described in Chapter 5A.
22 Remove the air cleaner assembly and intake duct as described in Chapter 4B.
23 Remove the engine management electronic control unit as described in Chapter 4B.
24 Slacken the retaining clips securing the charge air pipe to the turbocharger.
25 Release the retaining clip and disconnect

3.16 Slacken the retaining screw and release the EGR pipe clamp – 1.3 litre engines

the crankcase ventilation hose from the camshaft cover.
26 Undo the two charge air pipe retaining bolts, disengage the pipe from the turbocharger, then remove the pipe from the top of the engine.
27 Unclip the wiring loom cable-tie, undo the retaining screws/nut and remove the engine management electronic control unit bracket.
28 Undo the two nuts and remove the control unit bracket support frame.
29 Undo the bolts/nuts securing the rear charge air pipe to the inlet manifold and intercooler charge air pipe. Unclip the wiring harness and remove the charge air pipe. Recover the two gaskets.
30 Slacken the retaining clip and disconnect the coolant hose from the EGR valve.
31 Slacken the clamp and disconnect the charge air hose from the EGR valve housing.
32 Release the retaining clip and disconnect the coolant hose from the thermostat housing.
33 Undo the two bolts and detach the wiring harness bracket from the EGR valve housing.
34 Undo the retaining bolts and remove the engine lifting bracket from the left-hand end of the cylinder head.
35 Undo the two bolts securing the metal EGR pipe flange to the EGR valve housing. Separate the flange from the housing and recover the gasket.
36 Disconnect the wiring connector from the top of the EGR valve.
37 Undo the two bolts, noting the different bolt lengths, and remove the EGR valve and housing from the engine. Recover the gasket.
38 Refit the EGR valve assembly using the

3.42 Slacken the retaining clip and disconnect the air cleaner flexible intake hose from the charge air pipe – 1.7 litre Z17DTH engines

3.17 Undo the two bolts (arrowed) and remove the EGR valve and heat exchanger assembly – 1.3 litre engines

reversal of removal, but bearing in mind the following points:
a) *Thoroughly clean the mating faces and use a new gasket.*
b) *Tighten the mounting bolts to the specified torque.*
c) *Refit the charge air pipes using new gaskets.*
d) *Refit the battery tray and battery as described in Chapter 5A.*
e) *Refill the cooling system as described in Chapter 1B.*

EGR valve renewal – 1.7 litre Z17DTH engines

39 The exhaust gas recirculation valve is bolted to the rear, left-hand side of the cylinder head.
40 Remove the plastic cover over the top of the engine.
41 Drain the cooling system as described in Chapter 1B.
42 Slacken the retaining clip and disconnect the air cleaner flexible intake hose from the charge air pipe **(see illustration)**.
43 Release the wiring harness support clips from the plastic charge air pipe over the top of the engine **(see illustration)**.
44 Slacken the retaining clips securing the charge air pipe to the turbocharger.
45 Release the retaining clip and disconnect the crankcase ventilation hose from the camshaft cover **(see illustration)**.
46 Open the clip and detach the fuel hose from the charge air pipe, then undo the two charge air pipe retaining bolts. Disengage the pipe from the turbocharger, then remove the pipe from the top of the engine.

3.43 Release the clips and cable-ties (arrowed) securing the wiring harness to the charge air pipe – 1.7 litre Z17DTH engines

3.45 Release the retaining clip (arrowed) and disconnect the crankcase ventilation hose – 1.7 litre Z17DTH engines

47 Undo the six bolts securing the rear charge air pipe to the throttle housing and inlet manifold. Remove the charge air pipe and recover the gaskets **(see illustrations)**.

48 Remove the battery and battery tray as described in Chapter 5A.

49 Remove the throttle housing as described in Chapter 4B.

50 Undo the retaining bolts and remove the engine lifting bracket from the left-hand end of the cylinder head.

51 Disconnect the wiring connector from the top of the EGR valve.

52 Slacken the retaining clip and disconnect the coolant hose from the EGR valve.

53 Undo the two bolts securing the metal EGR pipe flange to the EGR valve housing. Separate the flange from the housing and recover the gasket.

54 Undo the two bolts, noting the different bolt lengths, and remove the EGR valve and housing from the engine. Recover the gasket.

55 Refit the EGR valve assembly using the reversal of removal, but bearing in mind the following points:

a) *Thoroughly clean the mating faces and use a new gasket.*
b) *Tighten the mounting bolts to the specified torque.*
c) *Refit the throttle housing as described in Chapter 4B.*
d) *Refit the charge air pipes using new gaskets.*
e) *Refit the battery tray and battery as described in Chapter 5A.*
f) *Refill the cooling system as described in Chapter 1B.*

EGR valve heat exchanger renewal – 1.3 litre engines

56 Remove the EGR valve as described previously.

57 Release the retaining clips and disconnect the two coolant hoses from the heat exchanger.

58 Undo the three bolts and separate the heat exchanger from the EGR valve. Recover the gasket.

59 Refitting is the reverse of removal using a new gasket and tightening the retaining bolts to the specified torque.

EGR valve heat exchanger renewal – 1.7 litre Z17DTH engines

60 Drain the cooling system as described in Chapter 1B.

61 Remove the plastic cover over the top of the engine.

62 Slacken the retaining clip and disconnect the air cleaner flexible intake hose from the charge air pipe **(see illustration 3.42)**.

63 Release the wiring harness support clips from the plastic charge air pipe over the top of the engine **(see illustration 3.43)**.

64 Slacken the retaining clips securing the charge air pipe to the turbocharger.

65 Release the retaining clip and disconnect the crankcase ventilation hose from the camshaft cover **(see illustration 3.45)**.

66 Open the clip and detach the fuel hose from the charge air pipe, then undo the two charge air pipe retaining bolts. Disengage the pipe from the turbocharger, then remove the pipe from the top of the engine.

67 Unclip the vacuum hose from the oil dipstick guide tube support bracket, and release the dipstick guide tube from the bracket. Undo the two bolts and remove the bracket from the camshaft cover.

68 Release the retaining clips and disconnect the upper and lower coolant hoses from the EGR valve heat exchanger. Undo the two bolts at each end of the metal EGR pipe, securing the pipe flanges to the exhaust manifold and EGR valve housing. Undo the retaining bolt and detach the EGR valve heat exchanger bracket from the front of the camshaft housing. Remove the EGR valve heat exchanger/pipe assembly from the engine and collect the two flange gaskets.

69 Refitting is the reverse of removal, bearing in mind the following points:

a) *Thoroughly clean the mating faces of the pipe flanges and use new gaskets.*
b) *Tighten the flange retaining bolts to the specified torque.*
c) *Refill the cooling system as described in Chapter 1B.*

4 Catalytic converter – general information and precautions

1 The catalytic converter is a reliable and simple device which needs no maintenance in itself, but there are some facts of which an owner should be aware if the converter is to function properly for its full service life.

Petrol engines

a) *DO NOT use leaded petrol or LRP in a car equipped with a catalytic converter – the lead will coat the precious metals, reducing their converting efficiency and will eventually destroy the converter.*
b) *Always keep the ignition and fuel systems well-maintained in accordance with the manufacturer's schedule.*
c) *If the engine develops a misfire, do not drive the car at all (or at least as little as possible) until the fault is cured.*
d) *DO NOT push- or tow-start the car – this will soak the catalytic converter in unburned fuel, causing it to overheat when the engine does start.*
e) *DO NOT switch off the ignition at high engine speeds.*
f) *DO NOT use fuel or engine oil additives – these may contain substances harmful to the catalytic converter.*
g) *DO NOT continue to use the car if the engine burns oil to the extent of leaving a visible trail of blue smoke.*
h) *Remember that the catalytic converter operates at very high temperatures. DO NOT, therefore, park the car in dry undergrowth, over long grass or piles of dead leaves after a long run.*
i) *Remember that the catalytic converter is FRAGILE – do not strike it with tools during servicing work.*
j) *In some cases a sulphurous smell (like that of rotten eggs) may be noticed from the exhaust. This is common to many catalytic converter-equipped cars and once the car has covered a few thousand miles the problem should disappear.*
k) *The catalytic converter, used on a well-maintained and well-driven car, should last for between 50 000 and 100 000 miles – if the converter is no longer effective it must be renewed.*

Diesel engines

2 Refer to the information given in parts f, g, h, i and k of the petrol engines information given above.

3.47a Undo the six bolts then remove the rear charge air pipe . . .

3.47b . . . and recover the gaskets – 1.7 litre Z17DTH engines

Chapter 5 Part A:
Starting and charging systems

Contents

Degrees of difficulty

Easy, suitable for novice with little experience	Fairly easy, suitable for beginner with some experience	Fairly difficult, suitable for competent DIY mechanic	Difficult, suitable for experienced DIY mechanic	Very difficult, suitable for expert DIY or professional

Specifications

Engine identification

Engine type	Manufacturer's engine code*
Petrol engines:	
1.4 litre (1364 cc) DOHC 16-valve	Z14XEP
1.6 litre (1598 cc):	
SOHC 8-valve..	Z16SE
DOHC 16-valve......................................	Z16XE and Z16XEP
1.8 litre (1796 cc) DOHC 16-valve	Z18XE
Diesel engines:	
1.3 litre (1248 cc) DOHC 16-valve	Z13DTJ
1.7 litre (1686 cc) DOHC 16-valve	Y17DT and Z17DTH

* For details of engine code location, see 'Vehicle identification' in the Reference Chapter.

General

Electrical system type .... 12 volt negative earth

Battery

Type .... Lead-acid, 'maintenance-free' (sealed for life)
Battery capacity.. 36, 44, 55 or 60 Ah (depending on model)
Charge condition:
  Poor .... 12.5 volts
  Normal .... 12.6 volts
  Good... 12.7 volts

Alternator

Type .... Bosch or Delco-Remy
Regulated voltage .... 13.7 to 14.7 volts (approximately)

Starter motor

Type .... Pre-engaged, Delco-Remy or Valeo

Torque wrench settings

	Nm	lbf ft
Alternator fixings:		
Petrol engines:		
Alternator-to-mounting bracket bolts/nuts...................	35	26
Alternator mounting bracket-to-cylinder block bolts...........	35	26
Support bracket to inlet manifold (Z16SE engines)............	20	15
Diesel engines:		
Alternator-to-mounting bracket bolts/nuts:		
1.3 litre engines.........................	22	16
1.7 litre engines (M8 bolt)............................	19	14
1.7 litre engines (M10 bolt)...........................	46	34
Auxiliary drivebelt tensioner:		
1.4 litre petrol engines:		
M8 bolt...	20	15
M10 bolt..	55	41
1.6 litre petrol engines:		
Z16SE and Z16XE.............................	35	26
Z16XEP..	50	37
1.8 litre petrol engines	35	26
Diesel engines	50	37
Auxiliary drivebelt idler pulley retaining bolt....................	38	28
Glow plugs:		
1.3 litre diesel engines...............................	10	7
1.7 litre diesel engines...............................	18	13
Oil pressure warning light switch:		
1.4 litre petrol engines...............................	20	15
1.6 litre petrol engines:		
Z16SE and Z16XE.............................	30	22
Z16XEP..	20	15
1.8 litre petrol engines	30	22
1.3 litre diesel engines...............................	32	24
1.7 litre diesel engines...............................	20	15
Roadwheel bolts..	110	81
Starter motor:		
Petrol engines..	25	18
1.3 litre diesel engines...................................	25	18
1.7 litre diesel engines:		
Lower bolt...	38	28
Upper bolt...	60	44

1 General information, precautions and battery disconnection

General information

The engine electrical system consists mainly of the charging and starting systems. Because of their engine-related functions, these components are covered separately from the body electrical devices such as the lights, instruments, etc (which are covered in Chapter 12). On petrol engine models refer to Part B for information on the ignition system.

The electrical system is of 12 volt negative earth type.

The battery is of the maintenance-free (sealed for life) type, and is charged by the alternator, which is belt-driven from the crankshaft pulley.

The starter motor is of pre-engaged type incorporating an integral solenoid. On starting, the solenoid moves the drive pinion into engagement with the flywheel ring gear before the starter motor is energised. Once the engine has started, a one-way clutch prevents the motor armature being driven by the engine until the pinion disengages.

Further details of the various systems are given in the relevant Sections of this Chapter. While some repair procedures are given, the usual course of action is to renew the component concerned.

Precautions

It is necessary to take extra care when working on the electrical system to avoid damage to semi-conductor devices (diodes and transistors), and to avoid the risk of personal injury. In addition to the precautions given in *Safety first!* at the beginning of this manual, observe the following when working on the system:

• *Always remove rings, watches, etc, before working on the electrical system.* Even with the battery disconnected, capacitive discharge could occur if a component's live terminal is earthed through a metal object. This could cause a shock or nasty burn.

• *Do not reverse the battery connections.* Components such as the alternator, electronic control units, or any other components having semi-conductor circuitry could be irreparably damaged.

• *If the engine is being started using jump leads and a slave battery, connect the batteries positive-to-positive and negative-to-negative (see Jump starting).* This also applies when connecting a battery charger but in this case both of the battery terminals should first be disconnected.

• *Never disconnect the battery terminals, the alternator, any electrical wiring or any test instruments when the engine is running.*

• *Do not allow the engine to turn the alternator when the alternator is not connected.*

• *Never test for alternator output by flashing the output lead to earth.*

• *Never use an ohmmeter of the type incorporating a hand-cranked generator for circuit or continuity testing.*

• *Always ensure that the battery negative lead is disconnected when working on the electrical system.*

• *Before using electric-arc welding equipment on the car, disconnect the battery, alternator and components such as the fuel injection/ignition electronic control unit to protect them from the risk of damage.*

Battery disconnection

Refer to the precautions listed in *Disconnecting the battery* in the Reference Chapter.

2 Electrical fault finding – general information

Refer to Chapter 12.

3 Battery – testing and charging

Testing

Traditional and low maintenance battery

1 If the vehicle covers a small annual mileage, it is worthwhile checking the specific gravity of the electrolyte every three months to determine the state of charge of the battery. Use a hydrometer to make the check and compare the results with the following table. Note that the specific gravity readings assume an electrolyte temperature of 15°C; for every 10°C below 15°C subtract 0.007. For every 10°C above 15°C add 0.007.

| | Ambient temperature | |
	above 25°C	below 25°C
Fully-charged	1.210 to 1.230	1.270 to 1.290
70% charged	1.170 to 1.190	1.230 to 1.250
Discharged	1.050 to 1.070	1.110 to 1.130

2 If the battery condition is suspect, first check the specific gravity of electrolyte in each cell. A variation of 0.040 or more between any cells indicates loss of electrolyte or deterioration of the internal plates.

3 If the specific gravity variation is 0.040 or more, the battery should be renewed. If the cell variation is satisfactory but the battery is discharged, it should be charged as described later in this Section.

Maintenance-free battery

4 Where a 'sealed for life' maintenance-free battery is fitted, topping-up and testing of the electrolyte in each cell is not possible. The condition of the battery can therefore only be tested using a battery condition indicator or a voltmeter.

5 Later models are fitted with a maintenance-free battery with a built-in 'magic-eye' charge condition indicator. The indicator is located in the top of the battery casing, and indicates the condition of the battery from its colour (see illustration). If the indicator shows green, then the battery is in a good state of charge. If the indicator turns darker, eventually to black, then the battery requires charging, as described later in this Section. If the indicator shows clear/

yellow, then the electrolyte level in the battery is too low to allow further use, and the battery should be renewed. Do not attempt to charge, load or jump start a battery when the indicator shows clear/yellow.

All battery types

6 If testing the battery using a voltmeter, connect the voltmeter across the battery and compare the result with those given in the Specifications under 'charge condition'. The test is only accurate if the battery has not been subjected to any kind of charge for the previous six hours. If this is not the case, switch on the headlights for 30 seconds, then wait four to five minutes before testing the battery after switching off the headlights. All other electrical circuits must be switched off, so check that the doors and tailgate are fully shut when making the test.

7 If the voltage reading is less than 12.2 volts, then the battery is discharged, whilst a reading of 12.2 to 12.4 volts indicates a partially-discharged condition.

8 If the battery is to be charged, remove it from the vehicle (Section 4) and charge it as described later in this Section.

Charging

Note: *The following is intended as a guide only. Always refer to the manufacturer's recommendations (often printed on a label attached to the battery) before charging a battery.*

Traditional and low maintenance battery

9 Charge the battery at a rate of 3.5 to 4 amps and continue to charge the battery at this rate until no further rise in specific gravity is noted over a four hour period.

10 Alternatively, a trickle charger charging at the rate of 1.5 amps can safely be used overnight.

11 Specially rapid 'boost' charges which are claimed to restore the power of the battery in 1 to 2 hours are not recommended, as they can cause serious damage to the battery plates through overheating.

12 While charging the battery, note that the temperature of the electrolyte should never exceed 38°C.

Maintenance-free battery

13 This battery type takes considerably longer to fully recharge than the standard type, the time taken being dependent on the extent of discharge, but it will take anything up to three days.

14 A constant voltage type charger is required, to be set, when connected, to 13.9 to 14.9 volts with a charger current below 25 amps. Using this method, the battery should be usable within three hours, giving a voltage reading of 12.5 volts, but this is for a partially-discharged battery and, as mentioned, full charging can take considerably longer.

15 If the battery is to be charged from a

3.5 Battery condition indicator (arrowed)

fully-discharged state (condition reading less than 12.2 volts), have it recharged by your Vauxhall/Opel dealer or local automotive electrician, as the charge rate is higher and constant supervision during charging is necessary.

4 Battery and battery tray – removal and refitting

Note: *Refer to 'Disconnecting the battery' in the Reference Chapter before proceeding.*

Battery

Removal

1 The battery is located at the front, left-hand side of the engine compartment.

2 Disconnect the lead at the negative (–) terminal by slackening the retaining nut and removing the terminal clamp (see illustration). Note that the battery negative (–) and positive (+) terminal connections are stamped on the battery case.

3 Disconnect the lead at the positive (+) terminal by lifting the plastic terminal cover, slackening the retaining nut and removing the terminal clamp (see illustration).

4 On the front facing side of the battery, unscrew the bolt and remove the retaining clamp. If necessary, lift the relay box out of the mounting bracket on the battery tray for improved access to the retaining clamp bolt (see illustrations).

5 Carefully lift the battery from its location and

4.2 Unscrew the battery negative (–) terminal retaining nut, then lift the terminal clamp off the battery post

4.3 Lift the plastic terminal cover, unscrew the (+) retaining nut, then lift the terminal clamp off the battery post

4.4a Unscrew the bolt (arrowed) and remove the battery retaining clamp

4.4b If necessary, lift the relay box out of the mounting bracket on the battery tray

remove it from the car. Make sure the battery is kept upright at all times.

Refitting

Note: *As a precaution, before refitting the battery check that all doors are unlocked.*

6 Refitting is a reversal of removal, but smear petroleum jelly on the terminals after reconnecting the leads to reduce corrosion, and always reconnect the positive lead first, followed by the negative lead.

Battery tray

Removal

7 Remove the battery as described previously.

8 Release the wiring harness cable-ties from the battery tray and move the harness to one side **(see illustration)**.

9 If not already done, lift the relay box out of the mounting bracket on the battery tray.

10 On diesel engine models, remove the fuel filter from the crash box on the battery tray as described in Chapter 1B. Note that it is not necessary to disconnect the fuel hoses, but just release them from the retaining clips and ties.

11 On diesel engine models, lift the two tabs on the base of the battery tray using a small screwdriver and detach the pre/post-heating system control unit from the underside of the tray **(see illustration)**.

12 Undo the two retaining bolts and two retaining nuts remove the battery tray from the engine compartment **(see illustrations)**.

Refitting

13 Refitting is a reversal of removal.

4.8 Release the clips and cable-ties from the battery tray and move the wiring harness to one side

4.11 On diesel engine models, lift the two tabs on the battery tray base and detach the pre/post-heating system control unit

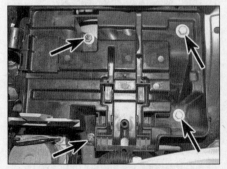

4.12a Undo the two retaining bolts and two retaining nuts (arrowed) . . .

4.12b . . . and remove the battery tray from the engine compartment

5 Charging system – testing

Note: *Refer to the precautions given in 'Safety first!' and in Section 1 of this Chapter before starting work.*

1 If the ignition no-charge warning light fails to illuminate when the ignition is switched on, first check the alternator wiring connections for security. If satisfactory, check that the warning light bulb has not blown, and that the bulbholder is secure in its location in the instrument panel. If the light still fails to illuminate, check the continuity of the warning light feed wire from the alternator to the bulbholder. If all is satisfactory, the alternator is at fault, and should be renewed, or taken to an auto-electrician for testing and repair.

2 If the ignition warning light illuminates when the engine is running, stop the engine and check the condition of the auxiliary drivebelt (see Chapter 1A or 1B) and that the alternator connections are secure. If all is so far satisfactory, have the alternator checked by an auto-electrician for testing and repair.

3 If the alternator output is suspect even though the warning light functions correctly, the regulated voltage may be checked as follows.

4 Connect a voltmeter across the battery terminals, and start the engine.

5 Increase the engine speed until the voltmeter reading remains steady; the reading should be approximately 12 to 13 volts, and no more than 14 volts.

6 Switch on as many electrical accessories (eg, the headlights, heated rear window and heater blower) as possible, and check that the alternator maintains the regulated voltage at around 13.5 to 14.5 volts.

7 If the regulated voltage is not as stated, the fault may be due to worn brushes, weak brush springs, a faulty voltage regulator, a faulty diode, a severed phase winding, or worn or damaged slip-rings. The alternator should be renewed or taken to an auto-electrician for testing and repair.

6 Auxiliary drivebelt –
removal and refitting

Refer to Chapter 1A or 1B.

7 Auxiliary drivebelt tensioner
– removal and refitting

Removal

1 Firmly apply the handbrake, then jack up the front of the car and support it securely on axle stands (see *Jacking and vehicle support*). Remove the right-hand front road- wheel.
2 Remove the air cleaner assembly and air intake duct as described in the relevant Part of Chapter 4.
3 Remove the auxiliary drivebelt as described in the relevant Part of Chapter 1.

1.4 litre petrol engines

4 Unscrew the upper and lower mounting bolts, and withdraw the tensioner pulley and spring assembly **(see illustration)**.

1.6 litre Z16SE and Z16XE, and 1.8 litre petrol engines

5 Unscrew the pivot bolt and withdraw the tensioner pulley and spring housing **(see illustration)**.

1.6 litre Z16XEP petrol engines

6 Remove the crankshaft pulley as described in Chapter 2C.
7 Undo the central mounting bolt, and remove the tensioner assembly from the engine **(see illustration)**.

1.3 litre diesel engines

8 Unscrew the tensioner body retaining bolt and withdraw the tensioner assembly **(see illustration)**.

1.7 litre diesel engines

9 On Z17DTH engines, remove the alternator as described in Section 8.
10 On models equipped with air conditioning, undo the auxiliary drivebelt idler pulley retaining bolt and remove the pulley **(see illustration)**.
11 On Y17DT engines, undo the central mounting bolt and remove the tensioner assembly from the alternator mounting bracket.
12 On Z17DTH engines, undo the tensioner mounting stud retaining nut at the rear of the alternator mounting bracket and remove the tensioner assembly from the mounting bracket.

Refitting

13 Refitting is a reversal of removal, bearing in mind the following points:

7.4 Auxiliary drivebelt tensioner mounting bolts – 1.4 litre petrol engines

a) *Tighten all mounting bolts/nuts to the specified torque.*
b) *On 1.3 litre diesel engines, ensure that the lug on the tensioner body engages with the corresponding hole on the cylinder block as the tensioner is refitted (see illustration).*
c) *On 1.7 litre Z17DTH diesel engines, refit the alternator as described in Section 8.*
d) *On 1.6 litre Z16XEP petrol engines, refit the crankshaft pulley as described in Chapter 2C.*
e) *Refit the auxiliary drivebelt as described in the relevant Part of Chapter 1.*
f) *Refit the air cleaner assembly and air intake duct as described in the relevant Part of Chapter 4.*

7.7 Auxiliary drivebelt tensioner mounting bolt (arrowed) – 1.6 litre Z16XEP petrol engines

7.10 Remove the auxiliary drivebelt idler pulley retaining bolt (arrowed) – 1.7 litre diesel engines

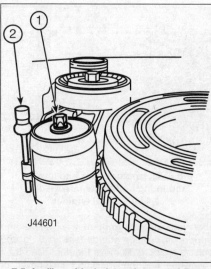

J44601

7.5 Auxiliary drivebelt tensioner – 1.6 litre Z16SE and Z16XE, and 1.8 litre petrol engines

  1 Pivot bolt   *2 Locking bolt*

8 Alternator –
removal and refitting

Removal

1.4 litre petrol engines

1 The alternator is located on the rear of the cylinder block. First, apply the handbrake,

7.8 Unscrew the tensioner body retaining bolt and withdraw the tensioner assembly – 1.3 litre diesel engines

7.13 Ensure that the lug on the tensioner body (arrowed) engages with the cylinder block – 1.3 litre diesel engines

8.6 Alternator upper and lower mounting bolts/nuts (arrowed) – 1.4 litre petrol engines

then jack up the front of the vehicle and support it on axle stands (see *Jacking and vehicle support*). Remove the right-hand front roadwheel and the wheel arch liner cover for access to the right-hand side of the engine.

2 Disconnect the battery negative terminal (refer to *Disconnecting the battery* in the Reference Chapter).

3 Release the tension on the auxiliary drivebelt and lock the tensioner in the released position as described in the auxiliary drivebelt renewal procedure in Chapter 1A. Note that it is not necessary to completely remove the drivebelt, as this would entail removal of the right-hand engine mounting bracket. With the drivebelt tension released, slip the belt off the alternator pulley.

4 Unscrew the auxiliary drivebelt tensioner lower mounting bolt and pivot the tensioner away from the alternator

5 Unscrew the two nuts and disconnect the alternator wiring connectors.

6 Unscrew the upper and lower mounting bolts/nuts and withdraw the alternator downwards from the block **(see illustration)**.

1.6 litre Z16SE petrol engines

7 The alternator is located on the rear of the cylinder block. First, apply the handbrake, then jack up the front of the vehicle and support it on axle stands (see *Jacking and vehicle support*). Remove the right-hand front roadwheel and the wheel arch liner cover for access to the right-hand side of the engine.

8 Disconnect the battery negative terminal

(refer to *Disconnecting the battery* in the Reference Chapter).

9 Remove the air cleaner assembly and air intake duct as described in Chapter 4A.

10 Remove the auxiliary drivebelt as described in Chapter 1A.

11 Slacken and remove the mounting bolts and remove the support bracket from the alternator to the inlet manifold.

12 Disconnect the oil pressure switch and oxygen sensor wiring connectors and move the cables to one side.

13 Remove the rubber covers (where fitted) from the alternator terminals, then unscrew the retaining nuts and disconnect the wiring from the rear of the alternator.

14 Release the wiring harness and cables from the clips on the alternator mounting bracket.

15 Slacken and remove the bolts securing the alternator mounting bracket to the cylinder block, then manoeuvre the alternator and bracket assembly upwards and out of position **(see illustration)**.

16 Undo the bolt securing the alternator to its mounting bracket and separate the two components **(see illustration)**.

1.6 litre Z16XE and 1.8 litre petrol engines

17 The alternator is located on the rear of the cylinder block. First, apply the handbrake, then jack up the front of the vehicle and support it on axle stands (see *Jacking and vehicle support*). Remove the right-hand front roadwheel and the wheel arch liner cover for access to the right-hand side of the engine.

18 Disconnect the battery negative terminal (refer to *Disconnecting the battery* in the Reference Chapter).

19 Remove the plastic cover from the top of the engine.

20 Remove the air cleaner assembly and air intake duct as described in Chapter 4A.

21 Remove the auxiliary drivebelt as described in Chapter 1A.

22 Unscrew the pivot bolt and withdraw the tensioner pulley and spring housing **(see illustration 7.5)**.

23 Disconnect the camshaft sensor wiring connector and unclip the wiring from the support bracket.

24 Unscrew the upper alternator mounting bolt and the two mounting bracket bolts.

25 Unclip the brake pipe and fuel pipe from the support bracket beneath the alternator then remove the support bracket.

26 Disconnect the oil pressure switch wiring connector and move the cable to one side.

27 Unscrew the nut from the alternator lower mounting bolt.

28 Slacken and remove the three bolts securing the alternator mounting bracket to the cylinder block, then manoeuvre the alternator and bracket assembly out of position **(see illustration 8.15)**.

29 Remove the alternator lower mounting bolt, then separate the alternator from the mounting bracket.

30 Remove the rubber covers (where fitted) from the alternator terminals, then unscrew the two retaining nuts and disconnect the wiring from the rear of the alternator.

31 Remove the alternator out from under the wheel arch.

1.6 litre Z16XEP petrol engines

32 The alternator is located on the rear of the cylinder block. First, apply the handbrake, then jack up the front of the vehicle and support it on axle stands (see *Jacking and vehicle support*). Remove the right-hand front roadwheel and the wheel arch liner cover for access to the right-hand side of the engine.

33 Disconnect the battery negative terminal (refer to *Disconnecting the battery* in the Reference Chapter).

34 Remove the auxiliary drivebelt as described in Chapter 1A.

35 Unscrew the nuts and disconnect the two wires from the rear of the alternator.

36 Unscrew the lower mounting bolt, slacken the upper mounting bolt and withdraw the alternator out from under the wheel arch.

1.3 litre diesel engines

37 The alternator is located on the rear of the cylinder block. First, apply the handbrake, then jack up the front of the vehicle and support it on axle stands (see *Jacking and vehicle support*). Remove the right-hand front roadwheel and the wheel arch liner cover for access to the right-hand side of the engine.

38 Disconnect the battery negative terminal (refer to *Disconnecting the battery* in the Reference Chapter).

39 Remove the auxiliary drivebelt as described in Chapter 1B.

40 Unscrew the nuts and disconnect the wires from the rear of the alternator.

41 Unscrew the upper mounting bolt and the two lower mounting bolts, then withdraw the alternator downwards from the block **(see illustration)**.

1.7 litre diesel engines

42 The alternator is located on the front of the cylinder block. First, apply the handbrake, then jack up the front of the vehicle and support it on axle stands (see

8.15 Alternator mounting bracket bolts (arrowed) – 1.6 litre Z16SE petrol engines

8.16 Withdraw the alternator lower mounting bolt – 1.6 litre Z16SE petrol engines

Jacking and vehicle support). Remove the right-hand front roadwheel and the wheel arch liner cover for access to the right-hand side of the engine.

43 Disconnect the battery negative terminal (refer to *Disconnecting the battery* in the Reference Chapter).

44 Remove the auxiliary drivebelt as described in Chapter 1B.

45 Disconnect the wiring connector at the oil level sensor.

46 Unscrew the oil feed pipe to the vacuum pump on the rear of the alternator, and unclip the oil return pipe **(see illustration)**. Be prepared for oil spillage.

47 Undo the nut and disconnect the alternator wiring connector **(see illustration)**.

48 Unscrew the alternator upper mounting bolt and unscrew the nut from the lower mounting bolt.

49 Prise the bottom of the alternator out of the mounting bracket and remove the lower mounting bolt.

50 Unscrew the union nut and disconnect the brake servo vacuum pipe from the vacuum pump.

51 Disconnect the wiring plug at the rear of the alternator, then manoeuvre the alternator, complete with vacuum pump, out from under the car.

Refitting

52 Refitting is a reversal of removal, but tighten all mounting bolts to the specified torque (where given). Refit the auxiliary drivebelt as described in the relevant Part of Chapter 1.

9 Alternator – testing and overhaul

If the alternator is thought to be suspect, it should be removed from the vehicle and taken to an auto-electrician for testing. Most auto electricians will be able to supply and fit brushes at a reasonable cost. However, check on the cost of repairs before proceeding as it may prove more economical to obtain a new or exchange alternator.

10 Starting system – testing

Note: *Refer to the precautions given in 'Safety first!' and in Section 1 of this Chapter before starting work.*

1 If the starter motor fails to operate when the ignition key is turned to the appropriate position, the possible causes are as follows:
 a) *The engine immobiliser is faulty.*
 b) *The battery is faulty.*
 c) *The electrical connections between the switch, solenoid, battery and starter motor are somewhere failing to pass*

8.41 Alternator mounting bolts (arrowed) – 1.3 litre diesel engines

the necessary current from the battery through the starter to earth.
 d) *The solenoid is faulty.*
 e) *The starter motor is mechanically or electrically defective.*

2 To check the battery, switch on the headlights. If they dim after a few seconds, this indicates that the battery is discharged – recharge (see Section 3) or renew the battery. If the headlights glow brightly, operate the starter switch while watching the headlights. If they dim, then this indicates that current is reaching the starter motor, therefore the fault must lie in the starter motor. If the lights continue to glow brightly (and no clicking sound can be heard from the starter motor solenoid), this indicates that there is a fault in the circuit or solenoid – see the following paragraphs. If the starter motor turns slowly when operated, but the battery is in good condition, then this indicates either that the starter motor is faulty, or there is considerable resistance somewhere in the circuit.

3 If a fault in the circuit is suspected, disconnect the battery leads (including the earth connection to the body), the starter/solenoid wiring and the engine/transmission earth strap. Thoroughly clean the connections, and reconnect the leads and wiring. Use a voltmeter or test light to check that full battery voltage is available at the battery positive lead connection to the solenoid. Smear petroleum jelly around the battery terminals to prevent corrosion – corroded connections are among

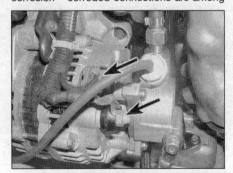
8.47 Disconnect the wiring plug and unbolt the wiring connector (arrowed) – 1.7 litre diesel engines

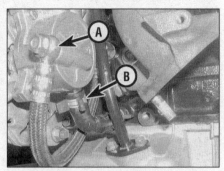
8.46 Vacuum pump oil feed pipe (A) and return pipe (B) – 1.7 litre diesel engines

the most frequent causes of electrical system faults.

4 If the battery and all connections are in good condition, check the circuit by disconnecting the switched feed wire from the solenoid (the thinner wire). Connect a voltmeter or test light between the wire end and a good earth (such as the battery negative terminal), and check that the wire is live when the ignition switch is turned to the 'start' position. If it is, then the circuit is sound – if not, there is a fault in the ignition/starter switch or wiring.

5 The solenoid contacts can be checked by connecting a voltmeter or test light between the battery positive feed connection on the starter side of the solenoid and earth. When the ignition switch is turned to the 'start' position, there should be a reading or lighted bulb, as applicable. If there is no reading or lighted bulb, the solenoid is faulty and should be renewed.

6 If the circuit and solenoid are proved sound, the fault must lie in the starter motor. In this event, it may be possible to have the starter motor overhauled by a specialist, but check on the cost of spares before proceeding, as it may prove more economical to obtain a new or exchange motor.

11 Starter motor – removal and refitting

Removal

Petrol engines

1 Disconnect the battery negative terminal (refer to *Disconnecting the battery* in the Reference Chapter).

2 Apply the handbrake, then jack up the front of the vehicle and support it on axle stands (see *Jacking and vehicle support*).

3 Where applicable, disconnect the oxygen sensor wiring connector, then undo the two bolts and remove the inlet manifold support bracket.

4 Unscrew the two nuts and disconnect the battery positive cable and the starter trigger wire from the starter **(see illustration)**.

5 Unscrew the nut and disconnect the earth cable from the starter mounting bolt.

11.4 Battery positive cable connection on the starter motor (arrowed) – petrol engines

11.9 Working through the access hole, unscrew and remove the starter upper mounting bolt – 1.3 litre diesel engines

11.12 Battery positive cable connection on the starter motor (arrowed) – 1.3 litre diesel engines

6 Unscrew the two mounting bolts and withdraw the starter motor from the rear of the engine.

1.3 litre diesel engines

7 Remove the battery and battery tray as described in Section 4.
8 Extract the rubber plug (where fitted) at the top of the transmission bellhousing for access to the starter upper mounting bolt.
9 Using a long socket bit inserted through the access hole, unscrew and remove the upper mounting bolt **(see illustration)**. Take great care not to drop the bolt in the bellhousing.
10 Apply the handbrake, then jack up the front of the vehicle and support it on axle stands (see *Jacking and vehicle support*).
11 Unscrew the bolt and detach the earth cable from the cylinder block, then undo the bolt and detach the wiring harness bracket.
12 Undo the two nuts and disconnect the wiring from the starter solenoid **(see illustration)**.
13 Unscrew the lower mounting bolt and withdraw the starter motor from the engine.

1.7 litre Y17DT diesel engines

14 Remove the battery and battery tray as described in Section 4.
15 Unscrew and remove the starter motor upper mounting bolt.
16 Apply the handbrake, then jack up the front of the vehicle and support it on axle stands (see *Jacking and vehicle support*).
17 Extract the retaining spring clip and disconnect the gearchange linkage from the shift guide bracket. Unscrew the retaining bolt and remove the shift guide bracket.
18 Unscrew the retaining nut and remove the earth lead from the starter motor lower mounting bolt.
19 Disconnect the wiring connector from the crankshaft sensor located below the starter motor.
20 Slacken the retaining clip and detach the oil filter housing oil return hose from the rear of the cylinder block. Be prepared for oil spillage.
21 Unscrew the two bolts and detach the atmospheric pressure sensor bracket.
22 Slacken and remove the retaining nut and screw and disconnect the wiring from the starter motor solenoid.

23 Unscrew the lower mounting bolt and manipulate the starter motor out from underneath the engine.

1.7 litre Z17DTH diesel engines

24 Remove the battery and battery tray as described in Section 4.
25 Unscrew and remove the starter motor upper mounting bolt.
26 Apply the handbrake, then jack up the front of the vehicle and support it on axle stands (see *Jacking and vehicle support*).
27 Remove the complete exhaust system as described in Chapter 4B.
28 Unscrew the retaining nut and remove the earth lead from the starter motor lower mounting bolt.
29 Slacken and remove the retaining nut and screw and disconnect the wiring from the starter motor solenoid.
30 Unscrew the lower mounting bolt and manipulate the starter motor out from underneath the engine.

Refitting

31 Refitting is a reversal of removal tightening the retaining bolts to the specified torque. Ensure all wiring is correctly routed and its retaining nuts are securely tightened.

12 Starter motor – testing and overhaul

If the starter motor is thought to be suspect, it should be removed from the vehicle and

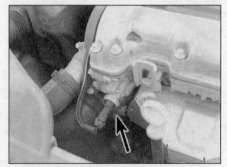

14.1 Oil pressure warning light switch location (arrowed) – 1.4 litre petrol engines

taken to an auto-electrician for testing. Most auto-electricians will be able to supply and fit brushes at a reasonable cost. However, check on the cost of repairs before proceeding as it may prove more economical to obtain a new or exchange motor.

13 Ignition switch – removal and refitting

1 The ignition switch is integral with the steering column lock, and removal and refitting is described in Chapter 10.

14 Oil pressure warning light switch – removal and refitting

Removal

1.4 litre petrol engines

1 The oil pressure warning light switch is screwed into the front right-hand side of the cylinder head **(see illustration)**.
2 Pull back the cover and disconnect the wiring from the switch.
3 Place some cloth rags beneath the switch, then unscrew the switch from the block. Be prepared for oil spillage, and if the switch is to be left removed from the engine for any length of time, plug the switch aperture

1.6 litre Z16SE and Z16XE, and 1.8 litre petrol engines

4 The oil pressure warning light switch is screwed into the rear of the oil pump housing which is located on the right-hand end of the engine, on the end of the crankshaft.
5 Firmly apply the handbrake, then jack up the front of the car and support it securely on axle stands (see *Jacking and vehicle support*).
6 Disconnect the wiring connector then unscrew the switch and recover the sealing washer. Be prepared for oil spillage, and if the switch is to be left removed from the engine for any length of time, plug the switch aperture **(see illustration)**.

1.6 litre Z16XEP petrol engines

7 The oil pressure warning light switch is

screwed into the front right-hand side of the cylinder block.

8 Firmly apply the handbrake, then jack up the front of the car and support it securely on axle stands (see *Jacking and vehicle support*).

9 On models equipped with air conditioning, refer to Chapter 3 and unbolt the air conditioning compressor from the cylinder block **without disconnecting the refrigerant lines**. Support the compressor to one side for access to the oil pressure warning light switch.

10 Disconnect the wiring connector then unscrew the switch and recover the sealing washer. Be prepared for oil spillage, and if the switch is to be left removed from the engine for any length of time, plug the switch aperture.

1.3 litre diesel engines

11 The oil pressure warning light switch is screwed into the front left-hand end of the cylinder head. To gain access, remove the plastic cover from the top of the engine.

12 Pull back the cover and disconnect the wiring from the switch.

13 Place some cloth rags beneath the switch, then unscrew the switch from the block. Be prepared for oil spillage, and if the switch is to be left removed from the engine for any length of time, plug the switch aperture

1.7 litre diesel engines

14 The oil pressure warning light switch is screwed into the left-hand end of the cylinder block, below and slightly to the rear of the thermostat housing. To improve access to the switch, remove the battery and battery tray as described in Section 4.

15 Disconnect the wiring connector by pulling, then unscrew the switch. Be prepared for oil spillage, and if the switch is to be left removed from the engine for any length of time, plug the switch aperture **(see illustration)**.

Refitting

16 Refitting is a reversal of removal, but tighten the switch to the specified torque.

15 Oil level sensor –
removal and refitting

Note: *An oil level sensor is not fitted to 1.4 litre petrol engines.*

Removal

1.6 litre Z16SE and Z16XE, and 1.8 litre petrol engines

1 The oil level sensor is located on the front face of the engine sump.

2 Firmly apply the handbrake, then jack up the front of the car and support it securely on axle stands (see *Jacking and vehicle support*).

3 Drain the engine oil into a clean container then refit the drain plug and tighten it to the specified torque (see Chapter 1A).

4 Disconnect the wiring connector from the sensor.

14.6 Oil pressure warning light switch location – 1.6 litre Z16SE and Z16XE, and 1.8 litre petrol engines

5 Unscrew the retaining bolts then ease the sensor out from the sump and remove it along with its sealing ring/washer. Discard the sealing ring/washer, a new one should be used on refitting **(see illustration)**.

1.6 litre Z16XEP petrol engines and 1.3 litre diesel engines

6 The oil level sensor is located inside the sump which must first be removed (see the relevant Part of Chapter 2).

7 With the sump removed, slide off the retaining clip and free the sensor wiring connector from the sump **(see illustration)**.

8 Where fitted, undo the retaining bolts and remove the oil baffle plate from inside the sump **(see illustration)**.

15.5 Remove the oil level sensor and remove the seal – 1.6 litre Z16SE and Z16XE, and 1.8 litre petrol engines

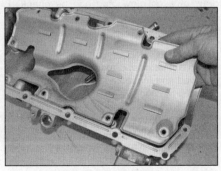

15.8 Undo the retaining bolts and remove the oil baffle plate – 1.6 litre Z16XEP petrol and 1.3 litre diesel engines

14.15 Oil pressure warning light switch – 1.7 litre diesel engines

9 Note the correct routing of the wiring then undo the retaining bolts and remove the sensor assembly from the sump **(see illustration)**. Check the wiring connector seal for signs or damage and renew if necessary.

1.7 litre diesel engines

10 The oil level sensor is located inside the sump main casting. To gain access, remove the sump lower pan from the main casting as described in Chapter 2E.

11 Disconnect the sensor wiring connector, then slide off the external retaining clip and free the sensor wiring connector from the sump main casting.

12 Note the correct routing of the wiring then undo the retaining bolts and remove the

15.7 Slide off the retaining clip (arrowed) and free the sensor wiring connector from the sump – 1.6 litre Z16XEP petrol and 1.3 litre diesel engines

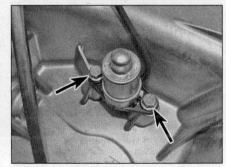

15.9 Undo the retaining bolts (arrowed) and remove the oil level sensor from the sump – 1.6 litre Z16XEP petrol and 1.3 litre diesel engines

17.3 Disconnect the wiring from the glow plugs (No 1 glow plug arrowed) – 1.3 litre diesel engines

sensor assembly from the sump main casting. Check the wiring connector seal for signs or damage and renew if necessary.

Refitting

1.6 litre Z16SE and Z16XE, and 1.8 litre petrol engines

13 Refitting is the reverse of removal ensuring the wiring is correctly routed and securely reconnected. On completion refill the engine with oil (see Chapter 1A).

1.6 litre Z16XEP petrol engines and all diesel engines

14 Prior to refitting remove all traces of locking compound from the sensor retaining bolt and sump threads. Apply a drop of fresh locking compound to the bolt threads and lubricate the wiring connector seal with a smear of engine oil.

15 Fit the sensor, making sure the wiring is correctly routed, and securely tighten its retaining bolts. Ease the wiring connector through the sump, taking care not to damage its seal, and secure it in position with the retaining clip.

16 Ensure the sensor is correctly refitted then, where applicable, refit the oil baffle plate.

17 Refit the sump or sump lower pan as described in the relevant Part of Chapter 2.

16 Pre/post-heating system (diesel engines) – description and testing

Description

1 Each cylinder of the engine is fitted with a heater plug (commonly called a glow plug) screwed into it. The plugs are electrically-operated before and during start-up when the engine is cold. Electrical feed to the glow plugs is controlled via the pre/post-heating system control unit.

2 A warning light in the instrument panel tells the driver that pre/post-heating is taking place. When the light goes out, the engine is ready to be started. The voltage supply to the glow plugs continues for several seconds after the light goes out. If no attempt is made to start, the timer then cuts off the supply, in order to avoid draining the battery and overheating the glow plugs.

3 The glow plugs also provide a 'post-heating' function, whereby the glow plugs remain switched on after the engine has started. The length of time 'post-heating' takes place is also determined by the control unit, and is dependent on engine temperature.

4 The fuel filter is fitted with a heating element to prevent the fuel 'waxing' in extreme cold temperature conditions and to improve combustion. The heating element is an integral part of the fuel filter housing and is controlled by the pre/post-heating system control unit.

Testing

5 If the system malfunctions, testing is ultimately by substitution of known good units, but some preliminary checks may be made as follows.

6 Connect a voltmeter or 12 volt test lamp between the glow plug supply cable and earth (engine or vehicle metal). Make sure that the live connection is kept clear of the engine and bodywork.

7 Have an assistant switch on the ignition, and check that voltage is applied to the glow plugs. Note the time for which the warning light is lit, and the total time for which voltage is applied before the system cuts out. Switch off the ignition.

8 At an underbonnet temperature of 20°C, typical times noted should be approximately 3 seconds for warning light operation. Warning light time will increase with lower temperatures and decrease with higher temperatures.

9 If there is no supply at all, the control unit or associated wiring is at fault.

10 To locate a defective glow plug, disconnect the wiring connector from each plug.

11 Use a continuity tester, or a 12 volt test lamp connected to the battery positive terminal, to check for continuity between each glow plug terminal and earth. The resistance of a glow plug in good condition is very low (less than 1 ohm), so if the test lamp does not light or the continuity tester shows a high resistance, the glow plug is certainly defective.

12 If an ammeter is available, the current draw of each glow plug can be checked. After an initial surge of 15 to 20 amps, each plug should draw 12 amps. Any plug which draws much more or less than this is probably defective.

13 As a final check, the glow plugs can be removed and inspected as described in the following Section.

17 Glow plugs (diesel engines) – removal, inspection and refitting

Caution: *If the pre/post-heating system has just been energised, or if the engine has been running, the glow plugs will be very hot.*

Removal

1.3 litre engines

1 The glow plugs are located at the front of the cylinder head above the exhaust manifold.

2 Disconnect the battery negative terminal (refer to *Disconnecting the battery* in the Reference Chapter), then lift off the engine cover.

3 Disconnect the wiring from the glow plugs by squeezing the connectors with thumb and forefinger, and pulling them from the plugs **(see illustration)**.

4 Unscrew the glow plugs and remove them from the cylinder head.

1.7 litre engines

5 The glow plugs are located at the rear of the cylinder head above the inlet manifold.

6 Disconnect the battery negative terminal (refer to *Disconnecting the battery* in the Reference Chapter).

7 Remove the air cleaner assembly and air intake ducts as described in Chapter 4B.

8 Slacken the retaining clips securing the charge air pipe to the turbocharger and air cleaner intake duct.

9 Remove the engine electronic control unit as described in Chapter 4B.

10 On Z17DTH engines, disconnect the wiring connectors at the fuel injectors.

11 Unscrew the two bolts and one nut, or the four bolts, unclip the wiring harness and remove the engine electronic control unit mounting bracket.

12 Disconnect the wiring from the glow plugs by squeezing the connectors with thumb and forefinger, and pulling them from the plugs.

13 Unscrew the glow plugs and remove them from the cylinder head.

Inspection

14 Inspect each glow plug for physical damage. Burnt or eroded glow plug tips can be caused by a bad injector spray pattern. Have the injectors checked if this type of damage is found.

15 If the glow plugs are in good physical condition, check them electrically using a 12 volt test lamp or continuity tester as described in the previous Section.

16 The glow plugs can be energised by applying 12 volts to them to verify that they heat up evenly and in the required time. Observe the following precautions.

a) *Support the glow plug by clamping it carefully in a vice or self-locking pliers. Remember it will become red-hot.*

b) *Make sure that the power supply or test lead incorporates a fuse or overload trip to protect against damage from a short-circuit.*

c) *After testing, allow the glow plug to cool for several minutes before attempting to handle it.*

17 A glow plug in good condition will start to glow red at the tip after drawing current for 5 seconds or so. Any plug which takes much longer to start glowing, or which starts glowing in the middle instead of at the tip, is defective.

Refitting

18 Carefully refit the plugs and tighten to the specified torque. Do not overtighten, as this can damage the glow plug element. Push the electrical connectors firmly onto the glow plugs.

19 The remainder of refitting is a reversal of removal, checking the operation of the glow plugs on completion.

18 Pre/post-heating system control unit (diesel engines) – removal and refitting

Removal

1 The pre/post-heating system control unit is located on the left-hand side of the engine compartment where it is mounted underneath the battery tray.

2 Remove the battery and battery tray as described in Section 4.

3 Disconnect the wiring connector from the base of the control unit and remove the unit from the engine compartment.

Refitting

4 Refitting is a reversal of removal.

Notes

Chapter 5 Part B:
Ignition system – petrol engines

Contents

Degrees of difficulty

Easy, suitable for novice with little experience	**Fairly easy,** suitable for beginner with some experience	**Fairly difficult,** suitable for competent DIY mechanic	**Difficult,** suitable for experienced DIY mechanic	**Very difficult,** suitable for expert DIY or professional

Specifications

General

System type	Distributorless ignition system
System application:	
1.4 litre engines	Bosch Motronic ME 7.6.1
1.6 litre engines	GM Multec-S
1.8 litre engines	Simtec 71.5
Location of No 1 cylinder	Timing chain/timing belt end of engine
Firing order	1-3-4-2

Torque wrench setting	**Nm**	**lbf ft**
Ignition module retaining screws	8	6

1 Ignition system – general information

The ignition system is integrated with the fuel injection system to form a combined engine management system under the control of one electronic control unit (ECU) – See Chapter 4A for further information. The ignition side of the system is of the distributorless type, and consists of the ignition module and the knock sensor.

On 1.6 litre SOHC engines, the ignition module is actually a four output ignition coil. The module consists of two separate HT coils which supply two cylinders each (one coil supplies cylinders 1 and 4, and the other cylinders 2 and 3). Under the control of the ECU, the module operates on the 'wasted spark' principle, ie, each spark plug sparks twice for every cycle of the engine, once on the compression stroke and once on the exhaust stroke.

On 1.4, 1.6 and 1.8 litre DOHC engines, the ignition module consists of four ignition coils, one per cylinder, in one casing mounted directly above the spark plugs. This module eliminates the need for any HT leads as the

coils locate directly onto the relevant spark plug. The ECU uses its inputs from the various sensors to calculate the required ignition advance setting and coil charging time.

The knock sensor is mounted onto the cylinder block and informs the ECU when the engine is 'pinking' under load. The sensor is sensitive to vibration and detects the knocking which occurs when the engine starts to 'pink' (pre-ignite). The knock sensor sends an electrical signal to the ECU which in turn retards the ignition advance setting until the 'pinking' ceases.

The ignition system operates under the overall control of the engine management electronic control unit. The systems comprise various sensors (whose inputs also provide data to control the fuel injection system), and the electronic control unit, in addition to the ignition module and spark plugs. Details of the system sensors and the electronic control unit are given in Chapter 4A.

The electronic control unit selects the optimum ignition advance setting based on the information received from the various sensors, and fires the relevant ignition coil accordingly. The degree of advance can thus be constantly varied to suit the prevailing engine operating conditions.

 Warning: Due to the high voltages produced by the electronic ignition system, extreme care must be taken when working on the system with the ignition switched on. Persons with surgically-implanted cardiac pacemaker devices should keep well clear of the ignition circuits, components and test equipment.

2 Ignition system – testing

1 If a fault appears in the engine management system, first ensure that all the system wiring connectors are securely connected and free of corrosion. Ensure that the fault is not due to poor maintenance; ie, check that the air cleaner filter element is clean, the spark plugs are in good condition and correctly gapped, the cylinder compression pressures are correct and that the engine breather hoses are clear and undamaged, referring to Chapters 1A, 2A, 2B and 2C for further information.
2 If these checks fail to reveal the cause of the problem, the vehicle should be taken to a suitably-equipped Vauxhall/Opel dealer or

2.2a Unclip and remove the trim panel beneath the handbrake lever . . .

2.2b . . . for access to the diagnostic socket (arrowed)

3.1 Ignition module – 1.6 litre SOHC engines

engine management diagnostic specialist for testing. A diagnostic socket is located in the centre console, to which a fault code reader or other suitable test equipment can be connected **(see illustrations)**. By using the code reader or test equipment, the engine management ECU can be interrogated, and any stored fault codes can be retrieved. This will allow the fault to be quickly and simply traced, alleviating the need to test all the system components individually, which is a time-consuming operation that carries a risk of damaging the ECU.

3 The only ignition system checks which can be carried out by the home mechanic are those described in Chapter 1A relating to the spark plugs. If necessary, the system wiring and wiring connectors can be checked as described in Chapter 12, ensuring that the ECU wiring connector(s) have first been disconnected.

3 Ignition module – removal and refitting

Removal

1.6 litre SOHC engines

1 Disconnect the wiring connector and HT leads from the ignition module **(see illustrations)**. The module HT lead terminals are numbered (the leads should also be numbered) with their respective cylinder number to avoid confusion on refitting.

2 Slacken and remove the retaining screws and remove the ignition module from the end of the cylinder head.

1.4, 1.6 and 1.8 litre DOHC engines

3 Where applicable, remove the oil filler cap and unscrew the two bolts securing the plastic

cover over the top of the engine. Lift off the cover and refit the oil filler cap.

4 On 1.6 litre Z16XEP engines, unclip the wiring trough from the left-hand end of the cylinder head.

5 The ignition module is mounted at the top of the engine, between the inlet and exhaust camshaft casings. Disconnect the wiring connector at the left-hand end of the module **(see illustration)**.

6 On 1.4 litre and 1.6 litre Z16XEP engines, remove the cover from the ignition module by sliding it towards the transmission and lifting off **(see illustration)**.

7 Undo the retaining bolts, and lift the module up and out of position **(see illustration)**. If the module proves reluctant to separate from the spark plugs, insert two long 8 mm bolts into the threaded holes in the top of the module, and pull up on the bolts to free the module from the plugs.

8 With the module removed, check the condition of the sealing grommets and renew if necessary **(see illustration)**.

Refitting

9 Refitting is the reversal of removal, tightening the retaining screws to the specified torque.

4 Ignition timing – checking and adjustment

Due to the nature of the ignition system, the ignition timing is constantly being monitored and adjusted by the engine management ECU.

The only way in which the ignition timing can be checked is by using specialist diagnostic test equipment connected to the engine management system diagnostic socket. No adjustment of the ignition timing is possible. Should the ignition timing be incorrect, then a fault is likely to be present in the engine management system.

5 Knock sensor – removal and refitting

Refer to the procedures contained in Chapter 4A.

3.5 Disconnect the wiring connector from the module

3.6 Remove the ignition module cover by sliding it towards the transmission and lifting off

3.7 Undo the retaining bolts, and lift the module up and out of position

3.8 Check the condition of the sealing grommets and renew if necessary

Chapter 6
Clutch

Contents

Degrees of difficulty

Easy, suitable for novice with little experience	Fairly easy, suitable for beginner with some experience	Fairly difficult, suitable for competent DIY mechanic	Difficult, suitable for experienced DIY mechanic	Very difficult, suitable for expert DIY or professional

Specifications

Engine identification

Engine type	Manufacturer's engine code*
Petrol engines:	
1.4 litre (1364 cc) DOHC 16-valve	Z14XEP
1.6 litre (1598 cc):	
SOHC 8-valve.	Z16SE
DOHC 16-valve.	Z16XE and Z16XEP
1.8 litre (1796 cc) DOHC 16-valve	Z18XE
Diesel engines:	
1.3 litre (1248 cc) DOHC 16-valve	Z13DTJ
1.7 litre (1686 cc) DOHC 16-valve	Y17DT and Z17DTH

* For details of engine code location, see 'Vehicle identification' in the Reference Chapter.

Type	Single dry plate with diaphragm spring, hydraulically-operated

Friction disc

Diameter:	
1.4 litre petrol engines	200 mm
1.6 litre petrol engines:	
Z16SE and Z16XE engines:	
Standard transmission	200 mm
Easytronic transmission	205 mm
Z16XEP engines:	
F13 standard transmission.	200 mm
F17+ standard and Easytronic transmission	205 mm
1.8 litre petrol engines	205 mm
1.3 litre diesel engines	216 mm
1.7 litre diesel engines:	
Y17DT engines	205 mm
Z17DTH engines.	228 mm
New lining thickness:	
Petrol engines.	7.65 mm
Diesel engines:	
1.3 litre engines.	7.20 mm
1.7 litre engines:	
Y17DT engines	7.65 mm
Z17DTH engines	8.40 mm

Torque wrench settings

	Nm	lbf ft
ABS hydraulic modulator mounting bracket bolts	20	15
Clutch master cylinder and mounting plate retaining nuts.	20	15
Pressure plate retaining bolts:		
M6 bolts	12	9
M7 bolts	15	11
M8 bolts	28	21
Release cylinder mounting bolts	5	4

1 General information

The clutch consists of a friction disc, a pressure plate assembly, and the hydraulic release cylinder (which incorporates the release bearing); all of these components are contained in the large cast-aluminium alloy bellhousing, sandwiched between the engine and the transmission.

The friction disc is fitted between the engine flywheel and the clutch pressure plate, and is allowed to slide on the transmission input shaft splines.

The pressure plate assembly is bolted to the engine flywheel. When the engine is running, drive is transmitted from the crankshaft, via the flywheel, to the friction disc (these components being clamped securely together by the pressure plate assembly) and from the friction disc to the transmission input shaft.

To interrupt the drive, the spring pressure must be relaxed. This is achieved using a hydraulic release mechanism which consists of the master cylinder, the release cylinder and the pipe/hose linking the two components. Depressing the pedal pushes on the master cylinder pushrod which hydraulically forces the release cylinder piston against the pressure plate spring fingers. This causes the springs to deform and releases the clamping force on the friction disc.

The clutch is self-adjusting and requires no manual adjustment.

Semi-automatic clutch

Models equipped with the Easytronic MTA (Manual Transmission with Automatic shift), are fitted with a semi-automatic clutch. The clutch may be operated either fully automatically or semi-automatically by means of the gear selector lever. There is no conventional clutch pedal fitted.

The Easytronic system essentially consists of a conventional manual gearbox and clutch fitted with electrical and hydraulic controls, the clutch being operated by a clutch module attached to the side of the transmission casing. Refer to Chapter 7B for more information. The clutch component removal and refitting procedures are included in this Chapter as they are very similar to those for the standard manual transmission.

2 Clutch hydraulic system – bleeding

Note: *On models equipped with the Easytronic transmission, the following manual method of bleeding the clutch is not possible since the hydraulic control unit is integral with the transmission. On these models, bleeding is carried out using the Vauxhall/Opel TECH2 diagnostic instrument, therefore this work should be entrusted to a Vauxhall/Opel dealer.*

⚠️ *Warning: Hydraulic fluid is poisonous; wash off immediately and thoroughly in the case of skin contact, and seek immediate medical advice if any fluid is swallowed or gets into the eyes. Certain types of hydraulic fluid are flammable, and may ignite when allowed into contact with hot components; when servicing any hydraulic system, it is safest to assume that the fluid is flammable, and to take precautions against the risk of fire as though it is petrol that is being handled. Hydraulic fluid is also an effective paint stripper, and will attack plastics; if any is spilt, it should be washed off immediately, using copious quantities of fresh water. Finally, it is hygroscopic (it absorbs moisture from the air) – old fluid may be contaminated and unfit for further use. When topping-up or renewing the fluid, always use the recommended type, and ensure that it comes from a freshly-opened sealed container.*

General information

1 The correct operation of any hydraulic system is only possible after removing all air from the components and circuit; this is achieved by bleeding the system.

2 The manufacturer's stipulate that the system must be initially bled by the 'back-bleeding' method using Vauxhall/Opel special bleeding equipment. This entails connecting a pressure bleeding unit containing fresh brake fluid, to the release cylinder bleed screw, with a collecting vessel connected to the brake fluid master cylinder reservoir. The pressure bleeding unit is then switched on, the bleed screw is opened and hydraulic fluid is delivered under pressure, backwards, to be expelled from the reservoir into the collecting vessel. Final bleeding is then carried out in the conventional way.

3 In practice, this method would normally only be required if new hydraulic components have been fitted, or if the system has been completely drained of hydraulic fluid. If the system has only been disconnected to allow component removal and refitting procedures to be carried out, such as removal and refitting of the transmission (for example for clutch replacement) or engine removal and refitting, then it is quite likely that normal bleeding will be sufficient.

2.8 Clutch bleed screw (arrowed)

4 Our advice would therefore be as follows:
a) *If the hydraulic system has only been partially disconnected, try bleeding by the conventional methods described in paragraphs 10 to 15, or 16 to 19.*
b) *If the hydraulic system has been completely drained and new components have been fitted, try bleeding by using the pressure bleeding method described in paragraphs 20 to 22.*
c) *If the above methods fail to produce a firm pedal on completion, it will be necessary to 'back-bleed' the system using Vauxhall/Opel bleeding equipment, or suitable alternative equipment as described in paragraphs 23 to 28.*

5 During the bleeding procedure, add only clean, unused hydraulic fluid of the recommended type; never re-use fluid that has already been bled from the system. Ensure that sufficient fluid is available before starting work.

6 If there is any possibility of incorrect fluid being already in the system, the hydraulic circuit must be flushed completely with uncontaminated, correct fluid.

7 If hydraulic fluid has been lost from the system, or air has entered because of a leak, ensure that the fault is cured before continuing further.

8 The bleed screw is located in the hose end fitting which is situated on the top of the transmission housing **(see illustration)**. On some models, access to the bleed screw is limited and it may be necessary to jack up the front of the vehicle and support it on axle stands so that the screw can be reached from below, or remove the battery and battery tray as described in Chapter 5A, so that the screw can be reached from above.

9 Check that all pipes and hoses are secure, unions tight and the bleed screw is closed. Clean any dirt from around the bleed screw.

Bleeding procedure

Conventional method

10 Collect a clean glass jar, a suitable length of plastic or rubber tubing which is a tight fit over the bleed screw, and a ring spanner to fit the screw. The help of an assistant will also be required.

11 Unscrew the master cylinder fluid reservoir cap (the clutch shares the same fluid reservoir as the braking system), and top the master cylinder reservoir up to the upper (MAX) level line. Ensure that the fluid level is maintained at least above the lower level line in the reservoir throughout the procedure.

12 Remove the dust cap from the bleed screw. Fit the spanner and tube to the screw, place the other end of the tube in the jar, and pour in sufficient fluid to cover the end of the tube.

13 Have the assistant fully depress the clutch pedal several times to build-up pressure, then maintain it on the final downstroke.

14 While pedal pressure is maintained, unscrew the bleed screw (approximately one turn) and allow the compressed fluid and

3.4 Disconnect the fluid supply hose (arrowed) from the clutch master cylinder

air to flow into the jar. The assistant should maintain pedal pressure and should not release it until instructed to do so. When the flow stops, tighten the bleed screw again, have the assistant release the pedal slowly, and recheck the reservoir fluid level.

15 Repeat the steps given in paragraphs 13 and 14 until the fluid emerging from the bleed screw is free from air bubbles. If the master cylinder has been drained and refilled allow approximately five seconds between cycles for the master cylinder passages to refill.

Using a one-way valve kit

16 As their name implies, these kits consist of a length of tubing with a one-way valve fitted, to prevent expelled air and fluid being drawn back into the system; some kits include a translucent container, which can be positioned so that the air bubbles can be more easily seen flowing from the end of the tube.

17 The kit is connected to the bleed screw, which is then opened.

18 The user returns to the driver's seat, depresses the clutch pedal with a smooth, steady stroke, and slowly releases it; this is repeated until the expelled fluid is clear of air bubbles.

19 Note that these kits simplify work so much that it is easy to forget the clutch fluid reservoir level; ensure that this is maintained at least above the lower level line at all times.

Pressure-bleeding method

20 These kits are usually operated by the reservoir of pressurised air contained in the spare tyre. However, note that it will probably be necessary to reduce the pressure to a lower

3.7a Using a small screwdriver depress the tabs each side . . .

3.5 Extract the retaining clip (arrowed) and disconnect the hydraulic pipe from the master cylinder connector

level than normal; refer to the instructions supplied with the kit.

21 By connecting a pressurised, fluid-filled container to the clutch fluid reservoir, bleeding can be carried out simply by opening the bleed screw and allowing the fluid to flow out until no more air bubbles can be seen in the expelled fluid.

22 This method has the advantage that the large reservoir of fluid provides an additional safeguard against air being drawn into the system during bleeding.

'Back-bleeding' method

23 The following procedure describes the bleeding method using Vauxhall/Opel equipment. Alternative equipment is available and should be used in accordance with the maker's instructions.

24 Connect the pressure hose (MKM-6174-1) to the bleed screw located in the hose end fitting situated on the top of the transmission housing **(see illustration 2.8)**. Connect the other end of the hose to a suitable pressure bleeding device set to operate at approximately 2.0 bar.

25 Attach the cap (MKM-6174-2) to the master cylinder reservoir, and place the hose in a collecting vessel.

26 Switch on the pressure bleeding equipment, open the bleed screw, and allow fresh hydraulic fluid to flow from the pressure bleeding unit, through the system and out through the top of the reservoir and into the collecting vessel. When fluid, free from air bubbles appears in the reservoir, close the bleed screw and switch off the bleeding equipment.

3.7b . . . and release the retaining clip (arrowed) securing the master cylinder pushrod to the clutch pedal

27 Disconnect the bleeding equipment from the bleed screw and reservoir.

28 Carry out a final conventional bleeding procedure as described in paragraphs 10 to 15, or 16 to 19.

All methods

29 When bleeding is complete, no more bubbles appear and correct pedal feel is restored, tighten the bleed screw securely (do not overtighten). Remove the tube and spanner, and wash off any spilt fluid. Refit the dust cap to the bleed screw.

30 Check the hydraulic fluid level in the master cylinder reservoir, and top-up if necessary (see *Weekly checks*).

31 Discard any hydraulic fluid that has been bled from the system; it will not be fit for re-use.

32 Check the operation of the clutch pedal. If the clutch is still not operating correctly, air must still be present in the system, and further bleeding is required. Failure to bleed satisfactorily after a reasonable repetition of the bleeding procedure may be due to worn master cylinder/release cylinder seals.

3 Master cylinder – removal and refitting

Note: *This procedure does not apply to models fitted with the Easytronic transmission.*

Removal

1 Remove the windscreen cowl panel as described in Chapter 11.

2 Unscrew the brake/clutch hydraulic fluid reservoir filler cap, and top-up the reservoir to the MAX mark (see *Weekly checks*). Place a piece of polythene over the filler neck, and secure the polythene with the filler cap. This will minimise brake fluid loss during subsequent operations.

3 Remove all traces of dirt from the outside of the master cylinder and the brake/clutch hydraulic fluid reservoir, then position some cloth beneath the cylinder to catch any spilt fluid.

4 Disconnect the fluid supply hose from the clutch master cylinder **(see illustration)**.

5 Extract the retaining clip securing the hydraulic pipe connector to the end fitting on the master cylinder **(see illustration)**. Release the bulkhead seal and withdraw the hydraulic pipe and seal from the master cylinder and bulkhead. Plug the pipe connector and master cylinder end fitting to minimise fluid loss and prevent the entry of dirt. Gently squeeze the two legs of the retaining clip together, and re-insert the clip into the pipe connector.

6 From inside the car, remove the lower trim panel under the facia on the driver's side as described in Chapter 11. Release the retaining clip and remove the driver's side footwell air duct.

7 Disconnect the return spring from the clutch pedal, then remove the retaining clip securing the master cylinder pushrod to the clutch pedal **(see illustrations)**.

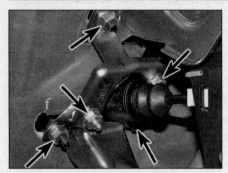

3.8 Master cylinder and mounting plate retaining nuts (arrowed)

8 Unscrew the two nuts securing the master cylinder to the mounting plate, and the three nuts securing the mounting plate to the pedal bracket **(see illustration)**. Withdraw the master cylinder and mounting plate from the pedal bracket and remove them from inside the car.

9 If the master cylinder is faulty it must be renewed; overhaul of the unit is not possible.

Refitting

10 Manoeuvre the master cylinder and mounting plate into position whilst ensuring that the pushrod aligns correctly with the pedal. Fit the five master cylinder and mounting plate retaining nuts and tighten them to the specified torque.

11 Secure the master cylinder pushrod to the clutch pedal with the retaining clip.

12 Refit the return spring to the clutch pedal.

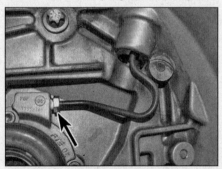

4.2 Clutch release cylinder hydraulic pipe union nut (arrowed)

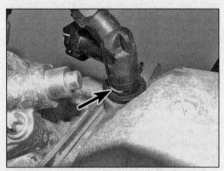

4.5 Extract the retaining clip (arrowed) and remove the hydraulic hose end fitting from the fastening sleeve

13 Refit the footwell air duct and the lower facia panel on the driver's side as described in Chapter 11.

14 Press the hydraulic pipe back connector onto the master cylinder end fitting ensuring that the pipe audibly engages and is securely retained.

15 Reconnect the fluid supply hose to the master cylinder.

16 Bleed the clutch hydraulic system as described in Section 2.

17 On completion, refit the windscreen cowl panel as described in Chapter 11.

4 Release cylinder – removal and refitting

Note 1: Due to the amount of work necessary to remove and refit clutch components, it is usually considered good practice to renew the clutch friction disc, pressure plate assembly and release cylinder as a matched set, even if only one of these is actually worn enough to require renewal. It is also worth considering the renewal of the clutch components on a preventative basis if the engine and/or transmission have been removed for some other reason.

Note 2: Refer to the warning concerning the dangers of asbestos dust at the beginning of Section 6.

Note 3: On models equipped with the Easytronic transmission, Vauxhall/Opel TECH2 diagnostic equipment will be required to bleed

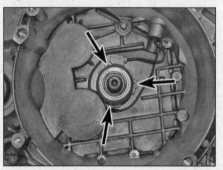

4.3 Clutch release cylinder retaining bolts (arrowed)

4.10 Make sure the lug (arrowed) on the fastening sleeve is located correctly in the transmission housing

the clutch hydraulic system and carry out a clutch Contact Point Determination program. If this equipment is not available, the following procedure should be entrusted to a Vauxhall/ Opel dealer.

Removal

1 Unless the complete engine/transmission unit is to be removed from the car and separated for major overhaul (see Chapter 2F), the clutch release cylinder can be reached by removing the transmission only, as described in Chapter 7A or 7B.

2 Wipe clean the outside of the release cylinder then slacken the union nut and disconnect the hydraulic pipe **(see illustration)**. Wipe up any spilt fluid with a clean cloth.

3 Unscrew the three retaining bolts and slide the release cylinder off from the transmission input shaft **(see illustration)**. Remove the sealing ring which is fitted between the cylinder and transmission housing, and discard it; a new one must be used on refitting. Whilst the cylinder is removed, take care not to allow any debris to enter the transmission unit.

4 The release cylinder is a sealed unit and cannot be overhauled. If the cylinder seals are leaking or the release bearing is noisy or rough in operation, then the complete unit must be renewed.

5 To remove the hydraulic pipe, extract the retaining clip and remove the hydraulic hose end fitting from the fastening sleeve on top of the transmission housing **(see illustration)**. Gently squeeze the legs of the retaining clip together and re-insert the clip back into position in the end fitting.

6 Using a small screwdriver, carefully spread the retaining lugs of the fastening sleeve to release the hydraulic pipe connection, and remove the pipe from inside the transmission housing. Check the condition of the sealing ring on the hydraulic pipe and renew if necessary.

7 If required, the fastening sleeve can be removed by squeezing the lower retaining lugs together with pointed-nose pliers, then withdrawing the sleeve upwards and out of the transmission. Note that if the fastening sleeve is removed, a new one must be obtained for refitting.

Refitting

8 Ensure the release cylinder and transmission mating surfaces are clean and dry and fit the new sealing ring to the transmission recess.

9 Lubricate the release cylinder seal with a smear of transmission oil then carefully ease the cylinder along the input shaft and into position. **Note:** *Vauxhall/Opel technicians use a special tapered sleeve on the input shaft to prevent damage to the seal. If necessary, wrap suitable tape around the end of the shaft. Ensure the sealing ring is still correctly seated in its groove then refit the release cylinder retaining bolts and tighten them to the specified torque.*

10 If removed, fit the new fastening sleeve,

engaging the lug on the sleeve with the cut-out in the housing **(see illustration)**. Ensure that the sleeve can be felt to positively lock in position.

11 Insert the hydraulic pipe into the fastening sleeve until the end fitting can be felt to positively lock in position.

12 Reconnect the hydraulic pipe to the release cylinder, tightening its union nut to the specified torque.

13 Refit the hydraulic hose end fitting to the fastening sleeve ensuring that it is positively retained by its clip.

14 Refit the transmission unit as described in Chapter 7A or 7B.

15 On models equipped with a conventional transmission, bleed the clutch hydraulic system as described in Section 2.

16 On models equipped with the Easytronic transmission, bleed the clutch hydraulic system and carry out a clutch Contact Point Determination program using Vauxhall/Opel TECH2 diagnostic equipment.

5 Clutch pedal –
removal and refitting

1 The clutch pedal is an integral part of the brake pedal and mounting bracket assembly and cannot be individually removed. Removal and refitting details for the brake pedal and mounting bracket assembly are contained in Chapter 9.

6 Clutch assembly –
removal, inspection and refitting

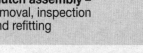

⚠️ *Warning: Dust created by clutch wear and deposited on the clutch components may contain asbestos, which is a health hazard. DO NOT blow it out with compressed air, or inhale any of it. DO NOT use petrol or petroleum-based solvents to clean off the dust. Brake system cleaner or methylated spirit should be used to flush the dust into a suitable receptacle. After the clutch components are wiped clean with rags, dispose of the contaminated rags and cleaner in a sealed, marked container.*

Note 1: *To prevent possible damage to the ends of the pressure plate diaphragm spring fingers, Vauxhall/Opel recommend the use of a special jig (KM-6263) to remove the clutch assembly, however, with care it is possible to carry out the work without the jig.*

Note 2: *On models equipped with the Easytronic transmission, Vauxhall/Opel TECH2 diagnostic equipment will be required to carry out a clutch Contact Point Determination program after the transmission has been refitted. If this equipment is not available, the following procedure should be entrusted to a Vauxhall/Opel dealer.*

Removal

1 Unless the complete engine/transmission unit is to be removed from the car and separated for major overhaul (see Chapter 2F), the clutch can be reached by removing the transmission as described in Chapter 7A or 7B.

2 Before disturbing the clutch, use chalk or a marker pen to mark the relationship of the pressure plate assembly to the flywheel.

3 At this stage, Vauxhall/Opel technicians fit the special jig KM-6263 to the rear of the engine and compress the diaphragm spring fingers until the friction disc is released **(see illustrations)**. The pressure plate mounting bolts are then unscrewed, and the jig spindle backed off.

4 If the jig is not available, progressively unscrew the pressure plate retaining bolts in diagonal sequence by half a turn at a time, until spring pressure is released and the bolts can be unscrewed by hand.

5 Remove the pressure plate assembly and collect the friction disc, noting which way round the disc is fitted. It is recommended that new pressure plate retaining bolts are obtained.

Inspection

Note: *Due to the amount of work necessary to remove and refit clutch components, it is usually considered good practice to renew the clutch friction disc, pressure plate assembly and release cylinder as a matched set, even if only one of these is actually worn enough to require renewal. It is also worth considering the renewal of the clutch components on a preventative basis if the engine and/or transmission have been removed for some other reason.*

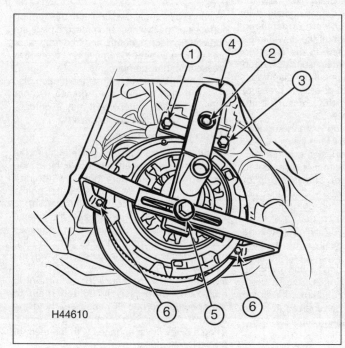
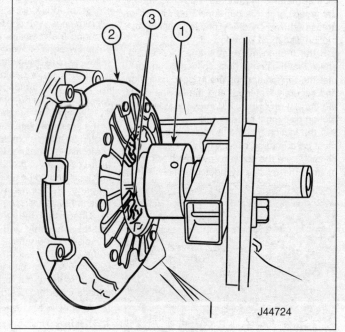

6.3a Vauxhall special jig KM-6263 for removing the clutch pressure plate and friction disc

1, 3 and 6 Bolts securing the jig to the engine
2 and 5 Bolts for adjusting the jig to the centre of the crankshaft

6.3b Thrust piece (1) in contact with the diaphragm spring fingers (3) of the pressure plate (2)

6.15 Mount a large bolt and washer into a vice, then fit the pressure plate over it

6.16 Fit large washers and a nut to the bolt and hand-tighten

6.17a Tighten the nut until the spring adjuster is free to turn . . .

6.17b . . . then open up the jaws of suitable pliers to compress the springs

6 When cleaning clutch components, read first the warning at the beginning of this Section; remove dust using a clean, dry cloth, and working in a well-ventilated atmosphere.

7 Check the friction disc facings for signs of wear, damage or oil contamination. If the friction material is cracked, burnt, scored or damaged, or if it is contaminated with oil or grease (shown by shiny black patches), the friction disc must be renewed.

8 If the friction material is still serviceable, check that the centre boss splines are unworn, that the torsion springs are in good condition and securely fastened, and that all the rivets are tight. If any wear or damage is found, the friction disc must be renewed.

9 If the friction material is fouled with oil, this must be due to an oil leak from the crankshaft oil seal, from the sump-to-cylinder block joint, or from the release cylinder assembly (either

6.21 The lettering 'transmission side' or 'Getriebeseite' on the friction disc must point towards the transmission

the main seal or the sealing ring). Renew the crankshaft oil seal or repair the sump joint as described in the appropriate Part of Chapter 2, before installing the new friction disc. The clutch release cylinder is covered in Section 4.

10 Check the pressure plate assembly for obvious signs of wear or damage; shake it to check for loose rivets, or worn or damaged fulcrum rings, and check that the drive straps securing the pressure plate to the cover do not show signs of overheating (such as a deep yellow or blue discoloration). If the diaphragm spring is worn or damaged, or if its pressure is in any way suspect, the pressure plate assembly should be renewed.

11 Examine the machined bearing surfaces of the pressure plate and of the flywheel; they should be clean, completely flat, and free from scratches or scoring. If either is discoloured from excessive heat, or shows signs of cracks, it should be renewed – although minor damage of this nature can sometimes be polished away using emery paper.

12 Check that the release cylinder bearing rotates smoothly and easily, with no sign of noise or roughness. Also check that the surface itself is smooth and unworn, with no signs of cracks, pitting or scoring. If there is any doubt about its condition, the clutch release cylinder should be renewed (it is not possible to renew the bearing separately).

Refitting

13 On certain models, the clutch pressure plate is unusual, as there is a pre-adjustment mechanism to compensate for wear in the friction disc (this is termed by Vauxhall/Opel

as a self-adjusting clutch (SAC), which is slightly ambiguous as all clutches fitted to these models are essentially self-adjusting). However, this mechanism must be reset before refitting the pressure plate. A new plate may be supplied preset, in which case this procedure can be ignored.

14 A large diameter bolt (M14 at least) long enough to pass through the pressure plate, a matching nut, and several large diameter washers, will be needed for this procedure. Mount the bolt head in the jaws of a sturdy bench vice, with one large washer fitted.

15 Offer the plate over the bolt, friction disc surface facing down, and locate it centrally over the bolt and washer – the washer should bear on the centre hub **(see illustration)**.

16 Fit several further large washers over the bolt, so that they bear on the ends of the spring fingers, then add the nut and tighten by hand to locate the washers **(see illustration)**.

17 The purpose of the procedure is to turn the plate's internal adjuster disc so that the three small coil springs visible on the plate's outer surface are fully compressed. Tighten the nut just fitted until the adjuster disc is free to turn. Using a pair of thin-nosed, or circlip pliers, in one of the three windows in the top surface, open the jaws of the pliers to turn the adjuster disc anti-clockwise, so that the springs are fully compressed **(see illustrations)**.

18 Hold the pliers in this position, then unscrew the centre nut. Once the nut is released, the adjuster disc will be gripped in position, and the pliers can be removed. Take the pressure plate from the vice, and it is ready to fit.

19 On reassembly, ensure that the friction surfaces of the flywheel and pressure plate are completely clean, smooth, and free from oil or grease. Use solvent to remove any protective grease from new components.

20 Lightly grease the teeth of the friction disc hub with high melting-point grease. Do not apply too much, otherwise it may eventually contaminate the friction disc linings.

Using the Vauxhall jig

21 Fit the special Vauxhall guide bush to the centre of the crankshaft, and locate the friction disc on it, making sure that the lettering 'transmission side' or 'Getriebeseite' points towards the transmission **(see illustration)**.

22 Locate the pressure plate on the special centring pins on the flywheel, then compress the diaphragm spring fingers with the jig, until the friction disc is in full contact with the flywheel.

23 Insert new pressure plate retaining bolts, and progressively tighten them to the specified torque. If necessary, hold the flywheel stationary while tightening the bolts, using a screwdriver engaged with the teeth of the starter ring gear.

24 Back off the jig spindle so that the diaphragm spring forces the pressure plate against the friction disc and flywheel, then remove the jig and guide bush from the engine.

25 Refit the transmission as described in Chapter 7A or 7B.

Without using the Vauxhall jig

26 Locate the friction disc on the flywheel, making sure that the lettering 'transmission side' or 'Getriebeseite' points towards the transmission **(see illustration 6.21)**.

27 Refit the pressure plate assembly, aligning the marks made on dismantling (if the original pressure plate is re-used). Fit new pressure plate bolts, but tighten them only finger-tight so that the friction disc can still be moved **(see illustration)**.

28 The friction disc must now be centralised so that, when the transmission is refitted, its input shaft will pass through the splines at the centre of the friction disc.

29 Centralisation can be achieved by passing a screwdriver or other long bar through the friction disc and into the hole in the crankshaft.

6.27 Fit the pressure plate assembly over the friction disc

The friction disc can then be moved around until it is centred on the crankshaft hole. Alternatively, a clutch-aligning tool can be used to eliminate the guesswork; these can be obtained from most accessory shops **(see illustration)**.

6.29 Centralise the friction disc using a clutch aligning tool or similar

30 When the friction disc is centralised, tighten the pressure plate bolts evenly and in a diagonal sequence to the specified torque setting.

31 Refit the transmission as described in Chapter 7A or 7B.

Chapter 7 Part A:
Manual transmission

Contents

Degrees of difficulty

Easy, suitable for novice with little experience 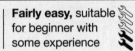	Fairly easy, suitable for beginner with some experience	Fairly difficult, suitable for competent DIY mechanic	Difficult, suitable for experienced DIY mechanic	Very difficult, suitable for expert DIY or professional

Specifications

Engine identification

Engine type	Manufacturer's engine code*
Petrol engines:	
1.4 litre (1364 cc) DOHC 16-valve	Z14XEP
1.6 litre (1598 cc):	
SOHC 8-valve	Z16SE
DOHC 16-valve	Z16XE and Z16XEP
1.8 litre (1796 cc) DOHC 16-valve	Z18XE
Diesel engines:	
1.3 litre (1248 cc) DOHC 16-valve	Z13DTJ
1.7 litre (1686 cc) DOHC 16-valve	Y17DT and Z17DTH

* For details of engine code location, see 'Vehicle identification' in the Reference Chapter.

General

Type	Five forward speeds and one reverse, synchromesh on all forward gears. Integral differential
Manufacturer's designation:	
Petrol engine models:	
1.4 litre engines	F13
1.6 litre engines:	
Z16SE engines	F13
Z16XE engines	F17+
Z16XEP engines up to 2008	F17+
Z16XEP engines from 2008	F13+
Diesel engine models:	
1.3 litre engines	F17+
1.7 litre engines:	
Y17DT engines	F17+
Z17DTH engines	F23

Gear ratios

F13 and F17+ (close ratio) transmissions:
1st	3.73:1
2nd	2.14:1
3rd	1.41:1
4th	1.12:1
5th	0.89:1
Reverse	3.31:1

F13, F13+ and F17+ (wide ratio) transmissions:
1st	3.73:1
2nd	1.96:1
3rd	1.32:1
4th	0.95:1
5th	0.76:1
Reverse	3.31:1

F23 (wide ratio) transmissions:
1st	3.57:1
2nd	1.88:1
3rd	1.19:1
4th	0.84:1
5th	0.68:1
Reverse	3.30:1

Final drive ratios

1.4 litre petrol engines	4.29:1
1.6 and 1.8 litre petrol engines	3.94:1
1.3 litre diesel engines	3.94:1

1.7 litre diesel engines:
F17+ transmissions	3.94:1
F23 transmissions	3.84:1

Torque wrench settings

	Nm	lbf ft

F13, F13+ and F17+ transmissions

Differential housing cover plate bolts:
	Nm	lbf ft
Alloy plate	18	13
Steel plate	30	22
Engine/transmission mountings	See the relevant Part of Chapter 2	
Engine-to-transmission bolts	See the relevant Part of Chapter 2	
Gear lever housing bolts	22	16

Gearchange mechanism selector rod clamp bolt:
	Nm	lbf ft
Stage 1	12	9
Stage 2	Angle-tighten a further 225°	

Oil level plug:
	Nm	lbf ft
Stage 1	4	3
Stage 2	Angle-tighten a further 45° to 180°	
Reversing light switch	20	15
Roadwheel bolts	110	81

F23 transmissions

	Nm	lbf ft
Engine/transmission mountings	See the relevant Part of Chapter 2	
Engine-to-transmission bolts	See the relevant Part of Chapter 2	
Oil drain plug	35	26
Oil filler plug	35	26
Oil level plug	35	26

Oil seal carrier-to-differential:
	Nm	lbf ft
Stage 1	20	15
Stage 2	Angle-tighten a further 45°	
Reversing light switch	20	15
Roadwheel bolts	110	81

1 General information

The transmission is contained in a cast-aluminium alloy casing bolted to the engine's left-hand end, and consists of the gearbox and final drive differential – often called a transaxle.

Drive is transmitted from the crankshaft via the clutch to the input shaft, which has a splined extension to accept the clutch friction disc, and rotates in sealed ball-bearings. From the input shaft, drive is transmitted to the output shaft, which rotates in a roller bearing at its right-hand end, and a sealed ball-bearing at its left-hand end. From the output shaft, the drive is transmitted to the differential crownwheel, which rotates with the differential case and planetary gears, thus driving the sun gears and driveshafts. The rotation of the planetary gears on their shaft allows the inner roadwheel to rotate at a slower speed than the outer roadwheel when the car is cornering.

The input and output shafts are arranged side-by-side, parallel to the crankshaft and driveshafts, so that their gear pinion teeth are in constant mesh. In the neutral position, the output shaft gear pinions rotate freely, so that drive cannot be transmitted to the crownwheel.

Gear selection is via a floor-mounted lever and either a rod-operated, or cable-operated selector linkage mechanism. The selector linkage cause the appropriate selector fork to move its respective synchro-sleeve along the shaft, to lock the gear pinion to the synchro-hub. Since the synchro-hubs are splined to the output shaft, this locks the pinion to the shaft, so that drive can be transmitted. To ensure that gearchanging can be made quickly and quietly, a synchromesh system is fitted to all forward gears, consisting of baulk rings and spring-loaded fingers, as well as the gear pinions and synchro-hubs. The synchromesh cones are formed on the mating faces of the baulk rings and gear pinions.

2 Transmission oil – level check, draining and refilling

F13, F13+ and F17+ transmissions

Level check

1 Position the vehicle over an inspection pit, on vehicle ramps, or jack it up and support it securely on axle stands (see *Jacking and vehicle support*), but make sure that it is level. The oil must be checked before the car is driven, or at least 5 minutes after the engine has been switched off. If the oil is checked immediately after driving the car, some of the oil will remain distributed around the transmission components, resulting in an inaccurate level reading.

2 Wipe clean the area around the level plug. The level plug is located behind the driveshaft inner joint on the left-hand side of the transmission **(see illustration 2.16)**. Unscrew the plug and clean it.

3 The oil level should reach the lower edge of the level plug aperture. If topping-up is necessary, wipe clean the area around the reversing light switch, and remove the switch as described in Section 7.

4 Add the specified grade of oil given in *Lubricants and fluids*, through the reversing light switch aperture, until it reaches the bottom of the level plug aperture. Allow any excess oil to drain, then refit and tighten the level plug to the specified torque.

5 Refit the reversing light switch with reference to Section 7.

6 Where applicable, refit the engine undertray, then lower the vehicle to the ground.

Draining

Caution: If the procedure is to be carried out on a hot transmission unit, take care not to burn yourself on the hot exhaust or the transmission/engine unit.

Note: *A new differential lower cover plate gasket will be required for this operation.*

7 This operation is much more efficient if the car is first taken on a journey of sufficient length to warm the engine/transmission up to normal operating temperature.

8 Position the vehicle over an inspection pit, on vehicle ramps, or jack it up and support it securely on axle stands (see *Jacking and vehicle support*), but make sure that it is level.

9 Since the transmission oil is not renewed as part of the manufacturer's maintenance schedule, no drain plug is fitted to the transmission. If for any reason the transmission needs to be drained, the only way of doing so is to remove the differential lower cover plate.

10 Refer to the relevant Part of Chapter 2, remove the engine/transmission rear mounting/torque link.

11 Wipe clean the area around the differential cover plate and position a suitable container underneath the cover.

12 Evenly and progressively slacken and remove the retaining bolts then withdraw the cover plate and allow the transmission oil to drain into the container **(see illustration)**. Remove the gasket and discard it; a new one should be used on refitting.

13 Allow the oil to drain completely into the container. If the oil is hot, take precautions against scalding. Remove all traces of dirt and oil from the cover and transmission mating surfaces and wipe clean the inside of the cover plate.

14 Once the oil has finished draining, ensure the mating surfaces are clean and dry then refit the cover plate to the transmission unit, complete with a new gasket. Refit the retaining bolts and evenly and progressively tighten them to the specified torque.

15 Refit the engine/transmission rear mounting/torque link as described in the relevant Part of Chapter 2.

Refilling

16 Wipe clean the area around the level plug. The level plug is located behind the driveshaft inner joint on the left-hand side of the transmission **(see illustration)**. Unscrew the plug and clean it.

17 The transmission is refilled via the reversing light switch aperture **(see illustration)**. Wipe clean the area around the reversing light switch, and remove the switch as described in Section 7. Refill the transmission with the specified grade of oil given in *Lubricants and fluids*, until it reaches the bottom of the level plug aperture. Allow any excess oil to drain, then refit and tighten the level plug to the specified torque.

18 Refit the reversing light switch with reference to Section 7, then lower the vehicle to the ground.

2.12 Differential cover plate securing bolts (arrowed) – F13, F13+ and F17+ transmissions

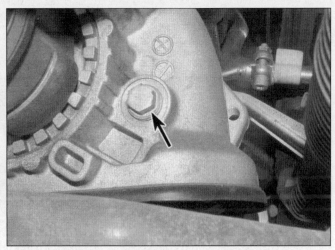

2.16 Transmission oil level plug (arrowed) – F13, F13+ and F17+ transmissions

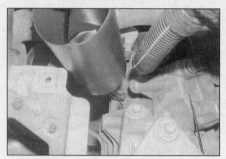

2.17 Fill the transmission through the reversing light switch aperture – F13, F13+ and F17+ transmissions

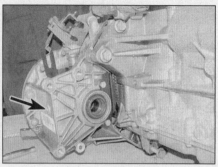

2.29 Transmission oil level plug (arrowed) – F23 transmissions

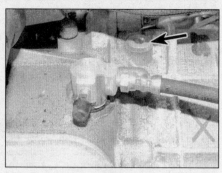

2.30 Transmission oil filler plug (arrowed) – F23 transmissions

F23 transmissions

Level check

19 Position the vehicle over an inspection pit, on vehicle ramps, or jack it up and support it securely on axle stands (see *Jacking and vehicle support*), but make sure that it is level. The oil must be checked before the car is driven, or at least 5 minutes after the engine has been switched off. If the oil is checked immediately after driving the car, some of the oil will remain distributed around the transmission components, resulting in an inaccurate level reading.

20 Wipe clean the area around the level plug located on the rear of the differential housing **(see illustration 2.29)**. Unscrew the plug and clean it.

21 The oil level should reach the lower edge of the level plug aperture. If topping-up is necessary, wipe clean the area around the filler plug on the top of the casing and unscrew the plug **(see illustration 2.30)**. To gain access to the plug, lift the fuel filter out of the crash box and position it to one side.

22 Add the specified grade of oil given in *Lubricants and fluids*, through the filler plug aperture, until it reaches the bottom of the level plug aperture. Allow any excess oil to drain, then refit and tighten the level plug to the specified torque.

23 Refit the oil filler plug and tighten it to the specified torque. Lower the vehicle to the ground and refit the fuel filter to the crash box.

Draining

Caution: If the procedure is to be carried out on a hot transmission unit, take care not to burn yourself on the hot exhaust or the transmission/engine unit.

24 This operation is much more efficient if the car is first taken on a journey of sufficient length to warm the engine/transmission up to normal operating temperature.

25 Position the vehicle over an inspection pit, on vehicle ramps, or jack it up and support it securely on axle stands (see *Jacking and vehicle support*), but make sure that it is level.

26 Wipe clean the area around the drain plug, located below the left-hand driveshaft, and position a suitable container under the plug.

27 Undo the drain plug and allow the oil to drain.

28 Once the oil has finished draining, refit the drain plug with a new sealing washer where applicable, and tighten the plug to the specified torque.

Refilling

29 Wipe clean the area around the level plug located on the rear of the differential housing **(see illustration)**. Unscrew the plug and clean it.

30 The transmission is refilled via the oil filler plug on the top of the casing **(see illustration)**. To gain access to the plug, lift the fuel filter out of the crash box and position it to one side.

31 Wipe clean the area around the plug and unscrew it. Refill the transmission with the specified grade of oil given in *Lubricants and fluids*, until it reaches the bottom of the level

plug aperture. Allow any excess oil to drain, then refit and tighten the level plug to the specified torque.

32 Refit the oil filler plug and tighten it to the specified torque, then lower the vehicle to the ground.

33 Refit the fuel filter to the crash box.

3 Gearchange linkage/ mechanism – adjustment

F13, F13+ and F17+ transmissions

Note: *A 5 mm drill bit or metal rod will be required to carry out this procedure.*

1 Adjustment of the gearchange linkage/ mechanism should only be needed if the mechanism has been disconnected or removed. The mechanism is adjusted at the clamp bolt which secures the selector rod to the transmission linkage at the rear of the engine compartment. Access is best from under the vehicle.

2 Apply the handbrake, then jack up the front of the vehicle and support it on axle stands (see *Jacking and vehicle support*). Remove the engine undertray, where fitted.

3 Slacken the gearchange selector rod clamp bolt which is situated at the front of the rod **(see illustration)**. Do not remove the bolt completely.

4 From inside the vehicle, unclip the gear lever gaiter from the centre console, then fold the gaiter up over the gear lever knob.

5 Push the gear lever to the left in neutral, then insert a 5 mm drill bit or metal rod through the special hole in the lever base to lock it in the adjusting position **(see illustration)**.

6 Working in the engine compartment, with the selector mechanism in neutral, turn the selector shaft anti-clockwise against the spring pressure towards the third gear position, and lock the selector mechanism by pressing in the spring-loaded locking pin which is located on the top of the transmission unit **(see illustration)**. Ensure that the locking pin is pressed fully in so that the spring is completely compressed.

7 With both the lever and transmission locked

3.3 Gearchange selector rod clamp bolt and nut (arrowed) – F13, F13+ and F17+ transmissions

3.5 Insert a 5 mm drill or punch (arrowed) through the lever base and into the locating hole – F13, F13+ and F17+ transmissions

in position, tighten the selector rod clamp bolt to the specified Stage 1 torque, then through the Stage 2 angle.

8 Remove the locking rod from the gear lever and check the operation of the gearchange mechanism; the transmission locking pin will automatically release when the lever is moved into the reverse position.

9 Ensure the transmission locking pin has released, then lower the vehicle to the ground.

10 Check that all gears can be engaged easily, first with the engine off, then with the engine running and the clutch disengaged.

11 On completion, refit the gear lever gaiter to the centre console.

F23 transmissions

12 From inside the vehicle, unclip the gear lever gaiter from the centre console, then fold the gaiter up over the gear lever knob.

13 Using a small screwdriver, open the clamping piece on the end of each selector cable as far as the notch. Opening them any further may damage the clamping pieces **(see illustrations)**.

14 In the engine compartment, set the gearchange selector on the transmission to the 'neutral' position.

15 Working back inside the car, position the gear lever in the 'neutral' position, and lock it there by pushing in the clamp **(see illustration)**.

16 Lock both gearshift cable clamping pieces by pushing them down, then pull out the clamp to unlock the gear lever.

17 Check that all gears can be engaged easily, first with the engine off, then with the engine running and the clutch disengaged.

18 On completion, refit the gear lever gaiter to the centre console.

4 Gearchange mechanism (F13, F13+ and F17+ transmissions) – removal and refitting

1 The gearchange mechanism consists of the gear lever, the selector rod and the linkage assembly on the transmission. The lever and selector rod and the linkage assembly can be removed separately.

Gear lever

Note: *To remove the gear lever, it is necessary to destroy the ball socket. Obtain a new socket before carrying out the work.*

Removal

2 Ensure that the lever is in neutral, then carefully unclip the edge of the gear lever gaiter from the centre console. There are two retaining lugs at the front and two at the rear of the centre console aperture. Pull the gaiter upwards over the gear lever knob, then release the cable-tie and remove it completely.

3 Using a screwdriver, depress the tabs at the bottom of the gear lever housing to release the ball socket from the housing **(see illustration)**.

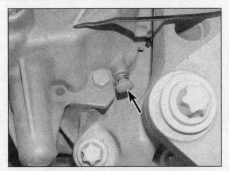

3.6 Lock the selector mechanism by pressing in the spring-loaded locking pin (arrowed) – F13, F13+ and F17+ transmissions

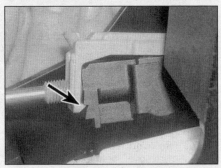

3.13b . . . until the lug (arrowed) rests on the notch – F23 transmissions

Pull up the gear lever together with the ball socket.

4 Using a screwdriver, lever the ball socket from the bottom of the gear lever **(see illustration)**. Note that this will destroy the socket.

5 Withdraw the gear lever from the selector rod guide.

Refitting

6 Wipe clean all lubricant from the bearing surfaces of the gear lever and guide, then apply new silicone grease to the surfaces.

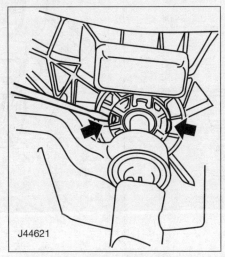

4.3 Depress the tabs at the bottom of the gear lever housing to release the ball socket from the housing

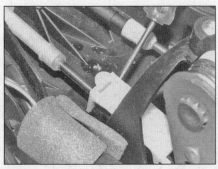

3.13a Using a small screwdriver, open the clamping piece on the end of each selector cable . . .

3.15 Lock the gear lever in 'neutral' by pushing in the clamp with a screwdriver – F23 transmissions

7 Insert the gear lever through the selector rod guide, then press the new ball socket firmly onto the end of the gear lever until it engages. Note that the lugs on the ball end must be aligned with the grooves of the ball socket **(see illustration)**.

8 Align the gear lever with the selector rod guide, then press the ball socket firmly into the housing. Note that the retaining clips must be heard to engage.

9 Refit the gaiter to the gear lever, using a new cable-tie, then clip the edge of the gaiter

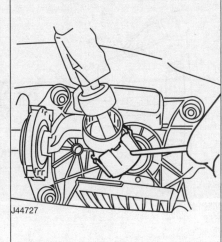

4.4 Lever the ball socket from the bottom of the gear lever

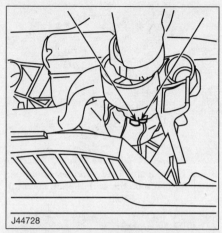

4.7 The lugs on the ball end must be aligned with the grooves of the ball socket

firmly into the centre console. To prevent any subsequent noise, the loose end of the cable-tie should be cut off.

Lever housing and selector rod

Removal

10 Apply the handbrake, then jack up the front of the vehicle and support it on axle stands (see *Jacking and vehicle support*).
11 Reach up behind the transmission and slacken the gearchange selector rod clamp bolt which is situated at the front of the rod **(see illustration 3.3)**. Do not remove the bolt completely. Push the selector rod rearwards and separate it from the shift guide.
12 Prise the gaiter from the bulkhead and withdraw from the selector rod.
13 Remove the centre console as described in Chapter 11.
14 Unscrew the nut and release the wiring

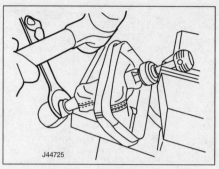

4.21 Driving the knob from the gear lever

trough from the left-hand side of the gear lever housing.
15 Unscrew the four bolts, then withdraw the gear lever housing and selector rod assembly from the vehicle.
16 If necessary, the selector rod may be removed from the housing.

Refitting

17 Clean the bush guide in the housing, and apply some silicone grease. Insert the selector rod through the guide.
18 The remaining refitting procedure is a reversal of removal, tightening the housing mounting bolts securely, and adjusting the linkage as described in Section 3.

Gear lever knob

Renewal

19 Using a small screwdriver, carefully prise the position indicator plate from the top of the gear lever knob.
20 Remove the gear lever as described earlier in this Section.
21 Make sure you note the fitted position of the knob, and also check that the pressure

spring fitted below the knob stays in place. Mount the gear lever in a soft-jawed vice, then drive the knob from the lever using a suitable spanner and mallet **(see illustration)**.
22 Locate the new knob on the lever and drive into position with the mallet. The distance from the lower edge of the lever guide to the lower edge of the stop lever with reverse gear button lock applied must be between 8.0 and 10.0 mm **(see illustration)**.
23 Refit the gear lever as described earlier in this Section.
24 Place the position indicator plate on the gear lever knob with the tab and knob groove aligned with each other, then press firmly into position.

Gearchange shift guide

Removal

25 Apply the handbrake, then jack up the front of the vehicle and support it on axle stands (see *Jacking and vehicle support*).
26 On diesel engine models, remove the battery and battery tray as described in Chapter 5A.
27 Reach up behind the transmission and slacken the gearchange selector rod clamp bolt which is situated at the front of the rod **(see illustration 3.3)**. Do not remove the bolt completely. Push the selector rod rearwards and separate it from the shift guide.
28 Remove the two clips and disconnect the linkage from the shift guide brackets.
29 Depress the retaining spring and lever out the pin. Detach the universal joint from the shift rod **(see illustration)**.
30 Withdraw the shift pivot together with the shift guide.

Refitting

31 Refitting is a reversal of removal, but adjust the linkage as described in Section 3.

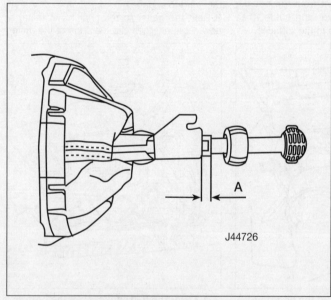

4.22 Correct position of the gear lever knob

A = 8.0 to 10.0 mm

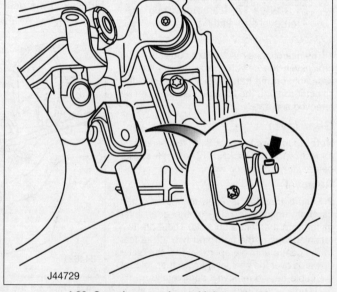

4.29 Gearchange universal joint removal

Arrow shows position of hollow pin retaining spring

5 Gearchange mechanism (F23 transmissions) – removal and refitting

Gear lever housing

Removal

1 Remove the centre console as described in Chapter 11.

2 Using a small screwdriver, open the clamping piece on the end of each selector cable as far as the notch. Opening them any further may damage the clamping pieces **(see illustrations 3.13a and 3.13b)**.

3 Note the fitted locations of the two cables, then depress the lugs on the sides of the outer cable ends and lift the outer cables from the gear lever housing **(see illustration)**.

4 Move the two selector cables forward to disengage the inner cables from the gear lever clamping pieces.

5 Undo the four retaining bolts and lift the gear lever housing from the floor **(see illustration)**.

6 If required, the cable clamping pieces attached to the gear lever can be carefully prised from their position using a forked tool. No further dismantling of the assembly is recommended.

Refitting

7 If previously removed, attached the cable clamping pieces to the base of the lever using a pair of pliers.

8 Position the gear lever housing on the floor, insert the securing bolts and tighten securely.

9 Engage the selector inner cables with the clamping pieces, then refit the outer cables to the gear lever housing. Do not lock the clamping pieces at this stage.

10 Carry out the gearchange mechanism adjustment procedure, as described in Section 3.

11 Refit the centre console as described in Chapter 11.

Selector cables

Removal

12 Carry out the operations described in paragraphs 1 to 4 above.

13 Remove the battery and battery tray as described in Chapter 5A.

14 Working in the engine compartment, note the fitted locations of the cables at their transmission attachments.

15 Using a suitable forked tool, release the inner cable end fittings from the transmission selector levers **(see illustration)**.

16 Pull back the retaining sleeves and detach the outer cables from the mounting bracket on the transmission **(see illustration)**.

17 Apply the handbrake, then jack up the front of the vehicle and support it on axle stands (see *Jacking and vehicle support*).

18 Release the rubber grommet at the cable entry point on the engine compartment bulkhead, then pull the cables (complete with

5.3 Depress the lugs on the sides of the outer cable ends and lift the cables from the gear lever housing

5.15 Release the inner cable end fittings from the transmission selector levers

grommet) out of the bulkhead and into the engine compartment.

Refitting

19 Push the selector cables through the bulkhead passage from the engine compartment and locate the rubber grommet back into position in the bulkhead.

20 Lower the vehicle to the ground.

21 Refit the outer cables to the mounting bracket on the transmission.

22 Engage the inner cable end fittings with the transmission selector levers, squeezing them together with pliers if necessary.

23 Engage the selector inner cables with the clamping pieces, then refit the outer cables to the gear lever housing. Do not lock the clamping pieces at this stage.

24 Carry out the gearchange mechanism adjustment procedure, as described in Section 3.

6.4 Prising out a driveshaft oil seal

5.5 Undo the four retaining bolts (arrowed) and lift the gear lever housing from the floor

5.16 Pull back the retaining sleeves and detach the outer cables from the transmission mounting bracket

25 If not already done, refit the battery tray and battery as described in Chapter 5.

26 Refit the centre console as described in Chapter 11.

6 Oil seals – renewal

Driveshaft oil seals

1 Firmly apply the handbrake, then jack up the front of the car and support it securely on axle stands (see *Jacking and vehicle support*). Where fitted, remove the engine undertray.

2 Drain the transmission oil as described in Section 2.

3 Remove the driveshaft/intermediate shaft as described in Chapter 8.

4 Note the correct fitted depth of the seal in its housing then carefully prise it out of position using a large flat-bladed screwdriver **(see illustration)**.

5 Remove all traces of dirt from the area around the oil seal aperture, then apply a smear of grease to the outer lip of the new oil seal. Ensure the seal is correctly positioned, with its sealing lip facing inwards, and tap it squarely into position, using a suitable tubular drift (such as a socket) which bears only on the hard outer edge of the seal **(see illustration)**. Ensure the seal is fitted at the same depth in its housing that the original was.

6 Refit the driveshaft/intermediate shaft as described in Chapter 8.

6.5 Fitting a new driveshaft oil seal using a socket as a tubular drift

7 Refill the transmission with the specified type and amount of oil, as described in Section 2.

Input shaft oil seal

8 The input shaft oil seal is an integral part of the clutch release cylinder; if the seal is leaking the complete release cylinder assembly must be renewed. Before condemning the release cylinder, check that the leak is not coming from the sealing ring which is fitted between the cylinder and the transmission housing; the sealing ring can be renewed once the release cylinder assembly has been removed. Refer to Chapter 6 for removal and refitting details.

7 Reversing light switch – testing, removal and refitting

F13, F13+ and F17+ transmissions

Testing

1 The reversing light circuit is operated by a plunger-type switch, mounted on the upper/front of the transmission casing.
2 To test the switch, disconnect the wiring, and use a suitable meter or a battery-and-bulb test circuit to check for continuity between the switch terminals. Continuity should only exist when reverse gear is selected. If this is not the case, and there are no obvious breaks or other damage to the wires, the switch is faulty and must be renewed.

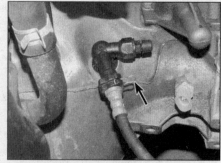

8.6 Prise out the clip (arrowed) to disconnect the clutch hydraulic hose from the release cylinder pipe

Removal

3 The reversing light switch is located on the front of the transmission casing, and is accessible from the left-hand side of the engine compartment or from beneath the vehicle.
4 Disconnect the wiring from the switch, then unscrew the switch from the transmission. Recover the O-ring seal.

Refitting

5 Refitting is a reversal of removal, but tighten the switch to the specified torque.

F23 transmissions

6 The reversing light circuit is controlled by a plunger-type switch screwed into the rear of the transmission above the left-hand driveshaft.
7 To gain access to the switch, firmly apply the handbrake, then jack up the front of the car and support it securely on axle stands (see *Jacking and vehicle support*).

Testing

8 Proceed as described in paragraph 2 above.

Removal

9 Disconnect the wiring connector, then unscrew the switch and remove it from the transmission casing along with its sealing washer.

Refitting

10 Fit a new sealing washer to the switch, then screw it back into position in the rear of the transmission housing and tighten it to the specified torque. Reconnect the wiring connector, then test the operation of the circuit.
11 On completion, lower the vehicle to the ground.

8 Manual transmission – removal and refitting

Note: *This is an involved procedure, and it may well prove easier to remove the transmission complete with the engine as an assembly (see Chapter 2F), then separate the transmission. However, this Section describes removing the transmission leaving the engine in position. Suitable equipment will be required to support the engine and transmission, and the help of an assistant will be required.*

Removal

1 Apply the handbrake, then jack up the front of the vehicle and support it on axle stands (see *Jacking and vehicle support*). Allow sufficient working room to remove the transmission from under the left-hand side of the engine compartment. Remove both front roadwheels and the engine top cover where fitted.
2 Remove the air cleaner housing and intake ducts (see the relevant Part of Chapter 4).

3 Remove the battery and battery tray as described in Chapter 5A.
4 Drain the transmission oil as described in Section 2 or be prepared for oil loss as the transmission is removed.
5 Remove the filler cap from the brake/clutch fluid reservoir on the bulkhead, then tighten it onto a piece of polythene. This will reduce the loss of fluid when the clutch hydraulic hose is disconnected. Alternatively, fit a hose clamp to the flexible hose next to the clutch hydraulic connection on the transmission housing.
6 Place some cloth rags beneath the hose, then prise out the retaining clip securing the clutch hydraulic pipe/hose end fitting to the top of the transmission bellhousing and detach the end fitting from the transmission **(see illustration)**. Gently squeeze the two legs of the retaining clip together and re-insert the retaining clip back into position in the end fitting. Discard the sealing ring from the pipe end; a new sealing ring must be used on refitting. Plug/cover both the union and pipe ends to minimise fluid loss and prevent the entry of dirt into the hydraulic system. **Note:** *Whilst the hose/pipe is disconnected, do not depress the clutch pedal.*
7 With reference to Section 7, disconnect the wiring from the reversing light switch.
8 Attach a suitable hoist and lifting tackle to the lifting bracket(s) located on the left-hand side of the cylinder head, and support the weight of the engine/transmission.
9 Refer to Chapter 10 and remove the front subframe.
10 Working as described in Chapter 8, disconnect the inner ends of both driveshafts from the differential and intermediate shaft, then remove the intermediate shaft. There is no need to disconnect the driveshafts from the swivel hub. Support the driveshafts by suspending them with wire or string – do not allow the driveshafts to hang down under their own weight, or the joints may be damaged.
11 Refer to Section 4 or 5, as applicable and disconnect the gearchange linkage/cables from the transmission.
12 Unscrew and remove the upper bolts securing the transmission to the rear of the engine. Where necessary, pull up the coolant hoses and secure them away from the transmission using plastic cable-ties.
13 Place a jack with a block of wood beneath the transmission, and raise the jack to take the weight of the transmission.
14 Unbolt the left-hand engine/transmission mounting bracket from the transmission with reference to the relevant Part of Chapter 2.
15 Unbolt and remove the front and rear engine/transmission mounting torque link brackets with reference to the relevant Part of Chapter 2.
16 Lower the left-hand side of the engine/transmission making sure that the coolant hoses and wiring harnesses are not stretched.
17 Slacken and remove the remaining bolts securing the transmission to the engine and sump flange. Note the correct fitted positions

of each bolt, and the relevant brackets, as they are removed to use as a reference on refitting. Make a final check that all components have been disconnected, and are positioned clear of the transmission so that they will not hinder the removal procedure.

18 With the help of an assistant, carefully withdraw the transmission (and adapter plate on diesel engine models) from the engine. Take care not to allow the weight of the transmission to hang on the input shaft otherwise the clutch friction disc hub may be damaged. Note that there are two locating dowels which may be tight, and it may be necessary to rock the transmission from side-to-side to release it from them. Once the transmission is free, lower the jack and manoeuvre the unit out from under the car.

Refitting

19 Commence refitting by positioning the transmission on the trolley jack beneath the engine compartment. With the help of an assistant, raise the transmission and locate it on the engine, making sure that the input shaft engages accurately with the splines of the friction disc hub. With the transmission located on the dowels, insert all of the retaining bolts and tighten to the specified torque.

20 The remaining refitting procedure is a reversal of removal, noting the following points:

a) *Tighten all nuts and bolts to the specified torque (where given).*

b) *Renew the driveshaft oil seals (see Section 6) before refitting the driveshafts.*

c) *Refit the front subframe assembly with reference to Chapter 10.*

d) *Fit a new sealing ring to the transmission clutch hydraulic pipe before clipping the hose/pipe end fitting into position. Ensure the end fitting is securely retained by its clip then bleed the hydraulic system as described in Chapter 6.*

e) *Refill the transmission with the specified type and quantity of oil, as described in Section 2.*

f) *On completion, adjust the gearchange linkage/mechanism as described in Section 3.*

9 Manual transmission overhaul – general information

1 Overhauling a manual transmission unit is a difficult and involved job for the DIY home mechanic. In addition to dismantling and reassembling many small parts, clearances must be precisely measured and, if necessary, changed by selecting shims and spacers. Internal transmission components are also often difficult to obtain, and in many instances, extremely expensive. Because of this, if the transmission develops a fault or becomes noisy, the best course of action is to have the unit overhauled by a specialist repairer, or to obtain an exchange reconditioned unit.

2 Nevertheless, it is not impossible for the more experienced mechanic to overhaul the transmission, provided the special tools are available, and the job is done in a deliberate step-by-step manner, so that nothing is overlooked.

3 The tools necessary for an overhaul include internal and external circlip pliers, bearing pullers, a slide hammer, a set of pin punches, a dial test indicator, and possibly a hydraulic press. In addition, a large, sturdy workbench and a vice will be required.

4 During dismantling of the transmission, make careful notes of how each component is fitted, to make reassembly easier and more accurate.

5 Before dismantling the transmission, it will help if you have some idea what area is malfunctioning. Certain problems can be closely related to specific areas in the transmission, which can make component examination and renewal easier. Refer to the *Fault finding* Section of this manual for more information.

Chapter 7 Part B:
Easytronic transmission

Contents

Degrees of difficulty

Easy, suitable for novice with little experience | **Fairly easy,** suitable for beginner with some experience | **Fairly difficult,** suitable for competent DIY mechanic | **Difficult,** suitable for experienced DIY mechanic | **Very difficult,** suitable for expert DIY or professional

Specifications

General

Type .... Five forward speeds and one reverse, automatic or manual selection. Integral differential
Manufacturer's designation .... F17+ MTA

Gear ratios

1.6 litre Z16XE and 1.8 litre petrol engines:
    1st. 3.73:1
    2nd 1.96:1
    3rd 1.30:1
    4th. 0.95:1
    5th. 0.76:1
    Reverse................................ 3.31:1
1.6 litre Z16XEP petrol engines:
    1st. 3.73:1
    2nd 2.14:1
    3rd 1.32.1
    4th. 0.89:1
    5th. 0.64:1
    Reverse................................ 3.31:1

Final drive ratios

1.6 litre Z16XE and 1.8 litre petrol engines..... 3.94:1
1.6 litre Z16XEP petrol engines 4.19:1

Torque wrench settings

	Nm	lbf ft
Clutch module with MTA control unit	11	8
Differential housing cover plate:		
Alloy plate	18	13
Steel plate	30	22
Engine/transmission mountings	See Chapter 2C	
Engine-to-transmission bolts	See Chapter 2C	
Transmission oil level plug:		
Stage 1	4	3
Stage 2	Angle-tighten a further 45° to 180°	
Transmission shift module	11	8
Transmission vent plug:		
Stage 1	4	3
Stage 2	Angle-tighten a further 45° to 135°	

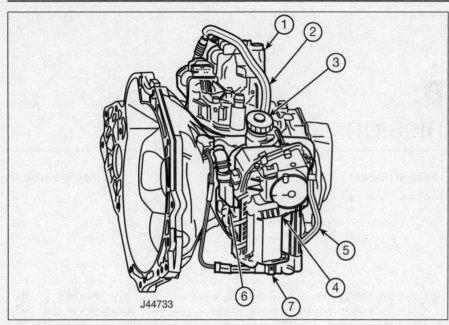

1.1 Easytronic (MTA) transmission

1 Transmission shift module
2 Wiring harness
3 Hydraulic fluid reservoir
4 Clutch control module
5 Hydraulic supply line to clutch control module
6 Wiring harness for clutch control module
7 Hydraulic pressure line to clutch release cylinder

1 General information

1 The Easytronic MTA transmission (Manual Transmission Automatic-shift) is essentially a conventional manual transmission with the addition of a clutch module and shift module, used in conjunction with a self-adjusting clutch plate **(see illustration)**.
2 The description of the MTA transmission is basically as for the manual transmission given in Chapter 7A, but with an electronically-operated hydraulic clutch control module and gear selection module. The transmission can be switched between fully automatic and manual mode, even while driving.

3 The clutch control module incorporates its own master cylinder and pushrod, which is operated electrically by a worm gear.
4 The gear selection module is fitted with a shifting motor and a selector motor, which together position the selector lever to move the selector forks in the transmission. It is located in exactly the same position as the gear selection cover fitted to the conventional manual transmission.
5 Since the transmission is electronically-controlled, in the event of a problem, in the first instance the vehicle should be taken to a Vauxhall/Opel dealer or diagnostic specialist who will have the TECH2 diagnostic equipment (or equivalent) necessary to pin-point the faulty area. Note also that if the transmission assembly, shift module or clutch module

are renewed, the vehicle must be taken to a Vauxhall/Opel dealer or diagnostic specialist in order to have the fault memory erased and new parameters programmed into the ECU.

2 Transmission oil – draining and refilling

Note: *Changing the transmission oil is not a specified service operation, however, it may be considered necessary if the vehicle has covered a high mileage or if a new transmission is being fitted. No drain plug is fitted.*

Draining

1 Apply the handbrake, then jack up the front of the vehicle and support it on axle stands (see *Jacking and vehicle support*).
2 Refer to Chapter 2C and remove the engine/transmission rear mounting/torque link.
3 Place a container under the differential cover plate. Unscrew the securing bolts and withdraw the cover plate, allowing the transmission oil to drain into the container **(see illustration)**. Recover the gasket and, if necessary, renew it.
4 Refit the differential cover plate together with the gasket, and tighten the securing bolts to the specified torque. Refit the rear engine/transmission mounting torque link and tighten the bolts to the specified torque.

Refilling

5 Wipe clean the area around the level plug. The level plug is located behind the driveshaft inner joint on the left-hand side of the transmission **(see illustration)**. Unscrew the plug and clean it.
6 The transmission is refilled through the vent on top of the transmission. Wipe clean the area around the vent, then unscrew and remove it. Refill the transmission with the specified grade of oil given in *Lubricants and fluids*, until it reaches the bottom of the level plug aperture. Allow any excess oil to drain, then refit and tighten the level plug. **Note:** *When new, the transmission is originally filled by weight, and the level may be 20 mm below the level hole.*

2.3 Differential cover plate securing bolts (arrowed)

2.5 Transmission oil filler/level plug (arrowed)

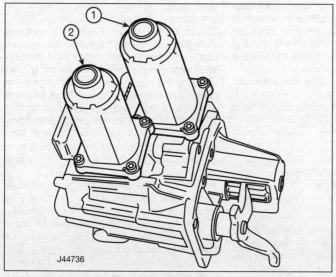

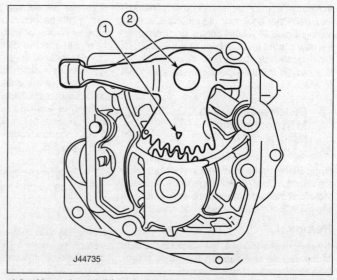

4.4 Shift motor (1) and selector motor (2) on the transmission shift module

4.6a Neutral mark (1) and shift lever shaft (2) on the transmission shift module

7 Refit and tighten the vent, then lower the vehicle to the ground.

3 Selector lever assembly – removal and refitting

Removal

1 Remove the centre console as described in Chapter 11.
2 Disconnect the wiring connector on the selector lever assembly.
3 Unscrew the four bolts securing the selector lever housing to the floor. Lift the housing up and out of its location and remove it from the car.

Refitting

4 Refitting is a reversal of removal.

4 Transmission shift module – removal and refitting

Removal

1 Switch on the ignition, then depress the footbrake pedal and move the selector lever to position N. Switch off the ignition.
2 Disconnect the two wiring plugs and release the harness from the support cable-ties on the top of the transmission.
3 Unbolt and remove the transmission shift module from the top of the transmission. To do this, lift it and tilt it slightly forwards before removing. Recover the gasket.
4 If the module cannot be removed because of internal jamming, unbolt the selector motor followed by the shifting motor (see illustration), and use a screwdriver to move

the selector lever to its neutral position first. The selector motor is the uppermost unit.
Note: *The manufacturers recommend that the shift module assembly is never re-used if dismantled.*

Refitting

5 Clean the gasket faces of the module and transmission, and obtain a new gasket.
6 Make sure that the selector lever is in neutral by checking that the mark on the segment is aligned with the pinion tooth. Check also that the lever is fully extended so that the annular groove is visible. The shift forks in the transmission must also be in neutral – use a screwdriver to move them if necessary (see illustrations).
7 Refit the shift module together with a new gasket, then insert the bolts and tighten to the specified torque.
8 Reconnect the wiring and secure with new cable-ties.

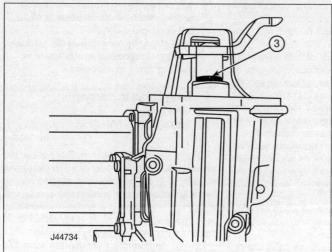

4.6b Groove (3) visible when the shift module is in neutral

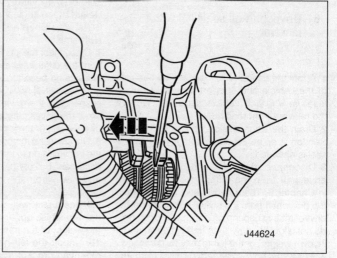

4.6c Using a screwdriver to move the transmission shift forks into neutral

9 Finally, it may be necessary to have a Vauxhall/Opel dealer or diagnostic specialist reprogramme all volatile control unit memories. If a new control unit has been fitted, a Vauxhall/Opel dealer or diagnostic specialist must programme the unit specifically for the model to which it is fitted.

5 Clutch module with MTA control unit – removal and refitting

Note: *Bleeding the module is carried out using the Vauxhall/Opel TECH2 diagnostic instrument, therefore this work should be entrusted to a Vauxhall/Opel dealer or diagnostic specialist.*

Removal

1 Apply the handbrake, then jack up the front of the vehicle and support it on axle stands (see *Jacking and vehicle support*).
2 Disconnect the wiring from the Easytronic transmission control unit and release it from the cable-tie supports.
3 Place a suitable container beneath the front of the transmission to catch spilt hydraulic fluid.
4 Fit a hose clamp to the hydraulic hose leading from the hydraulic fluid reservoir to the clutch control unit, then disconnect the hose.
5 Disconnect the hydraulic quick-release pressure hose from the clutch control unit.
6 Unscrew the mounting bolts and remove the module from the transmission.

Refitting

7 Refitting is a reversal of removal, but tighten the mounting bolts to the specified torque. Make sure that the quick-release pressure hose is fully engaged – it must make an audible sound. Bleed the hydraulic circuit. Finally, it may be necessary to reprogramme all volatile control unit memories. If a new control unit has been fitted, a Vauxhall/Opel dealer or diagnostic specialist must programme the unit specifically for the model to which it is fitted.

6 Driveshaft oil seals – renewal

1 Apply the handbrake, then jack up the front of the vehicle and support it on axle stands (see *Jacking and vehicle support*). Remove the relevant front roadwheel.
2 Drain the transmission oil as described in Section 2 or be prepared for oil loss as the seal is changed.
3 Disconnect the inner end of the relevant driveshaft from the differential as described in Chapter 8. There is no need to disconnect the driveshaft from the swivel hub. Support the driveshaft by suspending it with wire or string – do not allow the driveshaft to hang down under its own weight, or the joints may be damaged.
4 Prise the now-exposed oil seal from the differential housing, using a screwdriver or similar instrument.

5 Smear the sealing lip of the new oil seal with a little transmission oil, then using a metal tube or socket of suitable diameter, drive the new seal into the differential casing until the outer surface of the seal is flush with the outer surface of the differential casing.
6 Reconnect the driveshaft to the differential as described in Chapter 8.
7 Refill or top-up the transmission oil level with reference to Section 2.
8 Refit the roadwheel, then lower the vehicle to the ground.

7 Easytronic transmission – removal and refitting

Note: *This is an involved procedure, and it may well prove easier to remove the transmission complete with the engine as an assembly (see Chapter 2F), then separate the transmission. However, this Section describes removing the transmission leaving the engine in position. Suitable equipment will be required to support the engine and transmission, and the help of an assistant will be required.*

Removal

1 Apply the handbrake, then jack up the front of the vehicle and support it on axle stands (see *Jacking and vehicle support*). Allow sufficient working room to remove the transmission from under the left-hand side of the engine compartment. Remove both front roadwheels and the engine top cover where fitted.
2 Remove the air cleaner housing and intake ducts (see Chapter 4A).
3 Drain the transmission oil as described in Section 2 or be prepared for oil loss as the transmission is removed.
4 Disconnect the wiring from the Easytronic transmission control unit and release it from the cable-tie supports.
5 Attach a suitable hoist and lifting tackle to the lifting bracket(s) located on the left-hand side of the cylinder head, and support the weight of the engine/transmission.
6 Refer to Chapter 10 and remove the front subframe.
7 Disconnect the inner ends of both driveshafts from the differential as described in Chapter 8. There is no need to disconnect the driveshafts from the swivel hub. Support the driveshafts by suspending them with wire or string – do not allow the driveshafts to hang down under their own weight, or the joints may be damaged.
8 Unscrew and remove the upper bolts securing the transmission to the rear of the engine. Where necessary, pull up the coolant hoses and secure them away from the transmission using plastic cable-ties.
9 Place a jack with a block of wood beneath the transmission, and raise the jack to take the weight of the transmission.
10 Unbolt the left-hand engine/transmission mounting bracket from the transmission with reference to Chapter 2C.
11 Unbolt and remove the front and rear

engine/transmission mounting torque link brackets with reference to Chapter 2C.
12 Lower the left-hand side of the engine/transmission making sure that the coolant hoses and wiring harnesses are not stretched.
13 Slacken and remove the remaining bolts securing the transmission to the engine and sump flange. Note the correct fitted positions of each bolt, and the relevant brackets, as they are removed to use as a reference on refitting. Make a final check that all components have been disconnected, and are positioned clear of the transmission so that they will not hinder the removal procedure.
14 With the help of an assistant, carefully withdraw the transmission from the engine. Take care not to allow the weight of the transmission to hang on the input shaft otherwise the clutch friction disc hub may be damaged. Note that there are two locating dowels which may be tight, and it may be necessary to rock the transmission from side-to-side to release it from them. Once the transmission is free, lower the jack and manoeuvre the unit out from under the car.

Refitting

15 Commence refitting by positioning the transmission on the trolley jack beneath the engine compartment. With the help of an assistant, raise the transmission and locate it on the engine, making sure that the input shaft engages accurately with the splines of the friction disc hub. With the transmission located on the dowels, insert all of the retaining bolts and tighten to the specified torque.
16 The remaining refitting procedure is a reversal of removal, noting the following points:
a) Tighten all nuts and bolts to the specified torque (where given).
b) Renew the driveshaft oil seals (see Section 6) before refitting the driveshafts.
c) Refit the front subframe assembly with reference to Chapter 10.
d) Refit the air cleaner housing and intake ducts with reference to Chapter 4A.
e) Refill or top-up the transmission with the specified type and quantity of oil, as described in Section 2.
f) Finally, it may be necessary to have a dealer or diagnostic specialist reprogramme all volatile control unit memories.

8 Easytronic transmission overhaul – general information

In the event of a fault occurring on the transmission, it is first necessary to determine whether it is of an electrical, mechanical or hydraulic nature, and to achieve this, special test equipment is required. It is therefore essential to have the work carried out by a Vauxhall/Opel dealer if a transmission fault is suspected.

Do not remove the transmission from the car for possible repair before professional fault diagnosis has been carried out, since most tests require the transmission to be in the vehicle.

Chapter 8
Driveshafts

Contents

Degrees of difficulty

Easy, suitable for novice with little experience	Fairly easy, suitable for beginner with some experience	Fairly difficult, suitable for competent DIY mechanic	Difficult, suitable for experienced DIY mechanic	Very difficult, suitable for expert DIY or professional

Specifications

Type
Driveshaft type . . . . Solid steel shafts with inner and outer constant velocity (CV) joints. Right-hand driveshaft incorporating intermediate shaft on certain models

Lubrication (overhaul only – see text)
Lubricant type/specification . . . . Use only special grease supplied in sachets with gaiter kits – joints are otherwise pre-packed with grease and sealed

Torque wrench settings

	Nm	lbf ft
Anti-roll bar connecting link retaining nut*	65	48
Driveshaft retaining nut:*		
Stage 1	120	89
Stage 2	Slacken the nut completely	
Stage 3	20	15
Stage 4	Angle-tighten through a further 90°	
Intermediate shaft support bracket bolts	55	41
Lower arm balljoint clamp bolt nut*	60	44
Roadwheel bolts	110	81

* Use new nuts/bolts.

2.2 Extract the split pin from the driveshaft retaining nut

1 General information

Drive is transmitted from the differential to the front wheels by means of two solid steel driveshafts of unequal length. The right-hand driveshaft is longer than the left-hand one, due to the position of the transmission unit.

Both driveshafts are splined at their outer ends to accept the wheel hubs, and are threaded so that each hub can be fastened by a large nut. The inner end of each driveshaft is splined to accept the differential sun gear. On some models, a vibration damper is attached to the right-hand driveshaft.

Constant velocity (CV) joints are fitted to each end of the driveshafts, to ensure the

smooth and efficient transmission of drive at all the angles possible as the roadwheels move up-and-down with the suspension, and as they turn from side-to-side under steering. The outer constant velocity joints are of the ball-and-cage type and the inner constant velocity joints may be of the ball-and-cage type or tripod type.

On 1.7 litre Z17DTH diesel engine models, the right-hand driveshaft has an intermediate shaft attached to the rear of the cylinder block.

2 Driveshafts – removal and refitting

Note: *A new driveshaft retaining nut, split pin, inner joint circlip, lower arm balljoint clamp bolt nut and anti-roll bar connecting link retaining nut will be needed for refitting. The driveshaft outer joint splines may be a tight fit in the hub and it is possible that a puller/extractor will be required to draw the hub assembly off the driveshaft during removal.*

Removal

1 Firmly apply the handbrake, then jack up the front of the car and support it securely on axle stands (see *Jacking and vehicle support*). Remove the relevant front roadwheel.
2 Extract the split pin from the driveshaft retaining nut **(see illustration)**.
3 Refit at least two roadwheel bolts to the

front hub, and tighten them securely. Have an assistant firmly depress the brake pedal to prevent the front hub from rotating, then using a socket and extension bar, slacken the driveshaft retaining nut. Alternatively, a tool can be fabricated from two lengths of steel strip (one long, one short) and a nut and bolt; the nut and bolt forming the pivot of a forked tool. Bolt the tool to the hub using two wheel bolts, and hold the tool to prevent the hub from rotating as the driveshaft retaining nut is undone **(see illustration)**.
4 Unscrew the driveshaft retaining nut, and remove the washer.
5 Unscrew and remove the nut securing the anti-roll bar connecting link to the suspension strut, while holding the link stub on the flats provided with a further spanner **(see illustration)**. Release the link from the strut and move it to one side.
6 Unscrew and remove the lower arm balljoint clamp bolt nut, and withdraw the clamp bolt from the swivel hub **(see illustration)**.
7 Use a chisel or screwdriver as a wedge to expand the lower portion of the swivel hub **(see illustration)**.
8 Using a lever, push down on the lower arm to free the balljoint from the swivel hub **(see illustration)**, then move the swivel hub to one side and release the balljoint, taking care not to damage the balljoint rubber boot.
9 The swivel hub must now be freed from the end of the driveshaft. It may be possible to pull the hub off the driveshaft, but if the end of the driveshaft is tight in the hub, temporarily refit the driveshaft retaining nut to protect the driveshaft threads, then tap the end of the driveshaft with a soft-faced hammer while pulling outwards on the swivel hub **(see illustrations)**. Alternatively, use a suitable puller to press the driveshaft through the hub. Support the driveshaft by suspending it with wire or string; **Do not** *allow the driveshaft to hang down under its own weight, or the joints may be damaged.*
10 Position a container beneath the transmission to catch any oil that may be spilt.
11 Using a stout bar, release the inner end of the driveshaft from the differential or intermediate shaft. Lever between the constant velocity joint and differential housing, or between the

2.3 Using a fabricated tool to hold the front hub stationary whilst the driveshaft retaining nut is slackened

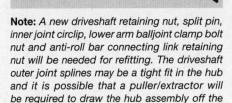

2.5 Unscrew the nut securing the connecting link to the anti-roll bar, while holding the link stub with a further spanner

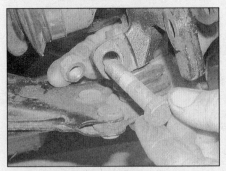

2.6 Unscrew the retaining nut and withdraw the clamp bolt from the swivel hub

2.7 Use a chisel or screwdriver as a wedge to expand the lower portion of the swivel hub

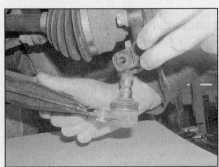

2.8 Push down the lower suspension arm to free the balljoint from the swivel hub

2.9a Use a soft-faced hammer to drive the driveshaft from the hub splines . . .

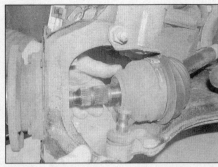

2.9b . . . then pull the swivel hub outwards

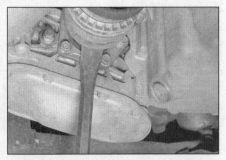

2.11 Using a stout bar, release the inner end of the driveshaft from the differential or intermediate shaft

2.21 Refit the washer and a new retaining nut

2.22a Insert a new split pin . . .

2.22b . . . and secure in position by bending over the split pin ends

constant velocity joint and intermediate shaft support bracket, to release the driveshaft retaining circlip **(see illustration)**.

12 Withdraw the driveshaft, ensuring that the constant velocity joints are not placed under excessive strain, and remove the driveshaft from beneath the vehicle. Whilst the driveshaft is removed, plug or tape over the differential aperture to prevent dirt entry.

Caution: Do not allow the vehicle to rest on its wheels with one or both driveshaft(s) removed, as damage to the wheel bearing(s) may result. If the vehicle must be moved on its wheels, clamp the wheel bearings using a long threaded rod and spacers to take the place of the outer driveshaft joint through the hub.

Refitting

13 Before refitting the driveshaft, examine the oil seal in the transmission housing and renew it if necessary as described in the relevant Part of Chapter 7.

14 Remove the circlip from the end of the driveshaft inner joint splines or intermediate shaft and discard it. Fit a new circlip, making sure it is correctly located in the groove.

15 Thoroughly clean the driveshaft splines, intermediate shaft splines (where applicable), and the apertures in the transmission and hub assembly. Apply a thin film of grease to the oil seal lips, and to the driveshaft splines and shoulders. Check that all gaiter clips are securely fastened.

16 Offer up the driveshaft, and engage the inner joint splines with those of the differential sun gear or intermediate shaft, taking care

not to damage the oil seal. Push the joint fully into position, then check that the circlip is correctly located and securely holds the joint in position. If necessary, use a soft-faced mallet or drift to drive the driveshaft inner joint fully into position.

17 Align the outer constant velocity joint splines with those of the hub, and slide the joint back into position in the hub.

18 Using a lever, push down on the lower suspension arm, then relocate the balljoint and release the arm. Make sure that the balljoint stub is fully entered in the swivel hub.

19 Insert the balljoint clamp bolt to the swivel hub, so that its threads are facing to the rear of the vehicle. Fit a new nut to the clamp bolt, and tighten it to the specified torque setting.

20 Locate the anti-roll bar connecting link on the suspension strut, fit a new retaining nut and tighten the nut to the specified torque.

21 Refit the washer to the end of the driveshaft, then screw on a new nut. Using the method employed on removal to prevent rotation, tighten the new driveshaft retaining nut through the stages given in the Specifications at the start of this Chapter **(see illustration)**.

22 With the nut correctly tightened, secure it in position with a new split pin **(see illustrations)**. If the holes in the driveshaft are not aligned with any of the slots in the nut, loosen **(do not tighten)** the nut by the *smallest possible amount* until the split pin can be inserted.

23 Refit the roadwheel, then lower the vehicle to the ground and tighten the roadwheel bolts to the specified torque.

24 Check and if necessary top-up the transmission oil level, using the information given in the relevant part of Chapter 7.

3 Intermediate shaft – removal and refitting

Removal

1 Remove the right-hand driveshaft as described in Section 2.

2 Place a suitable container beneath the differential, to collect escaping transmission oil/fluid when the intermediate shaft is withdrawn.

3 Undo the two bolts securing the intermediate shaft support bracket to the cylinder block **(see illustration)**. Pull the intermediate shaft out of the transmission and remove the shaft from under the car.

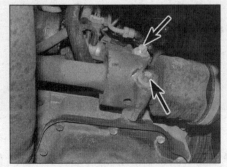

3.3 Intermediate shaft support bracket retaining bolts (arrowed)

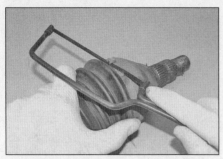

5.2 Release the rubber gaiter retaining clips by cutting through them using a hacksaw

Refitting

4 Before refitting the intermediate shaft, examine the oil seal in the transmission housing and renew it if necessary as described in the relevant Part of Chapter 7.

5 Remove the circlip from the end of the intermediate shaft and discard it. Fit a new circlip, making sure it is correctly located in the groove.

6 Thoroughly clean the driveshaft splines, the intermediate shaft splines, and the aperture in the transmission. Apply a thin film of grease to the oil seal lips, and to the driveshaft and intermediate shaft splines and shoulders.

7 Insert the intermediate shaft into the transmission, engaging the splines with the differential sun gear, taking care not to damage the oil seal.

8 Refit the two bolts securing the intermediate shaft support bracket to the cylinder block. Tighten the bolts to the specified torque.

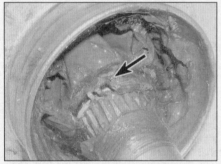

5.5 Outer CV joint snap-ring (arrowed)

5.6b If an external snap-ring is fitted, use circlip pliers to expand the snap-ring as the joint is removed

5.3 Cut the gaiter open using a suitable knife and remove it from the driveshaft

9 Refit the right-hand driveshaft as described in Section 2.

4 Intermediate shaft bearing – renewal

Note: *A hydraulic press, together with tubes and mandrels of suitable diameters will be needed for this operation. A new bearing, retaining circlip and O-ring will also be required.*

1 Remove the intermediate shaft as described in Section 3.

2 Remove the circlip and O-ring from the end of the intermediate shaft.

3 Using circlip pliers, extract the circlip securing the intermediate shaft bearing in the support bracket and withdraw the shaft and bearing from the support bracket.

5.6a Sharply strike the edge of the outer joint to drive it off the end of the shaft

5.7 Removing the circlip from the groove in the driveshaft splines

4 Extract the circlip securing the bearing to the intermediate shaft.

5 Support the underside of the bearing on the press bed and press the intermediate shaft downwards out of the bearing.

6 Suitably support the intermediate shaft on the press bed and position the new bearing on the shaft with the groove on the outer race towards the driveshaft end of the intermediate shaft.

7 Using a suitable tube in contact with the bearing inner race, press the bearing fully onto the intermediate shaft. Fit a new bearing retaining circlip to the intermediate shaft.

8 Locate the intermediate shaft support bracket in place over the bearing and refit the circlip.

9 Place a new O-ring on the intermediate shaft, then refit the shaft as described in Section 3.

5 Driveshaft rubber gaiters – renewal

Ball-and-cage type joints

1 Remove the driveshaft from the car as described in Section 2, then secure the shaft in a vice equipped with soft jaws.

2 Release the rubber gaiter inner and outer retaining clips by cutting through them using a junior hacksaw **(see illustration)**. Spread the clips and remove them from the gaiter.

3 Slide the rubber gaiter down the shaft to expose the CV joint or, alternatively, cut the gaiter open using a suitable knife and remove it from the driveshaft **(see illustration)**.

4 Using old rags, clean away as much of the old grease as possible from the CV joint. It is advisable to wear disposable rubber gloves during this operation.

5 The CV joint will be retained on the driveshaft either by an external snap-ring, or by an internal circlip **(see illustration)**. If an external snap-ring is fitted, use circlip pliers to expand the snap-ring as the CV joint is removed.

6 Using a mallet, sharply strike the edge of the joint to drive it off the end of the shaft **(see illustrations)**.

7 Once the joint has been removed, extract the snap-ring from the joint, or remove the circlip from the groove in the driveshaft splines **(see illustration)**. A new snap-ring or circlip must be fitted on reassembly.

8 If still in place, withdraw the rubber gaiter from the driveshaft.

9 With the CV joint removed from the driveshaft, wipe away the remaining grease (do not use any solvent) to allow the joint components to be inspected.

10 Move the inner splined driving member from side-to-side, to expose each ball in turn at the top of its track. Examine the balls for cracks, flat spots, or signs of surface pitting.

11 Inspect the ball tracks on the inner and outer members. If the tracks have widened, the balls will no longer be a tight fit. At the same time, check the ball cage windows for wear or cracking between the windows.

12 If, on inspection, any of the constant velocity joint components are found to be worn or damaged, it will be necessary to renew the complete joint assembly. If the joint is in satisfactory condition, obtain a repair kit consisting of a new gaiter and retaining clips, a constant velocity joint snap-ring or circlip, and the correct type and quantity of grease **(see illustration)**.

13 Slide the new rubber gaiter and retaining clips onto the driveshaft **(see illustration)**.

14 Fit a new snap-ring to the constant velocity joint, or a new circlip to the groove in the driveshaft, as applicable **(see illustrations)**.

15 Pack the joint with the grease supplied in the repair kit **(see illustration)**. Work the grease well into the bearing tracks whilst twisting the joint, and fill the rubber gaiter with any excess.

16 Using a soft-faced mallet, tap the joint onto the driveshaft until the snap-ring or circlip engages in its groove **(see illustration)**. Make sure that the joint is securely retained, by pulling on the joint, not the shaft.

17 Ease the gaiter over the joint, and ensure that the gaiter lips are correctly located in the grooves on both the driveshaft and constant velocity joint. Lift the outer sealing lip of the gaiter, to equalise air pressure within the gaiter.

18 Pull the large gaiter retaining clip as tight as possible, and locate the hooks on the clip in their slots. Remove any slack in the gaiter retaining clip by carefully compressing the raised section of the clip. In the absence of the special tool, a pair of side-cutters may be used. Secure the small retaining clip using the same procedure **(see illustrations)**.

19 Check that the constant velocity joint moves freely in all directions, then refit the driveshaft to the car as described in Section 2.

Inner tripod type joints

20 Remove the driveshaft from the car as described in Section 2.

21 Release the rubber gaiter inner and outer retaining clips by cutting through them using a junior hacksaw. Spread the clips and remove them from the gaiter.

22 Slide the rubber gaiter down the shaft to expose the CV joint or, alternatively, cut the gaiter open using a suitable knife and remove it from the driveshaft.

23 With the rubber gaiter released from the joint, mark the joint outer member in relation to the driveshaft, to ensure correct refitting.

24 Where fitted, remove the retaining plate from inside the joint outer member, then withdraw the joint outer member from the tripod and driveshaft. It may be necessary to tap the outer member free using a soft-faced mallet to release it from the tripod. As the outer member is withdrawn,

5.12 Components required for driveshaft gaiter renewal

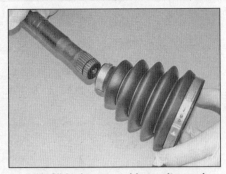

5.13 Slide the new rubber gaiter and retaining clips onto the driveshaft

5.14a Fit a new snap-ring to the constant velocity joint . . .

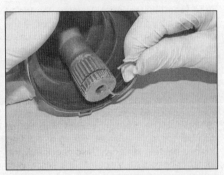

5.14b . . . or a new circlip to the groove in the driveshaft

take precautions to prevent the bearing rollers falling off the tripod. Wipe away all excess grease and, if necessary, wrap tape around the tripod joint to secure the rollers in position.

25 Prise the circlip from the end of the driveshaft, then using a punch, paint or a suitable marker pen, make alignment marks between the tripod joint and driveshaft, and also identify which way round the tripod is

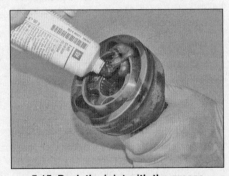

5.15 Pack the joint with the grease supplied in the repair kit

5.16 Tap the joint onto the driveshaft until the snap-ring or circlip engages in its groove

5.18a Secure the large gaiter retaining clip in position by compressing the raised section of the clip

5.18b The small inner retaining clip is secured in the same way

5.25a Prise the circlip from the end of the driveshaft. . .

5.25b . . . then make alignment marks between the tripod joint and the driveshaft

fitted **(see illustrations)**. Remove the tripod joint assembly from the end of the shaft, if the joint is a tight fit, it may be necessary to use a puller to draw it off the shaft – if a puller is used, take great care not to damage the rollers.

26 Slide the gaiter off the end of the driveshaft.

27 Where applicable, remove the tape from the joint, and wipe away as much of the old grease as possible (do not use any solvent).

28 Check the spider, rollers and outer member for signs of wear, pitting or scuffing on their bearing surfaces. Also check that the spider rollers rotate smoothly and easily, with no traces of roughness.

29 If any of the constant velocity joint components are found to be worn or damaged, it will be necessary to renew the complete joint assembly. If the joint is in satisfactory condition, obtain a repair kit consisting of a new gaiter and retaining clips, circlips, and the correct type and quantity of grease.

30 Clean the driveshaft, and tape over the splines on its inner end to protect the new gaiter as it is fitted.

31 Slide the new gaiter onto the driveshaft then remove the tape from the driveshaft end.

32 If necessary, again wind tape around the tripod to retain the rollers then, with the previously-made marks on the tripod and driveshaft aligned, push the tripod onto the driveshaft splines. If necessary use a soft-faced mallet to drive the tripod fully onto the splines. Secure the tripod in position using the new circlip, making sure that the circlip locates correctly in the driveshaft groove.

33 Where applicable, remove the tape from around the tripod, then work the grease

supplied with the repair kit fully into the roller bearings. Fill the joint outer member with any excess grease.

34 Locate the outer member over the tripod, tapping it into position if necessary, making sure that the previously-made marks are aligned. Where fitted, refit and attach the retaining plate to the joint outer member.

35 Slide the gaiter along the driveshaft, and locate it in the recesses on the driveshaft and joint outer member.

36 Ensure that the gaiter is not twisted or distorted, then carefully lift the lip of the gaiter at the outer member end to equalise air pressure in the gaiter.

37 Fit the large metal retaining clip to the gaiter. Remove any slack in the gaiter retaining clip by carefully compressing the raised section of the clip. In the absence of the special tool, a pair of side-cutters may be used. Secure the small retaining clip using the same procedure.

38 The driveshaft can now be refitted to the car as described in Section 2.

<table>
<tr><td>6</td><td>**Driveshaft joint –** checking and renewal</td><td></td></tr>
</table>

Checking

1 First carry out the checks described in Chapter 1A or 1B, to reveal if there is any wear in one of the driveshaft joints.

2 Check that the split pin is in position and the driveshaft nut is tight. If in doubt, the only alternative is to obtain a new nut and

split pin, then fit and tighten the nut using the procedures described in Section 2. Once tightened, secure the nut in position with the new split pin. Repeat this check on the other driveshaft nut.

3 Road test the vehicle, and listen for a metallic clicking noise from the front as the vehicle is driven slowly in a circle on full-lock. If evident, this indicates wear in the outer constant velocity joint which must be renewed.

4 To check for wear on the inner joint, apply the handbrake then jack up the front of the vehicle and support it on axle stands (see *Jacking and vehicle support*). Attempt to move the inner end of the driveshaft up-and-down, then hold the joint with one hand and attempt to rotate the driveshaft with the other. If excessive wear is evident, the joint must be renewed. **Note:** *If vibration, consistent with roadspeed, is felt through the car when accelerating, there is a possibility of wear in the inner constant velocity joints.*

Renewal

5 To renew the constant velocity joint, follow the procedures in Section 5. If the old gaiter is going to be re-used, it can be left on the driveshaft, take care not to damage the gaiter when removing the retaining clips.

<table>
<tr><td>7</td><td>**Vibration damper (right-hand driveshaft) –** removal and refitting</td><td></td></tr>
</table>

Note: *On some models a vibration damper is fitted to the right-hand driveshaft **(see illustration)**. The vibration damper can only be separated from the driveshafts that are made by GKN. On any other make of driveshaft the complete driveshaft will have to be renewed, if there is a fault with the vibration damper.*

Removal

1 Remove the driveshaft from the car as described in Section 2.

2 Remove the transmission side constant velocity joint and gaiter as described in Section 5.

3 Clean around the vibration damper, then mark the damper's fitted position on the driveshaft.

4 Cut the retaining clip from around the collar of the vibration damper and discard it, a new one will be required on refitting.

5 Spray the shaft with penetrating oil, and pull the vibration damper from the driveshaft.

Refitting

6 Refitting is a reversal of removal, bearing in mind the following points:

a) Fit the vibration damper to the driveshaft using the measurement shown **(see illustration)**.

b) Refit the constant velocity joint to the driveshaft as described in Section 5.

c) Refit the the driveshaft to the vehicle as described in Section 2.

7.0 Vibration damper fitted to the right-hand driveshaft on certain models

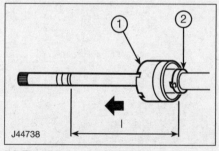

7.6 The vibration damper (1) must be secured in position with a new retaining clip (2)

Dimension I = 22.5 cm ± 5 mm

Chapter 9
Braking system

Contents

Degrees of difficulty

Easy, suitable for novice with little experience	Fairly easy, suitable for beginner with some experience	Fairly difficult, suitable for competent DIY mechanic	Difficult, suitable for experienced DIY mechanic	Very difficult, suitable for expert DIY or professional

Specifications

Front brakes

Type	Ventilated disc, with single-piston sliding caliper
Disc diameter:	
1.4 litre and 1.6 litre SOHC petrol models	260.0 mm
All other models	280.0 mm
Disc thickness:	
1.4 litre and 1.6 litre SOHC petrol models:	
New..	24.0 mm
Minimum..	21.0 mm
All other models:	
New..	25.0 mm
Minimum..	22.0 mm
Maximum disc run-out....................................	0.11 mm
Brake pad friction material minimum thickness...................	2.0 mm

Rear disc brakes

Type	Solid disc, with single-piston sliding caliper
Disc diameter:	
1.4 litre and 1.6 litre SOHC petrol models	240.0 mm
All other models	264.0 mm
Disc thickness:	
New	10.0 mm
Minimum..	8.0 mm
Maximum disc run-out....................................	0.13 mm
Brake pad friction material minimum thickness...................	2.0 mm

ABS system type

Up to model year 2005....................................	ABS 5.3
Model year 2005 onward	ABS 8.0

Torque wrench settings

	Nm	lbf ft
ABS hydraulic modulator mounting bracket bolts	20	15
ABS hydraulic modulator-to-mounting bracket nuts	10	7
Brake caliper bleed screws:		
Front caliper	7	5
Rear caliper	10	7
Brake caliper guide or guide pin bolts:*		
Front caliper	28	21
Rear caliper	25	18
Brake caliper mounting bracket bolts	100	74
Brake fluid pipe unions.	16	12
Brake hydraulic hose banjo union bolts.	40	30
Brake master cylinder retaining nuts*.	15	11
Brake pedal mounting bracket bolts/nuts	20	15
Brake proportioning valve adjustment piece locking screw.	12	9
Brake proportioning valve retaining bolts.	20	15
Clutch master cylinder and mounting plate retaining nuts.	20	15
Handbrake lever retaining nuts	10	7
Roadwheel bolts.	110	81
Vacuum pump mounting bolts (1.3 litre diesel engine models):		
Stage 1	6	4
Stage 2	20	15
Vacuum servo unit mounting nuts	20	15

Use new fastenings

1 General information

The braking system is of servo-assisted, dual-circuit hydraulic type split diagonally. The arrangement of the hydraulic system is such that each circuit operates one front and one rear brake from a tandem master cylinder. Under normal circumstances, both circuits operate in unison. However, in the event of hydraulic failure in one circuit, full braking force will still be available at two wheels.

All models are fitted with front and rear disc brakes. The disc brakes are actuated by single-piston sliding type calipers, which ensure that equal pressure is applied to each disc pad.

An Anti-lock Braking System (ABS) is fitted as standard equipment to most models and is optionally available on all others. On higher specification models, the ABS may also incorporate traction control or an electronic stability program. Refer to Section 18 for further information on ABS operation.

Models not fitted with ABS are equipped with a rear brake proportioning valve. The valve controls the hydraulic fluid pressure applied to the rear brakes under braking, according to vehicle load. This prevents premature lock-up of the rear brakes when the vehicle is only lightly loaded.

The cable-operated handbrake provides an independent mechanical means of rear brake application.

⚠ *Warning: When servicing any part of the system, work carefully and methodically; also observe scrupulous cleanliness when overhauling any part of the hydraulic system. Always renew components (in axle sets, where applicable) if in doubt about their condition,* and use only genuine Vauxhall/Opel parts, or at least those of known good quality. Note the warnings given in 'Safety first!' and at relevant points in this Chapter concerning the dangers of asbestos dust and hydraulic fluid.

2 Hydraulic system – bleeding

⚠ *Warning: Hydraulic fluid is poisonous; wash off immediately and thoroughly in the case of skin contact, and seek immediate medical advice if any fluid is swallowed or gets into the eyes. Certain types of hydraulic fluid are inflammable, and may ignite when allowed into contact with hot components; when servicing any hydraulic system, it is safest to assume that the fluid is inflammable, and to take precautions against the risk of fire as though it is petrol that is being handled. Hydraulic fluid is also an effective paint stripper, and will attack plastics; if any is spilt, it should be washed off immediately, using copious quantities of fresh water. Finally, it is hygroscopic (it absorbs moisture from the air) – old fluid may be contaminated and unfit for further use. When topping-up or renewing the fluid, always use the recommended type, and ensure that it comes from a freshly-opened sealed container.*

General

1 The correct operation of any hydraulic system is only possible after removing all air from the components and circuit; this is achieved by bleeding the system.

2 During the bleeding procedure, add only clean, unused hydraulic fluid of the recommended type; never re-use fluid that has already been bled from the system. Ensure that sufficient fluid is available before starting work.

3 If there is any possibility of incorrect fluid being already in the system, the brake components and circuit must be flushed completely with uncontaminated, correct fluid, and new seals should be fitted to the various components.

4 If hydraulic fluid has been lost from the system, or air has entered because of a leak, ensure that the fault is cured before proceeding further.

5 Park the vehicle over an inspection pit or on car ramps. Alternatively, apply the handbrake then jack up the front and rear of the vehicle and support it on axle stands (see Jacking and vehicle support). For improved access with the vehicle jacked up, remove the roadwheels.

6 Check that all pipes and hoses are secure, unions tight and bleed screws closed. Clean any dirt from around the bleed screws.

7 Unscrew the master cylinder reservoir cap, and top the master cylinder reservoir up to the MAX level line; refit the cap loosely, and remember to maintain the fluid level at least above the MIN level line throughout the procedure, otherwise there is a risk of further air entering the system.

8 There are a number of one-man, do-it-yourself brake bleeding kits currently available from motor accessory shops. It is recommended that one of these kits is used whenever possible, as they greatly simplify the bleeding operation, and also reduce the risk of expelled air and fluid being drawn back into the system. If such a kit is not available, the basic (two-man) method must be used, which is described in detail below.

Caution: Vauxhall recommend using a pressure bleeding kit for this operation (see paragraphs 24 to 27).

9 If a kit is to be used, prepare the vehicle as described previously, and follow the kit manufacturer's instructions, as the procedure may vary slightly according to the type being used; generally, they are as outlined below in the relevant sub-section.

10 Whichever method is used, the same sequence should be followed (paragraphs 11 and 12) to ensure the removal of all air from the system.

Bleeding sequence

11 If the system has been only partially disconnected, and suitable precautions were taken to minimise fluid loss, it should only be necessary to bleed that part of the system (ie, the primary or secondary circuit). If the master cylinder or main brake lines have been disconnected, then the complete system must be bled.

12 If the complete system is to be bled, then it should be done in the following sequence:
   a) Left-hand rear brake.
   b) Right-hand rear brake.
   c) Left-hand front brake.
   d) Right-hand front brake.

Bleeding

Basic (two-man) method

13 Collect together a clean glass jar, a suitable length of plastic or rubber tubing which is a tight fit over the bleed screw, and a ring spanner to fit the screw. The help of an assistant will also be required.

14 Remove the dust cap from the first bleed screw in the sequence (see illustrations). Fit the spanner and tube to the screw, place the other end of the tube in the jar, and pour in sufficient fluid to cover the end of the tube.

15 Ensure that the master cylinder reservoir fluid level is maintained at least above the MIN level line throughout the procedure.

16 Have the assistant fully depress the brake pedal several times to build-up pressure, then maintain it on the final downstroke.

17 While pedal pressure is maintained, unscrew the bleed screw (approximately one turn) and allow the compressed fluid and air to flow into the jar. The assistant should maintain pedal pressure, following it down to the floor if necessary, and should not release it until instructed to do so. When the flow stops, tighten the bleed screw again, have the assistant release the pedal slowly, and recheck the reservoir fluid level.

18 Repeat the steps given in paragraphs 16 and 17 until the fluid emerging from the bleed screw is free from air bubbles. If the master cylinder has been drained and refilled, and air is being bled from the first screw in the sequence, allow approximately five seconds between cycles for the master cylinder passages to refill.

19 When no more air bubbles appear, securely tighten the bleed screw, remove the tube and spanner, and refit the dust cap. Do not overtighten the bleed screw.

20 Repeat the procedure on the remaining

2.14a Remove the dust caps from the front . . .

2.14b . . . and rear bleed screws

screws in the sequence, until all air is removed from the system and the brake pedal feels firm again.

Using a one-way valve kit

21 As the name implies, these kits consist of a length of tubing with a one-way valve fitted, to prevent expelled air and fluid being drawn back into the system; some kits include a translucent container, which can be positioned so that the air bubbles can be more easily seen flowing from the end of the tube.

22 The kit is connected to the bleed screw, which is then opened. The user returns to the driver's seat, depresses the brake pedal with a smooth, steady stroke, and slowly releases it; this is repeated until the expelled fluid is clear of air bubbles.

23 Note that these kits simplify work so much that it is easy to forget the master cylinder reservoir fluid level; ensure that this is maintained at least above the MIN level line at all times.

Using a pressure-bleeding kit

24 These kits are usually operated by a reservoir of pressurised air contained in the spare tyre. However, note that it will probably be necessary to reduce the pressure to a lower level than normal; refer to the instructions supplied with the kit.

25 By connecting a pressurised, fluid-filled container to the master cylinder reservoir, bleeding can be carried out simply by opening each screw in turn (in the specified sequence), and allowing the fluid to flow out until no more air bubbles can be seen in the expelled fluid.

26 This method has the advantage that the large reservoir of fluid provides an additional safeguard against air being drawn into the system during bleeding.

27 Pressure-bleeding is particularly effective when bleeding 'difficult' systems, or when bleeding the complete system at the time of routine fluid renewal.

All methods

28 When bleeding is complete, and firm pedal feel is restored, wash off any spilt fluid, securely tighten the bleed screws, and refit the dust caps.

29 Check the hydraulic fluid level in the master cylinder reservoir, and top-up if necessary (see Weekly checks).

30 Discard any hydraulic fluid that has been bled from the system; it will not be fit for re-use.

31 Check the feel of the brake pedal. If it feels at all spongy, air must still be present in the system, and further bleeding is required. Failure to bleed satisfactorily after a reasonable repetition of the bleeding procedure may be due to worn master cylinder seals.

3 Hydraulic pipes and hoses – renewal

Note: Before starting work, refer to the note at the beginning of Section 2 concerning the dangers of hydraulic fluid.

1 If any pipe or hose is to be renewed, minimise fluid loss by first removing the master cylinder reservoir cap and screwing it down onto a piece of polythene. Alternatively, flexible hoses can be sealed, if required, using a proprietary brake hose clamp. Metal brake pipe unions can be plugged (if care is taken not to allow dirt into the system) or capped immediately they are disconnected. Place a wad of rag under any union that is to be disconnected, to catch any spilt fluid.

2 If a flexible hose is to be disconnected, unscrew the brake pipe union nut before removing the spring clip which secures the hose to its mounting bracket. Where applicable, unscrew the banjo union bolt securing the hose to the caliper and recover the copper washers.

3 To unscrew union nuts, it is preferable to obtain a brake pipe spanner of the correct size; these are available from most motor accessory shops. Failing this, a close-fitting open-ended spanner will be required, though if the nuts are tight or corroded, their flats may be rounded-off if the spanner slips. In such a case, a self-locking wrench is often the only way to unscrew a stubborn union, but it follows that the pipe and the damaged nuts must be renewed on reassembly. Always clean a union and surrounding area before disconnecting it. If disconnecting a component with more than one union, make a careful note of the connections before disturbing any of them.

4 If a brake pipe is to be renewed, it can be obtained, cut to length and with the union nuts and end flares in place, from Vauxhall/Opel dealers. All that is then necessary is to bend it to shape, following the line of the original, before fitting it to the car. Alternatively, most

motor accessory shops can make up brake pipes from kits, but this requires very careful measurement of the original, to ensure that the new one is of the correct length. The safest answer is usually to take the original to the shop as a pattern.

5 On refitting, do not overtighten the union nuts.

6 When refitting hoses to the calipers, always use new copper washers and tighten the banjo union bolts to the specified torque. Make sure that the hoses are positioned so that they will not touch surrounding bodywork or the roadwheels.

7 Ensure that the pipes and hoses are correctly routed, with no kinks, and that they are secured in the clips or brackets provided. After fitting, remove the polythene from the reservoir, and bleed the hydraulic system as described in Section 2. Wash off any spilt fluid, and check carefully for fluid leaks.

4 Front brake pads – renewal

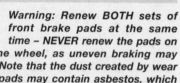

Warning: Renew BOTH sets of front brake pads at the same time – NEVER renew the pads on only one wheel, as uneven braking may result. Note that the dust created by wear of the pads may contain asbestos, which is a health hazard. Never blow it out with compressed air, and do not inhale any of it. An approved filtering mask should be worn when working on the brakes. DO NOT use petroleum-based solvents to clean brake parts – use brake cleaner or methylated spirit only.

1 Apply the handbrake, then jack up the front of the vehicle and support it on axle stands (see *Jacking and vehicle support*). Remove the front roadwheels.

2 Follow the accompanying photos (illustrations 4.2a to 4.2v) for the actual pad renewal procedure, bearing in mind the additional points below. Be sure to stay in order and read the caption under each illustration. Note that if the old pads are to be refitted, ensure that they are identified so that they can be returned to their original positions.

3 After removing the caliper from the mounting bracket, support it on top of the brake disc. Do not allow the caliper to hang unsupported on the flexible brake hose.

4 If the original brake pads are still serviceable, carefully clean them using a clean, fine wire brush or similar, paying particular attention to the sides and back of the metal backing plate. Clean out the grooves in the friction material, and pick out any large embedded particles of dirt or debris. Carefully clean the pad locations in the caliper body/mounting bracket.

5 Prior to fitting the pads, check that the guide bolts are a snug fit in the caliper mounting bracket. Inspect the dust seal around the piston for damage, and the piston for evidence of fluid leaks, corrosion or damage. If attention to any of these components is necessary, refer to Section 7.

6 If new brake pads are to be fitted, the caliper piston must be pushed back into the cylinder to allow for the extra pad thickness.

Either use a G-clamp or similar tool, or use suitable pieces of wood as levers. Clamp off the flexible brake hose leading to the caliper then connect a brake bleeding kit to the caliper bleed screw. Open the bleed screw as the piston is retracted, the surplus brake fluid will then be collected in the bleed kit vessel **(see illustration 4.2l)**. Close the bleed screw just before the caliper piston is pushed fully into the caliper. This should ensure no air enters the hydraulic system. **Note:** *The ABS unit contains hydraulic components that are very sensitive to impurities in the brake fluid. Even the smallest particles can cause the system to fail through blockage. The pad retraction method described here prevents any debris in the brake fluid expelled from the caliper from being passed back to the ABS hydraulic unit, as well as preventing any chance of damage to the master cylinder seals.*

7 With the brake pads installed, depress the brake pedal repeatedly, until normal (non-assisted) pedal pressure is restored, and the pads are pressed into firm contact with the brake disc.

8 Repeat the above procedure on the remaining front brake caliper.

9 Refit the roadwheels, then lower the vehicle to the ground and tighten the roadwheel bolts to the specified torque setting.

10 Check the hydraulic fluid level as described in *Weekly checks*.

Caution: New pads will not give full braking efficiency until they have bedded-in. Be prepared for this, and avoid hard braking as far as possible for the first hundred miles or so after pad renewal.

4.2a Push in the caliper piston by levering the caliper body towards the outside of the vehicle

4.2b Release the legs of the retaining spring from the caliper body . . .

4.2c . . . then remove the spring from the caliper mounting bracket

4.2d Remove the dust cap from the lower and upper guide bolts . . .

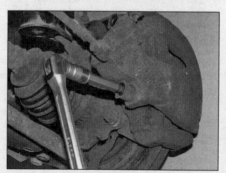

4.2e Unscrew the lower guide bolt . . .

4.2f . . . and the upper guide bolt

4.2g Lift the caliper off the mounting bracket

4.2h Remove the outer pad from the caliper mounting bracket . . .

4.2i . . . and the inner pad from the caliper piston, noting that it is retained by a spring clip attached to the pad backing plate

4.2j Measure the thickness of the pad friction material. If any are worn down to the specified minimum, or fouled with oil or grease, all four pads must be renewed

4.2k Brush the dust and dirt from the caliper piston and mounting bracket

4.2l If new pads are to be fitted, before refitting the caliper, push back the caliper piston whilst opening the bleed screw

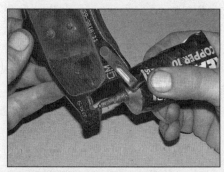

4.2m Apply a little high melting-point copper brake grease to the contact areas on the edges of the pad backing plate . . .

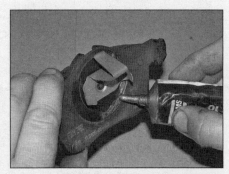

4.2n . . . and in the centre of the backing plate

4.2o Fit the inner pad to the caliper, ensuring that its clip is correctly located in the caliper piston

4.2p Fit the outer pad to the caliper mounting bracket, ensuring that its friction material is facing the brake disc

4.2q Slide the caliper into position in the mounting bracket

4.2r Fit the guide bolts . . .

4.2s . . . tighten the guide bolts to the specified torque . . .

4.2t . . . then refit the dust caps

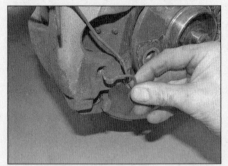

4.2u Locate the retaining spring legs into the holes in the caliper . . .

4.2v . . . then hold the legs in place and locate the spring behind the lugs on the mounting bracket

5 Rear brake pads – renewal

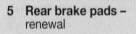

Warning: Renew BOTH sets of rear brake pads at the same time – NEVER renew the pads on only one wheel, as uneven braking may result. Note that the dust created by wear of the pads may contain asbestos, which is a health hazard. Never blow it out with compressed air, and do not inhale any of it. An approved filtering mask should be worn when working on the brakes. DO NOT use petroleum-based solvents to clean brake parts – use brake cleaner or methylated spirit only.

1 Chock the front wheels then jack up the rear of the car and securely support it on axle stands (see *Jacking and vehicle support*). Remove the rear roadwheels.

2 Slacken the handbrake cable adjuster at the handbrake lever as described in Section 14, paragraphs 11 and 12.

3 Follow the accompanying photos **(illustrations 5.3a to 5.3u)** for the actual pad renewal procedure, bearing in mind the additional points below. Be sure to stay in order and read the caption under each illustration. Note that if the old pads are to be refitted, ensure that they are identified so that they can be returned to their original positions.

4 If the original brake pads are still serviceable, carefully clean them using a clean, fine wire brush or similar, paying particular attention to the sides and back of the metal backing plate. Clean out the grooves in the friction material, and pick out any large embedded particles of dirt or debris. Carefully clean the pad locations in the caliper body/mounting bracket.

5 Prior to fitting the pads, check that the guide bolts are a snug fit in the caliper

mounting bracket. Brush the dust and dirt from the caliper and piston, but do not inhale it, as it is injurious to health. Inspect the dust seal around the piston for damage, and the piston for evidence of fluid leaks, corrosion or damage. If attention to any of these components is necessary, refer to Section 8.

6 If new brake pads are to be fitted, it will be necessary to retract the piston fully into the caliper bore by rotating it in a clockwise direction. This can be achieved by using sturdy circlip pliers, noting that as well as being turned, the piston has to be pressed in very firmly. Special tools are readily available to achieve this with less effort. While the caliper is being retracted, clamp off the flexible brake hose leading to the caliper then connect a brake bleeding kit to the caliper bleed screw. Open the bleed screw as the piston is retracted, the surplus brake fluid will then be collected in the bleed kit vessel **(see illustration 5.3l)**. Close the bleed screw just before the caliper piston is pushed fully into the caliper. This should ensure no air enters the hydraulic system. **Note:** *The ABS unit contains hydraulic components that are very sensitive to impurities in the brake fluid. Even the smallest particles can cause the system to fail through blockage. The pad retraction method described here prevents any debris in the brake fluid expelled from the caliper from being passed back to the ABS hydraulic unit, as well as preventing any chance of damage to the master cylinder seals.*

7 With the brake pads installed, depress the brake pedal repeatedly, until normal (non-assisted) pedal pressure is restored, and the pads are pressed into firm contact with the brake disc.

8 Repeat the above procedure on the remaining rear brake caliper.

9 Adjust the handbrake cable as described in Chapter 1A or 1B after fitting both sets of brake pads.

10 Refit the roadwheels, then lower the vehicle to the ground and tighten the roadwheel bolts to the specified torque setting.

11 Check the hydraulic fluid level as described in *Weekly checks*.

Caution: New pads will not give full braking efficiency until they have bedded-in. Be prepared for this, and avoid hard braking as far as possible for the first hundred miles or so after pad renewal.

5.3a Using a screwdriver, push the handbrake operating lever downwards, and detach the cable end fitting from the lever

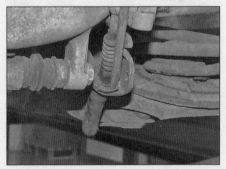

5.3b Prise out the handbrake outer cable retaining clip . . .

5.3c . . . and withdraw the handbrake cable from the caliper bracket

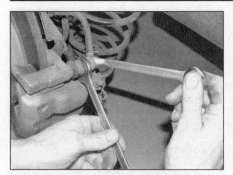

5.3d Unscrew the upper guide pin bolt while counterholding the guide pin with a second spanner

5.3e Unscrew the lower guide pin bolt in the same way

5.3f Lift the caliper off the mounting bracket and suspend it from a suitable place under the wheel arch using a cable-tie or similar

5.3g Remove the inner pad . . .

5.3h . . . and outer pad from the caliper mounting bracket

5.3i Remove the lower guide plate . . .

5.3j . . . and upper guide plate from the caliper mounting bracket

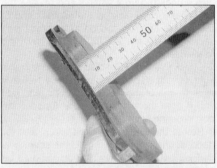

5.3k Measure the thickness of the pad friction material. If any are worn down to the specified minimum, or fouled with oil or grease, all four pads must be renewed

5.3l Using a caliper retracting tool to retract the piston as far as the stop

5.3m Once the piston is fully retracted, unscrew it slightly until the next piston cut-out (arrowed) is visible through the front of the caliper

5.3n Brush the dust and dirt from the caliper, piston and mounting bracket, then fit the lower guide plate . . .

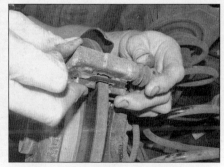

5.3o . . . and upper guide plate to the caliper mounting bracket

5.3p Apply a little high melting-point copper brake grease to the pad backing plate contact areas on the guide plates

5.3q If present remove the protective film from the pad backing plate, then fit the inner pad to the caliper mounting bracket . . .

5.3r . . . followed by the outer pad

5.3s Slide the caliper into position in the mounting bracket

5.3t Refit the upper and lower guide pin bolts and tighten them to the specified torque

5.3u Refit the handbrake cable to the mounting bracket and secure with the retaining clip, then reconnect the cable end to the caliper lever

6 Brake disc –
inspection, removal and refitting

Note: *Before starting work, refer to the warning at the beginning of Section 4 or 5 concerning the dangers of asbestos dust. If either disc requires renewal, both should be renewed at the same time together with new pads, to ensure even and consistent braking.*

Inspection

1 Remove the wheel trim, then loosen the roadwheel bolts. If checking a front disc, apply the handbrake, and if checking a rear

disc, chock the front wheels and release the handbrake, then jack up the relevant end of the vehicle and support on axle stands (see *Jacking and vehicle support*). Remove the roadwheel.

2 Check that the brake disc securing screw is tight, then fit a spacer approximately 10.0 mm thick to one of the roadwheel bolts, and refit and tighten the bolt in the hole opposite the disc securing screw.

3 Rotate the brake disc, and examine it for deep scoring or grooving. Light scoring is normal, but if excessive, the disc should be removed and either renewed or machined (within the specified limits) by an engineering works. The minimum thickness is given in the Specifications at the start of this Chapter.

4 Using a dial gauge, or a flat metal block and feeler blades, check that the disc run-out does not exceed the figure given in the Specifications. Measure the run-out 10.0 mm in from the outer edge of the disc.

5 If the disc run-out is excessive, remove the disc as described later, and check that the disc-to-hub surfaces are perfectly clean. Refit the disc and check the run-out again.

6 If the run-out is still excessive, the disc should be renewed.

7 To remove a disc, proceed as follows.

Front disc

Removal

8 Remove the roadwheel bolt and spacer used when checking the disc.

9 Unbolt and remove the front brake caliper complete with disc pads and mounting bracket, and suspend it from the coil spring using a cable-tie **(see illustrations).**

10 Remove the securing screw and withdraw the disc from the hub. **(see illustrations).**

Refitting

11 Refit the disc, making sure that the mating faces of the disc and hub are perfectly clean, and apply a little locking fluid to the threads of the securing screw.

12 Refit the caliper mounting bracket complete with caliper and pads, and tighten the bolts to the specified torque.

6.9a Unbolt and remove the front brake caliper complete with disc pads and mounting bracket . . .

6.9b . . . and suspend it from the coil spring using a cable-tie

Rear disc

Removal

13 Where applicable, remove the roadwheel bolt and spacer used when checking the disc.
14 Remove the rear brake pads as described in Section 5.
15 Undo the two bolts securing the caliper mounting bracket to the hub carrier and remove the mounting bracket.
16 Remove the securing screw and withdraw the disc from the hub **(see illustrations)**.

Refitting

17 Refit the disc, making sure that the mating faces of the disc and hub are perfectly clean, and apply a little locking fluid to the threads of the securing screw.
18 Refit the caliper mounting bracket and tighten the bolts to the specified torque.
19 Refit the brake pads as described in Section 5.

7 Front brake caliper – removal, overhaul and refitting

Note: *New brake hose copper washers will be required when refitting. Before starting work, refer to the note at the beginning of Section 2 concerning the dangers of hydraulic fluid, and to the warning at the beginning of Section 4 concerning the dangers of asbestos dust.*

Removal

1 Apply the handbrake, then jack up the front of the vehicle and support it on axle stands (see *Jacking and vehicle support*). Remove the roadwheel.
2 Minimise fluid loss by first removing the master cylinder reservoir cap and screwing it down onto a piece of polythene. Alternatively, use a brake hose clamp to clamp the flexible hose leading to the brake caliper.
3 Clean the area around the caliper brake hose union. Unscrew and remove the union bolt, and recover the copper sealing washer from each side of the hose union. Discard the washers; new ones must be used on refitting. Plug the hose end and caliper hole, to minimise fluid loss and prevent the ingress of dust and dirt into the hydraulic system.
4 Remove the brake pads as described in Section 4, then remove the caliper from the vehicle.

Overhaul

5 With the caliper on the bench, wipe it clean with a cloth rag.
6 Withdraw the partially-ejected piston from the caliper body, and remove the dust seal. The piston can be withdrawn by hand, or if necessary pushed out by applying compressed air to the brake hose union hole. Only low pressure should be required, such as is generated by a foot pump.
7 Using a small screwdriver, carefully remove the piston seal from the groove in the

6.10a Remove the securing screw . . .

6.10b . . . and withdraw the disc from the hub

6.16a Remove the securing screw (arrowed)

6.16b . . . and withdraw the disc from the hub

caliper, taking care not to mark the bore **(see illustration)**.
8 Carefully press the guide bushes out of the caliper body.
9 Thoroughly clean all components, using only methylated spirit or clean hydraulic fluid. Never use mineral-based solvents such as petrol or paraffin, which will attack the rubber components of the hydraulic system. Dry the components using compressed air or a clean, lint-free cloth. If available, use compressed air to blow clear the fluid passages.

⚠ *Warning: Wear eye protection when using compressed air.*

10 Check all components, and renew any that are worn or damaged. If the piston and/or cylinder bore are scratched excessively, renew the complete caliper body. Similarly check the

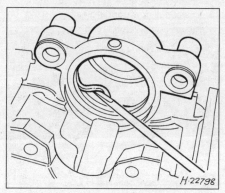
7.7 Removing the piston seal from the caliper body

condition of the guide bushes and bolts; both bushes and bolts should be undamaged and (when cleaned) a reasonably tight sliding fit. If there is any doubt about the condition of any component, renew it.
11 If the caliper is fit for further use, obtain the necessary components from your Vauxhall/Opel dealer. Renew the caliper seals and dust covers as a matter of course; these should never be re-used.
12 On reassembly, ensure that all components are absolutely clean and dry.
13 Dip the piston and the new piston seal in clean hydraulic fluid, and smear clean fluid on the cylinder bore surface.
14 Locate the new seal in the cylinder bore groove, using only the fingers to manipulate it into position.
15 Fit the new dust seal to the piston, then insert the piston into the cylinder bore using a twisting motion to ensure it enters the seal correctly. Locate the dust seal in the body groove, and push the piston fully into the caliper bore.
16 Insert the guide bushes into position in the caliper body.

Refitting

17 Refit the brake pads as described in Section 4, together with the caliper which at this stage will not have the hose attached.
18 Position a new copper sealing washer on each side of the hose union, and connect the brake hose to the caliper. Ensure that the hose is correctly positioned against the caliper body lug, then install the union bolt and tighten it to the specified torque setting.

19 Remove the brake hose clamp or polythene, and bleed the hydraulic system as described in Section 2. Note that, providing the precautions described were taken to minimise brake fluid loss, it should only be necessary to bleed the relevant front brake circuit.

20 Refit the roadwheel, then lower the vehicle to the ground and tighten the roadwheel bolts to the specified torque.

8 Rear brake caliper – removal, overhaul and refitting

Note 1: *Before starting work, refer to the note at the beginning of Section 2 concerning the dangers of hydraulic fluid, and to the warning at the beginning of Section 5 concerning the dangers of asbestos dust.*

Note 2: *Due to the integral handbrake operating mechanism incorporated in the caliper piston, it is not possible to fully dismantle the caliper. Only the guide pins, guide pin bushes and dust seals can be individually renewed. Check the availability of new parts before proceeding.*

Removal

1 Chock the front wheels, then jack up the rear of the vehicle and support on axle stands (see *Jacking and vehicle support*). Remove the roadwheel.

2 Minimise fluid loss by first removing the master cylinder reservoir cap and screwing it down onto a piece of polythene. Alternatively, use a brake hose clamp to clamp the flexible hose leading to the brake caliper.

3 Clean the area around the caliper brake hose union. Unscrew and remove the union bolt, and recover the copper sealing washer from each side of the hose union **(see illustration)**. Discard the washers; new ones must be used on refitting. Plug the hose end and caliper hole, to minimise fluid loss and prevent the ingress of dust and dirt into the hydraulic system.

4 Remove the brake pads as described in Section 5, then remove the caliper from the vehicle.

Overhaul

5 With the caliper on the bench, wipe it clean with a cloth rag.

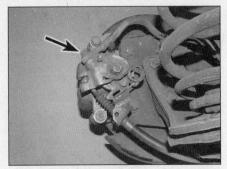

8.3 Rear caliper brake hose union bolt (arrowed)

6 Using a small screwdriver, carefully prise out the dust seal from the caliper, taking care not to damage the piston.

7 Carefully press the guide pin bushes out of the caliper body.

8 Further dismantling of the caliper is not possible as individual parts are not available separately.

9 Thoroughly clean all components, using only methylated spirit or clean hydraulic fluid. Dry the components using a clean, lint-free cloth.

10 Check the condition of the exposed portion of the caliper piston. If the piston and/or cylinder bore are scratched excessively or corroded, renew the complete caliper body. Similarly check the condition of the guide pin bushes, guide pins and bolts; the bushes, guide pins and bolts should be undamaged and (when cleaned) the guide pins a reasonably tight sliding fit in the bushes. If there is any doubt about the condition of any component, renew it.

11 If the caliper is fit for further use, obtain the necessary components from your Vauxhall/Opel dealer. Renew the caliper dust cover as a matter of course; it should never be re-used.

12 Fit the new dust seal to the piston, then locate the dust seal in the caliper body groove.

13 Insert the guide pin bushes into position in the caliper body.

Refitting

14 Refit the brake pads as described in Section 5, together with the caliper which at this stage will not have the hose attached.

15 Position a new copper sealing washer on

each side of the hose union, and connect the brake hose to the caliper. Ensure that the hose is correctly positioned against the caliper body lug, then install the union bolt and tighten it to the specified torque setting.

16 Remove the brake hose clamp or polythene, and bleed the hydraulic system as described in Section 2. Note that, providing the precautions described were taken to minimise brake fluid loss, it should only be necessary to bleed the relevant rear brake circuit.

17 Refit the roadwheel, then lower the vehicle to the ground and tighten the roadwheel bolts to the specified torque.

9 Master cylinder – removal and refitting

Note: *Before starting work, refer to the warning at the beginning of Section 2 concerning the dangers of hydraulic fluid.*

Removal

1 Remove the windscreen cowl panel and the bulkhead closure panel as described in Chapter 11.

2 Remove the master cylinder reservoir cap, and siphon the hydraulic fluid from the reservoir. **Note:** *Do not siphon the fluid by mouth, as it is poisonous; use a syringe or an old hydrometer.* Alternatively, open any convenient bleed screw in the system, and gently pump the brake pedal to expel the fluid through a plastic tube connected to the screw (see Section 2).

3 Extract the horseshoe-shaped retaining clip and withdraw the master cylinder reservoir from the mounting bracket **(see illustrations)**. Disconnect the clutch master cylinder hydraulic hose and the brake fluid level sensor wiring connector from the reservoir, then place the reservoir to one side.

4 Place cloth rags beneath the master cylinder to collect escaping brake fluid. Identify the brake lines for position, then unscrew the union nuts and move the lines to one side. Tape over or plug the line outlets.

5 Unscrew the mounting nuts and withdraw the master cylinder from the vacuum servo unit **(see illustration)**. Take care not to spill fluid on the vehicle paintwork.

9.3a Extract the horseshoe-shaped retaining clip . . .

9.3b . . . and withdraw the master cylinder reservoir from the mounting bracket

9.5 Brake master cylinder mounting nuts (arrowed)

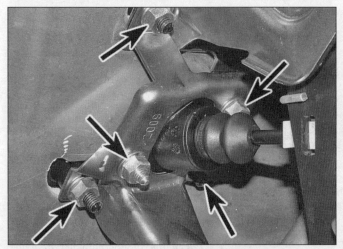

10.5 Clutch master cylinder and mounting plate retaining nuts (arrowed)

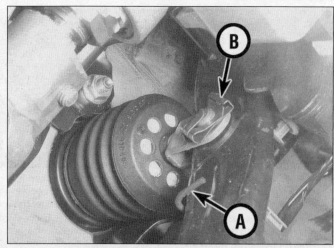

10.6 Unhook the pedal return spring (A) then slide off the spring clip (B) and withdraw the clevis pin

6 Remove the master cylinder and reservoir from the car.

7 If necessary, unscrew the retaining bolt and detach the fluid hose mounting block from the side of the master cylinder. Remove the two fluid hose seals from the master cylinder ports and obtain new seals for refitting.

8 No further dismantling of the master cylinder is possible as the internal components are not available separately.

Refitting

9 If the reservoir has been detached from the master cylinder, lubricate the new fluid hose seals with clean brake hydraulic fluid and push the new seals into position. Attach the fluid hose mounting block to the side of the master cylinder and secure the block with the retaining bolt.

10 Fit the master cylinder to the servo unit, ensuring that the servo unit pushrod enters the master cylinder piston centrally. Fit the retaining nuts and tighten them to the specified torque setting.

11 Refit the brake lines and tighten the union nuts securely.

12 Reconnect the clutch master cylinder hydraulic hose and the brake fluid level sensor wiring connector to the reservoir, then place the reservoir in position on the mounting

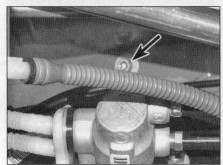

10.7 Undo the screw (arrowed) securing the pedal mounting bracket to the bulkhead

bracket. Refit the horshoe-shaped retaining clip.

13 Refit the bulkhead closure panel and the windscreen cowl panel as described in Chapter 11.

14 Remove the reservoir filler cap and top-up the reservoir with fresh hydraulic fluid to the MAX mark (see *Weekly checks*).

15 Bleed the hydraulic systems as described in Section 2 and Chapter 6 then refit the filler cap. Thoroughly check the operation of the brakes and clutch before using the vehicle on the road.

10 Brake pedal – removal and refitting

Note 1: *The brake pedal (and, where applicable, the clutch pedal) are an integral part of the pedal mounting bracket assembly and cannot be individually removed. Should renewal of the pedal(s), due to wear of the pivot bushes or the pedal itself, be required, it will be necessary to renew the complete mounting bracket assembly.*

Note 2: *This is a complicated operation that entails removal of the complete facia and facia crossmember. Before starting, read through the entire procedure to familiarise yourself with the work involved and the complications that may be encountered.*

Removal

1 Remove the windscreen cowl panel and bulkhead closure panel as described in Chapter 11.

2 Remove the complete facia and facia cross-member as described in Chapter 11.

3 From inside the car, disconnect the wiring connectors from the brake stop-light switch and, where fitted, the clutch pedal switch. Release the wiring harness from the clips and cable-ties on the pedal mounting bracket.

4 Disconnect the return spring from the clutch

pedal, then remove the retaining clip securing the master cylinder pushrod to the clutch pedal. To do this, depress the tab on each side of the clip using two screwdrivers, while at the same time, pushing the clip forward, out of the clutch pedal.

5 Unscrew the two nuts securing the clutch master cylinder to the mounting plate, and the three nuts securing the mounting plate to the pedal bracket **(see illustration)**.

6 Unhook the return spring from the brake pedal, then slide off the spring clip, and withdraw the clevis pin securing the pedal to the servo unit pushrod **(see illustration)**.

7 Working in the engine compartment, undo the screw located above the brake vacuum servo unit, securing the pedal mounting bracket to the bulkhead **(see illustration)**.

8 Working back inside the car, undo the four nuts securing the pedal mounting bracket to the bulkhead.

9 Make a final check that the various wiring harnesses have been released from their clips and ties on the pedal mounting bracket. Withdraw the mounting bracket rearward away from the bulkhead and remove the pedal and mounting bracket assembly from the car.

10 With the pedal mounting bracket removed, if required, the brake stop-light switch and clutch pedal switch (where fitted) can be removed as described in Section 15.

Refitting

11 If removed, refit the brake stop-light switch and clutch pedal switch (where fitted) as described in Section 15.

12 Locate the pedal mounting bracket assembly back in position on the bulkhead, ensuring that the vacuum servo unit pushrod and clutch master cylinder pushrod correctly engage with the respective pedals.

13 Refit the pedal mounting bracket retaining nuts and clutch master cylinder and mounting plate retaining nuts, and tighten to the specified torque.

14 Working in the engine compartment, refit

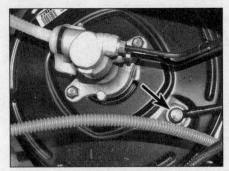

11.5 Carefully ease the vacuum hose (arrowed) out of the servo unit rubber grommet

and tighten the screw securing the pedal mounting bracket to the bulkhead.

15 Apply a smear of multipurpose grease to the clevis pin then align the servo unit pushrod with the brake pedal hole and insert the pin. Secure the pin in position with the retaining clip, making sure it is correctly located in the groove. Refit the return spring to the pedal.

16 Secure the clutch master cylinder pushrod to the clutch pedal with the retaining clip, then refit the return spring to the clutch pedal.

17 Reconnect the brake stop-light switch and, where fitted, the clutch switch wiring connectors. Secure the wiring harness with the clips and new cable-ties.

18 Refit the facia crossmember, facia, bulkhead closure panel and windscreen cowl panel as described in Chapter 11.

11 Vacuum servo unit – testing, removal and refitting

Testing

1 With the engine off, depress the footbrake several times to exhaust the vacuum. Now start the engine, keeping the pedal firmly depressed. As the engine starts, there should be a noticeable 'give' in the brake pedal as the vacuum builds-up. Allow the engine to run for at least two minutes, then switch it off. The brake pedal should now feel normal, but further applications should result in the pedal feeling firmer, the pedal stroke decreasing with each application.

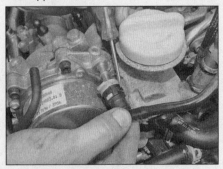

12.4 Disconnect the vacuum hose quick-release fitting at the vacuum pump

11.10 Slacken and remove the two nuts (arrowed) securing the servo unit to the pedal mounting bracket

2 If the servo does not operate as described, first inspect the servo unit check valve as described in Section 12.

3 If the servo unit still fails to operate satisfactorily, the fault lies within the unit itself. Repairs to the unit are not possible; if faulty, the servo unit must be renewed.

Removal

4 Remove the brake master cylinder as described in Section 9.

5 Carefully ease the vacuum hose out of the servo unit, taking care not to displace the sealing grommet (see illustration).

6 Remove the windscreen wiper motor and linkage as described in Chapter 12.

7 Remove the lower trim panel beneath the facia on the driver's side as described in Chapter 11.

8 Release the expanding rivet and remove the driver's side footwell air duct.

9 Unhook the return spring from the brake pedal, then slide off the spring clip, and withdraw the clevis pin securing the pedal to the servo unit pushrod (see illustration 10.6).

10 Slacken and remove the two diagonally-opposite nuts securing the servo unit to the pedal mounting bracket (see illustration).

11 Return to the engine compartment, and lift the servo unit out of position.

Refitting

12 Locate the vacuum servo unit in position on the bulkhead ensuring that the servo unit pushrod locates correctly around the brake pedal. Refit the two nuts and tighten them to the specified torque.

13 Apply a smear of multipurpose grease to the clevis pin then align the servo unit pushrod with the brake pedal hole and insert the pin. Secure the pin in position with the retaining clip, making sure it is correctly located in the groove.

14 Refit the driver's side footwell air duct, then refit the facia trim panels as described in Chapter 11.

15 Refit the windscreen wiper motor and linkage as described in Chapter 12.

16 Refit the vacuum hose to the servo grommet, ensuring that the hose is correctly seated.

17 Refit the brake master cylinder as described in Section 12.

12 Vacuum servo unit check valve and hose – removal, testing and refitting

Removal

1 Remove the windscreen cowl panel and the bulkhead closure panel as described in Chapter 11.

2 Carefully ease the vacuum hose out of the servo unit, taking care not to displace the sealing grommet (see illustration 11.5).

3 Where fitted, remove the plastic cover over the top of the engine.

4 Disconnect the hose quick-release fitting from the inlet manifold (petrol engines) or vacuum pump (diesel engines) (see illustration).

5 Release the rubber grommet from the bulkhead, then remove the hose and check valve from the car.

Testing

6 Examine the check valve and hose for signs of damage, and renew if necessary. The valve may be tested by blowing through it in both directions. Air should flow through the valve in one direction only – when blown through from the servo unit end. If air flows in both directions, or not at all, renew the valve and hose as an assembly.

7 Examine the servo unit rubber sealing grommet for signs of damage or deterioration, and renew as necessary.

Refitting

8 Refitting is a reversal of removal ensuring that the quick-release connector audibly locks in position, and that the hose is correctly seated in the servo grommet.

9 On completion, start the engine and check that there are no air leaks.

13 Handbrake lever – removal and refitting

Removal

1 Disconnect the battery negative terminal (refer to *Disconnecting the battery* in the Reference Chapter).

2 Remove the centre console as described in Chapter 11.

3 Ensure that the handbrake lever is released (off).

4 Disconnect the wiring connector from the handbrake lever warning light switch. Release the cable from the support.

5 Undo the handbrake cable adjuster nut and release the cable from the handbrake lever (see illustration).

6 Undo the four retaining nuts, unclip the lever from the support plate and remove the handbrake lever assembly from inside the car (see illustration).

Refitting

7 Refitting is the reverse of removal, but adjust the handbrake as described in Chapter 1A or 1B, and refit the centre console as described in Chapter 11.

14 Handbrake cables – removal and refitting

Removal

1 The handbrake cable consists of two sections, a short front (primary) section which connects the lever to the compensator plate, and the main cables (secondary) section which links the compensator plate to the rear brake calipers. Each section can be removed individually as follows.

Primary (front) cable

2 Chock the front wheels then jack up the rear of the car and securely support it on axle stands (see *Jacking and vehicle support*). Ensure that the handbrake lever is released (off).
3 Remove the centre console as described in Chapter 11.
4 Undo the handbrake cable adjuster nut and release the cable from the handbrake lever **(see illustration 13.6)**.
5 Release the cable from the guide on the mounting plate where necessary.
6 Remove the complete exhaust system as described in Chapter 4A or 4B.
7 Unscrew the nuts and remove the exhaust heat shield from the underbody.
8 Detach the front cable from the compensator plate by twisting it through 90°.
9 Release the grommet from the lever mounting plate, and withdraw the front cable from the vehicle. Remove the grommet from the cable.

Secondary (main) cable

Note: The secondary cables are supplied as one part, together with the compensator plate.
10 Chock the front wheels then jack up the rear of the car and securely support it on axle stands (see *Jacking and vehicle support*). Remove both rear roadwheels.
11 From inside the vehicle, unclip the handbrake lever gaiter from the centre console and slide the gaiter up the lever **(see illustration)**.
12 Move the handbrake lever to the fully released position, then turn the cable adjuster nut anti-clockwise to remove all tension from the cables **(see illustration 13.6)**.
13 Working on each side in turn, use a screwdriver to push the handbrake operating lever on the brake caliper downwards, and detach the cable end fitting from the lever **(see illustration)**.
14 Prise out the handbrake outer cable retaining clip and withdraw the handbrake cable from the caliper bracket **(see illustrations)**.

13.5 Undo the handbrake cable adjuster nut (arrowed) and release the cable from the handbrake lever

15 Remove the complete exhaust system as described in Chapter 4A or 4B.
16 Unscrew the nuts and remove the exhaust heat shield from the underbody.
17 Detach the front cable from the compensator plate by twisting it through 90°.
18 Release the main cable sections from the supports on the rear axle and fuel tank, and withdraw the cable from under the vehicle.

Refitting

19 Refitting is a reversal of the removal procedure, but adjust the handbrake as described in Chapter 1A or 1B. Make sure that the fitting on the rear of the front cable locates correctly in the compensator plate. Also make sure that the protective sleeve on the front cable is firmly located over the bead next to the compensator plate.

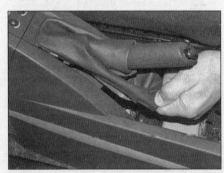

14.11 Unclip the gaiter from around the handbrake lever

14.14a Prise out the handbrake outer cable retaining clip . . .

13.6 Handbrake lever retaining nuts (arrowed)

15 Stop-light switch – removal, refitting and adjustment

Removal

1 The stop-light switch is located on the brake pedal bracket in the driver's footwell.
2 Remove the lower trim panel beneath the facia on the driver's side as described in Chapter 11.
3 Release the expanding rivet and remove the driver's side footwell air duct.
4 Disconnect the wiring connector at the stop-light switch.
5 Push the brake pedal down, pull out the brake switch actuating pin, then unclip the

14.13 Push the handbrake operating lever on the brake caliper downwards, and detach the cable end fitting from the lever

14.14b . . . and withdraw the handbrake cable from the caliper bracket

15.5a Pull out the centre actuating pin arrowed (switch removed for clarity) . . .

locking sleeve from around the actuating pin (see illustrations).

6 Release the securing clips and pull the switch to disengage it from the pedal mounting bracket.

Refitting and adjustment

7 With the actuating pin pulled out, and the locking sleeve unclipped, refit the switch to the pedal bracket.

8 Secure the switch with the locking sleeve.

9 Release the brake pedal and the pedal will automatically adjust the position of the actuating pin.

10 Reconnect the wiring connector, then refit the facia footwell trim panel as described in Chapter 11.

16 Handbrake warning light switch – removal and refitting

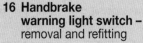

Removal

1 Remove the centre console as described in Chapter 11.

2 Disconnect the wiring connector from the warning light switch on the side of the handbrake lever.

3 Unscrew the mounting bolt and remove the switch from the handbrake lever bracket.

Refitting

4 Refitting is a reversal of removal.

17 Brake proportioning valve – removal, refitting and adjustment

Removal

1 Chock the front wheels, then jack up the rear of the vehicle, and support it securely on axle stands (see *Jacking and vehicle support*).

2 Minimise fluid loss by first removing the master cylinder reservoir cap and screwing it down onto a piece of polythene.

3 Wipe clean the area around the brake pipe union nuts on the brake proportioning valve. Identify the brake pipes for position, then unscrew the four union nuts and move the pipes to one side. Tape over or plug the line outlets.

15.5b . . . and unclip the locking sleeve

4 Undo the two bolts securing the valve to the mounting bracket. Unhook the tension spring from the bracket on the rear axle and remove the valve from under the car.

Refitting and adjustment

5 Refitting is a reversal of removal, but tighten the retaining bolts to the specified torque and bleed the brake hydraulic system as described in Section 2. Finally, adjust the proportioning valve as follows.

6 The vehicle should be empty with a maximum of half a tank of fuel. The rear wheels must be on the ground so that the weight of the vehicle is on the rear suspension. Alternatively, the rear wheels can be lowered onto car ramps.

7 Move the operating lever on the valve forward and backward and check for smooth operation. If there is any sign of binding or roughness when moving the lever, renew the valve.

8 Slacken the locking screw on the sliding adjustment piece on the end of the tension spring. Move the adjustment piece forward or backward as necessary so that all free play is removed from the spring. Hold the adjustment piece in this position and tighten the locking screw to the specified torque.

9 On completion, lower the vehicle to the ground (if applicable).

18 Anti-lock Braking and Traction Control systems – general information

ABS is fitted as standard equipment to most models and is optionally available on all others. On higher specification models, the ABS may also incorporate traction control or an electronic stability program as additional safety features.

The ABS system comprises a hydraulic modulator and electronic control unit together with four wheel speed sensors. The hydraulic modulator contains the electronic control unit (ECU), the hydraulic solenoid valves (one set for each brake) and the electrically-driven pump. The purpose of the system is to prevent the wheel(s) locking during heavy braking. This is achieved by automatic release of the brake on the relevant wheel, followed by re-application of the brake.

The solenoid valves are controlled by the ECU, which itself receives signals from the four wheel speed sensors which monitor the speed of rotation of each wheel. By comparing these signals, the ECU can determine the speed at which the vehicle is travelling. It can then use this speed to determine when a wheel is decelerating at an abnormal rate, compared to the speed of the vehicle, and therefore predicts when a wheel is about to lock. During normal operation, the system functions in the same way as a conventional braking system.

If the ECU senses that a wheel is about to lock, it operates the relevant solenoid valve(s) in the hydraulic unit, which then isolates from the master cylinder the relevant brake(s) on the wheel(s) which is/are about to lock, effectively sealing-in the hydraulic pressure.

If the speed of rotation of the wheel continues to decrease at an abnormal rate, the ECU operates the electrically-driven pump which pumps the hydraulic fluid back into the master cylinder, releasing the brake. Once the speed of rotation of the wheel returns to an acceptable rate, the pump stops, and the solenoid valves switch again, allowing the hydraulic master cylinder pressure to return to the caliper, which then re-applies the brake. This cycle can be carried out many times a second.

The action of the solenoid valves and return pump creates pulses in the hydraulic circuit. When the ABS system is functioning, these pulses can be felt through the brake pedal.

On models with traction control, the ABS hydraulic modulator incorporates an additional set of solenoid valves which operate the traction control system. The system operates at speeds up to approximately 30 mph using the signals supplied by the wheel speed sensors. If the ECU senses that a driving wheel is about to lose traction, it prevents this by momentarily applying the relevant front brake. The ABS ECU also communicates with the engine management ECU during traction control operation. In severe cases of traction loss the engine management ECU will reduce engine power to assist with traction recovery.

The electronic stability program (ESP) is a further development of ABS and traction control. Using additional sensors to monitor steering wheel position, vehicle yaw rate, acceleration and deceleration, in conjunction with the ABS sensors, the ECU can intervene under conditions of vehicle instability. Using the signals from the various sensors, the ECU can determine driver intent (steering wheel position, throttle position, vehicle speed and engine speed). From the sensor inputs from the wheel speed sensors, yaw rate sensors and acceleration sensors the ECU can calculate whether the vehicle is responding to driver input, or whether an unstable driving situation is occurring. If instability is detected, the ECU will intervene by applying or releasing the relevant front or rear brake, in conjunction with a power reduction, until vehicle stability returns.

The operation of the ABS, traction control, and stability programs is entirely dependent on electrical signals. To prevent the system responding to any inaccurate signals, a built-in safety circuit monitors all signals received by the ECU. If an inaccurate signal or low battery voltage is detected, the system is automatically shut down, and the relevant warning light on the instrument panel is illuminated to inform the driver that the system is not operational. Normal braking is still available, however.

If a fault develops in the ABS/traction control/ESP system, the vehicle must be taken to a Vauxhall/Opel dealer for fault diagnosis and repair.

19 Anti-lock Braking and Traction Control system components – removal and refitting

Note 1: *Faults on the ABS system can only be diagnosed using Vauxhall/Opel diagnostic equipment or compatible alternative equipment.*
Note 2: *Before starting work, refer to the note at the beginning of Section 2 concerning the dangers of hydraulic fluid.*

Hydraulic modulator

Removal

1 Remove the battery and battery tray as described in Chapter 5A.
2 Undo the retaining screw and release the plastic rivet securing the cooling system expansion tank to the front crossmember **(see illustrations)**.
3 Release the retaining clip, and withdraw the expansion tank from the front crossmember **(see illustrations)**. Place the tank to one side.
4 Minimise fluid loss by first removing the master cylinder reservoir cap and screwing it down onto a piece of polythene.
5 Pull out the locking bar and disconnect the wiring harness plug from the ABS ECU on the hydraulic modulator.
6 Note and record the fitted position of the brake pipes at the modulator, then unscrew the union nuts and release the pipes. As a precaution, place absorbent rags beneath the brake pipe unions when unscrewing them. Suitably plug or cap the disconnected unions to prevent dirt entry and fluid loss.
7 Unscrew the two retaining nuts and remove the hydraulic modulator from the mounting bracket.

Refitting

8 Refitting is the reverse of the removal procedure, noting the following points:
 a) *Tighten the modulator retaining nuts to the specified torque.*
 b) *Refit the brake pipes to their respective locations, and tighten the union nuts to the specified torque.*
 c) *Ensure that the wiring is correctly routed, and that the ECU wiring harness plug is firmly pressed into position and secured with the locking bar.*

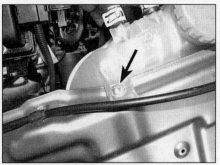

19.2a Undo the retaining screw (arrowed) . . .

19.3a . . . squeeze together the legs of the guide clip . . .

 d) *Refit the battery tray and battery as described in Chapter 5A.*
 e) *On completion, bleed the complete hydraulic system as described in Section 2. Ensure that the system is bled in the correct order, to prevent air entering the modulator return pump.*

Electronic control unit (ECU)

Note: *At the time of writing, no information was available for removal and refitting of the ECU on systems incorporating an electronic stability program (ESP). This work should therefore be entrusted to a Vauxhall/Opel dealer.*

Removal

9 Remove the hydraulic modulator from the car as described previously in this Section.
10 On the ABS 5.3 ECU, remove the cable connector from the base of the ECU.
11 Undo the six retaining screws (ABS 5.3), or four retaining screws (ABS 8.0), noting the

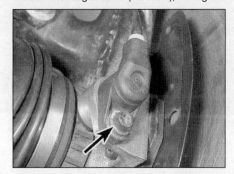

19.19a Undo the retaining bolt (arrowed) . . .

19.2b . . . and extract the plastic rivet securing the expansion tank to the crossmember . . .

19.3b . . . and withdraw the expansion tank from the crossmember

locations of the longer screws, and carefully withdraw the ECU from the base of the hydraulic modulator. Note that new retaining screws will be required for refitting.
12 Thoroughly clean the mating face of the hydraulic modulator and also check the condition of the ECU gasket. If the gasket is damaged it will be necessary to obtain a new ECU.

Refitting

13 Carefully place the ECU in position, keeping it square and level.
14 Fit the new retaining screws and lightly tighten in a diagonal sequence. Where applicable, refit the cable connector.
15 On completion, refit the hydraulic modulator as described previously in this Section.

Front wheel speed sensors

Removal

16 Disconnect the battery negative terminal (refer to *Disconnecting the battery* in the Reference Chapter).
17 Firmly apply the handbrake, then jack up the front of the car and support it securely on axle stands (see *Jacking and vehicle support*). Remove the appropriate front roadwheel.
18 Trace the wheel speed sensor wiring back to its wiring connector on the inner wheel arch, and release it from its retaining clip. Disconnect the connector, and work back along the sensor wiring, freeing it from all the relevant retaining clips and ties.
19 Slacken and remove the bolt securing the sensor to the swivel hub, and remove the sensor and lead assembly from the vehicle **(see illustrations)**.

19.19b . . . and remove the front wheel speed sensor

20.3 Disconnect the quick-release fitting (arrowed) and detach the servo unit vacuum hose – 1.3 litre engines

20.4 Undo the two mounting bolts (arrowed) and remove the pump from the camshaft housing – 1.3 litre engines

Refitting

20 Ensure that the sensor and swivel hub sealing faces are clean, then fit the sensor to the hub. Refit the retaining bolt, and tighten it securely.

21 Ensure that the sensor wiring is correctly routed, and retained by all the necessary clips. Reconnect it to its wiring connector, and fit the connector into the retaining clip.

22 Refit the roadwheel, then lower the vehicle to the ground and tighten the roadwheel bolts to the specified torque.

Rear wheel speed sensors

23 The rear wheel speed sensors are an integral part of the hub bearings and cannot be separated.

24 Refer to Chapter 10 for rear hub bearing removal and refitting procedures.

Yaw rate sensor

Note: *The yaw rate sensor is only fitted to vehicles with electronic stability control (ESP). The sensor is located beneath the centre console, just forward of the handbrake lever.*

Removal

25 Disconnect the battery negative terminal

(refer to *Disconnecting the battery* in the Reference Chapter).

26 Remove the centre console as described in Chapter 11.

27 Disconnect the sensor wiring connector, then undo the two bolts and remove the sensor from the car.

Refitting

28 Refitting is the reverse of the removal procedure.

Steering angle sensor

29 The steering angle sensor is an integral part of the airbag wiring contact unit on the steering column. Removal and refitting details for the airbag wiring contact unit are contained in Chapter 12.

20 Vacuum pump (diesel engine models) – removal and refitting

Removal

1.3 litre engines

1 Remove the plastic cover over the top of the engine.

2 Remove the battery and battery tray as described in Chapter 5A.

3 Disconnect the quick-release fitting and detach the servo unit vacuum hose from the pump **(see illustration)**. Disconnect the smaller vacuum hose from the outlet on the side of the pump.

4 Undo the two mounting bolts and remove the pump from the camshaft housing **(see illustration)**. Recover the gasket.

1.7 litre engines

5 Remove the alternator as described in Chapter 5A.

6 Undo the three retaining bolts and remove the vacuum pump from the rear of the alternator. Remove the O-ring seal.

Refitting

7 Refitting is a reversal of removal, but clean the mating faces of the pump and camshaft housing or alternator, and fit a new gasket or O-ring as applicable. Tighten the mounting bolts to the specified torque (where given).

Chapter 10
Suspension and steering

Contents

Degrees of difficulty

Easy, suitable for novice with little experience	**Fairly easy,** suitable for beginner with some experience	**Fairly difficult,** suitable for competent DIY mechanic	**Difficult,** suitable for experienced DIY mechanic	**Very difficult,** suitable for expert DIY or professional

Specifications

Front suspension

Type . . . . Independent, with MacPherson struts, gas-filled shock absorbers and anti-roll bar

Rear suspension

Type . . . . Semi-independent torsion beam, with trailing arms, coil springs and telescopic shock absorbers.

Steering

Type . . . . Rack-and-pinion with electric power steering (EPS)

Front and rear hub bearings

Bearing play (maximum). . . . . 0.1 mm
Bearing radial run-out. . . . . 0.04 mm
Bearing lateral run-out . . . . 0.05 mm

Torque wrench settings

	Nm	lbf ft
Front suspension		
Anti-roll bar clamp bolts......................................	20	15
Balljoint-to-lower arm bolts/nuts*.............................	55	41
Brake caliper mounting bracket-to-swivel hub bolts..............	100	74
Driveshaft retaining nut:*		
Stage 1...	120	89
Stage 2...	Slacken the nut completely	
Stage 3...	20	15
Stage 4...	Angle-tighten a further 90°	
Front subframe mounting bolts:*		
Stage 1...	90	66
Stage 2...	Angle-tighten a further 45°	
Stage 3...	Angle-tighten a further 15°	
Link rod-to-strut nut*.......................................	65	48
Link rod-to-anti-roll bar nut*................................	65	48
Lower arm balljoint clamp bolt nut*...........................	60	44
Lower arm pivot bolts/nut to front subframe:*		
Stage 1...	90	66
Stage 2...	Angle-tighten a further 75°	
Stage 3...	Angle-tighten a further 15°	
Lower arm-to-inner front bush bolts/nuts*.....................	55	41
Suspension strut piston rod upper mounting nut*...............	50	37
Suspension strut-to-swivel hub bolts:*		
Stage 1...	80	59
Stage 2...	Angle-tighten a further 60°	
Stage 3...	Angle-tighten a further 15°	
Suspension strut upper mounting nut..........................	55	41
Wheel speed sensor retaining bracket bolt.....................	8	6
Rear suspension		
Brake hydraulic line union nuts..............................	16	12
Hub bearing assembly to trailing arm:*		
Stage 1...	50	37
Stage 2...	Angle-tighten a further 30°	
Stage 3...	Angle-tighten a further 15°	
Shock absorber:		
To body...	90	66
To trailing arm.....................................	130	96
Torsion beam front mounting bracket:*		
Centre bolt:		
Stage 1...	90	66
Stage 2...	Angle-tighten a further 60°	
Stage 3...	Angle-tighten a further 15°	
Bracket-to-underbody bolts:*		
Stage 1...	90	66
Stage 2...	Angle-tighten a further 30°	
Stage 3...	Angle-tighten a further 15°	
Steering		
Airbag unit to steering wheel................................	8	6
EPS motor-to-steering column.................................	10	7
Intermediate shaft-to-steering pinion clamp bolt nut*.........	24	18
Steering column mounting bolts...............................	20	15
Steering column-to-intermediate shaft clamp bolt:		
Stage 1	24	18
Stage 2	Angle tighten a further 60°	
Steering gear-to-front subframe bolts:*		
Stage 1	45	33
Stage 2	Angle tighten a further 45°	
Stage 3	Angle tighten a further 15°	
Steering wheel bolt*...	30	22
Track rod inner balljoint to steering rack...................	70	52
Track rod end locknut..	50	37
Track rod end-to-swivel hub nut*.............................	35	26
Roadwheels		
Roadwheel bolts..	110	81

* Use new fasteners

1 General information

The independent front suspension is of the MacPherson strut type, incorporating coil springs and integral telescopic shock absorbers. The MacPherson struts are located by transverse lower suspension arms, which utilise rubber inner mounting bushes, and incorporate a balljoint at the outer ends. The front swivel hubs, which carry the hub bearings, brake calipers and disc assemblies, are bolted to the MacPherson struts, and connected to the lower arms via the balljoints. A front anti-roll bar is fitted, which has link rods with balljoints at each end to connect it to the strut.

The rear suspension is of semi-independent type, consisting of a torsion beam and trailing arms, with double-conical coil springs and telescopic shock absorbers. The front ends of the trailing arms are attached to the vehicle underbody by horizontal bushes, and the rear ends are located by the shock absorbers, which are bolted to the underbody at their upper ends. The coil springs are mounted independently of the shock absorbers, and act directly between the trailing arms and the underbody. Each rear wheel bearing, hub and stub axle assembly is manufactured as a sealed unit, and cannot be dismantled.

The steering column is linked to the steering gear by an intermediate shaft. The intermediate shaft has a universal joint fitted to its upper end, and is secured to the column by a clamp bolt. The lower end of the intermediate shaft is attached to the steering gear pinion by means of a universal joint and clamp bolts.

The rack-and-pinion type steering gear is mounted on the front subframe, and is connected by two track rods, with balljoints at their outer ends, to the steering arms projecting rearwards from the swivel hubs. The track rod ends are threaded, to facilitate adjustment.

Electric power-assisted steering is fitted as standard, whereby an electric motor, drivegear assembly and torque sensor incorporated in the steering column provide a variable degree

2.2 Extract the split pin from the driveshaft retaining nut

of power assistance according to roadspeed. The system is controlled by an electronic control unit with self-diagnostic capability, integral with the electric motor.

2 Front swivel hub – removal and refitting

Note: *A new driveshaft retaining nut, lower arm balljoint clamp bolt and nut, suspension strut-to-swivel hub nuts and bolts and a new track rod end retaining nut will be needed for refitting. The driveshaft outer joint splines may be a tight fit in the hub and it is possible that a puller/extractor will be required to draw the hub assembly off the driveshaft during removal.*

Removal

1 Firmly apply the handbrake, then jack up the front of the car and support it securely on axle stands (see *Jacking and vehicle support*). Remove the relevant front roadwheel.
2 Extract the split pin from the driveshaft retaining nut and discard it; a new one must be used on refitting **(see illustration)**.
3 Refit at least two roadwheel bolts to the front hub, and tighten them securely. Have an assistant firmly depress the brake pedal to prevent the front hub from rotating, then using a socket and extension bar, slacken the driveshaft retaining nut. Alternatively, a tool can be fabricated from two lengths of steel strip (one long, one short) and a nut and bolt;

2.3 Using a fabricated tool to hold the front hub stationary whilst the driveshaft retaining nut is slackened

the nut and bolt forming the pivot of a forked tool. Bolt the tool to the hub using two wheel bolts, and hold the tool to prevent the hub from rotating as the driveshaft retaining nut is undone **(see illustration)**.
4 Unscrew the driveshaft retaining nut, and remove the washer. Discard the nut and washer; new ones must be used on refitting.
5 Remove the front brake disc and the ABS wheel speed sensor as described in Chapter 9.
6 Unscrew the nut securing the track rod end to the steering arm on the swivel hub, then use a balljoint separator tool to remove the track rod end **(see illustration)**. Discard the nut; it should be renewed whenever it is disturbed.
7 Unscrew the nut and remove the clamp bolt securing the front suspension lower arm balljoint to the swivel hub **(see illustration)**. Note that a new clamp bolt and nut will be required for refitting.
8 Use a chisel or screwdriver as a wedge to expand the lower portion of the swivel hub **(see illustration)**.
9 Using a lever, push down on the suspension lower arm to free the balljoint from the swivel hub, then move the swivel hub to one side and release the arm, taking care not to damage the balljoint rubber boot. It is advisable to place a protective cover over the rubber boot such as the plastic cap from an aerosol can, suitably cut to fit.
10 Slacken and remove the two nuts and bolts securing the suspension strut to the

2.6 Use a balljoint separator tool to remove the track rod end

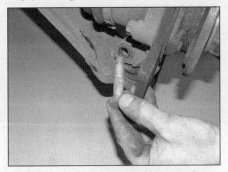

2.7 Unscrew the nut and remove the clamp bolt securing the lower arm balljoint to the swivel hub

2.8 Use a chisel or screwdriver as a wedge to expand the lower portion of the swivel hub

2.10 Slacken and remove the two nuts and bolts securing the suspension strut to the swivel hub

swivel hub **(see illustration)**. Discard the nuts and bolts; they should be renewed whenever they are disturbed.

11 Carefully pull the swivel hub assembly outwards, and withdraw the driveshaft outer constant velocity joint from the hub assembly. If necessary, the shaft can be tapped out of the hub using a soft-faced mallet. Alternatively, use a suitable puller to press the driveshaft through the hub. Support the driveshaft by suspending it with wire or string, and do not allow it to hang under its own weight. Remove the hub assembly from the vehicle.

Refitting

12 Ensure that the driveshaft outer constant velocity joint and hub splines are clean, then slide the hub onto the driveshaft splines. Fit the new driveshaft retaining nut, tightening it by hand only at this stage.

13 Engage the swivel hub with the suspension strut, and insert the new bolts from the front of the strut so that their threads are facing to the rear. Fit the new nuts, tightening them by hand only at this stage.

14 Locate the lower arm balljoint in the swivel hub. Insert the new clamp bolt from the front of the swivel hub, so that its threads are facing to the rear. Fit the new nut to the clamp bolt, and tighten it to the specified torque.

15 With the hub correctly located, tighten the strut-to-swivel hub bolts to the specified torque and through the specified angles given in the Specifications, using a torque wrench and angle-tightening gauge.

16 Engage the track rod end in the swivel

hub, then fit the new retaining nut and tighten it to the specified torque.

17 Refit the ABS wheel speed sensor, the brake disc, brake caliper and pads as described in Chapter 9.

18 Using the method employed on removal to prevent rotation, tighten the driveshaft retaining nut through the stages given in the Specifications.

19 With the nut correctly tightened, secure it in position with a new split pin. If the holes in the driveshaft are not aligned with any of the slots in the nut, loosen **(do not tighten)** the nut by the *smallest possible amount* until the split pin can be inserted.

20 Refit the roadwheel, then lower the vehicle to the ground and tighten the roadwheel bolts to the specified torque.

---

3 Front hub bearings – checking and renewal

Note: *The bearing is sealed, pre-adjusted and pre-lubricated. Never overtighten the driveshaft nut beyond the specified torque setting in an attempt to 'adjust' the bearing.*

Checking

1 Firmly apply the handbrake, then jack up the front of the car and support it securely on axle stands (see *Jacking and vehicle support*). Remove the roadwheel.

2 A dial test indicator (DTI) will be required to measure the amount of play in the bearing. Locate the DTI on the suspension strut and zero the probe on the brake disc.

3 Lever the hub in and out and measure the amount of play in the bearing.

4 To measure the bearing lateral and radial run-out, undo the two bolts securing the brake caliper mounting bracket to the swivel hub. Slide the mounting bracket, complete with brake caliper and pads off the brake disc, and tie it to the coil spring using wire or a cable-tie.

5 Undo the securing screw and remove the brake disc from the wheel hub.

6 To check the lateral run-out, locate the DTI on the suspension strut and zero the probe on the front face of the hub flange. Rotate the hub and measure the run-out.

7 To check the radial run-out, zero the DTI

probe on the upper face of the extended portion at the centre of the hub. Rotate the hub and measure the run-out.

8 If the play or run-out exceeds the specified amounts, renew the hub bearing as described below.

9 If the bearing is satisfactory, refit the brake disc and tighten its retaining screw securely.

10 Slide the brake pads, caliper and mounting bracket over the disc and into position on the swivel hub. Fit the two caliper mounting bracket retaining bolts and tighten them to the specified torque (see Chapter 9).

11 Refit the roadwheel, then lower the vehicle to the ground and tighten the roadwheel bolts to the specified torque.

Renewal

Note: *A press will be required to dismantle and rebuild the assembly; if such a tool is not available, a large bench vice and spacers (such as large sockets) will serve as an adequate substitute. The bearing's inner races are an interference fit on the hub; if the inner race remains on the hub flange when it is pressed out of the swivel hub, a knife-edged bearing puller will be required to remove it.*

12 Remove the swivel hub assembly as described in Section 2.

13 Align the holes in the hub and undo the screws, to remove the brake disc shield from the hub **(see illustration)**.

14 Support the swivel hub securely on blocks or in a vice. Using a tubular spacer/socket which bears only on the inner end of the hub flange, press the hub flange out of the bearing. If the bearing's outboard inner race remains on the hub, remove it using a bearing puller – see note above **(see illustration)**.

15 Extract the bearing retaining circlip from each side of the swivel hub assembly **(see illustration)**.

16 Using a drift or tubular spacer which bears only on the inner race, press the complete bearing assembly out of the swivel hub **(see illustration)**.

17 Thoroughly clean the hub and swivel hub, removing all traces of dirt and grease. Polish away any burrs or raised edges which might hinder reassembly. Check both assemblies for cracks or any other signs of wear or damage, and renew as necessary. Renew the circlip regardless of its apparent condition.

3.13 Disc shield retaining screws are accessed through holes in the hub flange

3.14 Using a socket to drift out the hub flange out from the bearing

3.15 Use circlip pliers to remove the circlip

3.16 Using a drift to remove the bearing from the swivel hub

3.19 Use a threaded rod and spacers to press the bearing squarely into position . . .

3.20 . . . then refit the circlip securely into the groove (arrowed)

3.21 Using a threaded rod and spacers/ sockets to press the hub flange into the bearing

3.22 Refit the disc shield to the hub assembly

18 On reassembly, apply a light film of oil to the bearing outer race and hub flange shaft, to aid installation of the bearing. Remove all traces of old thread-locking compound from the disc shield retaining screw holes, ideally by running a tap of the correct size and pitch through them.
19 Securely support the swivel hub, refit the inner circlip and locate the bearing in the hub. Press the bearing fully into position, ensuring that it enters the hub squarely, using the old wheel bearing or a tubular spacer which bears only on the bearing outer race **(see illustration)**.
20 Once the bearing is correctly seated, secure the bearing in position with the outer circlip. Make sure that the circlip is correctly located in its groove **(see illustration)**.
21 Securely support the swivel hub in a vice, then locate the hub flange into the bearing inner race. Press the flange into the swivel hub bearing, using a tubular spacer/sockets and threaded rod, until it seats against the hub shoulder **(see illustration)**. Check that the hub flange rotates freely, and wipe off any excess oil or grease.
22 Fit the disc shield to the hub assembly **(see illustration)**, and apply a few drops of thread-locking compound to the retaining screws. Fit the screws, and tighten them securely.
23 Refit the swivel hub assembly as described in Section 2.

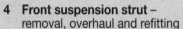

4 Front suspension strut –
removal, overhaul and refitting

Note: *New strut-to-swivel hub bolts and nuts, upper mounting nut and anti-roll bar link rod nut, will be required for refitting. Ideally, both front suspension struts should be renewed at the same time in order to maintain good steering and suspension characteristics.*

Removal

1 For access to the strut upper mounting, remove the windscreen cowl panel as described in Chapter 11.
2 Firmly apply the handbrake, then jack up the front of the car and support it securely on axle stands (see *Jacking and vehicle support*). Remove the appropriate roadwheel.
3 Unscrew the retaining nut and disconnect

the anti-roll bar link rod from the strut, discard it; a new one should be used on refitting. Use a spanner on the flats to hold the link while the nut is being loosened **(see illustration)**.
4 On models with ABS, release the front

4.3 Unscrew the nut and disconnect the anti-roll bar link rod from the strut

4.5a Undo the two retaining nuts . . .

wheel speed sensor wiring from the bracket on the suspension strut **(see illustration)**.
5 Slacken and remove the two nuts and bolts securing the suspension strut to the swivel hub **(see illustrations)**. Discard both nuts and

4.4 On models with ABS, release the front wheel speed sensor wiring from the bracket on the strut

4.5b . . . then remove the bolts securing the suspension strut to the swivel hub

4.6a Unscrew the suspension strut upper mounting nut . . .

4.6b . . . and remove the retaining plate

4.7 Release the strut from the swivel hub, and withdraw it from under the wheel arch

bolts; these must be renewed whenever they are disturbed.

6 Support the front strut assembly then, from within the engine compartment, remove the plastic cap (where fitted) from the upper strut mounting. Unscrew the suspension strut upper mounting nut and remove the retaining plate **(see illustrations)**. Discard the nut; a new one should be used on refitting.

7 Release the strut from the swivel hub, and withdraw it from under the wheel arch **(see illustration)**.

Overhaul

Note 1: *A spring compressor tool will be required for this operation. Before overhaul, mark the position of each component in relationship with each other for reassembly.*

Note 2: *A new piston rod nut will be required for reassembly.*

8 With the suspension strut resting on a bench, or clamped in a vice, fit a spring compressor tool, and compress the coil spring to relieve the pressure on the spring seats. Ensure that the compressor tool is securely located on the spring, in accordance with the tool manufacturer's instructions.

9 Mark the position of the spring relative to the top and bottom mountings, then counterhold the strut piston rod with an Allen key or suitable bit and unscrew the piston rod nut **(see illustration)**.

10 Remove the strut upper mounting, support bearing with upper spring seat, buffer and coil spring from the strut. If necessary, remove the upper spring seat from the support bearing **(see illustrations)**.

11 With the strut assembly now completely dismantled, examine all the components for wear, damage or deformation. Renew any of the components as necessary.

12 Examine the strut for signs of fluid leakage.

Check the strut piston for signs of pitting along its entire length, and check the strut body for signs of damage. While holding it in an upright position, test the operation of the strut by moving the piston through a full stroke, and then through short strokes of 50 to 100 mm. In both cases, the resistance felt should be smooth and continuous. If the resistance is jerky or uneven or if there is any visible sign of wear or damage to the strut, renewal is necessary.

13 If any doubt exists as to the condition of the coil spring, carefully remove the spring compressors and check the spring for distortion and signs of cracking. Renew the spring if it is damaged or distorted, or if there is any doubt as to its condition.

14 Inspect all other components for damage or deterioration, and renew any that are suspect.

15 With the spring compressed with the compressor tool, locate the spring on the strut making sure that it is correctly seated

4.9 Counterhold the strut piston rod with an Allen key or suitable bit, and unscrew the piston rod nut

4.10a Remove the strut upper mounting . . .

4.10b . . . support bearing with upper spring seat . . .

4.10c . . . and the buffer and coil spring from the strut

4.10d If necessary, remove the upper spring seat from the support bearing

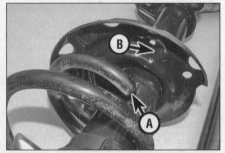

4.15 Locate the spring on the strut making sure that its lower end (A) is against the raised stop (B)

with its lower end against the raised stop **(see illustration)**.

16 Refit the buffer, support bearing and upper spring seat. Position the support bearing so that the lug on the side of the bearing is aligned with the raised stop on the lower spring seat **(see illustration)**.

17 Refit the strut upper mounting and the new piston rod nut. Tighten the nut to the specified torque while counterholding the piston rod.

18 Slowly slacken the spring compressor tool to relieve the tension in the spring. Check that the lower end of the spring locates correctly against the stop on the spring seat and the lug on the support bearing remains aligned as described in paragraphs 15 and 16. If necessary, turn the spring and the support bearing so that the components locate correctly before the compressor tool is removed. Remove the compressor tool when the spring is fully seated.

Refitting

19 Manoeuvre the strut assembly into position, ensuring that the top mounting is correctly located in the inner wing panel. Fit the upper mounting plate and new retaining nut, and tighten the nut finger-tight only at this stage.

20 Engage the swivel hub with the suspension strut, and insert the new bolts from the front of the strut so that their threads are facing to the rear. Fit the new nuts and tighten them to the specified torque and through the specified angles given in the Specifications, using a torque wrench and angle-tightening gauge.

21 Refit the anti-roll bar link rod to the strut and screw on the new retaining nut. Use a spanner on the flats to hold the link, while the nut is being tightened to the specified torque setting.

22 Where applicable, refit the ABS wheel speed sensor wiring to the bracket on the strut.

23 Refit the roadwheel, then lower the vehicle to the ground and tighten the roadwheel bolts to the specified torque.

24 With the vehicle standing on its wheels, tighten the strut upper mounting nut to the specified torque.

25 Refit the windscreen cowl panel as described in Chapter 11.

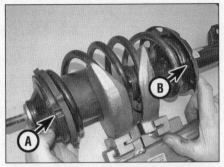

4.16 Position the support bearing so that the lug (A) on the side of the bearing is aligned with the raised stop (B) on the lower spring seat

5 Front suspension lower arm – removal, overhaul and refitting

Note: *When refitting, new pivot bolt/nuts, and new lower arm-to-balljoint nut/bolt, will be required.*

Removal

1 Firmly apply the handbrake, then jack up the front of the car and support it securely on axle stands (see *Jacking and vehicle support*). Remove the appropriate front roadwheel.

2 Unscrew and remove the lower arm balljoint clamp bolt nut, and withdraw the clamp bolt from the swivel hub, noting which way round it is fitted **(see illustration)**. Discard the clamp bolt and nut; new ones must be used on refitting.

3 Using a suitable lever, push down the lower arm to separate the balljoint from the swivel hub. When releasing the lower arm, take care not to damage the balljoint rubber boot; if necessary protect it with a piece of card or plastic. **Note:** *If the balljoint stub is tight in the swivel hub, use a screwdriver or cold chisel as a wedge to force the clamp apart.*

4 Unscrew the nut and withdraw the pivot bolt securing the front of the lower arm to the front subframe **(see illustration)**. Discard the bolt/nut; new ones should be used on refitting.

5 Unscrew the nut and withdraw the bolt securing the rear of the lower arm to the front subframe **(see illustration)**. Discard the bolt/

nut; new ones should be used on refitting. Remove the lower arm from the vehicle.

Overhaul

6 Thoroughly clean the lower arm and the area around the arm mountings, removing all traces of dirt and underseal if necessary. Check carefully for cracks, distortion, or any other signs of wear or damage, paying particular attention to the pivot bushes. If rear bush renewal is necessary, the lower arm should be taken to a Vauxhall/Opel dealer or suitably-equipped garage. A hydraulic press and spacers are required to press the bushes out of the arm, and to install the new ones. To renew the lower arm balljoint or front inner bush see Section 6.

Refitting

7 Offer up the lower arm, aligning the inner end of the arm with its mountings, insert new pivot bolts and nuts to the front and rear mounting points. **Note:** *Only tighten the mounting bolts/nuts hand-tight at this stage.*

8 Locate the lower balljoint stub fully in the bottom of the swivel hub, then refit the clamp bolt and tighten to the specified torque. Make sure the bolt head is facing the front of the vehicle.

9 Refit the roadwheel, lower the vehicle to the ground, and tighten the roadwheel bolts to specified torque setting.

10 The lower arm inner mounting bolts/nuts can now be tightened through the various stages given in the Specifications at the start of this Chapter.

6 Front lower arm balljoint and inner front bush – removal and refitting

Balljoint

Note: *The original balljoint is riveted to the lower arm; service replacements are bolted in position.*

Removal

1 Remove the front suspension lower arm as described in Section 5. **Note:** *If the fitted balljoint is a service replacement, it is not necessary to completely remove the arm*

5.2 Slacken and remove the nut and clamp bolt . . .

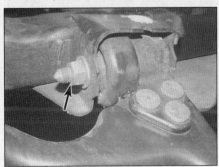

5.4 . . . the front lower arm pivot bolt (arrowed) . . .

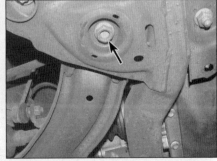

5.5 . . . and the rear lower arm retaining bolt (arrowed)

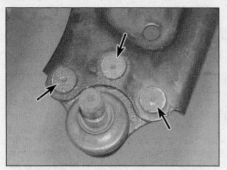

6.2 Drill out the balljoint securing rivets (arrowed) using a 12mm drill bit

but only to disconnect the balljoint from the bottom of the swivel hub then unbolt the old balljoint.

2 Mount the lower arm in a vice, then drill the heads from the three rivets that secure the balljoint to the lower arm, using a 12.0 mm diameter drill **(see illustration)**.

3 If necessary, tap the rivets from the lower arm, then remove the balljoint.

4 Clean any rust from the rivet holes, and apply rust inhibitor.

Refitting

5 The new balljoint must be fitted using three special bolts, spring washers and nuts, available from a Vauxhall/Opel parts stockists.

6 Ensure that the balljoint is fitted the correct way up, noting that the securing nuts are positioned on the underside of the lower arm. Tighten the nuts to the specified torque.

7 Refit the front suspension lower arm as described in Section 5.

Inner front bush (Hydro-bush)

Note: The original front bush is riveted to the lower arm; service replacements are bolted in position.

Removal

8 Remove the front lower arm assembly as described in Section 5 and mount the arm in a vice.

9 Using a 12.0 mm drill bit, drill the heads from the three rivets which hold the bush to the lower arm **(see illustration)**.

10 If necessary, tap the rivets from the lower arm, then remove the bush.

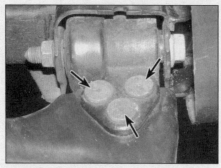

6.9 Drill out the front bush securing rivets (arrowed) using a 12mm drill bit

11 Clean any rust from the rivet holes, and apply rust inhibitor.

Refitting

12 The new bush must be fitted using three special bolts, spring washers and nuts, available from a Vauxhall/Opel parts stockists.

13 Align the new bush with the lower arm, then insert the new special bolts from the top downwards through the lower arm. Fit the new nuts to the bolts, tightening them to the specified torque.

14 Refit the front lower arm assembly as described in Section 5.

7 Front subframe – removal and refitting

Note: Vauxhall/Opel technicians use special jigs to ensure that the subframe is correctly aligned. Without the use of these tools it is important to note the position of the subframe accurately before removal.

Removal

1 Jack up the front and rear of the car and support it securely on axle stands (see *Jacking and vehicle support*). Preferably, position the car over an inspection pit, or on a lift. The help of an assistant will be needed for this procedure.

2 Set the front wheels in the straight-ahead position, then remove the ignition key and lock the column by turning the steering wheel as required. Remove both front roadwheels

and remove the lower liner from the right-hand wheel arch.

3 Remove the front bumper as described in Chapter 11.

4 Where fitted, remove the plastic cover over the top of the engine.

5 Remove the air cleaner assembly and intake ducts, and the complete exhaust system as described in the relevant Part of Chapter 4.

6 In the driver's footwell, unscrew the nut and remove the bolt securing the bottom of the steering column intermediate shaft to the steering gear pinion. Use paint or a suitable marker pen to make alignment marks between the intermediate shaft and the steering gear pinion, then pull the shaft from the pinion and position to one side **(see illustration)**.

7 Use cable-ties to secure the top mountings on each side of the radiator to prevent the radiator dropping when the subframe is removed.

8 Connect a hoist to the engine/transmission assembly and support its weight. If available, the type of support bar which locates in the engine compartment side channels is to be preferred, as this will ensure correct repositioning during refitting. Connect the hoist chains to the lifting brackets on the cylinder head.

9 Disconnect the steering track rod ends from the swivel hubs by unscrewing the nuts and using a balljoint separator tool **(see illustration)**.

10 Unscrew the nuts and disconnect the anti-roll bar link rods from the struts on both sides. Use a further spanner to hold the studs while the nuts are being loosened **(see illustration)**.

11 Unscrew and remove the lower arm balljoint clamp bolt nut, and withdraw the clamp bolt from the swivel hub on each side, noting which way round they are fitted **(see illustration)**. Discard the clamp bolt nuts; new ones must be used on refitting.

12 Using a suitable lever, push down the lower arms to separate the balljoints from the swivel hubs. When releasing the lower arms, take care not to damage the balljoint rubber boots; if necessary protect them with a piece of card or plastic. **Note:** *If the balljoint stub*

7.6 Unscrew the clamp bolt nut (arrowed) then disconnect the intermediate shaft from the steering gear pinion

7.9 Using a balljoint separator tool to free the balljoint

7.10 Holding the joint stub with an open-ended spanner, while removing the retaining nut

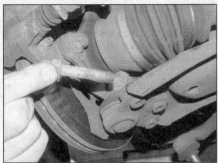

7.11 Withdraw the clamp bolt, and free the lower arm balljoint from the swivel hub

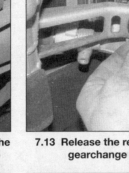

7.13 Release the retaining clip from the gearchange guide bracket

7.15 Undo the nut (arrowed) and remove the mounting bolt from the front torque link

To ensure correct repositioning, we bolted two lengths of metal bar to the subframe (one each side) and marked their positions on the underbody.

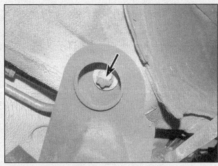

7.18a Unscrew the rear mounting bolts (one side arrowed) . . .

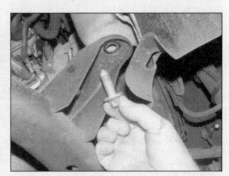

7.18b . . . and the front mounting bolts (one side shown)

is tight in the swivel hub, use a screwdriver or cold chisel as a wedge to force the clamp apart.

13 On manual transmission models with a rod-type gearchange mechanism, remove the retaining clip and release the gearchange guide bracket (see illustration).

14 Undo the three bolts and detach the rear engine mounting/torque link bracket from the transmission.

15 Slacken and remove the nut securing the front engine mounting/torque link to the subframe bracket. Withdraw the through-bolt (see illustration).

16 Support the subframe with a length of wood on a trolley jack. Ideally, a purpose-made cradle should be used. Enlist the help of an assistant.

17 Accurately mark the position of the subframe and mounting bolts to ensure correct refitting (see Haynes Hint). Note that Vauxhall/Opel technicians use a special jig with guide pins located through the alignment holes in the subframe and underbody.

18 Unscrew and remove the four subframe mounting bolts and carefully lower the subframe to the ground (see illustrations). As the subframe is lowered, make sure there are no cables or wiring still attached.

19 Remove the lower suspension arms from the subframe with reference to Section 5, the anti-roll bar with reference to Section 8, the rear engine mounting with reference to the

relevant Part of Chapter 2, and the steering gear with reference to Section 19.

Refitting

20 Refitting is a reversal of removal, bearing in mind the following points:

a) Ensure that the radiator lower mounting pegs engage correctly in the subframe brackets as the subframe is refitted.

b) Tighten all nuts and bolts to the specified torque and, where necessary, in the stages given. Note that new nuts/bolts should be used on all disturbed fittings.

c) Make sure that the subframe is correctly aligned with the underbody before fully tightening the mounting bolts.

d) Refer to the procedures contained in Section 16 when connecting the steering column intermediate shaft to the steering gear pinion.

8.4 Undo the link rod retaining nut (arrowed) from the end of the anti-roll bar

8 Front anti-roll bar – removal and refitting

Note: It is recommended that all mounting nuts and bolts are renewed when refitting.

Removal

1 Firmly apply the handbrake, then jack up the front of the car and support it securely on axle stands (see Jacking and vehicle support).

2 Remove the front subframe assembly as described in Section 7.

3 Prior to removal of the anti-roll bar, mark the position of each anti-roll bar mounting clamp rubber.

4 Unscrew the retaining nut and disconnect the link rod from the ends of the anti-roll bar, discard the retaining nut; a new one should be used on refitting (see illustration). Use a spanner on the flats to hold the link while the nut is being loosened.

5 Unscrew the two bolts from each mounting clamp, and remove the clamp (see illustration). As the last clamp is removed, support the anti-roll bar and remove it from the subframe.

6 Inspect the mounting clamp rubbers for signs of damage and deterioration, and renew if necessary (see illustration).

Refitting

7 Align the mounting rubbers with the marks made on the anti-roll bar prior to removal.

8 Refit the anti-roll bar to the subframe, and fit

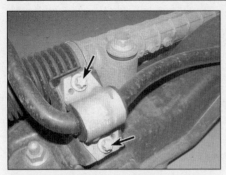

8.5 Unscrew and remove the anti-roll bar clamp retaining bolts (arrowed)

the mounting clamps. Ensure that the clamp half is correctly engaged with the anti-roll bar rubbers, then tighten each clamp retaining bolt, by hand only at this stage.

9 With the two clamps loosely installed, check the position of the anti-roll bar to the marks made on removal, then tighten the clamp bolts to the specified torque setting.

10 Refit the link rods to the ends of the anti-roll bar using new retaining nuts, tighten to the specified torque setting.

11 Refit the front subframe assembly as described in Section 7.

12 Refit the roadwheels if not already done, then lower the vehicle to the ground and tighten the roadwheel bolts to the specified torque.

9 Rear hub bearings – checking and renewal

Note: *The rear hub bearing and integral ABS wheel speed sensor is a sealed unit and no repairs are possible. If the bearing is worn or the speed sensor is faulty, a new bearing assembly must be obtained.*

Checking

1 Chock the front wheels then jack up the rear of the car and securely support it on axle stands (see *Jacking and vehicle support*). Remove the roadwheel.

2 Remove the brake disc as described in Chapter 9.

3 A dial test indicator (DTI) will be required

9.11 Disconnecting the ABS wiring from the inside of the rear hub

8.6 Remove and inspect the mounting clamp rubbers

to measure the amount of radial and lateral run-out in the bearing. Zero the indicator on the outer edge of the hub flange.

4 Lever the hub in and out and measure the amount of play in the bearing.

5 To measure lateral run-out, locate the probe on the surface of the hub which contacts the disc. To measure radial run-out, locate the probe on the outer perimeter of the hub so that it is pointing towards the centre of the hub.

6 Slowly turn the hub and note the maximum amount of run-out. If the run-out exceeds the amounts given in the Specifications, renew the hub bearing unit as described below.

7 Remove the indicator and refit the brake disc with reference to Chapter 9.

8 Refit the roadwheel, then lower the vehicle to the ground and tighten the roadwheel bolts to the specified torque.

Renewal

Note: *New hub bearing retaining nuts will be required for refitting.*

9 Chock the front wheels then jack up the rear of the car and securely support it on axle stands (see *Jacking and vehicle support*). Remove the roadwheel.

10 Remove the rear brake disc as described in Chapter 9.

11 Disconnect the wiring for the ABS wheel speed sensor located on the inside of the bearing assembly **(see illustration)**.

12 Support the bearing assembly and unscrew the four mounting nuts on the inside of the trailing arm. Withdraw the bearing and brake shield from the rear trailing arm. Note

10.3 Unscrew and remove the shock absorber lower mounting bolt from the trailing arm . . .

that the locating studs are spaced so that the bearing will only fit in one position.

13 Thoroughly clean the trailing arm, bearing unit and brake shield mating faces, then place the shield in position on the bearing unit.

14 Refit the bearing unit and brake shield to the trailing arm, and screw on four new retaining nuts.

15 Tighten the retaining nuts progressively to the specified Stage 1 torque setting using a torque wrench, and then through the specified Stage 2 and Stage 3 angles, using an angle tightening gauge.

16 Reconnect the ABS wheel speed sensor wiring connector.

17 Refit the rear brake disc as described in Chapter 9.

10 Rear shock absorber – removal, inspection and refitting

Note: *Always renew shock absorbers in pairs to maintain good road handling.*

Removal

1 Chock the front wheels then jack up the rear of the car and securely support it on axle stands (see *Jacking and vehicle support*). Remove the rear roadwheels.

2 Using a trolley jack, slightly raise the trailing arm on the relevant side.

3 Unscrew and remove the shock absorber lower mounting bolt from the trailing arm **(see illustration)**.

4 Support the shock absorber, then unscrew and remove the upper mounting bolt and withdraw the shock absorber from the underbody bracket **(see illustration)**.

Inspection

5 The shock absorber can be tested by clamping the lower mounting eye in a vice, then fully extending and compressing the shock absorber several times. Any evidence of jerky movement or lack of resistance indicates the need for renewal.

6 Examine the mounting rubbers in the shock absorber for excessive wear.

7 If the shock absorber or its mounting rubbers are worn excessively, renew the complete shock absorber.

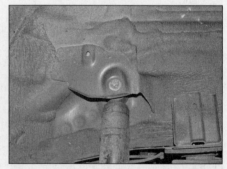

10.4 . . . and the upper mounting bolt from the underbody bracket

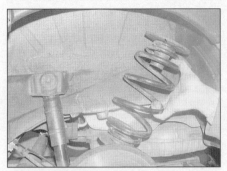

11.5a Remove the rear coil spring, together with the spring seats . . .

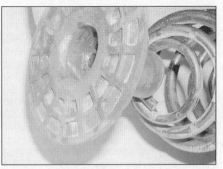

11.5b . . . then remove the upper spring seat . . .

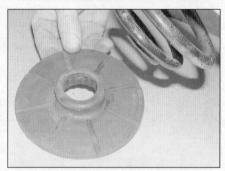

11.5c . . . and lower spring seat

Refitting

8 Refitting is a reversal of removal, but tighten the mounting bolts to the specified torque.

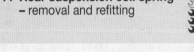
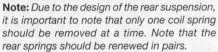

11 Rear suspension coil spring – removal and refitting

Note: *Due to the design of the rear suspension, it is important to note that only one coil spring should be removed at a time. Note that the rear springs should be renewed in pairs.*

Removal

1 Chock the front wheels then jack up the rear of the car and securely support it on axle stands (see *Jacking and vehicle support*). Remove the rear roadwheels.
2 Using a trolley jack, slightly raise the trailing arm on the relevant side.
3 Unscrew and remove the shock absorber lower mounting bolt from the trailing arm **(see illustration 10.3)**.
4 Carefully lower the trailing arm as far as possible without straining the brake flexible hoses leading to the rear brakes.
5 Remove the coil spring and spring seats from the underbody and trailing arm, and withdraw from under the vehicle. Note that the upper spring seat incorporates a damper buffer **(see illustrations)**.

Refitting

6 Refitting is a reversal of removal, but note the following points.
  a) *Ensure that the spring locates correctly*

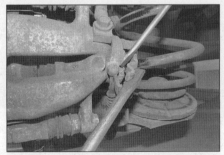

12.4 Push the handbrake operating lever on the brake caliper downwards, and detach the cable end fitting from the lever

on the upper and lower seats, as well as on the trailing arm and underbody.
  b) *Tighten the shock absorber lower mounting bolt to the specified torque.*
  c) *If both springs are being renewed, repeat the procedure on the remaining side of the vehicle.*

12 Rear suspension torsion beam and trailing arms – removal and refitting

Note: *New front mounting bracket retaining bolts will be required for refitting.*

Removal

1 Chock the front wheels then jack up the rear of the car and securely support it on axle stands (see *Jacking and vehicle support*). Remove the rear roadwheels.
2 From inside the vehicle, unclip the hand-

12.2 Unclip the gaiter from around the handbrake lever

12.5a Prise out the handbrake outer cable retaining clip . . .

brake lever gaiter from the centre console and slide the gaiter up the lever **(see illustration)**.
3 Move the handbrake lever to the fully-released position, then turn the cable adjuster nut anti-clockwise to remove all tension from the cables **(see illustration)**.
4 Working on each side in turn, use a screwdriver to push the handbrake operating lever on the brake caliper downwards, and detach the cable end fitting from the lever **(see illustration)**.
5 Prise out the handbrake outer cable retaining clip and withdraw the handbrake cable from the caliper bracket **(see illustrations)**. Detach the handbrake outer cables from the support brackets on the trailing arms and torsion beam.
6 Undo the two bolts each side securing the brake hydraulic hose and, where applicable, the ABS wheel speed sensor wiring harness support brackets to the trailing arms.
7 Where applicable, disconnect the wiring for

12.3 Handbrake cable adjuster nut (arrowed)

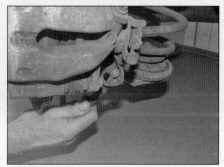

12.5b . . . and withdraw the handbrake cable from the caliper bracket

12.14 Rear suspension torsion beam front mounting bracket

the ABS wheel speed sensors located on the inside of the bearing assembly.

8 On vehicles without ABS, unhook the brake proportioning valve tension spring from the bracket on the rear axle.

9 Unbolt and remove the rear brake caliper on each side, complete with disc pads and mounting bracket, and suspend it from a suitable place under the wheel arch using wire or cable-ties.

10 On vehicles with xenon headlights, unclip the range control operating rod from the ball-pin on the rear axle.

11 Support the weight of the torsion beam and trailing arms using two trolley jacks. Alternatively, one trolley jack and a length of wood may be used, but the help of an assistant will be required.

12 Unscrew the lower mounting bolts and detach both shock absorbers from the torsion beam.

13 Carefully lower the torsion beam until it is possible to remove the coil springs and spring seats. Note that the upper spring seats incorporate buffers.

14 Make sure that the torsion beam is supported, then unscrew and remove the front mounting bracket bolts from the underbody **(see illustration)**. Note that new bolts will be required for refitting.

15 Lower the torsion beam to the ground and remove it from under the vehicle.

16 The remaining brake components can be removed from the trailing arms, referring to the relevant Sections of Chapter 9. The hub bearing units can be removed with reference to Section 9.

17 If necessary, the front mounting brackets can be removed after unscrewing the retaining nut and withdrawing the centre through-bolt. Note that a new nut and bolt will be required for refitting. Renewal of the front mounting bushes is a complex operation requiring numerous special tools and a hydraulic press. Bush renewal should therefore be entrusted to a Vauxhall/Opel dealer.

Refitting

18 Refit any components that were removed from the torsion beam, referring to the relevant Sections of this Chapter and Chapter 9, as applicable. If the front mounting brackets were removed from the trailing arms, refit the brackets using new nuts and bolts, but only tighten the nuts lightly at this stage.

19 Check the condition of the threads in the front mounting bracket captive nuts on the underbody. If necessary, use a tap to clean out the threads.

20 Support the torsion beam on the trolley jacks, and position the assembly under the rear of the vehicle.

21 Raise the jacks, and fit the new mounting bracket bolts. Do not fully-tighten the bolts at this stage.

22 If the front mounting brackets have been removed from the trailing arms, position the torsion beam so that the distance between the coil spring contact surfaces on the trailing arms and underbody is 177.0 ± 10.0 mm. With the torsion beam in this position, tighten the front mounting bracket centre bolts on each side to the specified torque and angle settings in the stages given.

23 Fully tighten the front mounting bracket-to-underbody bolts to the specified torque and angle settings in the stages given.

24 Locate the upper and lower seats on the coil springs, then refit the springs on the torsion beam.

25 Raise the torsion beam until the shock absorber lower mounting bolts can be inserted. Tighten the bolts to the specified torque.

26 On vehicles with xenon headlights, refit the range control operating rod to the ball-pin on the rear axle.

27 Refit the rear brake caliper on each side, complete with disc pads and mounting

bracket, and tighten the mounting bracket bolts to the specified torque (see Chapter 9).

28 On vehicles without ABS, attach the brake proportioning valve tension spring to the bracket on the rear axle

29 Refit the brake hydraulic pipes and flexible hoses together with the retaining plates and tighten the union nuts to the specified torque.

30 Where applicable, reconnect the wiring to the ABS wheel speed sensors.

31 Reconnect the handbrake cables to the caliper levers and fit the cables in the supports.

32 Adjust the handbrake cable as described in Chapter 1A or 1B, then refit the handbrake lever gaiter to the centre console.

33 Refit the roadwheels and lower the vehicle to the ground.

13 Steering wheel – removal and refitting

 Warning: Make sure that the airbag safety recommendations given in Chapter 12 are followed, to prevent personal injury.

Note: *A new steering wheel retaining bolt will be required for refitting.*

Removal

1 Remove the airbag as described in Chapter 12.

2 Set the front wheels in the straight-ahead position, then lock the column in position after removing the ignition key.

3 Disconnect the wiring harness connector for the steering wheel switches **(see illustration)**.

4 Unscrew the Torx retaining bolt securing the steering wheel to the column **(see illustration)**.

5 Check that there are alignment marks between the steering column shaft and steering wheel **(see illustration)**. If no marks are visible, centre punch the wheel and column shaft to ensure correct alignment when refitting.

6 Grip the steering wheel with both hands and carefully rock it from side-to-side to release it from the splines on the steering column. As the steering wheel is being removed, guide the wiring for the airbag through the aperture

13.3 Disconnect the wiring harness connector for the steering wheel switches

13.4 Unscrew the steering wheel retaining bolt (arrowed)

13.5 Alignment marks (arrowed) between the steering column shaft and steering wheel

in the wheel, taking care not to damage the wiring connectors **(see illustration)**.

Refitting

7 Refit the steering wheel, aligning the marks made prior to removal. Route the airbag wiring connectors through the steering wheel aperture. **Note:** *Make sure the guide lugs on the steering wheel centre hub locate correctly with the contact unit on the steering column, and that the two arrows on the contact unit are aligned.*
8 Clean the threads in the steering column, coat the new retaining bolt threads with locking compound, then fit the bolt and tighten to the specified torque.
9 Reconnect the wiring connector for the steering wheel switches.
10 Release the steering lock, and refit the airbag as described in Chapter 12.

---

14 Ignition switch/ steering column lock – removal and refitting

---

Removal

1 Disconnect the battery negative terminal (refer to *Disconnecting the battery* in the Reference Chapter).
2 Remove the steering column shrouds as described in Chapter 11.
3 Remove the windscreen wiper switch by releasing the upper and lower lugs and sliding the switch out of its mounting bracket **(see illustration)**.

Lock cylinder

4 Remove the rubber trim from around the lock cylinder. Insert the ignition key into the ignition switch/lock, and turn it to position I.
5 Insert a thin rod into the hole in the lock housing, press the rod to release the detent spring, and pull out the lock cylinder using the key **(see illustration)**.

Ignition switch wiring block

6 Release the securing clip and disconnect the wiring connector from the ignition switch wiring block **(see illustration)**.
7 Press the two lugs in (one at each side) and slide the switch wiring block down out of its mounting bracket **(see illustration)**.

14.6 Release the locking clip (arrowed) and disconnect the wiring connector

---

13.6 Guide the wiring for the airbag through the aperture in the wheel

Refitting

Lock cylinder

8 With the wiring block in position, press the steering locking pin downwards using a thin screwdriver, until it engages **(see illustration)**.
9 Ensure that the centre of the ignition switch wiring block is correctly aligned with the lock cylinder rod flats. If necessary, rotate the switch centre using a suitable screwdriver.
10 Insert the ignition switch/lock into the lock housing, while the key is in position I, and push it in until the detent spring clicks into position. Check the operation of the lock cylinder and steering lock.
11 Refit the windscreen wiper switch and the rubber trim around the lock cylinder.
12 Refit the steering column shrouds as described in Chapter 11.

14.3 Depress the retaining clips (arrowed) and slide the combination switch out from the column

14.7 Depress the retaining clips (arrowed) and slide the wiring block downwards and out from the column

---

Ignition switch wiring block

13 Slide the switch wiring block back up into its mounting bracket on the steering column, making sure it is located correctly.
14 Reconnect the wiring connector to switch wiring block.
15 Refit the ignition/lock cylinder as described in paragraphs 8 to 12.

---

15 Steering column – removal and refitting

Note: *It is recommended that all mounting nuts and bolts are renewed when refitting.*

Removal

1 Remove the EPS motor as described in Section 17.
2 Remove the steering wheel as described in Section 13.
3 Remove the airbag wiring contact unit as described in Chapter 12.
4 Release the securing clips and disconnect the wiring connectors from the ignition switch wiring block, the immobiliser control unit and the horn contact, then release the wiring cables from the steering column **(see illustrations)**.
5 Using paint or similar, make alignment marks between the steering column and intermediate shaft, then slacken and remove the clamp bolt securing the intermediate shaft to the steering column **(see illustration)**.

14.5 Insert a thin rod (arrowed) into the hole in the lock housing to release the detent spring

14.8 Align the lock cylinder recess (arrowed) in the switch housing

15.4a Release the locking clip (arrowed) and disconnect the wiring connector from the switch . . .

15.4b . . . and the immobiliser control unit

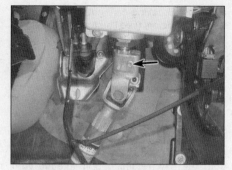

15.5 Remove the clamp bolt (arrowed) securing the intermediate shaft to the steering column

15.7a Undo the two lower mounting bolts (arrowed) . . .

15.7b . . . and two upper mounting bolts (arrowed) securing the column to the facia crossmember

6 If applicable, make sure the steering column adjustment handle is in the locked position.

7 Unscrew the two lower mounting bolts and two upper mounting bolts securing the steering column to the facia crossmember **(see illustrations)**.

8 Release the column assembly from its mountings, then detach it from the intermediate shaft and remove it from the vehicle. DO NOT release the steering lock while the steering column is off the vehicle, as it will alter the position of the angular adjustment setting for refitting.

Refitting

9 Manoeuvre the steering column into position, and engage it with the intermediate shaft universal joint, aligning the marks made on removal.

10 Refit the column upper and lower mounting bolts. Tighten all bolts by hand only at this stage.

11 Align the intermediate shaft bolt hole with the steering column shaft cut-out so that the clamp bolt can be slid into position (use thread-locking compound). Tighten the bolt by hand only.

12 With the steering column in position, tighten the column mounting bolts to the specified torque.

13 Tighten the intermediate shaft upper clamp bolt to the specified torque setting.

14 Reconnect the wiring connectors to the ignition switch wiring block, the immobiliser control unit and the horn contact, then secure the wiring cables to the steering column.

15 Refit the airbag wiring contact unit as described in Chapter 12.

16 Refit the steering wheel as described in Section 13.

17 Refit the EPS motor as described in Section 17.

16 Steering column intermediate shaft – removal and refitting

Note: *Vauxhall/Opel use a special tool (locating pin) to set the intermediate shaft length compensator when refitting.*

Removal

1 Set the front wheels in the straight-ahead position. Remove the ignition key and allow the steering lock to engage.

2 Remove the steering column shrouds as described in Chapter 11.

3 Remove the lower trim panel beneath the facia on the driver's side as described in Chapter 11.

4 If there are no alignment marks on the joints, use paint or a suitable marker pen to make alignment marks between the intermediate shaft joints and the steering column and steering gear shafts.

5 Slacken and remove the upper clamp bolt, and the lower clamp bolt and nut **(see illustrations)**. Discard the nut from the lower joint, as a new one will be required when refitting.

6 Disengage the shaft universal joint from the steering column, then slide the shaft from the steering gear pinion and remove it from the vehicle.

Inspection

7 The steering column intermediate shaft incorporates a telescopic safety section, in the event of a front-end crash, the shaft shortens on the splines and prevents the steering wheel injuring the driver. Inspect the intermediate shaft universal joint for excessive wear or damage. If either joint is worn or damaged in any way, the complete shaft assembly must be renewed.

Refitting

8 Check that the front wheels are still in the straight-ahead position, and that the steering wheel is correctly positioned.

9 Aligning the marks made on removal, locate the upper universal joint onto the steering column.

10 Install the steering column upper clamp

16.5a Remove the intermediate shaft upper clamp bolt (arrowed) . . .

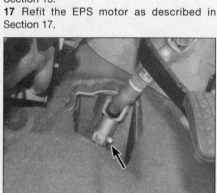

16.5b . . . and the lower clamp bolt (arrowed)

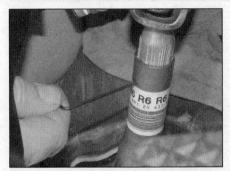

16.11 Locate the hole in the length compensator, then insert the locating pin

bolt (use thread-locking compound) and tighten to the specified torque setting.
11 Aligning the marks made on removal, locate the lower universal joint onto the steering gear pinion. Push the joint down onto the steering gear pinion until the hole in the length compensator is in line, then insert the locating pin (Vauxhall/Opel tool No KM-6181) **(see illustration)**. If the Vauxhall/Opel tool is not available, a suitable drill bit or a length of welding rod can be used.
12 Install the lower clamp bolt and new retaining nut, then tighten to the specified torque setting.
13 Remove the Vauxhall tool (locating pin) from the intermediate shaft, after the lower retaining bolt has been tightened in the correct position.
14 The remainder of refitting is a reverse of the removal procedure

17 Electric Power Steering (EPS) components – removal and refitting

EPS motor

Removal

1 Disconnect the battery negative terminal (refer to *Disconnecting the battery* in the Reference Chapter).
2 Set the front wheels in the straight-ahead position. Remove the ignition key and allow the steering lock to engage.
3 Remove the steering column shrouds as described in Chapter 11.
4 Remove the lower trim panel beneath the facia on the driver's side as described in Chapter 11.
5 Release the expanding rivet and remove the driver's side footwell air duct.
6 Disconnect the wiring connectors from the EPS control unit and release the wiring harness from the cable clips on the EPS motor **(see illustration)**.
7 Undo the two retaining bolts and remove the EPS motor and control unit assembly from the steering column.
8 No further dismantling of the EPS motor or control unit is possible and no components are separately available.

Refitting

9 Refitting is a reverse of the removal procedure

EPS control unit

10 The EPS control unit is attached to the EPS motor. Removal and refitting procedures are as described previously in this Section. Note that the control unit is not available as a separate component.

18 Steering gear rubber gaiters – renewal

1 Remove the relevant track rod end as described in Section 20.
2 Accurately mark the position of the track rod end securing locknut on the track rod, then unscrew the locknut.
3 Remove the inner and outer securing clips (see illustration), then slide the gaiter off the end of the track rod.
4 Thoroughly clean the track rod, then slide the new gaiter into position. Note that a groove is provided in the track rod for the outer end of the gaiter to locate in.
5 Fit the gaiter securing clips, using new clips if necessary, making sure that the gaiter is not twisted.
6 Refit the track rod end securing locknut to its original position as marked on removal.
7 Refit the track rod end as described in Section 20.
8 Have the front wheel toe-setting checked

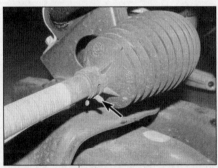

18.3a Release the gaiter outer retaining clip (arrowed) . . .

19.3a Undo the steering gear right-hand mounting bolt (arrowed) . . .

17.6 Disconnect the wiring connectors from the EPS control unit

and adjusted at the earliest opportunity – see Section 22 for general information.

19 Steering gear – removal and refitting

Note: *New steering gear-to-subframe nuts, bolts and washers will be required when refitting.*

Removal

1 Firmly apply the handbrake, then jack up the front of the car and support it securely on axle stands (see *Jacking and vehicle support*). Remove both front roadwheels.
2 Remove the front subframe as described in Section 7.
3 Slacken and remove the two bolts, nuts and washers securing the steering gear to the subframe **(see illustrations)**, then remove the

18.3b . . . and inner retaining clip (arrowed)

19.3b . . . and left-hand mounting bolt (arrowed)

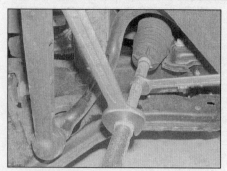

20.2 Hold the track rod stationary while loosening the track rod end securing locknut

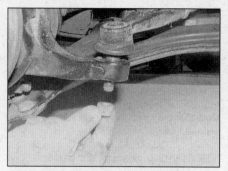

20.3 Unscrew the balljoint nut securing the track rod end to the steering arm on the swivel hub

20.4 Disconnect the track rod end from the steering arm on the swivel hub using a balljoint separator tool

steering gear from the subframe. Discard the bolts, nuts and washers as new ones will be required when refitting.

4 If a new steering gear is to be fitted, then the track rod ends will need to be removed from each end of the steering track rod arms (see Section 20).

Inspection

5 Examine the steering gear assembly for signs of wear or damage, and check that the rack moves freely throughout the full length of its travel, with no signs of roughness or excessive free play between the steering gear pinion and rack. Should any wear or damage be detected, it will be necessary to obtain a complete new steering gear assembly. The only components which can be renewed individually are the steering gear gaiters, the track rod ends and the track rods. Steering gear gaiter, track rod end and track rod renewal procedures are covered in Sections 18, 20 and 21 respectively.

Refitting

6 Refitting is a reverse of the removal procedure, bearing in mind the following points:

a) Set the steering gear in the straight-ahead position prior to refitting the front subframe.

b) Refit the front subframe as described in Section 7.

c) On completion, have the front wheel toe-setting checked and adjusted at the earliest opportunity – see Section 22 for general information.

20 Track rod end – removal and refitting

Note: A new track rod end retaining nut will be needed for refitting.

Removal

1 Apply the handbrake, then jack up the front of the vehicle, and support securely on axle stands (see Jacking and vehicle support). Remove the relevant roadwheel.

2 Loosen the track rod end securing locknut on the track rod a quarter turn, while holding

the track rod stationary with a second spanner on the flats provided **(see illustration)**. If necessary, use a wire brush to remove rust from the nut and threads, and lubricate the threads with penetrating oil before unscrewing the nut. As an additional check, measure the visible amount of threads on the track rod using vernier calipers. This will ensure the track rod end is refitted in the same position.

3 Unscrew and remove the balljoint nut securing the track rod end to the steering arm on the swivel hub **(see illustration)**.

4 Disconnect the track rod end balljoint from the steering arm on the swivel hub using a balljoint separator tool, taking care not to damage the balljoint boot **(see illustration)**.

5 Unscrew the track rod end from the track rod, counting the number of turns necessary to remove it and taking care not to disturb the locknut.

Refitting

6 Screw the track rod end onto the track rod the number of turns noted during removal. Check that the visible amount of threads on the track rod is as previously-noted.

7 Insert the track rod end into the steering arm on the swivel hub, then fit the nut and tighten to the specified torque. If the balljoint stud turns as the nut is being tightened, press down on the track rod end to force the stud into the arm.

8 Tighten the track rod end securing locknut on the track rod while holding the track rod stationary with a second spanner on the flats provided. If possible, tighten the nut to the specified torque using a special crow's-foot adapter for the torque wrench.

9 Refit the roadwheel, then lower the vehicle to the ground, and tighten the wheelbolts to the specified torque.

10 Have the front wheel toe-setting checked and adjusted at the earliest opportunity – see Section 22 for general information.

21 Track rod – renewal

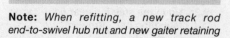

Note: When refitting, a new track rod end-to-swivel hub nut and new gaiter retaining

clips will be required. Vauxhall/Opel use a special socket to tighten the track rod inner balljoint to the end of the steering rack.

1 Remove the track rod end as described in Section 20.

2 Release the retaining clips, and slide the steering gear gaiter off the end of the track rod as described in Section 18.

3 Turn the steering onto full lock, so that the rack protrudes from the steering gear housing on the relevant side, slide the cover (where fitted) off the inner balljoint.

4 Prevent the rack from rotating using an open-ended spanner located on the rack flats, then unscrew and remove the track rod inner balljoint from the end of the steering rack. Where fitted remove any spacers/washers noting the correct position for refitting.

5 Remove the track rod assembly, and examine the track rod inner balljoint for signs of slackness or tight spots. Check that the track rod itself is straight and free from damage. If necessary, renew the track rod; it is also recommended that the steering gear gaiter/dust cover is renewed.

6 Where applicable, locate the spacer on the end of the steering rack, and screw the balljoint into the end of the steering rack. Tighten the track rod inner balljoint to the specified torque, whilst retaining the steering rack with an open-ended spanner.

7 Install the steering gaiter and track rod end as described in Sections 18 and 20.

22 Wheel alignment and steering angles – general information

Definitions

1 A car's steering and suspension geometry is defined in four basic settings – all angles are expressed in degrees (toe settings are also expressed as a measurement); the steering axis is defined as an imaginary line drawn through the axis of the suspension strut, extended where necessary to contact the ground.

2 Camber is the angle between each roadwheel and a vertical line drawn through its centre and tyre contact patch, when viewed from the front or rear of the car. Positive camber is when the roadwheels are tilted outwards from the vertical at the top; negative camber is when they are tilted inwards. The camber angle is not adjustable.

3 Castor is the angle between the steering axis and a vertical line drawn through each roadwheel's centre and tyre contact patch, when viewed from the side of the car. Positive castor is when the steering axis is tilted so that it contacts the ground ahead of the vertical; negative castor is when it contacts the ground

behind the vertical. The castor angle is not adjustable.

4 Toe is the difference, viewed from above, between lines drawn through the roadwheel centres and the car's centre-line. 'Toe-in' is when the roadwheels point inwards, towards each other at the front, while 'toe-out' is when they splay outwards from each other at the front.

5 The front wheel toe setting is adjusted by screwing the track rod in or out of its track rod ends, to alter the effective length of the track

rod assembly. The rear wheel toe setting is not adjustable.

Checking and adjustment

6 Due to the special measuring equipment necessary to check the wheel alignment and steering angles, and the skill required to use it properly, the checking and adjustment of these settings is best left to a Vauxhall/Opel dealer or similar expert. Note that most tyre-fitting shops now possess sophisticated checking equipment.

Chapter 11
Bodywork and fittings

Contents

Degrees of difficulty

Easy, suitable for novice with little experience ✎

Fairly easy, suitable for beginner with some experience ✎

Fairly difficult, suitable for competent DIY mechanic ✎

Difficult, suitable for experienced DIY mechanic ✎

Very difficult, suitable for expert DIY or professional ✎

Specifications

Torque wrench settings	Nm	lbf ft
Seat belts:		
Front tensioners	35	26
Front mountings	20	15
Rear mountings	35	26
Seats:		
Front seats	20	15
Rear seats	26	19

1 General information

The bodyshell is made of pressed-steel sections, and is available as a 5-door mini multi-purpose vehicle (MPV). Most components are welded together, but some use is made of structural adhesives; the front wings are bolted on.

The bonnet, doors, and some other vulnerable panels, are made of zinc-coated metal, and are further protected by being coated with an anti-chip primer, prior to being sprayed.

Extensive use is made of plastic materials, mainly on the interior, but also in exterior components. The front and rear bumpers are injection-moulded from a synthetic material which is very strong and yet light. Plastic components such as wheel arch liners are fitted to the underside of the vehicle, to improve the body's resistance to corrosion.

2 Maintenance – bodywork and underframe

The general condition of a vehicle's body-work is the one thing that significantly affects its value. Maintenance is easy, but needs to be regular. Neglect, particularly after minor damage, can lead quickly to further deterioration and costly repair bills. It is important also to keep watch on those parts of the vehicle not immediately visible, for instance the underside, inside all the wheel arches, and the lower part of the engine compartment.

The basic maintenance routine for the bodywork is washing – preferably with a lot of water, from a hose. This will remove all the loose solids which may have stuck to the vehicle. It is important to flush these off in such a way as to prevent grit from scratching the finish. The wheel arches and underframe need washing in the same way, to remove any accumulated mud, which will retain moisture and tend to encourage rust. Paradoxically enough, the best time to clean the underframe and wheel arches is in wet weather, when the mud is thoroughly wet and soft. In very wet weather, the underframe is usually cleaned of large accumulations automatically, and this is a good time for inspection.

Periodically, except on vehicles with a wax-based underbody protective coating, it is a good idea to have the whole of the underframe of the vehicle steam-cleaned, engine compartment included, so that a thorough inspection can be carried out to see what minor repairs and renovations are necessary. Steam-cleaning is available at many garages, and is necessary for the removal of the accumulation of oily grime, which sometimes is allowed to become thick in certain areas. If steam-cleaning facilities are not available, there are some excellent grease solvents available which can be brush-applied; the dirt can then be simply hosed off. Note that these methods should not be used on vehicles with wax-based underbody protective coating, or the coating will be removed. Such vehicles should be inspected annually, preferably just prior to Winter, when the underbody should be washed down, and any damage to the wax coating repaired. Ideally, a completely fresh coat should be applied. It would also be worth considering the use of such wax-based protection for injection into door panels, sills, box sections, etc, as an additional safeguard against rust damage, where such protection is not provided by the vehicle manufacturer.

After washing paintwork, wipe off with a chamois leather to give an unspotted clear finish. A coat of clear protective wax polish will give added protection against chemical pollutants in the air. If the paintwork sheen has dulled or oxidised, use a cleaner/polisher combination to restore the brilliance of the shine. This requires a little effort, but such dulling is usually caused because regular washing has been neglected. Care needs to be taken with metallic paintwork, as special non-abrasive cleaner/polisher is required to avoid damage to the finish. Always check that the door and ventilator opening drain holes and pipes are completely clear, so that water can be drained out. Brightwork should be treated in the same way as paintwork. Windscreens and windows can be kept clear of the smeary film which often appears, by the use of proprietary glass cleaner. Never use any form of wax or other body or chromium polish on glass.

3 Maintenance of upholstery and carpets – general

Mats and carpets should be brushed or vacuum-cleaned regularly, to keep them free of grit. If they are badly stained, remove them from the vehicle for scrubbing or sponging, and make quite sure they are dry before refitting. Seats and interior trim panels can be kept clean by wiping with a damp cloth. If they do become stained (which can be more apparent on light-coloured upholstery), use a little liquid detergent and a soft nail brush to scour the grime out of the grain of the material. Do not forget to keep the headlining clean in the same way as the upholstery. When using liquid cleaners inside the vehicle, do not over-wet the surfaces being cleaned. Excessive damp could get into the seams and padded interior, causing stains, offensive odours or even rot.

If the inside of the vehicle gets wet accidentally, it is worthwhile taking some trouble to dry it out properly, particularly where carpets are involved. Do not leave oil or electric heaters inside the vehicle for this purpose.

4 Minor body damage – repair

Minor scratches

If the scratch is very superficial, and does not penetrate to the metal of the bodywork, repair is very simple. Lightly rub the area of the scratch with a paintwork renovator, or a very fine cutting paste, to remove loose paint from the scratch, and to clear the surrounding bodywork of wax polish. Rinse the area with clean water.

Apply touch-up paint to the scratch using a fine paint brush; continue to apply fine layers of paint until the surface of the paint in the scratch is level with the surrounding paintwork. Allow the new paint at least two weeks to harden, then blend it into the surrounding paintwork by rubbing the scratch area with a paintwork renovator or a very fine cutting paste. Finally, apply wax polish.

Where the scratch has penetrated right through to the metal of the bodywork, causing the metal to rust, a different repair technique is required. Remove any loose rust from the bottom of the scratch with a penknife, then apply rust-inhibiting paint to prevent the formation of rust in the future. Using a rubber or nylon applicator, fill the scratch with bodystopper paste. If required, this paste can be mixed with cellulose thinners to provide a very thin paste which is ideal for filling narrow scratches. Before the stopper-paste in the scratch hardens, wrap a piece of smooth cotton rag around the top of a finger. Dip the finger in cellulose thinners, and quickly sweep it across the surface of the stopper-paste in the scratch; this will ensure that the surface of the stopper-paste is slightly hollowed. The scratch can now be painted over as described earlier in this Section.

Dents

When deep denting of the vehicle's bodywork has taken place, the first task is to pull the dent out, until the affected bodywork almost attains its original shape. There is little point in trying to restore the original shape completely, as the metal in the damaged area will have stretched on impact, and cannot be reshaped fully to its original contour. It is better to bring the level of the dent up to a point which is about 3 mm below the level of the surrounding bodywork. In cases where the dent is very shallow anyway, it is not worth trying to pull it out at all. If the underside of the dent is accessible, it can be hammered out gently from behind, using a mallet with a wooden or plastic head. Whilst doing this, hold a suitable block of wood firmly against the outside of the panel, to absorb the impact from the hammer blows and thus prevent a large area of the bodywork from being 'belled-out'.

Should the dent be in a section of the bodywork which has a double skin, or some other factor making it inaccessible from behind, a different technique is called for. Drill several small holes through the metal inside the area – particularly in the deeper section. Then screw long self-tapping screws into the holes, just sufficiently for them to gain a good purchase in the metal. Now the dent can be pulled out by pulling on the protruding heads of the screws with a pair of pliers.

The next stage of the repair is the removal of the paint from the damaged area, and from an inch or so of the surrounding 'sound' bodywork. This is accomplished most easily by using a wire brush or abrasive pad on a power drill, although it can be done just as effectively by hand, using sheets of abrasive paper. To complete the preparation for filling, score the surface of the bare metal with a screwdriver or the tang of a file, or alternatively, drill small holes in the affected area. This will provide a really good 'key' for the filler paste.

To complete the repair, see the Section on filling and respraying.

Rust holes or gashes

Remove all paint from the affected area, and from an inch or so of the surrounding 'sound' bodywork, using an abrasive pad or a wire brush on a power drill. If these are not available, a few sheets of abrasive paper will do the job most effectively. With the paint removed, you will be able to judge the severity of the corrosion, and therefore decide whether to renew the whole panel (if this is possible) or to repair the affected area. New body panels are not as expensive as most people think, and it is often quicker and more satisfactory to fit a new panel than to attempt to repair large areas of corrosion.

Remove all fittings from the affected area, except those which will act as a guide to the original shape of the damaged bodywork (eg headlight shells etc). Then, using tin snips or a hacksaw blade, remove all loose metal and any other metal badly affected by corrosion. Hammer the edges of the hole inwards, in order to create a slight depression for the filler paste.

Wire-brush the affected area to remove the powdery rust from the surface of the remaining metal. Paint the affected area with rust-inhibiting paint, if the back of the rusted area is accessible, treat this also.

Before filling can take place, it will be necessary to block the hole in some way. This can be achieved by the use of aluminium or plastic mesh, or aluminium tape.

Aluminium or plastic mesh, or glass-fibre matting, is probably the best material to use for a large hole. Cut a piece to the approximate size and shape of the hole to be filled, then position it in the hole so that its edges are below the level of the surrounding bodywork. It can be retained in position by several blobs of filler paste around its periphery.

Aluminium tape should be used for small or very narrow holes. Pull a piece off the roll, trim it to the approximate size and shape required, then pull off the backing paper (if used) and stick the tape over the hole; it can be overlapped if the thickness of one piece is insufficient. Burnish down the edges of the tape with the handle of a screwdriver or similar, to ensure that the tape is securely attached to the metal underneath.

Filling and respraying

Before using this Section, see the Sections on dent, deep scratch, rust holes and gash repairs.

Many types of bodyfiller are available, but generally speaking, those proprietary kits which contain a tin of filler paste and a tube of resin hardener are best for this type of repair. A wide, flexible plastic or nylon applicator will be found invaluable for imparting a smooth and well-contoured finish to the surface of the filler.

Mix up a little filler on a clean piece of card or board – measure the hardener carefully (follow the maker's instructions on the pack), otherwise the filler will set too rapidly or too slowly. Using the applicator, apply the filler paste to the prepared area; draw the applicator across the surface of the filler to achieve the correct contour and to level the surface. As soon as a contour that approximates to the correct one is achieved, stop working the paste – if you carry on too long, the paste will become sticky and begin to 'pick-up' on the applicator. Continue to add thin layers of filler paste at 20-minute intervals, until the level of the filler is just proud of the surrounding bodywork.

Once the filler has hardened, the excess can be removed using a metal plane or file. From then on, progressively-finer grades of abrasive paper should be used, starting with a 40-grade production paper, and finishing with a 400-grade wet-and-dry paper. Always wrap the abrasive paper around a flat rubber, cork, or wooden block – otherwise the surface of the filler will not be completely flat. During the smoothing of the filler surface, the wet-and-dry paper should be periodically rinsed in water. This will ensure that a very smooth finish is imparted to the filler at the final stage.

At this stage, the 'dent' should be surrounded by a ring of bare metal, which in turn should be encircled by the finely 'feathered' edge of the good paintwork. Rinse the repair area with clean water, until all of the dust produced by the rubbing-down operation has gone.

Spray the whole area with a light coat of primer – this will show up any imperfections in the surface of the filler. Repair these imperfections with fresh filler paste or bodystopper, and once more smooth the surface with abrasive paper. Repeat this spray-and-repair procedure until you are satisfied that the surface of the filler, and the feathered edge of the paintwork, are perfect. Clean the repair area with clean water, and allow to dry fully.

The repair area is now ready for final spraying. Paint spraying must be carried out in a warm, dry, windless and dust-free atmosphere. This condition can be created artificially if you have access to a large indoor working area, but if you are forced to work in the open, you will have to pick your day very carefully. If you are working indoors, dousing the floor in the work area with water will help to settle the dust which would otherwise be in the atmosphere. If the repair area is confined to one body panel, mask off the surrounding panels; this will help to minimise the effects of a slight mis-match in paint colours. Bodywork fittings (eg chrome strips, door handles etc) will also need to be masked off. Use genuine masking tape, and several thicknesses of newspaper, for the masking operations.

Before commencing to spray, agitate the aerosol can thoroughly, then spray a test area (an old tin, or similar) until the technique is mastered. Cover the repair area with a thick coat of primer; the thickness should be built up using several thin layers of paint, rather than one thick one. Using 400-grade wet-and-dry paper, rub down the surface of the primer until it is really smooth. While doing this, the work area should be thoroughly doused with water, and the wet-and-dry paper periodically rinsed in water. Allow to dry before spraying on more paint.

Spray on the top coat, again building up the thickness by using several thin layers of paint. Start spraying at one edge of the repair area, and then, using a side-to-side motion, work until the whole repair area and about 2 inches of the surrounding original paintwork is covered. Remove all masking material 10 to 15 minutes after spraying on the final coat of paint.

Allow the new paint at least two weeks to harden, then, using a paintwork renovator, or a very fine cutting paste, blend the edges of the paint into the existing paintwork. Finally, apply wax polish.

Plastic components

With the use of more and more plastic body components by the vehicle manufacturers (eg bumpers, spoilers, and in some cases major body panels), rectification of more serious damage to such items has become a matter of either entrusting repair work to a specialist in this field, or renewing complete components. Repair of such damage by the DIY owner is not really feasible, owing to the cost of the equipment and materials required for effecting such repairs. The basic technique involves making a groove along the line of the crack in the plastic, using a rotary burr in a power drill. The damaged part is then welded back together, using a hot-air gun to heat up and fuse a plastic filler rod into the groove. Any excess plastic is then removed, and the area rubbed down to a smooth finish. It is important that a filler rod of the correct plastic is used, as body components can be made of a variety of different types (eg polycarbonate, ABS, polypropylene).

Damage of a less serious nature (abrasions, minor cracks etc) can be repaired by the DIY owner using a two-part epoxy filler repair material. Once mixed in equal proportions, this is used in similar fashion to the bodywork filler used on metal panels. The filler is usually cured in twenty to thirty minutes, ready for sanding and painting.

If the owner is renewing a complete component himself, or if he has repaired it with epoxy filler, he will be left with the problem of finding a suitable paint for finishing which is compatible with the type of plastic used. At one time, the use of a universal paint was not possible, owing to the complex range of plastics encountered in body component applications. Standard paints, generally speaking, will not bond to plastic or rubber satisfactorily. However, it is now possible to obtain a plastic body parts finishing kit which consists of a pre-primer treatment, a primer and coloured top coat. Full instructions are normally supplied with a kit, but basically, the method of use is to first apply the pre-primer to the component concerned, and allow it to dry for up to 30 minutes. Then the primer is applied, and left to dry for about an hour before finally applying the special-coloured top coat. The result is a correctly-coloured component, where the paint will flex with the plastic or rubber, a property that standard paint does not normally possess.

5 Major body damage repair – general

Where serious damage has occurred, or large areas need renewal due to neglect, it means that complete new panels will need welding-in, and this is best left to professionals. If the damage is due to impact, it will also be necessary to check completely the alignment of the bodyshell, and this can only be carried out accurately by a Vauxhall/Opel dealer or accident repair specialist, using special jigs. If the body is left misaligned, it is primarily dangerous as the car will not handle properly, and secondly, uneven stresses will be imposed on the steering, suspension and possibly transmission, causing abnormal wear, or complete failure, particularly to such items as the tyres.

6 Front bumper – removal and refitting

Removal

1 Firmly apply the handbrake, then jack up the front of the car and support it securely on axle stands (see *Jacking and vehicle support*).

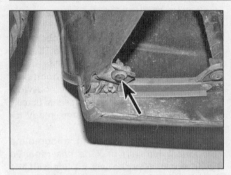

6.2a Undo the lower screw (arrowed) each side . . .

6.2b . . . and upper screw (arrowed) each side securing the front bumper to the wheel arch liners

6.3 Unscrew the two screws (arrowed) securing the top of the top of the bumper to the bumper frame

6.4a Withdraw the centre pins . . .

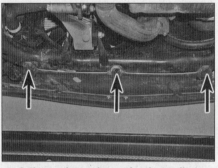

6.4b . . . then release the three clips (arrowed) securing the bottom of the bumper to the vehicle body

6.5a Release the sides of the bumper from the guides and withdraw the bumper from its location

2 Working under the wheel arch, undo the four screws (two on each side) securing the lower corners and sides of the bumper to the wheel arch liner **(see illustrations)**.

3 Unscrew the two screws securing the top of the top of the bumper to the bumper frame **(see illustration)**. On early models, lift out the air deflection panel over the top of the radiator.

4 Withdraw the centre pins, then release the three clips securing the bottom of the bumper to the vehicle body **(see illustrations)**.

5 With the aid of an assistant, release the sides of the bumper from the guides and withdraw the bumper from its location. Where applicable, disconnect the wiring connectors from the air conditioning temperature sensor and foglights **(see illustrations)**.

Refitting

6 Refitting is a reversal of the removal procedure, ensuring that all bumper fasteners are securely tightened.

6.5b Where applicable, disconnect the wiring connectors from the air conditioning temperature sensor (arrowed) . . .

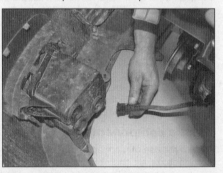

6.5c . . . and the foglights

7 Rear bumper – removal and refitting

Removal

1 Open the tailgate, and undo the four screws securing the top of the bumper to the vehicle **(see illustration)**.

2 From under the wheel arch on each side, undo the bumper upper retaining screw, then withdraw the centre pin and remove the lower plastic retaining clip **(see illustration)**.

3 Withdraw the centre pins, then remove the two plastic retaining clips securing the bottom of the bumper to the vehicle body **(see illustration)**.

4 With the aid of an assistant, release the sides of the bumper from the guides and

7.1 Undo the four screws securing the top of the rear bumper to the vehicle

7.2 From under the wheel arch on each side, undo the bumper upper retaining screw

withdraw the bumper from its location **(see illustrations)**. Disconnect the wiring connector as the bumper is being removed.

Refitting

5 Refitting is a reverse of the relevant removal procedure, ensuring that all disturbed fasteners are securely tightened. Before finally bolting the bumper in position, ensure that any wiring is securely connected.

8 Bonnet – removal, refitting and adjustment

Removal

1 Open the bonnet, and have an assistant support it. It may be useful to mark the outline position of each bonnet hinge relative to the bonnet (using a pencil or felt-tip pen), to use as a guide on refitting.
2 Disconnect the windscreen washer jet hose then undo the four bonnet retaining bolts, two each side **(see illustration)**. With the help of an assistant, carefully lift the bonnet clear. Store the bonnet out of the way, in a safe place.
3 Inspect the hinge for signs of wear or damage. If hinge renewal is necessary, the lower hinge bolts (three each side) will need to be removed from the inner wing panel. To gain access, remove the windscreen cowl panel as described in Section 20.

Refitting and adjustment

4 With the aid of an assistant, offer up the bonnet, and loosely fit the retaining bolts. Align the hinges with the marks made on removal, then tighten the retaining bolts securely.
5 Close the bonnet, and check for alignment with the adjacent panels. If necessary, slacken the bonnet support bolts, and realign the bonnet to suit. Once the bonnet is correctly aligned, securely tighten the bolts.
6 Once the bonnet is correctly aligned, check that the bonnet fastens and releases in a satisfactory manner, and if necessary adjust the lock striker as described in Section 10.

9 Bonnet release cable – removal and refitting

Removal

1 Remove the side sill front trim panel on the driver's side as described in Section 24.
2 Remove the windscreen cowl panel as described in Section 20.
3 Remove the bonnet lock spring as described in Section 10.
4 Insert a small screwdriver through the gap between the release handle and mounting bracket, to depress the detent lugs **(see illustrations)**. With the lug depressed, lift the release handle off the mounting bracket.

7.3 Remove the two plastic retaining clips (arrowed) securing the bottom of the bumper to the vehicle body

7.4b ... and withdraw the bumper from its location

5 Detach the outer cable from the release handle frame, then slip the inner cable end fitting out of the lever **(see illustrations)**.
6 Release the cable from the support clips and brackets in the engine compartment,

9.4a Insert a small screwdriver through the gap between the bonnet release handle and mounting bracket ...

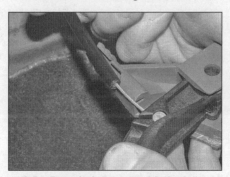

9.5a Detach the outer cable from the release handle frame ...

7.4a Release the sides of the bumper from the guides ...

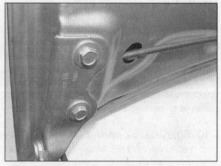

8.2 Bonnet retaining bolts

then withdraw the cable through the rubber grommet and into the passenger compartment. As an aid to refitting, tie a length of string to the cable before removing it and leave the string in position ready for refitting.

9.4b ... to depress the detent lugs (shown with handle removed)

9.5b ... then slip the inner cable end fitting out of the lever

10.3a Disengage the bonnet lock spring leg from the front crossmember . . .

Refitting

7 Refitting is a reversal of removal, but tie the string to the end of the cable, and use the string to pull the cable into position. Ensure that the cable is routed as noted before removal, and make sure that the grommet is correctly seated. On completion, refit the windscreen cowl panel and the interior trim panel as described in Section 20 and 24.

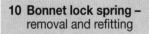

10 Bonnet lock spring –
removal and refitting

Removal

1 The bonnet is held in its locked position with a strong spring which engages with the striker on the front edge of the bonnet. The release cable is connected to the end of the spring.

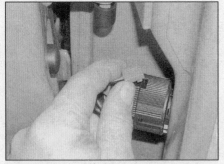

11.2a Pull out the locking clip . . .

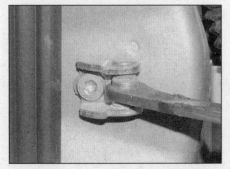

11.3 The front door check arm pivot is attached to the A-pillar with a Torx bolt

10.3b . . . slide the other end off the release cable and remove the spring from the crossmember

2 The striker may be removed from the bonnet by unscrewing the locknut, however measure its fitted length first as a guide to refitting it.
3 To remove the lock spring, disengage the spring leg from the front crossmember, slide the other end of the spring off the release cable and remove the spring from the crossmember **(see illustrations)**.

Refitting

4 Refitting is a reversal of removal.

11 Door –
removal, refitting and adjustment

Front door

Removal

1 To remove a door, open it fully and support it

11.2b . . . then twist the collar and pull the connector from the socket

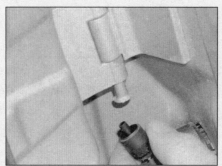

11.4 Removing the plastic covers from the front door hinge pins

under its lower edge on blocks or axle stands covered with pads of rag.
2 Disconnect the wiring connector from the front edge of the door. To release the connector, pull out the locking clip, then twist the collar and pull the connector from the socket in the door **(see illustrations)**.
3 Unscrew the Torx bolt securing the door check arm pivot to the A-pillar **(see illustration)**.
4 Where applicable, remove the plastic covers from the hinge pins **(see illustration)** then drive out the pins using a punch. Have an assistant support the door as the pins are driven out, then withdraw the door from the vehicle. If renewing a door, transfer all the serviceable fixings to the new door.

Refitting

5 Refitting is a reversal of removal.

Adjustment

6 The door hinges are welded onto the door frame and the body pillar, so that there is no provision for adjustment or alignment.
7 If the door can be moved up and down on its hinges due to wear in the hinge pins or their holes, it may be possible to drill out the holes and fit slightly oversize pins. Consult a Vauxhall/Opel dealer for further advice.
8 Door closure may be adjusted by altering the position of the lock striker on the body pillar, using an Allen key or a hexagon bit **(see illustration)**.

Rear door

Removal

9 Disconnect the wiring connector from the front edge of the door **(see illustration)**. To release the connector, twist the locking collar, then pull the connector from the socket in the door.
10 Unscrew the Torx bolt securing the door check arm pivot to the B-pillar **(see illustration)**.
11 Where applicable, remove the plastic covers from the hinge pins **(see illustration)** then drive out the pins using a punch. Have an assistant support the door as the pins are driven out, then withdraw the door from the vehicle. If renewing a door, transfer all the serviceable fixings to the new door.

11.8 Front door lock striker on the B-pillar

Refitting

12 Refitting is a reversal of removal.

Adjustment

13 The door hinges are welded onto the door frame and the body pillar, so that there is no provision for adjustment or alignment.

14 If the door can be moved up and down on its hinges due to wear in the hinge pins or their holes, it may be possible to drill out the holes and fit slightly oversize pins. Consult a Vauxhall/Opel dealer for further advice.

15 Door closure may be adjusted by altering the position of the lock striker on the body pillar, using an Allen key or a hexagon bit **(see illustration)**.

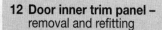

12 Door inner trim panel – removal and refitting

Removal

Front door

1 Fully lower the door window.

2 On models with electrically-operated mirrors, carefully prise out the mirror control switch from the exterior mirror inner trim panel and disconnect the switch wiring connector **(see illustration)**.

3 Carefully unclip the exterior mirror inner trim panel from the door. On models with manually-operated mirrors, it will be necessary to pull the knob off the adjusting lever in order to remove the panel **(see illustration)**.

4 Where a manual window regulator is fitted, locate a cloth rag between the handle and the trim panel and pull it back and forth to release the spring clip. Alternatively use a proprietory regulator spring clip removal tool **(see illustrations)**. Remove the handle from the splined shaft and refit the spring clip to the handle.

5 Lift the inner door lock handle, and carefully prise the handle trim cover out from the door trim panel **(see illustration)**. Disconnect the speaker wiring connector.

6 Where applicable, unclip the electric window switch assembly from the door trim panel, then disconnect the wiring connector **(see illustrations)**.

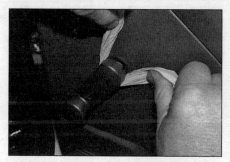

12.4a Locate a cloth rag between the handle and the trim panel and pull it back and forth to release the spring clip . . .

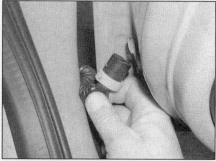

11.9 Disconnecting the wiring from the front edge of the rear door

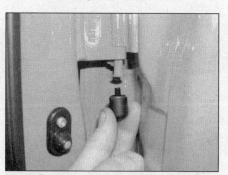

11.11 Removing the plastic covers from the rear door hinge pins

7 Carefully prise the window inner sealing strip from the top edge of the door trim panel **(see illustration)**.

12.2 Carefully prise out the mirror control switch from the exterior mirror inner trim panel

12.4b . . . alternatively use a proprietory regulator spring clip removal tool

11.10 Rear door check arm

11.15 Rear door lock striker on the C-pillar

8 Carefully prise off the trim cap and undo the screw in the door grab handle aperture **(see illustrations)**.

12.3 Unclip the exterior mirror inner trim panel from the door

12.5 Lift the inner door lock handle, and carefully prise the handle trim cover out from the door trim panel

12.6a Where applicable, unclip the electric window switch assembly from the door trim panel . . .

12.6b . . . then disconnect the wiring connector

12.7 Prise the window inner sealing strip from the top edge of the door trim panel

12.8a Prise off the trim cap . . .

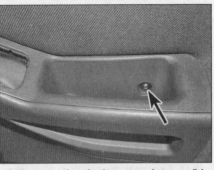

12.8b . . . and undo the screw (arrowed) in the door grab handle aperture

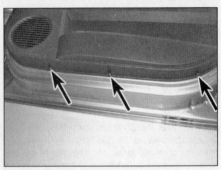

12.9a Undo the three lower trim panel securing screws (arrowed) . . .

9 Undo the three lower trim panel securing screws and the front upper trim panel securing screw **(see illustrations)**.

10 Using a wide-bladed screwdriver or removal tool, carefully prise the bottom and sides of the panel away from door to release the internal clips **(see illustration)**. Lift the panel upward to release it from the window aperture.

Rear door

11 Fully lower the door window.

12 Carefully unclip the inner triangular trim panel from the door **(see illustration)**.

13 Carefully prise the window inner sealing strip from the top edge of the door trim panel.

14 Where a manual window regulator is fitted, locate a cloth rag between the handle and the trim panel and pull it back and forth to release the spring clip. Alternatively use a proprietory regulator spring clip removal tool **(see illustrations 12.4a and 12.4b)**. Remove the handle from the splined shaft then remove the circular spacer **(see illustration)**. Refit the spring clip to the handle.

15 Lift the inner door lock handle, and carefully prise the handle trim cover out from the door trim panel **(see illustration)**. Disconnect the speaker wiring connector (where fitted).

12.9b . . . and the front upper trim panel securing screw (arrowed)

12.10 Prise the bottom and sides of the panel away from door to release the internal clips

12.12 Carefully unclip the inner triangular trim panel from the door

12.14 Remove the handle from the splined shaft then remove the circular spacer

12.15 Lift the inner door lock handle, and carefully prise the handle trim cover out from the door trim panel

12.16a Prise off the trim cap . . .

12.16b . . . and undo the screw (arrowed) in the door grab handle aperture

12.17a Undo the lower trim panel securing screw (arrowed) . . .

16 Carefully prise off the trim cap and undo the screw in the door grab handle aperture **(see illustrations)**.
17 Undo the lower trim panel securing screw and the upper trim panel securing screw **(see illustrations)**.
18 Using a wide-bladed screwdriver or removal tool, carefully prise the bottom and sides of the panel away from the door to release the internal clips **(see illustration)**. Lift the panel upward to release it from the window aperture.

Refitting

19 Refitting is the reverse of the relevant removal procedure.

12.17b . . . and the upper trim panel securing screw (arrowed)

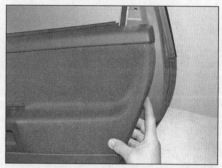

12.18 Prise the bottom and sides of the panel away from the door to release the internal clips

13 Door handle and lock components – removal and refitting

Removal

Front interior handle

1 Remove the door inner trim panel as described in Section 12.
2 Peel the polythene weathershield away from the door to gain access to the inner handle components **(see illustration)**.
3 Slide the inner handle forward to release it from the door panel **(see illustration)**.
4 Detach the operating cable from the handle lever, and remove the inner handle from the door.

Front exterior handle

5 Remove the door inner trim panel as

described in Section 12, then peel back the weathershield **(see illustration 13.2)**.
6 With the window fully raised, disconnect the wiring connector from the central locking

unit, then undo the lower retaining bolt and upper retaining nut and remove the shield from around the door locking mechanism **(see illustrations)**.

13.2 Peel the polythene weathershield away from the door

13.3 Slide the inner handle forward to release it from the door panel

13.6a Disconnect the wiring connector from the central locking unit . . .

13.6b . . . undo the lower retaining bolt (arrowed) . . .

13.6c . . . and upper retaining nut (arrowed) . . .

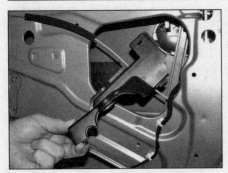

13.6d . . . and remove the shield from around the door locking mechanism

13.7 Undo the retaining nut and remove the exterior handle shell from inside the door

13.8 Unclip the exterior handle and remove it from the door

13.10a Extract the circlip from the rear of the lock cylinder . . .

13.10b . . . remove the lock lever . . .

described above, then unhook the link rod from the exterior door handle shell.

10 Extract the circlip from the rear of the lock cylinder, and remove the lever and springs, note the fitted position of the lever and springs for refitting **(see illustrations)**.

11 Using a 2 mm diameter pin punch, tap out the roll-pin securing the lock housing to the handle shell **(see illustration)**.

12 Insert the key into the lock cylinder, turn the lock housing anti-clockwise and carefully remove the lock cylinder upwards out of the housing **(see illustration)**.

13 Remove the key, then withdraw the lock barrel from the housing, taking care the tumblers do not fall out of the barrel **(see illustrations)**.

14 If the collar is removed from the lock shell, note the position for refitting. Make sure the two ball-bearings and locating ring are located correctly when refitting **(see illustrations)**.

7 Unclip the lock cylinder operating rod from the lock assembly, undo the retaining nut and remove the exterior handle shell from inside the door **(see illustration)**.

8 Unclip the exterior handle from the door

panel, and remove the handle from the outside of the door **(see illustration)**.

Front lock cylinder

9 Remove the exterior door handle as

13.10c . . . outer spring . . .

13.10d . . . and inner spring

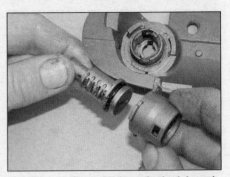

13.11 Using a pin punch, tap out the roll-pin securing the lock housing to the handle shell

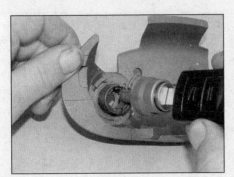

13.12 Remove the lock cylinder out of the housing

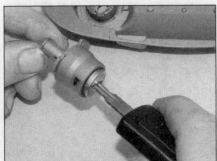

13.13a Remove the key . . .

13.13b . . . then withdraw the lock barrel from the housing

13.14a Remove the collar from the lock shell . . .

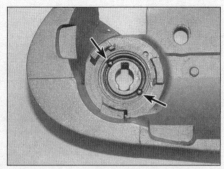

13.14b . . . then the ball-bearings (arrowed) . . .

13.14c . . . and the locating ring

13.16 Undo the three lock assembly retaining screws (arrowed)

13.17a Release the outer cable (arrowed) from the lock body . . .

13.17b . . . then disengage the inner cable from the lock lever

Front lock assembly

15 Remove the exterior door handle as described previously.

16 Undo the three retaining screws, and manoeuvre the lock assembly to gain access to the operating cables **(see illustration)**.

17 Release the outer cables from the lock body, then disengage the inner cables from the lock levers **(see illustrations)**.

18 Withdraw the lock assembly from the door frame.

Rear interior handle

19 Remove the door inner trim panel as described in Section 12.

20 Peel the polythene weathershield away from the door to gain access to the inner handle components **(see illustration 13.2)**.

21 Release the operating rod from the plastic guide on the door **(see illustration)**.

22 Slide the inner handle forward to release it from the door panel **(see illustration 13.3)**.

23 Detach the operating rod from the handle lever, and remove the inner handle from the door **(see illustration)**.

Rear exterior handle

24 Remove the door inner trim panel as described in Section 12, and peel back the weathershield **(see illustration 13.2)**.

25 Wind the window fully down, and release the window sealing strip from the rear of the door and window guide **(see illustration)**.

26 Undo the two window guide retaining bolts, free the upper part of the guide from the door, and manoeuvre the window guide down and out from the door **(see illustrations)**.

27 Wind the window fully up, then undo the two nuts, and free the mounting plate assembly from the rear of the handle **(see illustrations)**.

28 Unclip the exterior handle from the door panel, and withdraw the handle from the outside of the door

29 Unclip the operating link rod and remove the exterior handle **(see illustration)**.

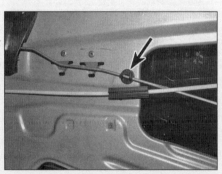

13.21 Release the operating rod from the plastic guide (arrowed) on the door

13.23 Detach the operating rod from the handle lever, and remove the inner handle

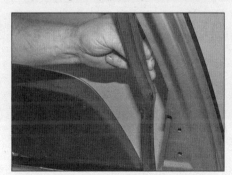

13.25 Release the window sealing strip from the rear of the door and window guide

13.26a Undo the window guide upper retaining bolt (arrowed) . . .

13.26b ... and lower retaining bolt (arrowed) ...

13.26c ... free the upper part of the guide from the door ...

13.26d ... and manoeuvre the window guide down and out from the door

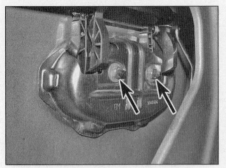

13.27a Undo the two nuts (arrowed) ...

13.27b ... and remove the mounting plate assembly from the rear of the handle

13.29 Unclip the operating link rod and remove the exterior handle

Rear lock assembly

30 Remove the interior handle as described previously.

31 Remove the rear window guide as described in paragraphs 25 and 26.

32 Release the retaining clip and detach the central locking wiring harness from the door **(see illustration)**.

33 Undo the three screws securing the lock to the door **(see illustration)**.

34 Disengage the exterior handle operating rod from the plastic bush on the lock lever and withdraw the lock out through the door aperture **(see illustrations)**.

35 Slide the locking clip out and disconnect the central locking wiring connector from the lock assembly **(see illustration)**.

36 Release the cable from the lock assembly by unclipping the outer cable and disconnecting the inner cable from the operating lever on the lock assembly **(see illustration)**. The link rod can be removed by pivoting the retaining clip away from the link rod, and freeing the link rod from the lever on the lock assembly.

Refitting

37 Refitting is the reverse of the removal sequence, noting the following points:
 a) If a lock cylinder has been removed, on refitting ensure that all the components

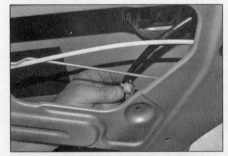

13.32 Release the retaining clip and detach the central locking wiring harness from the door

13.33 Undo the three screws (arrowed) securing the lock to the door

13.34a Disengage the exterior handle operating rod from the plastic bush (arrowed) on the lock lever ...

13.34b ... and withdraw the lock out through the door aperture

13.35 Slide the locking clip out and disconnect the wiring connector from the lock assembly

are refitted in the correct position, as noted on removal and are securely held in place by the circlip. Check the operation of the lock cylinder, making sure that the spring returns the cylinder to its central position, before refitting the handle shell to the door.

b) Ensure that all link rods are securely held in position by their retaining clips.

c) Apply grease to all lock and link rod pivot points.

d) Before installing the relevant trim panel, thoroughly check the operation of all the door lock handles and, where necessary, the central locking system, and ensure that the weathershield is correctly positioned.

e) Make sure the polythene weathershield fitted behind the trim panel is undamaged and perfectly sealed to the door around its complete contact area. If a perfect seal cannot be made, renew the weathershield.

14 Door window glass and regulator – removal and refitting

Removal

1 Remove the door inner trim panel as described in Section 12.

2 Peel the polythene weathershield away from the door to gain access to the door lock components **(see illustration 13.2)**. Proceed as described under the relevant sub-heading.

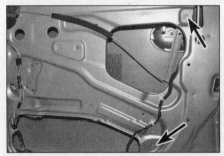

14.5 Drill out the two rivets (arrowed) securing the rear window guide rail to the door

14.11 Carefully prise the window outer sealing strip up and off the top edge of the door

13.36 Unclip the outer cable and disconnect the inner cable from the operating lever

Front window glass

Note: *A pop-rivet gun and suitable rivets will be required when refitting. The rivet heads should be approximately 4.8 mm in diameter and 11 mm in length.*

3 Remove the door exterior mirror as described in Section 17.

4 Carefully prise the window outer sealing strip up and off the top edge of the door.

5 Raise the window fully, then using an 8.5 mm drill bit, drill out the two rivets securing the rear window guide rail to the door **(see illustration)**. Take great care not to damage the door panel.

6 Free the window guide from the door, and manoeuvre the guide down and out from the door.

7 Support the window glass and undo the two bolts securing the window glass to the regulator **(see illustration)**.

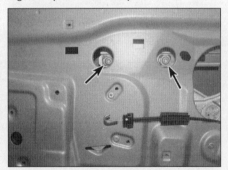

14.7 Undo the two bolts (arrowed) securing the window glass to the regulator

14.14a Free the window guide (arrowed) from the regulator mechanism . . .

8 Lower the window glass and partially remove the window sealing strip from the rear of the door.

9 Tilt the window glass and remove it up and out of the door.

Rear window glass

10 Carefully unclip the outer triangular trim panel from the door **(see illustration)**.

11 Carefully prise the window outer sealing strip up and off the top edge of the door **(see illustration)**.

12 Wind the window fully down, and release the window sealing strip from the rear of the door and window guide **(see illustration 13.25)**.

13 Undo the two window guide retaining bolts, free the upper part of the guide from the door, and manoeuvre the window guide down and out from the door **(see illustrations 13.26a to 13.26d)**.

14 Tilt the window glass forwards, and free the window guide from the regulator mechanism (it may be necessary to raise the window mechanism slightly to disengage the window guide). The glass can then be manoeuvred out from the door **(see illustrations)**.

Front regulator

Note: *A pop-rivet gun and suitable rivets will be required when refitting. The rivet heads should be approximately 4.8 mm in diameter and 11 mm in length.*

15 On models with electric windows, remove the door loudspeaker as described in Chapter 12.

16 With the window set in the raised position, secure the window glass in position, then

14.10 Unclip the outer triangular trim panel from the door

14.14b . . . then manoeuvre the glass out from the door

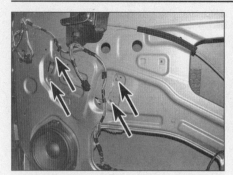

14.18a Drill out the four front rivets (arrowed) . . .

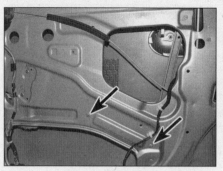

14.18b . . . and two centre rivets securing the regulator to the front door

14.21 Drill out the six rivets securing the regulator assembly to the rear door

undo the two bolts securing the window glass to the regulator **(see illustration 14.7)**.
17 On models with electric windows, reach through the loudspeaker aperture and disconnect the regulator motor wiring connector.
18 Using an 8.5 mm drill bit, drill out the six rivets securing the regulator assembly to the door, taking great care not to damage the door panel **(see illustrations)**.
19 With all the rivets removed, manoeuvre the regulator assembly out through the door aperture.

Rear regulator

Note: *A pop-rivet gun and suitable rivets will be required when refitting. The rivet heads should be approximately 4.8 mm in diameter and 11 mm in length.*
20 Remove the rear window glass as described in paragraphs 10 to 14.
21 Using an 8.5 mm drill bit, drill out the six rivets securing the regulator assembly to the door, taking great care not to damage the door panel **(see illustration)**.
22 With all the rivets removed, disengage the regulator from the two upper locating lugs and manoeuvre the regulator out through the door aperture.

Refitting

23 Refitting is the reverse of the removal procedure, noting the following points:
a) *Where the regulator or guide rail has been removed, remove the remains of the old rivets before fitting the regulator or guide*

rail to the door. Engage the regulator in position on the door, and secure it with new pop-rivets.
b) *Check the window moves smoothly and easily up-and-down, without any sign of tight spots. If the window movement is stiff, trace and rectify the cause. On the front window, movement is adjustable by slackening the regulator guide bolts and moving them in the slotted holes. Find the position where the window movement is the easiest, then securely tighten the bolts.*
c) *Refit the weathershield, making sure it is securely stuck to the door, then install the trim panel as described in Section 12.*

15 Tailgate and support struts – removal and refitting

Tailgate

Removal

1 Disconnect the battery negative terminal (refer to *Disconnecting the battery* in the Reference Chapter).
2 Remove the luggage compartment upper side trim panel on the left-hand side, as described in Section 24.
3 Disconnect the tailgate wiring harness connector, then unclip the harness from the D-pillar **(see illustration)**.
4 Release the rubber grommet from the roof

frame and withdraw the wiring harness from the roof.
5 Undo the two bolts and withdraw the high-level stop-light from the tailgate **(see illustration)**.
6 Disconnect the tailgate washer hose from the washer jet on the high-level stop-light **(see illustration)**.
7 Tie a suitable length of string to the washer hose end, release the rubber grommet from the roof frame then withdraw the hose. When the end of the hose appears, untie the string and leave it in position in the tailgate; it can then be used to draw the hose back into position when refitting.
8 Have an assistant support the tailgate, then disconnect the tops of the support struts by prising out the spring clips with a small screwdriver. Lower the struts to the body.
9 Extract the clips and carefully drive out the hinge pins, from outside to inside, using a small drift, while the assistant supports the tailgate **(see illustration)**. Withdraw the tailgate from the body.

Refitting

10 Refitting is a reversal of removal, but apply a little grease to the pivots, and check that when closed the tailgate is positioned centrally within the body aperture and flush with the surrounding bodywork. If necessary, adjust the position of the rubber supports so that the tailgate is flush with the surrounding bodywork. After making adjustments, check that the striker enters the lock centrally and if necessary loosen the striker bolts to reposition it. Tighten the bolts on completion.

15.3 Disconnect the tailgate wiring harness connector (arrowed), then unclip the harness from the D-pillar

15.5 Undo the two bolts (arrowed) and withdraw the high-level stop-light from the tailgate

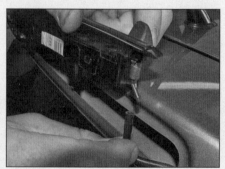

15.6 Disconnect the tailgate washer hose from the washer jet on the high-level stop-light

Support struts

Removal

11 Support the tailgate in the open position using a suitable piece of wood, or with the help of an assistant.
12 Raise the spring clips, and pull the support strut off its balljoint mountings on the tailgate and vehicle body **(see illustration)**.

Refitting

13 Refitting is a reversal of removal.

15.9 Extract the clips (arrowed) and carefully drive out the tailgate hinge pins

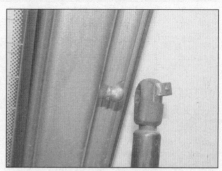

15.12 Lift the retaining clips and free the support strut from its balljoints

---

16 Tailgate lock components – removal and refitting

Removal

1 Remove the retaining screw trim caps at the base of the tailgate upper trim panel on each side. Undo the two retaining screws then remove the panel by prising it free at the sides, then at the centre to release the nine internal retaining clips **(see illustrations)**.
2 Undo the two screws in the grab handle apertures and the two screws at the base of the tailgate securing the lower trim panel to the tailgate **(see illustration)**.
3 Pull the lower trim panel away from the tailgate to release the twelve internal retaining clips and remove the panel from the tailgate **(see illustration)**.
4 Proceed as described under the relevant sub-heading.

Lock assembly

5 From inside the tailgate, release the retaining clip by pivoting it away from the link rod, and detach the rod from the lock assembly.
6 Slacken and remove the four screws, and remove the lock from inside the tailgate **(see illustration)**.

Lock actuator

7 From inside the tailgate, release the retaining clip by pivoting it away from the link rod, and detach the rod from the lock assembly.
8 Disconnect the wiring connector from the lock actuator **(see illustration)**.
9 Undo the three retaining screws and remove the lock actuator from the tailgate.

16.1a Remove the trim caps at the base of the tailgate upper trim panel on each side, then undo the two retaining screws

Exterior handle

10 Undo the two nuts securing the exterior handle to the tailgate **(see illustration)**.

11 Withdraw the exterior handle from

16.2 Undo the four screws (arrowed) securing the lower trim panel to the tailgate

16.1b Prise the panel free at the sides, then at the centre to release the internal clips

outside the tailgate and disconnect the wiring connector.

Refitting

12 Refitting is a reverse of the removal procedure.

16.3 Pull the lower trim panel away from the tailgate to release the internal clips

16.6 Undo the four screws and remove the lock from inside the tailgate

16.8 Disconnect the wiring connector (arrowed) from the lock actuator

16.10 Exterior handle retaining nuts

17 Exterior mirror and associated components – removal and refitting

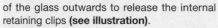

Mirror assembly

Removal

1 On models with electrically-operated mirrors, carefully prise out the mirror control switch from the exterior mirror inner trim panel and disconnect the switch wiring connector (see illustration 12.2).
2 Carefully unclip the exterior mirror inner trim panel from the door. On models with manually-operated mirrors, it will be necessary to pull the knob off the adjusting lever in order to remove the panel (see illustration 12.3).
3 On electrically-operated mirrors, disconnect the wiring connector to the mirror assembly (see illustration).
4 Undo the three retaining bolts, and remove the mirror assembly from the outside of the door (see illustration).

Refitting

5 Refitting is the reverse of removal.

Mirror glass

Removal

6 Push in the upper inner (nearest the door) corner of the glass so that the lower outer corner of the glass is forced out from the centre.
7 Using a plastic wedge, prise the outer edge of the glass outwards to release the internal retaining clips (see illustration).
8 Withdraw the mirror glass and, where applicable, disconnect the wiring connectors (see illustration).

Refitting

9 Refitting is the reverse of removal. Carefully press the mirror glass into the housing until the retaining clips are engaged.

Mirror cover

Removal

10 Remove the mirror glass as described previously.
11 Carefully disengage the four retaining lugs and remove the cover from the mirror body (see illustrations).

Refitting

12 Refitting is the reverse of removal.

Mirror switch

13 Refer to Chapter 12.

18 Windscreen, tailgate and fixed window glass – general information

These areas of glass are secured by the tight fit of the weatherstrip in the body aperture, and are bonded in position with a special adhesive. The removal and refitting of these areas of fixed glass is a difficult, messy and time-consuming task, which is considered beyond the scope of the home mechanic. It is difficult, unless one has plenty of practice, to obtain a secure, waterproof fit. Furthermore, the task carries a high risk of breakage; this applies especially to the laminated glass windscreen. In view of this, owners are strongly advised to have this sort of work carried out by one of the many specialist windscreen fitters, or a Vauxhall/Opel dealer.

19 Sunroof – general information

A manual or electric sunroof was offered as an optional extra on most models, and is fitted as standard equipment on some models.

Due to the complexity of the sunroof mechanism, considerable expertise is needed to repair, renew or adjust the sunroof components successfully. Removal of the sunroof first requires the headlining to be removed, which is a complex and tedious operation in itself, and not a task to be undertaken lightly (see Section 24). Therefore, any problems with the sunroof should be referred to a Vauxhall/Opel dealer.

On models with an electric sunroof, if the motor fails to operate, first check the relevant fuse. If the fault cannot be traced and rectified, the sunroof can be opened and closed manually using a screwdriver to turn the motor spindle. To gain access to the motor spindle, carefully prise out the trim cover situated at the rear of the sunroof.

17.3 On electrically-operated mirrors, disconnect the mirror wiring connector

17.4 Undo the three retaining bolts (arrowed) and remove the mirror assembly from the door

17.7 Prise the outer edge of the glass outwards to release the internal retaining clips

17.8 Withdraw the mirror glass and disconnect the wiring connectors

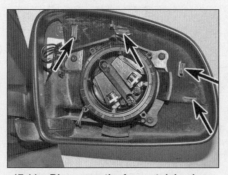

17.11a Disengage the four retaining lugs (arrowed) . . .

17.11b . . . and remove the cover from the mirror body

20.4 Pull up the rubber weatherseal from the flange at the rear of the engine compartment

Press in the central part of the motor spindle as far as possible with the screwdriver, and turn the spindle to move the sunroof to the required position.

20 Body exterior fittings –
removed and refitting

Radiator grille

1 Open the bonnet and undo the radiator grille retaining screws.
2 Release the retaining clips and remove the grille.
3 Refitting is the reverse of removal.

Windscreen cowl panel

4 Open the bonnet and pull up the rubber weatherseal from the flange at the rear of the engine compartment (see illustration).
5 Remove the windscreen wiper arms as described in Chapter 12.
6 Undo the six retaining screws and lift out the cowl panel (see illustrations).
7 Refitting is the reverse of removal. Ensure that the windscreen washer hose locates in the slot in the cowl panel as the panel is placed in position.
8 On completion, refit the windscreen wiper arms as described in Chapter 12.

Bulkhead closure panel

9 Remove the windscreen cowl panel as described previously.
10 Detach the fusebox from its location on the inside of the closure panel (see illustration).

20.11b . . . the two centre retaining screws (arrowed) . . .

20.6a Undo the six retaining screws . . .

11 Undo the six bolts securing the closure panel to the bulkhead (see illustrations).
12 Lift the closure panel upward to disengage the lower flange from the bulkhead, then move it forward and lift it out of the engine compartment (see illustration).
13 Refitting is the reverse of removal.

Wheel arch liners and body under-panels

14 The various plastic covers fitted to the underside of the vehicle are secured in position by a mixture of screws, nuts and retaining clips, and removal will be fairly obvious on inspection. Work methodically around the liner/panel, removing its retaining screws and releasing its retaining clips until it is free to be removed from the underside of the vehicle. Most clips used on the vehicle, with the exception of the fasteners which are used to secure the wheel arch liners, are

20.10 Detach the fusebox from the bulkhead closure panel

20.11c . . . and the two left-hand retaining screws (arrowed)

20.6b . . . and lift out the windscreen cowl panel

simply prised out of position. The wheel arch liner clips are released by tapping their centre pins through the clip, and then removing the outer section of the clip; new clips will be required on refitting if the centre pins are not recovered.
15 When refitting, renew any retaining clips that may have been broken on removal, and ensure that the panel is securely retained by all the relevant clips, nuts and screws. Vauxhall/Opel also recommend that plastic nuts (where used) are renewed, regardless of their apparent condition, whenever they are disturbed.

Body trim strips and badges

16 The various body trim strips and badges are held in position with a special adhesive tape. Removal requires the trim/badge to be heated, to soften the adhesive, and then cut away from the surface. Due to the high risk of

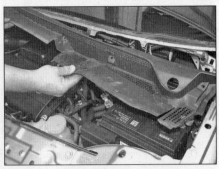

20.11a Undo the two right-hand retaining screws (arrowed) . . .

20.12 Lift the bulkhead closure panel upward and out of the engine compartment

21.2 Lift off the plastic cover from the wiring connector under the seat

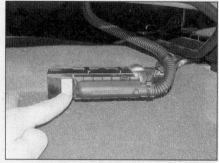

21.3a On early models, release the locking clip . . .

21.3b . . . and disconnect the seat wiring harness connector

21.4a On later models, remove the red locking plate . . .

21.4b . . . then pull the locking bar fully out and disconnect the seat wiring harness connector

21.5 Undo the seat retaining bolt (arrowed) from the front of both seat guide rails

damage to the vehicle's paintwork during this operation, it is recommended that this task should be entrusted to a Vauxhall/Opel dealer.

21 Seats – removal and refitting

⚠️ **Warning: The front seats are equipped with seat belt tensioners, and side airbags may be built into the outer sides of the seats. The seat belt tensioners and side airbags may cause injury if triggered accidentally. If the tensioner has been triggered due to a sudden impact or accident, the unit must be renewed, as it cannot be reset. If a seat is to be disposed of, the tensioner must be triggered before the seat is removed from the vehicle. Due to safety considerations,** *tensioner renewal or seat disposal must be entrusted to a Vauxhall dealer. Where side airbags are fitted, refer to Chapter 12 for the precautions which should be observed when dealing with an airbag system.*

1 Disconnect the battery negative terminal (refer to *Disconnecting the battery* in the Reference Chapter). Wait 2 minutes for the capacitors to discharge, before working on the seat electrics.

Front seat

Removal

2 Slide the seat adjustment fully to the rear, then lift off the plastic cover from the wiring connector under the seat **(see illustration)**.

3 On early models, disconnect the seat wiring connector by pressing the yellow release button until the red locking bar slides out. Pull the locking bar fully out and disconnect the connector **(see illustrations)**.

4 On later models, disconnect the seat wiring connector by first removing the red locking plate. Pull the locking bar fully out and disconnect the connector **(see illustrations)**.

5 Slacken and remove the seat retaining bolts from the front of the seat guide rails **(see illustration)**.

6 Slide the seat fully forwards, then unclip the cover over the seat belt mounting on the seat. Undo the seat belt lower mounting bolt **(see illustrations)**.

7 Slacken and remove the seat retaining bolts from rear of the guide rails and lift the seat out of the vehicle **(see illustration)**.

Refitting

8 Refitting is a reverse of the removal procedure, noting the following points:

a) *Remove all traces of old thread-locking compound from the threads of the seat retaining bolts, and clean the threaded*

21.6a Unclip the cover over the seat belt mounting on the seat . . .

21.6b . . . then undo the seat belt lower mounting bolt (arrowed)

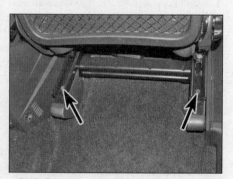

21.7 Seat rear retaining bolts (arrowed)

21.9a Extract the trim cap . . .

21.9b . . . and undo the rear seat belt lower mounting bolt (arrowed) from the rear seat

21.10a Lift up the plastic flap and unscrew the seat front mounting bolt trim covers on each side . . .

21.10b . . . then remove the covers

21.11 Undo the seat retaining bolts (arrowed) from the front of the seat guide rails

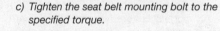

21.13 Undo the rear guide rail retaining bolts (arrowed)

holes in the vehicle floor, ideally by running a tap of the correct size and pitch down them.

b) Apply a suitable thread-locking compound to the threads of the seat bolts. Refit the bolts, and tighten them to the specified torque.

c) Reconnect the seat wiring block connector making sure it has locked securely, then reconnect the battery negative terminal.

Rear outer seat

Removal

9 Extract the trim cap and undo the rear seat belt lower mounting bolt from the rear seat **(see illustrations)**.
10 Lift up the plastic flap and unscrew the seat front mounting bolt trim covers on each side, then remove the covers **(see illustrations)**.
11 Slacken and remove the seat retaining

bolts from the front of the seat guide rails **(see illustration)**.
12 Reposition the seat as necessary for access to the seat guide rail rear retaining bolts.
13 Undo the rear guide rail retaining bolts and lift the seat out of the vehicle **(see illustration)**.

Refitting

14 Refitting is a reverse of the removal procedure, noting the following points:
a) Remove all traces of old thread-locking compound from the threads of the seat retaining bolts, and clean the threaded holes in the vehicle floor, ideally by running a tap of the correct size and pitch down them.
b) Apply a suitable thread-locking compound to the threads of the seat bolts. Refit the bolts, and tighten them to the specified torque.

c) Tighten the seat belt mounting bolt to the specified torque.

Rear centre seat

Removal

15 Lift off the plastic covers over the centre seat front mounting bolts, then undo the two mounting bolts **(see illustrations)**.
16 Bring the seat to the cargo position to expose the rear seat belt mountings.
17 Undo the mounting nuts and release the rear seat belt buckles on the left-hand and right-hand sides **(see illustration)**.
18 Undo the two rear mounting bolts and carefully remove the rear seat from the vehicle.

Refitting

19 Refitting is a reverse of the removal procedure, noting the following points:
a) Remove all traces of old thread-locking compound from the threads of the seat

21.15a Lift off the plastic covers over the centre seat front mounting bolts . . .

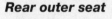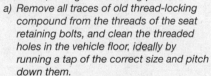

21.15b . . . then undo the two mounting bolts (arrowed)

21.17 Undo the mounting nut (arrowed) and release the rear seat belt buckles on both sides

23.3 Front seat belt upper mounting bolt (arrowed)

retaining bolts, and clean the threaded holes in the vehicle floor, ideally by running a tap of the correct size and pitch down them.

b) Apply a suitable thread-locking compound to the threads of the seat bolts. Refit the bolts, and tighten them to the specified torque setting.

c) Tighten the seat belt buckle mounting nuts to the specified torque.

22 Front seat belt tensioning mechanism – general information

All models covered in this manual are fitted with a front seat belt pyrotechnic tensioner system. The system is designed to instantaneously take up any slack in the seat belt in the case of a sudden frontal impact,

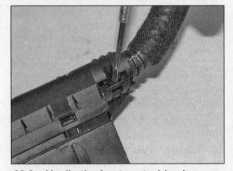

23.8a Unclip the front seat wiring harness connector cover . . .

23.9a Depress the two tabs on the side of the belt tensioner wiring plug . . .

23.4a Remove the trim from the outside of the door pillar . . .

therefore reducing the possibility of injury to the front seat occupants. Each front seat is fitted with its own system, the components of which are mounted in the seat frame.

The seat belt tensioner is triggered by a front or rear impact causing a deceleration of six times the force of gravity or greater. Lesser impacts will not trigger the system.

When the system is triggered, a pretensioned spring draws back the seat belt via a cable which acts on the seat belt stalk. The cable can move by up to 80.0 mm, which therefore reduces the slack in the seat belt around the shoulders and waist of the occupant by a similar amount.

There is a risk of injury if the system is triggered inadvertently when working on the vehicle, and it is therefore strongly recommended that any work involving the seat belt tensioner system is entrusted to a Vauxhall/Opel dealer. Refer to the warning

23.8b . . . and remove the cover from the connector

23.9b . . . and withdraw the plug from the main connector

23.4b . . . and undo the seat belt reel retaining nut using a deep socket

given at the beginning of Section 21 before contemplating any work on the front seats.

23 Seat belt components – removal and refitting

Front belt and reel

Removal

1 Remove the side sill inner trim panel as described in Section 24.

2 Slide the front seat fully forwards, then unclip the cover over the seat belt mounting on the seat. Undo the seat belt lower mounting bolt **(see illustrations 21.6a and 21.6b)**.

3 Undo the seat belt upper mounting bolt **(see illustration)**.

4 Prise the cover from the lower outside of the B-pillar for access to the front seat belt reel mounting nut. Using a 13 mm socket, 65 mm deep on the inside, unscrew the nut taking care not to drop it inside the B-pillar **(see illustrations)**. Note that an extension pin is provided to enable the nut to be removed safely.

5 With the nut removed, remove the reel from the inside of the pillar.

Refitting

6 Refitting is a reversal of removal, but tighten the mounting bolts to the specified torque.

Front belt stalk and tensioner

Removal

7 Remove the front seat as described in Section 21.

8 Unclip the front seat wiring harness connector cover and remove the cover from the connector **(see illustrations)**.

9 Depress the two tabs on the side of the tensioner wiring plug and withdraw the plug from the main connector **(see illustrations)**.

10 Unclip the tensioner trim cover, then undo the retaining bolt and remove the tensioner from the seat **(see illustrations)**.

Refitting

11 Refitting is a reverse of the removal procedure, noting the following points:

a) Remove all traces of old thread-locking compound from the thread of the

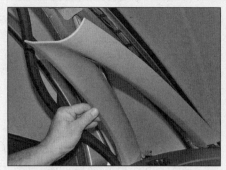

24.6 Pull the trim panel away from the A-pillar to release the five retaining clips

24.11 Starting at the top, prise the upper trim panel away from the B-pillar

24.13 Release the seat belt guide at the rear of the panel

B-pillar

Upper trim panel

8 Slide the front seat fully forwards, then unclip the cover over the seat belt mounting on the seat. Undo the seat belt lower mounting bolt (see illustrations 21.6a and 21.6b).
9 Pull off the front door weather strip in the vicinity of the B-pillar trim panel.
10 On models with side airbags, prise out the plastic cover at the top of the panel and undo the retaining screw now exposed.
11 Starting at the top, prise the upper trim panel away from the B-pillar (see illustration).
12 To separate the upper trim panel from the lower trim panel, depress the tongue at the base of the lower panel, then release the retaining tabs at each side, while pulling the upper panel away.

13 Release the seat belt guide at the rear of the panel, then feed the seat belt through the opening and remove the panel from the car (see illustration).
14 Refitting is a reversal of removal, but tighten the seat belt retaining bolt to the specified torque. On models with side airbags, apply a suitable thread-locking compound to the threads of the panel upper retaining screw and tighten the screw securely.

Lower trim panel

15 Remove the side sill inner trim panel as described later in this Section.
16 Remove the sound deadening pad from the inside of the side sill inner trim panel.
17 Release the two retaining tabs and withdraw the lower B-pillar panel from the side sill panel.
18 Refitting is a reversal of removal.

Side sill

Inner trim panel

19 Remove the B-pillar upper trim panel and the luggage compartment side trim panel as described elsewhere in this Section.
20 Open the front and rear doors and pull the weatherstrip away from the B-pillar and the lower part of the door apertures.
21 Starting at the top, prise the upper trim panel away from the B-pillar to release the three retaining clips.
22 Prise off the retaining pin securing the panel clip to the seat belt inertia reel.
23 Pull the panel away from the sill to release the ten retaining clips and remove the side sill inner trim panel together with the B-pillar lower trim panel from the car (see illustration). If necessary, the B-pillar lower trim panel can be separated as described previously.
24 Refitting is a reversal of removal.

Front trim panel

25 Pull the weatherstrip away from the lower part of the front door aperture.
26 Carefully prise out the trim cap from the trim panel and undo the retaining nut now exposed (see illustration).
27 Pull up the front edge of the side sill inner trim panel to provide clearance for removal of the front trim panel.
28 Pull the trim panel away from the A-pillar to release the retaining clips and remove it from the car (see illustration).
29 Refitting is a reversal of removal.

Luggage compartment

Upper side trim panel

Note: On models with side airbags, the upper side trim panel is in two sections. On models without side airbags, the side trim panel is a single section. The procedures are the same for both types.

30 On models with side airbags, prise out the plastic cover at the top of the panel and undo the retaining screw now exposed.
31 Extract the trim cap and undo the rear seat belt lower mounting bolt from the rear seat (see illustrations 21.9a and 21.9b).
32 Starting at the top, pull the panel away to release the internal clips, then lift the rear of the panel up to disengage the lower lugs (see illustration).

24.23 Pull the panel away from the sill to release the ten retaining clips

24.26 Prise out the trim cap from the trim panel and undo the retaining nut now exposed

24.28 Pull the trim panel away from the A-pillar to release the retaining clips

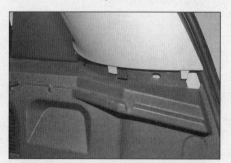

24.32 Pull the upper side trim panel away, then lift the rear of the panel up to disengage the lower lugs (arrowed)

24.37a Undo the lower side trim panel lower retaining screws . . .

24.37b . . . and upper retaining screws (arrowed)

24.38a Pull the panel away to disengage the three retaining clips at the front (arrowed) . . .

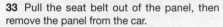

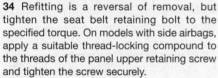

24.38b . . . and the single clip at the rear (arrowed)

24.41 Undo the four tailgate aperture trim panel retaining screws

24.42 Pull the panel away to release the internal clips, and remove the panel from the car

33 Pull the seat belt out of the panel, then remove the panel from the car.

34 Refitting is a reversal of removal, but tighten the seat belt retaining bolt to the specified torque. On models with side airbags, apply a suitable thread-locking compound to the threads of the panel upper retaining screw and tighten the screw securely.

Lower side trim panel

35 Remove the luggage compartment upper side trim panel and the tailgate aperture lower centre trim panel as described elsewhere in this Section.

36 Undo the four push-button nuts at the front of the luggage compartment floor cover and remove the floor cover.

37 Undo the six retaining screws (left-hand side panel) or five retaining screws (right-hand side panel) and unclip the two lower plastic pushbuttons **(see illustrations)**.

38 Pull the panel away to disengage the three retaining clips at the front and the single clip at the rear **(see illustrations)**. If working on the left-hand panel, disconnect the interior light wiring connectors. Remove the panel from the car.

39 Refitting is a reversal of removal.

Tailgate aperture lower centre trim panel

40 Open the tailgate.

41 Undo the four panel retaining screws **(see illustration)**.

42 Pull the panel away to release the internal clips, and remove the panel from the car **(see illustration)**.

43 Refitting is a reversal of removal.

Carpets

44 The passenger compartment floor carpet is in one piece, and is secured at its edges by screws or clips, usually the same fasteners used to secure the various adjoining trim panels.

45 Carpet removal and refitting is reasonably straightforward, but very time-consuming. All adjoining trim panels must be removed first, as must components such as the seats, the centre console and seat belt lower anchorages.

Headlining

46 The headlining is clipped to the roof, and can only be withdrawn once all fittings such as the grab handles, sunvisors, sunroof (if fitted), windscreen and rear quarter windows

25.3a Carefully prise out the rear ashtray/ stowage compartment from the rear of the centre console . . .

and related trim panels have been removed, and the door, tailgate and sunroof aperture sealing strips have been prised clear.

47 Note that headlining removal requires considerable skill and experience if it is to be carried out without damage, and is therefore best entrusted to an expert.

Interior mirror

48 Press the retaining clip at the top of the interior mirror mounting bracket, then carefully release the interior mirror in the downwards direction to remove it from the windscreen.

49 Refitting is the reverse of removal.

25 Centre console – removal and refitting

Removal

1 From under the facia, remove the driver's side lower centre trim panel and passenger's side lower trim panel as described in Section 26.

2 Remove the lower centre storage compartment from the facia as described in Section 26.

3 Carefully prise out the rear ashtray/stowage compartment from the rear of the console. Disconnect the cigarette lighter/accessory socket wiring connector and remove the compartment **(see illustrations)**.

4 Detach the rear audio unit from the centre console and disconnect the wiring connectors **(see illustrations)**.

5 Lift out the trim panel beneath the handbrake

25.3b . . . then disconnect the cigarette lighter/accessory socket wiring connector (arrowed)

25.4a Detach the rear audio unit from the centre console . . .

25.4b . . . and disconnect the wiring connectors

25.5a Lift out the trim panel beneath the handbrake lever . . .

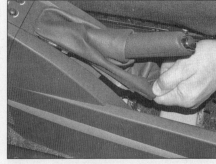

25.5b . . . then unclip the handbrake lever gaiter from the centre console

25.6 Unclip the gear lever gaiter from the console, then fold the gaiter up over the gear lever knob

lever, then unclip the handbrake lever gaiter from the centre console (see illustrations).

6 Unclip the gear lever gaiter, or Easytronic selector lever surround, from the centre console, then fold the gaiter up over the gear lever knob/selector (see illustration).

7 Undo the retaining screws at the front and centre of the centre console (see illustration).

8 Extract the trim caps and undo the two retaining screws at the rear of the console (see illustration).

9 Pull the handbrake lever up as far as it will

go, then manipulate the centre console up and out of its location.

Refitting

10 Refitting is the reverse of removal.

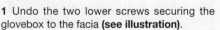
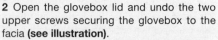

26 Facia panel components – removal and refitting

Glovebox

Removal

1 Undo the two lower screws securing the glovebox to the facia (see illustration).

2 Open the glovebox lid and undo the two upper screws securing the glovebox to the facia (see illustration).

3 Withdraw the glovebox from the facia, disconnect the glovebox light wiring connector

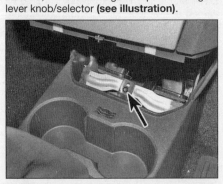

25.7a Undo the retaining screw (arrowed) at the front of the centre console . . .

25.7b . . . and in the centre of the console (arrowed)

25.8 Extract the trim caps and undo the two retaining screws at the rear of the console

26.1 Undo the two lower screws (arrowed) securing the glovebox to the facia

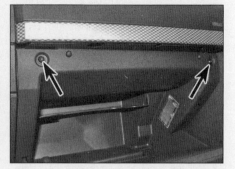

26.2 Open the glovebox lid and undo the two upper screws (arrowed)

26.3 Withdraw the glovebox from the facia and disconnect the glovebox light wiring connector

26.5 Undo the retaining screw and remove the steering column height adjuster handle

26.6 Prise up the upper shroud to release the two retaining tabs at the front, then disengage the rear lugs

26.7a Undo the upper screw each side (arrowed) . . .

26.7b . . . and the lower screw (arrowed) securing the lower shroud to the steering column

26.8a Prise free the circular trim panel around the ignition switch . . .

and remove the glovebox from the car (**see illustration**).

Refitting

4 Refitting is a reversal of removal.

Steering column shrouds

Removal

5 Undo the retaining screw and remove the steering column height adjuster handle (**see illustration**).

6 Carefully prise up the upper shroud to release the two retaining tabs at the front. Disengage the rear lugs and lift off the upper shroud (**see illustration**).

7 Undo the two upper screws and one lower screw securing the lower shroud to the steering column (**see illustrations**).

8 Carefully prise free the circular trim panel around the ignition switch, then remove the lower shroud from the steering column (**see illustrations**).

Refitting

9 Refitting is a reversal of removal.

Driver's side lower trim panel

Removal

10 Remove the steering column shrouds as described previously.

11 Undo the two lower screws securing the lower trim panel to the facia (**see illustration**).

12 Lower the panel at the bottom, disengage the two upper lugs and remove the panel from the facia (**see illustration**).

Refitting

13 Refitting is a reversal of removal.

Driver's side lower centre trim panel

Removal

14 Undo the two screws securing the trim panel to the base of the facia (**see illustration**).

26.8b . . . then remove the lower shroud from the steering column

26.12 Lower the panel at the bottom, then disengage the upper lugs (arrowed)

15 Disengage the rear of the panel from the centre console and remove the panel from under the facia.

Refitting

16 Refitting is a reversal of removal.

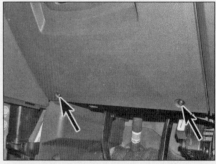

26.11 Undo the two lower screws (arrowed) securing the lower trim panel to the facia

26.14 Undo the two screws (arrowed) securing the lower centre trim panel to the base of the facia

26.18 Pull the panel away from the facia at the top to disengage the upper lugs, then release the panel from the side clips

26.20 Remove the decorative trim strip from the front of the storage compartment

26.21a Undo the two screws (arrowed) . . .

26.21b . . . and remove the storage compartment from the base of the facia

Passenger's side lower trim panel

Removal

17 Remove the glovebox as described previously.

26.23 Undo the two screws (arrowed) securing the ashtray housing to the facia

18 Pull the trim panel away from the facia at the top to disengage the two upper locating lugs, then release the panel from the clips at the side (see illustration). Remove the panel from under the facia.

Refitting

19 Refitting is a reversal of removal.

Lower centre storage compartment

Removal

20 Remove the decorative trim strip from the front of the storage compartment (see illustration).
21 Undo the two screws and remove the storage compartment from the base of the facia (see illustrations).

Refitting

22 Refitting is a reversal of removal.

Ashtray housing

Removal

23 Open the ashtray and undo the two screws securing the housing to the facia (see illustration).
24 Withdraw the ashtray housing from the facia, disconnect the cigarette lighter wiring connector and remove the housing from the car.

Refitting

25 Refitting is a reversal of removal.

Centre switch/vent panel

Removal

26 Remove the driver's side lower trim panel as described previously.
27 Undo the two upper screws securing the instrument panel surround to the facia.
28 Undo the instrument panel surround lower securing screw each side (see illustrations).
29 Pull the surround away from the facia to release the upper and lower retaining clips, and remove the surround (see illustration).
30 Open the glovebox and undo the two screws securing the decorative strip to the facia. Using a plastic spatula, carefully prise free the decorative strip to release the internal retaining clips (see illustrations).
31 Undo the two screws securing the centre switch/vent panel to the facia (see illustration).
32 Push the centre switch vent panel down and pull it away from the facia to release the upper retaining lugs and side retaining clip.

26.28a Undo the instrument panel surround lower securing screw on the right-hand side (arrowed) . . .

26.29 Pull the surround away from the facia to release the upper and lower retaining clips

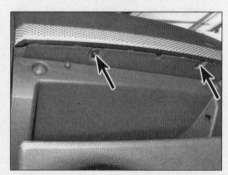

26.28b . . . and on the left-hand side (arrowed)

26.30a Undo the two screws (arrowed) securing the decorative strip to the facia . . .

26.30b ... carefully prise free the decorative strip to release the internal retaining clips

33 Withdraw the panel from the facia, disconnect the wiring connector and remove the panel **(see illustration)**.

Refitting

34 Refitting is a reversal of removal.

Complete facia assembly

Note: *This is an involved operation entailing the removal of numerous components and assemblies, and the disconnection of a multitude of wiring connectors. Make notes on the location of all disconnected wiring, or attach labels to the connectors, to avoid confusion when refitting.*

Removal

35 Disconnect the battery negative terminal (refer to *Disconnecting the battery* in the Reference Chapter).
36 Remove the A-pillar trim panels on both sides as described in Section 24.

26.43a Extract the plastic rivets and remove the footwell air duct on the driver's side ...

26.45b ... and release the fusebox from the facia

26.31 Undo the two screws (arrowed) securing the centre switch/vent panel to the facia

37 Remove the side sill inner trim panel and side sill front trim panel on both sides as described in Section 24.
38 Remove the centre console as described in Section 25.
39 Remove the steering wheel as described in Chapter 10.
40 Remove the heater control assembly as described in Chapter 3.
41 Remove the following facia panels as described previously in this Section:
a) Glovebox.
b) Steering column shrouds.
c) Driver's side lower trim panel.
d) Driver's side lower centre trim panel.
e) Passenger's side lower trim panel.
f) Lower centre storage compartment.
g) Ashtray housing.
h) Centre switch/vent panel.
42 Remove the following components as described in Chapter 12:

26.43b ... and passenger's side

26.46 Prise up the trim at the front of the facia, just sufficiently to gain access to the three upper retaining bolts

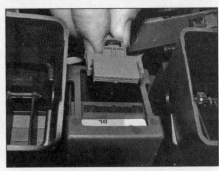

26.33 Withdraw the panel from the facia and disconnect the wiring connector

a) Instrument panel.
b) Clock/multifunction display unit.
c) Lighting switch assembly.
d) Steering column switches.
43 Extract the plastic rivets and remove the footwell air duct on the driver's and passenger's side **(see illustrations)**.
44 On models with electronic climate control, carefully prise out the sun sensor from the top of the facia and disconnect the wiring connector.
45 Remove the fusebox cover, undo the retaining screw and release the fusebox from the facia **(see illustrations)**.
46 Using a plastic spatula, carefully prise up the trim at the front of the facia, just sufficiently to gain access to the three facia upper retaining bolts **(see illustration)**.
47 Undo the following fasteners securing the facia to the mounting brackets **(see illustrations)**:
a) 3 bolts at the top.

26.45a Undo the retaining screw (arrowed) ...

26.47a Undo the 3 facia retaining bolts at the top (arrowed) ...

26.47b . . . 1 bolt (arrowed) at the left-hand and right-hand side . . .

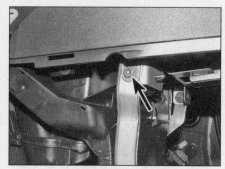

26.47c . . . 2 bolts (one arrowed) at the left-hand and right-hand centre brackets

26.47d . . . 1 bolt each side (arrowed) at the lower left-hand and right-hand corners of the facia

26.55a Undo the upper bolt (arrowed) . . .

26.55b . . . and lower bolt (arrowed) securing the facia crossmember to the A-pillar on each side

b) 1 bolt at the left-hand and right-hand side.

c) 2 bolts at the centre brackets.

d) 1 bolt each side at the lower left-hand and right-hand corners of the facia.

48 With the help of an assistant, carefully lift the facia from its location. Check that all wiring has been disconnected, then remove the facia from the car.

Refitting

49 Refitting is a reversal of removal ensuring that all wiring is correctly reconnected and all mountings securely tightened.

Facia crossmember

Note: *This is an involved operation entailing the disconnection of a multitude of wiring connectors. Make notes on the location of all disconnected wiring, or attach labels to the connectors, to avoid confusion when refitting.*

Removal

50 Remove the facia as described previously in this Section.

51 Remove the steering column as described in Chapter 10.

52 Remove the passenger's airbag as described in Chapter 12.

53 Undo the bolts securing the crossmember centre supports to the floor brackets.

54 Disconnect all remaining earth cables and wiring connections, making careful notes as to their locations. Release the wiring harness's from the relevant cable ties.

55 From outside the car, undo the two bolts securing the crossmember to the A-pillar on each side **(see illustrations)**.

56 With the help of an assistant, check that all wiring has been disconnected, then remove the crossmember from the car.

Refitting

57 Refitting is a reversal of removal ensuring that all wiring is correctly reconnected and all mountings securely tightened.

Chapter 12
Body electrical systems

Contents

Degrees of difficulty

Easy, suitable for novice with little experience | **Fairly easy,** suitable for beginner with some experience | **Fairly difficult,** suitable for competent DIY mechanic | **Difficult,** suitable for experienced DIY mechanic | **Very difficult,** suitable for expert DIY or professional

Specifications

System type . . . . 12 volt negative earth

Bulbs* — **Wattage**

Direction indicator 21
Direction indicator side repeater 5
Foglight:
   Front 55
   Rear 21
Headlight 55
Instrument panel:
   Illumination 2
   Warning lights 1.2
Interior lights. 10
Number plate light 10
Reversing light 21
Sidelight 5
Stop/tail-light 21/5

***** *Note: The bulb wattage information given is for guidance only as no actual wattage information is provided by Vauxhall/Opel. The wattage is stamped on the base or side of the bulb.*

1 General information and precautions

⚠️ **Warning: Before carrying out any work on the electrical system, read through the precautions given in 'Safety first!' at the beginning of this manual, and in Chapter 5A.**

1 The electrical system is of the 12 volt negative earth type. Power for the lights and all electrical accessories is supplied by a lead-acid type battery, which is charged by the engine-driven alternator.

2 This Chapter covers repair and service procedures for the various electrical components not associated with the engine. Information on the battery, alternator and starter motor can be found in Chapter 5A.

3 It should be noted that, prior to working on any component in the electrical system, the battery negative terminal should first be disconnected, to prevent the possibility of electrical short-circuits and/or fires.

Caution: Before proceeding, refer to 'Disconnecting the battery' in the Reference Chapter for further information.

2 Electrical fault finding – general information

Note: *Refer to the precautions given in 'Safety first!' and in Section 1 before starting work. The following tests relate to testing of the main electrical circuits, and should not be used to test delicate electronic circuits (such as the anti-lock braking system or fuel injection system), particularly where an electronic control unit is used.*

General

1 A typical electrical circuit consists of an electrical component, any switches, relays, motors, fuses, fusible links or circuit breakers related to that component, and the wiring and connectors which link the component to both the battery and the vehicle body. To help to pinpoint a problem in an electrical circuit, wiring diagrams are shown at the end of this Chapter.

2 Before attempting to diagnose an electrical fault, first study the appropriate wiring diagram to obtain a complete understanding of the components included in the particular circuit concerned. The possible sources of a fault can be narrowed down by noting if other components related to the circuit are operating properly. If several components or circuits fail at one time, the problem is likely to be related to a shared fuse or earth connection.

3 Electrical problems usually stem from simple causes, such as loose or corroded connections, a faulty earth connection, a blown fuse, a melted fusible link, or a faulty relay (refer to Section 3 for details of testing relays). Inspect the condition of all fuses, wires and connections in a problem circuit before testing the components. Use the wiring diagrams to determine which terminal connections will need to be checked in order to pinpoint the trouble-spot.

4 The basic tools required for electrical fault finding include a circuit tester or voltmeter (a 12 volt bulb with a set of test leads can also be used for certain tests); a self-powered test light (sometimes known as a continuity tester); an ohmmeter (to measure resistance); a battery and set of test leads; and a jumper wire, preferably with a circuit breaker or fuse incorporated, which can be used to bypass suspect wires or electrical components. Before attempting to locate a problem with test instruments, use the wiring diagram to determine where to make the connections.

5 To find the source of an intermittent wiring fault (usually due to a poor or dirty connection, or damaged wiring insulation), a 'wiggle' test can be performed on the wiring. This involves wiggling the wiring by hand to see if the fault occurs as the wiring is moved. It should be possible to narrow down the source of the fault to a particular section of wiring. This method of testing can be used in conjunction with any of the tests described in the following sub-Sections.

6 Apart from problems due to poor connections, two basic types of fault can occur in an electrical circuit – open-circuit, or short-circuit.

7 Open-circuit faults are caused by a break somewhere in the circuit, which prevents current from flowing. An open-circuit fault will prevent a component from working, but will not cause the relevant circuit fuse to blow.

8 Short-circuit faults are caused by a 'short' somewhere in the circuit, which allows the current flowing in the circuit to 'escape' along an alternative route, usually to earth. Short-circuit faults are normally caused by a breakdown in wiring insulation, which allows a feed wire to touch either another wire, or an earthed component such as the bodyshell. A short-circuit fault will normally cause the relevant circuit fuse to blow.

Finding an open-circuit

9 To check for an open-circuit, connect one lead of a circuit tester or voltmeter to either the negative battery terminal or a known good earth.

10 Connect the other lead to a connector in the circuit being tested, preferably nearest to the battery or fuse.

11 Switch on the circuit, bearing in mind that some circuits are live only when the ignition switch is turned to a particular position.

12 If voltage is present (indicated either by the tester bulb lighting or a voltmeter reading, as applicable), this means that the section of the circuit between the relevant connector and the battery is problem-free.

13 Continue to check the remainder of the circuit in the same fashion.

14 When a point is reached at which no voltage is present, the problem must lie between that point and the previous test point with voltage. Most problems can be traced to a broken, corroded or loose connection.

Finding a short-circuit

15 To check for a short-circuit, first disconnect the load(s) from the circuit (loads are the components which draw current from a circuit, such as bulbs, motors, heating elements, etc).

16 Remove the relevant fuse from the circuit, and connect a circuit tester or voltmeter to the fuse connections.

17 Switch on the circuit, bearing in mind that some circuits are live only when the ignition switch is turned to a particular position.

18 If voltage is present (indicated either by the tester bulb lighting or a voltmeter reading, as applicable), this means that there is a short-circuit.

19 If no voltage is present, but the fuse still blows with the load(s) connected, this indicates an internal fault in the load(s).

Finding an earth fault

20 The battery negative terminal is connected to 'earth' – the metal of the engine/transmission unit and the car body – and most systems are wired so that they only receive a positive feed, the current returning via the metal of the car body. This means that the component mounting and the body form part of that circuit. Loose or corroded mountings can therefore cause a range of electrical faults, ranging from total failure of a circuit, to a puzzling partial fault. In particular, lights may shine dimly (especially when another circuit sharing the same earth point is in operation), motors (eg, wiper motors or the radiator cooling fan motor) may run slowly, and the operation of one circuit may have an apparently-unrelated effect on another. Note that on many vehicles, earth straps are used between certain components, such as the engine/transmission and the body, usually where there is no metal-to-metal contact between components, due to flexible rubber mountings, etc.

21 To check whether a component is properly earthed, disconnect the battery, and connect one lead of an ohmmeter to a known good earth point. Connect the other lead to the wire or earth connection being tested. The resistance reading should be zero; if not, check the connection as follows.

22 If an earth connection is thought to be faulty, dismantle the connection, and clean back to bare metal both the bodyshell and the wire terminal or the component earth connection mating surface. Be careful to remove all traces of dirt and corrosion, then use a knife to trim away any paint, so that a clean metal-to-metal joint is made. On reassembly, tighten the joint fasteners securely; if a wire terminal is being refitted, use serrated washers between the terminal

3.2 Release the fusebox cover by pulling it out at the bottom and lifting off

3.3a Lift up the plastic flap on the windscreen cowl panel . . .

3.3b . . . press the tab on the side of the fusebox lid . . .

and the bodyshell, to ensure a clean and secure connection. When the connection is remade, prevent the onset of corrosion in the future by applying a coat of petroleum jelly or silicone-based grease. Alternatively, at regular intervals, spray on a proprietary ignition sealer or a water-dispersant lubricant.

3 Fuses and relays – general information

Fuses

1 The main fuses are located in the fusebox inside the car, adjacent to the glovebox, or below the lighting switch, depending on model year. Additional maxi-fuses are located in the engine compartment , below the windscreen on the left-hand side.

2 To gain access to the main fuses, release the fusebox cover by pulling it out at the bottom and lifting off **(see illustration)**.

3 To gain access to the maxi-fuses in the engine compartment, lift up the plastic flap on the windscreen cowl panel. Press the tab on the side of the fusebox lid and lift off the lid for access to the fuses **(see illustrations)**.

4 To remove a fuse, first switch off the circuit concerned (or the ignition), then pull the fuse out of its terminals **(see illustration)**. The wire within the fuse is clearly visible; if the fuse is blown, it will be broken or melted.

5 Always renew a fuse with one of an identical rating; never use a fuse with a different rating from the original, nor substitute anything else. Never renew a fuse more than once without tracing the source of the trouble. The fuse rating is stamped on top of the fuse; note that the fuses are also colour-coded for easy recognition.

6 If a new fuse blows immediately, find the cause before renewing it again; a short to earth as a result of faulty insulation is most likely. Where a fuse protects more than one circuit, try to isolate the defect by switching on each circuit in turn (if possible) until the fuse blows again. Always carry a supply of spare fuses of each relevant rating on the vehicle, a spare of each rating should be clipped into the base of the fusebox.

3.3c . . . and lift off the lid for access to the fuses

Relays

7 Most of the relays are located in the engine compartment relay box situated below the windscreen on the left-hand side. To gain access, remove the windscreen cowl panel as described in Chapter 11, then undo the three screws and lift off the relay box cover. Remove the relevant relay by pulling it out of its contacts.

8 On some models, additional relays are located in a second relay box attached to the battery tray at the front of the engine compartment.

0 If a circuit or system controlled by a relay develops a fault and the relay is suspect, operate the system; if the relay is functioning, it should be possible to hear it click as it is energised. If this is the case, the fault lies with the components or wiring of the system. If

4.3a Depress the retaining clips (arrowed) and slide out the switch . . .

3.4 Switch off the circuit concerned (or the ignition), then pull the fuse out of its terminals

the relay is not being energised, then either the relay is not receiving a main supply or a switching voltage, or the relay itself is faulty. Testing is by the substitution of a known good unit, but be careful; while some relays are identical in appearance and in operation, others look similar but perform different functions.

4 Switches – removal and refitting

Note: *Disconnect the battery negative terminal (refer to 'Disconnecting the battery' in the Reference Chapter) before removing any switch, and reconnect the terminal after refitting.*

Ignition switch/ steering column lock

1 Refer to Chapter 10.

Steering column switches

2 Remove the steering column shrouds as described in Chapter 11.

3 Depress the retaining clips, and release the relevant switch assembly from the column bracket. Disconnect the wiring connector, and remove the switch assembly from the vehicle **(see illustrations)**. If necessary, remove the opposite switch assembly in the same way.

4 Refitting is a reversal of the removal procedure, making sure the wiring connector is fitted correctly.

4.3b . . . then release the securing clip (arrowed) and disconnect the wiring connector

4.5a Press the switch knob in and turn it to the appropriate position . . .

4.5b . . . then withdraw the switch assembly from the facia

4.10a Depress the tabs on each side of the switch using a screwdriver . . .

4.10b . . . then withdraw the switch from the panel

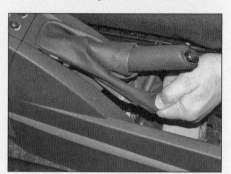

4.13 Unclip the cover from around the handbrake lever . . .

Lighting switch

5 With the light switch knob in the off position, press the knob in and turn it to the AUTO position (vehicles with automatic dipped beam activation), or to the vertical position (sidelights 'on'). The switch assembly internal catch is now unlocked and the switch assembly can be withdrawn from the facia (see illustrations). Once the switch is released, turn the switch off.

6 Release the locking catch and disconnect the switch wiring connector.

7 Note that the switch assembly cannot be dismantled; if any of its functions are faulty, the complete assembly must be renewed.

8 Reconnect the wiring connector and push the switch back into the facia.

Hazard warning light switch and seat heater switches

9 The hazard warning light switch and, where fitted, the seat heater switches are located in the centre switch/vent panel in the facia. Begin by removing the centre switch/vent panel as described in Chapter 11.

10 With the panel on the bench, use a screwdriver or similar tool inserted down the side of the switch from the rear, to depress the tabs on each side of the switch. With the tabs released, withdraw the switch from the panel (see illustrations). Note that the hazard warning light switch and, where fitted, the seat heater switches are a single assembly and are not available separately.

11 Refit the switch by pushing it back into the vent panel until the tabs engage, then refit the panel as described in Chapter 11.

Heated rear window switch and blower motor switch

12 The heated rear window and blower motor switches are an integral part of the heater control assembly. Removal and refitting procedures are contained in Chapter 3.

Handbrake warning light switch

13 Lift out the trim panel from the base of the centre console, then unclip the cover from around the handbrake lever (see illustration).

14 Disconnect the wiring connector, then undo the retaining bolt and remove the switch from the handbrake lever mounting bracket (see illustration).

15 Install the new switch, securely tightening its retaining bolt and refit the wiring connector. Refit the handbrake lever cover and console trim panel.

Stop-light switch

16 Refer to Chapter 9.

Courtesy light switch

17 Open the relevant door, then undo the switch retaining screw. Withdraw the switch from the pillar, disconnecting its wiring connector as it becomes accessible (see illustrations). Tie a

4.14 Undo the retaining bolt (arrowed) and remove the switch from the handbrake lever bracket

4.17a Undo the retaining screw (arrowed) . . .

4.17b . . . and withdraw the switch from the door pillar, then disconnect its wiring connector

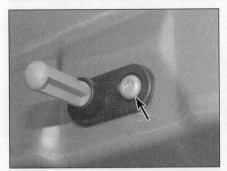

4.20 Undo the retaining screw (arrowed) and withdraw the switch

4.22a Carefully prise out the switch assembly, taking care not to damage the door trim panel . . .

4.22b . . . then disconnect the wiring connector and remove the switch

4.30 Carefully release the switch cover from both horn switches in the steering wheel

4.31a Disconnect the wiring connector (arrowed) . . .

4.31b . . . and remove both horn switches as an assembly

piece of string to the wiring, to prevent it falling back into the door pillar.

18 Refitting is a reverse of the removal procedure.

Luggage area light switch

19 The luggage area light switch is fitted to the bottom of the tailgate.

20 Undo the retaining screw, then withdraw the switch and disconnect it from its wiring connector **(see illustration)**. Tie a piece of string to the wiring, to prevent it falling back into the tailgate.

21 Refitting is a reverse of the removal procedure.

Electric window switches

22 Carefully prise out the switch assembly, taking care not to damage the door trim panel and remove the switch assembly. Disconnect the wiring connector and remove the switch **(see illustrations)**.

23 Refitting is the reverse of removal, ensuring that the wiring is correctly routed inside the door pocket.

Electric mirror switch

24 Carefully prise out the switch from the door trim panel, then disconnect the switch wiring connector, and remove the switch from the vehicle.

25 Refitting is the reverse of removal.

Electric sunroof switch

26 Carefully prise the sunroof switch out of position, and disconnect it from its wiring connector.

27 When refitting, connect the wiring connector, and clip the switch back into position.

Air conditioning system switch

28 The air conditioning system control switch is an integral part of the heating/ventilation control unit, and cannot be removed. Should the switch become faulty, the complete control unit assembly must be renewed (see Chapter 3).

Horn switches

29 Remove the driver's airbag as described in Section 22.

30 Using a small screwdriver, carefully release the switch cover from both horn switches in the steering wheel **(see illustration)**.

31 Unclip the switches from the steering wheel, disconnect the wiring connector and remove both switches as an assembly **(see illustrations)**.

32 Refit the wiring connector, the switches and the switch covers, then refit the airbag as described in Section 22.

Radio remote control switches

33 Remove the driver's airbag as described in Section 22.

34 Undo the two screws securing each switch unit to the steering wheel **(see illustration)**.

35 Release the switches from their locations in the steering wheel and remove both switches as an assembly **(see illustration)**.

36 Refit the switches then refit the airbag as described in Section 22.

4.34 Undo the two screws (arrowed) securing each remote control switch unit to the steering wheel . . .

4.35 . . . then remove both switches as an assembly

5.8 Disconnect the wiring connector . . .

5 Bulbs (exterior lights) – renewal

General

1 Whenever a bulb is renewed, note the following points:
a) Make sure the switch is in the OFF position for the bulb you are working on.
b) Remember that if the light has just been in use, the bulb may be extremely hot.
c) Always check the bulb contacts and holder, ensuring that there is clean metal-to-metal contact between the bulb and its live(s) and earth. Clean off any corrosion or dirt before fitting a new bulb.
d) Wherever bayonet-type bulbs are fitted, ensure that the live contact(s) bear firmly against the bulb contact.

5.14a Remove the sidelight bulbholder from the headlight unit . . .

5.16 Release the front indicator bulbholder from the headlight unit . . .

5.9 . . . release the retaining clip and withdraw the headlight bulb

e) Always ensure that the new bulb is of the correct rating, and that it is completely clean before fitting it; this applies particularly to headlight/foglight bulbs.

Halogen headlight – pre-2005 model year

Note 1: If working on the right-hand headlight unit, remove the air cleaner assembly and intake duct (see Chapter 4A or 4B). If working on the left-hand headlight unit, remove the relay box from the battery tray. Even with the adjacent components removed, access to the bulbs is extremely limited, if not impossible, and it is recommended that the relevant headlight unit is removed for bulb renewal (see Section 7).

Note 2: The lower bulb in the headlight unit is the dipped beam bulb and the upper bulb is the main beam bulb.

5.14b . . . and withdraw the capless bulb

5.17 . . . and remove the bayonet-fit bulb from the bulbholder

Dipped beam

2 Remove the cover from the rear of the headlight unit.
3 Rotate the bulbholder anti-clockwise and remove it from the headlight unit.
4 Withdraw the bulb from the bulbholder. When handling the new bulb, use a tissue or clean cloth to avoid touching the glass with the fingers; moisture and grease from the skin can cause blackening and rapid failure of this type of bulb. If the glass is accidentally touched, wipe it clean using methylated spirit.
5 Fit the new bulb to the bulbholder then insert the bulbholder into the headlight unit so that the two lugs on the bulb base engage with the recesses in the headlight unit.
6 Turn the bulbholder fully clockwise, then refit the cover to the rear of the headlight unit. Refit the headlight unit (Section 7), or any components removed for access.

Main beam

7 Remove the cover from the rear of the headlight unit.
8 Disconnect the wiring connector from the bulb **(see illustration)**.
9 Push the retaining spring clip forward then swivel it to one side to disengage the retaining lugs. Withdraw the bulb from the rear of the headlight unit **(see illustration)**.
10 When handling the new bulb, use a tissue or clean cloth to avoid touching the glass with the fingers; moisture and grease from the skin can cause blackening and rapid failure of this type of bulb. If the glass is accidentally touched, wipe it clean using methylated spirit.
11 Install the new bulb, ensuring that its locating tabs are correctly located in the headlight unit cut-outs. Secure the bulb with the spring clip and reconnect the wiring connector.
12 Refit the cover to the rear of the headlight unit. Refit the headlight unit (Section 7), or any components removed for access.

Front sidelight

13 Remove the cover behind the headlight main beam bulb.
14 Withdraw the sidelight bulbholder from the rear of the headlight unit. The bulb is of the capless (push-fit) type, and can be removed by simply pulling it out of the bulbholder **(see illustrations)**.
15 Refit the cover to the rear of the headlight unit. Refit the headlight unit (Section 7), or any components removed for access.

Front indicator

16 Twist the indicator bulbholder anti-clockwise, and remove it from the rear of the headlight unit **(see illustration)**.
17 The bulb is a bayonet-fit in the holder, and can be removed by pressing it and twisting in an anti-clockwise direction **(see illustration)**.
18 Refitting is a reverse of the removal procedure. On completion, Refit the headlight unit (Section 7), or any components removed for access.

5.19 Turn the plastic cover anti-clockwise and remove it from the rear of the headlight unit

5.20 Push the bulb base sideways and withdraw the bulb from the headlight unit

5.21 Hold the bulb by its base and disconnect the wiring connector

Halogen headlight – 2005 model year onwards

Note 1: *If working on the right-hand headlight unit, remove the air cleaner assembly and intake duct (see Chapter 4A or 4B). If working on the left-hand headlight unit, remove the relay box from the battery tray. Even with the adjacent components removed, access to the bulbs is extremely limited, if not impossible, and it is recommended that the relevant headlight unit is removed for bulb renewal (see Section 7).*

Note 2: *The lower bulb in the headlight unit is the dipped beam bulb and the upper bulb is the main beam bulb.*

Dipped beam

19 Turn the plastic cover anti-clockwise and remove it from the rear of the headlight unit **(see illustration)**.

20 Push the bulb base sideways and withdraw the bulb from the headlight unit **(see illustration)**.

21 Hold the bulb by its base and disconnect the wiring connector **(see illustration)**. When handling the new bulb, use a tissue or clean cloth to avoid touching the glass with the fingers; moisture and grease from the skin can cause blackening and rapid failure of this type of bulb. If the glass is accidentally touched, wipe it clean using methylated spirit.

22 Fit the new bulb to the headlight unit ensuring that the tab on the bulb base engages with the slot in the headlight unit. Reconnect the wiring connector.

5.24 Turn the plastic cover anti-clockwise and remove it from the rear of the headlight unit

23 Refit the cover to the rear of the headlight unit. Refit the headlight unit (Section 7), or any components removed for access.

Main beam

24 Turn the plastic cover anti-clockwise and remove it from the rear of the headlight unit **(see illustration)**.

25 Disconnect the wiring connector from the rear of the bulb **(see illustration)**.

26 Disengage the legs of the retaining spring clip from the lugs on the bulb by pushing the clip down and swivelling it to the side. Lift the bulb out of the headlight unit **(see illustrations)**. When handling the new bulb, use a tissue or clean cloth to avoid touching the glass with the fingers; moisture and grease from the skin can cause blackening and rapid failure of this type of bulb. If the glass is accidentally touched, wipe it clean using methylated spirit.

5.25 Disconnect the wiring connector from the rear of the bulb

27 Fit the new bulb to the headlight unit and secure with the spring clip. Reconnect the wiring connector.

28 Refit the cover to the rear of the headlight unit. Refit the headlight unit (Section 7), or any components removed for access.

Front sidelight

29 Remove the main beam plastic cover from the rear of the headlight unit **(see illustration 5.24)**.

30 Withdraw the sidelight bulbholder from the rear of the headlight unit. The bulb is of the capless (push-fit) type, and can be removed by simply pulling it out of the bulbholder **(see illustrations)**.

31 Refitting is a reverse of the removal procedure. On completion, Refit the headlight unit (Section 7), or any components removed for access.

5.26a Disengage the legs of the retaining spring clip from the lugs on the bulb . . .

5.26b . . . then lift the bulb out of the headlight unit

5.30a Remove the sidelight bulbholder from the headlight unit . . .

5.30b . . . and withdraw the capless bulb

5.32 Release the front indicator bulbholder from the headlight unit . . .

5.33 . . . and remove the bayonet-fit bulb from the bulbholder

Front indicator

32 Twist the indicator bulbholder anti-clockwise, and remove it from the rear of the headlight unit **(see illustration)**.

33 The bulb is a bayonet-fit in the holder, and can be removed by pressing it and twisting in an anti-clockwise direction **(see illustration)**.

34 Refit the cover to the rear of the headlight unit. Refit the headlight unit (Section 7), or any components removed for access.

Xenon headlight

⚠️ **Warning: Xenon dipped beam headlights operate at very high voltage. Do not touch the associated wiring when the headlights are switched on.**

Note: *On the Xenon type headlight unit, the lower bulb is the dipped beam bulb and the upper bulb is the main beam bulb.*

Dipped beam

35 Remove the headlight unit as described in Section 7.

36 Undo the three screws and remove the safety cover from the rear of the headlight.

37 Compress the legs of the retaining spring clip and pivot the clip off the xenon starter unit and bulb assembly. Withdraw the starter unit and bulb assembly from the rear of the headlight unit.

38 Disconnect the wiring connector and remove the xenon starter unit and bulb assembly. Note that the starter unit and bulb are a single unit and cannot be separated.

39 Refitting is the reverse of the removal

procedure. On completion, refit the headlight unit as described in Section 7.

Main beam

40 Remove the headlight unit as described in Section 7.

41 Remove the cover from the rear of the headlight unit.

42 Disconnect the wiring connector from the bulb.

43 Push the retaining spring clip forward then swivel it to one side to disengage the retaining lugs. Withdraw the bulb from the rear of the headlight unit.

44 When handling the new bulb, use a tissue or clean cloth to avoid touching the glass with the fingers; moisture and grease from the skin can cause blackening and rapid failure of this type of bulb. If the glass is accidentally touched, wipe it clean using methylated spirit.

45 Install the new bulb, ensuring that its locating tabs are correctly located in the headlight unit cut-outs. Secure the bulb with the spring clip and reconnect the wiring connector.

46 Refit the cover to the rear of the unit, then refit the headlight unit as described in Section 7.

Front sidelight

Note: *If working on the right-hand headlight unit, remove the air cleaner assembly and intake duct (see Chapter 4A or 4B). If working on the left-hand headlight unit, remove the relay box from the battery tray. Even with the adjacent components removed, access to the bulbs is extremely limited, if not impossible, and it is recommended that the relevant headlight unit is removed for bulb renewal (see Section 7).*

47 Remove the main beam cover from the rear of the headlight unit.

48 Withdraw the sidelight bulbholder from the rear of the headlight unit. The bulb is of the capless (push-fit) type, and can be removed by simply pulling it out of the bulbholder.

49 Refitting is the reverse of the removal procedure, ensuring that the bulbholder is fully engaged. On completion, refit the headlight unit as described in Section 7.

Front indicator

Note: *If working on the right-hand headlight unit, remove the air cleaner assembly and intake duct (see Chapter 4A or 4B). If working on the left-hand headlight unit, remove the relay box from the battery tray. Even with the adjacent components removed, access to the bulbs is extremely limited, if not impossible, and it is recommended that the relevant headlight unit is removed for bulb renewal (see Section 7).*

50 Twist the bulbholder anti-clockwise, and remove it from the rear of the headlight unit.

51 The bulb is a bayonet-fit in the holder, and can be removed by pressing it and twisting in an anti-clockwise direction.

52 Refitting is a reverse of the removal procedure. On completion, refit the headlight unit (Section 7), or any components removed for access.

Indicator side repeater

53 Carefully prise the rear edge of the indicator side repeater light out from the wing, if necessary using a suitable plastic wedge, taking great care not damage the painted finish of the wing **(see illustration)**.

5.53 Carefully prise the rear edge of the side repeater light out from the wing

5.54a Withdraw the light unit from the wing . . .

5.54b . . . pull the bulbholder out of the light unit . . .

5.54c . . . and withdraw the capless bulb

5.57 Twist the cover and free it from the foglight unit

5.58 Release the spring clip and withdraw the foglight bulb from the light unit

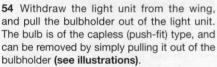

5.59 Disconnect the wiring connector and remove the bulb

5.64a Undo the two upper screws (arrowed) . . .

5.64b . . . and two lower screws (arrowed)

54 Withdraw the light unit from the wing, and pull the bulbholder out of the light unit. The bulb is of the capless (push-fit) type, and can be removed by simply pulling it out of the bulbholder **(see illustrations)**.

55 Refitting is a reverse of the removal procedure.

Front foglight

56 Firmly apply the handbrake, then jack up the front of the vehicle and support it securely on axle stands (see *Jacking and vehicle support*).

57 Twist the cover and free it from the foglight unit **(see illustration)**.

58 Release the spring clip and withdraw the foglight bulb from the light unit **(see illustration)**.

59 Disconnect the wiring connector and remove the bulb **(see illustration)**.

60 When handling the new bulb, use a tissue or clean cloth to avoid touching the glass with the fingers; moisture and grease from the skin can cause blackening and rapid failure of this type of bulb. If the glass is accidentally touched, wipe it clean using methylated spirit.

61 Connect the wiring connector to the new bulb.

62 Insert the new bulb, making sure it is correctly located, and secure it in position with the spring clip.

63 Refit the cover to the rear of the unit then lower the vehicle to the ground.

Rear light cluster

64 Open the tailgate and undo the four retaining screws from the rear light unit **(see illustrations)**.

65 Withdraw the light unit from the rear wing and disconnect the wiring connector **(see illustration)**. Take care not to allow the wiring harness to fall back inside the rear wing.

66 Undo the two screws securing the bulbholder to the light unit **(see illustration)**.

67 Press the two tabs at the base of the bulb-holder and disengage the lower part of the bulbholder from the light unit **(see illustration)**.

68 Release the bulbholder upper retaining tab from the light unit and remove the bulbholder **(see illustration)**.

5.65 Withdraw the light unit from the rear wing and disconnect the wiring connector

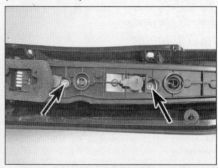

5.66 Undo the two screws (arrowed) securing the bulbholder to the light unit

5.67 Press the two tabs (arrowed) and disengage the lower part of the bulbholder from the light unit

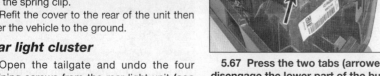

5.68 Release the upper retaining tab (arrowed) from the light unit and remove the bulbholder

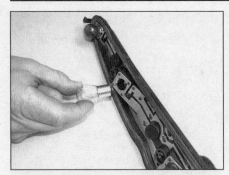

5.69 Remove the relevant bayonet-fit bulb from the bulbholder

5.72 Twist the bulbholder anti-clockwise, and remove it from the light unit

5.73 The bulb is a bayonet-fit in the holder

5.75 Carefully prise the light unit out from the tailgate

5.76a Twist the bulbholder to remove it from the light unit . . .

5.76b . . . and remove the push-fit bulb

69 The relevant bulb can then be renewed; all bulbs have a bayonet-fitting (see illustration). Note that the stop/tail-light bulb has offset locating pins, to prevent it being installed incorrectly.

70 Refitting is a reverse of the removal procedure, ensuring that the light unit locates securely into position.

Rear foglight

71 Remove the rear light cluster as described previously in paragraphs 64 and 65.

72 Twist the bulbholder anti-clockwise, and remove it from the light unit (see illustration).

73 The bulb is a bayonet-fit in the holder (see illustration).

74 Refitting is a reverse of the removal procedure.

Number plate light

75 Using a small flat-bladed screwdriver,

carefully prise the light unit out from the tailgate (see illustration).

76 Twist the bulbholder to remove it from the light unit, and remove the push-fit bulb (see illustration).

77 Refitting is a reverse of the removal procedure.

High-level stop-light

78 The high-level stop-light bulbs are of the LED (light emitting diode) type and cannot be individually renewed. Remove the complete light unit as described in Section 7.

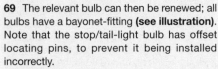

6 Bulbs (interior lights) – renewal

General

1 Refer to Section 5, paragraph 1.

Front courtesy light

Without map reading lights

2 Using a suitable screwdriver, carefully prise the light unit out of position, and release the bulb from the light unit contacts (see illustrations).

3 Install the new bulb, ensuring that it is securely held in position by the contacts, and clip the light unit back into position.

With map reading lights

4 Using a small flat-bladed screwdriver, carefully prise the light unit out from its surround. Disconnect the wiring connector, and remove the light (see illustration).

5 Unclip the lens from the light unit, and release the bulb from its contacts (see illustrations).

6 Install the new bulb, ensuring that it is securely held in position by the contacts, and clip the lens back into position.

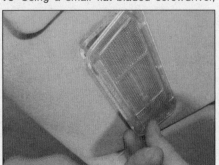

6.2a Carefully prise the courtesy light unit out of position . . .

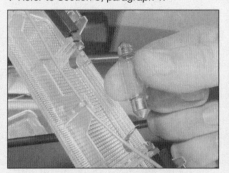

6.2b . . . and release the festoon bulb from its wiring contacts

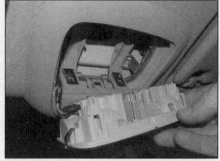

6.4 Release the interior light unit from the surround trim

6.5a Unclip the lens from the light unit . . .

6.5b . . . and remove the capless bulb

6.11a Carefully prise the light unit out of position . . .

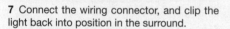
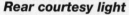

6.11b . . . and release the bulb from the light unit contacts

6.14 Removing an instrument panel illumination bulb

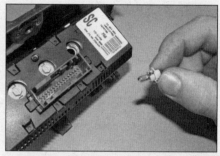

6.18 Twist the relevant bulbholder anti-clockwise, and withdraw it from the rear of the display unit

7 Connect the wiring connector, and clip the light back into position in the surround.

Rear courtesy light

8 Using a suitable screwdriver, carefully prise the right-hand side of the light unit out of position, and withdraw the light unit.
9 Release the locking plate and disconnect the wiring connector. Remove the relevant bulb from the light unit.
10 Install the new bulb, ensuring that it is securely held in position by the contacts. Refit the wiring connector and locking plate, then clip the light unit back into position.

Luggage compartment light and glovebox light

11 Using a suitable screwdriver, carefully prise the light unit out of position, and release the bulb from the light unit contacts **(see illustrations)**.
12 Install the new bulb, ensuring that it is securely held in position by the contacts, and clip the light unit back into position.

Instrument illumination and warning lights

13 Remove the instrument panel as described in Section 9.
14 Twist the relevant bulbholder anti-clockwise, and withdraw it from the rear of the panel **(see illustration)**.
15 All bulbs are integral with their holders. Be very careful to ensure that the new bulbs are of the correct rating, the same as those removed.
16 Refit the bulbholder to the rear of the

instrument panel, then refit the instrument panel as described in Section 9.

Clock illumination and multi-function display illumination

17 Remove the clock/multi-function display unit as described in Section 10.
18 Twist the relevant bulbholder anti-clockwise, and withdraw it from the rear of the display unit **(see illustration)**. The bulbs are integral with their holders.
19 Refit the bulbholder to the rear of the unit, then refit the unit as described in Section 10.

Heater control panel illumination

20 Withdraw the heater control panel as described in Chapter 3, so that access to the front of the panel can be gained. Note that there is no need to remove the panel

6.22 Carefully prise free and remove the cover over the heater control panel illumination bulbs

completely; the control cables can be left attached.
21 Pull off the control knob for the heater blower motor.
22 Carefully prise free and remove the cover over the illumination bulbs **(see illustration)**.
23 Withdraw the relevant bulb from the control panel. To aid removal, use a tight-fitting piece of rubber or plastic tube pushed over the bulb **(see illustration)**.
24 Refit the bulb cover and blower motor knob, then refit the control panel as described in Chapter 3.

Switch illumination

25 All the switches are fitted with illumination bulbs; some are also fitted with a bulb to show when the circuit concerned is operating. These bulbs are an integral part of the switch assembly, and cannot be obtained separately.

6.23 Withdraw the relevant bulb from the control panel

7.2a Undo the upper bolts (arrowed) . . .

7.2b . . . and the lower bolt (arrowed) . . .

7.2c . . . withdraw the headlight unit . . .

7.2d . . . and disconnect the wiring connector

7.3a Remove the cover from the rear of the headlight unit . . .

7.3b . . . rotate the adjustment motor clockwise to free it from the headlight unit . . .

7 Exterior light units – removal and refitting

Note: *Disconnect the battery negative terminal (refer to 'Disconnecting the battery' in the Reference Chapter) before removing any light unit, and reconnect the terminal after refitting.*

Headlight

⚠️ *Warning: Xenon dipped beam headlights operate at very high voltage. Do not touch the associated wiring when the headlights are switched on.*

1 Remove the front bumper as described in Chapter 11.
2 Undo the three retaining bolts and withdraw the headlight unit from the vehicle. Disconnect the wiring connectors from rear of the headlight unit as it is withdrawn **(see illustrations)**.

7.3c . . . then unclip the balljoint from the rear of the light reflector and disconnect the wiring connector

3 On models fitted with halogen type headlight units, the headlight beam adjustment motor can be removed and refitted as follows. On all other headlight types the motor is an integral part of the light unit. Remove the cover from the rear of the headlight unit, then rotate the adjustment motor clockwise to free the motor from the rear of the headlight unit. Unclip the balljoint from the rear of the light reflector and disconnect the wiring connector **(see illustrations)**.
4 On refitting, align the motor balljoint with the light unit socket, and clip it into position. Engage the motor assembly with the light unit, and twist it anti-clockwise to secure it in position.
5 Refitting is a reverse of the removal procedure. On completion, check the headlight beam alignment using the information given in Section 8.

Front indicator light

6 The front direction indicator lights are

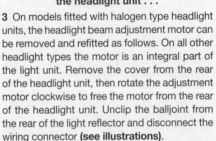

7.11a Front foglight lower retaining screws (arrowed) . . .

integral with the headlight units. Removal and refitting is as described above.

Indicator side repeater light

7 Carefully prise the rear edge of the indicator side repeater light out from the wing, if necessary using a suitable plastic wedge, taking great care not damage the painted finish of the wing **(see illustration 5.53)**.
8 Withdraw the light unit from the wing, and disconnect its wiring connector. Tie a piece of string to the wiring, to prevent it falling back into the wing.
9 On refitting, connect the wiring connector, and clip the light unit back into position.

Front foglight

10 Remove the front bumper as described in Chapter 11.
11 Undo the three foglight retaining screws and remove the light unit from the bumper **(see illustrations)**.

7.11b . . . and upper retaining screw (arrowed)

12 Refit the light unit to the bumper, and securely tighten its retaining screws.
13 Secure the front bumper in position, then adjust the foglight aim through the hole in the bumper to the side of the foglight.

Rear light cluster

14 Open the tailgate and remove the four retaining screws from the rear light unit **(see illustrations 5.64a and 5.64b)**.
15 Withdraw the light unit from the rear wing and disconnect the wiring connector **(see illustration 5.65)**. Take care not to allow the wiring harness to fall back inside the rear wing.
16 Refitting is the reverse of the removal sequence, ensuring that the light unit locates securely into position.

Number plate light

17 Using a small flat-bladed screwdriver, carefully prise the light out from the tailgate and disconnect it from the wiring connectors **(see illustration 5.75)**.
18 Refitting is a reversal of removal.

High-level stop-light

19 Open the tailgate and undo the two high-level stop-light retaining bolts **(see illustration)**.
20 Withdraw the light unit from the tailgate, disconnect the wiring connector and tailgate washer hose, then remove the light unit **(see illustration)**.
21 Refitting is a reversal of removal.

8 Headlight beam alignment – general information

1 Accurate adjustment of the headlight beam is only possible using optical beam-setting equipment, and this work should therefore be carried out by a Vauxhall/Opel dealer or suitably-equipped workshop.
2 For reference, the headlights can be adjusted using the adjuster assemblies fitted to the top of each light unit. The inner adjuster alters the horizontal position of the beam. The outer adjuster alters the vertical aim of the beam.
3 Some models have an electrically-operated headlight beam adjustment system, controlled

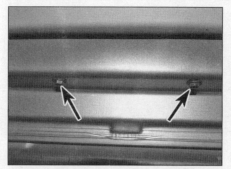
7.19 Undo the two high-level stop-light retaining bolts (arrowed)

via a switch in the facia. The recommended settings are as follows:
0 *Front seat(s) occupied*
1 *All seats occupied*
2 *All seats occupied, and load in luggage compartment*
3 *Driver's seat occupied and load in the luggage compartment*
Note: *When adjusting the headlight aim, ensure that the switch is set to position 0.*

9 Instrument panel – removal and refitting

Note: *The instrument panel is a complete assembly, and no dismantling of the instrument panel is possible. The only additional work possible is the renewal of a bulb (see Section 6).*

9.4a Undo the instrument panel surround lower securing screw on the right-hand side (arrowed) . . .

9.5 Pull the surround away from the facia to release the upper and lower retaining clips

9.6a Undo the instrument panel lower securing screw on the right-hand side (arrowed) . . .

7.20 Withdraw the light unit from the tailgate and disconnect the wiring connector and tailgate washer hose

Removal

1 Disconnect the battery negative terminal (refer to *Disconnecting the battery* in the Reference Chapter).
2 Remove the steering column shrouds and the driver's side lower trim panel as described in Chapter 11.
3 Undo the two upper screws securing the instrument panel surround to the facia.
4 Undo the instrument panel surround lower securing screw each side **(see illustrations)**.
5 Pull the surround away from the facia to release the upper and lower retaining clips, and remove the surround **(see illustration)**.
6 Unscrew the two retaining screws from the base of the instrument panel **(see illustrations)**.
7 Depress the panel upper retaining clip, and withdraw the instrument panel from the facia.

9.4b . . . and on the left-hand side (arrowed)

9.6b . . . and on the left-hand side (arrowed)

9.7a Depress the panel upper retaining clip, and withdraw the instrument panel from the facia

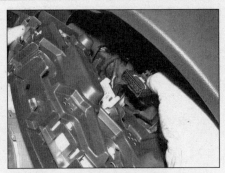

9.7b Disconnect the wiring connector and remove the panel

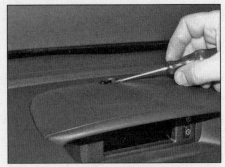

10.2a Carefully prise up the trim cap from the centre of the facia . . .

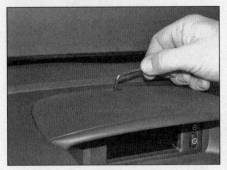

10.2b . . . and undo the retaining screw beneath

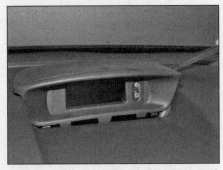

10.3 Carefully prise the display unit out of the facia

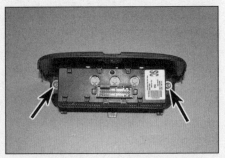

10.5 Undo the two retaining screws (arrowed) and separate the display unit from the surround

Disconnect the wiring connector and remove the panel (see illustrations).

Refitting

8 Refitting is a reversal of removal.

10 Clock/multi-function display components – removal and refitting

Removal

1 Disconnect the battery negative terminal (refer to *Disconnecting the battery* in the Reference Chapter).
2 Carefully prise up the trim cap from the centre of the facia and undo the retaining screw below (see illustrations).
3 Using a plastic spatula or similar tool,

carefully prise the display unit out of the facia (see illustration).
4 Disconnect the wiring connector and remove the unit from the car.
5 If necessary, undo the two retaining screws and separate the display unit from the surround (see illustration).

Refitting

6 Refitting is a reversal of removal.

11 Horn – removal and refitting

Note: *Depending on engine type and model year, the horn may be located above the radiator on the right-hand side, or under the front bumper on the left-hand side.*

Removal

1 If the horn is located under the front bumper, firmly apply the handbrake, then jack up the front of the vehicle and support it securely on axle stands (see *Jacking and vehicle support*).
2 Undo the retaining nut and remove the horn, disconnecting its wiring connectors as they become accessible (see illustration).

Refitting

3 Refitting is the reverse of removal.

12 Wiper arm – removal and refitting

Windscreen wiper arm

Removal

1 Operate the wiper motor, then switch it off so that the wiper arm returns to the at-rest (parked) position.

HAYNES HiNT *Stick a piece of masking tape along the edge of the wiper blade, to use as an alignment aid on refitting.*

2 Extract the wiper arm spindle nut cover, slacken and remove the spindle nut and collect the washer (see illustrations).
3 Lift the blade off the glass, and pull the wiper arm off its spindle (see illustration).

11.2 Horn retaining nut (arrowed)

12.2a Extract the wiper arm spindle nut cover . . .

12.2b ... then undo the spindle nut and collect the washer

12.3 Lift the blade off the glass, and pull the wiper arm off its spindle

12.8 Tailgate wiper arm spindle nut

If necessary, the arm can be levered off the spindle using a suitable flat-bladed screwdriver. **Note:** *If both windscreen wiper arms are to be removed at the same time, mark them for identification. The arms are not interchangeable.*

Refitting

4 Ensure that the wiper arm and spindle splines are clean and dry, then refit the arm to the spindle, aligning the wiper blade with the tape fitted on removal.

5 If the basic wiper arm setting dimension has been lost, position the arms as follows:

Driver's side (lower arm) – position the blade approximately 2.5 cm above the rubber lip of the windscreen cowl panel.
Passenger's side (upper arm) – position the blade approximately 6.0 cm above the rubber lip of the windscreen cowl panel.

6 Refit the spindle washer and nut, tightening the nut securely, then refit the nut cover back in position.

Tailgate wiper arm

Removal

7 Operate the wiper motor, then switch it off so that the wiper arm returns to the at-rest (parked) position.

8 Lift up the wiper arm spindle nut cover, then slacken and remove the spindle nut **(see illustration)**.

9 Lift the blade off the glass, and pull the wiper arm off its spindle. If necessary, the arm can be levered off the spindle using a suitable flat-bladed screwdriver.

Refitting

10 Ensure that the wiper arm and spindle splines are clean and dry, then refit the arm to the spindle, aligning the wiper blade parallel with the lower edge of the tailgate window.

11 Refit the spindle nut, tightening the nut securely, then refit the nut cover back in position.

13 Windscreen wiper motor and linkage – removal and refitting

Removal

1 Disconnect the battery negative terminal (refer to *Disconnecting the battery* in the Reference Chapter).

2 Remove the windscreen cowl panel and the bulkhead closure panel as described in Chapter 11.

3 Lift off the cover over the brake hydraulic fluid reservoir, then extract the horseshoe-shaped clip securing the reservoir to the mounting bracket. Withdraw the reservoir from the mounting bracket and place it to one side **(see illustrations)**.

4 Disconnect the wiper motor wiring connector, then release the wiring harness from the bracket on the scuttle **(see illustration)**.

5 Undo the six bolts securing the wiper motor and linkage to the scuttle mountings **(see illustrations)**.

6 Remove the wiper motor and linkage assembly out from the vehicle **(see illustration)**.

7 If necessary, unscrew the retaining nut from the motor shaft. Free the wiper linkage arm from the shaft, then remove the three motor retaining bolts. Release the cable-ties and separate the motor and linkage.

13.3a Extract the horseshoe-shaped retaining clip ...

13.3b ... then withdraw the brake hydraulic fluid reservoir from the mounting bracket and place it to one side

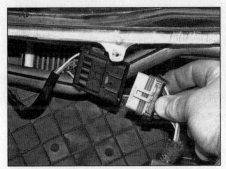

13.4 Disconnect the wiper motor wiring connector

13.5a Undo the wiper linkage right-hand retaining bolts ...

13.5b ... centre retaining bolts ...

13.5c . . . and left-hand retaining bolts

Refitting

8 If the linkage arm has been removed from the wiper motor shaft, temporarily reconnect the motor wiring connector. Switch on the windscreen wipers, then switch them off again and allow the motor to stop at the park position. Disconnect the motor wiring connector.

9 Refit the motor to the linkage and securely tighten the motor retaining bolts. Locate the linkage arm on the motor shaft so that it is positioned centrally between the two arrows on the linkage frame **(see illustration)**. Refit and tighten the linkage arm retaining nut, then resecure the wiring harness with new cable-ties.

10 Manoeuvre the motor and linkage assembly back into position in the vehicle. Refit the retaining bolts, and tighten them securely.

11 Reconnect the wiper motor wiring

14.2a Remove the trim caps at the base of the tailgate upper trim panel on each side, then undo the two retaining screws

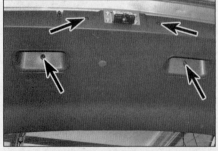

14.3 Undo the four screws (arrowed) securing the lower trim panel to the tailgate

13.6 Remove the wiper motor and linkage assembly out from the vehicle

connector then refit the brake fluid reservoir and secure with the retaining clip.

12 Refit the bulkhead closure panel and windscreen cowl panel as described in Chapter 11.

13 Install both the wiper arms as described in Section 12, and reconnect the battery negative terminal.

14 Tailgate wiper motor – removal and refitting

Removal

1 Remove the wiper arm as described in Section 12.

2 Open the tailgate and remove the retaining screw trim caps at the base of the tailgate upper trim panel on each side. Undo the two retaining screws then remove the panel by

14.2b Prise the panel free at the sides, then at the centre to release the internal clips

14.4 Pull the lower trim panel away from the tailgate to release the internal clips

13.9 Locate the linkage arm on the motor shaft centrally between the two arrows stamped on the linkage frame

prising it free at the sides, then at the centre to release the nine internal retaining clips **(see illustrations)**.

3 Undo the two screws in the grab handle apertures and the two screws at the base of the tailgate securing the lower trim panel to the tailgate **(see illustration)**.

4 Pull the lower trim panel away from the tailgate to release the twelve internal retaining clips and remove the panel from the tailgate **(see illustration)**.

5 Disconnect the wiper motor wiring connector, and release the wiring from any relevant retaining clips.

6 Slacken and remove the wiper motor mounting bolts and remove the wiper motor **(see illustration)**. Where applicable, recover any spacers from the motor mounting bracket, and slide the inner mounting rubber off the motor spindle.

7 Examine the motor mounting rubbers for signs of damage or deterioration, and renew as necessary.

Refitting

8 Where applicable, slide the inner mounting rubber onto the motor spindle, and ensure that any rubbers are correctly fitted to the motor mountings.

9 Refit the wiper motor mounting bolts and tighten them securely.

10 Reconnect the wiper motor wiring connector.

11 Refit the trim panels to the tailgate, ensuring they are securely retained by all of the screws and clips.

12 Refit the wiper arm as described in Section 12.

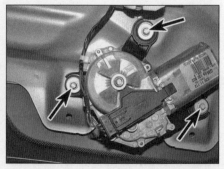

14.6 Tailgate wiper motor mounting bolts (arrowed)

15 Windscreen/tailgate washer system components – removal and refitting

Washer system reservoir

1 Remove the windscreen cowl panel and the bulkhead closure panel as described in Chapter 11.

2 Unscrew the nut securing the washer reservoir to the scuttle bracket.

3 Manipulate the reservoir up and out of its position. Disconnect the wiring connector from the washer pump, then disconnect the hose(s) from the base of the pump and remove the reservoir from the vehicle. Wash off any spilt fluid with cold water.

4 Refitting is the reverse of removal, ensuring that the washer hose(s) are securely connected. On completion, refit the bulkhead closure panel and windscreen cowl panel as described in Chapter 11.

Washer pump

5 Remove the washer reservoir as described above.

6 Tip out the contents of the reservoir, then carefully ease the pump out from the reservoir and recover its sealing grommet.

7 Refitting is the reverse of removal, using a new sealing grommet if the original one shows signs of damage or deterioration. On completion, refit the bulkhead closure panel and windscreen cowl panel as described in Chapter 11.

Windscreen washer jets

8 Open the bonnet and ease the top of the washer jet from its location, then disengage the lower retaining lugs **(see illustrations)**.

9 Disconnect the nozzle from its fluid hose, and remove it from the vehicle.

10 Refitting is the reverse of removal.

Tailgate washer jet

11 Remove the high-level stop-light as described in Section 7.

12 Using pointed-nose pliers, depress the tabs on the side of the washer jet and withdraw the jet from the high-level stop-light **(see illustrations)**.

13 Refitting is the reverse of removal.

16 Radio/cassette/CD player – removal and refitting

Note: *The following removal and refitting procedure is for the range of radio/cassette/CD units which Vauxhall/Opel fit as standard equipment. Removal and refitting procedures of non-standard units may differ slightly.*

Removal

1 All the radio/cassette/CD players fitted by Vauxhall/Opel have DIN standard fixings.

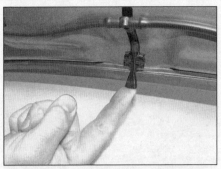
15.8a Ease the top of the windscreen washer jet from its location . . .

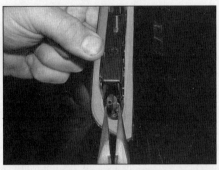
15.12a Depress the tabs on the side of the tailgate washer jet . . .

Two special tools, obtainable from most car accessory shops, are required for removal. Alternatively, suitable tools can be fabricated from 3 mm diameter wire, such as welding rod.

2 Disconnect the battery negative terminal (refer to *Disconnecting the battery* in the Reference Chapter).

3 Insert the tools into the holes on the front of the unit, and push them until they snap into place. The radio/cassette/CD player can then be slid out of the facia **(see illustration)**.

4 Disconnect the wiring and aerial connections at the rear of the unit, and remove the unit from the car **(see illustration)**.

Refitting

5 To refit the radio/cassette/CD player, reconnect the wiring and simply push the unit into the facia until the retaining lugs snap into place. On completion, reconnect the battery

16.3 Insert the tools and withdraw the radio/cassette/CD player from the facia

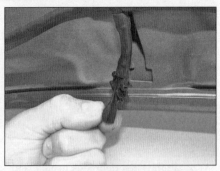
15.8b . . . then disengage the lower retaining lugs

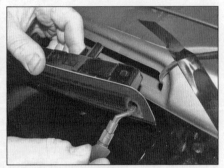
15.12b . . . and withdraw the jet from the high-level stop-light

and enter the radio security code, where applicable.

17 Speakers – removal and refitting

Small (treble) speaker

1 Lift the inner door lock handle, and carefully prise the handle trim cover out from the door trim panel **(see illustration)**.

2 Disconnect the speaker wiring connector then remove the speaker from the trim cover **(see illustrations)**.

3 Refitting is the reverse of removal.

Large (bass) speaker

4 Remove the front door inner trim panel as described in Chapter 11.

5 Undo the retaining screws, then free the

16.4 Disconnect the wiring and aerial connections at the rear of the unit

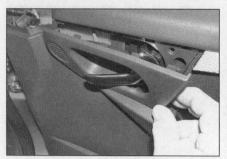

17.1 Lift the inner door lock handle, and carefully prise the handle trim cover out from the door trim panel

17.2a Disconnect the speaker wiring connector . . .

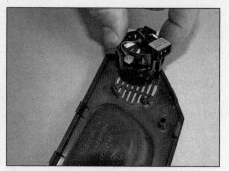

17.2b . . . then remove the speaker from the trim cover

speaker from the door. Disconnect the wiring connectors and remove the speaker **(see illustrations)**.

6 Refitting is the reverse of removal.

18 Radio aerial – removal and refitting

1 Where required, the aerial mast can be unscrewed from the base unit.
2 Removal of the base unit entails removal of the headlining, which is a complicated operation, considered to be outside the scope of this manual. Therefore, any problems relating to the aerial base unit or wiring should be entrusted to a Vauxhall/Opel dealer.

19 Anti-theft alarm system – general information

Note: *This information is applicable only to the anti-theft alarm system fitted by Vauxhall/Opel as standard equipment.*
1 Most models in the range are fitted with an anti-theft alarm system as standard equipment. The alarm is automatically armed and disarmed when the deadlocks are operated using the driver's door lock or remote control key. The alarm has switches on all the doors (including the tailgate), the bonnet, the radio/cassette/CD player and the ignition and starter circuits. If the tailgate, bonnet or any of the doors are opened whilst the alarm is set, the alarm

horn will sound and the hazard warning lights will flash. The alarm also has an immobiliser function which makes the ignition and starter circuits inoperable whilst the alarm is triggered.
2 The alarm system performs a self-test every time it is switched on; this test takes approximately 10 seconds. During the self-test, the LED (light emitting diode) in the hazard warning light switch will come on. If the LED flashes, then either the tailgate, bonnet or one of the doors is open, or there is a fault in the circuit. After the initial 10-second period, the LED will flash to indicate that the alarm is switched on. On unlocking the driver's door lock, the LED will illuminate for approximately 1 second, then go out, indicating that the alarm has been switched off.
3 With the alarm set, if the tailgate is unlocked, the tailgate switch sensing will automatically be switched off, but the door and bonnet switches will still be active. Once the tailgate is shut and locked again, the tailgate switch sensing will be switched back on after approximately 10 seconds.
4 Should the alarm system develop a fault, the vehicle should be taken to a Vauxhall dealer for examination.

20 Heated front seat components – general information

On models with heated front seats, a heater mat is fitted to both the seat back and seat cushion. Renewal of either heater mat involves peeling back the upholstery, removing the old

mat, sticking the new mat in position and then refitting the upholstery. Note that upholstery removal and refitting requires considerable skill and experience if it is to be carried out successfully, and is therefore best entrusted to your Vauxhall/Opel dealer. In practice, it will be very difficult for the home mechanic to carry out the job without ruining the upholstery.

21 Airbag system – general information and precautions

General information
A driver's airbag is fitted as standard equipment on all models. The airbag is fitted in the steering wheel centre pad. Additionally, a passenger's airbag located in the facia, side airbags located in the front seats, and curtain airbags located in the headlining are optionally available.
The system is armed only when the ignition is switched on, however, a reserve power source maintains a power supply to the system in the event of a break in the main electrical supply. The steering wheel and facia airbags are activated by a 'g' sensor (deceleration sensor), and controlled by an electronic control unit located under the centre console. The side airbags and curtain airbags are activated by severe side impact and operate independently of the main system. A separate electrical supply, control unit and sensor is provided for the side/curtain airbags on each side of the car.
The airbags are inflated by a gas generator, which forces the bag out from its location in the steering wheel, facia, seat back frame, or headlining.

Precautions
⚠️ **Warning: The following precautions must be observed when working on vehicles equipped with an airbag system, to prevent the possibility of personal injury.**
General precautions
The following precautions **must** be observed when carrying out work on a vehicle equipped with an airbag:
a) *Do not disconnect the battery with the engine running.*

17.5a Undo the retaining screws (arrowed) . . .

17.5b . . . remove the speaker and disconnect the wiring connector

b) Before carrying out any work in the vicinity of the airbag, removal of any of the airbag components, or any welding work on the vehicle, de-activate the system as described in the following sub-Section.

c) Do not attempt to test any of the airbag system circuits using test meters or any other test equipment.

d) If the airbag warning light comes on, or any fault in the system is suspected, consult a Vauxhall dealer without delay. **Do not** attempt to carry out fault diagnosis, or any dismantling of the components.

Precautions when handling an airbag

a) Transport the airbag by itself, bag upward.

b) Do not put your arms around the airbag.

c) Carry the airbag close to the body, bag outward.

d) Do not drop the airbag or expose it to impacts.

e) Do not attempt to dismantle the airbag unit.

f) Do not connect any form of electrical equipment to any part of the airbag circuit.

Precautions when storing an airbag

a) Store the unit in a cupboard with the airbag upward.

b) Do not expose the airbag to temperatures above 80ºC.

c) Do not expose the airbag to flames.

d) Do not attempt to dispose of the airbag – consult a Vauxhall/Opel dealer.

e) Never refit an airbag which is known to be faulty or damaged.

De-activation of airbag system

The system must be de-activated before carrying out any work on the airbag components or surrounding area:

a) Switch on the ignition and check the operation of the airbag warning light on the instrument panel. The light should illuminate when the ignition is switched on, then extinguish.

b) Switch off the ignition.

c) Remove the ignition key.

d) Switch off all electrical equipment.

e) Disconnect the battery negative terminal (refer to 'Disconnecting the battery' in the Reference Chapter).

f) Insulate the battery negative terminal and the end of the battery negative lead to prevent any possibility of contact.

g) Wait for at least two minutes before carrying out any further work. Wait at least ten minutes if the airbag warning light did not operate correctly.

Activation of airbag system

To activate the system on completion of any work, proceed as follows:

a) Ensure that there are no occupants in the vehicle, and that there are no loose objects around the vicinity of the steering wheel. Close the vehicle doors and windows.

b) Ensure that the ignition is switched off

then reconnect the battery negative terminal.

c) Open the driver's door and switch on the ignition, without reaching in front of the steering wheel. Check that the airbag warning light illuminates briefly then extinguishes.

d) Switch off the ignition.

e) If the airbag warning light does not operate as described in paragraph c), consult a Vauxhall/Opel dealer before driving the vehicle.

22 Airbag system components – removal and refitting

> **Warning: Refer to the precautions given in Section 21 before attempting to carry out work on any of the airbag components.**

1 De-activate the airbag system as described in the previous Section, then proceed as described under the relevant heading.

Driver's airbag

2 With the steering wheel in the straight-ahead position, undo the two retaining screws from the rear of the steering wheel (see illustration).

3 Carefully lift the airbag assembly away from the steering wheel, release the locking pin and disconnect the wiring connector from the rear of the unit (see illustrations). Note that the airbag must not be knocked or dropped, and should be stored the correct way up, with its padded surface uppermost.

22.3a Lift the airbag away from the steering wheel . . .

22.3c . . . and disconnect the wiring connector from the rear of the unit

22.2 Undo the two airbag retaining screws from the rear of the steering wheel

4 Refitting is a reversal of the removal procedure. Make sure the locking pin is secure in the wiring block connector, then tighten the airbag retaining screws securely.

Passenger's airbag

5 Disconnect the battery negative terminal (refer to *Disconnecting the battery* in the Reference Chapter).

6 Remove the glovebox as described in Chapter 11.

7 Undo the screws securing the airbag to the mounting brackets, and withdraw the airbag out through the glovebox aperture. Note that the airbag must not be knocked or dropped, and should be stored the correct way up (as mounted in the vehicle).

8 Release the locking pin and disconnect the airbag wiring plug from the side of the unit (see illustration).

9 Refitting is a reversal of the removal

22.3b . . . release the locking pin . . .

22.8 Release the locking pin and disconnect the wiring plug from the side of the passenger's airbag

22.18 Depress the retaining clips (arrowed)
and slide out the switch

22.19 Disconnect the wiring connector
from the back of the contact unit

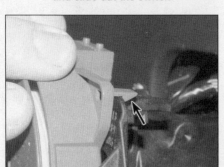

22.20a Release the securing lugs (one
arrowed) . . .

22.20b . . . and withdraw the contact unit
from the steering column

procedure. Make sure the locking pin is secure in the wiring block connector, then tighten the airbag retaining screws securely.

Side airbags

10 The side airbags are located internally within the front seat back and no attempt should be made to remove them. Any suspected problems with the side airbag system should be referred to a Vauxhall/Opel dealer.

Curtain airbags

11 The curtain airbags are located behind the headlining above the doors on each side and no attempt should be made to remove them. Any suspected problems with the curtain airbag system should be referred to a Vauxhall/Opel dealer.

Airbag control unit

12 Remove the centre console as described in Chapter 11.
13 Disconnect the control unit wiring connector, then undo the retaining nuts and remove the control unit from the vehicle.

Note the fitted position of the control unit – the arrow on the top of the unit is facing forwards.
14 Refitting is the reverse of removal. If a new control unit is being installed, the vehicle must be taken to a Vauxhall/Opel dealer for the control unit to be reprogrammed at the earliest possible opportunity. **Note:** *The airbag system will not be operational until the new control unit is reprogrammed; this will be indicated by the warning light in the instrument panel being illuminated.*

Airbag wiring contact unit

15 Disconnect the battery negative terminal (refer to *Disconnecting the battery* in the Reference Chapter) and wait for 2 minutes.
16 Remove the steering wheel as described in Chapter 10.
17 Remove the steering column shrouds as described in Chapter 11.
18 Depress the retaining clips, and release the left- and right-hand combination switches from the column. Release the securing clips and disconnect the wiring connectors, then remove the switches from the vehicle **(see illustration)**.
19 Release the retaining clip and disconnect the wiring connector from the contact unit **(see illustration)**.
20 Unclip the four securing lugs and slide the contact unit from the top of the steering column. DO NOT turn the contact unit centre, as it is set in the vehicle straight-ahead position for refitting **(see illustrations)**.
21 Refitting is the reverse of removal noting the following points:
   a) If a new contact unit is being installed, remove the transport lock (sticker) before refitting, this locks the contact unit in the centre position ready for refitting.
   b) Press the contact unit on squarely, taking care not to damage the securing lugs.

Vauxhall Meriva wiring diagrams

Diagram 1

 WARNING: This vehicle is fitted with a supplemental restraint system (SRS) consisting of a combination of driver (and passenger) airbag(s), side impact protection airbags and seatbelt pre-tensioners. The use of electrical test equipment on any SRS wiring systems may cause the seatbelt pre-tensioners to abruptly retract and airbags to explosively deploy, resulting in potentially severe personal injury. Extreme care should be taken to correctly identify any circuits to be tested to avoid choosing any of the SRS wiring in error.
For further information see airbag system precautions in body electrical systems chapter.
Note: The SRS wiring harness can normally be identified by yellow and/or orange harness or harness connectors.

Key to symbols

Bulb	
Switch	
Fuse/Fusible link	F26
Resistor	
Variable resistor	
Variable resistor	

Wire splice, soldered joint, or unspecified connector
Connecting wires
Diode
Light-emitting diode
Item number *12*
Motor/pump
Heating element

Solenoid actuator
Earth point and location E7
Dashed outline denotes part of a larger item, containing in this case an electronic or solid state device (pins 43 and 44 of a single connector designated x45). x45/43 x45/44
Wire colour (red with black tracer) Rd/Bk

Passenger compartment fusebox 5

F1 7.5A Central control unit
F2 5A Immobiliser, hazard warning lights, exterior lighting, horn
F3 30A Headlight washer system
F4 - Spare
F5 - Spare
F6 - Spare
F7 10A Starter, Diesel engine controller
F8 15A Horn
F9 20A Fuel injection, fuel pump
F10 20A Direction indicators, body control unit
F11 20A Audio system, info display, infotainment system
F12 7.5A Heated rear window, electric mirrors
F13 10A Central locking, alarm
F14 15A Petrol engine control
　　7.5A Diesel engine control
F15 10A Engine control unit
　　15A Z17DTH engine
F16 20A Accessory socket, cigar lighter
F17 - Spare
F18 - Spare
F19 20A Central locking
F20 5A Interior lighting
F21 15A Windscreen washer
F22 20A Rear electric windows
F23 20A Sunroof
F24 5A Alarm
F25 15A Rear wiper
F26 15A Ignition system, engine electronics
F27 5A Engine controller, airbag, ESP, reversing lights
F28 7.5A Air conditioning
F29 20A Front LH electric window
F30 5A Number plate light
F31 7.5A Engine control
　　10A Z17DTH engine
F32 20A Front RH electric window
F33 5A Body control unit, immobiliser, control indicators
F34 30A Front wiper
F35 5A Interior lighting, power steering, information display
F36 15A Stop light, ABS, ESP
F37 20A Cigar lighter, auxiliary heater
F38 15A LH heated seat
F39 15A RH heated seat
F40 5A Headlight levelling
F41 15A Reversing lights
F42 5A Engine cooling, front foglights
F43 5A LH parking light
F44 5A RH parking light
F45 10A Rear fog lights
F46 15A Front fog lights
F47 20A Towbar, accessory socket
F48 - Spare
F49 - Spare

F50 30A Diesel filter heater
F51 15A LH headlight dip beam (xenox)
　　10A LH headlight dip beam (halogen)
F52 15A RH headlight dip beam (xenox)
　　10A RH headlight dip beam (halogen)
F53 5A Sunroof, electric windows, audio system, mirrors
F54 10A LH main beam
F55 10A RH main beam
F56 -

Engine fusebox 4

F1 30A Heater blower
F2 50A Power steering
F3 40A ABS
F4 60A Easytronic Diesel
　　80A Pre-heating system
F5 30A Heated rear window
F6 40A Engine cooling fan (Y17DT)
　　50A Engine cooling fan (Z17DTH)
F7 30A Starter
F8 40A Engine cooling fan (petrol models)

Earth locations

E1 On transmission tunnel, between front seats
E2 On transmission tunnel, in front of rear seat
E3 On transmission tunnel, in front of rear seat
E4 RH footwell, lower 'A' pillar
E5 LH luggage compartment, behind rear light
E6 Inside tailgate
E7 RH luggage compartment, behind rear light
E8 LH engine compartment, front longitudinal member
E9 LH engine compartment, inner wing
E10 Behind battery
E11 On rear of engine
E12 On rear of engine

H47151

Wire colours

Bk	Black	**Pk**	Pink
Ye	Yellow	**Vt**	Violet
Bu	Blue	**Og**	Orange
Bn	Brown	**Wh**	White
Gn	Green	**Lgn**	Light Green
Gy	Grey	**Lbu**	Light Blue
Pu	Purple	**Dgn**	Dark Green
Bg	Beige	**DBu**	Dark Blue
Rd	Red		

* models without ESP

Key to items

1 Battery
2 Alternator
3 Starter motor
4 Engine fusebox
5 Passenger fusebox
6 Ignition switch
7 Body control control unit
8 Starter relay
9 Steering wheel contact unit
10 Horn relay

11 Horn switch
12 LH horn
13 RH horn
14 Engine cooling fan relay A
15 Engine cooling fan relay B
17 Engine cooling fan relay D
18 Engine cooling fan relay A
20 Engine cooling fan resistors
21 Instrument cluster

Diagram 2

H47152

Starting & charging

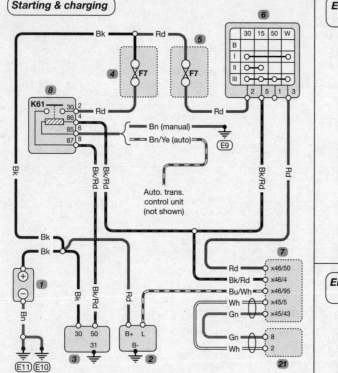

Horn

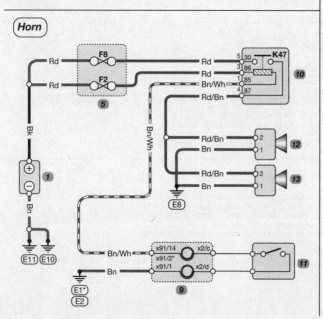

Engine cooling fan - variation 1

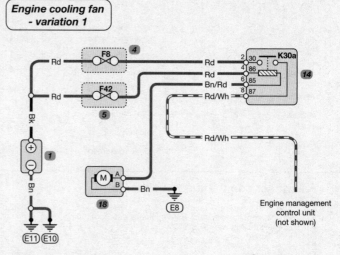

Engine cooling fan - variation 2

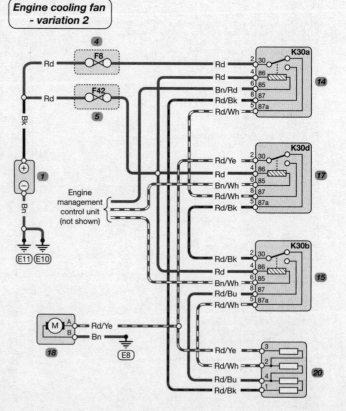

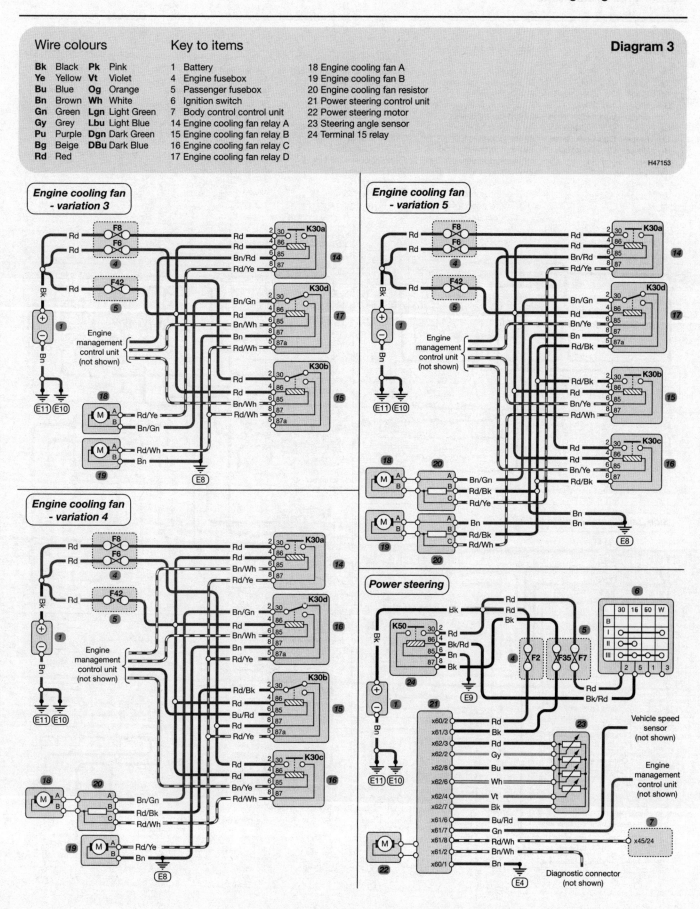

Wire colours

Bk	Black	Pk	Pink
Ye	Yellow	Vt	Violet
Bu	Blue	Og	Orange
Bn	Brown	Wh	White
Gn	Green	Lgn	Light Green
Gy	Grey	Lbu	Light Blue
Pu	Purple	Dgn	Dark Green
Bg	Beige	DBu	Dark Blue
Rd	Red		

Key to items

1 Battery
4 Engine fusebox
5 Passenger fusebox
6 Ignition switch
7 Body control control unit
14 Engine cooling fan relay A
15 Engine cooling fan relay B
16 Engine cooling fan relay C
17 Engine cooling fan relay D
18 Engine cooling fan A
19 Engine cooling fan B
20 Engine cooling fan resistor
21 Power steering control unit
22 Power steering motor
23 Steering angle sensor
24 Terminal 15 relay

Diagram 3

H47153

Engine cooling fan - variation 3

Engine cooling fan - variation 5

Engine cooling fan - variation 4

Power steering

Diagram 4

Wire colours

Bk	Black	**Pk**	Pink
Ye	Yellow	**Vt**	Violet
Bu	Blue	**Og**	Orange
Bn	Brown	**Wh**	White
Gn	Green	**Lgn**	Light Green
Gy	Grey	**Lbu**	Light Blue
Pu	Purple	**Dgn**	Dark Green
Bg	Beige	**DBu**	Dark Blue
Rd	Red		

Key to items

1 Battery
5 Passenger fusebox
6 Ignition switch
7 Body control control unit
21 Instrument cluster
24 Terminal 15 relay
27 Rear cigar lighter
28 Front accessory socket
29 Rear accessory socket
30 Light switch
  a = side/headlight
  b = indicator
  c = front fog light
  d = rear fog light
31 Number plate light relay
32 LH side light relay
33 RH side light relay
34 LH number plate light
35 RH number plate light
36 LH headlight unit
  a = side light
37 RH headlight unit
  (as above)
38 LH rear light unit
  a = tail light
  b = stop light
  c = reversing light
39 RH rear light unit
  (as above)
40 Reversing light relay (auto.)
41 Reversing light switch (manual)
42 Stop light switch
43 High level stop light
44 Front fog light relay
45 Rear fog light relay
46 LH front fog light
47 RH front fog light
48 RH rear fog light
49 Front cigar lighter

H47154

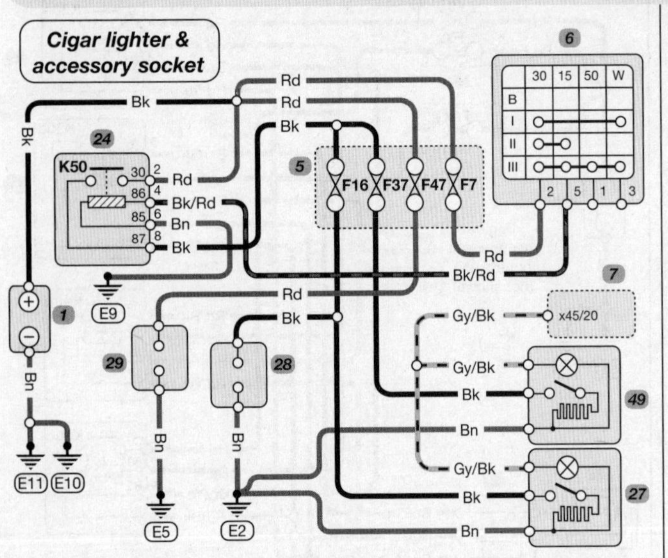

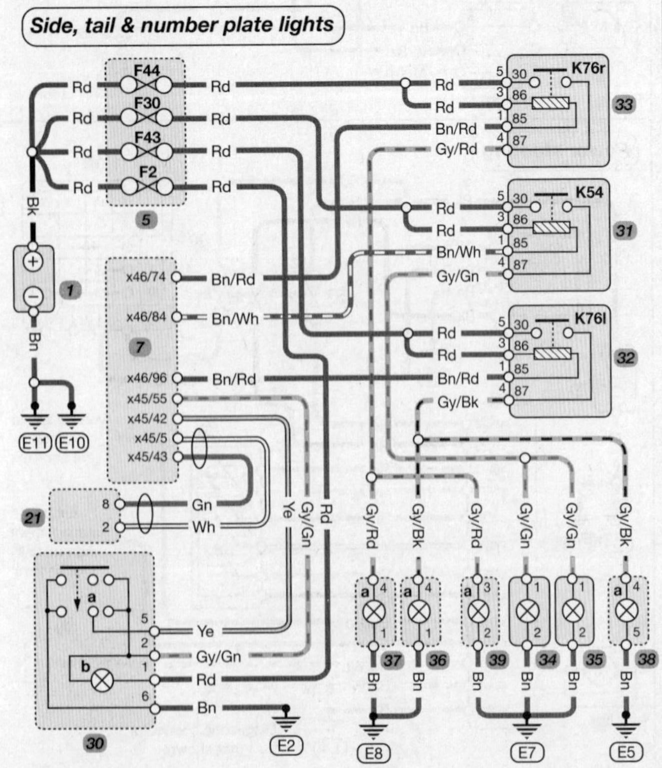

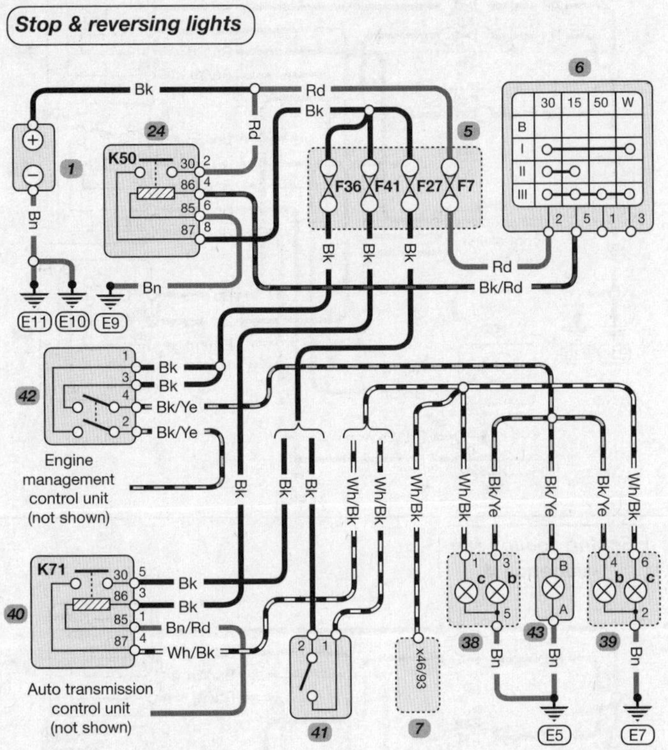

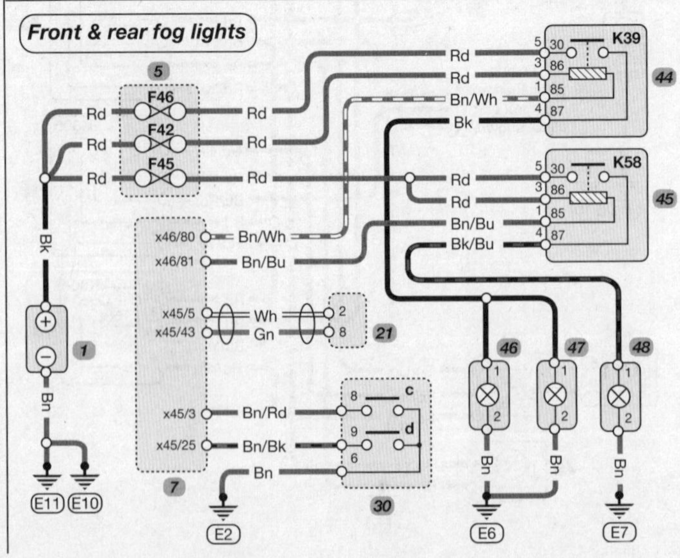

Wire colours

Bk	Black	**Pk**	Pink
Ye	Yellow	**Vt**	Violet
Bu	Blue	**Og**	Orange
Bn	Brown	**Wh**	White
Gn	Green	**Lgn**	Light Green
Gy	Grey	**Lbu**	Light Blue
Pu	Purple	**Dgn**	Dark Green
Bg	Beige	**DBu**	Dark Blue
Rd	Red		

Key to items

1 Battery
5 Passenger fusebox
6 Ignition switch
7 Body control control unit
21 Instrument cluster
24 Terminal 15 relay
30 Light switch
  a = side/headlight
  b = indicator
  e = headlight adjuster
36 LH headlight unit
  b = dip beam (non xenon)
  c = high beam
  d = dip beam (xenon)

e = headlight levelling actuator
f = direction indicator
37 RH headlight unit
  (as above)
38 LH rear light unit
  d = direction indicator
39 RH rear light unit
  (as above)
50 Dip beam relay
51 Main beam relay
52 Steering column switch unit
  a = dip/main
  b = direction indicators
53 Headlight levelling control unit

54 Direction indicator relay
55 Hazard warning/seat heating switch
  a = hazrd warning switch
56 LH direction indicator side repeater
57 RH direction indicator side repeater

Diagram 5

H47155

Headlights

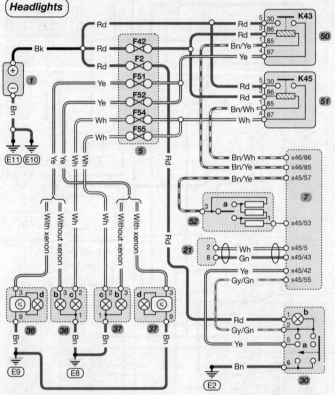

Direction indicators & hazard warning lights

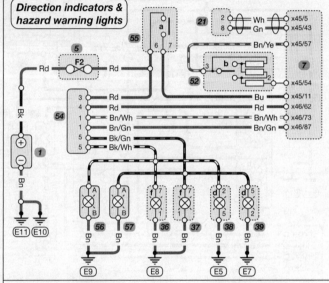

Headlight levelling - models without xenon

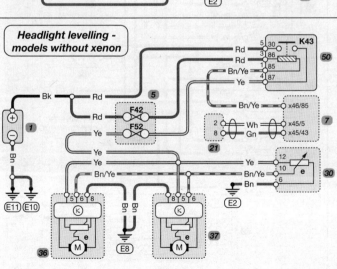

Headlight levelling - models with xenon

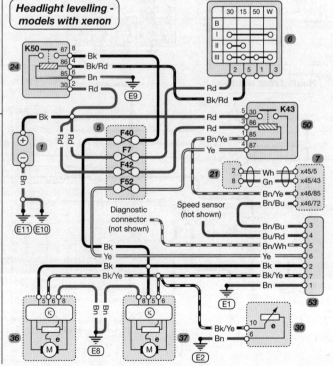

Wire colours

Bk	Black	Pk	Pink
Ye	Yellow	Vt	Violet
Bu	Blue	Og	Orange
Bn	Brown	Wh	White
Gn	Green	Lgn	Light Green
Gy	Grey	Lbu	Light Blue
Pu	Purple	Dgn	Dark Green
Bg	Beige	DBu	Dark Blue
Rd	Red		

Key to items

1 Battery
4 Engine fusebox
5 Passenger fusebox
6 Ignition switch
7 Body control control unit
21 Instrument cluster
24 Terminal 15 relay
60 Front interior light
  a = airbag indicator
  b = interior light
  c = map reading light
61 Rear interior light

62 Glove box light/switch
63 Luggage compartment light
64 Luggage compartment light switch
65 Driver's door switch
66 Passenger's door switch
67 LH rear door switch
68 RH rear door switch
69 Front wiper motor
70 Rear wiper motor
71 Headlight washer pump
72 Front/rear washer pump
73 Headlight washer relay

74 Rear wiper relay
75 Front wiper relay 1
76 Front wiper relay 2
77 Rear washer relay
78 Front washer relay
79 Wash/wipe switch
  a = front wash/wipe
  b = rear wash wipe
80 Heated rear window relay
81 Heated rear window
82 Heater assembly
  a = heated rear window switch

Diagram 6

H47156

Interior lighting

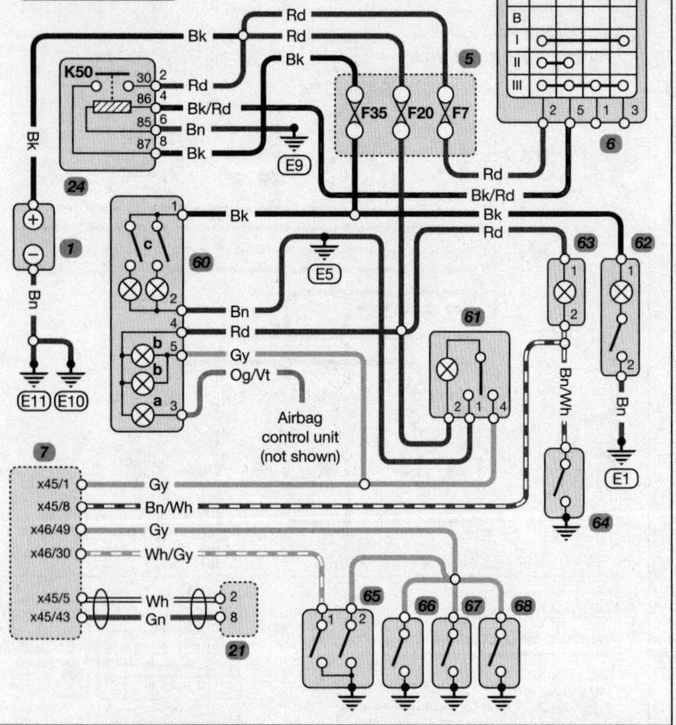

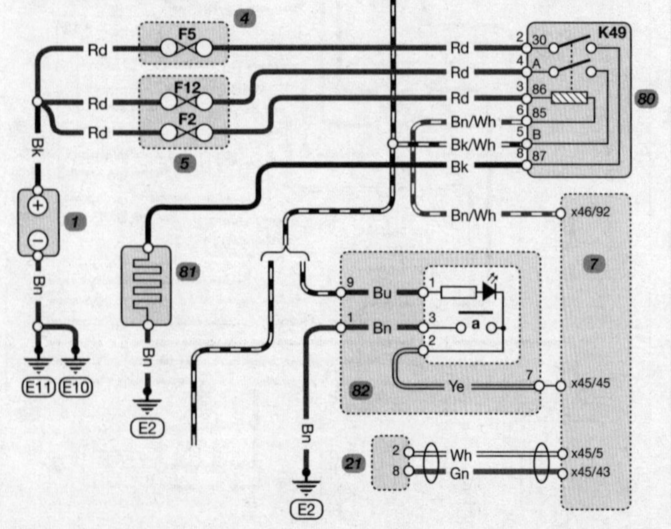

Wash/wipe

Heated rear window

See diagram 8
Heated mirrors

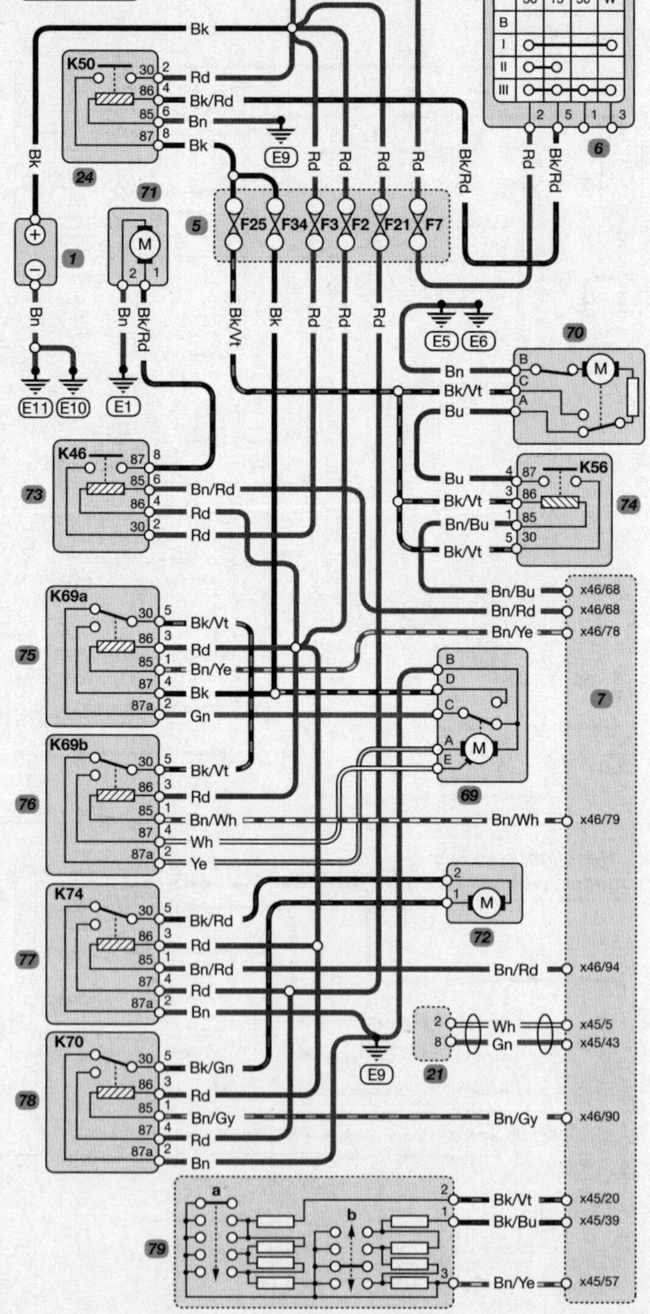

Wire colours

Bk	Black	**Pk**	Pink
Ye	Yellow	**Vt**	Violet
Bu	Blue	**Og**	Orange
Bn	Brown	**Wh**	White
Gn	Green	**Lgn**	Light Green
Gy	Grey	**Lbu**	Light Blue
Pu	Purple	**Dgn**	Dark Green
Bg	Beige	**DBu**	Dark Blue
Rd	Red		

Key to items

1 Battery
4 Engine fusebox
5 Passenger fusebox
6 Ignition switch
7 Body control control unit
21 Instrument cluster
   a = airbag warning light
   b = engine warning light
   c = control unit
   d = instrument illumination
24 Terminal 15 relay

82 Heater assembly
   b = heater blower switch
   c = switch illumination
   d = heater blower motor
   e = heater blower resistors
   f = air conditioning switch
   g = recirculation actuator
   h = recirculation switch
85 Terminal 15a relay
86 Compressor clutch relay
87 Compressor clutch

88 Low brake fluid switch
89 Handbrake switch
90 Outside air temperature sensor
91 Multi-information display
92 Triple infomation display

Diagram 7

H47157

Air conditioning

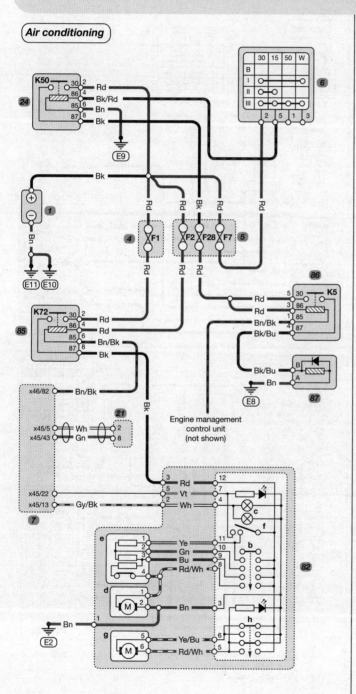

Instrument cluster & information display

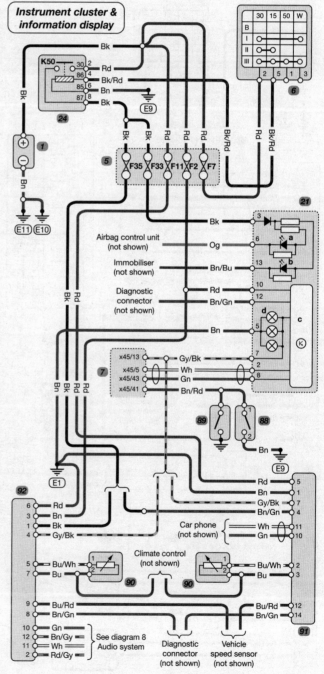

Wire colours

Bk	Black	**Pk**	Pink
Ye	Yellow	**Vt**	Violet
Bu	Blue	**Og**	Orange
Bn	Brown	**Wh**	White
Gn	Green	**Lgn**	Light Green
Gy	Grey	**Lbu**	Light Blue
Pu	Purple	**Dgn**	Dark Green
Bg	Beige	**DBu**	Dark Blue
Rd	Red		

Key to items

1 Battery
5 Passenger fusebox
6 Ignition switch
7 Body control control unit
9 Steering wheel contact unit
21 Instrument cluster
95 Audio remote controls
96 Twin audio
97 Roof antenna
98 Audio unit
99 LH front door speaker
100 LH front tweeter

101 RH front speaker
102 RH front tweeter
103 LH rear door speaker
104 LH rear tweeter
105 RH rear door speaker
106 RH rear tweeter
107 Sunroof switch
  a = front roof switch
  b = rear roof switch
108 Front sunroof motor
109 Rear sunroof motor

110 Mirror adjustment switch
  a = mirror adjustment
  b = mirror selection
  c = mirror retraction
111 Driver's mirror assembly
  a = retraction motor
  b = mirror adjustment motors
  c = heating element
112 Passenger's mirror assembly
  (as above)
113 Mirror retraction control unit

Diagram 8

H47158

Audio system

Sunroof

Electric mirrors

See diagram 7
Triple info.
display

Vehicle
speed
sensor
(not shown)

Diagnostic
connector
(not shown)

Carphone
(not shown)

Carphone/
navigation
(not shown)

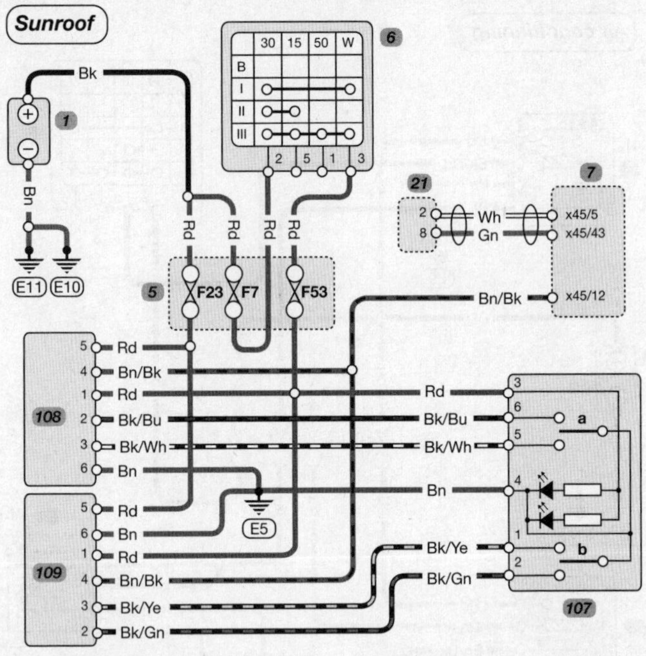

See diagram 6
Heated rear
window

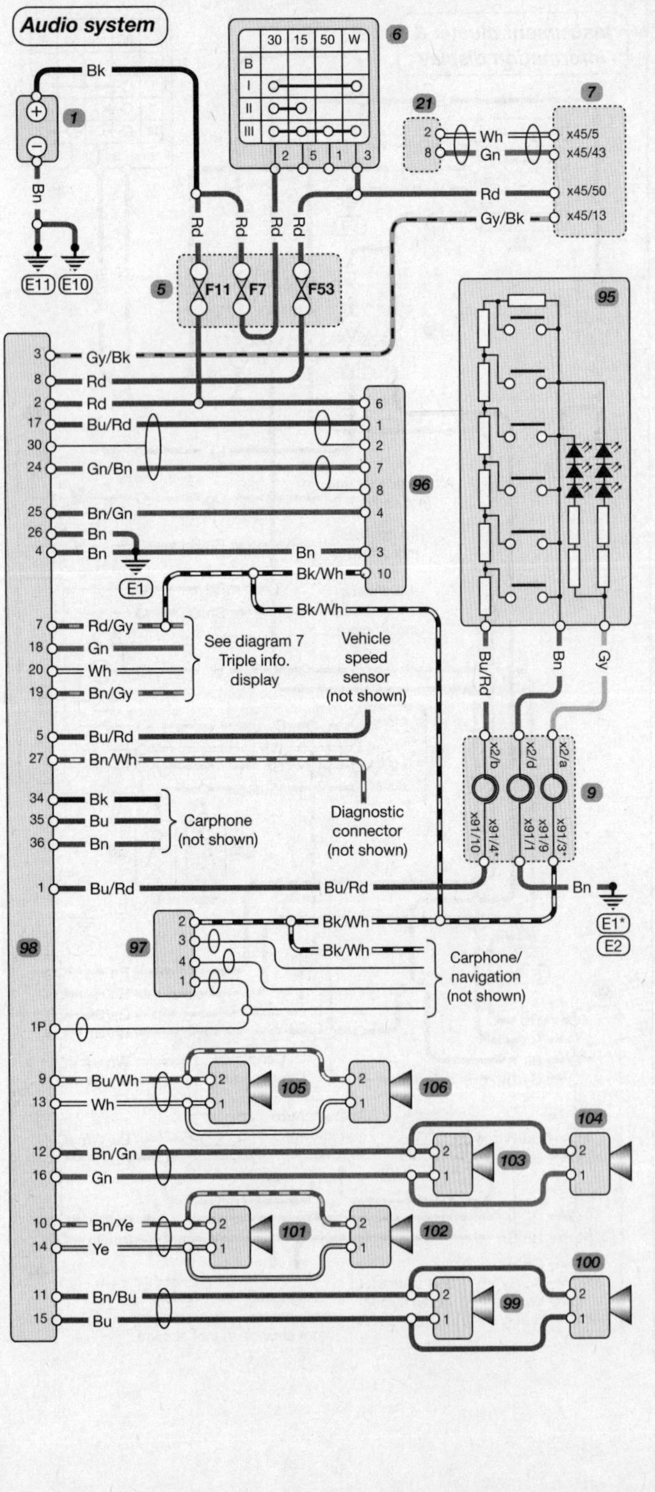

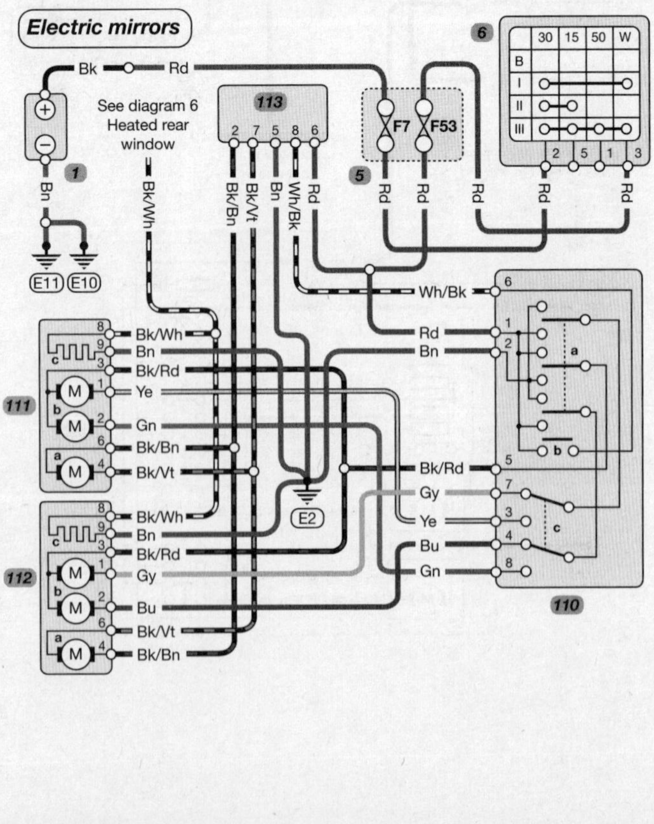

Wire colours

Bk	Black	Pk	Pink
Ye	Yellow	Vt	Violet
Bu	Blue	Og	Orange
Bn	Brown	Wh	White
Gn	Green	Lgn	Light Green
Gy	Grey	Lbu	Light Blue
Pu	Purple	Dgn	Dark Green
Bg	Beige	DBu	Dark Blue
Rd	Red		

Key to items

1   Battery
5   Passenger fusebox
6   Ignition switch
7   Body control control unit
9   Steering wheel contact unit
21   Instrument cluster
115   Driver's electric window motor
116   Passenger's electric window motor
117   LH rear electric window motor
118   RH rear electric window motor
119   Passenger's electric window door switch
120   LH rear electric window door switch
121   RH rear electric window door switch

122   Electric window master switch
    a = rear window isolation switch
    b = RH rear door switch
    c = LH rear door switch
    d = switch illumination
    e = driver's door switch
    f = passenger's door switch
123   Driver's door 'lock' relay
124   Door 'unlock relay'
125   Door 'deadlock' relay
126   Door 'lock' relay
127   Fuel filler flap relay
128   Driver's door lock

129   Tailgate lock
130   LH rear door lock
131   RH rear door lock
132   Passenger's door lock
133   Fuel filler flap lock

Diagram 9

H47159

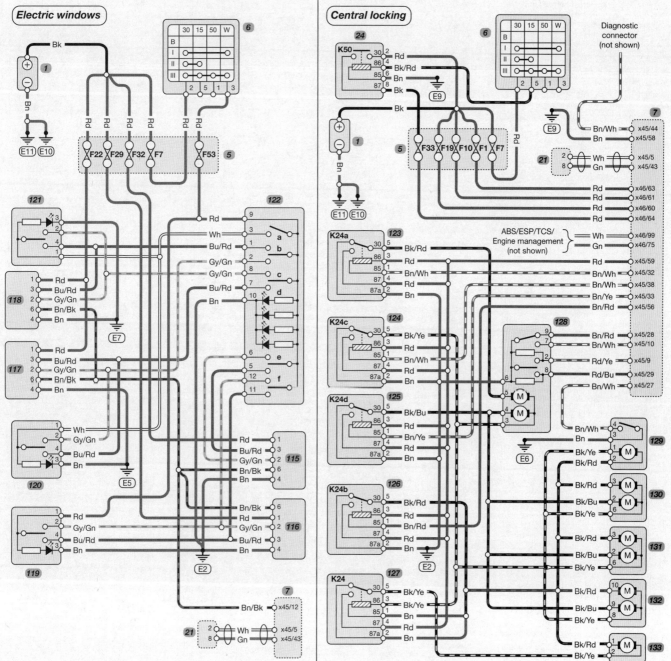

Electric windows

Central locking

Notes

Reference REF•1

Dimensions and weights

Note: *All figures are approximate and may vary according to model. Refer to manufacturer's data for exact figures.*

Dimensions

Overall length	4042 mm
Overall width (including door mirrors)	1952 mm
Overall height (unladen)	1624 mm
Wheelbase	2630 mm
Turning circle diameter (wall to wall)	10.42 metres
Front track*	1429 mm
Rear track*	1420 mm
Ground clearance*	122 mm

* Approximate values

Weights

Kerb weight	1350 to 1418 kg
Gross vehicle weight	Refer to information contained on the vehicle identification plate
Maximum roof load (including weight of rack)	100 kg

Fuel economy

Although depreciation is still the biggest part of the cost of motoring for most car owners, the cost of fuel is more immediately noticeable. These pages give some tips on how to get the best fuel economy.

Working it out

Manufacturer's figures

Car manufacturers are required by law to provide fuel consumption information on all new vehicles sold. These 'official' figures are obtained by simulating various driving conditions on a rolling road or a test track. Real life conditions are different, so the fuel consumption actually achieved may not bear much resemblance to the quoted figures.

How to calculate it

Many cars now have trip computers which will

display fuel consumption, both instantaneous and average. Refer to the owner's handbook for details of how to use these.

To calculate consumption yourself (and maybe to check that the trip computer is accurate), proceed as follows.

1. Fill up with fuel and note the mileage, or zero the trip recorder.
2. Drive as usual until you need to fill up again.
3. Note the amount of fuel required to refill the tank, and the mileage covered since the previous fill-up.
4. Divide the mileage by the amount of fuel used to obtain the consumption figure.

For example:

    Mileage at first fill-up (a) = 27,903
    Mileage at second fill-up (b) = 28,346
    Mileage covered (b - a) = 443
    Fuel required at second fill-up = 48.6 litres

The half-completed changeover to metric units in the UK means that we buy our fuel

in litres, measure distances in miles and talk about fuel consumption in miles per gallon. There are two ways round this: the first is to convert the litres to gallons before doing the calculation (by dividing by 4.546, or see Table 1). So in the example:

    48.6 litres ÷ 4.546 = 10.69 gallons
    443 miles ÷ 10.69 gallons = 41.4 mpg

The second way is to calculate the consumption in miles per litre, then multiply that figure by 4.546 (or see Table 2).

So in the example, fuel consumption is:

    443 miles ÷ 48.6 litres = 9.1 mpl
    9.1 mpl x 4.546 = 41.4 mpg

The rest of Europe expresses fuel consumption in litres of fuel required to travel 100 km (l/100 km). For interest, the conversions are given in Table 3. In practice it doesn't matter what units you use, provided you know what your normal consumption is and can spot if it's getting better or worse.

Table 1: conversion of litres to Imperial gallons

litres	1	2	3	4	5	10	20	30	40	50	60	70
gallons	0.22	0.44	0.66	0.88	1.10	2.24	4.49	6.73	8.98	11.22	13.47	15.71

Table 2: conversion of miles per litre to miles per gallon

miles per litre	5	6	7	8	9	10	11	12	13	14
miles per gallon	23	27	32	36	41	46	50	55	59	64

Table 3: conversion of litres per 100 km to miles per gallon

litres per 100 km	4	4.5	5	5.5	6	6.5	7	8	9	10
miles per gallon	71	63	56	51	47	43	40	35	31	28

Maintenance

A well-maintained car uses less fuel and creates less pollution. In particular:

Filters

Change air and fuel filters at the specified intervals.

Oil

Use a good quality oil of the lowest viscosity specified by the vehicle manufacturer (see *Lubricants and fluids*). Check the level often and be careful not to overfill.

Spark plugs

When applicable, renew at the specified intervals.

Tyres

Check tyre pressures regularly. Under-inflated tyres have an increased rolling resistance. It is generally safe to use the higher pressures specified for full load conditions even when not fully laden, but keep an eye on the centre band of tread for signs of wear due to over-inflation.

When buying new tyres, consider the 'fuel saving' models which most manufacturers include in their ranges.

Driving style

Acceleration

Acceleration uses more fuel than driving at a steady speed. The best technique with modern cars is to accelerate reasonably briskly to the desired speed, changing up through the gears as soon as possible without making the engine labour.

Air conditioning

Air conditioning absorbs quite a bit of energy from the engine – typically 3 kW (4 hp) or so. The effect on fuel consumption is at its worst in slow traffic. Switch it off when not required.

Anticipation

Drive smoothly and try to read the traffic flow so as to avoid unnecessary acceleration and braking.

Automatic transmission

When accelerating in an automatic, avoid depressing the throttle so far as to make the transmission hold onto lower gears at higher speeds. Don't use the 'Sport' setting, if applicable.

When stationary with the engine running, select 'N' or 'P'. When moving, keep your left foot away from the brake.

Braking

Braking converts the car's energy of motion into heat – essentially, it is wasted. Obviously some braking is always going to be necessary, but with good anticipation it is surprising how much can be avoided, especially on routes that you know well.

Carshare

Consider sharing lifts to work or to the shops. Even once a week will make a difference.

Electrical loads

Electricity is 'fuel' too; the alternator which charges the battery does so by converting some of the engine's energy of motion into electrical energy. The more electrical accessories are in use, the greater the load on the alternator. Switch off big consumers like the heated rear window when not required.

Freewheeling

Freewheeling (coasting) in neutral with the engine switched off is dangerous. The effort required to operate power-assisted brakes and steering increases when the engine is not running, with a potential lack of control in emergency situations.

In any case, modern fuel injection systems automatically cut off the engine's fuel supply on the overrun (moving and in gear, but with the accelerator pedal released).

Gadgets

Bolt-on devices claiming to save fuel have been around for nearly as long as the motor car itself. Those which worked were rapidly adopted as standard equipment by the vehicle manufacturers. Others worked only in certain situations, or saved fuel only at the expense of unacceptable effects on performance, driveability or the life of engine components.

The most effective fuel saving gadget is the driver's right foot.

Journey planning

Combine (eg) a trip to the supermarket with a visit to the recycling centre and the DIY store, rather than making separate journeys.

When possible choose a travelling time outside rush hours.

Load

The more heavily a car is laden, the greater the energy required to accelerate it to a given speed. Remove heavy items which you don't need to carry.

One load which is often overlooked is the contents of the fuel tank. A tankful of fuel (55 litres / 12 gallons) weighs 45 kg (100 lb) or so. Just half filling it may be worthwhile.

Lost?

At the risk of stating the obvious, if you're going somewhere new, have details of the route to hand. There's not much point in achieving record mpg if you also go miles out of your way.

Parking

If possible, carry out any reversing or turning manoeuvres when you arrive at a parking space so that you can drive straight out when you leave. Manoeuvering when the engine is cold uses a lot more fuel.

Driving around looking for free on-street parking may cost more in fuel than buying a car park ticket.

Premium fuel

Most major oil companies (and some supermarkets) have premium grades of fuel which are several pence a litre dearer than the standard grades. Reports vary, but the consensus seems to be that if these fuels improve economy at all, they do not do so by enough to justify their extra cost.

Roof rack

When loading a roof rack, try to produce a wedge shape with the narrow end at the front. Any cover should be securely fastened – if it flaps it's creating turbulence and absorbing energy.

Remove roof racks and boxes when not in use – they increase air resistance and can create a surprising amount of noise.

Short journeys

The engine is at its least efficient, and wear is highest, during the first few miles after a cold start. Consider walking, cycling or using public transport.

Speed

The engine is at its most efficient when running at a steady speed and load at the rpm where it develops maximum torque. (You can find this figure in the car's handbook.) For most cars this corresponds to between 55 and 65 mph in top gear.

Above the optimum cruising speed, fuel consumption starts to rise quite sharply. A car travelling at 80 mph will typically be using 30% more fuel than at 60 mph.

Supermarket fuel

It may be cheap but is it any good? In the UK all supermarket fuel must meet the relevant British Standard. The major oil companies will say that their branded fuels have better additive packages which may stop carbon and other deposits building up. A reasonable compromise might be to use one tank of branded fuel to three or four from the supermarket.

Switch off when stationary

Switch off the engine if you look like being stationary for more than 30 seconds or so. This is good for the environment as well as for your pocket. Be aware though that frequent restarts are hard on the battery and the starter motor.

Windows

Driving with the windows open increases air turbulence around the vehicle. Closing the windows promotes smooth airflow and

reduced resistance. The faster you go, the more significant this is.

And finally . . .

Driving techniques associated with good fuel economy tend to involve moderate acceleration and low top speeds. Be considerate to the needs of other road users who may need to make brisker progress; even if you do not agree with them this is not an excuse to be obstructive.

Safety must always take precedence over economy, whether it is a question of accelerating hard to complete an overtaking manoeuvre, killing your speed when confronted with a potential hazard or switching the lights on when it starts to get dark.

Conversion factors

Length (distance)

Inches (in)	x 25.4	= Millimetres (mm)	x 0.0394	= Inches (in)
Feet (ft)	x 0.305	= Metres (m)	x 3.281	= Feet (ft)
Miles	x 1.609	= Kilometres (km)	x 0.621	= Miles

Volume (capacity)

Cubic inches (cu in; in^3)	x 16.387	= Cubic centimetres (cc; cm^3)	x 0.061	= Cubic inches (cu in; in^3)
Imperial pints (Imp pt)	x 0.568	= Litres (l)	x 1.76	= Imperial pints (Imp pt)
Imperial quarts (Imp qt)	x 1.137	= Litres (l)	x 0.88	= Imperial quarts (Imp qt)
Imperial quarts (Imp qt)	x 1.201	= US quarts (US qt)	x 0.833	= Imperial quarts (Imp qt)
US quarts (US qt)	x 0.946	= Litres (l)	x 1.057	= US quarts (US qt)
Imperial gallons (Imp gal)	x 4.546	= Litres (l)	x 0.22	= Imperial gallons (Imp gal)
Imperial gallons (Imp gal)	x 1.201	= US gallons (US gal)	x 0.833	= Imperial gallons (Imp gal)
US gallons (US gal)	x 3.785	= Litres (l)	x 0.264	= US gallons (US gal)

Mass (weight)

Ounces (oz)	x 28.35	= Grams (g)	x 0.035	= Ounces (oz)
Pounds (lb)	x 0.454	= Kilograms (kg)	x 2.205	= Pounds (lb)

Force

Ounces-force (ozf; oz)	x 0.278	= Newtons (N)	x 3.6	= Ounces-force (ozf; oz)
Pounds-force (lbf; lb)	x 4.448	= Newtons (N)	x 0.225	= Pounds-force (lbf; lb)
Newtons (N)	x 0.1	= Kilograms-force (kgf; kg)	x 9.81	= Newtons (N)

Pressure

Pounds-force per square inch (psi; lbf/in^2; lb/in^2)	x 0.070	= Kilograms-force per square centimetre (kgf/cm^2; kg/cm^2)	x 14.223	= Pounds-force per square inch (psi; lbf/in^2; lb/in^2)
Pounds-force per square inch (psi; lbf/in^2; lb/in^2)	x 0.068	= Atmospheres (atm)	x 14.696	= Pounds-force per square inch (psi; lbf/in^2; lb/in^2)
Pounds-force per square inch (psi; lbf/in^2; lb/in^2)	x 0.069	= Bars	x 14.5	= Pounds-force per square inch (psi; lbf/in^2; lb/in^2)
Pounds-force per square inch (psi; lbf/in^2; lb/in^2)	x 6.895	= Kilopascals (kPa)	x 0.145	= Pounds-force per square inch (psi; lbf/in^2; lb/in^2)
Kilopascals (kPa)	x 0.01	= Kilograms-force per square centimetre (kgf/cm^2; kg/cm^2)	x 98.1	= Kilopascals (kPa)
Millibar (mbar)	x 100	= Pascals (Pa)	x 0.01	= Millibar (mbar)
Millibar (mbar)	x 0.0145	= Pounds-force per square inch (psi; lbf/in^2; lb/in^2)	x 68.947	= Millibar (mbar)
Millibar (mbar)	x 0.75	= Millimetres of mercury (mmHg)	x 1.333	= Millibar (mbar)
Millibar (mbar)	x 0.401	= Inches of water (inH$_2$O)	x 2.491	= Millibar (mbar)
Millimetres of mercury (mmHg)	x 0.535	= Inches of water (inH$_2$O)	x 1.868	= Millimetres of mercury (mmHg)
Inches of water (inH$_2$O)	x 0.036	= Pounds-force per square inch (psi; lbf/in^2; lb/in^2)	x 27.68	= Inches of water (inH$_2$O)

Torque (moment of force)

Pounds-force inches (lbf in; lb in)	x 1.152	= Kilograms-force centimetre (kgf cm; kg cm)	x 0.868	= Pounds-force inches (lbf in; lb in)
Pounds-force inches (lbf in; lb in)	x 0.113	= Newton metres (Nm)	x 8.85	= Pounds-force inches (lbf in; lb in)
Pounds-force inches (lbf in; lb in)	x 0.083	= Pounds-force feet (lbf ft; lb ft)	x 12	= Pounds-force inches (lbf in; lb in)
Pounds-force feet (lbf ft; lb ft)	x 0.138	= Kilograms-force metres (kgf m; kg m)	x 7.233	= Pounds-force feet (lbf ft; lb ft)
Pounds-force feet (lbf ft; lb ft)	x 1.356	= Newton metres (Nm)	x 0.738	= Pounds-force feet (lbf ft; lb ft)
Newton metres (Nm)	x 0.102	= Kilograms-force metres (kgf m; kg m)	x 9.804	= Newton metres (Nm)

Power

Horsepower (hp)	x 745.7	= Watts (W)	x 0.0013	= Horsepower (hp)

Velocity (speed)

Miles per hour (miles/hr; mph)	x 1.609	= Kilometres per hour (km/hr; kph)	x 0.621	= Miles per hour (miles/hr; mph)

Fuel consumption*

Miles per gallon, Imperial (mpg)	x 0.354	= Kilometres per litre (km/l)	x 2.825	= Miles per gallon, Imperial (mpg)
Miles per gallon, US (mpg)	x 0.425	= Kilometres per litre (km/l)	x 2.352	= Miles per gallon, US (mpg)

Temperature

Degrees Fahrenheit = (°C x 1.8) + 32   Degrees Celsius (Degrees Centigrade; °C) = (°F - 32) x 0.56

It is common practice to convert from miles per gallon (mpg) to litres/100 kilometres (l/100km), where mpg x l/100 km = 282

Spare parts are available from many sources, including maker's appointed garages, accessory shops, and motor factors. To be sure of obtaining the correct parts, it will sometimes be necessary to quote the vehicle identification number. If possible, it can also be useful to take the old parts along for positive identification. Items such as starter motors and alternators may be available under a service exchange scheme – any parts returned should be clean.

Our advice regarding spare parts is as follows.

Officially appointed garages

This is the best source of parts which are peculiar to your car, and which are not otherwise generally available (eg, badges, interior trim, certain body panels, etc). It is also the only place at which you should buy parts if the car is still under warranty.

Accessory shops

These are very good places to buy materials and components needed for the maintenance of your car (oil, air and fuel filters, light bulbs, drivebelts, greases, brake pads, touch-up paint, etc). Components of this nature sold by a reputable shop are usually of the same standard as those used by the car manufacturer.

Besides components, these shops also sell tools and general accessories, usually have convenient opening hours, charge lower prices, and can often be found close to home. Some accessory shops have parts counters where components needed for almost any repair job can be purchased or ordered.

Motor factors

Good factors will stock all the more important components which wear out comparatively quickly, and can sometimes supply individual components needed for the overhaul of a larger assembly (eg, brake seals and hydraulic parts, bearing shells, pistons, valves). They may also handle work such as cylinder block reboring, crankshaft regrinding, etc.

Engine reconditioners

These specialise in engine overhaul and can also supply components. It is recommended that the establishment is a member of the Federation of Engine Re-Manufacturers, or a similar society.

Tyre and exhaust specialists

These outlets may be independent, or members of a local or national chain. They frequently offer competitive prices when compared with a main dealer or local garage, but it will pay to obtain several quotes before making a decision. When researching prices, also ask what extras may be added – for instance fitting a new valve, balancing the wheel and tyre disposal all both commonly charged on top of the price of a new tyre.

Other sources

Beware of parts or materials obtained from market stalls, car boot sales, on-line auctions or similar outlets. Such items are not invariably sub-standard, but there is little chance of compensation if they do prove unsatisfactory. In the case of safety-critical components such as brake pads, there is the risk not only of financial loss, but also of an accident causing injury or death.

Second-hand components or assemblies obtained from a car breaker can be a good buy in some circumstances, but this sort of purchase is best made by the experienced DIY mechanic.

Vehicle identification

Modifications are a continuing and unpublished process in vehicle manufacture, quite apart from major model changes. Spare parts manuals and lists are compiled upon a numerical basis, the individual vehicle numbers being essential to correct identification of the component required.

Vauxhall/Opel use a 'Car pass' scheme for vehicle identification. This is a card which is issued to the customer when the car is first purchased. It contains important information, eg, VIN number, key number and radio code. It also includes a special code for diagnostic equipment, therefore it must be kept in a secure place and not in the vehicle.

When ordering spare parts, always give as much information as possible. Quote the car model, year of manufacture and vehicle identification and/or engine numbers as appropriate.

The *vehicle identification plate* is located in the right-hand side of the engine compartment, above the air cleaner housing and includes the Vehicle Identification Number (VIN), vehicle weight information and paint and trim colour codes. This information also appears on the right-hand front door B-pillar **(see illustration)**.

The *Vehicle Identification Number (VIN)* is given on the vehicle identification plate and is also stamped into the body floor panel between the right-hand front seat and the door sill panel **(see illustration)**; lift the flap in the carpet to see it.

The engine number is stamped on a horizontal flat located on the front of the cylinder block, at the transmission end. The first part of the engine number gives the engine code – eg, Z14XEP.

Engine codes

1.4 litre (1364 cc) DOHC 16-valve petrol engine Z14XEP
1.6 litre (1598 cc) petrol engine:
  SOHC 8-valve. Z16SE
  DOHC 16-valve. . . . . Z16XE and Z16XEP
1.8 litre (1796 cc) DOHC 16-valve petrol engine Z18XE
1.3 litre (1248 cc) DOHC 16-valve diesel engine Z13DTJ
1.7 litre (1686 cc) DOHC 16-valve diesel engine . . Y17DT and Z17DTH

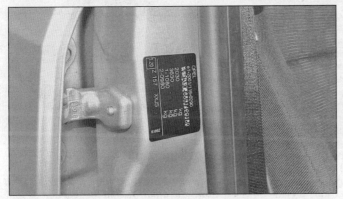

Vehicle Identification Number (VIN) plate attached to the front right-hand side door pillar

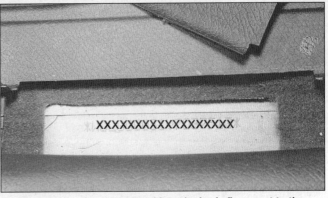

The VIN number is stamped into the body floor next to the right-hand front seat

Whenever servicing, repair or overhaul work is carried out on the car or its components, observe the following procedures and instructions. This will assist in carrying out the operation efficiently and to a professional standard of workmanship.

Joint mating faces and gaskets

When separating components at their mating faces, never insert screwdrivers or similar implements into the joint between the faces in order to prise them apart. This can cause severe damage which results in oil leaks, coolant leaks, etc upon reassembly. Separation is usually achieved by tapping along the joint with a soft-faced hammer in order to break the seal. However, note that this method may not be suitable where dowels are used for component location.

Where a gasket is used between the mating faces of two components, a new one must be fitted on reassembly; fit it dry unless otherwise stated in the repair procedure. Make sure that the mating faces are clean and dry, with all traces of old gasket removed. When cleaning a joint face, use a tool which is unlikely to score or damage the face, and remove any burrs or nicks with an oilstone or fine file.

Make sure that tapped holes are cleaned with a pipe cleaner, and keep them free of jointing compound, if this is being used, unless specifically instructed otherwise.

Ensure that all orifices, channels or pipes are clear, and blow through them, preferably using compressed air.

Oil seals

Oil seals can be removed by levering them out with a wide flat-bladed screwdriver or similar implement. Alternatively, a number of self-tapping screws may be screwed into the seal, and these used as a purchase for pliers or some similar device in order to pull the seal free.

Whenever an oil seal is removed from its working location, either individually or as part of an assembly, it should be renewed.

The very fine sealing lip of the seal is easily damaged, and will not seal if the surface it contacts is not completely clean and free from scratches, nicks or grooves. If the original sealing surface of the component cannot be restored, and the manufacturer has not made provision for slight relocation of the seal relative to the sealing surface, the component should be renewed.

Protect the lips of the seal from any surface which may damage them in the course of fitting. Use tape or a conical sleeve where possible. Where indicated, lubricate the seal lips with oil before fitting and, on dual-lipped seals, fill the space between the lips with grease.

Unless otherwise stated, oil seals must be fitted with their sealing lips toward the lubricant to be sealed.

Use a tubular drift or block of wood of the appropriate size to install the seal and, if the seal housing is shouldered, drive the seal down to the shoulder. If the seal housing is unshouldered, the seal should be fitted with its face flush with the housing top face (unless otherwise instructed).

Screw threads and fastenings

Seized nuts, bolts and screws are quite a common occurrence where corrosion has set in, and the use of penetrating oil or releasing fluid will often overcome this problem if the offending item is soaked for a while before attempting to release it. The use of an impact driver may also provide a means of releasing such stubborn fastening devices, when used in conjunction with the appropriate screwdriver bit or socket. If none of these methods works, it may be necessary to resort to the careful application of heat, or the use of a hacksaw or nut splitter device. Before resorting to extreme methods, check that you are not dealing with a left-hand thread!

Studs are usually removed by locking two nuts together on the threaded part, and then using a spanner on the lower nut to unscrew the stud. Studs or bolts which have broken off below the surface of the component in which they are mounted can sometimes be removed using a stud extractor.

Always ensure that a blind tapped hole is completely free from oil, grease, water or other fluid before installing the bolt or stud. Failure to do this could cause the housing to crack due to the hydraulic action of the bolt or stud as it is screwed in.

For some screw fastenings, notably cylinder head bolts or nuts, torque wrench settings are no longer specified for the latter stages of tightening, "angle-tightening" being called up instead. Typically, a fairly low torque wrench setting will be applied to the bolts/nuts in the correct sequence, followed by one or more stages of tightening through specified angles.

When checking or retightening a nut or bolt to a specified torque setting, slacken the nut or bolt by a quarter of a turn, and then retighten to the specified setting. However, this should not be attempted where angular tightening has been used.

Locknuts, locktabs and washers

Any fastening which will rotate against a component or housing during tightening should always have a washer between it and the relevant component or housing.

Spring or split washers should always be renewed when they are used to lock a critical component such as a big-end bearing retaining bolt or nut. Locktabs which are folded over to retain a nut or bolt should always be renewed.

Self-locking nuts can be re-used in non-critical areas, providing resistance can be felt when the locking portion passes over the bolt or stud thread. However, it should be noted that self-locking stiffnuts tend to lose their effectiveness after long periods of use, and should then be renewed as a matter of course.

Split pins must always be replaced with new ones of the correct size for the hole.

When thread-locking compound is found on the threads of a fastener which is to be re-used, it should be cleaned off with a wire brush and solvent, and fresh compound applied on reassembly.

Special tools

Some repair procedures in this manual entail the use of special tools such as a press, two or three-legged pullers, spring compressors, etc. Wherever possible, suitable readily-available alternatives to the manufacturer's special tools are described, and are shown in use. In some instances, where no alternative is possible, it has been necessary to resort to the use of a manufacturer's tool, and this has been done for reasons of safety as well as the efficient completion of the repair operation. Unless you are highly-skilled and have a thorough understanding of the procedures described, never attempt to bypass the use of any special tool when the procedure described specifies its use. Not only is there a very great risk of personal injury, but expensive damage could be caused to the components involved.

Environmental considerations

When disposing of used engine oil, brake fluid, antifreeze, etc, give due consideration to any detrimental environmental effects. Do not, for instance, pour any of the above liquids down drains into the general sewage system, or onto the ground to soak away. Many local council refuse tips provide a facility for waste oil disposal, as do some garages. You can find your nearest disposal point by calling the Environment Agency on 08708 506 506 or by visiting www.oilbankline.org.uk.

Note: It is illegal and anti-social to dump oil down the drain. To find the location of your local oil recycling bank, call 08708 506 506 or visit www.oilbankline.org.uk.

The jack supplied with the vehicle tool kit should only be used for changing roadwheels – see *Wheel changing* at the front of this manual. Ensure the jack head is correctly engaged before attempting to raise the vehicle. When carrying out any other kind of work, raise the vehicle using a hydraulic jack, and always supplement the jack with axle stands positioned under the vehicle jacking points.

When jacking up the vehicle with a trolley jack, position the jack head under one of the relevant jacking points (note that the jacking points for use with a hydraulic jack are different to those for use with the vehicle jack). Use a block of wood between the jack or axle stand and the sill – the block of wood should have a groove cut into it, in which the welded flange of the sill will locate. **Do not** jack the

vehicle under the sump or any of the steering or suspension components. Supplement the jack using axle stands **(see illustrations)**.

 Warning: Never work under, around, or near a raised vehicle, unless it is adequately supported in at least two places.

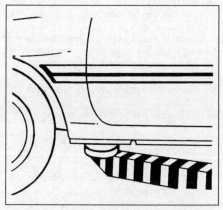

Front jacking point for hydraulic jack or axle stands

Rear jacking point for hydraulic jack or axle stands

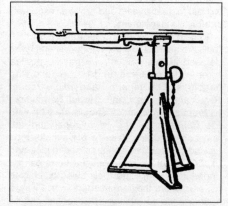

Axle stands should be placed under, or adjacent to, the jacking point (arrowed)

Disconnecting the battery

Numerous systems fitted to the vehicle require battery power to be available at all times, either to ensure their continued operation (such as the clock) or to maintain control unit memories which would be erased if the battery were to be disconnected. Whenever the battery is to be disconnected therefore, first note the following, to ensure that there are no unforeseen consequences of this action:

a) *First, on any vehicle with central locking, it is a wise precaution to remove the key from the ignition, and to keep it with you, so that it does not get locked in, if the central locking should engage accidentally when the battery is reconnected.*

b) *Depending on model and specification, the Vauxhall/Opel anti-theft alarm system may be of the type which is automatically activated when the vehicle battery is disconnected and/or reconnected. To prevent the alarm sounding on models so equipped, switch the ignition on, then off, and disconnect the battery within 15 seconds. If the alarm is activated when the battery is reconnected, switch the ignition on then off to deactivate the alarm.*

c) *If a security-coded audio unit is fitted, and the unit and/or the battery is*

disconnected, the unit will not function again on reconnection until the correct security code is entered. Details of this procedure, which varies according to the unit fitted, are given in the vehicle audio system operating instructions. Ensure you have the correct code before you disconnect the battery. If you do not have the code or details of the correct procedure, but can supply proof of ownership and a legitimate reason for wanting this information, a Vauxhall/Opel dealer may be able to help.

d) *The engine management electronic control unit is of the 'self-learning' type, meaning that as it operates, it also monitors and stores the settings which give optimum engine performance under all operating conditions. When the battery is disconnected, these settings are lost and the ECU reverts to the base settings programmed into its memory at the factory. On restarting, this may lead to the engine running/idling roughly for a short while, until the ECU has re-learned the optimum settings. This process is best accomplished by taking the vehicle on a road test (for approximately 15 minutes), covering all engine speeds and loads, concentrating mainly in the 2500 to 3500 rpm region.*

e) *On models with electric windows, it will be necessary to reprogramme the motors to restore the one-touch function of the buttons, after reconnection of the battery. To do this, fully close both front windows. With the windows closed, depress the up button of the driver's side window for approximately 5 seconds, then release it and depress the passenger side window up button for approximately 5 seconds.*

f) *On models with an electric sliding sunroof, it will be necessary to fully open and fully close the sunroof after battery reconnection, to recalibrate the sensors.*

g) *On models equipped with an electronic stability program (ESP), it will be necessary to recalibrate the steering angle sensor when the battery is reconnected. To do this, turn the steering wheel to the straight-ahead position. Switch on the ignition and turn the steering wheel to full left lock, then full right-lock. Return to the straight-ahead position and switch off the ignition.*

h) *On all models, when reconnecting the battery after disconnection, switch on the ignition and wait 10 seconds to allow the electronic vehicle systems to stabilise and re-initialise.*

Introduction

A selection of good tools is a fundamental requirement for anyone contemplating the maintenance and repair of a motor vehicle. For the owner who does not possess any, their purchase will prove a considerable expense, offsetting some of the savings made by doing-it-yourself. However, provided that the tools purchased meet the relevant national safety standards and are of good quality, they will last for many years and prove an extremely worthwhile investment.

To help the average owner to decide which tools are needed to carry out the various tasks detailed in this manual, we have compiled three lists of tools under the following headings: *Maintenance and minor repair, Repair and overhaul*, and *Special*. Newcomers to practical mechanics should start off with the *Maintenance and minor repair* tool kit, and confine themselves to the simpler jobs around the vehicle. Then, as confidence and experience grow, more difficult tasks can be undertaken, with extra tools being purchased as, and when, they are needed. In this way, a *Maintenance and minor repair* tool kit can be built up into a *Repair and overhaul* tool kit over a considerable period of time, without any major cash outlays. The experienced do-it-yourselfer will have a tool kit good enough for most repair and overhaul procedures, and will add tools from the *Special* category when it is felt that the expense is justified by the amount of use to which these tools will be put.

Maintenance and minor repair tool kit

The tools given in this list should be considered as a minimum requirement if routine maintenance, servicing and minor repair operations are to be undertaken. We recommend the purchase of combination spanners (ring one end, open-ended the other); although more expensive than open-ended ones, they do give the advantages of both types of spanner.

☐ *Combination spanners:*
  Metric - 8 to 19 mm inclusive
☐ *Adjustable spanner - 35 mm jaw (approx.)*
☐ *Spark plug spanner (with rubber insert) - petrol models*
☐ *Spark plug gap adjustment tool - petrol models*
☐ *Set of feeler gauges*
☐ *Brake bleed nipple spanner*
☐ *Screwdrivers:*
  Flat blade - 100 mm long x 6 mm dia
  Cross blade - 100 mm long x 6 mm dia
  Torx - various sizes (not all vehicles)
☐ *Combination pliers*
☐ *Hacksaw (junior)*
☐ *Tyre pump*
☐ *Tyre pressure gauge*
☐ *Oil can*
☐ *Oil filter removal tool (if applicable)*
☐ *Fine emery cloth*
☐ *Wire brush (small)*
☐ *Funnel (medium size)*
☐ *Sump drain plug key (not all vehicles)*

Repair and overhaul tool kit

These tools are virtually essential for anyone undertaking any major repairs to a motor vehicle, and are additional to those given in the *Maintenance and minor repair* list. Included in this list is a comprehensive set of sockets. Although these are expensive, they will be found invaluable as they are so versatile - particularly if various drives are included in the set. We recommend the half-inch square-drive type, as this can be used with most proprietary torque wrenches.

The tools in this list will sometimes need to be supplemented by tools from the *Special* list:

☐ *Sockets to cover range in previous list (including Torx sockets)*
☐ *Reversible ratchet drive (for use with sockets)*
☐ *Extension piece, 250 mm (for use with sockets)*
☐ *Universal joint (for use with sockets)*
☐ *Flexible handle or sliding T "breaker bar" (for use with sockets)*
☐ *Torque wrench (for use with sockets)*
☐ *Self-locking grips*
☐ *Ball pein hammer*
☐ *Soft-faced mallet (plastic or rubber)*
☐ *Screwdrivers:*
  Flat blade - long & sturdy, short (chubby), and narrow (electrician's) types
  Cross blade - long & sturdy, and short (chubby) types
☐ *Pliers:*
  Long-nosed
  Side cutters (electrician's)
  Circlip (internal and external)
☐ *Cold chisel - 25 mm*
☐ *Scriber*
☐ *Scraper*
☐ *Centre-punch*
☐ *Pin punch*
☐ *Hacksaw*
☐ *Brake hose clamp*
☐ *Brake/clutch bleeding kit*
☐ *Selection of twist drills*
☐ *Steel rule/straight-edge*
☐ *Allen keys (inc. splined/Torx type)*
☐ *Selection of files*
☐ *Wire brush*
☐ *Axle stands*
☐ *Jack (strong trolley or hydraulic type)*
☐ *Light with extension lead*
☐ *Universal electrical multi-meter*

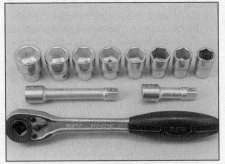

Sockets and reversible ratchet drive

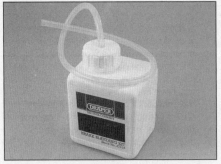

Brake bleeding kit

Torx key, socket and bit

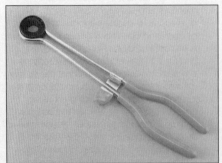

Hose clamp

Angular-tightening gauge

Special tools

The tools in this list are those which are not used regularly, are expensive to buy, or which need to be used in accordance with their manufacturers' instructions. Unless relatively difficult mechanical jobs are undertaken frequently, it will not be economic to buy many of these tools. Where this is the case, you could consider clubbing together with friends (or joining a motorists' club) to make a joint purchase, or borrowing the tools against a deposit from a local garage or tool hire specialist.

The following list contains only those tools and instruments freely available to the public, and not those special tools produced by the vehicle manufacturer specifically for its dealer network. You will find occasional references to these manufacturers' special tools in the text of this manual. Generally, an alternative method of doing the job without the vehicle manufacturers' special tool is given. However, sometimes there is no alternative to using them. Where this is the case and the relevant tool cannot be bought or borrowed, you will have to entrust the work to a dealer.

- [ ] Angular-tightening gauge
- [ ] Valve spring compressor
- [ ] Valve grinding tool
- [ ] Piston ring compressor
- [ ] Piston ring removal/installation tool
- [ ] Cylinder bore hone
- [ ] Balljoint separator
- [ ] Coil spring compressors (where applicable)
- [ ] Two/three-legged hub and bearing puller
- [ ] Impact screwdriver
- [ ] Micrometer and/or vernier calipers
- [ ] Dial gauge
- [ ] Tachometer
- [ ] Fault code reader
- [ ] Cylinder compression gauge
- [ ] Hand-operated vacuum pump and gauge
- [ ] Clutch plate alignment set
- [ ] Brake shoe steady spring cup removal tool
- [ ] Bush and bearing removal/installation set
- [ ] Stud extractors
- [ ] Tap and die set
- [ ] Lifting tackle

Buying tools

Reputable motor accessory shops and superstores often offer excellent quality tools at discount prices, so it pays to shop around.

Remember, you don't have to buy the most expensive items on the shelf, but it is always advisable to steer clear of the very cheap tools. Beware of 'bargains' offered on market stalls, on-line or at car boot sales. There are plenty of good tools around at reasonable prices, but always aim to purchase items which meet the relevant national safety standards. If in doubt, ask the proprietor or manager of the shop for advice before making a purchase.

Care and maintenance of tools

Having purchased a reasonable tool kit, it is necessary to keep the tools in a clean and serviceable condition. After use, always wipe off any dirt, grease and metal particles using a clean, dry cloth, before putting the tools away. Never leave them lying around after they have been used. A simple tool rack on the garage or workshop wall for items such as screwdrivers and pliers is a good idea. Store all normal spanners and sockets in a metal box. Any measuring instruments, gauges, meters, etc, must be carefully stored where they cannot be damaged or become rusty.

Take a little care when tools are used. Hammer heads inevitably become marked, and screwdrivers lose the keen edge on their blades from time to time. A little timely attention with emery cloth or a file will soon restore items like this to a good finish.

Working facilities

Not to be forgotten when discussing tools is the workshop itself. If anything more than routine maintenance is to be carried out, a suitable working area becomes essential.

It is appreciated that many an owner-mechanic is forced by circumstances to remove an engine or similar item without the benefit of a garage or workshop. Having done this, any repairs should always be done under the cover of a roof.

Wherever possible, any dismantling should be done on a clean, flat workbench or table at a suitable working height.

Any workbench needs a vice; one with a jaw opening of 100 mm is suitable for most jobs. As mentioned previously, some clean dry storage space is also required for tools, as well as for any lubricants, cleaning fluids, touch-up paints etc, which become necessary.

Another item which may be required, and which has a much more general usage, is an electric drill with a chuck capacity of at least 8 mm. This, together with a good range of twist drills, is virtually essential for fitting accessories.

Last, but not least, always keep a supply of old newspapers and clean, lint-free rags available, and try to keep any working area as clean as possible.

Micrometers

Dial test indicator ("dial gauge")

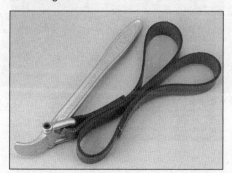
Oil filter removal tool (strap wrench type)

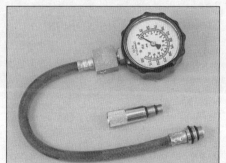
Compression tester

Fault code reader

This is a guide to getting your vehicle through the MOT test. Obviously it will not be possible to examine the vehicle to the same standard as the professional MOT tester. However, working through the following checks will enable you to identify any problem areas before submitting the vehicle for the test.

It has only been possible to summarise the test requirements here, based on the regulations in force at the time of printing. Test standards are becoming increasingly stringent, although there are some exemptions for older vehicles.

An assistant will be needed to help carry out some of these checks.

The checks have been sub-divided into four categories, as follows:

1 Checks carried out **FROM THE DRIVER'S SEAT**

2 Checks carried out **WITH THE VEHICLE ON THE GROUND**

3 Checks carried out **WITH THE VEHICLE RAISED AND THE WHEELS FREE TO TURN**

4 Checks carried out on **YOUR VEHICLE'S EXHAUST EMISSION SYSTEM**

---

1 Checks carried out **FROM THE DRIVER'S SEAT**

Handbrake

☐ Test the operation of the handbrake. Excessive travel (too many clicks) indicates incorrect brake or cable adjustment.
☐ Check that the handbrake cannot be released by tapping the lever sideways. Check the security of the lever mountings.

Footbrake

☐ Depress the brake pedal and check that it does not creep down to the floor, indicating a master cylinder fault. Release the pedal, wait a few seconds, then depress it again. If the pedal travels nearly to the floor before firm resistance is felt, brake adjustment or repair is necessary. If the pedal feels spongy, there is air in the hydraulic system which must be removed by bleeding.

☐ Check that the brake pedal is secure and in good condition. Check also for signs of fluid leaks on the pedal, floor or carpets, which would indicate failed seals in the brake master cylinder.
☐ Check the servo unit (when applicable) by operating the brake pedal several times, then keeping the pedal depressed and starting the engine. As the engine starts, the pedal will move down slightly. If not, the vacuum hose or the servo itself may be faulty.

Steering wheel and column

☐ Examine the steering wheel for fractures or looseness of the hub, spokes or rim.
☐ Move the steering wheel from side to side and then up and down. Check that the steering wheel is not loose on the column, indicating wear or a loose retaining nut. Continue moving the steering wheel as before, but also turn it slightly from left to right.
☐ Check that the steering wheel is not loose on the column, and that there is no abnormal movement of the steering wheel, indicating

wear in the column support bearings or couplings.

Windscreen, mirrors and sunvisor

☐ The windscreen must be free of cracks or other significant damage within the driver's field of view. (Small stone chips are acceptable.) Rear view mirrors must be secure, intact, and capable of being adjusted.

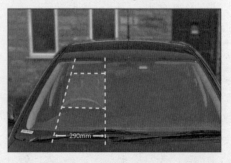

☐ The driver's sunvisor must be capable of being stored in the "up" position.

Seat belts and seats

Note: *The following checks are applicable to all seat belts, front and rear.*

☐ Examine the webbing of all the belts (including rear belts if fitted) for cuts, serious fraying or deterioration. Fasten and unfasten each belt to check the buckles. If applicable, check the retracting mechanism. Check the security of all seat belt mountings accessible from inside the vehicle.

☐ Seat belts with pre-tensioners, once activated, have a "flag" or similar showing on the seat belt stalk. This, in itself, is not a reason for test failure.

☐ The front seats themselves must be securely attached and the backrests must lock in the upright position.

Doors

☐ Both front doors must be able to be opened and closed from outside and inside, and must latch securely when closed.

2 Checks carried out WITH THE VEHICLE ON THE GROUND

Vehicle identification

☐ Number plates must be in good condition, secure and legible, with letters and numbers correctly spaced – spacing at (A) should be 33 mm and at (B) 11 mm.

☐ The VIN plate and/or homologation plate must be legible.

Electrical equipment

☐ Switch on the ignition and check the operation of the horn.

☐ Check the windscreen washers and wipers, examining the wiper blades; renew damaged or perished blades. Also check the operation of the stop-lights.

☐ Check the operation of the sidelights and number plate lights. The lenses and reflectors must be secure, clean and undamaged.

☐ Check the operation and alignment of the headlights. The headlight reflectors must not be tarnished and the lenses must be undamaged.

☐ Switch on the ignition and check the operation of the direction indicators (including the instrument panel tell-tale) and the hazard warning lights. Operation of the sidelights and stop-lights must not affect the indicators - if it does, the cause is usually a bad earth at the rear light cluster.

☐ Check the operation of the rear foglight(s), including the warning light on the instrument panel or in the switch.

☐ The ABS warning light must illuminate in accordance with the manufacturers' design. For most vehicles, the ABS warning light should illuminate when the ignition is switched on, and (if the system is operating properly) extinguish after a few seconds. Refer to the owner's handbook.

Footbrake

☐ Examine the master cylinder, brake pipes and servo unit for leaks, loose mountings, corrosion or other damage.

☐ The fluid reservoir must be secure and the fluid level must be between the upper (**A**) and lower (**B**) markings.

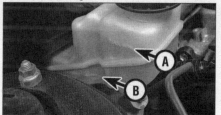

☐ Inspect both front brake flexible hoses for cracks or deterioration of the rubber. Turn the steering from lock to lock, and ensure that the hoses do not contact the wheel, tyre, or any part of the steering or suspension mechanism. With the brake pedal firmly depressed, check the hoses for bulges or leaks under pressure.

Steering and suspension

☐ Have your assistant turn the steering wheel from side to side slightly, up to the point where the steering gear just begins to transmit this movement to the roadwheels. Check for excessive free play between the steering wheel and the steering gear, indicating wear or insecurity of the steering column joints, the column-to-steering gear coupling, or the steering gear itself.

☐ Have your assistant turn the steering wheel more vigorously in each direction, so that the roadwheels just begin to turn. As this is done, examine all the steering joints, linkages, fittings and attachments. Renew any component that shows signs of wear or damage. On vehicles with power steering, check the security and condition of the steering pump, drivebelt and hoses.

☐ Check that the vehicle is standing level, and at approximately the correct ride height.

Shock absorbers

☐ Depress each corner of the vehicle in turn, then release it. The vehicle should rise and then settle in its normal position. If the vehicle continues to rise and fall, the shock absorber is defective. A shock absorber which has seized will also cause the vehicle to fail.

Exhaust system

☐ Start the engine. With your assistant holding a rag over the tailpipe, check the entire system for leaks. Repair or renew leaking sections.

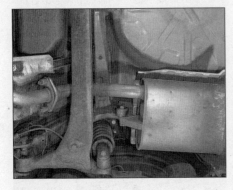

3 Checks carried out **WITH THE VEHICLE RAISED AND THE WHEELS FREE TO TURN**

Jack up the front and rear of the vehicle, and securely support it on axle stands. Position the stands clear of the suspension assemblies. Ensure that the wheels are clear of the ground and that the steering can be turned from lock to lock.

Steering mechanism

☐ Have your assistant turn the steering from lock to lock. Check that the steering turns smoothly, and that no part of the steering mechanism, including a wheel or tyre, fouls any brake hose or pipe or any part of the body structure.
☐ Examine the steering rack rubber gaiters for damage or insecurity of the retaining clips. If power steering is fitted, check for signs of damage or leakage of the fluid hoses, pipes or connections. Also check for excessive stiffness or binding of the steering, a missing split pin or locking device, or severe corrosion of the body structure within 30 cm of any steering component attachment point.

Front and rear suspension and wheel bearings

☐ Starting at the front right-hand side, grasp the roadwheel at the 3 o'clock and 9 o'clock positions and rock gently but firmly. Check for free play or insecurity at the wheel bearings, suspension balljoints, or suspension mount-ings, pivots and attachments.
☐ Now grasp the wheel at the 12 o'clock and 6 o'clock positions and repeat the previous inspection. Spin the wheel, and check for roughness or tightness of the front wheel bearing.

☐ If excess free play is suspected at a component pivot point, this can be confirmed by using a large screwdriver or similar tool and levering between the mounting and the component attachment. This will confirm whether the wear is in the pivot bush, its retaining bolt, or in the mounting itself (the bolt holes can often become elongated).

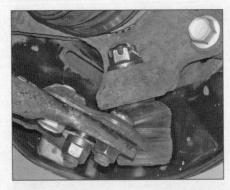

☐ Carry out all the above checks at the other front wheel, and then at both rear wheels.

Springs and shock absorbers

☐ Examine the suspension struts (when applicable) for serious fluid leakage, corrosion, or damage to the casing. Also check the security of the mounting points.
☐ If coil springs are fitted, check that the spring ends locate in their seats, and that the spring is not corroded, cracked or broken.
☐ If leaf springs are fitted, check that all leaves are intact, that the axle is securely attached to each spring, and that there is no deterioration of the spring eye mountings, bushes, and shackles.

☐ The same general checks apply to vehicles fitted with other suspension types, such as torsion bars, hydraulic displacer units, etc. Ensure that all mountings and attachments are secure, that there are no signs of excessive wear, corrosion or damage, and (on hydraulic types) that there are no fluid leaks or damaged pipes.
☐ Inspect the shock absorbers for signs of serious fluid leakage. Check for wear of the mounting bushes or attachments, or damage to the body of the unit.

Driveshafts
(fwd vehicles only)

☐ Rotate each front wheel in turn and inspect the constant velocity joint gaiters for splits or damage. Also check that each driveshaft is straight and undamaged.

Braking system

☐ If possible without dismantling, check brake pad wear and disc condition. Ensure that the friction lining material has not worn excessively, (A) and that the discs are not fractured, pitted, scored or badly worn (B).

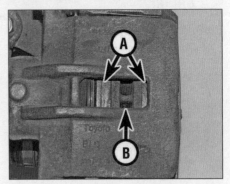

☐ Examine all the rigid brake pipes underneath the vehicle, and the flexible hose(s) at the rear. Look for corrosion, chafing or insecurity of the pipes, and for signs of bulging under pressure, chafing, splits or deterioration of the flexible hoses.
☐ Look for signs of fluid leaks at the brake calipers or on the brake backplates. Repair or renew leaking components.
☐ Slowly spin each wheel, while your assistant depresses and releases the footbrake. Ensure that each brake is operating and does not bind when the pedal is released.

□ Examine the handbrake mechanism, checking for frayed or broken cables, excessive corrosion, or wear or insecurity of the linkage. Check that the mechanism works on each relevant wheel, and releases fully, without binding.

□ It is not possible to test brake efficiency without special equipment, but a road test can be carried out later to check that the vehicle pulls up in a straight line.

Fuel and exhaust systems

□ Inspect the fuel tank (including the filler cap), fuel pipes, hoses and unions. All components must be secure and free from leaks.

□ Examine the exhaust system over its entire length, checking for any damaged, broken or missing mountings, security of the retaining clamps and rust or corrosion.

Wheels and tyres

□ Examine the sidewalls and tread area of each tyre in turn. Check for cuts, tears, lumps, bulges, separation of the tread, and exposure of the ply or cord due to wear or damage. Check that the tyre bead is correctly seated on the wheel rim, that the valve is sound and properly seated, and that the wheel is not distorted or damaged.

□ Check that the tyres are of the correct size for the vehicle, that they are of the same size

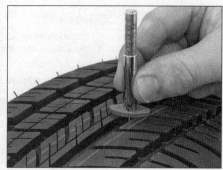

and type on each axle, and that the pressures are correct.

□ Check the tyre tread depth. The legal minimum at the time of writing is 1.6 mm over at least three-quarters of the tread width. Abnormal tread wear may indicate incorrect front wheel alignment.

Body corrosion

□ Check the condition of the entire vehicle structure for signs of corrosion in load-bearing areas. (These include chassis box sections, side sills, cross-members, pillars, and all suspension, steering, braking system and seat belt mountings and anchorages.) Any corrosion which has seriously reduced the thickness of a load-bearing area is likely to cause the vehicle to fail. In this case professional repairs are likely to be needed.

□ Damage or corrosion which causes sharp or otherwise dangerous edges to be exposed will also cause the vehicle to fail.

4 Checks carried out on YOUR VEHICLE'S EXHAUST EMISSION SYSTEM

Petrol models

□ The engine should be warmed up, and running well (ignition system in good order, air filter element clean, etc).

□ Before testing, run the engine at around 2500 rpm for 20 seconds. Let the engine drop to idle, and watch for smoke from the exhaust. If the idle speed is too high, or if dense blue or black smoke emerges for more than 5 seconds, the vehicle will fail. Typically, blue smoke signifies oil burning (engine wear); black smoke means unburnt fuel (dirty air cleaner element, or other fuel system fault).

□ An exhaust gas analyser for measuring carbon monoxide (CO) and hydrocarbons (HC) is now needed. If one cannot be hired or borrowed, have a local garage perform the check.

CO emissions (mixture)

□ The MOT tester has access to the CO limits for all vehicles. The CO level is measured at idle speed, and at 'fast idle' (2500 to 3000 rpm). The following limits are given as a general guide:

At idle speed – Less than 0.5% CO
At 'fast idle' – Less than 0.3% CO
Lambda reading – 0.97 to 1.03

□ If the CO level is too high, this may point to poor maintenance, a fuel injection system problem, faulty lambda (oxygen) sensor or catalytic converter. Try an injector cleaning treatment, and check the vehicle's ECU for fault codes.

HC emissions

□ The MOT tester has access to HC limits for all vehicles. The HC level is measured at 'fast idle' (2500 to 3000 rpm). The following limits are given as a general guide:

At 'fast idle' – Less then 200 ppm

□ Excessive HC emissions are typically caused by oil being burnt (worn engine), or by a blocked crankcase ventilation system ('breather'). If the engine oil is old and thin, an oil change may help. If the engine is running badly, check the vehicle's ECU for fault codes.

Diesel models

□ The only emission test for diesel engines is measuring exhaust smoke density, using a calibrated smoke meter. The test involves accelerating the engine at least 3 times to its maximum unloaded speed.

Note: *On engines with a timing belt, it is VITAL that the belt is in good condition before the test is carried out.*

□ With the engine warmed up, it is first purged by running at around 2500 rpm for 20 seconds. A governor check is then carried out, by slowly accelerating the engine to its maximum speed. After this, the smoke meter is connected, and the engine is accelerated quickly to maximum speed three times. If the smoke density is less than the limits given below, the vehicle will pass:

Non-turbo vehicles: 2.5m-1
Turbocharged vehicles: 3.0m-1

□ If excess smoke is produced, try fitting a new air cleaner element, or using an injector cleaning treatment. If the engine is running badly, where applicable, check the vehicle's ECU for fault codes. Also check the vehicle's EGR system, where applicable. At high mileages, the injectors may require professional attention.

Engine

- [ ] Engine fails to rotate when attempting to start
- [ ] Engine rotates, but will not start
- [ ] Engine difficult to start when cold
- [ ] Engine difficult to start when hot
- [ ] Starter motor noisy or excessively-rough in engagement
- [ ] Engine starts, but stops immediately
- [ ] Engine idles erratically
- [ ] Engine misfires at idle speed
- [ ] Engine misfires throughout the driving speed range
- [ ] Engine hesitates on acceleration
- [ ] Engine stalls
- [ ] Engine lacks power
- [ ] Engine backfires
- [ ] Oil pressure warning light illuminated with engine running
- [ ] Engine runs-on after switching off
- [ ] Engine noises

Cooling system

- [ ] Overheating
- [ ] Overcooling
- [ ] External coolant leakage
- [ ] Internal coolant leakage
- [ ] Corrosion

Fuel and exhaust systems

- [ ] Excessive fuel consumption
- [ ] Fuel leakage and/or fuel odour
- [ ] Excessive noise or fumes from exhaust system

Clutch

- [ ] Pedal travels to floor – no pressure or very little resistance
- [ ] Clutch fails to disengage (unable to select gears)
- [ ] Clutch slips (engine speed increases, with no increase in vehicle speed)
- [ ] Judder as clutch is engaged
- [ ] Noise when depressing or releasing clutch pedal

Manual transmission

- [ ] Noisy in neutral with engine running
- [ ] Noisy in one particular gear
- [ ] Difficulty engaging gears
- [ ] Jumps out of gear
- [ ] Vibration
- [ ] Lubricant leaks

Driveshafts

- [ ] Vibration when accelerating or decelerating
- [ ] Clicking or knocking noise on turns (at slow speed on full-lock)

Braking system

- [ ] Vehicle pulls to one side under braking
- [ ] Noise (grinding or high-pitched squeal) when brakes applied
- [ ] Excessive brake pedal travel
- [ ] Brake pedal feels spongy when depressed
- [ ] Excessive brake pedal effort required to stop vehicle
- [ ] Judder felt through brake pedal or steering wheel when braking
- [ ] Brakes binding
- [ ] Rear wheels locking under normal braking

Suspension and steering

- [ ] Vehicle pulls to one side
- [ ] Wheel wobble and vibration
- [ ] Excessive pitching and/or rolling around corners, or during braking
- [ ] Wandering or general instability
- [ ] Excessively-stiff steering
- [ ] Excessive play in steering
- [ ] Lack of power assistance
- [ ] Tyre wear excessive

Electrical system

- [ ] Battery will not hold a charge for more than a few days
- [ ] Ignition/no-charge warning light remains illuminated with engine running
- [ ] Ignition/no-charge warning light fails to come on
- [ ] Lights inoperative
- [ ] Instrument readings inaccurate or erratic
- [ ] Horn inoperative, or unsatisfactory in operation
- [ ] Windscreen wipers inoperative, or unsatisfactory in operation
- [ ] Windscreen washers inoperative, or unsatisfactory in operation
- [ ] Electric windows inoperative, or unsatisfactory in operation
- [ ] Central locking system inoperative, or unsatisfactory in operation

Introduction

The vehicle owner who does his or her own maintenance according to the recommended service schedules should not have to use this section of the manual very often. Modern component reliability is such that, provided those items subject to wear or deterioration are inspected or renewed at the specified intervals, sudden failure is comparatively rare. Faults do not usually just happen as a result of sudden failure, but develop over a period of time. Major mechanical failures in particular are usually preceded by characteristic symptoms over hundreds or even thousands of miles. Those components which do occasionally fail without warning are often small and easily carried in the vehicle.

With any fault-finding, the first step is to decide where to begin investigations. Sometimes this is obvious, but on other occasions, a little detective work will be necessary. The owner who makes half a dozen haphazard adjustments or replacements may be successful in curing a fault (or its symptoms), but will be none the wiser if the fault recurs, and ultimately may have spent more time and money than was necessary. A calm and logical approach will be found to be more satisfactory in the long run. Always take into account any warning signs or abnormalities that may have been noticed in the period preceding the fault – power loss, high or low gauge readings, unusual smells, etc – and remember that failure of components such as fuses or spark plugs may only be pointers to some underlying fault.

The pages which follow provide an easy-reference guide to the more common problems which may occur during the operation of the vehicle. These problems and their possible causes are grouped under headings denoting various components or systems, such as Engine, Cooling system, etc. The general Chapter which deals with the problem is also shown in brackets; refer to the relevant part of that Chapter for system-specific information. Whatever the fault, certain basic principles apply. These are as follows:

Verify the fault. This is simply a matter of being sure that you know what the symptoms are before starting work. This is particularly important if you are investigating a fault for someone else, who may not have described it very accurately.

Don't overlook the obvious. For example, if the vehicle won't start, is there fuel in the tank? (Don't take anyone else's word on this particular point, and don't trust the fuel gauge either!) If an electrical fault is indicated, look for loose or broken wires before digging out the test gear.

Cure the disease, not the symptom. Substituting a flat battery with a fully-charged one will get you off the hard shoulder, but if the underlying cause is not attended to, the new battery will go the same way. Similarly, changing oil-fouled spark plugs for a new set will get you moving again, but remember that the reason for the fouling (if it wasn't simply an incorrect grade of plug) will have to be established and corrected.

Don't take anything for granted. Particularly, don't forget that a 'new' component may itself be defective (especially if it's been rattling around in the boot for months), and don't leave components out of a fault diagnosis sequence just because they are new or recently-fitted. When you do finally diagnose a difficult fault, you'll probably realise that all the evidence was there from the start.

Consider what work, if any, has recently been carried out. Many faults arise through careless or hurried work. For instance, if any work has been performed under the bonnet, could some of the wiring have been dislodged or incorrectly routed, or a hose trapped? Have all the fasteners been properly tightened? Were new, genuine parts and new gaskets used? There is often a certain amount of detective work to be done in this case, as an apparently-unrelated task can have far-reaching consequences.

Diesel fault diagnosis

The majority of starting problems on small diesel engines are electrical in origin. The mechanic who is familiar with petrol engines but less so with diesel may be inclined to view the diesel's injectors and pump in the same light as the spark plugs and distributor, but this is generally a mistake.

When investigating complaints of difficult starting for someone else, make sure that the correct starting procedure is understood and is being followed. Some drivers are unaware of the significance of the preheating warning light – many modern engines are sufficiently forgiving for this not to matter in mild weather, but with the onset of winter, problems begin. Glow plugs in particular are often neglected – just one faulty plug will make cold-weather starting very difficult.

As a rule of thumb, if the engine is difficult to start but runs well when it has finally got going, the problem is electrical (battery, starter motor or preheating system). If poor performance is combined with difficult starting, the problem is likely to be in the fuel system. The low-pressure (supply) side of the fuel system should be checked before suspecting the injectors and high-pressure pump. The most common fuel supply problem is air getting into the system, and any pipe from the fuel tank forwards must be scrutinised if air leakage is suspected.

Engine

Engine fails to rotate when attempting to start

- ☐ Battery terminal connections loose or corroded (see *Weekly checks*)
- ☐ Battery discharged or faulty (Chapter 5A)
- ☐ Broken, loose or disconnected wiring in the starting circuit (Chapter 5A)
- ☐ Defective starter solenoid or ignition switch (Chapter 5A or 12)
- ☐ Defective starter motor (Chapter 5A)
- ☐ Starter pinion or flywheel ring gear teeth loose or broken (Chapter 2A, 2B, 2C, 2D, 2E or 5A)
- ☐ Engine earth strap broken or disconnected (Chapter 5A)
- ☐ Engine suffering 'hydraulic lock' (eg from water drawn into the engine after traversing flooded roads, or from a serious internal coolant leak) – consult a main dealer for advice

Engine rotates, but will not start

- ☐ Fuel tank empty
- ☐ Battery discharged (engine rotates slowly) (Chapter 5A)
- ☐ Battery terminal connections loose or corroded (see *Weekly checks*)
- ☐ Ignition components damp or damaged – petrol models (Chapter 1A or 5B)
- ☐ Immobiliser fault, or 'uncoded' ignition key being used (Chapter 12 or *Roadside repairs*)
- ☐ Broken, loose or disconnected wiring in the ignition circuit – petrol models (Chapter 1A or 5B)
- ☐ Worn, faulty or incorrectly-gapped spark plugs – petrol models (Chapter 1A)
- ☐ Preheating system faulty – diesel models (Chapter 5A)
- ☐ Fuel injection/engine management system fault (Chapter 4A, 4B or 4C)
- ☐ Air in fuel system – diesel models (Chapter 4B)
- ☐ Major mechanical failure (eg timing belt/chain snapped) (Chapter 2A, 2B, 2C, 2D or 2E)

Engine difficult to start when cold

- ☐ Battery discharged (Chapter 5A)
- ☐ Battery terminal connections loose or corroded (see *Weekly checks*)

- ☐ Worn, faulty or incorrectly-gapped spark plugs – petrol models (Chapter 1A)
- ☐ Other ignition system fault – petrol models (Chapter 1A or 5B)
- ☐ Preheating system faulty – diesel models (Chapter 5A)
- ☐ Fuel injection/engine management system fault (Chapter 4A, 4B or 4C)
- ☐ Wrong grade of engine oil used (*Weekly checks*, Chapter 1A or 1B)
- ☐ Low cylinder compression (Chapter 2A, 2B, 2C, 2D or 2E)

Engine difficult to start when hot

- ☐ Air filter element dirty or clogged (Chapter 1A or 1B)
- ☐ Fuel injection/engine management system fault (Chapter 4A, 4B or 4C)
- ☐ Low cylinder compression (Chapter 2A, 2B, 2C, 2D or 2E)

Starter motor noisy or excessively-rough in engagement

- ☐ Starter pinion or flywheel ring gear teeth loose or broken (Chapter 2A, 2B, 2C, 2D, 2E or 5A)
- ☐ Starter motor mounting bolts loose or missing (Chapter 5A)
- ☐ Starter motor internal components worn or damaged (Chapter 5A)

Engine starts, but stops immediately

- ☐ Loose or faulty electrical connections in the ignition circuit – petrol models (Chapter 1A or 5B)
- ☐ Vacuum leak at the throttle housing or inlet manifold – petrol models (Chapter 4A or 4B)
- ☐ Blocked injectors/fuel injection system fault (Chapter 4A or 4B)

Engine idles erratically

- ☐ Air filter element clogged (Chapter 1A or 1B)
- ☐ Vacuum leak at the throttle housing, inlet manifold or associated hoses – petrol models (Chapter 4A or 4C)
- ☐ Worn, faulty or incorrectly-gapped spark plugs – petrol models (Chapter 1A)
- ☐ Uneven or low cylinder compression (Chapter 2A, 2B, 2C, 2D or 2E)
- ☐ Camshaft lobes worn (Chapter 2A, 2B, 2C, 2D or 2E)
- ☐ Blocked injectors/fuel injection system fault (Chapter 4A, or 4B)

Engine (continued)

Engine misfires at idle speed

- [ ] Worn, faulty or incorrectly-gapped spark plugs – petrol models (Chapter 1A)
- [ ] Vacuum leak at the throttle housing, inlet manifold or associated hoses – petrol models (Chapter 4A or 4C)
- [ ] Blocked injectors/fuel injection system fault (Chapter 4A, 4B or 4C)
- [ ] Faulty injector(s) – diesel models (Chapter 4B)
- [ ] Uneven or low cylinder compression (Chapter 2A, 2B, 2C, 2D or 2E)
- [ ] Disconnected, leaking, or perished crankcase ventilation hoses (Chapter 4C)

Engine misfires throughout the driving speed range

- [ ] Fuel filter choked (Chapter 1A or 1B)
- [ ] Fuel pump faulty, or delivery pressure low – petrol models (Chapter 4A)
- [ ] Fuel tank vent blocked, or fuel pipes restricted (Chapter 4A or 4B)
- [ ] Vacuum leak at the throttle housing, inlet manifold or associated hoses – petrol models (Chapter 4A or 4C)
- [ ] Worn, faulty or incorrectly-gapped spark plugs – petrol models (Chapter 1A)
- [ ] Faulty injector(s) – diesel models (Chapter 4B)
- [ ] Faulty ignition module – petrol models (Chapter 5B)
- [ ] Uneven or low cylinder compression (Chapter 2A, 2B, 2C, 2D or 2E)
- [ ] Blocked injector/fuel injection system fault (Chapter 4A or 4B)
- [ ] Blocked catalytic converter (Chapter 4A, 4B or 4C)
- [ ] Engine overheating (Chapter 3)

Engine hesitates on acceleration

- [ ] Worn, faulty or incorrectly-gapped spark plugs – petrol models (Chapter 1A)
- [ ] Vacuum leak at the throttle housing, inlet manifold or associated hoses – petrol models (Chapter 4A or 4C)
- [ ] Blocked injectors/fuel injection system fault (Chapter 4A or 4B)
- [ ] Faulty injector(s) – diesel models (Chapter 4B)

Engine stalls

- [ ] Vacuum leak at the throttle housing, inlet manifold or associated hoses – petrol models (Chapter 4A or 4C)
- [ ] Fuel filter choked (Chapter 1A or 1B)
- [ ] Fuel pump faulty, or delivery pressure low – petrol models (Chapter 4A)
- [ ] Fuel tank vent blocked, or fuel pipes restricted (Chapter 4A or 4B)
- [ ] Blocked injectors/fuel injection system fault (Chapter 4A or 4B)
- [ ] Faulty injector(s) – diesel models (Chapter 4B)

Engine lacks power

- [ ] Air filter element blocked (Chapter 1A or 1B)
- [ ] Fuel filter choked (Chapter 1A or 1B)
- [ ] Fuel pipes blocked or restricted (Chapter 4A or 4B)
- [ ] Worn, faulty or incorrectly-gapped spark plugs – petrol models (Chapter 1A)
- [ ] Engine overheating (Chapter 3)
- [ ] Fuel tank level low – diesel models (Chapter 4B)
- [ ] Accelerator pedal position sensor faulty (Chapter 4A or 4B)
- [ ] Vacuum leak at the throttle housing, inlet manifold or associated hoses – petrol models (Chapter 4A or 4C)
- [ ] Blocked injectors/fuel injection system fault (Chapter 4A or 4B)
- [ ] Faulty injector(s) – diesel models (Chapter 4B)
- [ ] Fuel pump faulty, or delivery pressure low – petrol models (Chapter 4A)
- [ ] Uneven or low cylinder compression (Chapter 2A, 2B, 2C, 2D or 2E)
- [ ] Blocked catalytic converter (Chapter 4A, 4B or 4C)
- [ ] Brakes binding (Chapter 1A, 1B or 9)
- [ ] Clutch slipping (Chapter 6)

Engine backfires

- [ ] Vacuum leak at the throttle housing, inlet manifold or associated hoses – petrol models (Chapter 4A)
- [ ] Blocked injectors/fuel injection system fault (Chapter 4A or 4B)
- [ ] Blocked catalytic converter (Chapter 4A, 4B or 4C)
- [ ] Faulty ignition module – petrol models (Chapter 5B)

Oil pressure warning light illuminated with engine running

- [ ] Low oil level, or incorrect oil grade (see Weekly checks)
- [ ] Faulty oil pressure switch, or wiring damaged (Chapter 5A)
- [ ] Worn engine bearings and/or oil pump (Chapter 2A, 2B, 2C, 2D, 2E or 2F)
- [ ] High engine operating temperature (Chapter 3)
- [ ] Oil pump pressure relief valve defective (Chapter 2A, 2B, 2C, 2D or 2E)
- [ ] Oil pump pick-up strainer clogged (Chapter 2A, 2B, 2C, 2D or 2E)

Engine runs-on after switching off

- [ ] Excessive carbon build-up in engine (Chapter 2A, 2B, 2C, 2D or 2E)
- [ ] High engine operating temperature (Chapter 3)
- [ ] Fuel injection/engine management system fault (Chapter 4A, 4B or 4C)

Engine noises

Pre-ignition (pinking) or knocking during acceleration or under load

- [ ] Ignition timing incorrect/ignition system fault – petrol models (Chapter 1A or 5B)
- [ ] Incorrect grade of spark plug – petrol models (Chapter 1A)
- [ ] Incorrect grade of fuel (Chapter 4A or 4B)
- [ ] Knock sensor faulty – petrol models (Chapter 4A)
- [ ] Vacuum leak at the throttle housing, inlet manifold or associated hoses – petrol models (Chapter 4A or 4C)
- [ ] Excessive carbon build-up in engine (Chapter 2A, 2B, 2C, 2D or 2E)
- [ ] Fuel injection/engine management system fault (Chapter 4A, 4B or 4C)
- [ ] Faulty injector(s) – diesel models (Chapter 4B)

Whistling or wheezing noises

- [ ] Leaking inlet manifold or throttle housing gasket – petrol models (Chapter 4A)
- [ ] Leaking exhaust manifold gasket or pipe-to-manifold joint (Chapter 4A or 4B)
- [ ] Leaking vacuum hose (Chapter 4A, 4B, 4C or 9)
- [ ] Blowing cylinder head gasket (Chapter 2A, 2B, 2C, 2D or 2E)
- [ ] Partially blocked or leaking crankcase ventilation system (Chapter 4C)

Tapping or rattling noises

- [ ] Worn valve gear or camshaft (Chapter 2A, 2B, 2C, 2D or 2E)
- [ ] Ancillary component fault (coolant pump, alternator, etc) (Chapter 3, 5A, etc)

Knocking or thumping noises

- [ ] Worn big-end bearings (regular heavy knocking, perhaps less under load) (Chapter 2F)
- [ ] Worn main bearings (rumbling and knocking, perhaps worsening under load) (Chapter 2F)
- [ ] Piston slap – most noticeable when cold, caused by piston/bore wear (Chapter 2F)
- [ ] Ancillary component fault (coolant pump, alternator, etc) (Chapter 3, 5A, etc)
- [ ] Engine mountings worn or defective (Chapter 2A, 2B, 2C, 2D or 2E)
- [ ] Front suspension or steering components worn (Chapter 10)

Cooling system

Overheating

- [ ] Insufficient coolant in system (see *Weekly checks*)
- [ ] Thermostat faulty (Chapter 3)
- [ ] Radiator core blocked, or grille restricted (Chapter 3)
- [ ] Cooling fan faulty, or resistor pack fault (Chapter 3)
- [ ] Inaccurate coolant temperature sensor (Chapter 3)
- [ ] Airlock in cooling system (Chapter 1A, 1B or 3)
- [ ] Expansion tank pressure cap faulty (Chapter 3)
- [ ] Engine management system fault (Chapter 4A, 4B or 4C)

Overcooling

- [ ] Thermostat faulty (Chapter 3)
- [ ] Inaccurate coolant temperature sensor (Chapter 3)
- [ ] Cooling fan faulty (Chapter 3)
- [ ] Engine management system fault (Chapter 4A, 4B or 4C)

External coolant leakage

- [ ] Deteriorated or damaged hoses or hose clips (Chapter 1A or 1B)
- [ ] Radiator core or heater matrix leaking (Chapter 3)
- [ ] Expansion tank pressure cap faulty (Chapter 1A or 1B)
- [ ] Coolant pump internal seal leaking (Chapter 3)
- [ ] Coolant pump gasket leaking (Chapter 3)
- [ ] Boiling due to overheating (Chapter 3)
- [ ] Cylinder block core plug leaking (Chapter 2F)

Internal coolant leakage

- [ ] Leaking cylinder head gasket (Chapter 2A, 2B, 2C, 2D or 2E)
- [ ] Cracked cylinder head or cylinder block (Chapter 2A, 2B, 2C, 2D, 2E or 2F)

Corrosion

- [ ] Infrequent draining and flushing (Chapter 1A or 1B)
- [ ] Incorrect coolant mixture or inappropriate coolant type (see *Weekly checks*)

Fuel and exhaust systems

Excessive fuel consumption

- [ ] Air filter element dirty or clogged (Chapter 1A or 1B)
- [ ] Fuel injection system fault (Chapter 4A, 4B or 4C)
- [ ] Engine management system fault (Chapter 4A, 4B or 4C)
- [ ] Crankcase ventilation system blocked (Chapter 4C)
- [ ] Tyres under-inflated (see *Weekly checks*)
- [ ] Brakes binding (Chapter 1A, 1B or 9)
- [ ] Fuel leak, causing apparent high consumption (Chapter 1A, 1B, 4A or 4B)

Fuel leakage and/or fuel odour

- [ ] Damaged or corroded fuel tank, pipes or connections (Chapter 4A, 4B or 4C)
- [ ] Evaporative emissions system fault – petrol models (Chapter 4C)

Excessive noise or fumes from exhaust system

- [ ] Leaking exhaust system or manifold joints (Chapter 1A, 1B, 4A or 4B)
- [ ] Leaking, corroded or damaged silencers or pipe (Chapter 1A, 1B, 4A, 4B or 4C)
- [ ] Broken mountings causing body or suspension contact (Chapter 1A or 1B)

Clutch

Pedal travels to floor – no pressure or very little resistance

- [ ] Air in hydraulic system/faulty master or slave cylinder (Chapter 6)
- [ ] Faulty hydraulic release system (Chapter 6)
- [ ] Clutch pedal return spring detached or broken (Chapter 6)
- [ ] Broken diaphragm spring in clutch pressure plate (Chapter 6)

Clutch fails to disengage (unable to select gears)

- [ ] Air in hydraulic system/faulty master or slave cylinder (Chapter 6)
- [ ] Faulty hydraulic release system (Chapter 6)
- [ ] Clutch disc sticking on transmission input shaft splines (Chapter 6)
- [ ] Clutch disc sticking to flywheel or pressure plate (Chapter 6)
- [ ] Faulty pressure plate assembly (Chapter 6)
- [ ] Clutch release mechanism worn or incorrectly assembled (Chapter 6)

Clutch slips (engine speed increases, with no increase in vehicle speed)

- [ ] Faulty hydraulic release system (Chapter 6)
- [ ] Clutch disc linings excessively worn (Chapter 6)
- [ ] Clutch disc linings contaminated with oil or grease (Chapter 6)
- [ ] Faulty pressure plate or weak diaphragm spring (Chapter 6)

Judder as clutch is engaged

- [ ] Clutch disc linings contaminated with oil or grease (Chapter 6)
- [ ] Clutch disc linings excessively worn (Chapter 6)
- [ ] Faulty or distorted pressure plate or diaphragm spring (Chapter 6).
- [ ] Worn or loose engine or transmission mountings (Chapter 2A, 2B, 2C, 2D or 2E)
- [ ] Clutch disc hub or transmission input shaft splines worn (Chapter 6)

Noise when depressing or releasing clutch pedal

- [ ] Faulty hydraulic release system (Chapter 6)
- [ ] Worn or dry clutch pedal bushes (Chapter 6)
- [ ] Worn or dry clutch master cylinder piston (Chapter 6)
- [ ] Faulty pressure plate assembly (Chapter 6)
- [ ] Pressure plate diaphragm spring broken (Chapter 6)
- [ ] Broken clutch disc cushioning springs (Chapter 6)

Manual transmission

Note: *Fault finding for the Easytronic transmission should be entrusted to a Vauxhall/Opel dealer.*

Noisy in neutral with engine running

- [ ] Lack of oil (Chapter 7A)
- [ ] Input shaft bearings worn (noise apparent with clutch pedal released, but not when depressed) (Chapter 7A)*
- [ ] Clutch release bearing system (noise apparent with clutch pedal depressed, possibly less when released) (Chapter 6)

Noisy in one particular gear

- [ ] Worn, damaged or chipped gear teeth (Chapter 7A)*

Difficulty engaging gears

- [ ] Clutch fault (Chapter 6)
- [ ] Worn, damaged, or poorly-adjusted gearchange (Chapter 7A)
- [ ] Lack of oil (Chapter 7A)
- [ ] Worn synchroniser units (Chapter 7A)*

Jumps out of gear

- [ ] Worn, damaged, or poorly-adjusted gearchange (Chapter 7A)
- [ ] Worn synchroniser units (Chapter 7A)*
- [ ] Worn selector forks (Chapter 7A)*

Vibration

- [ ] Lack of oil (Chapter 7A)
- [ ] Worn bearings (Chapter 7A)*

Lubricant leaks

- [ ] Leaking driveshaft or selector shaft oil seal (Chapter 7A)
- [ ] Leaking housing joint (Chapter 7A)*
- [ ] Leaking input shaft oil seal (Chapter 7A)*

* Although the corrective action necessary to remedy the symptoms described is beyond the scope of the home mechanic, the above information should be helpful in isolating the cause of the condition, so that the owner can communicate clearly with a professional mechanic.

Driveshafts

Vibration when accelerating or decelerating

- [ ] Worn inner constant velocity joint (Chapter 8)
- [ ] Bent or distorted driveshaft (Chapter 8)
- [ ] Worn intermediate bearing (Chapter 8)

Clicking or knocking noise on turns (at slow speed on full-lock)

- [ ] Worn outer constant velocity joint (Chapter 8)
- [ ] Lack of constant velocity joint lubricant, possibly due to damaged gaiter (Chapter 8)

Braking system

Note: *Before assuming that a brake problem exists, make sure that the tyres are in good condition and correctly inflated, that the front wheel alignment is correct, and that the vehicle is not loaded with weight in an unequal manner. Apart from checking the condition of all pipe and hose connections, any faults occurring on the anti-lock braking system should be referred to a Vauxhall dealer for diagnosis.*

Vehicle pulls to one side under braking

- [ ] Worn, defective, damaged or contaminated brake pads on one side (Chapter 1A, 1B or 9)
- [ ] Seized or partially-seized brake caliper piston (Chapter 1A, 1B or 9)
- [ ] A mixture of brake pad lining materials fitted between sides (Chapter 1A, 1B or 9)
- [ ] Brake caliper mounting bolts loose (Chapter 9)
- [ ] Worn or damaged steering or suspension components (Chapter 1A, 1B or 10)

Noise (grinding or high-pitched squeal) when brakes applied

- [ ] Brake pad friction lining material worn down to metal backing (Chapter 1A, 1B or 9)
- [ ] Excessive corrosion of brake disc (may be apparent after the vehicle has been standing for some time (Chapter 1A, 1B or 9)
- [ ] Foreign object (stone chipping, etc) trapped between brake disc and shield (Chapter 1A, 1B or 9)

Excessive brake pedal travel

- [ ] Faulty master cylinder (Chapter 9)
- [ ] Air in hydraulic system (Chapter 9)
- [ ] Faulty vacuum servo unit (Chapter 9)

Brake pedal feels spongy when depressed

- [ ] Air in hydraulic system (Chapter 9)
- [ ] Deteriorated flexible rubber brake hoses (Chapter 1A, 1B or 9)
- [ ] Master cylinder mounting nuts loose (Chapter 9)
- [ ] Faulty master cylinder (Chapter 9)

Excessive brake pedal effort required to stop vehicle

- [ ] Faulty vacuum servo unit (Chapter 9)
- [ ] Faulty vacuum pump – diesel models (Chapter 9)
- [ ] Disconnected, damaged or insecure brake servo vacuum hose (Chapter 9)
- [ ] Primary or secondary hydraulic circuit failure (Chapter 9)
- [ ] Seized brake caliper piston (Chapter 9)
- [ ] Brake pads incorrectly fitted (Chapter 9)
- [ ] Incorrect grade of brake pads fitted (Chapter 9)
- [ ] Brake pad linings contaminated (Chapter 1A, 1B or 9)

Judder felt through brake pedal or steering wheel when braking

Note: *Under heavy braking on models equipped with ABS, vibration may be felt through the brake pedal. This is a normal feature of ABS operation, and does not constitute a fault*

- [ ] Excessive run-out or distortion of discs (Chapter 9)
- [ ] Brake pad linings worn (Chapter 1A, 1B or 9)
- [ ] Brake caliper mounting bolts loose (Chapter 9)
- [ ] Wear in suspension or steering components or mountings (Chapter 1A, 1B or 10)
- [ ] Front wheels out of balance (see *Weekly checks*)

Brakes binding

- [ ] Seized brake caliper piston (Chapter 9)
- [ ] Incorrectly-adjusted handbrake mechanism (Chapter 9)
- [ ] Faulty master cylinder (Chapter 9)

Rear wheels locking under normal braking

- [ ] Rear brake pad linings contaminated or damaged (Chapter 1 or 9)
- [ ] Rear brake discs/drums warped (Chapter 1A, 1B or 9)
- [ ] Rear brake pressure regulating valve faulty – where fitted (Chapter 9)

Suspension and steering

Note: Before diagnosing suspension or steering faults, be sure that the trouble is not due to incorrect tyre pressures, mixtures of tyre types, or binding brakes.

Vehicle pulls to one side

- ☐ Defective tyre (see *Weekly checks*)
- ☐ Excessive wear in suspension or steering components (Chapter 1A, 1B or 10)
- ☐ Incorrect front wheel alignment (Chapter 10)
- ☐ Accident damage to steering or suspension components (Chapter 1A or 1B)

Wheel wobble and vibration

- ☐ Front wheels out of balance (vibration felt mainly through the steering wheel) (see *Weekly checks*)
- ☐ Rear wheels out of balance (vibration felt throughout the vehicle) (see *Weekly checks*)
- ☐ Roadwheels damaged or distorted (see *Weekly checks*)
- ☐ Faulty or damaged tyre (see *Weekly checks*)
- ☐ Worn steering or suspension joints, bushes or components (Chapter 1A, 1B or 10)
- ☐ Wheel bolts loose (Chapter 1A or 1B)

Excessive pitching and/or rolling around corners, or during braking

- ☐ Defective shock absorbers (Chapter 1A, 1B or 10)
- ☐ Broken or weak spring and/or suspension component (Chapter 1A, 1B or 10)
- ☐ Worn or damaged anti-roll bar or mountings (Chapter 1A, 1B or 10)

Wandering or general instability

- ☐ Incorrect front wheel alignment (Chapter 10)
- ☐ Worn steering or suspension joints, bushes or components (Chapter 1A, 1B or 10)
- ☐ Roadwheels out of balance (see *Weekly checks*)
- ☐ Faulty or damaged tyre (see *Weekly checks*)
- ☐ Wheel bolts loose (Chapter 1A or 1B)
- ☐ Defective shock absorbers (Chapter 1A, 1B or 10)
- ☐ Electric power steering system fault (Chapter 10)

Excessively-stiff steering

- ☐ Seized steering linkage balljoint or suspension balljoint (Chapter 1A, 1B or 10)
- ☐ Incorrect front wheel alignment (Chapter 10)
- ☐ Steering rack damaged (Chapter 10)
- ☐ Electric power steering system fault (Chapter 10)

Excessive play in steering

- ☐ Worn steering column/intermediate shaft joints (Chapter 10)
- ☐ Worn track rod balljoints (Chapter 1A, 1B or 10)
- ☐ Worn steering rack (Chapter 10)
- ☐ Worn steering or suspension joints, bushes or components (Chapter 1A, 1B or 10)

Lack of power assistance

- ☐ Electric power steering system fault (Chapter 10)
- ☐ Faulty steering rack (Chapter 10)

Tyre wear excessive

Tyres worn on inside or outside edges

- ☐ Tyres under-inflated (wear on both edges) (see *Weekly checks*)
- ☐ Incorrect camber or castor angles (wear on one edge only) (Chapter 10)
- ☐ Worn steering or suspension joints, bushes or components (Chapter 1A, 1B or 10)
- ☐ Excessively-hard cornering or braking
- ☐ Accident damage

Tyre treads exhibit feathered edges

- ☐ Incorrect toe-setting (Chapter 10)

Tyres worn in centre of tread

- ☐ Tyres over-inflated (see *Weekly checks*)

Tyres worn on inside and outside edges

- ☐ Tyres under-inflated (see *Weekly checks*)

Tyres worn unevenly

- ☐ Tyres/wheels out of balance (see *Weekly checks*)
- ☐ Excessive wheel or tyre run-out
- ☐ Worn shock absorbers (Chapter 1A, 1B or 10)
- ☐ Faulty tyre (see *Weekly checks*)

Electrical system

Note: For problems associated with the starting system, refer to the faults listed under 'Engine' earlier in this Section.

Battery will not hold a charge for more than a few days

- ☐ Battery defective internally (Chapter 5A)
- ☐ Battery terminal connections loose or corroded (see *Weekly checks*)
- ☐ Auxiliary drivebelt worn or incorrectly adjusted (Chapter 1A or 1B)
- ☐ Alternator not charging at correct output (Chapter 5A)
- ☐ Alternator or voltage regulator faulty (Chapter 5A)
- ☐ Short-circuit causing continual battery drain (Chapter 5A or 12)

Ignition/no-charge warning light remains illuminated with engine running

- ☐ Auxiliary drivebelt broken, worn, or incorrectly adjusted (Chapter 1A or 1B)

- ☐ Internal fault in alternator or voltage regulator (Chapter 5A)
- ☐ Broken, disconnected, or loose wiring in charging circuit (Chapter 5A or 12)

Ignition/no-charge warning light fails to come on

- ☐ Warning light bulb blown (Chapter 12)
- ☐ Broken, disconnected, or loose wiring in warning light circuit (Chapter 5A or 12)
- ☐ Alternator faulty (Chapter 5A)

Lights inoperative

- ☐ Bulb blown (Chapter 12)
- ☐ Corrosion of bulb or bulbholder contacts (Chapter 12)
- ☐ Blown fuse (Chapter 12)
- ☐ Faulty relay (Chapter 12)
- ☐ Broken, loose, or disconnected wiring (Chapter 12)
- ☐ Faulty switch (Chapter 12)

Electrical system (continued)

Instrument readings inaccurate or erratic

Fuel or temperature gauges give no reading

- [ ] Faulty gauge sender unit (Chapter 3, 4A or 4B)
- [ ] Wiring open-circuit (Chapter 12)
- [ ] Faulty gauge (Chapter 12)

Fuel or temperature gauges give continuous maximum reading

- [ ] Faulty gauge sender unit (Chapter 3, 4A or 4B)
- [ ] Wiring short-circuit (Chapter 12)
- [ ] Faulty gauge (Chapter 12)

Horn inoperative, or unsatisfactory in operation

Horn operates all the time

- [ ] Horn push either earthed or stuck down (Chapter 12)
- [ ] Horn cable-to-horn push earthed (Chapter 12)

Horn fails to operate

- [ ] Blown fuse (Chapter 12)
- [ ] Cable or connections loose, broken or disconnected (Chapter 12)
- [ ] Faulty horn (Chapter 12)

Horn emits intermittent or unsatisfactory sound

- [ ] Cable connections loose (Chapter 12)
- [ ] Horn mountings loose (Chapter 12)
- [ ] Faulty horn (Chapter 12)

Windscreen wipers inoperative, or unsatisfactory in operation

Wipers fail to operate, or operate very slowly

- [ ] Wiper blades stuck to screen, or linkage seized or binding (Chapter 12)
- [ ] Blown fuse (Chapter 12)
- [ ] Battery discharged (Chapter 5A)
- [ ] Cable or connections loose, broken or disconnected (Chapter 12)
- [ ] Faulty relay (Chapter 12)
- [ ] Faulty wiper motor (Chapter 12)

Wiper blades sweep over too large or too small an area of the glass

- [ ] Wiper blades incorrectly fitted, or wrong size used (see Weekly checks)
- [ ] Wiper arms incorrectly positioned on spindles (Chapter 12)
- [ ] Excessive wear of wiper linkage (Chapter 12)
- [ ] Wiper motor or linkage mountings loose or insecure (Chapter 12)

Wiper blades fail to clean the glass effectively

- [ ] Wiper blade rubbers dirty, worn or perished (see Weekly checks)
- [ ] Wiper blades incorrectly fitted, or wrong size used (see Weekly checks)
- [ ] Wiper arm tension springs broken, or arm pivots seized (Chapter 12)
- [ ] Insufficient windscreen washer additive to adequately remove road film (see Weekly checks)

Windscreen washers inoperative, or unsatisfactory in operation

One or more washer jets inoperative

- [ ] Blocked washer jet
- [ ] Disconnected, kinked or restricted fluid hose (Chapter 12)
- [ ] Insufficient fluid in washer reservoir (see Weekly checks)

Washer pump fails to operate

- [ ] Broken or disconnected wiring or connections (Chapter 12)
- [ ] Blown fuse (Chapter 12)
- [ ] Faulty washer switch (Chapter 12)
- [ ] Faulty washer pump (Chapter 12)

Washer pump runs for some time before fluid is emitted from jets

- [ ] Faulty one-way valve in fluid supply hose (Chapter 12)

Electric windows inoperative, or unsatisfactory in operation

Window glass will only move in one direction

- [ ] Faulty switch (Chapter 12)

Window glass slow to move

- [ ] Battery discharged (Chapter 5A)
- [ ] Regulator seized or damaged, or in need of lubrication (Chapter 11)
- [ ] Door internal components or trim fouling regulator (Chapter 11)
- [ ] Faulty motor (Chapter 11)

Window glass fails to move

- [ ] Blown fuse (Chapter 12)
- [ ] Faulty relay (Chapter 12)
- [ ] Broken or disconnected wiring or connections (Chapter 12)
- [ ] Faulty motor (Chapter 11)

Central locking system inoperative, or unsatisfactory in operation

Complete system failure

- [ ] Remote handset battery discharged, where applicable (Chapter 1A or 1B)
- [ ] Blown fuse (Chapter 12)
- [ ] Faulty relay (Chapter 12)
- [ ] Broken or disconnected wiring or connections (Chapter 12)
- [ ] Faulty motor (Chapter 11)

Latch locks but will not unlock, or unlocks but will not lock

- [ ] Remote handset battery discharged, where applicable (Chapter 1A or 1B)
- [ ] Faulty master switch (Chapter 12)
- [ ] Broken or disconnected latch operating rods or levers (Chapter 11)
- [ ] Faulty relay (Chapter 12)
- [ ] Faulty motor (Chapter 11)

One solenoid/motor fails to operate

- [ ] Broken or disconnected wiring or connections (Chapter 12)
- [ ] Faulty operating assembly (Chapter 11)
- [ ] Broken, binding or disconnected latch operating rods or levers (Chapter 11)
- [ ] Fault in door latch (Chapter 11)

A

ABS (Anti-lock brake system) A system, usually electronically controlled, that senses incipient wheel lockup during braking and relieves hydraulic pressure at wheels that are about to skid.

Air bag An inflatable bag hidden in the steering wheel (driver's side) or the dash or glovebox (passenger side). In a head-on collision, the bags inflate, preventing the driver and front passenger from being thrown forward into the steering wheel or windscreen.

Air cleaner A metal or plastic housing, containing a filter element, which removes dust and dirt from the air being drawn into the engine.

Air filter element The actual filter in an air cleaner system, usually manufactured from pleated paper and requiring renewal at regular intervals.

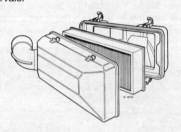

Air filter

Allen key A hexagonal wrench which fits into a recessed hexagonal hole.

Alligator clip A long-nosed spring-loaded metal clip with meshing teeth. Used to make temporary electrical connections.

Alternator A component in the electrical system which converts mechanical energy from a drivebelt into electrical energy to charge the battery and to operate the starting system, ignition system and electrical accessories.

Ampere (amp) A unit of measurement for the flow of electric current. One amp is the amount of current produced by one volt acting through a resistance of one ohm.

Anaerobic sealer A substance used to prevent bolts and screws from loosening. Anaerobic means that it does not require oxygen for activation. The Loctite brand is widely used.

Antifreeze A substance (usually ethylene glycol) mixed with water, and added to a vehicle's cooling system, to prevent freezing of the coolant in winter. Antifreeze also contains chemicals to inhibit corrosion and the formation of rust and other deposits that would tend to clog the radiator and coolant passages and reduce cooling efficiency.

Anti-seize compound A coating that reduces the risk of seizing on fasteners that are subjected to high temperatures, such as exhaust manifold bolts and nuts.

Asbestos A natural fibrous mineral with great heat resistance, commonly used in the composition of brake friction materials.

Asbestos is a health hazard and the dust created by brake systems should never be inhaled or ingested.

Axle A shaft on which a wheel revolves, or which revolves with a wheel. Also, a solid beam that connects the two wheels at one end of the vehicle. An axle which also transmits power to the wheels is known as a live axle.

Axleshaft A single rotating shaft, on either side of the differential, which delivers power from the final drive assembly to the drive wheels. Also called a driveshaft or a halfshaft.

B

Ball bearing An anti-friction bearing consisting of a hardened inner and outer race with hardened steel balls between two races.

Bearing The curved surface on a shaft or in a bore, or the part assembled into either, that permits relative motion between them with minimum wear and friction.

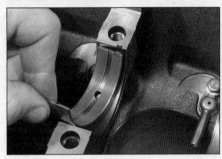

Bearing

Big-end bearing The bearing in the end of the connecting rod that's attached to the crankshaft.

Bleed nipple A valve on a brake wheel cylinder, caliper or other hydraulic component that is opened to purge the hydraulic system of air. Also called a bleed screw.

Brake bleeding Procedure for removing air from lines of a hydraulic brake system.

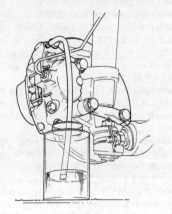

Brake bleeding

Brake disc The component of a disc brake that rotates with the wheels.

Brake drum The component of a drum brake that rotates with the wheels.

Brake linings The friction material which contacts the brake disc or drum to retard the vehicle's speed. The linings are bonded or riveted to the brake pads or shoes.

Brake pads The replaceable friction pads that pinch the brake disc when the brakes are applied. Brake pads consist of a friction material bonded or riveted to a rigid backing plate.

Brake shoe The crescent-shaped carrier to which the brake linings are mounted and which forces the lining against the rotating drum during braking.

Braking systems For more information on braking systems, consult the *Haynes Automotive Brake Manual*.

Breaker bar A long socket wrench handle providing greater leverage.

Bulkhead The insulated partition between the engine and the passenger compartment.

C

Caliper The non-rotating part of a disc-brake assembly that straddles the disc and carries the brake pads. The caliper also contains the hydraulic components that cause the pads to pinch the disc when the brakes are applied. A caliper is also a measuring tool that can be set to measure inside or outside dimensions of an object.

Camshaft A rotating shaft on which a series of cam lobes operate the valve mechanisms. The camshaft may be driven by gears, by sprockets and chain or by sprockets and a belt.

Canister A container in an evaporative emission control system; contains activated charcoal granules to trap vapours from the fuel system.

Canister

Carburettor A device which mixes fuel with air in the proper proportions to provide a desired power output from a spark ignition internal combustion engine.

Castellated Resembling the parapets along the top of a castle wall. For example, a castellated balljoint stud nut.

Castor In wheel alignment, the backward or forward tilt of the steering axis. Castor is positive when the steering axis is inclined rearward at the top.

Catalytic converter A silencer-like device in the exhaust system which converts certain pollutants in the exhaust gases into less harmful substances.

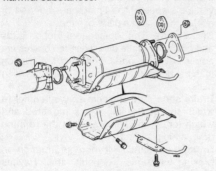

Catalytic converter

Circlip A ring-shaped clip used to prevent endwise movement of cylindrical parts and shafts. An internal circlip is installed in a groove in a housing; an external circlip fits into a groove on the outside of a cylindrical piece such as a shaft.

Clearance The amount of space between two parts. For example, between a piston and a cylinder, between a bearing and a journal, etc.

Coil spring A spiral of elastic steel found in various sizes throughout a vehicle, for example as a springing medium in the suspension and in the valve train.

Compression Reduction in volume, and increase in pressure and temperature, of a gas, caused by squeezing it into a smaller space.

Compression ratio The relationship between cylinder volume when the piston is at top dead centre and cylinder volume when the piston is at bottom dead centre.

Constant velocity (CV) joint A type of universal joint that cancels out vibrations caused by driving power being transmitted through an angle.

Core plug A disc or cup-shaped metal device inserted in a hole in a casting through which core was removed when the casting was formed. Also known as a freeze plug or expansion plug.

Crankcase The lower part of the engine block in which the crankshaft rotates.

Crankshaft The main rotating member, or shaft, running the length of the crankcase, with offset "throws" to which the connecting rods are attached.

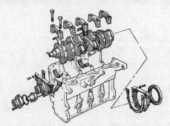

Crankshaft assembly

Crocodile clip See Alligator clip

D

Diagnostic code Code numbers obtained by accessing the diagnostic mode of an engine management computer. This code can be used to determine the area in the system where a malfunction may be located.

Disc brake A brake design incorporating a rotating disc onto which brake pads are squeezed. The resulting friction converts the energy of a moving vehicle into heat.

Double-overhead cam (DOHC) An engine that uses two overhead camshafts, usually one for the intake valves and one for the exhaust valves.

Drivebelt(s) The belt(s) used to drive accessories such as the alternator, water pump, power steering pump, air conditioning compressor, etc. off the crankshaft pulley.

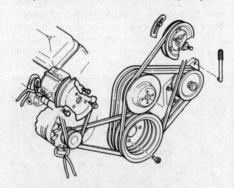

Accessory drivebelts

Driveshaft Any shaft used to transmit motion. Commonly used when referring to the axleshafts on a front wheel drive vehicle.

Drum brake A type of brake using a drum-shaped metal cylinder attached to the inner surface of the wheel. When the brake pedal is pressed, curved brake shoes with friction linings press against the inside of the drum to slow or stop the vehicle.

E

EGR valve A valve used to introduce exhaust gases into the intake air stream.

Electronic control unit (ECU) A computer which controls (for instance) ignition and fuel injection systems, or an anti-lock braking system. For more information refer to the *Haynes Automotive Electrical and Electronic Systems Manual*.

Electronic Fuel Injection (EFI) A computer controlled fuel system that distributes fuel through an injector located in each intake port of the engine.

Emergency brake A braking system, independent of the main hydraulic system, that can be used to slow or stop the vehicle if the primary brakes fail, or to hold the vehicle stationary even though the brake pedal isn't depressed. It usually consists of a hand lever that actuates either front or rear brakes mechanically through a series of cables and linkages. Also known as a handbrake or parking brake.

Endfloat The amount of lengthwise movement between two parts. As applied to a crankshaft, the distance that the crankshaft can move forward and back in the cylinder block.

Engine management system (EMS) A computer controlled system which manages the fuel injection and the ignition systems in an integrated fashion.

Exhaust manifold A part with several passages through which exhaust gases leave the engine combustion chambers and enter the exhaust pipe.

F

Fan clutch A viscous (fluid) drive coupling device which permits variable engine fan speeds in relation to engine speeds.

Feeler blade A thin strip or blade of hardened steel, ground to an exact thickness, used to check or measure clearances between parts.

Feeler blade

Firing order The order in which the engine cylinders fire, or deliver their power strokes, beginning with the number one cylinder.

Flywheel A heavy spinning wheel in which energy is absorbed and stored by means of momentum. On cars, the flywheel is attached to the crankshaft to smooth out firing impulses.

Free play The amount of travel before any action takes place. The "looseness" in a linkage, or an assembly of parts, between the initial application of force and actual movement. For example, the distance the brake pedal moves before the pistons in the master cylinder are actuated.

Fuse An electrical device which protects a circuit against accidental overload. The typical fuse contains a soft piece of metal which is calibrated to melt at a predetermined current flow (expressed as amps) and break the circuit.

Fusible link A circuit protection device consisting of a conductor surrounded by heat-resistant insulation. The conductor is smaller than the wire it protects, so it acts as the weakest link in the circuit. Unlike a blown fuse, a failed fusible link must frequently be cut from the wire for replacement.

G

Gap The distance the spark must travel in jumping from the centre electrode to the side electrode in a spark plug. Also refers to the spacing between the points in a contact breaker assembly in a conventional points-type ignition, or to the distance between the reluctor or rotor and the pickup coil in an electronic ignition.

Adjusting spark plug gap

Gasket Any thin, soft material - usually cork, cardboard, asbestos or soft metal - installed between two metal surfaces to ensure a good seal. For instance, the cylinder head gasket seals the joint between the block and the cylinder head.

Gasket

Gauge An instrument panel display used to monitor engine conditions. A gauge with a movable pointer on a dial or a fixed scale is an analogue gauge. A gauge with a numerical readout is called a digital gauge.

H

Halfshaft A rotating shaft that transmits power from the final drive unit to a drive wheel, usually when referring to a live rear axle.

Harmonic balancer A device designed to reduce torsion or twisting vibration in the crankshaft. May be incorporated in the crankshaft pulley. Also known as a vibration damper.

Hone An abrasive tool for correcting small irregularities or differences in diameter in an engine cylinder, brake cylinder, etc.

Hydraulic tappet A tappet that utilises hydraulic pressure from the engine's lubrication system to maintain zero clearance (constant contact with both camshaft and valve stem). Automatically adjusts to variation in valve stem length. Hydraulic tappets also reduce valve noise.

I

Ignition timing The moment at which the spark plug fires, usually expressed in the number of crankshaft degrees before the piston reaches the top of its stroke.

Inlet manifold A tube or housing with passages through which flows the air-fuel mixture (carburettor vehicles and vehicles with throttle body injection) or air only (port fuel-injected vehicles) to the port openings in the cylinder head.

J

Jump start Starting the engine of a vehicle with a discharged or weak battery by attaching jump leads from the weak battery to a charged or helper battery.

L

Load Sensing Proportioning Valve (LSPV) A brake hydraulic system control valve that works like a proportioning valve, but also takes into consideration the amount of weight carried by the rear axle.

Locknut A nut used to lock an adjustment nut, or other threaded component, in place. For example, a locknut is employed to keep the adjusting nut on the rocker arm in position.

Lockwasher A form of washer designed to prevent an attaching nut from working loose.

M

MacPherson strut A type of front suspension system devised by Earle MacPherson at Ford of England. In its original form, a simple lateral link with the anti-roll bar creates the lower control arm. A long strut - an integral coil spring and shock absorber - is mounted between the body and the steering knuckle. Many modern so-called MacPherson strut systems use a conventional lower A-arm and don't rely on the anti-roll bar for location.

Multimeter An electrical test instrument with the capability to measure voltage, current and resistance.

N

NOx Oxides of Nitrogen. A common toxic pollutant emitted by petrol and diesel engines at higher temperatures.

O

Ohm The unit of electrical resistance. One volt applied to a resistance of one ohm will produce a current of one amp.

Ohmmeter An instrument for measuring electrical resistance.

O-ring A type of sealing ring made of a special rubber-like material; in use, the O-ring is compressed into a groove to provide the sealing action.

Overhead cam (ohc) engine An engine with the camshaft(s) located on top of the cylinder head(s).

Overhead valve (ohv) engine An engine with the valves located in the cylinder head, but with the camshaft located in the engine block.

Oxygen sensor A device installed in the engine exhaust manifold, which senses the oxygen content in the exhaust and converts this information into an electric current. Also called a Lambda sensor.

P

Phillips screw A type of screw head having a cross instead of a slot for a corresponding type of screwdriver.

Plastigage A thin strip of plastic thread, available in different sizes, used for measuring clearances. For example, a strip of Plastigage is laid across a bearing journal. The parts are assembled and dismantled; the width of the crushed strip indicates the clearance between journal and bearing.

Plastigage

Propeller shaft The long hollow tube with universal joints at both ends that carries power from the transmission to the differential on front-engined rear wheel drive vehicles.

Proportioning valve A hydraulic control valve which limits the amount of pressure to the rear brakes during panic stops to prevent wheel lock-up.

R

Rack-and-pinion steering A steering system with a pinion gear on the end of the steering shaft that mates with a rack (think of a geared wheel opened up and laid flat). When the steering wheel is turned, the pinion turns, moving the rack to the left or right. This movement is transmitted through the track rods to the steering arms at the wheels.

Radiator A liquid-to-air heat transfer device designed to reduce the temperature of the coolant in an internal combustion engine cooling system.

Refrigerant Any substance used as a heat transfer agent in an air-conditioning system. R-12 has been the principle refrigerant for many years; recently, however, manufacturers have begun using R-134a, a non-CFC substance that is considered less harmful to the ozone in the upper atmosphere.

Rocker arm A lever arm that rocks on a shaft or pivots on a stud. In an overhead valve engine, the rocker arm converts the upward movement of the pushrod into a downward movement to open a valve.

Rotor In a distributor, the rotating device inside the cap that connects the centre electrode and the outer terminals as it turns, distributing the high voltage from the coil secondary winding to the proper spark plug. Also, that part of an alternator which rotates inside the stator. Also, the rotating assembly of a turbocharger, including the compressor wheel, shaft and turbine wheel.

Runout The amount of wobble (in-and-out movement) of a gear or wheel as it's rotated. The amount a shaft rotates "out-of-true." The out-of-round condition of a rotating part.

S

Sealant A liquid or paste used to prevent leakage at a joint. Sometimes used in conjunction with a gasket.

Sealed beam lamp An older headlight design which integrates the reflector, lens and filaments into a hermetically-sealed one-piece unit. When a filament burns out or the lens cracks, the entire unit is simply replaced.

Serpentine drivebelt A single, long, wide accessory drivebelt that's used on some newer vehicles to drive all the accessories, instead of a series of smaller, shorter belts. Serpentine drivebelts are usually tensioned by an automatic tensioner.

Serpentine drivebelt

Shim Thin spacer, commonly used to adjust the clearance or relative positions between two parts. For example, shims inserted into or under bucket tappets control valve clearances. Clearance is adjusted by changing the thickness of the shim.

Slide hammer A special puller that screws into or hooks onto a component such as a shaft or bearing; a heavy sliding handle on the shaft bottoms against the end of the shaft to knock the component free.

Sprocket A tooth or projection on the periphery of a wheel, shaped to engage with a chain or drivebelt. Commonly used to refer to the sprocket wheel itself.

Starter inhibitor switch On vehicles with an automatic transmission, a switch that prevents starting if the vehicle is not in Neutral or Park.

Strut See MacPherson strut.

T

Tappet A cylindrical component which transmits motion from the cam to the valve stem, either directly or via a pushrod and rocker arm. Also called a cam follower.

Thermostat A heat-controlled valve that regulates the flow of coolant between the cylinder block and the radiator, so maintaining optimum engine operating temperature. A thermostat is also used in some air cleaners in which the temperature is regulated.

Thrust bearing The bearing in the clutch assembly that is moved in to the release levers by clutch pedal action to disengage the clutch. Also referred to as a release bearing.

Timing belt A toothed belt which drives the camshaft. Serious engine damage may result if it breaks in service.

Timing chain A chain which drives the camshaft.

Toe-in The amount the front wheels are closer together at the front than at the rear. On rear wheel drive vehicles, a slight amount of toe-in is usually specified to keep the front wheels running parallel on the road by offsetting other forces that tend to spread the wheels apart.

Toe-out The amount the front wheels are closer together at the rear than at the front. On front wheel drive vehicles, a slight amount of toe-out is usually specified.

Tools For full information on choosing and using tools, refer to the *Haynes Automotive Tools Manual*.

Tracer A stripe of a second colour applied to a wire insulator to distinguish that wire from another one with the same colour insulator.

Tune-up A process of accurate and careful adjustments and parts replacement to obtain the best possible engine performance.

Turbocharger A centrifugal device, driven by exhaust gases, that pressurises the intake air. Normally used to increase the power output from a given engine displacement, but can also be used primarily to reduce exhaust emissions (as on VW's "Umwelt" Diesel engine).

U

Universal joint or U-joint A double-pivoted connection for transmitting power from a driving to a driven shaft through an angle. A U-joint consists of two Y-shaped yokes and a cross-shaped member called the spider.

V

Valve A device through which the flow of liquid, gas, vacuum, or loose material in bulk may be started, stopped, or regulated by a movable part that opens, shuts, or partially obstructs one or more ports or passageways. A valve is also the movable part of such a device.

Valve clearance The clearance between the valve tip (the end of the valve stem) and the rocker arm or tappet. The valve clearance is measured when the valve is closed.

Vernier caliper A precision measuring instrument that measures inside and outside dimensions. Not quite as accurate as a micrometer, but more convenient.

Viscosity The thickness of a liquid or its resistance to flow.

Volt A unit for expressing electrical "pressure" in a circuit. One volt that will produce a current of one ampere through a resistance of one ohm.

W

Welding Various processes used to join metal items by heating the areas to be joined to a molten state and fusing them together. For more information refer to the *Haynes Automotive Welding Manual*.

Wiring diagram A drawing portraying the components and wires in a vehicle's electrical system, using standardised symbols. For more information refer to the *Haynes Automotive Electrical and Electronic Systems Manual*.

Note: *References throughout this index are in the form "**Chapter number**" • "**Page number**". So, for example, 2C•15 refers to page 15 of Chapter 2C.*

Note: *References throughout this index are in the form "**Chapter number**" • "**Page number**". So, for example, 2C•15 refers to page 15 of Chapter 2C.*

*Note: References throughout this index are in the form "**Chapter number**" • "**Page number**". So, for example, 2C•15 refers to page 15 of Chapter 2C.*

Note: *References throughout this index are in the form* "**Chapter number**" • "**Page number**". *So, for example, 2C•15 refers to page 15 of Chapter 2C.*

Preserving Our Motoring Heritage

< The Model J Duesenberg Derham Tourster. Only eight of these magnificent cars were ever built – this is the only example to be found outside the United States of America

Almost every car you've ever loved, loathed or desired is gathered under one roof at the Haynes Motor Museum. Over 300 immaculately presented cars and motorbikes represent every aspect of our motoring heritage, from elegant reminders of bygone days, such as the superb Model J Duesenberg to curiosities like the bug-eyed BMW Isetta. There are also many old friends and flames. Perhaps you remember the 1959 Ford Popular that you did your courting in? The magnificent 'Red Collection' is a spectacle of classic sports cars including AC, Alfa Romeo, Austin Healey, Ferrari, Lamborghini, Maserati, MG, Riley, Porsche and Triumph.

A Perfect Day Out

Each and every vehicle at the Haynes Motor Museum has played its part in the history and culture of Motoring. Today, they make a wonderful spectacle and a great day out for all the family. Bring the kids, bring Mum and Dad, but above all bring your camera to capture those golden memories for ever. You will also find an impressive array of motoring memorabilia, a comfortable 70 seat video cinema and one of the most extensive transport book shops in Britain. The Pit Stop Cafe serves everything from a cup of tea to wholesome, home-made meals or, if you prefer, you can enjoy the large picnic area nestled in the beautiful rural surroundings of Somerset.

> John Haynes O.B.E., Founder and Chairman of the museum at the wheel of a Haynes Light 12.

< Graham Hill's Lola Cosworth Formula 1 car next to a 1934 Riley Sports.

The Museum is situated on the A359 Yeovil to Frome road at Sparkford, just off the A303 in Somerset. It is about 40 miles south of Bristol, and 25 minutes drive from the M5 intersection at Taunton.
Open 9.30am - 5.30pm (10.00am - 4.00pm Winter) 7 days a week, *except Christmas Day, Boxing Day and New Years Day*
Special rates available for schools, coach parties and outings Charitable Trust No. 292048